# Proposition 2½
# Its Impact on
# Massachusetts

# Proposition 2½ Its Impact on Massachusetts

A Report from the
**IMPACT: 2½ Project**
at the
Massachusetts Institute
of Technology

Edited by
Lawrence E. Susskind
Coedited by
Jane Fountain Serio

Oelgeschlager, Gunn & Hain,
Publishers, Inc.
Cambridge, Massachusetts

International Standard Book Number:    0-89946-174-3 (cloth)
                                      0-89946-175-1 (paper)

Library of Congress Catalog Card Number:   83-6298

Printed in the U.S.A.


Library of Congress Cataloging in Publication Data
Main entry under title:

Proposition 2½

   Includes index.

   1.   Real property tax--Massachusetts.   2.   Tax and expenditure
limitations--Massachusetts.   3.   Municipal finance--Massachusetts--
Case studies.   I. Susskind, Lawrence.
HJ4227.P76   1983      336'.014'744      83-6298
ISBN   0-89946-174-3
ISBN   0-89946-175-1 (pbk.)

# CONTENTS

## Part Four
## Analysis and Interpretation

# Preface

Proponents of Proposition 2 1/2 claimed that if their tax limitation measure passed, property tax rates would be cut dramatically, Massachusetts could end its untoward reliance on the municipal property tax, local officials would be forced to increase government productivity, and waste and corruption would be eliminated. Opponents of Proposition 2 1/2 made equally strong claims. They insisted that a tax limitation, as well as some of the other provisions of Proposition 2 1/2, would force curtailment of basic police and fire protection, eliminate many social service programs, discourage new real estate investment, require drastic cuts in expenditures for public education, necessitate the firing of tens of thousands of public employees, and bankrupt a number of communities already tottering on the verge of financial disaster. No doubt, both sides exaggerated. Even the most casual observer of Massachusetts politics, however, could not help but realize that the Commonwealth had reached a turning point. Public discontent with ever increasing property tax burdens and with the legislature's inability to respond effectively had finally boiled over.

Proposition 2 1/2 passed by a 59- to 41-percent margin in November 1980. Citizens for Limited Taxation and the Massachusetts High Technology Council (the prime backers of the referendum) claimed that the public had finally spoken -- demanding not only property tax relief but a reduction in the scope and scale of government activity as well. Opponents admitted that the voters wanted tax reform but did not agree that cuts in services or a redefinition of government's role were called for.

Proposition 2 1/2 took effect in January 1981. City councils, town meeting members, and other local officials had only a few months to prepare budgets for the next fiscal year (beginning July 1981). They faced numerous uncertainties as they tried to cope with mandated tax cuts and reductions in excise tax revenue. No one knew whether the state legislature would increase financial aid to local government. (In the end, this was not decided until after the beginning of the 1982 fiscal year.) No one knew whether cuts in federal aid to state and local governments contemplated in Washington would actually occur. Nor was it clear what powers cities and towns would be given to make up lost revenue by adopting new taxes or fees. Boston, for example, waited months while the legislature debated whether to permit the city to adopt new "local option" taxes. Public officials were not sure how voters would react to proposed service cuts. Some officials felt that the best strategy was to announce the harshest cuts possible in the hope that the resulting public outcry would move the legislature to increase aid to local government. Clearly, the voters wanted tax relief, but it was not at all obvious that they would stand for service cuts. The politicians moved cautiously.

For years Massachusetts communities simply totalled the annual budget increases requested by municipal department heads, added in wage increases negotiated with public employee unions, calculated the funds needed to cover the impact of inflation on fixed costs, and arrived at the figure that needed to be raised in taxes. After subtracting projected federal and state aid, the tax rate was set by dividing the assessed valuation of the community by the total that needed to be raised. In 1977, the state legislature imposed a four percent cap on annual local spending increases, but this was easily and often overriden by town meeting and city council votes. Proposition 2 1/2 turned the entire budget process upside down. The tax rate was fixed *first* (i.e., 2.5 percent of a community's fair market value). If a community's existing tax rate were higher than 2.5 percent, cuts of at least 15 percent a year in spending were required until the mandated level was reached. Proposition 2 1/2 imposed a simultaneous limit of 2.5 percent on annual levy (i.e., spending) increases -- regardless of the growth in property value attributable to new development. Override provisions were extrememly tough; all the loopholes were closed. Almost every city and town was forced to alter its normal budget process to meet the harsh realities of Proposition 2 1/2.

Proposition 13, California's tax limitation measure, was not nearly so onerous. In general, cities and towns in California met the one percent property tax rate limit without much difficulty. Substantial increments in state aid, especially for the cities required to take the largest cuts, eased the burden. (The state had a large revenue surplus on hand.) In Massachusetts, effective property tax rates as of 1980 averaged eight percent. Getting under the 2.5 percent limit clearly required several years of severe cutbacks. In addition, Proposition 2 1/2 cut automobile excise tax revenue in Massachusetts by almost 40 percent. There was no surplus for the state legislature to share with the cities and towns. The state could bail out cities only by cutting other state expenditures. Finally, Massachusetts failed to enact an aid formula keyed to the actual cutbacks mandated by Proposition 2 1/2. While the legislature eventually allocated $350 million in additional aid for cities and towns, the formula used to distribute this money rewarded some communities, restoring more than 100 percent of their losses, but hardly helped others at all.

In March 1981, a team of scholars based at the Department of Urban Studies and Planning at the Massachusetts Institute of Technology (MIT), initiated the IMPACT: 2 1/2 Project. More than two dozen professors (specialists in a variety of fields) from ten colleges and universities in the state, came together to monitor the impacts of Proposition 2 1/2. With funds from the Lincoln Institute of Land Policy, a nonprofit, educational institution in Cambridge, Massachusetts, as well as grants from several local and national foundations, the IMPACT: 2 1/2 Project team sought to provide a nonpartisan source of reliable information. Of course, none of the findings presented in this volume necessarily reflect the views or policies of the various institutions providing financial or in-kind support for the IMPACT: 2 1/2 Project.

Thirteen case study communities were selected for on-going monitoring. Sixty-one cities and towns were selected for annual statistical surveillance. An information system containing ten years of data on local revenues, local spending, public employment, service quality levels, and fiscal stability in all 351 cities and towns was constructed. The research team agreed at the outset that the impacts of Proposition 2 1/2 could not be understood apart from the longer term budgetary and public service trends during the prior decade. Graduate student staff from several universities undertook the laborious task of putting all the necessary data into the computer.

Many of the impacts of Proposition 2 1/2 will not be felt for several years; some that are immediately obvious will be impossible to interpret intelligently for several years. The impact of Proposition 2 1/2 on land and housing prices, for example, will take years to become clear. Decisions about what and how to cut in the first year, however, are easy to monitor and of enormous interest. Who decided what the local spending priorities should be? Which strategies and tactics were most effective in staving off cuts? Which interest groups gained or lost power in the budget process? Do strict tax limitations provoke a more thorough search for greater efficiency? Do tax cuts help eliminate waste and combat corruption? Can private and voluntary organizations be convinced to assume responsibility for services that are cut? Can localities find new non-property tax sources of revenue? Can the growing power of public employee unions be challenged effectively by municipal officials? Will affirmative action requirements be met in periods of cutbacks? Partial answers to these and related questions have begun to emerge.

There are, we believe, two major audiences for this first volume. One includes mostly residents of Massachusetts, particularly elected and appointed officials trying to cope with mandated cutbacks. This group is eager for impartial analysis and trustworthy information. The other audience consists mainly of scholars and policy analysts elsewhere in the country, trying to come to grips with taxcutting pressures in their own states. The results of Proposition 13 are inconclusive. The state bailout in California forestalled difficult cuts. Moreover, little, if any, systematic evaluation of the impacts of Proposition 13 is available. People elsewhere want to know what has happened and what might happen if something like Proposition 2 1/2 passes in their part of the country.

Thirteen case studies are presented in this first volume. Academic purists are sometimes put off by case study research, arguing that case studies are rarely representative (in a statistically significant sense) and often highly subjective in their presentation of the facts. The case studies in this volume definitely do *not* represent the experiences of all cities and towns in Massachusetts. We learned early in our research that the effects of Proposition 2 1/2 and local responses to the tax cutting mandate are incredibly varied. We selected communities likely to be hard hit by Proposition 2 1/2. While seeking case study communities distributed by size, income level, public spending propensities, and other demographic and organizational attributes, we concentrated on communities facing significant cubacks. How else could we study responses to tax limitations?

The fiscal and public employment trends prior to Proposition 2 1/2 discussed in this volume are based on federal and state data as well as information collected from our sample of 61 communities. Our in-depth case studies are based on extensive interviews with key officials and residents. We do not claim that our analyses are entirely objective. Everyone involved in the monitoring effort had personal predispositions and political leanings that were bound to shade their perceptions. Nevertheless, drafts of all the studies included in this volume have been reviewed by a range of individuals with as broad an array of viewpoints as exists in the state. Every individual quoted was given an opportunity to review statements attributed to him or her. We are confident that our presentation is as unbiased as possible.

Dozens of people helped to compile the studies in this volume. In each case study community alone, residents and officials gave generously of their time. At MIT and at other universities, colleagues provided advice and guidance on a regular basis. President Paul Gray of the Massachusetts Institute of Technology and President Derek Bok of Harvard University have both been enormously supportive of the IMPACT: 2 1/2 Project. We thank them for their assistance and applaud the universities' willingness to play a role in monitoring an extremely important public policy decision. We welcome the advice and suggestions of our readers, particularly those who are experiencing the impacts of Proposition 2 1/2 firsthand.

# Acknowledgments

A great many individuals and organizations, too many to name here, contributed in a variety of ways to the IMPACT: 2 1/2 Project and to the preparation of this book. Their interest and support are gratefully acknowledged.

Arlo Woolery and Charles Cook of the Lincoln Institute of Land Policy in Cambridge, Massachusetts have been especially supportive of the IMPACT: 2 1/2 Project. We appreciate the Lincoln Institute's continued support of this public educational joint venture.

We are also grateful for the financial assistance contributed to the IMPACT: 2 1/2 Project by the following organizations: the Davis Foundation; the Ford Foundation; Harvard University; the Hyams Trust Foundation; the Kendall Foundation; the Massachusetts Institute of Technology, particularly, the Department of Urban Studies and Planning, the Laboratory of Architecture and Planning, and the Undergraduate Research Opportunities Program; the M.I.T.–Harvard Joint Center for Urban Studies; the Permanent Charities Fund of Boston; the United States Department of Housing and Urban Development; the Urban Institute; and the Wyman–Gordon Foundation. The opinions expressed in this book do not necessarily represent the official policies of any of these organizations. We take responsibility for any errors of omission or commission.

Four individuals, without whose help this Project could not have proceeded, deserve special recognition. Argie Staples served as Project Administrator from the beginning of the Project until August 1982. She helped organize the team and orchestrate the first year's work. Donna McDaniel, Editor of the IMPACT: 2 1/2 Newsletter, provided editorial assistance with the case studies that appear in this volume. John Klensin provided crucial advice and instruction in the design and operation of our data management and word processing systems. Finally, Jane Fountain Serio, current Project Administrator and coeditor of this volume, provided the skill, energy and perseverance which brought this book to fruition. Her unflagging commitment to excellence inspired everyone else involved with the IMPACT: 2 1/2 Project.

# Introduction

We do not expect even the most devout followers of Proposition 2 1/2 to read this book from cover to cover. Therefore, some guidance is in order. The first part of the book outlines the mandate of Proposition 2 1/2 for those unfamiliar with all of its provisions (and subsequent amendments). Sherry Tvedt Davis's brief history of Proposition 2 1/2 puts the Massachusetts tax limitation movement in perspective. Alan Tosti's review of the amendments to Proposition 2 1/2 makes sense of the complicted do's and don'ts of the law. A list of the budget cuts mandated by Proposition 2 1/2 for each of the 351 cities and towns in the Commonwealth underscores the dramatically different situation facing each community.

Part Two reviews public employment and expenditure trends in Massachusetts over the five years prior to enactment of Proposition 2 1/2. Many readers may be surprised to learn that municipal spending levels were dropping even before the rise of the tax limitation movement in Massachusetts. The Introduction to the Trend Analysis highlights the key findings in Part Two. For readers who are not statistically inclined, the Introduction may be sufficient. The trends in public spending, local revenue collection, fiscal stability, public employment, and the state's reliance on user fees and charges are analyzed historically and comparatively; i.e., communities are compared over time as well as to each other. This second section of the book should be of special interest to municipal officials who want to compare their situation to the pressures faced by other communities. Scholars interested in the pressures that provoke tax limitation initiatives would be especially anxious to examine the pre-2 1/2 trends.

Part Three presents thirteen municipal case studies. Each case study emphasizes the political dynamics of the cutback planning process. Dramatic shifts in the budgetmaking power of various groups are clearly evident. The case studies provide a glimpse into the future -- noting the probable effects of some of the short-term remedies that have been adopted.

Part Four offers a series of interpretations. Lawrence Susskind and Cynthia Horan explain how and why the drastic cuts feared by the anti-Proposition 2 1/2 forces were avoided and summarizes the coping strategies used by the hardest hit communities. Katherine Bradbury, Helen Ladd, and Claire Christopherson are especially interested in the effects of budget cutbacks on public education. They also explore the overall shifts in the Commonwealth's tax system caused by Proposition 2 1/2. Rebecca Black examines the impact of Proposition 2 1/2 on labor relations in the public sector. While the experiences of case study communities vary dramatically, surprising consistencies emerge: public employee unions rarely formed local coalitions to fight off cutbacks; most public employees accepted less than the rate of inflation. Patricia McCarney analyzes the efforts of a number of cities and towns to replace lost property tax revenue by charging for municipal services previously provided at no charge to local taxpayers and by raising fees for sewer, water, and other services. Karl Kim analyzes the changes in municipal appropriation levels in seventeen case study communities. The pattern of cuts varied enormously, but Kim clearly demonstrates which services bore the brunt of the cuts. John Greiner and Harry Hatry of the Urban Institute present a detailed summary of local departmental efforts to enhance efficiency and productivity. While they identify some enormously creative and encouraging responses in a few localities, the overall record for the first year is disappointing. Jerome Rothenberg and Paul Smoke provide a synopsis of first year impacts, emphasizing possible explanations for the dramatically different experiences in each city and town.

The Appendix is substantial. Detailed information about every city and town with a population over 10,000 is presented in tabular form. These tables allow readers to answer their own questions about particular (sets of) communities.

We offer no recommendations or conclusions (although we were tempted). It is too soon to weigh the benefits and the costs. In a second volume of IMPACT: 2 1/2 reports, we will look closely at the topics of continuing concern: revaluation and the distribution of the property tax burden, classification as a response to the pressures of revaluation, the affirmative action implications of local hiring and firing practices, the changing nature of local political leadership in periods of cutbacks, the effects of spending cuts on the quality of municipal services, the impact of deferred maintenance on municipal infrastructure, the distributional effects of state aid, the interaction between cutbacks in federal aid and state tax limitations, the impact of Proposition 2 1/2 on the availability of social services -- particularly for the poor and the disadvantaged, the advantages and disadvantages of reprivatizing public services, and the effects of property tax limitation and service cuts on residential property values.

The general impression we have from interacting with local officials and residents is that the citizens of Massachusetts are a hardy bunch. They encounter each day's ups and downs with good humor and a continued commitment to doing their best. When we see their steadfastness we are encouraged to continue the task of impact monitoring, even though it can be grueling at times.

Part One

The Mandate of Proposition 2 1/2

Chapter 1

# A Brief History of Proposition 2 1/2

Sherry Tvedt Davis

In November 1980, Massachusetts voters approved by a three-to-two margin an initiative designed to reduce property taxes in "Taxachusetts" by 40 percent. In this era of budget cutbacks and government retrenchment at the federal level, it is interesting to examine the short history of the initiative, Proposition 2 1/2, to see how such a dramatic change in tax policy occurred.

An instrumental part of this change is the indirect initiative process. In Massachusetts there are two categories of initiatives: for a law and for a constitutional amendment. Initiatives are circulated in September of the year preceding the election. If sufficient signatures are collected, the initiative is entered as a bill into the legislative session in January. An initiative for a law, such as Proposition 2 1/2, may be enacted without appearing on the ballot if the legislature approves it. If the legislature votes against the initiative, the sponsors must collect an additional 10,000 signatures to place the proposal on the ballot. The legislature may also propose an alternative measure to appear on the ballot.

An initiative for an amendment must be voted on by two successive legislatures (i.e., with an election in between). If it does not receive more than one-fourth of the vote each time it does not appear on the ballot. The legislature may amend a constitutional initiative with the approval of the sponsors, but not a statutory initiative. The purpose of this cumbersome process is to allow the legislature to respond through alternatives, amendments and vetoes to the issues raised by initiatives and to temper extreme proposals. This process and the distinctions between the types of initiatives provide a backdrop for the Proposition 2 1/2 story.

Proposition 2 1/2's title is derived from its property tax limits. The law prohibits property taxes from exceeding 2.5 percent of the "full and fair" cash value of the local tax base. A city or town with a property tax rate that exceeded this limit in 1980 is required to reduce its property tax levy by 15 percent a year until the limit is reached. If the tax rate was below the limit in 1980, the tax levy is reduced to its 1979 value. After a city or town reaches its appropriate property tax limit, the tax levy may increase by no more than 2.5 percent a year. There are no exceptions for population growth, inflation or additions to the tax base.

A complex measure, Proposition 2 1/2 also alters procedures to prepare local budgets. Cities and towns are now required to use full value assessment. Although the state court ordered all cities and towns to reassess property at 100 percent of value in 1974, less than one-third had complied by 1980. The authority of city councils and town meetings to determine local expenditures is diminished, as any change in the tax levy or rate must be approved by voters. School committees have lost fiscal autonomy: school budgets may now be changed by city councils or town meetings. Binding arbitration for policemen and firemen has been repealed. The state may no longer require cities and towns to establish programs or enforce regulations without reimbursement. Finally, no county or special district may increase its assessments against a city or town by more than 4 percent a year.

Why did Massachusetts voters approve Proposition 2 1/2? A conventional explanation of this and other "taxpayers' revolts" is that voters want lower property taxes and smaller local government. And this explanation is attractive. It is what the initiative is designed to do, is the philosophy of the Citizens for Limited Taxation (CLT) who sponsored it, and is consistent with the budget- and tax-cutting policies of the Reagan Administration.

But this reason overlooks two incongruities that suggest a rival explanation. First, Proposition 2 1/2 is unlike the more than 40 taxing and spending limits proposed afer Proposition 13. Most of those approved by voters apply to state taxes and spending, and limit the growth of future rather than existing taxes. In fact, only Idaho and California voters have approved initiatives to reduce property taxes. In both states, this outcome can be directly related to rapidly rising residential assessments – a problem that did not exist in Massachusetts. And only Proposition 2 1/2 proposed substantial changes in local budget procedures and state–county–local fiscal relationships.

Second, in several surveys conducted prior to the election, Massachusetts voters indicated that they were satisfied with local officials and services. Many expressed deep apprehension about local service cutbacks. Most did not believe local governments were wasteful or corrupt. The passage of Proposition 2 1/2 is inconsistent with these expressed attitudes.

What, then, explains the vote in favor of Proposition 2 1/2? Massachusetts voters were frustrated with high taxes and a recalcitrant legislature that refused to enact tax reform or tax relief. Cities and towns relied heavily on the property tax: it was virtually their only "own source" revenue. In 1980, property taxes were 70 percent above the national average. The state government relies on a flat-rate income tax and a sales tax that some say exempts more than it taxes. In 1980, Massachusetts ranked 42nd among the states in the balanced use of taxes. For decades, special commissions, taxpayers groups, business organizations, and individuals have suggested taxing and spending controls, increased state aid, a graduated income tax, reduced property taxes, new sources of local revenue, user fees and restrictions on state mandates as means to reform the state tax structure and provide property tax relief. None has been enacted. By 1980, Proposition 2 1/2 was viewed, by supporters and many opponents, as the only chance to obtain control over taxes and expenditures. Many hoped that a vote in favor of the harsh measures would send a message to the legislature for tax reform. An analysis of the legislative history of Proposition 2 1/2 supports this explanation and reveals some problems that emerge when the initiative process is used to set tax policy.

In June 1978, just three days after California voters approved Proposition 13, four Republican legislators introduced the first version of Proposition 2 1/2 into the Massachusetts legislature. As only one month remained in the session, they combined several small property tax reform bills that had been defeated in the past and added a 2.5 percent tax rate limit. From this time forward, the legislature had several formal and informal opportunities to propose an alternative to Proposition 2 1/2 that would provide property tax relief without threatening fiscal chaos.

Soon after they filed Proposition 2 1/2, the legislators began to work with the Citizens for Limited Taxation (CLT), a small taxpayers organization founded in 1973 by individuals who wanted to reduce state and local taxes. In 1976, CLT led the campaign against a graduated income tax proposal on the ballot; it was defeated by a three-to-one margin. In 1977, CLT sponsored an initiative amendment to limit state spending to the average ratio of state expenditures to personal income for the past three years. More than two times the required 56,000 signatures were collected to place the "King Amendment" (named after CLT's president) on the 1978 legislative agenda for its first vote in a constitutional convention.

After Proposition 13 passed, there was considerable public pressure to address tax limits before they adjourned. In late June it granted approval to the King Amendment and allowed the first Proposition 2 1/2 to die in committee. In this way the legislature voted for possible limits on spending in the future but did not have to address property taxes. It was a symbolic, politically useful vote on the heels of Proposition 13 that did little to abate dissatisfaction with property taxes and the state tax structure.

In August, CLT and four other groups filed initiatives that proposed property tax limits ranging from one percent to 2.5 percent. CLT's initiative was disqualified by the attorney general, and no other group collected enough signatures to place the issue on the ballot. A nonbinding advisory question, however, did appear. It directed the legislature to vote in favor of legislation to reduce property taxes, increase state aid, and limit state and local tax increases. More than three out of four voters indicated that they favored such legislation – an obvious cry for property tax relief and a signal to the legislature to provide it.

When the legislature convened in January 1979, several bills to limit or reduce state and local taxes were pending. Despite November's vote, only one was enacted: Governor Edward J. King's tax cap. It required cities and towns, for the next two fiscal years only, to limit property tax increases to 4 percent of the previous year's levy. The cap excluded school budgets and permitted local overrides. As a tax limit, it was a stopgap measure at best.

As the legislature had not enacted substantial reforms, nine initiatives to limit or reduce state and local taxes were filed in August. In addition to CLT, initiatives were proposed by the Associated Industries of Massachusetts (AIM) and the Massachusetts High Technology Council (MHTC), the Massachusetts Taxpayers Foundation (MTF), a bipartisan group of state legislators, a coalition of public employee unions and neighborhood organizations, the Massachusetts Teachers Association (MTA), and the Republican leadership in the legislature. The large number and diversity of groups resorting to the initiative process to establish tax limits indicate the extent of the dissatisfaction.

In the early fall, CLT collaborated with AIM and MHTC. The two business groups were concerned that high taxes were hurting the state's ability to attract businesses and employees. They had jointly filed two initiatives similar to those sponsored by CLT. CLT needed financial resources for the campaign and the business groups needed volunteers to collect signatures. Thus, CLT circulated two petitions: an AIM–MHTC constitutional amendment and their own Proposition 2 1/2. More than 60,000 signatures for Proposition 2 1/2 and 59,000 for AIM–MHTC amendment were collected – barely enough to qualify each for the ballot.

Of the other groups, only MTA collected enough signatures to place its initiative on the ballot. MTA proposed property tax limits for the next four years equal to the previous year's levy plus an increase proportional to the growth in statewide personal income. It was not, however, a strong alternative to Proposition 2 1/2. It was temporary, had several exclusions, would not reduce property taxes, and required legislative appropriations.

When the legislature convened in January 1980, the tax limit issue was incorporated into four initiatives which had to be voted on before adjournment. The CLT and MTA initiatives had to be approved or the sponsors would have to collect additional signatures. The legislature also had to cast its first vote on the AIM–MHTC constitutional amendment and its second on the King Amendment. In addition, several legislators filed bills to limit state or local taxes and spending. Among these was a proposal from the Committee for the Responsible Limit (CRL), a group organized by more than 20 bipartisan legislators and the MTF. CRL hoped to argue for a moderate compromise tax limit during the 1980 legislative session that would diffuse support for Proposition 2 1/2.

Throughout the first half of the session, the legislature vetoed tax limits but did not attempt to propose alternatives. In early April, the House vetoed both the CLT and MTA initiatives; both groups collected the signatures required to place the measures on the ballot. Soon after, the CRL proposal was rejected. And in May, the legislature voted against the King Amendment. Several other tax limit bills were left to die in committee.

The legislature seemed to sidestep the AIM-MHTC amendment. In May, the Committee on Taxation gave it an unfavorable recommendation. It was widely acknowledged, however, that at least one-fourth of the legislators would vote in favor, enough to bring it before the next legislature in 1981 or 1982. The legislature was scheduled to vote on the amendment on May 14; the vote was rescheduled to May 28, then to June 11, June 18, June 25 and July 2. On July 5, the legislature adjourned without taking a vote on the amendment.

Before the end of the session, the Committee on Taxation proposed a tax limit to reduce the ratio of state and local taxes to personal income over time until it equaled the average for 17 competing industrial states. Named after its sponsor, the Cohen Amendment was not intended primarily to reduce property taxes but to make the state more "competitive." Nonetheless, it had the potential to remove the support of the business community from Proposition 2 1/2. Although the bill was passed in late June, it was rescheduled for a second vote. The legislature adjourned without taking the vote and the bill died.

Despite its defeat of all tax limit proposals, the "tabling" of the AIM-MHTC amendment, and its early adjournment, the legislature had one final chance to address tax limits before the November election. After considerable public protest, Governor King called the legislature back into constitutional convention in September. Before taking a vote on the AIM-MHTC amendment, however, the legislature substituted the Cohen Amendment by voice vote. The revised amendment was overwhelmingly approved. This action had a significant effect on the Proposition 2 1/2 campaign. AIM and MHTC agreed to the substitution because they did not want to lose their initiative or the support of the legislature on other issues. But the legislators surmised incorrectly that the business community would no longer support Proposition 2 1/2. Although AIM took a neutral position, MHTC announced its full support and backed its position with a $250,000 contribution to CLT -- a contribution crucial to the win in November.

There are several possible explanations as to why the Massachusetts legislature did not enact or propose moderate tax reforms as alternatives to Proposition 2 1/2. It is difficult to build a constituency for tax reform since reduced property taxes combined with higher sales and income taxes distribute costs and benefits of reform too thinly. An alternative on the ballot that did not explicitly offer large tax cuts like Proposition 2 1/2 might have angered voters. A second view is that voters no longer trusted the legislature to reform the tax system. After fiascos with the sales tax, the lottery and state aid -- all intended to reduce the property taxes -- many people feared that new taxes meant only higher total taxes, not lower property taxes. The Democratic leadership is also responsible for the stalemate as it refused to propose alternatives. Finally, there was resentment that voters might usurp the legislature's authority to set tax policy. If voters wanted to approve a fiscal nightmare, the reasoning went, they could live with the consequences.

On election day, voters were asked to choose between Proposition 2 1/2 and the status quo. Several opinion polls showed that voters supported the initiative because they felt property taxes were too high, not because they wanted smaller government or fewer services. More importantly, when given a choice, a majority preferred a more moderate alternative that restricted the growth of property taxes or slightly lowered them. But this alternative was not on the ballot, and in the three years prior to the election the legislature demonstrated that it would not enact such legislation. In the end, it is likely that the known benefits of a tax cut outweighed apprehensions about unknown future service cuts. Property taxes were unacceptably high; Proposition 2 1/2 gave voters the authority to lower them.

Proposition 2 1/2 also underscores a problem inherent in the initiative process. Tax cuts and tax reform are complex, multi-sided issues. They are properly accomodated through the legislative process where negotiation, compromise, vetoes and stalemates allow representation of minority interests. When proposed as an initiative, the question of designing and using tax limits is boiled down to a simple yes or no vote. In the case of Proposition 2 1/2, voters could not choose whether they wanted to reduce property taxes or merely limit their growth, whether they wanted limits on state taxes, or whether they were willing to authorize new sources of local revenue. Opponents could only campaign against the issue, they could not incorporate their concerns into law. Yet, ironically, CLT resorted to the initiative process because the legislative process -- the appropriate arena -- had failed to address voters' concerns about taxes satisfactorily. And it is the citizens who lose from this stalemate. They must now live with a conservative tax limit law that has the potential to drive cities and towns into fiscal crises, but without the law there may have been no relief from uncomfortably high property taxes.

Since the passage of Proposition 2 1/2, neither its costs nor its benefits have been as great as predicted. There are three principal reasons for this. First, although the initiative was passed in November 1980, it did not take effect until the beginning of the 1982 fiscal year, July 1981. Thus, the initiative has only been in effect a short time. Second, there was one uncontrolled variable in the tax limit: the value of the tax base in the year it was implemented. Cities and towns are now required to use full value property assessments. Most have reassessed property since the passage of Proposition 2 1/2 to ensure that they garnered the largest possible tax levy in the base year. Tax bases were traditionally undervalued, so the magnitude of the first-year cuts was reduced. Third, in the first year of 15 percent cutbacks, it was possible for many cities and towns to employ belt-tightening strategies without laying off employees. For example, reduced maintenance budgets, new user fees, unfilled vacant positions and frozen salaries allowed tough decisions about layoffs and program cutbacks to be deferred.

In addition, Proposition 2 1/2 has not significantly affected the policies of the state legislature or the governor. When local officials first approached the state house for fiscal aid in January 1981, they were accused of "saber rattling" with their predictions of budget cutbacks. The legislature begrudgingly passed an increased state aid bill for the next fiscal year only. The formula selected to allocate the state aid is not based on Proposition 2 1/2 revenue losses, but follows the formula used to allocate state lottery revenues. Thus, some cities and towns receive state aid several times their revenue losses, while others receive only a fraction. At this time, therefore, if is difficult to predict just how Proposition 2 1/2 will change the Massachusetts fiscal structure.

The major provisions of Proposition 2 1/2 are outlined in Table 1.1.

**Table 1.1**
**The Major Provisions of Proposition 2 1/2**

---

Limits the amount communities may tax to no more than 2.5 percent of the total fair cash value of all property.

Requires communities exceeding that limit to "roll back" the tax levy 15 percent a year until they meet the limit.

Limits increases in the property tax levy to 2.5 percent a year.

Limits motor vehicle excise taxes to $25 per thousand dollars of valuation.

Allows renters to itemize one-half of annual rent as a state income tax deduction.

Repeals school committee fiscal autonomy and compulsory and binding arbitration for public employees.

Prohibits unfunded state mandates.

Provides for local override of the levy limit by 2/3 of the voters in biennial general elections.

Limits outside agency assessments to the community to no more than 4 percent a year.

---

## Notes for Chapter 1

Reprinted with permission from the *National Civic Review,* November 1981.

Chapter 2

# Proposition 2 1/2 Amended: What Communities Can and Cannot Do

Alan Tosti

The passage of the Proposition 2 1/2 amendment package was intended to help end some of the problems municipalities faced in determining their FY83 appropriations. (The amendments to Proposition 2 1/2 are presented at the end of this chapter). Unfortunately, while some problems were solved new ones were created.

## Absolute Maximum Limit

The amendments set an absolute maximum levy limit of 2 1/2 percent of total property value. Even a successful override could not permit growth above that limit. Because of this, the maintenance of accurate, up-to-date values became more important than ever. The higher the full and fair cash value, the higher the maximum limit.

## Full and Fair Cash Valuation

Municipalities were supposed to determine their full and fair cash valuation as of January 1, 1982. Municipalities completing revaluation were told that they could use their new values as soon as they were ready. Most communities used a conservative updating of their 1980 state equalized values as recommended by the Department of Revenue (DOR).

Those municipalities with values certified by January 1, 1980 or 1981 were allowed to submit their updated values. Municipalities must update their assessments every two years. If a municipality is substantially under its maximum levy limit, this should be sufficient. But, if it is at, or very close to, the maximum limit ($25.00 per $1,000) it might be necessary to recertify its assessments to take advantage of property value growth.

## Percentage Limit

The percentage limit was set at either 2 1/2 or that percent which was in effect in either FY79 or FY81. Under no circumstances could it be greater than 2 1/2. Once a municipality had determined the appropriate percent, it could forget about 1979 or 1981. If the 1981 percent was chosen, the municipality was required get town meeting or city council approval. If the municipality chose the 1979 percent no action was required.

## Maximum Levy Limit

The maximum levy limit was obtained by multiplying the appropriate percentage by full and fair cash valuation. If the FY82 levy was above the limit, the municipality was required to reduce its FY82 levy by at least 15 percent or that lesser percentage necessary to reach its levy limit. This reduction could be reduced according to the override provisions.

If the FY82 levy was below this limit, municipalities were allowed to increase the FY82 levy by 2 1/2 percent or by that amount which would increase the levy to the limit. This could be increased (but not above the maximum limit) by other provisions of the law.

If the FY82 levy were at the limit, and property values were fully updated, the only possible opportunity to increase the levy was the vote on exempting debt and interest. But this was available only if the debt service were level or increasing.

## New Growth Allowed

The legislation allowed for additional taxes in municipalities below their maximum limit from new construction or substantial renovation which was being taxed for the first time. This new construction multiplied by the FY82 tax rate was permitted to be added to the FY83 levy limit (FY82 levy multiplied by 1.025) as long as the total did not exceed the maximum limit (full and fair cash value multiplied by 2 1/2 percent). New construction was a benefit to municipalities above their limits by increasing their full and fair cash value which thus reduced the amount they had to cut.

Once municipalities determined their levy limits, the next step was to determine all other sources of revenue. Many municipalities used their recapitulation sheets and worked backwards.

## Regional School Assessments

Chapter 744 is the state law which requires the regional school budget to be approved by two-thirds of the regional school committee and two-thirds of the local appropriating authorities. This required coordination among member communities to insure a thorough local review of the regional budget.

## Appropriations

Once these facts were known, the remainder was what was available for appropriation for operating budgets and warrant articles. The distribution between various departments can be a somewhat controversial process. To avoid controversy, many municipalities divided the revenue according to that department's share of the budget in the previous year. This was reasonable if all services have equal priority and if the demand for services is constant. These questions should be examined closely. Has school enrollment held steady? What has happened to the number of police and fire calls? Departments should be required to consider real needs, even before Proposition 2 1/2 cuts are taken into consideration.

## Override Timetable

An override means a return to the property tax. This was designed as a safety valve or a last resort, used only if state aid was not enough to preserve services demanded by the people. However, waiting for definite state aid figures meant postponing overrides until late in the fiscal year.

Whether to go to the override before or after the local appropriating authority acted was another debatable point. Many simply presented override questions at their regular election, saving the cost of a special election. If the override were before the appropriation process, the people were setting parameters for town meeting or council action; if it were held afterwards, the people were then being asked to approve the actions of the appropriating authority. This allowed for an exact amount to be put before the people, but required cutting budgets if the people rejected the override. One alternative was to set up certain appropriations that were voted contingent upon approval of the override.

The overrides themselves were modified to be more flexible than those of the original version of 2 1/2. They are also more complicated. The DOR guidelines specified suggested steps for these calculations.

## Override - Debt Service

The exemption of past debt service was particularly confusing and controversial. The interpretation of the amendments to Proposition 2 1/2 made the exemption less helpful than initially expected. In fact, municipalities below their 2 1/2 limit which exempted past debt service could have ended up with less revenue than if they had not asked for the override. The reason for this is that the instructions for calculating the exemption of debt service required a community to deduct the amount of debt service costs from the overall levy before applying the 2 1/2 percent increase to the remaining amount. This clearly acted to reduce the amount of allowable levy. In addition, other complicating questions have been raised which might further reduce the usefulness of the debt service exemption. This override needed to be studied very carefully. Communities were urged to explore fully the various ramifications of each option, the schedule of budget approval and the local financial picture before making a decision on overrides.

## Amendments to Proposition 2 1/2, December 1980

The December 1980 amendments to Proposition 2 1/2 are presented in the following section.

*Override*

With a 2/3 vote, Selectmen or City Councils can place the override question on the local ballot at a general or special election. (Originally, only the state legislature could do this for November general elections.) Initially, a 2/3 vote was required on the referendum to allow any upward revision of the tax limit. The new chapter includes certain overrides which may be determined by a simple majority and others which still require two-thirds.

*A simple majority* is needed if a community required to cut its levy 15 percent wants to reduce that cut to 7.5 percent; or if a community allowed to increase its levy by 2.5 percent wants to double that increase to 5 percent.

*A two-thirds vote* is required when a community which must cut its levy wants to reduce that cut to 0 (the vote applies to one year only); or when a community wants to allow more than 5 percent growth (although the total levy may never exceed 2.5 percent of full and fair valuation).

*The Base*

Communities may use either FY81 or FY79 levy percentages as the base for calculating their limit. (Initially, those below 2.5 percent in FY81 had to use their FY79 levies as the cap.)

*Economic Growth*

Communities may now expand levies in proportion to growth in the tax base brought about by new construction or substantial renovations -- but not simply from revaluation. (Substantial renovation is defined as a 50 percent increase in valuation.) Originally, the levy could grow only by 2.5 percent a year, regardless of any expansion in the tax base.

*Debt Exclusion*

A community may vote by a simple majority vote to exclude from its levy cap either pre-2 1/2 debt and interest or new debt and interest. (No exclusion was allowed initially.)

*Assessments*

The original cap of 4 percent growth on state, district, and regional assessments to municipalities is dropped to 2.5 percent, with the exception of optional services. (Regional schools, however, are not included in this amendment.)

*Fiscal Autonomy*

Although Proposition 2 1/2 removes the traditional fiscal autonomy of school committees, an amendment specifies that the committees retain line-item autonomy within the school appropriation.

*State Mandates*

An amendment limits the original prohibition against state laws imposing local costs to those adopted after January 1, 1981. It also limits prohibitions against state laws expanding property tax exemptions and state rules and regulations which impose local costs. A city or town may, however, adopt a state law or regulation even if it is not state funded.

*Bonding*

The state treasurer is authorized to pay amounts owed to bondholders in the event a municipality is unable to meet its obligation. (The amounts would be advanced against state aid.) A provision of savings bank law prohibiting investments in municipal bonds when there is an expenditure limit in place has been eliminated.

*Rental Deduction*

The rental deduction allowed on state income tax forms is limited to $2,500 for tax years 1982 and beyond and any deduction applies only to residences in Massachusetts.

*Other Provisions*

The Commissioner of Revenue is authorized to correct errors in the calculation of a community's tax rate and make appropriate adjustments. The State Auditor replaces a gubernatorial appointee on the Emergency Finance Board. Statutes regarding recision of locally accepted laws are revised.

Table 2.1 contains the FY82 municipal revenue losses mandated by Proposition 2 1/2.

## Table 2.1
## Municipal Revenue Losses Mandated by Proposition 2 1/2

| Municipality | 1980 Population | FY82 2 1/2 Revenue Loss | Municipality | 1980 Population | FY82 2 1/2 Revenue Loss |
|---|---|---|---|---|---|
| Abington | 13,517 | 1,231,433 | Bourne | 13,874 | 220,807 |
| Acton | 17,544 | 340,156 | Boxborough | 3,126 | 69,472 |
| Acushnet | 8,704 | 122,827 | Boxford | 5,374 | 128,714 |
| Adams | 10,381 | 138,121 | Boylston | 3,470 | 81,257 |
| Agawam | 26,271 | 965,386 | Braintree | 36,337 | 5,092,780 |
| Alford | 394 | 34,201 | Brewster | 5,226 | 63,759 |
| Amesbury | 13,971 | 1,220,966 | Bridgewater | 17,202 | 1,420,476 |
| Amherst | 33,229 | 820,105 | Brimfield | 2,318 | 37,530 |
| Andover | 26,370 | 460,806 | Brockton | 95,172 | 10,074,602 |
| Arlington | 48,219 | 6,019,822 | Brookfield | 2,397 | 218,827 |
| Ashburnham | 4,075 | 326,104 | Brookline | 55,072 | 8,376,611 |
| Ashby | 2,311 | 228,473 | Buckland | 1,864 | 18,377 |
| Ashfield | 1,458 | 68,805 | Burlington | 23,486 | 3,813,412 |
| Ashland | 9,165 | 854,544 | Cambridge | 95,322 | 13,483,855 |
| Athol | 10,634 | 622,655 | Canton | 18,182 | 2,529,687 |
| Attleboro | 34,196 | 3,492,858 | Carlisle | 3,306 | 59,512 |
| Auburn | 14,845 | 831,899 | Carver | 6,988 | 249,128 |
| Avon | 5,026 | 118,066 | Charlemont | 1,149 | 51,600 |
| Ayer | 6,993 | 254,883 | Charlton | 6,719 | 118,517 |
| Barnstable | 30,898 | 533,452 | Chatham | 6,071 | 109,928 |
| Barre | 4,102 | 86,165 | Chelmsford | 31,174 | 2,672,301 |
| Becket | 1,339 | 168,965 | Chelsea | 25,431 | 2,591,359 |
| Bedford | 13,067 | 169,434 | Cheshire | 3,124 | 204,393 |
| Belchertown | 8,339 | 138,892 | Chester | 1,123 | 24,982 |
| Bellingham | 14,300 | 779,722 | Chesterfield | 1,000 | 9,651 |
| Belmont | 26,100 | 261,142 | Chicopee | 55,112 | 4,482,843 |
| Berkley | 2,731 | 38,446 | Chilmark | 489 | 8,404 |
| Berlin | 2,215 | 157,875 | Clarksburg | 1,871 | 129,069 |
| Bernardston | 1,750 | 28,130 | Clinton | 12,771 | 1,072,856 |
| Beverly | 37,655 | 4,138,679 | Cohasset | 7,174 | 139,991 |
| Billerica | 36,727 | 4,100,698 | Colrain | 1,552 | 23,422 |
| Blackstone | 6,570 | 416,559 | Concord | 16,293 | 1,110,864 |
| Blandford | 1,038 | 68,730 | Conway | 1,213 | 19,490 |
| Bolton | 2,530 | 56,408 | Cummington | 657 | 8,288 |
| Boston | 562,994 | 88,017,787 | Dalton | 6,797 | 682,603 |

| Munici-pality | 1980 Popu-lation | FY82 2 1/2 Revenue Loss | Munici-pality | 1980 Popu-lation | FY82 2 1/2 Revenue Loss |
|---|---|---|---|---|---|
| Danvers | 24,100 | 405,434 | Granby | 5,380 | 101,838 |
| Dartmouth | 23,966 | 358,149 | Granville | 1,204 | 19,591 |
| Dedham | 25,298 | 2,306,259 | Gt Barrington | 7,405 | 71,649 |
| Deerfield | 4,517 | 105,767 | Greenfield | 18,436 | 1,954,574 |
| Dennis | 12,360 | 266,575 | Groton | 6,154 | 112,256 |
| Dighton | 5,352 | 64,236 | Groveland | 5,040 | 243,535 |
| Douglas | 3,730 | 307,377 | Hadley | 4,125 | 82,754 |
| Dover | 4,703 | 119,104 | Halifax | 5,513 | 400,307 |
| Dracut | 21,249 | 812,830 | Hamilton | 6,960 | 106,192 |
| Dudley | 8,717 | 168,253 | Hampden | 4,745 | 288,856 |
| Dunstable | 1,671 | 36,951 | Hancock | 643 | 19,740 |
| Duxbury | 11,807 | 1,812,835 | Hanover | 11,358 | 1,347,671 |
| E. Bridgewater | 9,945 | 997,780 | Hanson | 8,617 | 911,204 |
| E. Brookfield | 1,955 | 59,256 | Hardwick | 2,272 | 76,443 |
| E. Longmeadow | 12,905 | 227,697 | Harvard | 12,170 | 108,670 |
| Eastham | 3,472 | 34,605 | Harwich | 8,971 | 103,552 |
| Easthampton | 15,580 | 760,861 | Hatfield | 3,045 | 262,200 |
| Easton | 16,623 | 1,794,807 | Haverhill | 46,865 | 3,941,650 |
| Edgartown | 2,204 | 30,413 | Hawley | 280 | 22,930 |
| Egremont | 1,311 | 20,421 | Heath | 482 | 3,247 |
| Erving | 1,326 | 94,027 | Hingham | 20,339 | 1,718,711 |
| Essex | 2,998 | 53,177 | Hinsdale | 1,707 | 21,131 |
| Everett | 37,195 | 5,304,872 | Holbrook | 11,140 | 1,253,311 |
| Fairhaven | 15,759 | 706,442 | Holden | 13,336 | 303,181 |
| Fall River | 92,574 | 5,894,567 | Holland | 1,589 | 17,920 |
| Falmouth | 23,640 | 363,965 | Holliston | 12,622 | 1,593,056 |
| Fitchburg | 39,580 | 3,629,522 | Holyoke | 44,678 | 3,204,240 |
| Florida | 780 | 1,452 | Hopedale | 3,905 | 364,690 |
| Foxborough | 14,148 | 995,175 | Hopkinton | 7,114 | 152,894 |
| Framingham | 65,113 | 7,220,457 | Hubbardston | 1,797 | 34,536 |
| Franklin | 18,217 | 1,972,519 | Hudson | 16,408 | 1,802,595 |
| Freetown | 7,058 | 202,141 | Hull | 9,714 | 1,352,307 |
| Gardner | 17,900 | 836,789 | Huntington | 1,804 | 33,210 |
| Gay Head | 220 | 61,070 | Ipswich | 11,158 | 192,301 |
| Georgetown | 5,687 | 101,859 | Kingston | 7,362 | 491,168 |
| Gill | 1,259 | 13,615 | Lakeville | 5,931 | 89,828 |
| Gloucester | 27,768 | 918,120 | Lancaster | 6,334 | 96,533 |
| Goshen | 651 | 8,037 | Lanesborough | 3,131 | 320,553 |
| Gosnold | 63 | (2,052) | Lawrence | 63,175 | 4,398,876 |
| Grafton | 11,238 | 254,192 | Lee | 6,247 | 616,968 |

| Munici-pality | 1980 Popu-lation | FY82 2 1/2 Revenue Loss | Munici-pality | 1980 Popu-lation | FY82 2 1/2 Revenue Loss |
|---|---|---|---|---|---|
| Leicester | 9,446 | 168,622 | Monson | 7,315 | 351,851 |
| Lenox | 6,523 | 511,688 | Montague | 8,011 | 490,220 |
| Leominster | 34,508 | 2,370,233 | Monterey | 818 | 25,756 |
| Leverett | 1,471 | 15,511 | Montgomery | 637 | 12,105 |
| Lexington | 29,479 | 496,222 | Mt Washington | 93 | 1,205 |
| Leyden | 498 | 4,721 | Nahant | 3,947 | 68,310 |
| Lincoln | 7,098 | 101,116 | Nantucket | 5,087 | 58,503 |
| Littleton | 6,970 | 132,162 | Natick | 29,461 | 3,126,666 |
| Longmeadow | 16,301 | 367,717 | Needham | 27,901 | 631,112 |
| Lowell | 92,418 | 6,256,392 | New Ashford | 159 | 9,589 |
| Ludlow | 18,150 | 779,525 | New Bedford | 98,478 | 6,734,519 |
| Lunenberg | 8,405 | 908,852 | New Braintree | 671 | 8,954 |
| Lynn | 78,471 | 9,344,867 | New Marlborough | 1,160 | 24,204 |
| Lynnfield | 11,267 | 288,570 | New Salem | 688 | 11,712 |
| Malden | 53,386 | 5,245,983 | Newbury | 4,529 | 79,439 |
| Manchester | 5,424 | 73,944 | Newburyport | 15,900 | 1,673,560 |
| Mansfield | 13,453 | 187,838 | Newton | 83,622 | 13,635,435 |
| Marblehead | 20,126 | 375,814 | Norfolk | 6,363 | 89,397 |
| Marion | 3,932 | 67,544 | N.Adams | 18,063 | 199,406 |
| Marlborough | 30,617 | 2,769,626 | N.Andover | 20,129 | 385,654 |
| Marshfield | 20,916 | 2,216,328 | N.Attleborough | 21,095 | 1,837,007 |
| Mashpee | 3,700 | 34,467 | N.Brookfield | 10,568 | 90,721 |
| Mattapoisett | 5,597 | 85,826 | N.Reading | 11,455 | 261,087 |
| Maynard | 9,590 | 1,295,108 | Northampton | 29,286 | 2,385,273 |
| Medfield | 10,220 | 325,885 | Northborough | 12,246 | 221,681 |
| Medford | 58,076 | 6,414,184 | Northbridge | 4,150 | 180,094 |
| Medway | 8,447 | 1,053,113 | Northfield | 2,386 | 38,091 |
| Melrose | 30,055 | 3,334,957 | Norton | 12,690 | 1,233,324 |
| Mendon | 3,108 | 57,234 | Norwell | 9,182 | 1,360,481 |
| Merrimac | 4,451 | 244,034 | Norwood | 29,711 | 574,765 |
| Methuen | 36,701 | 1,060,793 | Oak Bluffs | 1,984 | 7,042 |
| Middleborough | 16,404 | 496,846 | Oakham | 994 | 19,415 |
| Middlefield | 385 | 4,704 | Orange | 6,844 | 455,210 |
| Middleton | 4,135 | 257,021 | Orleans | 5,306 | 81,267 |
| Milford | 23,390 | 2,305,287 | Otis | 963 | 14,016 |
| Millbury | 11,808 | 1,005,422 | Oxford | 11,680 | 951,045 |
| Millis | 6,908 | 594,753 | Palmer | 11,389 | 398,667 |
| Millville | 1,693 | 110,522 | Paxton | 3,762 | 90,771 |
| Milton | 25,860 | 3,294,947 | Peabody | 45,976 | 5,414,068 |
| Monroe | 179 | 1,445 | Pelham | 1,112 | 21,055 |

| Munici-pality | 1980 Popu-lation | FY82 2 1/2 Revenue Loss | Munici-pality | 1980 Popu-lation | FY82 2 1/2 Revenue Loss |
|---|---|---|---|---|---|
| Pembroke | 13,487 | 1,490,562 | Shrewsbury | 22,674 | 527,076 |
| Pepperell | 8,061 | 240,797 | Shutesbury | 1,049 | 13,190 |
| Peru | 633 | 61,702 | Somerset | 18,813 | 86,865 |
| Petersham | 1,024 | 32,029 | Somerville | 77,372 | 7,116,526 |
| Phillipston | 953 | 57,487 | S. Hadley | 4,137 | 986,336 |
| Pittsfield | 51,974 | 5,700,744 | Southampton | 16,339 | 75,124 |
| Plainsfield | 425 | 35,993 | Southborough | 6,193 | 152,063 |
| Plainsville | 5,857 | 128,646 | Southbridge | 16,665 | 250,770 |
| Plymouth | 35,913 | 733,813 | Southwick | 7,382 | 117,502 |
| Plympton | 1,974 | 24,717 | Spencer | 10,774 | 197,856 |
| Princeton | 2,425 | 56,097 | Springfield | 152,319 | 12,582,819 |
| Provincetown | 3,536 | 108,723 | Sterling | 5,440 | 103,957 |
| Quincy | 84,743 | 11,932,706 | Stockbridge | 2,328 | 32,983 |
| Randolph | 28,218 | 3,182,707 | Stoneham | 21,424 | 2,512,831 |
| Raynham | 9,085 | 385,467 | Stoughton | 26,710 | 2,158,958 |
| Reading | 22,678 | 1,436,787 | Stow | 5,144 | 105,031 |
| Rehoboth | 6,570 | 120,630 | Sturbridge | 5,976 | 96,433 |
| Revere | 42,423 | 4,944,817 | Sudbury | 14,027 | 630,280 |
| Richmond | 1,659 | 26,265 | Sunderland | 2,929 | 54,979 |
| Rochester | 3,205 | 40,310 | Sutton | 5,855 | 111,363 |
| Rockland | 15,695 | 1,400,688 | Swampscott | 13,837 | 1,492,978 |
| Rockport | 6,345 | 83,331 | Swansea | 15,461 | 189,606 |
| Rowe | 336 | (12,146) | Taunton | 45,001 | 3,248,933 |
| Rowley | 3,867 | 84,897 | Templeton | 6,070 | 310,177 |
| Royalston | 955 | 15,429 | Tewksbury | 24,635 | 2,633,195 |
| Russell | 1,570 | 30,141 | Tisbury | 2,972 | 54,855 |
| Rutland | 4,334 | 86,605 | Tolland | 235 | 5,987 |
| Salem | 38,220 | 4,623,826 | Topsfield | 5,709 | 144,005 |
| Salisbury | 5,973 | 90,931 | Townsend | 7,201 | 253,082 |
| Sandisfield | 720 | 5,788 | Truro | 1,486 | 22,066 |
| Sandwich | 8,727 | 670,907 | Tyngsborough | 5,683 | 97,895 |
| Saugus | 24,746 | 2,313,936 | Tyringham | 344 | 6,018 |
| Savoy | 644 | 6,232 | Upton | 3,886 | 327,588 |
| Scituate | 17,317 | 2,370,838 | Uxbridge | 8,374 | 201,688 |
| Seekonk | 12,269 | 196,161 | Wakefield | 24,895 | 3,082,340 |
| Sharon | 13,601 | 1,623,231 | Wales | 1,177 | 106,801 |
| Sheffield | 2,743 | 56,499 | Walpole | 18,859 | 1,144,443 |
| Shelburne | 2,002 | 91,830 | Waltham | 58,200 | 6,933,518 |
| Sherborn | 4,049 | 72,563 | Ware | 8,953 | 232,006 |
| Shirley | 5,124 | 275,519 | Wareham | 18,457 | 1,116,798 |

| Municipality | 1980 Population | FY82 2 1/2 Revenue Loss | Municipality | 1980 Population | FY82 2 1/2 Revenue Loss |
|---|---|---|---|---|---|
| Warren | 3,777 | 288,157 | Westhampton | 1,137 | 20,857 |
| Warwick | 603 | 61,207 | Westminster | 5,139 | 119,439 |
| Washington | 587 | 49,014 | Weston | 11,169 | 283,515 |
| Watertown | 34,384 | 4,484,985 | Westport | 13,763 | 188,038 |
| Wayland | 12,170 | 198,154 | Westwood | 13,212 | 1,063,208 |
| | | | | | |
| Webster | 14,480 | 255,274 | Weymouth | 55,601 | 5,880,823 |
| Wellesley | 27,209 | 436,567 | Whately | 1,341 | 20,923 |
| Wellfleet | 2,209 | 168,888 | Whitman | 13,534 | 1,387,585 |
| Wendell | 694 | 7,609 | Wilbraham | 12,053 | 1,114,017 |
| Wenham | 3,897 | 63,447 | Williamsburg | 2,237 | 123,095 |
| | | | | | |
| W.Boylston | 6,204 | 251,440 | Williamstown | 8,741 | 98,803 |
| W.Bridgewater | 6,359 | 760,085 | Wilmington | 17,471 | 2,441,743 |
| W.Brookfield | 3,026 | 149,409 | Winchendon | 7,019 | 127,456 |
| W.Newbury | 2,861 | 131,264 | Winchester | 20,701 | 1,511,238 |
| W.Springfield | 36,465 | 1,057,978 | Windsor | 598 | 12,580 |
| | | | | | |
| W.Stockbridge | 1,280 | 28,763 | Winthrop | 19,294 | 1,569,233 |
| W.Tisbury | 1,010 | 19,322 | Woburn | 36,626 | 4,128,474 |
| Westborough | 13,619 | 313,522 | Worcester | 161,799 | 6,318,309 |
| Westfield | 27,042 | 2,692,288 | Worthington | 932 | 85,715 |
| Westford | 13,434 | 943,379 | Wrentham | 7,580 | 384,236 |
| | | | Yarmouth | 18,449 | 371,361 |

**Part Two**

**Pre-Proposition 2 1/2 Trends**

# Chapter 3

# Introduction to Trend Analysis

## Impact: 2 1/2 Staff

## Introduction

The Impact: 2 1/2 Project staff examined fiscal and public employment trends in Massachusetts during the five year period immediately preceding the passage of Proposition 2 1/2. The results of this analysis provide a backdrop against which to analyze its first year impacts.

The analysis is based on findings from a carefully selected sample of sixty-one representative municipalities. (1) These cities and towns are representative along a variety of dimensions, making it possible to examine how particular municipal attributes are associated wih local fiscal variables.

This introduction describes the selection of the sample, the sources of data, and some of the problems inherent in the analysis. It also discusses the relationships among municipal attributes and their implications, the major findings, and and the implications of these findings.

## Selection of the Sample

The staff selected communities to monitor by grouping the 256 largest cities and towns in Massachusetts according to five characteristics, or attributes. Because the U.S. Census Bureau did not publish data in the 1970 Census of Population for communities with a population of less than 2,000, these smaller communities were initially ignored. (Four communities from this low population category were later added).

The five attributes used were 1980 population, 1970 average income, the first year (1982) percentage reduction in property tax revenue mandated by

Proposition 2 1/2, and the percentage change in the population from 1970 to 1980. Each of these attributes was subdivided into high, medium, and low levels after considering the actual distribution of cities and towns within each category. (2) In addition to sorting communities according to the five attributes geographic location was also taken into account. Tables 3.1–3.8 describe the sample in detail. (Tables 3.2–3.8 are located at the end of the chapter). Within these groups, 61 municipalities were chosen as representative of the Commonwealth's cities and towns.

**Table 3.1**
**Distribution of Sample by Attribute Groups**
(Number of Communities in Each Group in Parentheses)

| Attribute | Low Group | Middle Group | High Group | Average* |
|---|---|---|---|---|
| 1982 Revenue Gap** | -15% | -15-0% | 0-2.5% | -8.2% |
| | (13) | (31) | (17) | (256) |
| % Residential | <60% | 60-81% | >81% | 71% |
| Property | (14) | (27) | (20) | (256) |
| % Population | < 0% | 0-15% | >15% | 9.97% |
| Change, 1970-80 | (23) | (23) | (15) | (256) |
| | <6,800 | 6,800-27,000 | >27,000 | 22,204 |
| 1980 Population | (16) | (29) | (16) | (256) |
| 1970 Average Per- | <$9,400 | $9,400-12,000 | >$12,000 | $10,874 |
| sonal Income | (14) | (27) | (20) | (256) |

*This column reports the average of the attributes of the 256 Massachusetts communities surveyed in the 1970 Census.
**This is defined as:(1982 tax levy - 1981 tax levy)/1981 tax levy. A negative value indicates a required decrease in property tax revenues in 1982 relative to 1981, a positive value indicates that no such decrease was required, and that a municipality was able to increase its tax levy in 1982. The maximum negative value in the first year is 15 percent, while the maximum positive value is 2.5%.

## Data Sources

The data used come primarily from the U.S. Bureau of the Census. The 1977 data are from the 1977 Census of Governments, while data for the other four years are from the Census Bureau's Annual Survey of Governments. Some of the data in the fiscal stability report were provided by the Massachusetts Department of Revenue and the Massachusetts Taxpayers Foundation. Although the data are basically complete for the primary sample of 61 Massachusetts cities and towns, there are a few missing values. Every effort was made to fill in missing data, but it was not always possible.

Most of the attribute data come from the Census Bureau. Average 1970 personal income, 1970 population, and percentage of residential property are reported in the 1970 Census of Population. The 1980 population data are reported in the 1980 Census of Population. The Proposition 2 1/2 first year revenue gap was calculated from data obtained from the Massachusetts Department of Revenue.

## Data Reporting Issues

Massachusetts communities are quite diverse. They vary in size, density, wealth, land use, industrial mix, and in other ways. By design, the 61 sample communities reflect this diversity.

Along some standard dimensions -- population, average income, reported percentage of residential property, population growth rate, and presumed impact of Proposition 2 1/2 -- the sample is representative of Massachusetts communities. Along other dimensions it may not be. Unfortunately, there is no selection of communities perfectly representative along every dimension simultaneously.

The diversity of cities and towns extends to how they organize themselves, how various tasks are allocated, and whether some tasks are performed at all. For each major expenditure, revenue, or employment category, the sample communities divide into two groups -- those that participate in that category, and those that do not. This variation is reflected in the analysis by the mean and median values for all municipalities (ignoring the two group issue); the number of communities with zero values (i.e., those that do not participate in this category); the number of communities with nonzero values; and the mean and median values for the latter group. The discussion in the following chapters focuses on the means of the nonzero group. The full range of statistics is presented in sets of tables that are available from the IMPACT: 2 1/2 Project.

Problems also arise in examining the magnitude of changes from one year to another. This is a major problem in certain cases. For example, among the smaller communities, there are many employment categories with less than three or four people in them. A change from one year to the next, due to retirement, a vacancy, or the addition of an extra person (permanent or temporary), can make an enormous percentage difference, even an infinite one if the initial figure was zero. In examining certain figures, it is therefore probably best to ignore percentage changes for some of the smaller communities and categories even though we have reported them.

In certain cases, extremely high or low values exert a strong upward or downward influence on the mean. Some groups of communities are relatively small, but because there was no basis on which to assume that the data were distributed normally, or even symmetrically, extreme values were not removed before calculating the mean. Again, because the data were not symmetrical, it was not possible to report a measure of the symmetric spread (a standard deviation or the equivalent) that could convey much information.

Finally, the percentage change figure reported is not the percentage change between the means, but rather, the average percentage change. Thus, it is possible to have a small positive mean change between two years and a small negative average percentage change. One very extreme positive change value or one very extreme negative percentage change value would, for example, cause this situation to occur. In summary, the reader should assume that the reported values are overly sensitive to some changes and less sensitive to others. Two reported values should not be considered different unless the differences are large.

In order to deal with the three problems discussed above, the staff developed a set of rules for eliminating meaningless statistics or statistics that were open to substantial misinterpretation. Throughout the chapters in this section of the book such values have been replaced with an asterisk (*). An asterisk means that one of the three data problems mentioned above has arisen in the calculation of that statistic.

## Relationships Among the Attributes

The degree of correlation among the attributes (e.g., Do big cities tend to have low incomes?) is an important consideration in interpreting the results. Table 3.4 presents a correlation matrix for the five attributes used to cluster communities.

Although there is significant correlation among the attributes many are not terribly strong, and some are very weak. Nevertheless, all of the major relationships move in the expected direction: high population communities tend to have higher 2 1/2 revenue gaps, lower incomes, less residential property in the tax base, and declining populations. The strongest overall relationships are a positive one between average income and 2 1/2 revenue gap, a negative one between population and 2 1/2 revenue gap (i.e., higher population is associated with higher revenue losses), and a negative one between population and income.

Smaller communities are more likely to be wealthy and growing, and less likely to have been severely hit by Proposition 2 1/2. Larger communities, on the other hand, are more likely to have lower average incomes, higher losses due to Proposition 2 1/2, and declining populations. Again, these relationships are not very strong. There are clearly many exceptions to these general rules. For example, there are many small communities in the Commonwealth with low average incomes and a great deal of agricultural property in their tax bases (and hence less residential property). It is important to keep this in mind when interpreting some of the generalizations made in this section of the volume.

## Summary of Findings

This section summarizes and discusses some of the major findings of the expenditure, revenue, public employment, and fiscal stability monitoring reports. The individual reports should be consulted for more detail.

### Expenditure Trends

Current expenditures are reported per capita in constant dollars (adjusted for inflation). They are further specified by municipal function, such as schools, fire, government administration, police. etc., for FY80. Because of substantial annual variations in capital expenditures these are reported as a five year, FY76 to FY80, average.

While patterns of current expenditures vary across communities, the high expenditure items are similar for each municipality. Most spending is on schools, government administration, streets, and police and fire. Libraries, parks and recreation, and sanitation account for much lower budget shares. The expenditure report examined spending patterns in considerably more detail by type of community. Several trends emerged.

Between 1976 and 1980 total expenditures tended to be highest in communities with high populations, high Proposition 2 1/2 revenue losses, low income, and declining populations. These patterns held throughout the five year period under consideration. Most municipalities also decreased their real per capita expenditures from 1977 to 1980 although total current expenditures fluctuated significantly from year to year. High expenditure communities experienced the least of these fluctuations, a pattern worth remembering as more data about the post–Proposition 2 1/2 era become available.

The actual composition of municipal spending varied greatly across different types of communities. A number of trends are worth noting. For example, low income, high population, and declining population communities tended to spend the most (in real per capita terms) on all types of services except schools and roads. Higher income, higher growth, and low population communities spent significantly more on schools and roads. Another interesting pattern is that low income communities and those with high Proposition 2 1/2 revenue losses tended to spend more than other types of municipalities on general government administration.

### Revenue Trends

The composition of municipal revenues remained fairly stable during the 1976 to 1980 period, although certain types of communities decreased their reliance on intergovernmental (i.e., "outside") revenues. The only revenue source that declined substantially was federal aid. Although this decline occurred in most types of communities, it was most dramatic in low income communities, large communities, communities with declining populations, and those with a high Proposition 2 1/2 revenue loss. The only major increases occurred in the miscellaneous general revenue category. Although it seldom accounted for more than a few percent of total general revenue, real per capita miscellaneous general revenue increased significantly from 1976 to 1980 in all types of communities. The major source of this new revenue has been investment income; dramatic increases can be accounted for to some extent by higher interest rates earned by municipalities on temporarily idle cash and retirement funds.

Although the composition of municipal revenues remained fairly stable throughout the five year period preceding the passage of Proposition 2 1/2, the level of revenue did not. Real per capita total general revenue declined in most communities from 1976 to 1980, with the smallest declines occurring in low income, medium to high 2 1/2 gap, high population, and declining population communities. These figures suggest that the real per capita purchasing power of local governments in the Commonwealth declined in the five year period prior to the passage of Proposition 2 1/2.

The communities experiencing the smallest declines in real per capita revenue -- low income, high population, high 2 1/2 revenue loss, declining population -- tended to be some of the larger and poorer cities. This probably occurred because the real losses in federal aid in these communities tended to be offset by higher state aid and increased revenue from user fees and charges. It is also likely that these cities had greater fixed costs and were under greater political pressure to maintain contant per capita levels of spending.

The intergovernmental aid situation during this five year period merits further consideration. As noted earlier, the communities particularly affected by decreases in federal aid tended to be the larger, poorer, and declining communities – precisely those hit hardest by Proposition 2 1/2. Fortunately for these communities, state aid seems to have made up for some of the losses during the 1976 to 1980 period. Substantial decreases in state aid were experienced by small, higher income, and growing communities, and those communities with no 2 1/2 revenue loss. At the same time, significant increases in state aid were realized in many of the poorer, high population, high 2 1/2 loss communities, and those with declining populations. The net impact of decreasing federal aid and increasing state aid in needier communities is that they experienced no major change in the proportion of total general revenues accounted for by intergovernmental revenues from 1976 to 1980. In other types of communities, however, reliance on intergovernmental aid actually decreased because federal aid revenues decreased and state aid revenues either decreased or remained fairly constant.

*Public Employment Trends*

Total full-time employment declined in a majority of municipalities in the sample from 1976 to 1980. The most significant declines were sustained in large communities, in high Proposition 2 1/2 revenue loss communities, and in slow growth communities. In contrast, total part-time employment increased in all types of communities. The greatest increases in part–time employment occurred in medium–sized communities, low income communities, and those that suffered no revenue loss due to the tax limitation. These trends suggest that larger municipalities, many of which had existing fiscal problems, began implementing minor cutbacks in employment prior to the imposition of Proposition 2 1/2. The apparent substitution of part–time for full–time employees raises a question about how such substitution affected the level and quality of services.

Minor growth in full–time employment did occur in police, fire, and road service departments during this period of general decline. Growth tended to occur in low to medium population communities, moderate income communities, and those experiencing population growth. Full–time employment for schools, libraries, and parks and recreation tended to decrease, although changes were slight in the latter two categories. Small communities and those with a high percentage of residential property tended to experience the greatest cutbacks in teachers. The most significant losses in roads departments and parks departments occurred in larger and low income cities and towns. Administrative employment decreased slightly on average, except in communities with high Proposition 2 1/2 losses, larger communities, low income communities, and those with declining populations.

Although exceptions exist, full–time employment increases were systematically related to municipal characteristics. Moderate–sized and growing municipalities, as well as communities with high incomes, tended to increase certain types of municipal employment from 1976 to 1980. Conversely, large municipalities, municipalities with declining populations, and low income municipalities generally began cutting back during this period. Furthermore, many communities began to rely more heavily on part–time employment during the five years prior to Proposition 2 1/2.

*Fiscal Stability*

Several indices of fiscal stability were calculated. Basically, these measures examine local fiscal policies, such as long term debt and fixed costs, in relation to local revenue or fiscal capacity during the 1976 to 1980 period. For example, although long term debt remained a fairly constant proportion of equalized property value early in the period, it began to fall as 1981 approached. This suggests that even before Proposition 2 1/2 restricted total revenue, capital expenditures were being reduced in many municipalities. Cities and towns with the highest levels of debt, as a fraction of fiscal capacity, were high population, low income, and high Proposition 2 1/2 revenue loss communities.

Other measures of fiscal stability remained fairly constant over time and among communities. However, a few trends were discernible. For example, investment income as a proportion of total general revenue grew in all types of communities. Fixed costs remained a significant fraction of total general revenue, with the largest fractions found in high population and low income communities. Finally, certified free cash as a percentage of total general expenditures tended to decline in most types of communities during the period under consideration.

## Conclusions

The purpose of this trend analysis is to identify and characterize patterns of municipal fiscal behavior prior to the enactment of Proposition 2 1/2. Using a representative sample of communities and simple descriptive statistics, the staff was able to detect several important patterns, a few of which suggest that the first year impacts of Proposition 2 1/2 may perhaps do little more than continue trends that began six years before. Many Massachusetts cities and towns have been cutting back for at least several years.

What do these data suggest about the impact of Proposition 2 1/2? Given the limited scope of the analysis, this is difficult to answer with precision, but the trends associated with high revenue gap cities and towns can often be easily projected as revenues fall. For example, total employment in high gap communities was falling for several years prior to 1981, a situation the tax limitation is likely to exacerbate even with increased reliance on statewide revenue sources. Expenditures in aggregate must fall when alternative revenue sources do not fill the gap. Discretionary sources of revenues will be exploited more extensively than reported here, though these indirect responses may be difficult to monitor. It would be interesting to see, for example, how long-term capital investments, such as street maintenance and the funding of pension retirement obligations, vary as more immediate and pressing expenses become more difficult to fund with allocated monies.

Similarly, 2 1/2 can be expected to influence fiscal stability. With growing pressure to generate new revenue, there may be greater awareness and flexibility on the part of administrators for leveraging funds in financial markets. We observed this not to be the case prior to 1981. Long-term debt is also likely to fall, as municipalities tend to delay maintenance and large capital investments. With the elimination of most discretionary funds, fixed costs may increase as a proportion of own-source revenue. This will allow less local discretion each year in setting spending priorities.

Despite the uncertainty involved in making exact predictions about how communities will respond, voluntarily or involuntarily, to Proposition 2 1/2, one trend seems relatively clear: the towns hit hardest tend to be larger and have lower incomes. These are precisely the communities that tend to have the highest service needs, the lowest fiscal capability, and which have been cutting back in certain areas for years. The net effects of 2 1/2 on spending and employment in these cities depends on what happens on the revenue side. It is clear that these communities will be forced to reduce their reliance on the property tax. There is also evidence that federal aid has been dropping sharply. The unknown element is the extent to which state aid and alternative revenue sources will be able to offset the heavy revenue losses imposed by 2 1/2. Moreover, the direct effects of these losses will likely be masked by changes in the quality of services, in productivity, and in public expectations regarding the role of local government.

It is important to comment on the information these reports cannot provide, and on other kinds of questions this research has raised. The impact of the tax limitation, for example, will likely have differential effects on communities depending on the mandated changes in their fiscal base, changes in intergovernmental aid programs, as well as changes in expenditure patterns within each jurisdiction. While the period and the municipalities studied in this report give an idea how communities have responded to changes in the past, 2 1/2 represents an abrupt shift in the allocation of public monies among the cities and towns in the Commonwealth. Consequently, it is very difficult to forecast the magnitude of impacts. In part, this points up the need to develop more detailed analyses of the issues and trends identified here. Since capital expenditures are often planned and implemented over a long time horizon, it may be useful to group municipalities by characteristics that reflect longer term changes.

In short, the monitoring reports suggest a range of possible impacts of 2 1/2 on different types of communities. Detailed analyses are required to investigate the underlying connections between expenditures, population characteristics, fiscal capacity, and financial strategies of various kinds.

## Table 3.2
## 1980 Population

| Low (less than 6,800) | Medium (6,800-27,000) | High (more than 27,000) |
|---|---|---|
| Dalton | Amesbury | Arlington |
| Deerfield | Burlington | Cambridge |
| Dighton | Bridgewater | Chelmsford |
| Dover | Chelsea | Everett |
| Georgetown | Clinton | Framingham |
| Hatfield | Concord | Gloucester |
| Lynnfield | Dartmouth | New Bedford |
| Marion | Dennis | Norwood |
| New Marlborough | Dracut | Pittsfield |
| Pelham | Easthampton | Quincy |
| Petersham | Foxborough | Salem |
| Stow | Ipswich | Springfield |
| Sturbridge | Kingston | Watertown |
| Sutton | Leicester | Wellesley |
| Warwick | Longmeadow | Woburn |
| Wenham | Marshfield | Worcester |
| | Palmer | |
| | Rehoboth | |
| | Seekonk | |
| | Southwick | |
| | Stoneham | |
| | Walpole | |
| | Ware | |
| | Wayland | |
| | Webster | |
| | Westborough | |
| | Wilbraham | |
| | Winchendon | |
| | Whitman | |

## Table 3.3
## 1982 Revenue Gap (as a Percent of 1981 Tax Levy)

| High (-15%) | Medium (-15%-0%) | Low (0%-2.5%) |
|---|---|---|
| Burlington | Amesbury | Dartmouth |
| Cambridge | Arlington | Deerfield |
| Clinton | Bridgewater | Dennis |
| Dalton | Chelmsford | Dover |
| Easthampton | Chelsea | Ipswich |
| Everett | Concord | Leicester |
| Framingham | Dighton | Lynnfield |
| Hatfield | Dracut | Marion |
| New Bedford | Foxborough | New Marlborough |
| Springfield | Georgetown | Rehoboth |
| Stoneham | Gloucester | Seekonk |
| Watertown | Kingston | Southwich |
| Whitman | Longmeadow | Stow |
| | Marshfield | Sutton |
| | Norwood | Wenham |
| | Palmer | Westborough |
| | Pelham | Winchendon |
| | Petersham | |
| | Pittsfield | |
| | Quincy | |
| | Salem | |
| | Sturbridge | |
| | Walpole | |

## Table 3.4
## 1970 Average Personal Income

| Low (less than $9,400) | Medium ($9,400-$12,000) | High (more than $12,000) |
|---|---|---|
| Amesbury | Arlington | Burlington |
| Cambridge | Bridgewater | Chelmsford |
| Chelsea | Clinton | Concord |
| Dennis | Dalton | Dover |
| Everett | Dartmouth | Longmeadow |
| Gloucester | Deerfield | Lynnfield |
| New Bedford | Dighton | Marshfield |
| Pittsfield | Dracut | New Marlborough |
| Quincy | Easthampton | Norwood |
| Salem | Framingham | Pelham |
| Springfield | Foxborough | Petersham |
| Ware | Georgetown | Stow |
| Webster | Hatfield | Walpole |
| Worcester | Ipswich | Warwick |
| | Kingston | Wayland |
| | Leicester | Wellesley |
| | Marion | Wenham |
| | Palmer | Wilbraham |
| | Rehoboth | Winchendon |
| | Seekonk | |
| | Southwick | |
| | Stoneham | |
| | Sturbridge | |
| | Sutton | |
| | Watertown | |
| | Whitman | |
| | Woburn | |

## Table 3.5 Percent Residential Property (1970)

| Low (less than 60) | Medium (60-81) | High (more than 81) |
|---|---|---|
| Burlington | Bridgewater | Amesbury |
| Cambridge | Concord | Arlington |
| Chelsea | Dalton | Chelmsford |
| Clinton | Dartmouth | Dover |
| Deerfield | Dennis | Dracut |
| Dighton | Easthampton | Georgetown |
| Everett | Foxborough | Ipswich |
| Palmer | Gloucester | Leicester |
| Pittsfield | Hatfield | Longmeadow |
| Quincy | Kingston | Marshfield |
| Salem | Marion | New Marlborough |
| Springfield | New Bedford | Pelham |
| Watertown | Norwood | .Petersham |
| Woburn | Rehoboth | Warwick |
| | Seekonk | Wayland |
| | Stoneham | Wellesley |
| | Stow | Wenham |
| | Sturbridge | Wilbraham |
| | Southwick | Winchendon |
| | Sutton | |
| | Walpole | |
| | Ware | |
| | Webster | |
| | Westborough | |
| | Whitman | |
| | Worcester | |

## Table 3.6
### Percent Population Growth (1970–1980)

| Low (less than 0) | Medium (0-15) | High (more than 15) |
|---|---|---|
| Arlington | Burlington | Amesbury |
| Cambridge | Concord | Bridgewater |
| Chelmsford | Dighton | Deerfield |
| Chelsea | Dover | Dennis |
| Clinton | Framingham | Dracut |
| Dalton | Georgetown | Easthampton |
| Dartmouth | Hatfield | Kingston |
| Everett | Ipswich | Marshfield |
| Foxborough | Leicester | Pelham |
| Gloucester | Longmeadow | Rehoboth |
| New Bedford | Lynnfield | Southwick |
| Norwood | Marion | Stow |
| Palmer | New Bedford | Sturbridge |
| Pittsfield | New Marlborough | Sutton |
| Quincy | Petersham | Warwick |
| Salem | Seekonk | |
| Springfield | Stoneham | |
| Watertown | Walpole | |
| Wayland | Ware | |
| Webster | Wenham | |
| Wellesley | Westborough | |
| Woburn | Whitman | |
| Worcester | Winchendon | |

**Table 3.7**
**Geographic Distribution of Sample Communities**

| Location | Counties Included | Distribution of Sample |
|---|---|---|
| Western Massachusetts | Berkshire, Franklin, Hampden, Hampshire | 13 |
| Central | Worcester | 10 |
| Southeastern | Barnstable, Bristol, Dukes, Nantucket, Norfolk, Plymouth | 17 |
| Northeastern | Essex, Middlesex, Suffolk | 21 |

**Table 3.8**
**Attribute Correlation Matrix**

| | 1980 Population | 1970 Average Income | Residential Property(%) | Population Growth(%) | 1982 Revenue Gap |
|---|---|---|---|---|---|
| 1980 Population | 1.000 | | | | |
| 1970 Average Income | -0.402 | 1.000 | | | |
| Residential Property(%) | -0.343 | 0.526 | 1.000 | | |
| Population Growth(%) | -0.248 | -0.015 | 0.284 | 1.000 | |
| 1982 Revenue Gap | -0.466 | 0.323 | 0.405 | 0.060 | 1.000 |

Chapter 4

## Public Expenditure Patterns

### Impact: 2 1/2 Staff

## Introduction

This report explores local government expenditure patterns in Massachusetts during the five-year period preceding the passage of Proposition 2 1/2. In the first section current expenditures (i.e., allocations across different services for each community) are reviewed. The next section examines capital expenditures and presents some limited findings about the ways in which communities make capital expenditures. The final section contains a summary and suggests some directions for future research.

## Current Expenditures

For the purposes of this analysis, we have combined operating expenditures made with locally generated revenue, with intergovernmental expenditures. The annual values that we report represent per capita expenditures expressed in real terms, using the Boston urban wage earners Consumer Price Index (CPI-W).

Total per capita expenditures vary widely among the 61 communities. In 1980, total per capita expenditures ranged from $185.49 to $538.98. The range was similar in the other years.

We examined municipal expenditures for: schools, police, fire protection, sanitation, streets, parks, libraries, government administration, and "other" government functions. The "other" category is a residual expenditure category derived by subtracting all other functions from the total. Table 4.1 contains average per capita local expenditures for the 61-community sample.

## Table 4.1
### Per Capita Local Expenditures (Percentage of Total)

| Service | 1976 | 1980 |
|---|---|---|
| Local Schools | 59.1 | 58.1 |
| Police | 5.7 | 6.0 |
| Fire | 3.8 | 4.0 |
| Sanitation | 1.3 | 1.2 |
| Roads | 6.5 | 6.5 |
| Parks and Recreation | 1.9 | 1.9 |
| Libraries | 1.3 | 1.1 |
| Financial/General Administration | 13.4 | 14.7 |
| Other | 8.0 | 6.5 |
| Total | 100.0 | 100.0 |

### *1980 Operating Expenditures*

Communities spent the most on schools, government administration, and streets. Police and fire protection also accounted for a substantial portion of most local budgets. Municipalities spent the least, in terms of percentage of total expenditures, on libraries and parks. The "other" category of expenditures varied tremendously from community to community.

*Population.* Total expenditures were highest in the largest communities. These communities spent, on the average, more on all services except schools and streets. Small and medium-size communities spent close to 60 percent of their total expenditures on schools. Larger communities spent 46 percent. Although the percentage difference is large, the differences between actual levels of spending are small. There was a substantial difference between small and large communities with regard to street expenditures. The smallest communities spent much more in actual terms and as a percentage of total spending on streets.

*2 1/2 Gap.* Expenditures patterns are similar in high gap and medium gap communities. No gap communities had the lowest level of total expenditures and the lowest per capita spending for virtually all functions except schools. Medium and high gap towns spent the most on government administration and "other" functions.

*Income.* Low income communities had the highest total expenditures and spent the most on all services except schools and streets. High income communities spent the most on schools ($221.36 per capita) and streets ($19.01 per capita). Medium income communities had the lowest total expenditures and tended to spend the least on most functions. Low income communities spent more than two times the amount of medium and high income communities on government administration ($85.14 per capita). Low income communities also had the highest expenditures on "other" functions.

*Residential Property.* Total expenditures were highest in communities with a low percentage of residential property. Spending in these communities was noticeably higher on fire protection, government administration, and "other" functions. These communities spent the least on schools in actual levels and as a percentage of total expenditures. Communities with a medium percentage of residential property had, overall, the lowest expenditures.

*Population Change.* Declining population communities had the highest total expenditures. These communities tended to spend more on all services except schools. Low growth communities spent the most on schools, in actual levels and as a percentage of total budget. Moderate growth communities had the lowest total expenditures, but spent the most on streets.

## Total Operating Expenditures, 1976-1980

The five-year trends in total current expenditures varied widely among communities. Since 1977, there has been a general decline in total expenditures among all communities. This decline was more pronounced among some communities than others. Most of the time, attribute groups retained their levels of spending, relative to the other groups.

*Population.* Over the five-year period, high population communities retained the highest level of total expenditures. The decline in total expenditures was most pronounced in medium and low population communities.

*2 1/2 Gap.* Over the five-year period, no gap communities retained the lowest total expenditures. Between 1976 and 1977, medium gap communities experienced a substantial increase in spending which put these communities above high gap communities in total spending. The level of spending in high gap communities changed the least.

*Income.* During the five-year period, low income communities had a more stable level of total expenditures than either high or moderate income communities Over this period, moderate income communities retained the lowest levels of total expenditures. Low and high income communities had similar levels of expenditures, although expenditures fluctuated more in high income than low income communities.

*Residential Property.* The decline in expenditures among high and moderate residential communities was more severe than in the low residential areas. The level of expenditures was lowest in moderately residential areas and highest in low residential areas.

*Population Change.* The declining population communities had the highest expenditures throughout the five-year period. Low and moderate growth communities experienced the sharpest declines in total expenditures, since 1977. Low and moderate growth communities decreased total expenditures in real terms, much more than declining communities.

School Operating Expenditures, 1976-1980

Per capita expenditures on schools for all types of communities was highest in 1976. Since 1977, there has been a general pattern of decline in school expenditures. This trend is similar to the trend in total current expenditures. For most of the attribute groupings, school spending in 1980 was similar to school spending in 1976.

Police Operating Expenditures, 1976-1980

Unlike school expenditures, police expenditures remained relatively stable over the five—year period. For most of the attribute groups, per capita police expenditures did not change dramatically. Consequently, expenditures in 1980 were similar to those in 1976.

Fire Operating Expenditures, 1976-1980

Fire expenditures during the period 1976–1980, increased slightly between 1976 and 1977 and decreased slightly after that. Although fire expenditures increased during the middle year periods, 1980 levels were very close, although slightly higher than in 1976.

Sanitation Operating Expenditures, 1976-1980

For most communities, sanitation expenditures were higher during the early part of the five—year period than during later years. Expenditures on sanitation were highest during 1977 and 1978. In general, per capita spending on sanitation changed little between 1976 and 1980.

Streets Operating Expenditures, 1976-1980

Expenditures for streets were highest in 1978. There was a gradual decline in spending from 1978, and 1980 expenditure levels are similar to those in 1976.

Parks & Recreation Operating Expenditures, 1976-1980

For most communities, spending on parks and recreation changed little over the five—year period. Spending tended to be highest during 1978.

Libraries Operating Expenditures, 1976-1980

We did not find strong trends in per capita library expenditures during the five—year period. In some communities, spending in 1976 was higher than in 1980; in other communities, the opposite -- higher spending in 1980 -- was true.

*Government Administration Operating Expenditures, 1976-1980*

In most instances, spending for government administration was higher in 1980 than it was in 1976.

## Capital Expenditures

The pattern of capital expenditures in the 61 primary site communities varied widely across service areas in each municipality as well as over time. Cities and towns often make capital expenditures on an erratic basis, but in line with a five- or seven-year plan. For this reason, there are large year to year variations in capital spending.

Because of these annual variations in capital expenditures, we decided to examine five-year annual per capita capital expenditures from FY76 to FY80. We then grouped these expenditures according to the community attributes described above.

Few clear trends in capital expenditures emerge. There are substantial differences between the non-zero mean and non-zero median values for the five-year period of capital expenditures, which suggests that community attributes have little bearing on the level of capital expenditures. (1)

Total capital expenditures tend to be higher in communities with large populations, large 2 1/2 gaps, low income, large non-residential property tax bases, and declining populations. There is no single type of capital expenditure that appears to be the largest, across all community types. During the five-year period, some communities made large capital expenditures on schools, while other communities made street improvements. Unlike the pattern in operating expenditures, in which schools routinely account for the largest share of total expenditures, capital expenditures over the five-year period vary much more widely.

## Summary

Operating expenditures vary from community to community. Generally, spending on schools, government administration, streets, police, and fire protection constitute large categories of expenditures across different types of communities. Spending on libraries, parks, and sanitation tends to be much lower. "Other" expenditures vary tremendously.

Per capita expenditures tend to be highest in communities with large population, 2 1/2 revenue gaps, low income, low percentages of residential property, and declining population. In general, these trends hold across the five-year period, 1976-1980. Most, but not all, communities have experienced a decline in real expenditures since 1977.

Throughout the 1976–1980 period, there were substantial fluctuations in levels of total operating expenditures. High expenditure communities experienced the least of these fluctuations and tended to have more stable levels of expenditure. The impact of Proposition 2 1/2 on these communities, as well as on those communities with lower spending levels, remains to be seen. How will high expenditure communities respond to 2 1/2, relative to those communities with lower expenditures? Changes in expenditure patterns among different types of communities should be the focus of future investigations.

Another topic that needs to be addressed more thoroughly, is the allocation of expenditures among various functions of government. Changes in the level of spending for various functions needs to be analyzed in a more systematic fashion. We need to understand more about year to year fluctuations in expenditures.

Our investigation revealed that different types of communities spent varying amounts on municipal services. Police expenditures tended to be most stable over the five-year period. School expenditures tended to decline, while most other service expenditures fluctuated, in real terms, between 1976 and 1980. One issue that arises in the aftermath of Proposition 2 1/2 is the definition and provision of "essential" services. The data from 1976 to 1980 do not suggest major shifts in level of expenditures among municipal services. Whether there will be a shift in expenditures favoring "essential" services remains to be seen.

Our analysis of capital expenditures indicates little more than the wide variation in how communities make such expenditures. Since capital expenditures occur over long periods, we need to select community attributes for cross-community comparisons that reflect long-term changes.

## Notes for Chapter 4

1. The tremendous variations in capital expenditures provides a strong argument for analyzing capital and operating expenditures separately. None of the five community attributes was strongly related to differences in capital expenditures. Differences in income, size, etc., may provide clues to the patterns of operating expenditures, but such community attributes offer little or no basis for sorting out different patterns in capital expenditures.

Chapter 5

## Sources of Local Revenues

### Impact: 2 1/2 Staff

## Introduction

This second trend analysis explores the changing sources of local government revenue in Massachusetts during the five-year period preceding the passage of Proposition 2 1/2. The second section discusses differences in the reliance on own-source and intergovernmental revenues among different types of communities, while the third section explores how different types of communities vary in their use of specific revenue sources. Differences in utility revenue as a share of total local revenue are examined in the fourth section. Changes over time in the use of specific sources of revenue are analyzed in the fifth section, and the final section summarizes the findings and suggests avenues for future research.

## Own-Source versus Intergovernmental Revenue

This section examines local revenues from own-sources and intergovernmental sources for the years 1976 and 1980. Communities were once again clustered by the same five attributes. A full set of cross tabulations were prepared.

### Major Trends

There was a decrease in reliance on intergovernmental aid from 1976 to 1980. The greatest decrease tended to occur in smaller towns. Larger and poor communities with declining populations exhibited very little change in their reliance on intergovernmental aid. This suggests that a substantial portion of total intergovernmental aid was, by 1980, still being channelled into the places that needed it the most. However, this is mostly due to the redistributive nature of the state aid formula in Massachusetts. Federal aid allocated during this period actually tended to flow in the opposite direction.

## Population

Low population municipalities dramatically decreased their dependence on intergovernmental aid from 1976 to 1980. In 1976, aid revenues accounted for an average of 30.4 percent of total revenue compared to 23.3 percent in 1980. Virtually no change in reliance on intergovernmental aid by medium population communities occurred from 1976 to 1980. A modest decrease from 28.4 percent to 26.6 percent occurred in high population communities.

## 2 1/2 Gap

Municipalities hit hardest by Proposition 2 1/2 decreased their reliance on intergovernmental aid revenues from 1976 to 1980 just slightly, with the average declining from 31 percent of total general revenue to 28 percent of total general revenue. Low to medium gap communities experienced an even smaller decline (from 30.7 to 29.8 percent). The most substantial decline in reliance on intergovernmental aid revenues was experienced by communities with no gap (i.e., no adverse impact of Proposition 2 1/2). Inter-governmental aid as a percentage of total general revenue for these communities declined from 30.5 percent in 1976 to 24.5 percent in 1980.

## Income

The fraction of total general revenue realized from intergovernmental aid remained stable in low income communities from 1976 to 1980. Moderate decreases occurred in both medium income and high income municipalities. The decline in the former was from 31.6 percent to 27.6 percent, while the decline in the latter was from 25.5 percent to 22.4 percent.

## Residential Property

Inter-governmental aid revenues declined slightly in importance for communities with a low percentage of residential property, falling from 31.0 percentt in 1976 to 29.3 percent in 1980. A similarly modest decline from 29.5 to 28.6 percent was experienced by municipalities with a high percentage of residential property. Medium residential property communities experienced a more substantial decrease in reliance on intergovernmental aid, with a drop from 30.2 percent of total general revenue in 1976 to 25.9 percent of total general revenue in 1980.

## Population Change

Municipalities with declining populations experienced no average change in reliance on intergovernmental aid from 1976 to 1980. In low to moderate growth communities average dependence on intergovernmental aid dropped from 29.6 to 24.7 percent during this time period. In high growth communities, the decline in intergovernmental aid as a percentage of total general revenue was from 32.0 percent in 1976 to 29.1 percent in 1980.

## The Composition of Municipal General Revenue

Total municipal revenue is made up of property tax revenue, other (nonproperty) tax revenue, federal aid, state aid, user charges, and miscellaneous general revenue (primarily revenue derived from investments and from the sale of property and other municipal assets). Table 5.1 presents per capita sources

**Table 5.1**
**Per Capita Sources of Local Revenues in Massachusetts, 1976 and 1980**
**(Percent of Total, 61 Community Average)**

| Sources of Revenue | 1976 | 1980 |
|---|---|---|
| Property Tax | 63.1 | 64.8 |
| Other Taxes | 0.5 | 0.5 |
| User Charges | 4.4 | 4.4 |
| State Aid | 25.2 | 24.6 |
| Federal Aid | 5.3 | 3.3 |
| Other General Revenue | 1.6 | 2.4 |
| Total General Revenue | 100.0 | 100.0 |

of local revenue for the 61-community sample.

*Major Trends*

The proportion of total revenue coming from the property tax, other taxes, and user charges remained fairly constant 1976 to 1980, with some minor exceptions. Some major changes occurred in the percentage of total general revenue represented by state and federal aid. State aid tended to decline in wealthier, smaller, growing, and no gap communities and to increase in poorer, larger, high gap, and declining population communities. Federal revenues have tended to decline in importance for most municipalities in our sample, but the most severe losses in federal aid tend to be in high population, low income, and high gap communities. Miscellaneous general revenue tended to increase in importance across most of the sample from 1976 to 1980, primarily because of increases in investment earnings achieved by local governments.

*The Property Tax*

Property tax revenue as a percentage of total general revenue remained fairly stable across most of our sample, ranging from a low of about 56.0 percent in low income communities to a high of about 72.0 percent in high income communities. In general, changes in this proportion from 1976 to 1980 were minor across all attributes. Seldom did the proportion grow or decline by more than a percentage point or two. Notable exceptions include low population communities where the growth was from 65.2 percent to 70.6 percent, and no gap communities, where the growth was from 63.5 percent to 69.6 percent. In general, there was a small average growth in reliance on the property tax except in medium gap, low income, and declining population communities. These were the trends before the implementation of Proposition 2 1/2.

*Other Taxes*

Average reliance on other taxes is very small in our sample, ranging from a low 0.3 percent to a high of 0.7 percent. This proportion stayed constant or rose very slightly from 1976 to 1980. Declines in reliance on other taxes occurred in high income, high residential property, and medium growth communities. Increases of more than 0.1 percent occurred only in medium residential property and high growth communities. Other taxes are clearly not a very significant source of revenue for Massachusetts cities and towns.

*User Charges*

User charges are another minor source of revenue which remained fairly constant as a proportion of total general revenue from 1976 to 1980. Most municipalities (across all attribute groups) experienced changes in this proportion of only a few tenths of a percent, with about half rising and half declining. The largest single change was a decrease from 5.5 percent to 4.6 percent in high population and growing communities. Low income and high population communities tend, on average, to make the greatest use of user charges.

*State Aid*

There has been a change in the percentage of total general revenues accounted for by state aid from 1976 to 1980. The range runs from about 19.0 percent to about 27.0 percent. During the period under consideration, state aid as a percentage of total general revenues increased in high population, high gap, and low income communities. This proportion tended to decrease in low population, no gap, medium to high income, and growing communities. These changes were generally not trivial, usually on the order of at least several percent of total general revenue. Thus, more state aid appeared to be going to the types of communities that needed it most in 1980.

*Federal Aid*

While state aid seems to have been flowing to communities that needed it in the 1976 to 1980 period, federal aid was moving in the opposite direction. In general, there was a cutback in federal aid as a percentage of total general revenue from 1976 to 1980. The only attribute groups in which a minor increase occurred were the high income communities and low to moderate gap communities. The most severe cutbacks actually occurred in the high population (from 7.5 percent to 3.9 percent), high gap (from 8.3 percent to 3.7 percent), low income (from 10.5 percent to 5.4 percent), and declining population (from 7.8 percent to 5.4 percent) communities. Thus, while most Massachusetts cities and towns experienced some decline in their reliance on federal aid, the communities hardest hit were the ones most in need of intergovernmental assistance.

## Miscellaneous General Revenue

Although miscellaneous general revenue (which consists primarily of investment income and sale of municipal assets) generally accounts for only a few percent of total general revenue, its importance has increased dramatically in percentage terms, often doubling in the period from 1976 to 1980. This proportion did not decline for any attribute group, although it did remain constant for low income communities. There is no discernible pattern. This increase in miscellaneous general revenue across all types of communities seems to be due primarily to major increases in investment income earned by the cities and towns in our sample.

## Utility Revenue as a Share of Total Revenue

The previous sections have examined the composition of general revenue, a category which traditionally excludes utility revenue. This section examines the relative importance of utility revenue.

## Major Trends

Utility revenue is not a major source of revenue in most communities in our sample. Utility revenue accounts for an average of 2 to 3 percent of total revenue in high gap, low income, low residential property, and high growth communities. In high population, low to moderate gap, high residential property, and moderate growth communities, utility revenue represents about 6 to 8 percent of total revenue. High income municipalities are most dependent on utility revenue (9.3 percent). By and large, utility revenue remained a fairly constant proportion of total revenue from 1976 to 1980. High gap communities were the only group to experience a slight average decline in reliance on utility revenue. Large average gains were registered only in the no gap group. Most of the other changes in utility revenue as a percentage of total revenue from 1976 to 1980 were small increases of several tenths of a percentage point.

## Population

Six of 16 low population, 24 of 29 medium population, and all 15 high population communities in our sample rely on utility revenues to provide some portion of their total revenues. The degree of reliance in 1980 did not seem to differ much among population groups, ranging from an average of 4.9 percent of total revenue in medium population communities to an average of 6.5 percent in high population communities. Utility revenue as a fraction of total revenue remained fairly constant (on average) in low population communities, and increased slightly (on average) in medium and high population communities.

## 2 1/2 Gap

Twelve of 13 high gap municipalities, 25 of 31 low to moderate gap municipalities, and 8 of 17 no gap communities in our sample receive some utility revenues. The average reliance in 1980 ranged from 2.7 percent of total revenues in high gap communities to 6.7 percent of total revenues in moderate gap communities. The average share of total revenues accounted for by utility revenue grew significantly from 4.2 percent to 5.9 percent in no gap communities, grew slightly from 6.3 percent to 6.7 percent in low to moderate gap communities, and declined slightly from 3.0 percent to 2.7 percent in high gap communities during the period 1976 to 1980.

## Income

Thirteen of 14 low income, 19 of 27 medium income, and 12 of 15 high income communities reported some reliance on utility revenues. The share of total revenues accounted for by utility revenue in 1980 ranged from 2.9 percent in low income communities to 9.3 percent in high income communities. This share remained fairly constant on average in low income communities from 1976 to 1980, and tended to grow slightly in medium and high income communities.

## Residential Property

Eleven of 14 low residential property communities, 21 of 27 medium residential property communities, and 12 of 15 high residential property communities in our sample had some degree of reliance on utility revenue. This reliance ranged from 2.6 percent of total revenues in low residential property communities to 7.9 percent of total revenues in high residential property communities in 1980. This percentage remained fairly stable in low and medium residential property communities from 1976 to 1980, while it tended to increase modestly in high residential property communities.

## Population Change

Some reliance on utility revenues was reported by 20 of the 23 declining population municipalities, 17 of 23 low to moderate growth communities, and 8 of 15 high growth communities in our sample. Utility revenue as a proportion of total revenue in 1980 ranged from an average 2.5 percent in high growth municipalities to an average of 6.9 percent in low to moderate growth communities. The proportion remained fairly stable on average in the high growth and declining population communities from 1976 to 1980, with very modest increases reported in the low to moderate growth communities.

## Changes in the Use of Specific Types of Revenue, 1976 to 1980

This section examines changes in the levels of selected real per capita revenue sources from 1976 to 1980 for our sample of Massachusetts cities and towns. Although we did experience some of the data problems discussed in the

Introduction to Trend Analysis, we were able to identify certain patterns of change among different types of cities and towns. This section is divided into subsections for each of the types of revenue examined. Within each subsection, there are six paragraphs. The first summarizes the major trends for that type of revenue, and the other five discuss how variations in each of the five attributes seem to affect the level of the type of revenue being discussed.

*Total General Revenue*

*Major Trends.* Real per capita total general revenue declined in the five-year period preceding the passage of Proposition 2 1/2. The greatest decline occurred in low population, no gap, high income, medium residential property, and high population growth communities. Conversely, the smallest decline tended to occur in medium to high population, medium to high gap, low income, and declining population communities. This suggests that the larger and poorer communities in Massachusetts have been under greater pressure to maintain constant (per capita) rates of spending. Smaller and wealthier communities have shown less of a tendency to keep their real purchasing power constant. The figures suggest real per capita purchasing power of local governments in the Commonwealth has continued to decline in the five-year period under consideration.

*Population.* The 16 low population municipalities experienced a mean decline of $24.99 (6.4 percent) in real per capita total general revenue from 1976 to 1980. The 29 medium population and 16 high population municipalities also experienced declines, with a $13.90 (3.4 percent) average decrease for the former category and a $17.71 (4.2 percent) average decrease for the latter category.

*2 1/2 Gap.* The 13 high gap and 17 no gap municipalities respectively averaged $16.42 (3.8 percent) and $52.85 (15.0 percent) declines in real per capita total general revenue from 1976 to 1980. The 31 low to moderate gap communities experienced an extremely modest gain of $.83 (1.1 percent).

*Income.* The 14 low income, 27 medium income, and 15 high income municipalities all experienced average declines in real per capita total general revenue from 1976 to 1980. The low income group averaged a $13.59 (3.3 percent) loss, while the medium and high income groups respectively averaged losses of $18.75 (4.5 percent) and $21.59 (5.7 percent).

*Residential Property.* The mean increase in real per capita total general revenues for the 14 low residential property municipalities was $.29 (1.6 percent). The 27 medium and 15 high residential property communities experienced average respective losses in real per capita total general revenue of $30.44 (8.3 percent) and $13.49 (3.4 percent).

*Population Change.* The 23 declining population municipalities averaged a loss of $8.00 (1.2 percent) in real per capita total general revenues from 1976 to 1980. The 23 low to moderate growth municipalities experienced an average loss of $19.04 (4.3 percent) and the 15 high growth municipalities experienced an average loss of $30.96 (9.4 percent) in real per capita total general revenues during this time period.

## Property Tax Revenue

*Major Trends.*    Real per capita property tax revenue declined in all 61 cities and towns in our sample. Although most of the differences were not very great, the largest decline tended to occur in medium to high population, no gap, and low income municipalities. There were also substantial average declines in medium residential property communities and communities with declining populations and high rates of growth. Obviously, no clear pattern emerges from these observations, although the most dramatic decline in real per capita property taxes was in low income municipalities.

*Population.*    Almost every community in our sample experienced a decline in real per capita property tax revenues from 1976 to 1980. All 16 low population communities experienced an average real decline of $2.33 (*) in property tax revenues. The 29 medium population and 16 high population communities also experienced an average decrease in real per capita property-tax revenues. The respective mean declines for these two categories were $9.57 (4.4 percent) and $12.99 (3.8 percent).

*2 1/2 Revenue Gap.*    The 13 high gap communities experienced an average decline in real per capita property tax revenues of $9.28 (2.8 percent). The 31 low to medium gap communities experienced an average decline of $4.35 (0.5 percent), while the 17 communities with no gap experienced the greatest average decline; $15.71 (7.1 percent).

*Income.*    The 14 low income communities had the greatest real per capita average decline in property tax revenues from 1976 to 1980. The figure here was $17.94 (5.6 percent). In contrast, the 27 medium income communities had an average decline of $6.16 (1.8 percent), while the 15 high income communities experienced an average decline of $5.98 (2.6 percent).

*Residential Property.*    The 14 low residential property communities tended to have a decline in real per capita property tax revenues from 1976 to 1980, with the average figure here being $5.77 (*). Medium residential property declined an average of $11.33 (4.6 percent) in a 27 municipalities. Localities having a high percentage of residential property experienced an average decrease in real per capita property tax revenue of $8.04 (3.4 percent).

*Population Change.*    The 23 communities with declining populations experienced an average decline of $12.25 (3.8 percent) in real per capita property tax revenues. In the 23 low to medium growth municipalities, the average decline was very small, $.83 (*), while in the 15 high growth communities, the mean decline was $14.78 (6.1 percent).

*Other (Nonproperty) Tax Revenue*

*Major Trends.* Most of the changes in real per capita nonproperty tax revenue from 1976 to 1980 are very small, generally under one dollar. These small changes often register as large percentage changes because other taxes are such a minor revenue source. High population, medium to high gap and low to medium income communities with moderate percentages of residential property, and declining population were most likely to experience an increase in reliance on real per capita other taxes. Decreases were more likely to occur in low to medium population, no gap, high income communities, with a high percentage of residential property and some population growth. There is, however, a great deal of variation across most attribute categories.

*Population.* The 16 low population communities experienced a mean gain of $.06 (6.8 percent) in real per capita nonproperty tax revenue from 1976 to 1980. The 29 medium population communities experienced a mean decline of $.20 (*), while the 16 high population communities experienced an average gain of $.30 (25.4 percent).

*2 1/2 Gap.* The 13 high gap communiies averaged a $.15 (22.9 percent) gain in real per capita other tax revenue from 1976 to 1980. A mean gain of $.16 (16.7 percent) was realized in the 31 low to moderate gap communities, while a mean loss of $.41 (*) was experienced by the 17 no gap communities.

*Income.* Average gains of $.34 (18.1 percent) and $.28 (34.6 percent) in real per capita other tax revenues were realized from 1976 to 1980 by the 14 low income and 27 medium income municipalities, respectively. The 15 high income communities experienced an average loss of $.70 (*) during this time period.

*Residential Property.* The 14 low residential property communities averaged a gain of $.09 (9.6 percent) in real per capita nonproperty tax revenue from 1976 to 1980. During the same period, the 27 medium residential property communities experienced an average gain of $.48 (44.2 percent) and 15 high residential property communities experienced an average loss of $.81 (8.2 percent).

*Population Change.* The 23 declining population communities experienced an average increase of $.11 (11.3 percent) in real per capita other tax revenue from 1976 to 1980. An average decline of $.52 (*) occurred in the 23 low to moderate growth municipalities, while the 15 high growth municipalities averaged a $.63 (48.1 percent) gain in real per capita nonproperty tax revenue.

*Federal Aid Revenue*

*Major Trends.* There was a clear and substantial decline in reliance on federal aid for most communities in our sample from 1976 to 1980. The decline is evident across almost every group in every attribute. There is no clear pattern of decline among different population and gap groups, although the middle groups in each of these attribute groups seem to have been the least affected. A very disturbing pattern, however, is that low income municipalities lost an average of $19.91 (45.8 percent) of real per capita federal aid from 1976 to 1980, while high income municipalities gained an average of $2.36 (16.4 percent) during the same period. Similarly, municipalities with a high percentage of residential property and high growth communities appear to have been affected the least by cutbacks in federal aid from 1976 to 1980.

*Population.*   Changes in the level of real federal aid per capita occurred in all 15 low population communities, all 29 medium population municipalities, and all 16 high population municipalities. The low population group experienced an average decline of $5.32 (69.7 percent). The medium population group experienced an average decline of $3.26 (*), while the high population municipalities experienced an average decline of $16.25 (56.5 percent).

*2 1/2 Gap.*   All 13 high gap municipalities experienced a change in real per capita federal aid from 1976 to 1980, with the mean figure being a decrease of $17.84 (60.7 percent). All 30 low to moderate gap communities also lost an average of $1.11 (*) in real per capita federal aid, while the mean loss in the high gap communities was $9.95 (65.3 percent).

*Income.*   The 14 low income communities and 27 medium income municipalities experienced average losses in real per capita federal aid of $19.91 (45.8 percent) and $5.26 (26.1 percent), respectively. The 15 high income municipalities, on the other hand, experienced an average increase of $2.36 (16.4 percent) in real per capita federal aid from 1976 to 1980.

*Residential Property.*   The 14 low residential property municipalities and the 27 medium residential property municipalities experienced average declines in real per capita federal aid from 1976 to 1980. The mean decline for the former category was $9.45 (*), while the mean decline for the latter category was $9.78 (58.8 percent). The 15 municipalities with a high percentage of residential property actually averaged an increase in real per capita federal aid of $.74 (20.4 percent).

*Population Change.*   The 23 communities with a declining population averaged a loss of $10.36 (*) in real per capita federal aid from 1976 to 1980. The 23 low to medium growth communities experienced an average loss of $9.03 (56.9 percent), while the 14 high growth communities made a modest average gain of $.82 (*).

## State Aid Revenue

*Major Trends.*   Some clear trends emerge from an examination of our state aid statistics. Substantial increases in real per capita state aid from 1976 to 1980 tended to occur in high population, high gap, low income, low residential· property, and declining population communities. On the other hand, substantial decreases tended to be experienced by low population, no gap, high income, medium to high residential property, and growing communities. The prime beneficiaries of state aid, thus, appear to have been some of the larger and poorer cities in 1980. The shift in real per capita state aid from 1976 to 1980 seems to have been away from the types of communities that are more likely to have the fiscal capacity to provide for themselves. This shift tended to favor the types of municipalities most likely to be under severe fiscal stress.

*Population.* The 16 low population municipalities experienced an average decrease of $21.78 (26.2 percent) in real per capita state aid from 1976 to 1980. The mean decline for the medium population municipalities was much smaller, with the figure here being $.61 (0.9 percent). The 16 high population municipalities increased their average reliance on state aid by $4.39 (10.8 percent).

*2 1/2 Gap.* The 13 high gap communities gained an average of $7.44 (13.6 percent) in real per capita state aid revenue from 1976 to 1980. There was, on average, not much change in state aid in the 31 low to moderate gap communities, with the mean gain being $.16 (2.0 percent). The 17 no gap communities experienced major declines in average real per capita state aid from 2976 to 1980, with the mean loss being $23.40 (30.1 percent).

*Income.* While the 14 low income municipalities made substantial average gains in real per capita state aid revenue from 1976 to 1980, the 27 medium and 15 high income municipalities experienced significant losses. The mean increase for the low income group was $20.86 (23.3 percent), while the medium and high income groups experienced average declines of $22.57 (10.3 percent) and $18.03 (22.0 percent), respectively.

*Residential Property.* The 14 low residential property municipalities gained an average of $7.87 (11.9 percent) in real per capita state aid revenues from 1976 to 1980. The medium and high residential property communities, on the other hand, experienced fairly major losses of state aid during this time period. The average decline for the former category was $10.83 (12.3 percent), while the average decline for the latter category was $7.25 (7.7 percent).

*Population Change.* An average gain of $9.91 (14.9 percent) in real per capita state aid was realized by the 23 declining population communities from 1976 to 1980. The 23 moderate and 15 high growth communities experienced respective average losses of $12.99 (15.7 percent) and $15.00 (16.9 percent) in real per capita state aid revenues.

## User Charges

*Major Trends.* Many of the communities in our sample experienced a very modest decline in real per capita income from user charges from 1976 to 1980. Declines were most likely to occur in no gap, high income, medium residential property, and high growth communities. Some Massachusetts municipalities also increased their reliance on real per capita user charges from 1976 to 1980. An increase was most likely to occur in high population, low to moderate gap, low income low residential property, and declining population communities. Many of the larger cities in the Commonwealth tended to fall into these latter categories. In a time of fiscal stress, with declining federal aid and declining tax bases, it seems reasonable that larger cities would attempt to tap an under-used revenue source such as user charges.

*Population.*   The 15 low population and 29 medium population municipalities experienced modest decreases in real per capita user charges of $.32 (*) and $.85 (*), respectively. The 16 high population communities, on the other hand, averaged a moderate increase of $3.04 (*) in real per capita user charges from 1976 to 1980.

*2 1/2 Gap.*   The 13 high gap municipalities averaged a modest decrease in real per capita user charges of $.96 (5.1 percent), while the low to medium gap communities made an average gain of $2.70 (15 percent). The no gap municipalities experienced an average decline of $2.91 (12 percent) in real per capita user charges during this time period.

*Income.*   The 14 low income municipalities averaged a $3.24 (2.8 percent) increase in real per capita user charges from 1976 to 1980. The 27 medium income and 15 high income municipalities experienced average decreases of $.42 (*) and $1.53 (7.9 percent), respectively.

*Resdential Property.*   The 14 low residential property communities and 15 high residential property communities experienced average increases in their reliance on real per capita user charges from 1976 to 1980. The former group averaged an increase of $4.46 (19.1 percent), while the latter group averaged an increase of $.49 (9.6 percent). The 27 medium residential property communities experienced an average decline of $2.18 (5.9 percent) in real per capita user charges during this time period.

*Population Change.*   The 23 municipalities with declining populations averaged a $2.27 (*) increase in real per capita user charges from 1976 to 1980, and the 23 low to moderate growth communities averaged a $.59 (*) increase. The 14 high growth communities experienced an average decrease of $3.34 (15.2 percent).

## *Miscellaneous General Revenue*

*Major Trends.*   Miscellaneous general revenue, which includes investment income, revenue derived from the sale of municipal assets, and all types of revenue not elsewhere classified, grew dramatically in percentage terms across most of our sample. The greatest average increases in real per capita terms tended to occur in low population, high gap, and medium income communities. The only noticeable decline tended to occur in some of the low income communities. This increase in real per capita miscellaneous general revenue is primarily attributable to an increase in municipal investment earnings.

*Population.*   Real per capita miscellaneous general revenue changed in all 16 low population, all 29 medium population, and all 16 high population municipalities. in our sample from 1976 to 1980. The mean increases for the respective categories were $4.22 (139.5 percent), $.50 (*), and $3.79 (81.4 percent).

*2 1/2 Gap.* Real per capita miscellaneous general revenue increased in the 13 high gap communities by an average of $4.07 (105 percent). All 31 medium to low gap municipalities and all 17 no gap municipalities also experienced a change. In the former category, there was a mean increase of $3.52 (92.6 percent), while in the latter category, there was a mean decrease of $.48 (*).

*Income.* The 14 low income municipalities experienced an average decrease of $.19 (*) in real per capita miscellaneous revenue from 1976 to 1980. All 27 medium income and all 15 high income municipalities also experienced a change. In the medium income category, there was an average increase of $4.37 (172.2 percent), while in the high income group, the average increase was $2.30 (76.1 percent).

*Residential Property.* A change in real per capita miscellaneous general revenue occurred in all 14 low residential property communities, all 27 medium residential communities, and all 15 high residential property communities. The respective increases for the three categories are $3.08 (88.4 percent), $3.19 (155 percent), and $1.38 (38.5 percent).

*Population Change.* The 23 municipalities with a declining population experienced an average increase in real per capita miscellaneous general revenue of $2.33 (62.5 percent) from 1976 to 1980. The 23 low to moderate growth municipalities experienced an average increase of $3.74 (97.9 percent) and the 15 high growth communities experienced an average increase of $.41 (159 percent).

## Summary

Two major trends clearly emerge from the preceding findings. report. The first is a general decline in the real per capita value of most municipal revenue sources in our sample from 1976 to 1980. The second is a decreased reliance on intergovernmental aid in the majority of communities in our sample during that time period. The first trend indicates that a deterioration of municipal purchasing power occurred in the Commonwealth in the five-year period immediately preceding the passage of Proposition 2 1/2. It remains to be seen how this trend has been affected by Proposition 2 1/2. The second trend raises a major question about the potential impact of Proposition 2 1/2. If certain communities are severely affected by decreasing intergovernmental revenues and have also had their ability to raise property tax revenue curtailed by Proposition 2 1/2, how will they adjust? Will they reduce municipal services, vote to override Proposition 2 1/2, attempt to diversify their own-source revenues, or hope to be bailed out by the state? This is one focus of our post-Proposition 2 1/2 research.

The composition of municipal revenue seems to have remained fairly stable during the 1976 to 1980 period for most revenue sources. The most dramatic decline occurred in the federal aid category. While this decline occurred across more types of communities, it was more pronounced in the larger, lower income, high 2 1/2 gap communities with declining populations. This raises significant questions about the potential impact of the major cutbacks in federal aid already implemented and recently proposed by the Reagan Administration. Will such cuts continue to affect severely the communities with the greatest need for intergovernmental aid? If so, which municipal services are most likely to be adversely affected?

Fortunately for the communities in fiscal distress, state aid in Massachusetts seems to have become more redistributive during the 1976 to 1980 period. Substantial decreases in state aid were experienced by small, higher income, growing communities, and those with no 2 1/2 gap. At the same time, significant increases in state aid were realized in many of the poorer, high 2 1/2 gap, high population communities, and those with declining populations. The net impact of decreasing federal aid and increasing state aid in the needier communities was that there were no major changes in the proportion of total general revenue accounted for by intergovernmental aid during the 1976 to 1980 period. However, the question remains: with federal aid on a dramatic decline, will state aid continue to make up the gap? If not, how are municipalities going to cope with the loss of intergovernmental revenue?

There is one final trend which merits attention. Although it seldom accounts for more than several percent of total general revenue, there was a very signficant increase in real per capita miscellaneous general revenue from 1976 to 1980. To some extent, this can be accounted for by dramatic increases in the rate of interest earned by municipalities on their investments. But it also raises another interesting question. To what extent have municipal officials been more aggressive in attempting to earn higher rates of return on their temporarily idle cash? Furthermore, what types of options in this area are open to local government managers? Since Proposition 2 1/2 will undoubtedly require creative managerial responses, research in this area might prove to be extremely useful.

Chapter 6

# Municipal Fiscal Stability

## Impact: 2 1/2 Staff

## Introduction

While there is bound to be disagreement over the indicators that ought to be used to characterize local fiscal stability, it is crucial that an attempt be made. These same indicators will be used to measure the impact of Proposition 2 1/2 on municipal fiscal stability during the post–2 1/2 period as well. Three sections follow. The first section discusses the indicators of fiscal stability used. The second section analyzes changes in fiscal stability in different types of communities. The final section presents our prognosis regarding the likely impacts of Proposition 2 1/2 on municipal fiscal stability.

## Synopsis of Indicators

Obviously, there is no standard or simple measure of municipal fiscal stress or stability. Therefore, our strategy was to develop a series of ratios (Table 6.1). Each ratio reflects one aspect of a community's financial management success or failure (although absolute standards of fiscal stress or wellbeing do not exist). Diversity in size, resource endowment, and service needs make it impossible to pronounce a community "sound" or "mismanaged" on the basis of such quantitative measures. This chapter is intended to identify trends and raise questions.

### Indicator 1. Investment Income

Investment income (as a proportion of total general revenue) indicates earnings on invested municipal funds. This figure includes interest received on

**Table 6.1**
**Fiscal Stability Indicators in Massachusetts, 1976 and 1980**
(61 Community Average)

| Ratio x 100* | 1976 | 1980 |
|---|---|---|
| 1. Investment Income/ | | |
|    Total General Revenue | 0.9 | 1.3 |
| 2. Long-term Debt Outstanding/ | | |
|    Equalized Property Valuation | 2.7 | 2.0 |
| 3. Fixed Costs/ | | |
|    Total General Revenue | 31.5 | 47.9 |
| 4. Revenues from User Fees and Charges/ | | |
|    Own-Source Revenues | 6.3 | 6.3 |
| 6. Certified Free Cash/ | | |
|    Total General Expenditures | 3.5 | 5.0 |

* Data for Ratio 5 (Uncollected Property Taxes/Equalized Property Valuation) is not presented.  See text for a discussion of major findings and problems associated with this ratio.

all government deposits and investment holdings and interest from investments in certificates of deposit, mini-certificates of deposit, repurchase agreements, treasury bills, the Massachusetts Municipal Depository Trust, and combination demand and savings accounts. The amount of income earned on investments is one useful indicator of effective financial management and contributes to a portrait of each community's fiscal stability. Investment income reflects the local treasurer's approach to maximizing the earning potential of otherwise "idle" cash.

*Indicator 2.  Long-term Capital Debt Outstanding*

Long-term capital debt outstanding refers to all bonds, mortgages and the like, with an original term of more than one year. Included are revenue obligations of the municipal government, and noninterest bearing, long-term debt. In order to compare debt obligations among communities, long-term capital debt outlays should be studied in relation to equalized valuation.

Equalized valuation (from 1976 through 1980) is the Department of Revenue's estimate of the market value of all locally taxable property. It is a measure generated to standardize the basis on which the assessed value of property is expressed. It provides a means of comparing all the state's cities and towns, for purposes of distributing state aid and apportioning county costs. While some progress has been made in bringing property tax assessments in Massachusetts in line with full and fair cash value (as constitutionally mandated) wide variation remains among locally generated assessed values. As of FY81, only 98 of the state's 351 cities and towns were assessing at 100 percent of full market value. Revaluation in the remaining 253 cities and towns is supposed to be completed by 1983.

Dividing debt by equalized valuation provides a way of evaluating different municipalities' capacity to meet fixed debt payments. The greater the proportion of long-term fixed debt to equalized valuation, the greater the possibility that a municipality is over-extended. A sharp jump in long-term debt outstanding is usually associated with pressure to raise the tax rate. We define fiscal stability, in part, as the ability to cover repayment of long-term fixed debt in the face of other service obligations.

### Indicator 3. Pension Obligations, Retirement Contributions, Debt Service, and State and County Charges

This indicator measures the fixed costs a municipality must cover each fiscal year. These costs are considered relative to total general revenue. The size of each component of fixed cost differs with the age and size of the work force, the amount of long-term debt incurred (both principal and interest payments), and charges imposed by the county and the state. Each municipality must accommodate these demands no matter how they vary from year to year.

### Indicator 4. Revenue from Fees and Charges

Generally, revenues from fees and user charges are the dollar amounts (payments) received from the public for the performance of specific services (e.g., sewer, water, or trash collection services). Essentially, the person benefitting from the service is charged. Revenues from fees and charges also include receipts from the sale of commodities and services (e.g., recreation services, parking meters, facilities, permits, licenses, or school lunches), but exclude revenue generated by municipal utilities. This source of income is examined in relation to local own source revenue of all kinds. Local own source revenue includes all revenue raised by the municipality, total general revenue, minus both state aid and direct federal aid. The greater the revenue generated from fees and user charges, the less dependent a municipality is likely to be on property taxes and motor vehicle excise taxes.

### Indicator 5. Uncollected Property Taxes

We thought, initially, that this would be a useful proxy of municipal management capability. This indicator was intended to describe tax collection practices as well as the frequency of tax delinquencies. Since property taxes constitute about 55 percent of Massachusetts' local revenues, tax collection is an important measure of a community's fiscal stability. Municipalities can choose to convert delinquent taxes into tax title claims before the end of the fiscal year. Hence, the figure submitted each year on the local balance sheet may not reflect the true level of uncollected property taxes through that year. It is therefore, almost impossible to determine which communities are most aggressive in collecting back taxes each year. From 1976 to 1980, the amount of uncollected property taxes for the sample of 61 communities ranged between .1 percent and 5.6 percent of equalized valuation. Tax collection is an on-going activity; thus, the amount of delinquent taxes reported at the end of any given year provides an inaccurate accounting. (1) The relatively small overall percentages of uncollected taxes suggest a high or unhealthy percentage of uncollected taxes in very few cases. The analysis using this indicator has been deleted from the pages that follow because of the difficulties involved in collecting meaningful data.

*Indicator 6.   Certified Free Cash*

Technically, certified free cash is money that has been appropriated, but not spent. From this surplus revenue, liabilities, such as real and personal taxes, are deducted and the remainder certified by the Massachusetts Department of Revenue at the end of the current fiscal year. (2)

Municipal managers may appropriate amounts from this certified free cash reserve to finance other municipal expenditures, to offset property taxes, or to serve as a hedge against unfavorable results during the current fiscal year. (3) Certified free cash has been used to minimize expensive short-term borrowing, and before Proposition 2 1/2 was enacted, it served as a hedge against the need to change the tax rate each year.

Credit rating agencies view certified free cash as a necessary component of a sound fiscal management strategy. Typically, it represents 3-5 percent of a municipality's total budget. What is important to the financial community is not always important to cities and towns. Floating a bond may be a rare undertaking in a small community. Hence, its credit rating may be of little significance. A consistent negative free cash balance (exhibited by several of the sample communities) may indicate a management approach that is indeed appropriate to that community. In short, low free cash reserves may not be an indicator of fiscal distress. It is difficult to generalize practices from our data: budgeting over or under resource capacity may be intentional; unanticipated events (e.g., a storm or a fire) may disrupt a municipality's budget. Certified free cash is evaluated in relation to total general expenditures to facilitate comparisons among communities.

## Findings

This section describes the findings after examining the changes occurring in each group of communities (sorted by attribute).

*Ratio 1.   Investment Income*

*Major Trends.*   Between 1976 and 1980, investment income rarely exceeded 1.5 percent of municipal total general revenue for the cities and towns in the sample. A dip in investment income in 1977 (between .4 and .8 percent of total general revenue) occurred in almost all communities in the sample. Thus, 1977 marks the year of lowest earnings. Throughout the other years, the amount of investment income fluctuated, perhaps indicating an unsystematic approach to investing idle cash.

Earning interest on income is a practice that has not been pursued to its fullest potential by any of the sample municipalities. Investment income of 1.5 percent of total revenue seems low. The increase in income earnings in 1980, across all groups and all attributes, indicates that municipal officials may be rethinking their investment strategies. Since Proposition 2 1/2 passed, municipal officials have sought new revenue sources. It will be important to follow the results of municipal investment practices over the next several years.

A unique aspect of this indicator (investment income as a proportion of total general revenue) is the growth in investment earnings across all categories of communities. What specific management practices lie behind this pattern of increases has not yet been determined. While these increases may reflect nothing more than changes in interest rates from year to year, it is certain that investment earnings are an untapped source of revenue for all communities.

*Analysis.* The smallest municipalities (population under 10,000) generated the lowest aggregate amount of earnings from invested income. By the end of 1980, however, this group had closed the gap with larger municipalities. The smallest communities increased their earned income from 1.0 percent of the total general revenue in 1977, to 1.5 percent of total general revenue in 1980.

Communities facing a large gap between their expected property tax revenue prior to Proposition 2 1/2 and the amount they were allowed to collect in 1980 (after the passage of Proposition 2 1/2) were those that generated the least investment income in 1980. In 1976, these communities were just about equal to no gap communities in earned income (in relation to total revenue), but by 1980, they were earning only half as much, on average, as no gap communities.

From 1976 to 1980, high income communities showed consistent increases in the amount of income earned from investments. The lowest income communities in the sample experienced an up-and-down pattern in investment earnings from year to year, ending up in 1980 only slightly ahead of their 1976 level of 0.8 percent of general revenue.

The fastest growing communities earned substantially less than stable or declining municipalities in 1976, but by 1980, rapidly growing cities and towns were earning slightly more in investment income than the others.

*Ratio 2.   Long-Term Debt Outstanding*

*Major Trends.*   Capital investment as indicated by long-term capital debt outstanding, remained relatively constant prior to the passage of Proposition 2 1/2. Decreases began to register in FY79. It may be that public officials, anticipating a revenue shortfall, began to defer capital investment to some degree. High interest rates -- part of the unstable fiscal climate -- may also have contributed to the general reluctance to initiate capital projects.

Overall, the proportion of long-term debt to municipal equalized valuation (a measure of potential taxing power) does not exceed 5.0 percent in the sample. High population, high gap, low income communities with declining population have consistently incurred the highest level of long-term, fixed debt, in some instances four and five times greater than in other communities.

*Analysis.*   In 1976, the largest communities had a ratio of long-term debt to equalized valuation about three times (3.9 percent) that of the smallest communities (1.3 percent). By 1980, this difference had dropped to two times (2.8 compared with 1.3 percent), still a considerable variation.

Between 1976 and 1980, high gap communities consistently maintained the largest amount of long-term debt in relation to equalized valuation. The most dramatic change occurred between the high gap and no gap communities. In 1976, the ratio was more than one-and-one-half times (3.6 percent) that of no gap communities (2.2 percent). By 1980, it had dropped for no gap communities to only .9 percent, while high gap communities incurred more than three times this debt level (3.1 percent).

In the sample, low income communities incurred the greatest level of long-term debt in relation to equalized valuation, peaking at 5.1 percent in 1977. The level of debt incurred among high and low income communities increases sharply over time. In 1976, debt was 3.6 percent of equalized valuation as compared to 2.8 percent for high income communities. As of 1980, the debt ratio of low income communities was two-and-one-half times (3.6 percent) that of high income communities (1.4 percent).

In 1976, communities losing population had a ratio of long-term debt to equalized valuation almost 1.2 times (3.2 percent) that of high growth communities (2.5 percent). In 1980, the high growth communities dropped substantially to a debt level of 1.5 percent, while communities with a declining population decreased their debt level to only 2.8 percent, a difference almost twice the level of high growth towns.

*Ratio 3.   Pension Obligations, Retirement Contributions, Debt Service
          and State and County Charges*

*Major Trends.*   Fixed costs, as defined in this ratio, make up between 24.1 percent and 52.4 percent of municipal total general revenue in Massachusetts. No gap, high income, and high percentage of residential property communities exhibit the lowest proportion of fixed costs to total general revenue (ranging from 27.2 to 43.4 percent). There was a decrease in the aggregate level of fixed costs experienced by all types of communities in 1979. No further analysis is possible without more detailed data concerning the components of fixed costs.

*Analysis.* Fixed costs in the largest communities in the sample were, on average, in 1976, just over 38 percent of total general revenue. In that same year, in the smallest communities, fixed costs accounted for 32.1 percent of general revenue. By 1980, these ratios had increased to 44.4 percent in small communities and had dropped to 32.9 percent in larger communities.

Fixed costs in the low income communities were, on average, in 1976, 37.6 percent of total general revenue. In that same year, in the high income communities, fixed costs accounted for 34.7 percent of the total general revenue. By 1980, these levels had decreased to 33.6 percent in the low income communities and 31.4 percent in the high income communities.

In 1976, fixed costs in communities with a low percentage of residential property was 41.1 percent in relation to total general revenue. Fixed costs in communities with a high percentage of residential property were, on average, just over 27 percent of total general revenue. By 1980, the level of fixed costs had substantially decreased for the low residential property communities to 34.3 percent, while high residential property communities increased their ratio of fixed costs to general revenue to just over 33.2 percent.

## Ratio 4.   Revenue from Fees and Charges

*Major Trends.* The municipalities most likely to employ user charges are high population, low income communities with a moderate percentage of residential property in their tax base, and a declining population. The highest proportion of fees and user charges to own-source revenue was 13.9 percent, while 10.0 percent was the most frequently observed proportion. Fees and user charges revenue is derived primarily from water and sewer and other infrastructure services. The proportion of own-source revenue derived from fees and user charges may have been too low throughout the baseline period to serve as anything more than a supplemental source of revenue, easing only slightly the municipal dependence on the property tax.

*Analysis.* High population communities raised almost three times as much of their own-source revenue from fees and charges as low population communities. In 1976, the proportion of own-source revenue raised from fees and charges in high population communities was 9.0 percent, while low population communities raised 3.6 percent. In 1980, the high population communities increased their proportion of revenue from fees and charges to 9.5 percent and low population communities dropped slightly to 3.3 percent.

Low income communities raised the highest proportion of own-source revenue from fees and charges, ranging between 12.9 and 13.9 percent. This level is more than three times the amount raised by the high income communities. In 1976, low income communities raised 13.3 percent of own-source revenue from fees and charges, which high income communities raised, on average, slightly more than 4.0 percent. By 1980, the low income communities increased their ratio slightly to 13.9 percent, while high income communities dropped slightly to 4.0 percent.

Between 1976 and 1980, there was only a slight difference in the amount of own-source revenue raised by fees and charges in communities losing or gaining population. In 1976, those communities losing population had a ratio of 7.4 percent, and those gaining population raised 8.3 percent of their own-source revenue from fees and charges. By 1980, communities losing population increased slightly to 7.8 percent and communities gaining population dropped to 6.4 percent.

## *Ratio 6. Certified Free Cash*

*Major Trends.* This indicator, when sorted across attributes, demonstrated significant variation. This, combined with the ambiguities surrounding the use of certified free cash as a buffer, makes it difficult to generalize about management behavior or make a determination as to a municipality's fiscal stress or health. However, evident in all groups, excluding low income communities, is a decrease in the proportion of certified free cash in relation to total general expenditures. This supports evidence cited earlier regarding the increasing reliance on asset surpluses in both fiscal year 1980 and fiscal year 1981, as municipalities faced increasing costs in an inflationary climate.

*Analysis.* Low income communities were the only ones to increase their percentage of certified free cash relative to general expenditures, between 1979 and 1980 by 0.7 percent. In 1976, the certified free cash in low income communities was less than half (1.6 percent) that of high income communities (3.3 percent). By 1980, the amount of certified free cash had increased to 4.6 percent for low income communities, compared to 5.1 percent for high income communities.

Between 1976 and 1980, low population communities maintained the highest proportion of certified free cash to total general expenditures. In 1976, the certified free cash in low population communities was 8.3 percent compared to only 2.7 percent for the high population communities. By 1980, the level of certified free cash had dropped to 5.1 percent for low income communities; for high income communities it had dropped to 2.2 percent.

In 1976, communities with declining population had almost five times the level of certified free cash (3.3 percent) as communities with an increasing population (.6 percent). By 1980, the difference between the two population groups was only 0.8 percent. Communities losing population had increased to 4.2 percent, while communities gaining population had increased it dramatically to 5.0 percent.

## Prognosis

With the passage of Proposition 2 1/2, investment income was expected to increase. Given the increased pressure on local officials to generate additional nonproperty tax revenue, surely new ways of leveraging funds will be found. Long-term debt is likely to decrease as communities defer maintenance and capital investment. With the elimination of discretionary expenditures, fixed costs are likely to increase as a fraction of total spending, while user fees and charges should increase as a proportion of own-source revenue. Finally, certified free cash will probably continue to decrease as communities struggle to live within tight appropriation levels.

In the five years prior to enactment of Proposition 2 1/2 the fiscal stability of large, high gap, low income, slow growth municipalities had already begun to show signs of strain. Indeed, all cities and towns were engaged in the difficult process of "belt-tightening." There is every reason to believe that Proposition 2 1/2 will merely accelerate these trends.

## Notes for Chapter 6

1. All data were collected by hand from balance sheets submitted by municipalities to the Massachusetts Department of Revenue at the end of each fiscal year. Where there were no balance sheets, computations were made from municipal reports, or, when necessary, by direct communication with municipal treasurers for both current and previous year data. However, there remains a high proportion of missing data because of the unique management and financial histories of several communities in the sample.

2. Certified free cash is the result of operations of the current fiscal year, as well as the cumulative surplus or deficit resulting from the operations of previous years.

3. Evidence exists in the aggregate to support this, as documented in Chapter 23 of this volume. In FY81, the total amount of cerified free cash for Massachusetts municipalities amounted to $180 million. By January of FY82, the total had been reduced to $120 million.

Chapter 7

# Public Employment

## Impact: 2 1/2 Staff

## Introduction

This report characterizes local government employment in Massachusetts during the five year period preceding the passage of Proposition 2 1/2. Included are discussions of differences in the composition of employment among different types of communities, changes in specific categories of employme,nt over time, a summary of our findings and a suggested agenda for future research.

## Composition of Total Full-Time and Total Part-Time Employment

This section examines the composition of total full-time and total part-time employment in our sample for the years 1976 and 1980. Table 7.1 presents public employment data for the 61-community sample average. Our intent is to describe how communities with different characteristics vary in their reliance on different types of employment. The major results are presented first, followed by sections discussing how communities with differences in population, the 2 1/2 gap, income, percentage of residential property in the tax base, and population change from 1970 to 1980 differ in their public employment patterns.

*Population.* Among the categories of full-time employment, teachers represent the largest proportion of total employment; the "other" category accounts for the second largest category; the police category is third. (1) This pattern holds true for all the groups in 1976 and 1980, with one exception. Smaller communities had more employees in roads departments than in the police category in 1976 and 1980. Middle size communities had a higher proportion of teachers in 1976 and 1980 than either small or large communities.

**Table 7.1**
**Public Employment in Massachusetts, 1976 and 1980**
**(Number of Employees, 61 Community Average)**

| Service | Part Time 1976 | Time 1980 | Full 1976 | Time 1980 |
|---|---|---|---|---|
| Local Schools | | | | |
|   Instructional | 328 | 315 | 34 | 46 |
|   Noninstructional | 154 | 94 | 60 | 77 |
| Police | 64 | 65 | 18 | 17 |
| Fire | 59 | 62 | 9 | 9 |
| Sanitation | 13 | 16 | 0 | 0 |
| Roads | 36 | 35 | 3 | 1 |
| Parks and Recreation | 14 | 13 | 11 | 7 |
| Libraries | 16 | 14 | 10 | 12 |
| Financial and | | | | |
|   General Administration | 30 | 32 | 8 | 9 |
|   Total | 812 | 793 | 174 | 208 |

The general distribution of employees among the categories shows no major change from 1976 to 1980.

The "other" category accounts for the largest proportion of part–time employees, with teachers second for all groups in 1976 and 1980. Police are third in medium and large communities in 1976 and 1980, while administration is third in small communities in 1976 and 1980. From 1976 to 1980, communities maintained or reduced their part–time employment for police, fire, roads, and administration, and increased part–time employment for teachers and "other." The data also indicate differences in the reliance on part–time employees between small communities and the two groups of larger communities. Medium and large communities have no part–time employees in fire or roads, and very few in administration. Small communities have no full–time employees in fire, and instead rely on part–time employment.

*2 1/2 Gap.* The distribution of full–time employees according to the gap attribute is similar to the pattern observed for other attributes. Teachers represent the largest category, with "other" and police following, for all groups in both 1976 and 1980. The one exception is that high gap communities had a slightly higher allocation for fire than police during 1976 and 1980. There is little variation among the groups except in the fire category, where high and low to medium gap communities allocated more to fire than no gap communities. From 1976 to 1980, all groups decreased their proportion of employment in the "other" category. Administration and roads remained relatively stable, while the proportion of full-time employment in fire, police, and teachers increased.

For part-time employment, the "other" category represents a majority of employment for all groups in 1976 and 1980. Teachers comprise the second largest category, with low to medium gap communities at a higher level than no gap or high gap communities. Police are the third largest category and account for a similar proportion of all groups in 1980. The only consistent change for all groups from 1976 to 1980 is an increase in part-time teacher employment. No gap communities increased employment for police and administration from 1976 to 1980. Police and administration declined for low to medium gap communities, while fire, roads, and "other" remained the same. High gap communities increased police and administration, while fire and "other" declined.

*Income.*  For full-time employment in all communities, teachers are the largest category, "other" is second, and police is third. The distribution varies with low income communities allocating less to teachers and more to fire, police, and "other" than either middle or upper income communities. Teachers account for greater than 50 percent of employment for middle and upper income communities in both 1976 and 1980. The most noticeable shift from 1976 to 1980 is that all groups allocate more to police and fire, and less to the "other" category.

The order of part-time employment for all groups in 1976 is 1) "other," 2) teachers, and 3) police. The one exception is that middle income communities had slightly more employment in the police than the teacher category. The most important change from 1976 to 1980 is a greater reliance on part-time teachers for all groups, with a decline of part-time employment in the "other" category. There were no part-time employees in roads or in fire, except for a small percentage (4.5 percent) in high income communities in 1976. Another variation by income group is evident in the administation category. Low income communities rely less on part-time employment than either middle or high income communities, although the full-time proportion of administration is similar across all groups in both years.

*Residential Property.*  The residential attribute data suggest the same pattern of distribution of full-time employees with teachers first, "other" second, and police, third for all groups in both 1976 and 1980. From 1976 to 1980, all groups allocate less to "other" and roads, and more to fire and police, while administration and teachers remain fairly stable. The most noticeable variation among the groups is that no gap communities, with a lower proportion of residential property than either low to medium or high gap communities, has a lower allocation for teachers. This variation is similar to that observed with the income attribute, where lower income communities had a lower proportion of full-time teachers than higher income communities.

The consistency among the groups holds true for the distribution of part-time employees: 1) "other," 2) teachers, and 3) police in 1976 and 1980 for all groups. From 1976 to 1980, the part-time employment of teachers increased proportionately for all groups, while declines occurred in administration and police for all groups. There was no part-time employment in roads or fire, except in high gap communities in 1976.

*Population Change.*    In 1976 and 1980, the order of full-time employment distribution for all groups was 1) teachers, 2) "other," and 3) police. Towns that lost population from 1970 to 1980 had much higher employment in the fire category in both years than communities that experienced growth. Towns that grew from 1970 to 1980 had higher employment in roads than either communities that declined or maintained their population. From 1976 to 1980, the "other" category declined for all groups, and teachers increased for all groups, although most noticeably in communities losing population. Growing communities increased their allocation of police and fire employment from 1976 to 1980.

Towns losing population distributed their part-time employment in 1976 and 1980 to 1) "other," 2) teachers, and 3) police. Stable and growing communities allocated slightly more employment to administration than police in both years. Again, there was very little part-time employment for either fire or roads in all groups. The greatest difference from 1976 to 1980 was the increased reliance on part-time teachers by all groups.

## Changes in Specific Categories of Municipal Employment, 1976 to 1980

This section examines changes in employment levels in specific municipal services from 1976 to 1980 for our sample of Massachusetts communities. While we did experience some of the measurement problems discussed in the Introduction to Trend Analysis, it has been possible to identify certain major patterns of change among the different types of communities.

As in the previous section, the analysis here is limited and essentially descriptive. Our purpose is to develop the raw data in order to give the reader a sense of the character of recent trends in local public employment.

A number of subsections follow, each describing the sample data for a major employment category: 1) total full-time and part-time; 2) full-time teachers; 3) full-time police; 4) full-time fire; 5) full-time road department; and 6) full-time other (administrative, library, and parks and recreation). Each sub-section has several parts. The first summarizes the major trends and the remainder isolate how differences in each of the attributes seem to affect the level of that employment type.

### Total Employment:    Full-Time and Part-Time

There has been a mild to moderate decline in total employment in the Massachusetts local public sector from 1976 to 1980. The larger decreases have tended to occur in high population, high gap, and medium to high income communities. There have also been average increases in low growth communities.

Because of wide fluctuations across communities within the same categories, however, the statistics on total full-time employment are difficult to interpret. The reported statistics do not indicate a discernable pattern among some of the attribute groups, but the overall trend is clearly one of decline in total employment.

There was, however, a large growth in part-time employment in our sample over the period. The greatest percentage increases tended to occur in the medium population, no gap, low income communities. These high part-time employee growth communities also tended to have a medium percentage of residential property and a high rate of population growth from 1976 to 1980. There was no major visible part-time employment decrease for communities in our sample.

*Population.* There was, on average, a decline in total full-time employment in communities in all three population categories. Fourteen of 16 low population communities experienced some change, with an average decline of 7.5 employees (*). All 29 communities in the medium population category and all 16 communities in the high population category had 1980 total employment levels that differed from their 1976 employment levels. The average change in the former category was −21.3 (3.1 percent), compared to −24.6 (1.4 percent) in the latter category.

All low population communities in our sample reported changes in part-time employment from 1976 to 1980. These communities increased an average of 8.5 part-time employees (19.4 percent). Twenty-eight of 29 medium population communities experienced a change, with a mean increase of 23.3 part-time employees (*). All 16 of the high population communities experienced a change in part-time employment. The average increase for this group was 81 part-time employees (18.2 percent).

*Population Change.* Municipalities with a declining population from 1970 to 1980 lost an average of 16.8 full-time employees (1.7 percent) during that time. Change occurred in 22 of the 23 communities with a declining population. Towns with moderate population growth lost an average of 35.5 full-time employees (*) and communities with high growth experienced a gain of 2.6 employees (*). Twenty-two of 23 communities in the moderate growth groups and all 25 of the communities in the high growth group experienced some change in full-time employment from 1976 to 1980.

Twenty-two of 23 communities in which population declined from 1970 to 1980 had a change in part-time employment from 1976 to 1980. The average increase here was 63.2 part-time employees (23.7 percent). In communities with no population change, the average increase was 17 part-time employees (24.0 percent). All communities in that category experienced change. The 15 population growth communities had a mean increase of 20.1 part-time employees (*).

*Income.* The measures of central tendency for the income groupings are severely affected by a few extreme values. The statistics indicate that low income communities added, on average, 1 full-time employee (1.3 percent), while medium income communities experienced an average decline of 24.5 employees (2.9 percent) and high income communities had an average decline of 29.3 employees (3.6 percent). Changes occurred in all 14 low income communities, 26 of 27 medium income communities, and all 15 high income communities.

All of the 14 low income communities in our sample changed the number of part-time employees over the period. The average increase was 106.7 (50 percent). The average increase in part-time employment for 26 of 27 medium income communities was 24 (*). In all of the 15 high income communities, part-time employment decreased on the average by 4.8 part-time employees (*).

*2 1/2 Gap.*   Twelve of 13 high gap communities changed their total full-time employment levels from 1976 to 1980. The mean decline was 46.5 (3.6 percent), compared to a decline of 16.8 (6.2 percent) in the low to moderate gap category and a decline of 3.0 (*) in the no gap category. Thirty of 31 communities in the middle group experienced some change, while all 17 communities in the no gap group revised their total full-time employment level.

A change in part-time employment occurred in 12 of 13 high gap communities with an average increase of 30.9 part-time employees (11 percent). The average increase in the medium to low gap communities was 44.8 part-time employees (25.8 percent). All 31 communities in this group had some change. All of the sampled communities with no gap added part-time employees in this time period, with an average change of 19 part-time employees (*).

*Residential Property.*   All 14 municipalities with a low percentage of residential property, 26 of 27 communities with intermediate levels of residential property, and all 15 communities with a high percentage of residential property reduced levels of total full-time employment on average. The mean changes for the low, intermediate, and high residential property groups were, respectively, −21.1 (0.2 percent), −23.0 (2.9 percent), and −11.3 (2.2 percent).

In the 14 communities with a low percentage of residential property, 13 had an average increase of 35.8 part-time employees (8.5 percent). All the communities in the intermediate group added, on average, 44.4 part-time employees (*). Those communities with a high percentage of residential property increased the number of part-time employees by an average of 25.5 (*).

## Full-Time Teachers

The majority of communities in our sample reported minor declines in full-time teacher employment from 1976 to 1980. The largest percentage decreases occurred in the smaller communities, and in those municipalities with a low proportion of residential property. Low percentage decreases were reported by high population communities, those with a gap ranging from low to high, and by communities that lost population or remained stable from 1970 to 1980. Slight increases occurred in only two groups: growing communities and communities with no 2 1/2 gap.

*Population and Population Change.* Eleven of 16 low population communities in our sample experienced a decline in full-time teacher employment. These communities decreased, on average, by 8.8 teachers (6.8 percent). An average change of 1.6 teachers occurred in 27 of 29 medium size communities. Of the large municipalities in our sample, 15 of 16 reported an average loss of 41.2 teachers (3.4 percent).

Small average percentage declines were reported by 21 of 23 declining population communities and 19 of 23 low to moderate growth communities. They lost, on average, 26.7 teachers (1.3 percent) and 12.9 teachers (1.9 percent), respectively. Thirteen of 15 growing communities showed an average gain of 3.8 teachers (0.2 percent).

*2 1/2 Gap.* Similar average percentage declines occurred in low to high gap communities in our sample. Eleven of 13 high gap communities reported a loss of 43.3 teachers (3.9 percent). Low to medium gap communities experienced an average decline of 10.9 teachers (3.5 percent) in 29 of 31 communities reporting a change. One of the few reported increases occurred in the no gap communities, with 13 of 17 municipalities showing an average increase of 2.7 (6 percent) teachers.

*Income.* Towns of all income levels reported a decline in full-time teachers. Twelve of 14 low income communities lost an average of 35.2 teachers (*). An average loss of 9.8 teachers (*) was reported by 24 of 27 moderate income communities. Fourteen of 15 high income communities lost an average of 6.8 full-time teachers (*).

## Full-Time Police

Overall, there was some minor to moderate growth in full-time police employment in our sample. The greatest percentage increase tended to occur in low population, medium to no gap, medium income communities. These high police growth communities also tended to have a higher percentage of residential property and a high rate of population growth from 1970 to 1980. On the other hand, the smallest percentage increases in full-time police employment, and in some cases, significant decreases, tended to occur in high population, high gap, low income communities with a low percentage of residential property and some decline in population. (2) This latter group basically consists of Massachusetts' larger cities.

*Population and Population Change.* Only 8 of 16 low population communities in our sample experienced a change in full-time police employment. These 8 increased an average of 2.0 policemen (25.3 percent). Twenty-five of 29 medium population communities experienced a mean increase of 1.5 policemen (8.1 percent). The 16 high population communities had an average increase of 1 policeman (3.7 percent).

The 23 communities in which population declined from 1970 to 1980 had an average increase of 0.4 (*) policemen, compared with 2.3 policement (12.0 percent) in the middle category and 2.4 policemen (19.0 percent) in the growing communities. Sixteen of 23 communities in the low to medium growth category and 10 of 15 communities in the high growth category, experienced changes in full-time police employment.

*2 1/2 Gap.*    A change in full-time police employment occurred in 12 of 13 high gap communities, with an average decrease of 2.6 policemen (*). The average increase in the medium to low gap communities was 3.2 policemen (11.6 percent). Twenty-four of the 29 communities in this group had some change. Eleven of the 17 communities with no gap added an average of 1.7 policemen (11.9 percent).

*Income.*    Thirteen of 14 low income communities changed the number of full-time policemen from 1976 to 1980. The average loss was 1.2 policemen (*), compared to an average gain of 2.6 policemen (15.3 percent) in the medium income communities. Twenty-one of 26 communities in the latter category experienced some change. In the 15 high income communities, 13 varied their employment of full-time policemen over this time period. The average increase was 2.2 policemen (9.3 percent).

*Full-Time Fire Employment*

The general trend in fire employment for our sample has been one of significant growth from 1976 to 1980. The largest relative increases occurred in communities with low to medium population, no gap, medium to high income, medium to high residential property, and medium to high growth. The smallest increases were usually in high population, high gap, low income, low residential property communities, that experienced population declines from 1970 to 1980. As with police employment, this negative growth group is representative of some of the larger cities in the Commonwealth.

*Population and Population Change.*    Of the 16 low population municipalities, 2 experienced an average increase of 2.5 (*) fire fighters. Twelve of 29 medium population municipalities had an average increase of 4 fire fighters (25.6 percent). All high population municipalities revised their full-time fire employment levels, by an average increase of 6.3 fire fighters (3.4 percent).

Eighteen of 23 municipalities decreasing in population had an average increase of 5.7 fire fighters (*). Nine of 13 low population change communities experienced a change, with an average growth of 2.5 fire fighters (24.6 percent). Of the 15 municipalities with population increases, 7 experienced a mean increase of 6.5 fire fighters (*).

*2 1/2 Gap.*    The average increase of full-time fire fighters in high gap municipalities was 5.3, with 8 of 13 municipalities experiencing some change. Twenty-one of 32 middle to low gap municipalities experienced an average increase of 4.8 fire fighters (8.1 percent). Only 4 of 17 no gap municipalities had a change in fire fighter employment, with an average increase of 5.7 fire fighters (*).

*Income.* Employment in 13 of 14 low income municipalities rose, on average, by 8 fire fighters (7.9 percent). Eleven of 27 middle income municipalities reported an average increase of 3 fire fighters (22.4 percent). Ten of 15 high income municipalities experienced an average growth of 4 fire fighters (18.7 percent).

## Full-Time Road Department Employment

A high number of communities in all attribute groups reported some change in full-time employment for road employees from 1976 to 1980. Employment growth, on average, was reported by medium-sized, no gap to medium gap, high income, stable and growing communities, and communities with a high proportion of residential property. Large municipalities with a high gap and a low proportion of residential property, and low income communities experienced declines, on average, in road employment.

*Population.* Eight of 16 small municipalities experienced a mean decline of .13 (*) road employees. An average increase of 0.6 road employees (7.7 percent) occurred in 25 of 29 middle-sized communities. Fourteen of 16 high population municipalities experienced an average decrease of 16.6 road employees (9.4 percent).

Twenty of 23 municipalities with declining populations lost an average of 11.8 road employees (6.4 percent). Municipalities with low to moderate population growth had average increases of 0.68 road employees (6.2 percent). Nineteen of 23 communities were in this group. Eight of 15 high growth municipalities reported an increase of 6.3 road employees (4 percent).

*2 1/2 Gap.* Eleven of 13 high gap communities experienced an average loss of 1 road employee (13 percent). Medium to low gap communities reported an average decrease of 8.9 road employees in 25 of 31 municipalities. An average increase of 1.5 road employees (18.3 percent) occurred in 11 of 17 no gap municipalities.

*Income.* Eleven of 13 low income municipalities had an average loss of 15.2 road employees (24.2 percent). Moderate income communities, with 19 of 27 experiencing a change, had a mean decrease of 6.3 road employees (6.1 percent). Fourteen of 15 high income communities gained an average of 5.1 road employees (34.2 percent).

## Full-Time Other Employment: Administrative, Library, Parks & Recreation

Changes in the level of administrative employment from 1976 to 1980 varied somewhat across the municipalities in our sample. High population, high gap, low income communities, with a low percentage of residential property and declining population were most likely to show an increase in administrators, but the average percentage growth is quite small. The communities with these attributes tended to be larger cities.

Library employment declined from 1976 to 1980 for the majority of municipalities that experienced changes in this category. The only slight increases occurred in small municipalities that grew in populatin from 1970 to 1980. These increases, however, were reported by a minority of communities in those groups. Several communities reported no change.

Employment for parks and recreation deparments tended to decline slightly in our sample. The largest decreases usually occurred in municipalities with medium to high populations, medium to low gaps, low average incomes, and medium levels of residential property. It is not clear from our data, however, that the pattern of parks and recreation employment cutbacks in our sample is meaningful. For the most part, the changes were quite small. The only exceptions to this trend were high income, and high residential property communities that experienced a moderate average increase in parks and recreation employment.

*Population and Population Change.*    Eleven of 16 low population municipalities in our sample underwent a change in full-time administrative employment. These 11 low population communities decreased on the average by 0.45 administrators (15.5 percent). Twenty-four of 29 medium population communities experienced a mean increase of 1.2 administrators (14 percent) over the period. Sixteen of the high population communities had an average increase of 4.1 administrators (3.6 percent).

Among small communities, 14 of 16 reported no change in library employment, while two reported an average increase of .5 (8.9 percent). Nineteen of 29 medium-sized communities experienced an average decrease of 1 library employee (0.6 percent). Fifteen of the 16 large municipalities in our sample lost an average of 5.4 library employees (*).

Two of 16 low population communities averaged an increase in park employment of 0.5 (*) over the period. Ten of 29 medium population communities decreased by an average of 1.8 full-time park employees (7.2 percent). Fourteen of 16 high population communities had an average loss of 1.7 park employees (*).

Twenty-two of 23 communities that lost population averaged an increase of 3.2 administrators (3.5 percent). Twenty such communities had a mean loss of 4 library employees (2.6 percent), while 18 lost an average of 1.7 park employees (*).

The 23 low growth communities reported no significant change in administrative employment, but 11 of these communities lost 2.2 library employees (2.8 percent) and 10 lost 1 park employee (*), on average.

Among the 15 high growth communities, 9 gained 2.2 administrative employees (*), 5 gained 1 library employees (32 percent), while 5 lost 2.2 park employees (*), on average.

*2 1/2 Gap.*   All 13 high gap communities experienced a change in the number of administrators, with an average increase of 3.6 administrators (4.9 percent). Twenty-four of 29 communities in the medium to low gap category had an average increase of 1.5 administrators (7.5 percent). The growth of administrators in communities with no gap was 0.6 administrators (*). Fourteen of 17 communities in our sample had some change.

Towns in all groups of the gap attribute decreased, on average, their library employment. Ten no gap communities reported no change, while seven reported an average loss of 0.86 library employees (29 percent). Twenty of the 31 medium gap communities reported an average loss of 1.3 library employees (6 percent). Nine of the 13 high gap communities experienced an average loss of 7.5 library employees (*).

Ten of 13 large gap municipalities rose by an average of 0.2 in full-time park employment (*). Thirteen of 29 medium to low gap municipalities lost an average of 2.7 park employees (4.3 percent). Five of the 17 no gap municipalities experienced a mean decrease of 0.6 in full-time park employment (*).

*Income.*   The average increase of administrators in 13 of 15 low income communities was 5.3 (5.6 percent). Moderate income communities experienced, on average, no significant change in the number of administrators. All high income municipalities in our sample had an average increase of 1.4 administrators (11.1 percent).

Twelve of 14 low income communities reported an average loss of 4 library employees (*). Fifteen of 27 moderate income communities experienced an average decrease of 2.3 library employees (6 percent). Eight of 15 high income communities lost an average of 2 library employees (10 percent).

Thirteen of 14 low income municipalities had a mean decline of 5.3 park employees (4.4 percent). Eleven of 17 middle income municipalities experienced an average decrease of 0.3 in full-time park employment (*). Eight of 15 high income municipalities had an average increase of 3 park employees (*).

## Summary

Total full-time employment generally declined in a majority of municipalities in our sample from 1976 to 1980. The largest average decreases occurred in large municipalities, in high 2 1/2 gap municipalities, and in slow growth municipalities. In contrast, total part-time employment increased without exception in the sampled communities from 1976 to 1980. High average increases occurred in medium-sized communities, low-income communities, and those with no gap. These trends confirm that larger municipalities, experiencing population losses and corresponding financial difficulties, began implementing minor cutbacks prior to Proposition 2 1/2. In addition, the substitution of part-time for full-time employees raises the interesting issue of how communities compare costs, and the level and quality of services, for the two employment types.

Two categories of full-time employment experienced minor growth during this period of general decline -- fire and police. The increases occurred in municipalities with certain attributes, namely, low to medium population, moderate income, moderate to high percentage of residential property and population growth. Employment for roads increased in municipalities with similar characteristics. Full-time employment for teachers, library and parks employees tended to decrease, although the average changes were small for the latter two categories. Small communities, and municipalities with a low percentage of residential property reported the largest average decreases in full-time teacher employment.

Even though exceptions exist, it seems clear that full-time employment increases and decreases are related to municipal characteristics. Moderate-sized, growing municipalities with a moderate to high income population and a moderate to high proportion of residential property, tended to increase certain types of municipal employment from 1976 to 1980. Conversely, large municipalities with declining populations, low incomes, and low proportions of residential property in their tax base tended to begin employment cutbacks during the period. It is clear that many municipalities also began to rely more on part-time employment.

The descriptive statistics presented in this report raise a number of important questions related to the ability of local governments to maintain an adequate level of public services. What types of further employment cutbacks will be necessary in order to cope with Proposition 2 1/2? Will the growing tendency to rely more heavily on part-time employment continue? What will happen to employment levels in the larger, low-income and high gap communities where greater than average employment cutbacks occurred before Proposition 2 1/2? Will employment in parks, recreation, and library activities continue to decline, and at what rate, now that Proposition 2 1/2 has tightened the fiscal squeeze on many cities and towns? What types of cooperative employment strategies among communities in such services as fire protection might evolve as a way of dealing with Proposition 2 1/2?

It is clear that local public employment in Massachusetts was beginning to decline during the 1976 to 1980 period, especially in certain service areas and certain types of communities. Further research is needed to explain this trend and its implications.

Chapter 8

## User Fees and Charges

Daniel M. Holland and Patricia McCarney

## Introduction

Proposition 2 1/2 has generated substantial interest in fees and charges as a means of financing the continued *supply* of public services. But, in fact, fees and charges also affect the *demand* for public services. If a service is made available at zero price (as is characteristic in the public sector), the "demand" or "need" for it is likely to be higher than it would be if a price reflecting true costs were imposed. Relative to what most people would be willing to pay for public goods they are "overprovided." Proposition 2 1/2 is partly aimed at depriving local officials of the resources with which to satisfy "excess demand." As Richard Bird has argued in *Charging for Public Services,* however, this will not assure that the resources that remain will be allocated efficiently. (1) User charges, by choking off excess demand, may aid in increasing the efficiency of allocation in the public sector.

There are reasons, then, to look at both supply and demand considerations in evaluating new-found local interest in user fees and charges in Massachusetts.

## Comparing Massachusetts with the U.S. Average

Before comparing Massachusetts with the U.S. average, the problems of aggregate comparisons should be acknowledged. In particular, it is important to point out that aggregate comparisons mask important variations in provisions of services, changing practices, institutional developments, allocations of governmental responsibility, and attitudes on the relative roles of public and private initiatives.

Massachusetts appears to underemploy user charges for public services. On a per capita basis state and local fees and charges came to $144 for the U.S. as a whole and only $116 for Massachusetts. As a percentage of personal income, these charges were only 1.7 percent in Massachusetts while equaling 2.3 percent for the U.S. as a whole. Fees and charges by states and local governments in the U.S. equalled 17.7 percent of revenue from own tax sources; in Massachusetts the comparable figure in 1980 was only 11.5 percent.

Were Massachusetts to achieve the nationwide average in these categories, hundreds of millions of additional dollars could be replaced.

| If Massachusetts Achieved Country-Wide Average of Current Charges | Increased Revenue (in millions) | Percentage Increase in Own Taxes Plus User Charges |
|---|---|---|
| Per capita | 161.7 | 2.5 |
| Percentage of personal income | 230.0 | 3.5 |
| Percentage of own taxes | 353.0 | 5.5 |

(Estimates based on FY77 data from U.S. Department of Commerce, Bureau of the Census, *1977 Census of Governments,*
Volume 4, Number 5.)

This is not to suggest that Massachusetts should seek to achieve these national averages. Indeed, a closer look at the Massachusetts-U.S. comparisons are needed. By any of the ratios in Table 8.1, the state government in Massachusetts employs user charges to about the same extent as other states. It is local governments that fall below the U.S. average.

Looking at per capita comparisons in more detail (Table 8.2) combined state and local charges in Massachusetts fall below the U.S. average for education, hospitals, sewage, sanitation, natural resources, and parks and recreation; and above the national average for housing and urban renewal, airports, and water transport and terminals. The same disparities appear when we consider current charges as a percentage of personal income. Of course, charges per capita or as a percentage of personal income could be below the national average in Massachusetts for one or both of two reasons: expenditures in a given category could be lower in Massachusetts or the proportion of total expenditures recouped through charges could be lower.

Let:
> Expenditures = E
> Population = P
> Charges = C

Then,
> $E/P$ x $C/E$ = $C/P$

Since the disparities between the U.S. average and the Commonwealth are the same in the percentage of Total Spending in Category columns as in Charges Per Capita and Percentage of Total Spending in Category columns, we have no way of determining the relative weights of these factors, except for Housing and Urban Renewal. There the percentage of total spending recouped by charges is below average but the per capita charge is above average.

On a per capita basis, the most pronounced shortfalls below the U.S. average are in sewage, sanitation other than sewage, and natural resources. With respect to charges for natural resources there is good reason for the Commonwealth to be lower than the average. Its minimal natural resource endowment gives the state less to charge for.

Comparisons between Massachusetts and the U.S. average for State expenditures (Table 8.3) or local expenditures (Table 8.4) are also ambiguous.

## Comparing Massachusetts with Some Other States

The relative underutilization of user charges in Massachusetts is confirmed by comparing the Commonwealth to several other states (i.e., New York, California, and Connecticut). Massachusetts is particularly low (again in terms of charges per capita) in fees for sewage, sanitation other than sewage, and for parks and recreation relative to Californa and New York.

*When charges levied are taken as a percentage of personal income,* Massachusetts appears to underemploy education charges (other than school lunch sales), hospital charges and once again, sewage charges, relative to the national total. When compared to other states, as in Table 8.5 (middle column) Massachusetts appears to be on par in education charges with our three other sample states, quite low relative to California in hospital and sewage charges, but higher in hospital charges relative to New York and Connecticut.

We have also made comparisons using the Financing Ratio, that is, current charges taken as a percentage of total spending. The Financing Ratio represents the percentage of current operations recovered through user charges. From this standpoint. Massachusetts again appears to underemploy user charges in both the sewage and sanitation other than sewage categories. In these two categories Massachusetts also has a very low performance relative to California (as indicated in Table 8.4).

Table 8.2 indicates that charges in Massachusetts for parks and recreation are below the U.S. average at 16.8 percent, and, as indicated in Table 8.5, well below Connecticut at 28.5 percent and California at 17.8 percent.

The "low charge" categories identified in the preceding discussion of state and local government are education (other than school lunch sales), hospitals, sewage, sanitation other than sewage, natural resources, and parks and recreation.

When education charges are examined further relative to the U.S. averages (Tables 8.3 and 8.4), the lag in Massachusetts appears to be accounted for by both state and local underutilization. This is clear both in terms of charges per capita and in terms of charges as a percentage of personal income. Both levels of government appear to be underemploying user charges (relative to the U.S. average) in education.

A different conclusion must be drawn for *hospitals.* Hospital charges per capita at the state level in Massachusetts are $19.90 compared to a U.S. average of $31.51. At the local level Massachusetts governments are performing almost at par with the national average. (Local charges per capita for hospitals in Massachusetts were $28.13 relative to the U.S. average of $28.32.) In addition, as Table 8.7 indicates, Massachusetts local governments are performing quite well in hospital charges per capita relative to California (31.51), New York ($20.25) and especially well relative to Connecticut ($3.22). Here it is at the state level that much of Massachusetts' low performance is explained. Massachusetts hospital charges per capita employed by the state were $2.87 relative to California at $13.11 per capita, Connecticut at $11.63 and New York at $7.63.

Still different conclusions must be reached for the remaining three "low-charge" categories. The underemployment of user charges in sewage, sanitation other than sewage, and, parks and recreation are accounted for by local not state decisions in Massachusetts.

Local governments in Massachusetts appear to underemploy charges for sewage relative to the U.S. average: charges per capita in Massachusetts are $3.36 versus $11.31 nationwide: in terms of charges as a percentage of personal income in Massachusetts 0.05 percent versus 0.18 percent for the nation as a whole; and in terms of the financing ratio in Massachusetts charges equal 55.5 percent of current sewage expenditures compared with the U.S. average of 106.4 percent. The underemployment of user charges in sewage provisions at the local level in Massachusetts is also identifiable relative to California and New York (Table 8.7).

With respect to the category *sanitation other than sewage,* it is the local level of governments in Massachusetts which accounts for the underemployment of user charges. Massachusetts local governments charges in this category are low relative to the U.S. average by all three measures (charges per capita, percentage of personal income, and percentage of total spending in the category or financing ratio). (See Tables 8.4 and 8.7).

Finally, with regard to *parks and recreation,* it is local governments in Massachusetts that account for the underemployment of current charges. State government is almost on par with the U.S. average and with the other three sample states. This finding is consistent across all three measures and for all three states. More specifically (Table 8.4) charges per capita by Massachusetts local governments amounted to 0.89 relative to the U.S. average of $2.93. When taken as a percentage of personal income, current charges in parks and recreation by Massachusetts local governments amounted to 0.01 percent relative to the U.S. at 0.05 percent. The financing ratio shows Massachusetts local governments' current charges equal to 7.4 percent of the total current spending on parks and recreation relative to 16.3 percent for the U.S. Massachusetts local governments were outperformed according to all three measures by local governments in California, New York and Connecticut.

We cite these averages as "suggestive." Individual cities and towns in the Commonwealth will also find "suggestive" their user charge performance relative to the average *within* Massachusetts.

## The Current State of Charging by Cities and Towns in Massachusetts

In Table 8.8 we present estimates of user charges per capita in Massachusetts. While population is not the ideal deflator, per capita amounts are more appropriate for comparisons than aggregate amounts. The data of the table cover the 150 cities and towns in the Commonwealth with population in excess of 10,000.

Very few cities and towns in Massachusetts have their own hospitals. The three largest cities -- Boston, Springfield, and Worcester -- do, but only a few of the municipalities of smaller size have their own hospitals for which they can charge. For the cities which have them, hospital charges are by far the largest current charge they levy. For almost all "Hospital" cities and towns, hospital charges are over 80 percent of total current charges. And for most cities and towns having them, hospital charges are at a level close to, and in some cases higher than, current expenditures on hospitals. (Current expenditures are essentially wages and salaries and related benefits). Current charges in "Hospital" cities and towns are high both because expenditures per capita are high and the ratio of charges to expenditures are high. The data show no systematic relation between city size and hospital charges per capita.

At the opposite extreme, almost all cities and towns, 148 out of 150 and all those with population over 20,000, impose current charges in connection with education. While city and town outlays per capita are generally higher for education than hospitals, per capita current charges for education are much lower than for hospitals, reflecting a much lower "financing" fraction -- i.e., ratio of current charges to total current outlays -- for education. Hospitals, we noted, generally have a charge-financing ratio for current expenditures of close to 1; in education the ratio is very low, ranging from 3.3 percent for the smallest towns in our sample to 1.6 percent for the largest cities. The data of Table 8.8 show declining educational charges per capita with increasing city size. This could reflect numerous factors: a lower proportion of school-age children to total population in larger cities and towns for one, or lower average income for families with school-age children in cities than in towns.

Current charges for education are broken down into three categories -- charges for school lunches, charges for tuition, and all other current charges for education. Virtually all cities levy a charge of some sort for school lunches and "other" educational charges, and over two-thirds charge to some extent for tuition.

For cities of all sizes the school lunch charge is by far the largest of the three categories. The same pattern observed for all current charges for education characterizes charges for school lunch and other educational charges, viz declining charges per capita reading from the smaller to larger cities. For most cities, ("hospital" cities are the exception) school lunch charges per capita exceed all other charges except sewerage.

Housing and urban renewal charges are levied by very few cities, and come to very modest amounts. Airport charges also are imposed by only a few cities. Their airports vary greatly in size and activies as reflected in the wide variation in airport charges per capita. Airport charges tend to cover a high proportion of current expenditures on airports -- varying from about 50 percent to over 100 percent.

It is usual to charge for parks and recreation. Three-quarters of the cities and towns in Massachusetts with over 10,000 in population employ them; and the proportion who charge for parks and recreation is about the same in all size classes. But the charge/expenditure ratio for parks and recreation is low, ranging from 5 to 10 percent and falling with city size.

For the vast majority of cities, sewerage charges per capita are the highest category of charge employed. There is no systematic relation between city size and sewerage charges per capita. And it is not clear that we would expect to find one. While, other things equal, we might expect economies of scale in sewerage plants and therefore sewerage charges per capita declining with city size, it is also likely that the larger a city's population the more substantial its sewerage plant and, therefore, the higher per capita sewerage charges.

Sewerage charges characteristically come to a multiple of current sewerage expenditures. How close they come to total outlays on sewerage systems, however, is quite a different matter, since a large portion of sewerage costs are "capital" rather than current. But by either measure sewerage services are probably characterized by a high "financing" ratio.

While over 60 percent of the towns and cities (with over 10,000 in population) in the Commonwealth levy sewerage charges, only 31 percent impose charges for sanitation other than sewerage which, presumably, is primarily garbage disposal services. The proportion of the cities charging for sanitation services other than sewerage rises with size of city, but the amount of the charge per capita does not; if anything it behaves the other way -- falling between $1.27 and $2.88, on average for cities with populations between 10,000 and 75,000 and $0.27 to $1.38 for the largest cities in the Commonwealth. The volume of garbage and waste increases more than proportionately with population density; this behavior of per capita charges, therefore, suggests a declining financing ratio for sanitation other than sewerage. And this is what the data indicate. Whereas the smallest towns (those between 10,000 and 20,000 in population) have a charge/expenditure ratio of 24 percent for Sanitation Other than Sewerage, sanitation charges in Springfield and Worcester, on average come to 9 percent of expenditures and in Boston only 1 percent.

Our data point up that parking and congestion are urban concerns. Less than half the towns and cities (with population over 10,000) in the Commonwealth impose charges for parking facilities. But the vast majority of the larger ones, say with populations over 25,000, have parking charges. And parking facilities charges per capita are very clearly a rising function of population size. While some parking charges are for facilities that require outlays, e.g. garages, much of the parking charge is simply a device for rationing scarce space. Therefore, the financing ratio for parking facilities runs between 1.5 and 9.

Not shown in the averages in Table 8.8 are the pronounced diversities around the averages in each category. These are suggestive of a "personal" factor at work. That some cities charge for a given service and others do not reflects among other factors the beliefs and personal influence of individual mayors, city managers, department heads and budget directors.

In Tables 8.9 and 8.10, discussed very briefly here, appear user charges per capita as of 1980, again for cities and towns in Massachusetts with population exceeding 10,000, but arrayed in Table 8.9 by equalized valuation of real property per capita and in Table 8.10 by personal income (as of 1970) per capita.

Other things equal, we should expect that the higher the equalized value per capita, the more could be raised from a given *rate* of property tax, the less, therefore, the reliance on user charges. But, of course, other things are not equal.

In Table 8.9 the seven communities that make up the highest equalized value class are wealthy small towns, primarily on the Cape. Because they are small they have no hospitals and spend relatively little on sewers. That they are primarily beach communities also explains their high per capita charges for Parks and Recreation and Airports. The high charge for Housing and Urban Renewal in the $25,000 and over equalized value group is due solely to a program in the town of Weston, evidently a special story.

It is surprising to see the higher valuation class communities failing to rely more heavily on the property tax and having per capita user charges for garbage and trash collection as high as communities with a lower property tax base per capita. However, a tradeoff exists between property tax and user charges in the decline in Other Current Charges reading from low to high Equalized Valuation Per Capita classes.

While, *a priori,* one would expect a positive association between per capita income and the level of charges (since citizens with higher incomes could be expected to pay more for services or to pay for more services) only for Education in Table 8.10 is this expectation borne out.

Clearly, further understanding of the determinants of user charges in Massachusetts to municipal finance awaits multivariate analysis.

## Willingness to Pay in Massachusetts

Public officials in Massachusetts see the need for more user charges. Economists have long advocated greater employment of user charges on grounds of economic efficiency. What does the public think?

Among Massachusetts residents there does not seem to be strong support for user charges as against taxes (those presently employed or alternative possibilities) for financing public services.

In their questionnaire survey (1980) of voters on Proposition 2 1/2, Helen Ladd and Julie Boatwright Wilson asked the following questions: "For each service I read, would you like to keep the financing the way it is now or see a greater share of the money come from local property taxes, from state income taxes, from state sales taxes, or a greater share from fees paid by users of the service." The results are summarized in Table 8.11.

For the three service areas that account for the large part of the typical budget a greater share for user charge financing as against the other choices was preferred by a very few: Police, 2.2%; Fire Fighting, 1.4%; Public Elementary and High School Education, 7.2%. Additional employment of user fees was most strongly supported for: Regular Garbage Pickup, 17.2%; Local Public Transportation, 25.7%; After School Programs such as Music and Athletics, 20.5%; Adult Education, 32.4%; and State and Community Colleges and Universities, 20.7%.

Relative preference for user charges for these services is reasonable, since their consumption involves externalities to a lesser degree than the other items listed in Table 8.11.

In no case is there really a mandate for user charges. Thus while 17 percent expressed a preference for more user charges in financing regular garbage pickup, 42 percent preferred more property tax and 30 percent the same revenue mix as at present. And twice as many preferred additional property tax to more user charges for after-school programs. That only 8 percent preferred more reliance on user charges for financing public parks and recreation (compared with 49 percent favoring more property tax) points up the limited possibilities of user charges, since recreation is a clear case of a service from which the benefit is primarily individual.

Incidentally, Massachusetts residents appeared to be properly perceptive of the inappropriateness of user charges for "redistributive" services, very low percentages favoring more reliance on user charges for financing: Mental Health Programs, 4.8%; Services for the Elderly, 2.9%; and Special Education for Children with Learning Problems, 5.9%.

We alert the reader that this sort of information is just the start of knowledge. Some of the categories are too broad to elicit meaningful answers. Instead of asking about "Police" generally, had the question been put with respect to special police details required to control traffic in connection with a private party, or fire department expense for ambulance service enjoyed by individuals, a higher proportion of respondents would undoubtedly have preferred user charges.

## Some Institutional and Legal Considerations

Federal income tax policy tends to favor taxes versus user charges, because state and local taxes are deductible by owner-occupiers in calculating taxable income for the Federal tax, but fees and charges are not. A similar bias exists in state aid formulae, which attempt to reward local governments for tax "effort" but do not take account of user charges in measuring tax effort. On the other hand, we note a point particularly important for capital cities and others impacted heavily by tax-exempt properties: organizations exempt from property taxes have to pay user fees.

In general, the academic supporters of user charges implicitly assume that prices will reflect marginal costs, which may exceed or fall short of average variable cost and average total cost. In fact, however, various constraints limit user charge formulae that can be employed. Local governments in Massachusetts, for example, have been constrained by law or custom (it is not clear which) to prices that recover no more than variable costs.

However, the law governing a municipality's imposition of user charges has been undergoing amendment during the last year. Since the passge of Proposition 2 1/2, the law has been shaped in such a way as to give the municipaliy more discretionary power in the institution of fees and charges. Whereas, before, fees and charges were set by statute, changes to the legislation now free the upper limit and allow a municipality much more discretion in establishing fee and charge levels.

Who in turn sets this fee at the municipal level is dependent upon the individual service category being considered. For example, for public hospital fees and charges, it is usually the hospital commissioner; for parking facilities, and water and sewer charges, it is often the selectmen or mayor; for recreation and parks fees, it is usually the department head and staff who set the charges; and for education, fees and charges are usually regulated by the school committee or the state depending on the various subcategories of education services.

In the late summer of 1981 legislation was passed extending the rights of cities and towns in Massachusetts to set up special revolving accounts supported by user charges. These revolving funds allow revenues raised from fees and charges for municipal services to be diverted directly back into those services instead of being put into the general fund. In other words, special revolving funds allow direct support of the service which generates the fees.

One specific area of legislation which has been amended is Section 20A of Chapter 59. Section 9 of Chapter 782 (Chapter 782 makes a number of substantial modifications to Proposition 2 1/2, i.e., Chapter 580 of the Acts of 1980) strikes the old Section 20A of Chapter 59 of the General laws and replaces it with the new section 20A. Whereas the original draft of Proposition 2 1/2 states that "no government entity shall make any charge or impose any fee for goods provided or services rendered in excess of the costs of furnishing such goods and or providing such service," in the new Section 20A as amended by Chapter 782, this passage has been dropped. As a result, the law is now silent with respect to what level a user charge may be set at. Restrictions do still exist however for counties, districts, and public authorities to set costs, charges and fees. And this presumably leaves cities and towns free to set user charges at, above or below cost as they choose.

But even were the courts to hold that the old provisions still apply, the constraints on user charges would be ambiguous. For there are many definitions of cost, among which may be designated variable costs, total costs, and marginal costs. In practice user charges have been set below all of these, i.e., have not covered even variable costs. Where attempts have been made at "full cost" recovery it is variable (or current) costs that were the benchmark. Rarely, if ever, have capital costs been taken into account in the design of user charges. In fact, however, an appropriate user charge, i.e., one that made for efficient resource allocations in the public sector, would be based on marginal cost, a criterion very infrequently employed in fees and charges. Charges based on marginal cost could fall short of or exceed total costs. Since "efficiency" is a major reason for user charges, and "efficiency" in this connection means charges based on marginal costs, these ambiguities in the law and its interpretation would have to be clarified if user charges and fees are to be employed appropriately.

The outstanding legal issue for municipalities now with respect to user charges and fees, concerns the definition of a fee versus a tax. The controversial question that has been before the courts in Massachusetts has been framed as: "When does a user fee become a tax?" This legal question had been avoided until opposition from the real estate community in Boston was raised against Mayor White's proposed special fire charge for high-rise buildings. This "special fee" was challenged as actually being a hidden "property tax" and put in question the legal right to fire protection. This has raised the necessity for a very clear definition of fees and charges. The distinction between a fee and a tax seems to be developing in terms of voluntarism. The current interpretation addresses the nature of a fee or charge as being voluntary and a tax as being involuntary. However, only preliminary reflection suggests the difficulty of such a distinction in these terms. Is payment of a water or sewage charge for example voluntary? That is, can the user choose not to pay for this service? It is the kind of questioning which not only reveals the difficulty of such a definition but which can also assist in formulating clearer statements about the nature of fees and charges, particularly in terms of their distinctiveness relative to a so-called "tax." The court decision passed in April 1982 determined Mayor White's fire charge to be a *tax* and thus to be "illegal."

Conclusion

The purpose of this paper has been to develop the background on user fees and charges, and the current "facts" in their employment by cities and towns in the Commonwealth. These "facts" consititute the benchmark against which to evaluate the emerging dynamics of the response, with respect to charges and fees, to Proposition 2 1/2.

The "facts" also serve to suggest some important factors to look for as we follow the experience with charges and fees over the next few years.

1. How important a source of finance charges will be for governments depends to an important extent on:
   a. The range of services they offer. Cities that run their own hospitals, for example, will levy charges on those who use them that are very large per capita, and will show up as having a high fee intesity. Removing current hospital charges from their totals, however, shows "hospital" cities and towns to be no more avid with respect to charges for other services than the other cities and towns in the Commonwealth.

   b. The fraction of outlays in a given service that charges recoup. For hospitals this fraction is about 1. For education, which virtually all cities and towns levy some charges for, the fraction is very low -- between .015 and .03. Charges for fire and police services are not tabulated separately in our data, but appear under "other." Police and fire outlays are a major component of the municipal budget, and probably have a financing ratio on the order of magnitude of education.

   c. The *degree* to which they charge relative to other cities and towns. If the largest cities in Massachusetts charge to the same degree (i.e., had the same financing ratios) as the smaller ones for Sanitation Services Other than Sewerage, they would have a perceptibly higher revenue from current charges.

2. Further work will be undertaken in developing the data for user charges from the IMPACT: 2 1/2 Project data base. Data in categories similar to the 1980 data presented above on the Masachusetts cities and towns will be developed annually 1970-1980. Trends and departures from trends in FY81 and FY82 will be studied. We will seek to "explain" the measures of fee intensity, with reference to various attributes of cities and towns such as population size, the range of services provided, per capita personal income levels and the level of spending (current expenditures) per capita.

From the research conducted up to this point, there is some indication that there are factors which contribute to fee intensity which will not be captured by the demographics and economic variables. It appears that the individual department heads for example, or the financial officers of the city or town, and other municipal officials having decision-making authority, are the key actors in setting up or operating a fee schedule. Personal attitudes and a kind of "business outlook" often determine whether user charges will be employed for any one service. Political variables related to the makeup of the town councils for example are also possible factors influencing the existing level or introduction of a user charge system. It is this kind of information which is not contained in the data and which indicates a further area of research to be undertaken, and which will be best attained through a case study approach.

For the study of user charges, therefore, four main questions must be addressed:

1.  What is happening in response to Proposition 2 1/2 with respect to charges and fees?
2.  Can a more extensive set of user charges be developed for education, police, and fire?
3.  How can cities and towns that fall below the average with respect to charges repair that deficiency?
4.  What is the process by which suitable activities for charges and fees are identified, schedules of fees and charges developed, and community consensus on employing them achieved?

In carrying out this research we will be concerned not simply with identifying areas to which charges might be applied, but also with the design of the charge. And we will extend our study to cover the factors affecting the decisions of those who make policy changes.

## Notes for Chapter 8

1. Richard M. Bird, *Charging for Public Services: A New Look at an Old Idea,* Canadian Tax Foundation, 1976.

TABLE 8.1
CURRENT CHARGES PER CAPITA, CURRENT CHARGES AS A
PERCENTAGE OF PERSONAL INCOME, AND FEE INTENSITY RATIOS
FOR THE UNITED STATES, MASSACHUSETTS, CONNECTICUT, NEW YORK, AND CALIFORNIA
(1976-77)

| Region | Current Charges Per Capita | | | Current Charges as a Percentage of Personal Income | | | Fee Intensity Percentage Total Revenue from Current Charges / Total Revenue from Own Taxes | | |
|---|---|---|---|---|---|---|---|---|---|
| | State & Local | State | Local | State & Local | State | Local | State & Local | State | Local |
| United States | $144 | $56 | $88 | 2.3 | 0.9 | 1.4 | 17.7 | 11.9 | 25.5 |
| Massachusetts | 116 | 53 | 62 | 1.7 | 0.8 | 0.9 | 11.5 | 10.4 | 12.6 |
| Connecticut | 92 | 55 | 37 | 1.3 | 0.8 | 0.5 | 10.4 | 11.7 | 8.9 |
| New York | 157 | 41 | 116 | 2.2 | 0.6 | 1.6 | 12.5 | 6.8 | 17.7 |
| California | 151 | 48 | 103 | 2.2 | 0.7 | 1.5 | 13.9 | 8.4 | 20.0 |

Source: U.S. Department of Commerce, Bureau of the Census, 1977 Census of Governments, Vol. 4, No. 5.

TABLE 8.2
CURRENT CHARGES: UNITED STATES AND MASSACHUSETTS COMPARED
STATE AND LOCAL
(1976-77)

| Current Charge By Type | Aggregate (in millions) | | Charge per Capita | | Percentage of Personal Income | | Percentage of* Total Spending In Category (Financing Ratio) | | Percentage of All Current Charges | |
|---|---|---|---|---|---|---|---|---|---|---|
| | U.S. | Mass | U.S. | Mass. | U.S. | Mass. | U.S. | Mass. | U.S. | Mass. |
| Total Current Charges | $31,273.1 | $665.4 | $144.06 | $115.19 | 2.27 | 1.74 | ---- | ---- | 100.0 | 100.0 |
| Education | 10,285.8 | 182.5 | 47.53 | 31.60 | .75 | .48 | 10.1 | 4.3 | 33.0 | 27.4 |
| -School Lunch Sales (Gross) | 1,609.4 | 51.3 | 7.44 | 8.89 | .12 | .13 | ---- | ---- | 5.2 | 7.7 |
| -Other | 8,676.4 | 131.2 | 40.09 | 22.71 | .63 | .34 | ---- | ---- | 27.8 | 19.7 |
| Hospital | 8,498.3 | 179.1 | 39.27 | 31.00 | .62 | .47 | 48.4 | 42.8 | 27.3 | 26.9 |
| Sewage | 2,450.5 | 19.6 | 11.53 | 3.39 | .18 | .05 | 102.5 | 44.6 | 7.9 | 3.0 |
| Sanitation other Than Sewage | 646.5 | 2.4 | 2.99 | .41 | .05 | .01 | 27.2 | 3.5 | 2.0 | 0.4 |
| Natural Resources | 522.1 | 6.2 | 2.41 | .11 | .04 | 0.00 | 12.9 | 2.1 | 1.7 | 0.1 |
| Parks & Recreation | 824.8 | 9.8 | 3.81 | 1.70 | .06 | .03 | 16.8 | 10.7 | 2.6 | 1.5 |
| Housing and Urban Renewal | 926.0 | 48.1 | 4.28 | 8.32 | .07 | .13 | 44.9 | 33.1 | 2.9 | 7.2 |
| Airport | 1,254.1 | 50.4 | 5.80 | 8.72 | .09 | .13 | 93.0 | 194.3 | 4.0 | 7.6 |
| Parking Facilities | 269.2 | 9.4 | 1.24 | 1.63 | .02 | .02 | 90.1 | 161.4 | 0.9 | 1.4 |
| Water Transport and Terminals | 580.3 | 20.3 | 2.68 | 3.51 | .04 | .05 | 76.6 | 78.9 | 1.9 | 3.0 |
| Other and Unallocatable | 4,915.3 | 143.3 | 22.72 | 24.80 | .36 | .37 | ---- | ---- | 15.8 | 21.5 |

* Where possible (i.e., Sewage and Housing and Urban Renewal), capital outlay has been deducted.
Source: U.S. Department of Commerce, Bureau of the Census, 1977 Census of Governments, Vol. 4, No. 5.

TABLE 8.3
CURRENT CHARGES: UNITED STATES AND MASSACHUSETTS COMPARED
STATE
(1976-77)

| Current Charge By Type | Aggregate (in millions) | | Charge per Capita | | Percentage of Personal Income | | Percentage of* Total Spending In Category (Financing Ratio) | | Percentage of All Current Charges | |
|---|---|---|---|---|---|---|---|---|---|---|
| | U.S. | Mass. | U.S. | Mass. | U.S. | Mass. | U.S. | Mass. | U.S. | Mass. |
| Total Current Charges | $12,076.1 | 6,817.7 | $55.81 | $52.77 | .88 | .80 | ---- | ---- | 100.0 | 100.0 |
| Education | 6,817.7 | 115.0 | 31.51 | 19.90 | .50 | .30 | 25.0 | 22.0 | 56.4 | 37.2 |
| -School Lunch Sales (Gross) | ---- | ---- | ---- | ---- | ---- | ---- | ---- | ---- | ---- | ---- |
| -Other | 6,817.7 | 115.0 | 31.51 | 19.90 | .50 | .30 | 25.0 | 22.0 | 56.4 | 37.2 |
| Hospital | 2,370.3 | 16.6 | 10.95 | 2.87 | .17 | .04 | 28.0 | 1.0 | 19.6 | 5.4 |
| Sewage | 3.7 | 0.2 | .02 | .03 | --** | --** | 4.0 | 7.0 | 0.3 | 0.1 |
| Sanitation other Than Sewage | 0.03 | ---- | ---- | ---- | ---- | ---- | ---- | ---- | ---- | ---- |
| Natural Resources | 365.7 | 0.6 | 1.69 | .10 | .03 | --** | 12.0 | 2.0 | 3.0 | 0.2 |
| Parks & Recreation | 191.5 | 4.7 | .88 | .81 | .01 | .01 | 19.0 | 21.0 | 1.6 | 1.5 |
| Housing and Urban Renewal | 44.3 | ---- | .21 | ---- | --** | --** | 52.0 | ---- | 0.4 | ---- |
| Airport | 141.2 | 49.9 | .65 | 8.51 | --** | .13 | 75.0 | 230.0 | 1.2 | 16.1 |
| Parking Facilities | ---- | ---- | ---- | ---- | ---- | ---- | ---- | ---- | ---- | ---- |
| Water Transport and Terminals | 167.7 | 20.2 | .78 | 3.50 | .01 | .05 | 65.0 | 80.0 | 1.4 | 6.6 |
| Other and Unallocatable | 1,974.0 | 98.5 | 9.12 | 17.50 | .14 | .26 | ---- | ---- | 16.4 | 32.3 |

* Where possible (i.e., Sewage and Housing and Urban Renewal), capital outlay has been deducted.
** Less than 0.01 percent.
Source: U.S. Department of Commerce, Bureau of the Census. 1977 Census of Governments, Vol. 4, No. 5.

TABLE 8.4
CURRENT CHARGES: UNITED STATES AND MASSACHUSETTS COMPARED
LOCAL
(1976-77)

| Current Charge By Type | Aggregate (in Millions) | | Charge Per Capita | | Percentage of Personal Income | | Percentage of* Total Spending in Category (Financing Ratio) | | Percentage of All Current Charges | |
|---|---|---|---|---|---|---|---|---|---|---|
| | U.S. | Mass. | U.S. | Mass. | U.S. | Mass. | U.S. | Mass. | U.S. | Mass. |
| Total Current Charges | $19,096.9 | $306.6 | 88.25 | $62.41 | 1.39 | 0.94 | ---- | ---- | 100.0 | 100.0 |
| Education | 3,468.1 | 67.5 | 14.64 | 11.69 | 0.25 | 0.18 | 4.5 | 2.9 | 18.2 | 18.7 |
| -School Lunch Sales (Gross) | 1,609.4 | 51.3 | 7.44 | 8.88 | 0.12 | 0.13 | ---- | ---- | 8.4 | 14.2 |
| -Other | 1,858.7 | 16.2 | 8.59 | 2.81 | 0.14 | 0.04 | ---- | ---- | 4.5 | 4.5 |
| Hospital | 6,128.0 | 162.5 | 28.32 | 28.13 | 0.45 | 0.43 | 68.7 | 88.3 | 32.1 | 45.1 |
| Sewage | 2,446.9 | 19.4 | 11.31 | 3.36 | 0.18 | 0.05 | 106.4 | 55.5 | 12.8 | 5.4 |
| Sanitation Other Than Sewage | 646.5 | 2.4 | 2.99 | .41 | 0.05 | 0.01 | 27.2 | 3.5 | 3.4 | 0.7 |
| Natural Resources | 156.4 | 0.05 | .72 | .01 | 0.01 | --** | 16.2 | 2.6 | 0.8 | 0.0 |
| Parks & Recreation | 633.3 | 5.1 | 2.93 | .89 | 0.05 | 0.01 | 16.3 | 7.4 | 3.3 | 1.4 |
| Housing and Urban Renewal | 881.6 | 48.1 | 4.07 | 8.32 | 0.06 | 0.13 | 44.6 | 33.1 | 4.6 | 13.3 |
| Airport | 1,113.0 | 1.2 | 5.14 | .20 | 0.08 | --** | 96.0 | 28.1 | 5.8 | 0.3 |
| Parking Facilities | 269.2 | 9.4 | 1.24 | 1.63 | 0.02 | 0.03 | 90.3 | 161.4 | 1.4 | 2.6 |
| Water Transport And Terminals | 412.6 | 0.06 | 1.91 | .01 | 0.03 | --** | 82.8 | 11.6 | 2.2 | 0.0 |
| Other and Unallocatable | 2,941.3 | 44.8 | 13.59 | 7.75 | 0.21 | 0.12 | ---- | ---- | 15.4 | 12.4 |

* Where possible (Sewage and Housing and Urban Renewal), capital outlay has been deducted.
** Less than 0.01 percent.
Source: U.S. Department of Commerce, Bureau of the Census, 1977 Census of Governments, Vol. 4, No. 5.

TABLE 8.5
CURRENT CHARGES: SELECTED STATES COMPARED
STATE AND LOCAL
(1976-77)

| Current Charge By Type | Charge Per Capita | | | | Percentage of Personal Income | | | | Percentage of Total Spending In Category (Financing Ratio)* | | | |
|---|---|---|---|---|---|---|---|---|---|---|---|---|
| | N.Y. | Calif. | Mass. | Conn. | N.Y. | Calif. | Mass. | Conn. | N.Y. | Calif. | Mass. | Conn. |
| Total Current Charges | $157.06 | $151.52 | $115.19 | $92.20 | 2.22 | 2.15 | 1.74 | 1.25 | ---- | ---- | ---- | ---- |
| Education | 35.99 | 35.29 | 31.60 | 31.83 | .51 | .50 | .48 | .43 | 6.5 | 6.2 | 4.3 | 7.2 |
| -School Lunch Sales (Gross) | 5.08 | 6.85 | 8.89 | 7.88 | .07 | .10 | .13 | .11 | ---- | ---- | ---- | ---- |
| -Other | 30.92 | 28.44 | 22.71 | 23.95 | .44 | .40 | .34 | .32 | ---- | ---- | ---- | ---- |
| Hospital | 27.88 | 44.25 | 31.00 | 14.85 | .39 | .63 | .47 | .20 | 22.3 | 55.3 | 42.8 | 28.2 |
| Sewage | 6.39 | 11.64 | 3.39 | 3.20 | .09 | .17 | .05 | .04 | 57.1 | 104.4 | 44.6 | 28.8 |
| Sanitation Other Than Sewage | 1.43 | 4.56 | .41 | .75 | .02 | .06 | .01 | .01 | 6.1 | 51.0 | 3.5 | 7.7 |
| Natural Resources | .08 | 10.18 | .11 | .06 | --** | .14 | .04 | --** | 1.5 | 27.7 | 2.1 | 1.2 |
| Parks & Recreation | 3.75 | 5.93 | 1.70 | 4.13 | .05 | .08 | .03 | .06 | 13.7 | 17.8 | 10.7 | 28.5 |
| Housing and Urban Renewal | 16.36 | 2.25 | 8.32 | 7.06 | .23 | .03 | .13 | .10 | 57.0 | 27.0 | 33.1 | 41.6 |
| Airport | 13.88 | 6.75 | 8.72 | 1.60 | .20 | .10 | .13 | .02 | 114.0 | 88.8 | 194.3 | 135.9 |
| Parking Facilities | 2.72 | 1.23 | 1.63 | 1.53 | .04 | .02 | .02 | .02 | 113.3 | 84.1 | 161.4 | 68.3 |
| Water Transport and Terminals | 3.35 | 5.66 | 3.51 | .12 | .05 | .08 | .05 | --** | 91.5 | 115.9 | 78.9 | 149.2 |
| Other and Unallocatable | 45.23 | 23.78 | 24.80 | 27.07 | .64 | .34 | .37 | .37 | ---- | ---- | ---- | ---- |

* Where possible, (i.e., Sewage and Housing and Urban Renewal), capital outlay has been deducted.
** Less than 0.01 percent.
Source: U.S. Department of Commerce, Bureau of the Census, 1977 Census of Governments, Vol. 4, No. 5.

TABLE 8.6
CURRENT CHARGES: SELECTED STATES COMPARED
BY STATE
(1976-77)

| Current Charge By Type | Charge Per Capita | | | | Percentage of Personal Income | | | | Percentage of Total Spending In Category (Financing Ratio)* | | | |
|---|---|---|---|---|---|---|---|---|---|---|---|---|
| | N.Y. | Calif. | Mass. | Conn. | N.Y. | Calif. | Mass. | Conn. | N.Y. | Calif. | Mass. | Conn. |
| Total Current Charges | $40.70 | $48.39 | $52.77 | $55.13 | .58 | .69 | .80 | .75 | ---- | ---- | ---- | ---- |
| Education | 16.91 | 23.50 | 19.90 | 21.12 | .24 | .33 | .30 | .29 | 18.3 | 18.5 | 22.0 | 21.5 |
| -School Lunch Sales (Gross) | ---- | ---- | ---- | ---- | ---- | ---- | ---- | ---- | ---- | ---- | ---- | ---- |
| -Other | 16.91 | 23.50 | 19.90 | 21.12 | .24 | .33 | .30 | .29 | ---- | ---- | ---- | ---- |
| Hospital | 7.63 | 13.11 | 2.87 | 11.63 | .11 | .19 | .04 | .16 | 12.4 | 50.0 | 1.0 | 23.6 |
| Sewage | ---- | .05 | .03 | ---- | ---- | --** | --** | ---- | ---- | 5.4 | 7.0 | ---- |
| Sanitation Other Than Sewage | ---- | ---- | ---- | ---- | ---- | ---- | ---- | ---- | ---- | ---- | ---- | ---- |
| Natural Resources | .04 | 6.39 | .10 | .06 | --** | .09 | --** | --** | 1.1 | 32.4 | 2.0 | 1.3 |
| Parks & Recreation | 1.03 | .71 | .81 | .29 | .02 | .01 | .01 | --** | 15.0 | 17.6 | 21.0 | 22.7 |
| Housing and Urban Renewal | 1.24 | .02 | ---- | ---- | .02 | ---- | ---- | ---- | 82.0 | 13.1 | ---- | ---- |
| Airport | .41 | ---- | 8.51 | 1.49 | .01 | ---- | .13 | .02 | 37.4 | ---- | 230.0 | 159.8 |
| Parking Facilities | ---- | ---- | ---- | ---- | ---- | ---- | ---- | ---- | ---- | ---- | ---- | ---- |
| Water Transport and Terminals | .09 | ---- | 3.50 | .12 | --** | ---- | .05 | --** | 8.5 | ---- | 80.0 | 191.7 |
| Other and Unallocatable | 13.32 | 4.61 | 17.50 | 20.41 | .19 | .07 | .26 | .28 | ---- | ---- | ---- | ---- |

* Where possible (i.e., Sewage and Housing and Urban Renewal), capital outlay has been deducted.
** Less than 0.01 percent.
Source: U.S. Department of Commerce, Bureau of the Census, 1977 Census of Governments, Vol. 4, No. 5.

TABLE 8.7
CURRENT CHARGES: SELECTED STATES COMPARED
LOCAL
(1976-77)

| Current Charge By Type | Charge Per Capita | | | | Percentage of Personal Income | | | | Percentage of Total Spending In Category (Financing Ratio)* | | | |
|---|---|---|---|---|---|---|---|---|---|---|---|---|
| | N.Y. | Calif. | Mass. | Conn. | N.Y. | Calif. | Mass. | Conn. | N.Y. | Calif. | Mass. | Conn. |
| Total Current Charges | $116.36 | $103.13 | $62.41 | $37.07 | 1.64 | 1.47 | .94 | .50 | ---- | ---- | ---- | ---- |
| Education | 19.08 | 11.79 | 11.69 | 10.71 | .27 | .17 | .18 | .15 | 4.2 | 2.7 | 2.9 | 3.1 |
| -School Lunch Sales (Gross) | 5.08 | 6.85 | 8.88 | 7.88 | .07 | .10 | .13 | .11 | ---- | ---- | ---- | ---- |
| -Other | 14.01 | 4.94 | 2.81 | 2.83 | .20 | .07 | .04 | .04 | ---- | ---- | ---- | ---- |
| Hospital | 20.25 | 31.15 | 28.13 | 3.22 | .29 | .44 | .43 | .04 | 31.8 | 57.9 | 88.3 | 94.9 |
| Sewage | 6.39 | 11.60 | 3.36 | 3.20 | .09 | .17 | .05 | .04 | 63.4 | 112.9 | 55.5 | 28.8 |
| Sanitation Other Than Sewage | 1.43 | 4.56 | .41 | .74 | .02 | .07 | .01 | .01 | 6.1 | 51.0 | 3.5 | 7.7 |
| Natural Resources | .04 | 3.79 | .01 | --- | --** | .05 | --** | ---- | 2.8 | 22.3 | 2.6 | ---- |
| Parks & Recreation | 2.71 | 5.22 | .89 | 3.84 | .04 | .07 | .01 | .05 | 13.2 | 17.9 | 7.4 | 29.1 |
| Housing and Urban Renewal | 15.11 | 2.23 | 8.32 | 7.06 | .21 | .03 | .13 | .10 | 55.6 | 272.6 | 33.1 | 43.2 |
| Airport | 13.47 | 6.75 | .20 | .10 | .19 | .10 | --** | --** | 121.6 | 89.3 | 28.1 | 43.3 |
| Parking Facilities | 2.72 | 1.23 | 1.63 | 1.52 | .04 | .02 | .03 | .02 | 113.3 | 84.1 | 161.4 | 68.3 |
| Water Transport and Terminals | 3.26 | 5.66 | .01 | ---- | .05 | .08 | --** | ---- | 127.4 | 115.9 | 11.6 | ---- |
| Other and Unallocatable | 31.91 | 19.17 | 7.75 | 6.66 | .45 | .27 | .12 | .09 | ---- | ---- | ---- | ---- |

* Where possible (i.e., Sewage and Housing and Urban Renewal), capital outlay has been deducted.
** Less than 0.01 percent.

Source: U.S. Department of Commerce, Bureau of the Census, 1977 Census of Governments, Vol. 4, No. 5.

## TABLE 8.8
### SUMMARY DATA ON FREQUENCY OF EMPLOYMENT OF USER CHARGES AND PER CAPITA AMOUNTS OF CHARGE FOR CITIES AND TOWNS EMPLOYING SAME, ARRAYED BY CITY SIZE, MASSACHUSETTS, 1980

| | 10,000< 20,000 | 20,000< 35,000 | 35,000< 50,000 | 50,000< 75,000 | 75,000< 100,000 | 100,000< 500,000 | 500,000 and over | All Over 10,000 No. Employing | All Over 10,000 % of Total |
|---|---|---|---|---|---|---|---|---|---|
| **Current Charges Per Capita** | | | | | | | | | |
| Health and Hospital | $157.06 (3) | $270.17 (17) | $198.96 (13) | $15.28 (11) | $204.51 (22) | $69.79 (100) | $177.24 (100) | 14 | 9 |
| Sewerage | 7.27 (49) | 9.56 (64) | 15.45 (81) | 9.27 (67) | 5.60 (78) | 8.48 (100) | 26.07 (100) | 91 | 61 |
| Parks and Recreation | 2.71 (69) | 2.02 (79) | 2.51 (75) | 1.66 (89) | 0.90 (78) | 1.64 (100) | 0.21 (100) | 12 | 75 |
| Housing/Urban Renewal | 7.24 (1) | 0 (0) | 0.67 (6) | 0.25 (11) | 0.53 (22) | 0.12 (100) | 2.23 (100) | 7 | 5 |
| Airport | 0.40 (6) | 11.44 (7) | 4.31 (31) | 0.72 (22) | 0.51 (22) | 2.01 (100) | 0 (0) | 18 | 12 |
| Parking Facilities | 0.68 (17) | 0.80 (52) | 0.97 (81) | 1.36 (67) | 2.39 (100) | 2.67 (100) | 11.60 (100) | 65 | 43 |
| Sanitation Other than Sewerage | 1.74 (18) | 1.27 (38) | 2.88 (31) | 2.00 (44) | 1.38 (67) | 1.13 (100) | 0.27 (100) | 47 | 31 |
| Education | 14.20 (97) | 13.01 (100) | 10.49 (100) | 11.37 (100) | 8.47 (100) | 6.61 (100) | 3.57 (100) | 48 | 99 |
| Other Current Charges | 5.67 (99) | 6.63 (100) | 8.96 (100) | 11.45 (100) | 9.10 (100) | 11.97 (100) | 6.85 (100) | 50 | 100 |
| **Utility Charges Per Capita** | | | | | | | | | |
| Water | 24.64 (75) | 25.41 (88) | 23.48 (100) | 27.00 (100) | 26.05 (100) | 35.35 (100) | 56.82 (100) | 27 | 85 |
| Electricity | 357.63 (10) | 380.51 (24) | 451.37 (31) | 0 (0) | 0 (0) | 0 (0) | 0 (0) | 23 | 15 |
| Gas | 37.56 (1) | 54.34 (2) | 129.17 (6) | 0 (0) | 0 (0) | 0 (0) | 0 (0) | 2 | 2 |

* Numbers in parentheses are percentage of all cities in each size class employing indicated charge. Source: Unpublished data from Governments' Division, Bureau of the Census, U.S. Department of Commerce.

## TABLE 8.9
### SUMMARY DATA ON FREQUENCY OF EMPLOYMENT OF USER CHARGES AND PER CAPITA AMOUNTS OF CHARGE FOR CITIES AND TOWNS EMPLOYING SAME, ARRAYED BY EQUALIZED VALUATION OF PROPERTY PER CAPITA, MASSACHUSETTS, 1980

| | < $9,500 | $9,500-12,499 | $12,500-14,999 | $15,000-24,999 | $25,000 and over |
|---|---|---|---|---|---|
| **Current Charges Per Capita** | | | | | |
| Health and Hospital | $139.72 (17)* | $195.75 (7) | $178.22 (3) | $202.88 (11) | $0 |
| Sewerage | 12.65 (60) | 8.36 (68) | 6.06 (69) | 11.41 (50) | 3.41 (43) |
| Parks and Recreation | 1.08 (74) | 1.69 (66) | 1.93 (69) | 1.91 (84) | 11.23 (100) |
| Housing and Urban Renewal | 0.73 (11) | 0.85 (2) | 0.25 (3) | 0 (0) | 7.25 (14) |
| Airport | 1.36 (26) | 1.69 (7) | 0.32 (10) | 0 (0) | 21.86 (29) |
| Parking Facilities | 1.45 (57) | 1.30 (49) | 1.51 (31) | 0.91 (34) | 1.01 (43) |
| Sanitation Other Than Sewerage | 1.61 (31) | 0.99 (27) | 1.98 (24) | 1.83 (42) | 2.11 (29) |
| Education | 8.71 (100) | 12.95 (100) | 13.62 (100) | 15.89 (100) | 13.47 (71) |
| Other Current Charges | 7.18 (97) | 7.01 (100) | 7.47 (100) | 6.60 (100) | 5.57 (100) |
| **Utility Charges Per Capita** | | | | | |
| Water | 23.16 (94) | 21.10 (83) | 25.68 (86) | 31.22 (79) | 31.70 (71) |
| Electricity | 464.12 (9) | 313.53 (17) | 450.09 (21) | 359.76 (18) | 0 (0) |
| Gas | 0 (0) | 83.36 (5) | 64.35 (3) | 0 (0) | 0 (0) |

* $ amounts in cells are charges per capita; numbers in ( ) are percentage of cities in each class emphasizing indicated charge.

Source: Unpublished data from Government's Division, Bureau of the Census, U.S. Department of Commerce.

TABLE 8.10

SUMMARY DATA ON FREQUENCY OF EMPLOYMENT OF USER CHARGES
AND PER CAPITA AMOUNTS OF CHARGE FOR CITIES AND TOWNS EMPLOYING SAME,
ARRAYED BY AVERAGE CITY AND TOWN INCOME (1970), MASSACHUSETTS
(USER CHARGE DATA AS OF 1980)

| | <$9,000 | $9,000-10,499 | $10,500-12,499 | $12,500-14,999 | $15,000 and over |
|---|---|---|---|---|---|
| Current Charges Per Capita | | | | | |
| Health and Hospital | $121.14 (19) | $274.58 (5) | $321.48 (5) | $1.04 (5) | $172.88 (12) |
| Sewerage | 12.28 (65) | 8.06 (61) | 6.78 (64) | 9.31 (58) | 11.94 (47) |
| Parks and Recreation | 1.20 (81) | 3.25 (66) | 2.88 (64) | 2.04 (79) | 1.90 (100) |
| Housing and Urban Renewal | 0.67 (16) | 0 (0) | 0 (0) | 0 (0) | 7.25 (6) |
| Airport | 1.48 (22) | 7.87 (16) | 1.23 (5) | 0.38 (5) | 0 (0) |
| Parking Facilities | 2.25 (70) | 0.56 (47) | 0.47 (28) | 0.55 (21) | 1.25 (35) |
| Sanitation Other Than Sewerage | 1.34 (46) | 1.83 (13) | 1.51 (26) | 2.04 (47) | 1.78 (35) |
| Education | 8.66 (100) | 13.08 (95) | 13.25 (100) | 16.33 (100) | 16.69 (100) |
| Other Current Charges | 8.46 (97) | 7.07 (100) | 5.46 (100) | 6.81 (100) | 7.17 (100) |
| Utility Charges Per Capita | | | | | |
| Water | 25.74 (92) | 22.26 (76) | 23.03 (87) | 32.33 (89) | 28.14 (76) |
| Electricity | 422.57 (11) | 309.24 (13) | 356.01 (15) | 483.23 (26) | 339.06 (18) |
| Gas | 0 (0) | 83.36 (5) | 64.35 (3) | 0 (0) | 0 (0) |

Source: Unpublished data from Government's Division, Bureau of the Census, U.S. Department of Commerce.

## Table 8.11
## Percentage Preferring Each Method of Financing Public Services

| Service Type | Keep Financing the Same | Greater Share of Money Should Come from: | | | | |
| --- | --- | --- | --- | --- | --- | --- |
| | | Local Proper- ty Tax | State Income Tax | State Sales Tax | User Fees | Other Sources |
| **Municipal Services** | | | | | | |
| Police | 24.4 | 50.7 | 16.6 | 5.2 | 2.2 | 0.9 |
| Firefighting | 30.6 | 51.0 | 11.6 | 4.9 | 1.4 | 0.5 |
| Regular Garbage Pickup | 29.7 | 41.7 | 6.4 | 3.8 | 17.2 | 1.2 |
| Local Public Parks & Recreation | 21.9 | 49.0 | 12.2 | 7.1 | 8.4 | 1.4 |
| Local Public Transportation | 17.3 | 18.2 | 23.3 | 12.4 | 25.7 | 3.1 |
| **School Related Services** | | | | | | |
| Public Elementary & High School Education | 20.3 | 34.1 | 28.4 | 8.5 | 7.2 | 1.5 |
| After School Programs Such as Music & Sports | 19.6 | 39.1 | 13.3 | 6.2 | 20.5 | 1.3 |
| Special Education for Children with Learning Disabilities | 16.9 | 15.2 | 48.4 | 12.1 | 5.9 | 1.5 |
| Adult Education | 19.8 | 20.3 | 19.6 | 6.6 | 32.4 | 1.3 |
| **Human Resources Services** | | | | | | |
| Mental Health Programs | 16.5 | 5.4 | 57.8 | 13.7 | 4.8 | 1.8 |
| Services for the Elderly | 24.3 | 16.1 | 42.4 | 13.1 | 2.9 | 1.2 |
| State & Community Colleges & Universities | 16.5 | 3.4 | 46.1 | 12.0 | 20.7 | 1.3 |
| **Legal Services** | | | | | | |
| Courts and Judges | 25.5 | 8.9 | 43.9 | 9.7 | 10.5 | 1.5 |
| **Public Assistance** | | | | | | |
| Welfare or other Public Assistance | 21.5 | 7.8 | 45.6 | 13.6 | 8.0 | 3.5 |

Source: Helen F. Ladd and Julie Boatwright Wilson, "Proposition 2 1/2: Explaining the Vote," Research Report R81-1, April 1981, John F. Kennedy School of Government, Harvard University, Cambridge, MA.

Part Three

Case Studies

# Chapter 9

## Amesbury: Linking Salaries to State Aid

Melvyn Colon

## Introduction

Amesbury is located on the Massachusetts–New Hampshire border. In the past decade, the town's population increased 22.7 percent to 13,971 (partly because Boston is less than one–hour away by car). Amesbury's location on highways I–95 and I–495 has attracted industry, and the town has developed an industrial park to accommodate it. Amesbury's Industrial and Development Commission estimates that 700 new jobs were created between 1975 and 1980 and reports that all space in the park has been leased.

Amesbury is more a working–class than a bedroom community. Average income in 1970 was $8,947. In 1977, most of the town's residents were employed as operatives, laborers, clerical workers, salespersons, and service workers.

There has been a great deal of public investment in Amesbury in the past two decades. Many school buildings were either built or rebuilt to accommodate students from two local parochial schools that closed in the early 1950's, and from the local high school that was destroyed by fire. The town built two new elementary schools, a new high school, renovated the burned–out high school, and converted it into a middle school. The town has also made periodic additions to its full–service hospital, established in 1926. These and other public investments have yielded a high debt per capita: $94.00 compared with a median of $50 for communities of similar size. But they have also generated more state and federal aid. As a result, Amesbury relies less on the property tax.

Like other towns, Amesbury has kept its property assessments low in order to maximize its state aid. The town revalued in 1971, but by 1978 its assessment ratio was 75 percent of full market value, and by 1981, the Massachusetts Taxpayers Foundation estimated it at 54 percent. (In 1981, Amesbury's $10,772 per capita equalized valuation was only 61 percent of the median per capita equalized valuation for towns of similar size.)

## The Gap

In FY81, Amesbury's property value was $81,506,000; the Department of Revenue's equalized valuation was $170,005,000. Town officials estimated that after revaluation, the town's property value would be $300 million. (Revaluation was supposed to be completed by late 1981.) If reassessment yielded a $300 million valuation, the FY82 property tax levy ($7.5 million) would substantially exceed the FY81 levy ($5.9 million). But the levy would be only $4.25 million if based on the state's $170 million equalized valuation. The first year's 15 percent reduction would be $885,000. Town officials also estimated a $300,000 loss in motor vehicle excise taxes, making a total revenue loss of $1.2 million.

Local officials drew up a budget without waiting for the completion of revaluation. FY82 fixed costs (including interest payments, debt payments, insurance, retirement, and pensions) totalled $1,793,171, and the town needed more than $100,000 to pay for revaluation and $64,000 to cover a deficit from FY81. In addition, four labor contracts had to be negotiated in FY82 (for police officers, fire fighters, public works and hospital employees). The Finance Committee and the Board of Selectmen decided to use the most conservative estimate and to make a 15 percent budget reduction in case the property tax levy turned out to be less than $5 million.

## The Budget Process

Many boards, committees, and other town officials are involved in the budget-making process in Amesbury -- the Finance Committee, the Board of Selectmen, the Wage and Personnel Board, the Town Accountant, the School Committee, the Board of the Department of Public Works, the trustees of the hospital, and the 200 representatives to Town Meeting. Many of these actors expect to set policy and exercise budget authority to such an extent that no body actually seems in control. Indeed, Amesbury's government -- especially its budget process -- is characterized by a fragmentation of responsibility. The Board of Selectmen coordinates policy-making between Town Meetings, but it is a relatively weak executive body because many important departments -- notably, the Department of Public Works and the hospital -- remain outside its authority. The appointed members of the Finance Committee figure more prominently in shaping the budget. They set overall budget priorities for all departments. In the first year of Proposition 2 1/2, members of the Finance Committee limited how much each department could spend -- a departure from past practices.

In December 1980, the Finance Committee directed all department heads to reduce their budgets 13.5 percent (a calculation derived by Michael Basque, the Town Accountant). The Committee wanted to study the effects of a 13.5 percent, across-the-board reduction in order to rank departmental services in order of importance. The Selectmen objected to across-the-board cuts. They wanted priorities established immediately. Selectmen Fournier strongly urged the Finance Committee to support public safety departments first. He thought sufficient money could be freed to protect police and fire fighters by reducing the number of warrant articles calling for capital or miscellaneous expenditures this year. He drew up a list of priorities that distinquished between important and unimportant warrant articles and urged the Finance Committee to abandon its "conservative" approach. The other Selectmen agreed with Fournier and asked department heads and board chairmen to keep warrant articles to a minimum. When the Finance Committee refused to modify its request for across-the-board cuts, the Selectmen asked department heads under their authority to submit three budgets -- one, level-funded; one, cut 7 percent; one, 15 percent. They intended to support the Police and Fire departments.

The School Department, which begins its budget deliberations in September, had already prepared preliminary budgets before Proposition 2 1/2 passed. In FY81, the department's budget was $5.4 million. A $750,000 cut, plus raises and rising fixed costs (a $250,000 increase, according to the Superintendent) amounted to an effective loss of $1 million for the FY82 school budget. Serving about 2,800 students, the School Department employs 270 people, of whom 180 are teachers. About three-quarters of the school budget represents salaries and wages. The School Committee held numerous hearings to encourage public participation. Parental concerns included cuts in athletic and reading programs, and potential increases in class sizes. With these in mind, the Committee submitted a preliminary budget to the Finance Committee in January, requesting a slight increase over the previous year's appropriation. But the Finance Committee insisted on a 13.5 percent reduction in the school budget.

The Police and Fire Chiefs submitted increased budgets for their departments. Because wages and salaries constitute 85-90 percent of their budgets, a 13.5 percent reduction required them to lay off employees, which they did not do. The Fire Chief had to comply with a contractual minimum manning provision (no fewer than five men per shift), but he made some reductions on equipment and maintenance items. He presented a budget of $580,157 to the Finance Committee, a $35,634 increase over the FY81 budget. The Police Chief used more discretion. He and three officers were scheduled to retire in FY82. The Chief postponed hiring replacements (saving $13,000) and made reductions in nonpersonnel budget items. However, his budget request ($612,722) was $26,000 greater than his FY81 budget.

When the Finance Committee began work on department budgets, it decided to postpone raises until state aid was distributed. Negotiated raises would not be funded and negotiations for raises were postponed until September. (An exception was made for three town officials whose raises had been approved at the previous Town Meeting.) This gave town officials considerable latitude, but labor's response was immediate. The DPW Board and its union, AFSCME, filed a grievance against the town for unfair labor practices. The union had already negotiated a contract for a 7 percent raise, ostensibly to take effect July 1st, but not if Town Meeting supported the Finance Committee's recommendation .

After two months, the Finance Committee agreed with Selectman Fournier to protect public safety departments from layoffs by paring down the number of warrant articles. But the Committee still reduced the Fire Department's request by $25,000 and the Police Department's by $12,000.

## Town Meeting

At the May Town Meeting, most of the Finance Committee's recommendations passed. Town Meeting approved major reductions in the School Department, the two layoffs, and minor budget reductions in the Department of Public Works. It also voted to postpone raises until Special Town Meeting in September. When raises were officially postponed, 15 nurses quit work at Amesbury's hospital. Hospital employees had just negotiated a 7 percent raise at one of the lowest paying hospitals in the state. To respond to this crisis, a Special Town Meeting in July awarded all hospital employees a raise of 8.5 percent to take effect in September. (The hospital has filled 13 of the 15 vacancies created that summer.) Town Meeting had reduced street lighting $50,000, or 50 percent of the budget, but town officials subsequently learned that this was illegal. The state Department of Utilities allows only a 10 percent reduction, hence, the street lighting budget had to be increased to comply with the law.

## State Aid

Amesbury received about $500,000 in additional state aid. In October, a Special Town Meeting allocated funds for raises. The Police Department and the DPW negotiated three-year contracts with yearly raises of 8, 7, and 6 percent. Selectman Fournier estimated the cost of raises at about $40,000 per department. A similar settlement is expected for the Fire Department, although minimum manning is still at issue.

The Special Town Meeting restored street lighting funds and allocated $215,000 to the School Department. The Superintendent used some of the money ($100,000) to fund transportation and utility costs. The remaining $115,000 was used to rehire employees, including nine teachers, a librarian, a counsellor, four cafeteria supervisors, a library aide, a teacher's aide, and two tutors.

## Impacts on the School Department

The School Committee prepared a final budget with a cut of $750,000. Seventy-five positions were eliminated, including 20 teachers, a psychologist, 2 nurses, 2 librarians, 2 assistant principals, about 30 teacher aides, and one-third of the coaching staff. The number of custodial and cafeteria employees was reduced. No funds were allocated for library or text book or equipment purchases. Junior high and high school freshman athletics were eliminated. Reductions were made in special education, Spanish, English, art, reading, music, and physical education. School lunch prices were raised.

In 1981, school officials were in the process of implementing recommendations made by the state auditors to upgrade Amesbury's special education programs, which required a large increase in the budget. School programs were reorganized and new employees were hired (three teachers, eight tutors, and eight teacher aides). The investment was intended to reduce the $250,000 paid in tuition and transportation to special schools for handicapped children. Because of the contractual provision limiting layoffs to nontenured teachers, some of these newly created positions were eliminated this year.

The School Superintendent anticipated major problems. He argued that the FY82 budget was so inadequate that schools might have to be closed in the spring. Unbudgeted costs had already been incurred to repair a leaky roof, and the Superintendent predicted that the allocation for heating buildings was insufficient. The transportation budget had been cut to provide only the legal minimum (to students living more than two miles from school); the Superintendent was concerned about the safety of students having to walk. He said he had hoped for more support from the Finance Committee for the schools, but noted the new activities of people interested in education in Amesbury. Teachers have been urging concerned businessmen to donate useful classroom materials, and an educational foundation has been established to seek corporate and federal support. The foundation has already sponsored a performance by a concert pianist to raise funds for school programs.

## Labor Relations

The unions had to negotiate contracts at budget–making time, when sentiment against public employees usually increases. Because of Proposition 2 1/2, money available to each department was limited, but after the nurses quit and the town negotiated an 8.5 percent raise for all hospital employees, other public employees benefited. Town officials would have difficulty negotiating raises below the 8.5 percent "standard" set. Although Amesbury's unions were more active as a result of Proposition 2 1/2, the Selectmen expected the elimination of binding arbitration to improve management's control. The Board of Selectmen has had especially difficult relations with the fire fighters union (a previous contract required four months of negotiations and binding arbitration). The Selectmen hoped to eliminate the minimum manning clause from the fire fighters' contract.

## Future Fiscal Policy

In FY82, Amesbury based its budget on a property tax levy of about $5.1 million. If property is revalued at more than $200 million, as seems likely, the town will be in compliance with Proposition 2 1/2 in FY83. But the Finance Committee and the Board of Selectmen are trying to establish a financial cushion with additional state aid in case further budget cuts are required in FY83. They may be if Amesbury loses some of its federal aid. As a result of reduced spending, the School Department may lose some Title I funds (currently $175,000) and Public Law 94-142 funds (currently $50,000) for handicapped children. Amesbury's hospital may also lose some of its revenue sharing funds (currently $500,000), which would have to be made up by the town.

In April 1982, Amesbury adopted the Town Manager form of government, a change that had been at issue for over a decade. The Town Manager is directly responsible for all town budgets, and the many elected boards and committees will lose much of their budget-making autonomy. Town officials hope a central executive will make the local government more accountable, efficient, responsive, and less "political."

## Summary

Because of Amsbury's low property assessment ratio in FY82, Proposition 2 1/2 had more of an impact on the town than it would have had otherwise. By far, the School Department suffered the most severe budget reductions, but also benefited most from increased state aid. It is highly likely that revaluation will save the town from another property tax levy reduction, but raises and possible federal reductions may make it necessary to do more budget-cutting in Amesbury during FY83.

Chapter 10

# Arlington: Setting Budget Priorities

Thomas Campbell

## Introduction

A town of 5.5 square miles, Arlington is 93 percent residential and depends heavily on the property tax for its revenues. In 1980, Arlington's commercial and industrial sector produced only 7.1 percent of its property tax revenues; its residential property produced 84 percent. The town's nearly all-white population increased about 1 percent a year between 1950 and 1970, to a high of 53,525. By 1980, the population had declined 10 percent to 48,2110.

Arlington has a reputation for well-managed and responsive government. The town's administrators and elected officials have instituted performance- and zero-based budgeting systems, conducted numerous citizen surveys and needs assessments, and reduced costs through energy conservation and other programs. Town officials have pursued an aggressive cash management policy, maintaining a high tax collection rate (99 percent), a strong deferred pension system, and a large amount of free cash carried from year to year. These policies, combined with a high level of public services, have resulted in a strong AA rating by Moody's Investment Service. In a report prepared for the Finance Committee, "Alternatives for Responding to Prop 2 1/2," the auditing firm of Ernst & Whinney complimented Arlington on its ability to provide efficient and professional services.

Arlington has a strong Town Manager form of government. Appointed by the five-member Board of Selectmen, the Manager is responsible for the supervision and administration of all departments, except the Selectmen, Treasurer, Comptroller, Finance Committee, Board of Assessors, and the Schools. (1) The Town Manager may reorganize, consolidate, and abolish departments. He makes appointments to boards and commissions, subject to the approval of

113

the Selectmen. The Manager makes the final decisions about department spending plans. He must present a budget to the Board of Selectmen by December 1st.

The Selectmen review the Manager's budget and hold public hearings with department heads. They must adopt a budget by December 21st. The Selectmen then forward the budget to the Finance Committee. This 21-member board is appointed by the Town Moderator (Harry McCabe); the Chairman of the Trust Fund (Kermit Streng); and the Chairman of the Finance Committee (Robert O'Neill). As advisor to the Town Meeting, the Finance Committee determines how much the town is able to spend and investigates departmental requests for increased expenditures. The Committee organizes subcommittees to work with department heads to analyze program needs and finance issues. The subcommittees hold hearings and draw up a report for the Town Meeting. The Town Meeting, a 250-person body, has final authority over all appropriations. The members, elected from each precinct, vote on warrant articles, comprised of line-item budget expenditures, as well as discretionary costs such as those involved in collective bargaining agreements.

As part of their financial analysis, Arlington town officials regularly compare the town with 18 other cities and towns located nearby, similar in size, wealth, and population. (2) Of these 19, Arlington ranks fourth highest in its reliance on the residential property tax (over 70 percent). In 1980, Arlington's total tax levy per capita was $608, ranking 7th lowest, well below the group's average of $665. Arlington ranks fifth lowest in spending per resident ($735) for municipal services -- $135 less than the group's average. Local expenditures since 1967 show that the town has not increased its spending as fast as other communities in the group, ranking sixth lowest. While per capita spending has increased 6.8 percent since 1971, every town department has had less money to spend than it had ten years ago as a result of inflation. The growth in the tax rate reflects a similar situation: Arlington's tax rate has risen from $51.80 per thousand of assessed value to $87.00 per thousand. However, after inflation has been taken into account, Arlington's taxes have actually decreased 14 percent.

Despite its generally recognized high performance management, Arlington's property has not been revalued since 1969. (The Massachusetts Taxpayers Foundation estimated a 59 percent assessment ratio for Arlington.) In June 1980, the town hired Clemingshaw, Inc. to revalue its property. Because of Proposition 2 1/2, town officials wanted the study completed in time to use a higher valuation for the 1982 budget. But the Board of Assessors and the firm successfully argued that rushing the deadline (April 1982) meant risking inaccurate assessments. In another effort to raise the value of the tax base in Arlington, town officials brought suit against the state (March 1981) over its $887 million equalized valuation of the town. Clemingshaw's sampling of 400 property sales indicated a valuation closer to $1.2 billion. The town lost this court challenge.

### The Gap

Basing its FY82 property tax levy on the state's equalized valuation ($887 million), the town lost $6.4 million, or 20 percent of its revenues. From a 1981 tax levy of $31.6 million, the law mandated a reduction of $4.6 million in property tax revenues and a $1.5 million (62 percent) reduction in the motor vehicle excise tax. If Arlington did not revalue its property, it would eventually lose 30 percent of its property tax levy ($9.4 million) to reach 2 1/2 percent of value. However, with a projected valuation of $1.2 billion, town officials do not expect further cutbacks after 100 percent revaluation (i.e., 2.5 percent of $1.2 billion yields a tax levy greater than FY82's $26.8 million levy). Through tough bargaining and a review of existing fiscal policies, Arlington's budget cutback was $2.5 million instead of $6.4 million. The substance of Arlington's FY82 budget process is how town officials managed to offset the town's revenue losses.

### Views on Proposition 2 1/2

Arlington's residents passed Proposition 2 1/2 by a three-to-two margin, despite the active opposition of local officials. In early September, the Selectmen formed an anti-Proposition 2 1/2 committee to distribute information door-to-door about the tax limitation measure and its potential consequences. Comprised of many local officials, unions, and the League of Women Voters, the committee attempted to persuade voters that Proposition 2 1/2 was not the best means of achieving tax relief and fiscal reform.

The Town Manager, Don Marquis, thought voters were as frustrated with the state government as they were with high local taxes. In a telephone survey of residents in January 1981, the Town Manager's office found that 88 percent of Arlington's residents supported reducing state expenditures and increasing local aid. Marquis campaigned statewide to obtain the support of other cities and towns for a resolution calling for increased state aid of $350 million and a cap on state expenditures at the 1981 level. In March, the Arlington Town Meeting passed a warrant article to that effect, 155-12.

Many town officials suggested that Proposition 2 1/2 passed because it offered a grab bag of attractive elements to almost every section of the population -- elderly homeowners, renters, those wanting more control of school budgets, and residents frustrated with inflation. Others believed that Proposition 2 1/2 offered taxpayers their only escape from spiralling public costs and higher taxes. The Chairman of the Selectmen, Bill Grannon, said, "2 1/2 expressed the citizens' belief that government can cut taxes and retain a representative set of services. And here in Arlington, through our budget process, they were right." But some officials claimed that the vote for Proposition 2 1/2 was not the result of rational choice, that voters did not know the consequences of service reductions.

Various people predict that the tax limitation measure will redefine the role of local government. The Town Manager, for instance, hoped local government would again concentrate primarily on protecting life and property. James Forte, an individual active in town affairs, agreed: "Citizens want the plumbing to work, the criminals arrested, the fires put out, and the garbage collected." A newly elected Selectmen, Charles Lyons, thought that "Prop 2 1/2 indicated that local government was not solving problems responsibly." He hoped town officials would now learn to work together. But the Head of the Human Resources Department, Arthur Johnson, did not think this would be the case. He predicted more conflicts as agencies competed for scarce resources.

## The Budget Process

Arlington residents pride themselves on the town's form of open government and their own involvement with town decision-making. The town has an active Citizen Involvement Committee and almost every town department has a citizen advisory board to oversee its affairs and make recommendations at Town Meeting. Most citizen influence on the 1982 budget was accomplished through these formal, long-established channels. Some lobbying took place at the Selectmen's budget hearings, when the Library Trustees and the Board of Youth Services demonstrated local support in an effort to restore cutbacks in those services. However, no interest groups or neighborhood associations made efforts to protest cutbacks or affect the course of the budget.

It was clear that the major fiscal decisions were made this year by a small group of men. As the budget developed, a few individuals formed a committee to reconcile budgetary conflicts and uncertainties. The School Superintendent, Town Manager, Treasurer, Comptroller, one of the Selectmen, and the Finance Committee Chairman set bottom line revenue and expenditure levels for various departments. Yet, these decisions were not made until late in the budget process when deadlines posed a threat to the continued operation of the town.

The politics of Arlington's budget process revolved around the distribution of budget responsibility among the town's officials. The Town Manager Act, which sets forth the functions of different departments, does not explicitly delegate responsibility for budget or service policy. Consequently, roles are often defined by precedent and by individual perceptions and actions. According to two Selectmen, their Board should establish a policy framework within which the Town Manager should work. However, through 15 years of managing Arlington, Don Marquis has established himself as a strong and independent Town Manager. The Selectmen believe Marquis has taken on too much responsibility. They want the Board to reassert its policy-making role. The Finance Committee, which evaluates departmental justifications for increased expenditures, played a lesser part in this year's budget process. The Committee's Chairman, Robert O'Neill, said the Committee's role was diminished because there were few such increases to evaluate this year. Many Committee members had hoped they would have more policy responsibility in a year of cutbacks.

## The FY82 Budget

By late summer 1980, the Town Manager had estimated how much budget-cutting Arlington would have to do if Proposition 2 1/2 passed. After estimating the revenue loss, he subtracted the town's "fixed costs" (30 percent of the budget for debt service, fuel costs, pension funding, and insurance) from the budget and estimated the percentage reduction from the remaining 70 percent (representing services). He added in increases in employees' salaries (at $100,000 per 1 percent increase -- although salaries were still under negotiation), and factored in a 12 percent inflation rate. He concluded that a 30 percent cut might be necessary.

Marquis hoped to avoid laying off employees. He estimated that for every two employees laid off, a third would have to be laid off to cover unemployment compensation benefits. He also felt that layoffs based on seniority would deny the town a choice between productive and less productive employees. The Town Manager thought that property revaluation would allow him to rehire people if layoffs could not be avoided.

When Proposition 2 1/2 passed, the Town Manager concentrated the $6.4 million reduction in services. In initial meetings with department heads, Marquis set forth the following guidelines: "All departments will take cuts; will avoid layoffs through wage freezes; will leave open positions vacant; will maintain all essential services." This general approach was agreed to by the Selectmen and members of the Finance Committee who also wanted to prevent layoffs and implement 2 1/2 with as little disruption to service as possible. Although Marquis realized that some services were more vital than others, he asked for across-the-board reductions. He hoped department heads would develop new cost-saving measures and productivity improvements.

To determine specific reductions, Marquis asked department heads to develop zero-based budgets, ranking services and specifying the cost of each. This was the first year department heads had used the zero-based budgeting procedure; previously, they had used a combination of performance-based and management-by-objective methods. The Town Manager reviewed the departmental priorities that emerged from the ranking process and eliminated the lowest ranking services until each budget was reduced by 30 percent. This "worst-case scenario" was publicized, revealing severe service cutbacks and layoffs: 28 policemen, 25 fire fighters, 150 school employees, 14 public works employees, and 97 other town employees. The Youth Consultation Center would be closed. The Town Manager pointed out that a 30 percent reduction was necessary only if all revenue factors (i.e., state aid, fees, revaluation) remained unchanged.

In fact, the FY82 revenue projection began to look more favorable. Shortly after Proposition 2 1/2 passed, Robert O'Neill, the Finance Committee Chairman, made a more liberal set of budget assumptions and concluded that the town needed to make a 20 percent budget cut. Among other things, O'Neill estimated an increase in parking meter revenues, receipts from the Assessor, and earnings on town investments due to higher interest rates. He assumed that fuel costs would level off. O'Neill was also concerned about the distribution of revenue between the school and town budgets. He subtracted "fixed costs" and warrant articles applicable to the town and school budgets, allocating 52 percent of town revenues to the School Department, 43 percent to all other departments, and 4.5 percent to warrant articles, based on the previous year's budget. Marquis, the School Superintendent, William Gibbs, and the Board of Selectmen agreed to this formula.

However, by the time the Manager was required to submit a budget to the Board of Selectmen (December 1980), nothing had actually occurred to increase FY82 revenues and the Manager submitted the "worst-case" budget. Although the Selectmen felt that Marquis was using the 30 percent cutback budget to further his statewide campaign to increase state aid, they, too, were faced with a December deadline and passed Marquis' budget on to the Finance Committee.

But the Selectmen still wanted to develop their own planning process. In February, they adopted a set of long- and short-term goals, including more citizen participation (primarily the work of William Grannon, founding Chairman of the Citizen's Involvement Committee). In March, the Selectmen developed a policy for implementing Proposition 2 1/2, based on these goals. The policy essentially restated the Town Manager's goals of preventing layoffs and retaining as much service capacity as possible. The Board based its cutback strategy on identifying whole departments as "critical" or "essential." The departments considered "critical" included police, fire, and public works; "essential" departments included general administration, legal, planning and community development, cemeteries, engineering, libraries, properties and natural resources, comptroller, purchasing, and personnel. However, the Board's March strategy to implement 2 1/2 was discarded as it began to conduct public hearings with department heads to consider budget reductions.

Because town officials remained uncertain about FY82 revenues, the Finance Committee recommended that Town Meeting (usually held in March) consider only nonmonetary warrants and adjourn until June 1st or until state aid became known. This was done, but the School Superintendent and the Town Manager were unable to postpone preparing for layoffs. Civil Service regulations and union contracts prohibit layoffs without sufficient notice. Therefore, termination notices were mailed to 150 school employees and notices were prepared for 130 town employees. The preparation was publicized over the opposition of the Selectmen.

In late April, a newly elected Selectman, Charles Lyons, made some new assumptions about FY82 revenues and suggested that a $2.5 million cut could be made instead of a $6.4 million cut. Lyons believed that town officials had not fully exploited all opportunities to reduce the impact of Proposition 2 1/2. With a June 1st deadline fast approaching, Lyons urged the formation of a task force to confirm revenues, identify the precise number of layoffs, and construct a more liberal budget.

In early May, the Selectmen agreed to organize a Budget and Revenue Task Force. Its members -- O'Neill, Lyons, Marquis, John Bilafer (Treasurer),

A.L. Minervini (Comptroller), and William Gibbs (School Superintendent) -- agreed with Lyons' proposals and set out to present a final budget to Town Meeting. In his effort to reduce the cutbacks, Lyons had made a number of important recommendations. In a memorandum to the Selectmen, he proposed using $3.7 million in free cash (instead of following the traditional practice of retaining half of the previous year's balance). Lyons had also received a "fairly firm" estimate of state aid from State Representative John Cusack ($1.5 million) which he incorporated into his proposal. (The $1.5 million estimate turned out to be quite close -- Arlington received $1.4 million.) In addition, the 15 percent tax reduction mandated by Proposition 2 1/2 meant that the amount required for the overlay account could be decreased commensurately, providing an additional $200,000 for expenditures. (3) Receipts from the sale of two schools for condominium development added $320,000. The Task Force caught the spirit of Lyons' reasoning before settling on total FY82 revenues.

Within a week of making the revenue decision, the Task Force completed a budget and forwarded it to the Finance Committee for Town Meeting. The key to getting the budget over its final hurdles was to convince the Finance Committee Chairman to use all of the town's free cash. Experience had shown that the town needed a buffer against unanticipated cost adjustments, and O'Neill opposed emptying the account. However, the Task Force voted in favor of its full use. O'Neill abided by the group's decision because its aim was to prevent layoffs and maintain services. O'Neill's support was essential because the Finance Committee had to approve the budget, and O'Neill had to defend it at Town Meeting. Finance Committee support looked problematic anyway because some members felt that the the Task Force had usurped their budgetary authority.

The School Superintendent and the Town Manager had only two or three days to revise departmental budgets after allocations had been determined. The additional revenue enabled the Town Manager to respond to public sentiment for funding the Youth Consultation Center. The School Superintendent had been making incremental cuts all along with the approval of the School Committee. In reviewing the final budget, the Finance Committee objected to the way it had been developed, but passed it on the strong recommendation of the Finance Committee Chairman.

## Town Meeting

Other than mild disagreements over the adequacy of wage and service levels, there have been few budget disputes at Town Meeting in the past. The Town Moderator recalled, "We used to just pass most of the warrant articles that were recommended by the Finance Committee, add up the appropriations, and set the tax rate." Again, this year, Town Meeting had few objections to the substance of the Proposition 2 1/2 budget. The Finance Committee Chairman argued that the budget contained no slack, that adjustments proposed for one department would create deficits in others. In other words, the message at Town Meeting was "don't tamper with it." Town Meeting members recognized that the budget was the product of much time and effort. The higher FY82 revenue eliminated conflict over the closing of the Youth Center and the branch library. Town Meeting welcomed the unexpectedly small reductions in fire, police, and public works. The Town Moderator, Harry McCabe, was relieved -- he had feared that pandemonium would erupt if disputes had been left to Town Meeting. However, some Finance Committee members and Town Meeting representatives argued that the budget had been railroaded through: Town Meeting members used to discuss line-item issues; this year, they considered only aggregate figures. Furthermore, they argued, Town Meeting usually takes about 25 sessions to pass a budget; this year, the budget passed in only 8 meetings. The unusual speed was indeed due to the persuasiveness of O'Neill and the other members of the Task Force, but the town also needed to have a budget in place by July 1st (end of the fiscal year) to continue operating.

The Town Meeting passed two budget provisions -- one with state aid, the other, without. The Task Force decided that $652,000 of the $1.4 million in state aid would be allocated for school salaries, $447,500 would fund the pension system, and $500,000 would cover raises negotiated in the current round of collective bargaining. The last decision made at Town Meeting was to adjourn until a Special Town Meeting could be held after the "cherry sheet" figures became final. This meeting, scheduled for July 13, had to be deferred until September 14 because the state budget had still not been passed.

At the September 14 Special Town Meeting, the Finance Committee Chairman reviewed the financial situation and presented a set of warrant articles dealing with the unappropriated $500,000 available for collective bargaining settlements. With state aid confirmed at $1.4 million, O'Neill projected an estimated FY82 tax rate of $73.60, down $13.40 from the FY81 rate of $87.00. The rate would be set officially on October 1st, once all appropriations from the Special Town Meeting were made final. The $500,000 set aside for raises had to be allocated at this meeting or it had to be used to reduce taxes. O'Neill again emphasized that no appropriation could be made which increased the tax rate, and that Town Meeting could only reduce budgets or appropriate expenditures from next year's revenues. O'Neill pointed out the riskiness of such an action because of the depletion of the town's usual buffer -- free cash. He raised this concern because he projected only $2 million in free cash from the FY81 budget, compared with the $3.7 million committed for FY82.

On the advice of the Town Counsel, John Maher, who is also the Collective Bargaining Agent, the Town Manager inserted warrant articles at the Meeting to bolster the town's bargaining position. Instead of allowing all unions to bargain freely for a share of the half-million, separate warrant articles were presented and passed which allocated a 3 percent raise and a 2 percent reserve for each union. (These proportions could be estimated because a 1 percent increase in salaries cost the town $100,000, limiting total possible pay increases to 5 percent.) Joe Roselli, President of the Fire Fighters union and a Town Meeting member, charged that this approach set an inadequate ceiling of 3 percent, threatened each union's bargaining position, and impeded collective bargaining. Other Town Meeting members agreed with his analysis.

Although Arlington's total cutbacks rounded out to 11 percent, much less than originally feared, the FY82 budget was not without its critics. Many felt that the Manager's continuous presentation of "worst case" budget from November until May, caused public employees undue stress. Although the Town Manager met with employees on a monthly basis to keep them informed of budget developments, some employees complained that the Manager continued to emphasize 30 percent reductions even after the Finance Committee Chairman projected a 20 percent cutback. Others thought the Manager should have presented the other cutback scenarios he had developed and encouraged more public involvement. According to one employee, "The rumor mill was ripe. Things could have been spelled out and made less uncertain." A number of Town Meeting members argued that more people should have examined the priorities that governed the cutbacks. From the outset, however, Marquis had not wanted cuts to be made public until they were more or less final.

Many department heads also felt left out of the budget process. They claimed their meetings with the Town Manager were solely informational. Critics argued that the zero-based budgets were just paper work that made budget-making competitive among department heads instead of cooperative. (One department head, in an effort to take the performance budget seriously, instituted careful performance and qualitative measures, but eliminated them upon discovering that other department heads had made no efforts to study performance.) A department head could set priorities for services within his or her department, but choices among departments were the prerogatives of the Town Manager, which reduced the ability of department heads to negotiate trade-offs.

Some town officials argued that the Town Manager's budget did not represent some well-known service preferences of Arlington's residents. In 1975 and 1979, the Selectmen and the Citizen Involvement Committee conducted surveys of over 450 residents to determine community preferences for town services. The Chairman of the Board of Selectmen, William Grannon, thought the Manager did not follow the results of the survey this year, and added that, "this type of data is ignored at one's own peril." The final budget did reflect many of the survey's results. However, the surveys indicated that citizens preferred distributing cutback losses over all services, instead of applying it only to community safety (61 percent) or human services (54 percent). Grannon developed this argument when the Town Manager eliminated funding for the Youth Consultation Center, which citizens wanted to maintain at current spending levels. Marquis argued that the Center could only be funded if town had enough revenue. However, Grannon and others still felt that the Town Manager wanted the Center closed.

## Summary of Impacts on the Town Budget

The final reduction in the town budget was $1.4 million. The town lost approximately 60 positions through attrition; departmental budget reductions ranged from 5 to 15 percent of previous spending levels. The Library Department absorbed the largest budget reduction -- 20 percent. The budget for Community Safety, an umbrella department for police and fire services, was reduced by 5.1 percent, which resulted in a loss of positions through attrition and some deferred equipment acquisitions. No positions were eliminated in the Fire Department and eight fire fighters will be rehired. The Human Resources Department was cut back 5 percent, most of which was borne by the Council on Aging, recreation services, and youth services. The Public Works Department was cut back 11 percent, and the Properties and Natural Resources Department absorbed a 13 percent cut. The General Administration budget was reduced by 6 percent. Although the Planning and Community Development Department was cut back 25 percent, the loss was not reflected in effort since planners' salaries were transferred from town funding to federal CDBG support. The School Department budget was reduced $1.1 million.

## Impacts on the Youth Consultation Center

In his initial budget, the Town Manager planned to eliminate the Youth Consultation Center. The Center's Director, Patsy Kramer, felt that the Manager's decision was motivated by the political expedient of cutting costs in a vulnerable area. Through public hearings and a lobbying campaign to save the service, Center officials found strong support from the Board of Selectmen and the Finance Committee. The issue was resolved through increased revenue, but the service was retained in July with a cut of 17 percent and was fully-funded at the September Town Meeting. Meanwhile, the Director is trying to qualify the Center for third party payments, and is seeking other funding sources.

## Impacts on the Libraries

Originally, the Town Manager proposed closing one library branch in order to preserve a full complement of library services and staff at the Central Library. The Director of Libraries agreed. Studies have shown that library use begins to decline beyond a 5-mile radius. Since the Central Library is located in the center of Arlington's 5.5 square miles, officials believed that closing the branch would inconvenience few residents. But the branch was located in the district of an influential Selectman, who argued that the Central Library was over-staffed. The branch remained open. The 20 percent cut in the Library budget resulted in a reduction of reference services at the Central Library.

## Impacts on the Police Department

The Police Chief believed that continued attrition would eventually have an adverse effect on police services in Arlington. He lost three patrolmen and a captain to early retirement and job changes -- these positions were eliminated. In dealing with these losses, the Chief tried to maintain as much patrol time as possible by reducing the hours spent on the "less essential," traffic supervisors program. But citizen support for assisting students at street crossings made that impossible.

## Impacts on the School Department

The original cut forecast for the School Department was nearly 25 percent, leaving a budget of $13.2 million. (The FY81 budget was $17.1 million.) In cutting back services, school officials tried to maintain as much classroom effort and as many student services as possible. The department had already eliminated 130 school positions over the last four years because of declining enrollment. It was also finishing a three-year contract with the teachers union, with pay increases built in. The potential for numerous layoffs appeared certain. The school department is required (by contract) to notify its personnel of layoffs by April 15th, and these notifications were mailed to 200 teaching and maintenance employees as of that date.

Going into the Town Meeting, school officials worked with a much improved, if still tentative, budget figure of $14.7 million. The School Department budget would be increased to $15.3 million, with state aid.

The enlarged budget allowed the School Superintendent to rehire some employees. About 120 school positions were lost, 40 of which were custodial and maintenance positions. Yet, the Superintendent thought that the impacts of Proposition 2 1/2 on the school system would be on-going. He argued that equipment must be replaced and repairs made sometime, if not in FY82. He was concerned about the long-term effect of declining school services, low morale among teachers, and the loss of younger teachers. He thought younger teachers added "spark" to the system. His general projection for the Arlington School Department was that "with multiple cutbacks, we can hold the line for awhile. But after a period, they will catch up with us and kids won't get the education they deserve."

## Impacts on Labor Relations

Proposition 2 1/2 cutbacks produced job uncertainty among public employees. Every union representative in Arlington mentioned the pride public employees take in their work. They felt that Proposition 2 1/2 represented a loss of faith in government doing a good job. Public employees are concerned about scaled-down pay increases, about promotion without accompanying pay increases, the loss of younger workers, and the new job insecurity. Some knew friends that developed ulcers or coworkers who quit for jobs in the private sector. Many pointed out that they had specifically chosen public service jobs over those in the private sector in order to have job security. Some employees now hold two jobs and are disillusioned by the lack of respect citizens have for their public employees.

For years, public labor relations in Arlington have been controversial. In the first round of bargaining after police and fire fighters were guaranteed binding arbitration, Arlington fire fighters were the first union in the state to take negotiations to the point of "last best offer" binding arbitration. The Town Manager took the case to court, not only because he disliked binding arbitration, but because he thought it was unconstitutional as well. The State

Supreme Judicial Court decided the case against the town. Since then, many negotiations have been drawn out. Management has offered pay packages that include 5 percent across-the-board increases and a merit pay increase of 2 percent, based on an employee's performance review, but police officers and fire fighters have increased their wages by 10 percent.

The Town Counsel is the town's collective bargaining agent. Each of the six unions in Arlington bargain separately with the Town Counsel, except for the Arlington Education Association which bargains with the School administration. Union representatives expressed frustration with this arrangement because the Town Manager makes final decisions and all bargaining positions are passed through him.

Initially, the six unions met to discuss working with town officials to make their views on Proposition 2 1/2 known. However, internal disagreement prevented the development of a labor coalition.

A difficult decision continues to be the wage-employment trade-off. Since town officials imposed a wage-freeze, the unions were directly confronted with the effects of a policy that retains employees at the expense of pay increases. Some union spokesmen felt that this policy would result in low wages in the future. Union spokesmen are not satisfied with the town's presentation of its ability to pay or the process town officials used to make cuts this year. They want management to make cuts among members of its own rank. They argued that it is unfair for lower level public employees to absorb the full impact of Proposition 2 1/2. Union spokesmen said the cuts would be endurable if management would reduce the inequities between union and management salaries, improve its own productivity, and cut back its own benefits. Union people want pay increases to accompany management's policy to prevent layoffs, but they prefer layoffs to pay decreases or stagnation.

Union spokesmen are frustrated that negotiations have been so drawn out. A number of unions have been in contract negotiations since October 1980 without progress or resolution. Union people want to know more about the town's resources, but complain that management keeps budget figures close to its chest. The largest union, local 680 AFSCME (involving six department budgets) could shut down the town with a strike, but no one thinks it would be a productive action to take. With the loss of binding arbitration, the fire fighters and police view a strike as a possibility only if difficult impasses remain unresolved.

Finally, union leaders are concerned about the consequences of layoffs by seniority. Older employees depend on younger ones, they argued, especially in police and fire departments. The younger ones carry the heavy loads and do the hard work of hauling hoses up ladders and taking night duty. For young officers seeking promotion, it would be extremely frustrating to prepare for promotional exams only to find positions closed at the top. One union president was concerned about the conflict and resentment that developed between young employees and older ones when layoffs seemed imminent. He warned of the dangers to unions in dealing with cutbacks: too many internal arguments, pitting employee against employee, union against union.

## Impacts on Development

As a residential town with little land left for new development, Arlington's planning strategy has been to revitalize its downtown area to attract business. In the past, Arlington's federal funds have been spent improving the general character of the town's central business area and to preserve its historical sites. One planner thought that only a reduction in federal funds would change this strategy. This year, the town faced a total loss of $1.2 million in CDBG funds because its population has declined below the federal elgibility requirement for funding (50,000). However, town officials successfully challenged Congress to extend funds for two more years to those towns that were previously receiving CDBG funds.

A local low-income tenants association in Menotomy Manor (a 178-unit public housing project of 750 residents) claimed that it had not received its "fair share" of the low-income funds allocated to it by the CDBG Act. Of the 1981 allocation of $1.2 million in CDBG funds, the tenants received $28,000, which is used to support day care and activities for youth. The President of the Association, Marilyn Murphy, believed that her group would have to become better organized and more politically involved in the future, if it were to compete with business and condominium development plans.

## Fees and User Charges

User charges and fees have presented Arlington with new and difficult choices. In his FY82 budget, the Town Manager explicitly discussed the pros and cons of user fees. On the positive side, charging for services resulted in a contribution from those who have tax-exempt property or non-residents. User charges prevent the town from subsidizing services not provided to the general public. To some extent, they measure the demand for a service. On the negative side, Marquis argued that fees set too high deprive low-income people of needed services. High fees also encourage people to avoid paying. Because fees can not be deducted from federal income tax, it costs the average homeowner less to pay for most services through municipal taxes.

Many town fees (e.g., for licenses and inspections) had not been changed since 1975. The town used a list of service fee limits compiled by the State Department of Revenue to guide it in setting new rates for services. The new rates were approved at the September 14th Town Meeting. In most cases, the new fees represented the state's maximum rates. Water and sewer charges were reviewed separately by town officials and state authorities. The town is a member of the Metropolitan District Commission. The MDC's fee changes will be mandatory and will be instituted next year, producing new revenues in FY83.

## Impacts on Capital Expenditures

The Town Manager's office developed a six-year projection of capital expenditures (for the 1980-81 Performance Budget) to avoid "crisis" spending and inordinate fluctuations in the tax rate. The Manager recommended that capital outlays increase from $1.2 million in 1981 to $2.2 million by 1986, which would increase the tax rate from $87 to $127. After Proposition 2 1/2 passed, the Town Manager asked department heads to defer all but their most critical outlays, which resulted in a 3.5 percent decrease in capital expenditures. However, a major portion of the decrease resulted from the purchase of a new computer system ($370,000) and a reduction of $200,000 in highway outlays. The Town Manager foresees larger outlays for maintenance if capital expenditures are deferred too long.

## Future Fiscal Policy

Many officials thought Arlington fared well in the first year of Proposition 2 1/2 budget cutting. However, there were competing predictions about the future. A member of the Finance Committee, Alan Tosti, warned that the town had "mortgaged its future" when it used all its free cash. But others, including Selectman Charles Lyons, thought the fiscal conservatism of the past prepared the town to work around tighter budgets. They believed that levying user charges for water and sewer services (adding $750,000 to the Proposition 2 1/2 levy), developing new efficiency measures, and reducing employee benefits would allow the town breathing room. In all, Arlington officials hoped the hardest task was over. Selectman Lyons said, "With so many factors determining the tax levy, we might have overcut this year, but I think we'll be alright in the future."

Everyone interviewed was concerned about the effects of inflation. Some hoped that President Reagan's economic policies would slow inflation. But an equal number were pessimistic. They feared that federal budget cuts combined with inflation would make things difficult ahead.

Most town officials favored some type of tax reform, ranging from further increases in local aid, to a more progressive tax structure. Some favored amending Proposition 2 1/2 to allow towns to increase expenditures by 5 instead of 2 1/2 percent. James Forte, the Chairman of the Citizen Involvement Committee, advocated setting up a state task force to review tax options and plan a new tax structure to be implemented by stages.

The Town Meeting voted to form a Town Government Reorganization Committee to search for new ways to improve delivery of services. The Finance Committee had commissioned a $27,000 study of public efficiency and general town management. Members of the Town Meeting voted to follow it through. However, department heads claimed that these studies are redundant, that Ernst & Whinney's, "Alternatives for Responding to 2 1/2," was only a composite of already well-known public productivity improvements. They argued that most of these were already in effect in Arlington. They hoped to conduct a public relations campaign to regain the support of Arlington residents for maintaining the town's high quality services.

## Summary

Past fiscal conservatism and new revenues enabled Arlington to survive the first year of Proposition 2 1/2 with less extensive cutbacks than originally anticipated. Proposition 2 1/2 forced town officials to make an overall review of past policies and the town's administrative structure. The cutbacks exacerbated differences among town officials over budgetary power and responsibility. Although the formation of the Budget and Revenue Task Force created some controversy and resentment, this kind of centralized, cross–administrative coordination was essential in dealing with Proposition 2 1/2. But critics argue that the test of this centralized budget process will be the local government's interest in keeping open the lines of communication and providing high quality services, along with adequate working conditions and reasonable salaries.

## Notes for Chapter 10

1. In 1981, the Town Manager had authority over 550 town employees, while the School Superintendent supervised 693 employees.

2. Communities in the Comparative Analysis Group: Arlington, Belmont, Brookline, Cambridge, Concord, Framingham, Malden, Medford, Melrose, Milton, Natick, Needham, Newton, Quincy, Waltham, Watertown, Wellesley, Weymouth, Winchester.

3. The overlay account is the amount raised by the Assessors, in excess of appropriations and other charges, to cover abatements and to avoid fractions. This account had previously been considered a "fixed cost," determined by the Assessors. The reduction in property taxes lowered the amount of potential abatements that would be necessary.

Chapter 11

# Bridgewater: Drawing the Lines for a Budget Battle

Melvyn Colon

## Introduction

Bridgewater is a moderate–income, residential community of about 14,000, located halfway between New Bedford and Boston. Incorporated in 1656, the town is one of the oldest in the state and was once a small manufacturing center. Today, Bridgewater has little commercial or industrial activity. However, the completion of Route 495 -- which will make the town the hub of a wheel connecting Providence, Boston, and Cape Cod -- promises to attract new development. In fact, Bridggewater has been growing rapidly. Its population increased 59 percent between 1950 and 1975, and 34 percent in the past ten years.

## Revenues After 2 1/2

According to the Massachusetts Department of Revenue, Bridgewater had a full and fair cash value of $219,559,000 in 1981. Under the terms of Proposition 2 1/2, Bridgewater's allowable tax levy in FY82 was $5,772,101. Bridgewater raised $6,790,000 in property taxes in FY81. The town had to reduce its tax levy by 15 percent in FY82, and has to reduce taxes by $283,126 in FY83. Bridgewater also lost approximately $450,000 in motor vehicle excise taxes in FY81. Although the town received $541,375 in federal aid in 1980, according to the *Annual Town Report* town officials expect to lose at least $50,000 in Title I funds because of proposed federal budget cuts. However, they estimated that Bridgewater would receive $2,219,445 in state aid in FY82, an increase of $23,670 over FY81's award. Bridgewater began revaluation in July 1981, a process that was to be completed in October 1982. Meanwhile, the state's equalized valuation for the town increased from $219 million to $233 million, which precludes further levy reductions. Town officials expect the new town value, which they hope to use for FY83 tax billing, to be higher than $233 million.

## The Budget Process

Formal budget making in Bridgewater involves the Selectmen, the Finance Committee (known as the Advisory Board in Bridgewater), the Wage and Personnel Board, department heads, the School Committee, and the Town Accountant. The three Selectmen in Bridgewater, Chairman Donald Buron, John Hickey, and David Canepa, played a leading role in the 1982 budget–making process. The Selectmen in Bridgewater oversee all town departments except the School Department. Each selectman serves as a liason to one of the three major town departments. (Buron works with the Highway Deparment, Canepa with the Fire Department, and Hickey with the Police Department.) This year, the board of Selectmen instituted monthly meetings with department heads and participated actively in drawing up departmental budgets, setting priorities, and determining specific cus. The Selectmen's close working relations with the Wage and Personnel Board resulted in its support for their many controversial personnel decisions.

The inexperience of this year's Advisory Board -- last year, most of its members resigned -- contributed to the Selectmen's influential position. It is the responsibility of the Advisory Board to review all money articles and all budgets, and to make recommendations to the open Town Meeting. But relations between the Advisory Board and Town Accountant George Belcher broke down early in the budget process and there was little further communication between them. The Advisory Board was unable to gain access to or information from the Town Accountant. Advisory Board members argued that Belcher simply refused to cooperate with them. But the Selectmen argued that Belcher simply intimidated and harassed Belcher. They instructed him not to attend meetings unless accompanied by a Selectman or the Town Counsel. Whatever the causes, the rift left the Advisory Board without information on town finances until late in the budget process. Therefore, the Advisory Board relied on the Selectmen for most of their budget information.

In addition, the Advisory Board received the Wage and Personnel Board's budget and other sections of the town budget only seven days before the Town Meeting, scheduled for June 23rd. The Selectmen had already reviewed the budget, but the Advisory Board held long meetings into the night in order to be ready for Town Meeting. It succeeded in reviewing the budgets in time to make a full set of recommendations to Town Meeting, although many of the figures in the warrant were penciled in at the last minute.

The Selectmen were most influential. Two of them agreed on many issues and tended to vote together. They presented a unified front in defending their policies. This was nowhere more evident than in their dispute with the Police Chief: the selectmen's budget passed despite the Chief's strenuous objection and the opposition of the third Selectman.

## Preparation of Department Budgets

During the month and a half after Proposition 2 1/2 passed, the Selectmen tried to determine how much revenue would actually be lost. In December, the legislature decided that the motor vehicle excise tax reduction would take effect in FY81, which meant the loss of $450,000.

After the full financial impact of Proposition 2 1/2 was known, the Selectmen implemented the following policies to effect the necessary cutbacks: 1) all town departments, including the School Department, were asked to return 3-4 percent of their FY81 budgets to make up the excise tax loss; 2) the Selectmen imposed a hiring freeze; 3) overtime was banned except in emergencies and departments had to make weekly reports on their use of overtime; 4) two committees were formed, one to review the ambulance service and the other to investigate the cost of street lighting; 5) Selectman Canepa announced that anyone who proposed an increase in departmental appropriations at Town Meeting would be asked to specify which department budget would be cut to pay for it; and 6) town officials decided to sell a town-owned house and two fire trucks. The fire trucks were sold for $30,000.

In January, the Selectmen decided to require a 15 percent reduction in all departmental budgets. They were not certain how this cut would affect individual departments, but they feared that, with fixed costs rising $103,000 in FY82, a 15 percent cut might not be sufficient. An important factor affecting each department's ability to absorb a 15 percent cut was the proportion of its budget devoted to personnel. Selectman Canepa estimated that 91 percent of the Fire Department's budget was devoted to personnel, 83 percent of the Police Department's budget, but only 40 percent of the Highway Department's budget. And indeed, the large town departments submitted preliminary budgets with differential cuts: the Police Department proposed a 9 percent cut, the Fire Department presented a budget reduced 6 percent. But the Highway Department's preliminary budget was cut the Selectmen's prescribed 15 percent. Because the School Department began its budget process before the vote on 2 1/2, school officials simply guessed what limits might be set on their budget. Accordingly, they asked the Regional School District Superintendent to submit three budgets -- one, level-funded, one cut by 15 percent, and one cut by 30 percent.

From January to June, department heads and town boards negotiated over budgets. This stage was dominated by the Board of Selectmen. The Board developed service priorities with public safety first. A deep cut in either the Police or Fire department budgets would reduce their personnel and impair their ability to maintain service levels. The Selectmen asked the Highway Department Superintendent to make further substantial cuts. A second priority was thus specified: the Selectmen intended to reduce nonpersonnel expenditures before laying off employees.

## Impacts on the Highway Department

With the first mandate from the Selectmen to reduce his budget 15 percent, the head of the Highway Department established a priority system to repair only the most badly damaged roads. When the Selectmen requested further cuts, the department head felt unable to comply. The Selectmen then made additional budget cuts. They postponed or eliminated purchases of capital equipment and laid off two men. In all, the Highway department budget was reduced 28 percent.

## Impacts on the Police Department

Police Chief William Ferioli mounted the strongest opposition to the selectmen's budget. He felt that He managed his department well and should not have to make personnel cuts. Over the years, he had opposed the management and personnel policies of two of the three Selectmen. Since he did not want to lay off personnel, and, in fact, wanted to fill two open positions despite the hiring freeze, he made his reduction in overtime and equipment.

The Police Chief attempted to develop the support of the electorate and the Advisory Board. He courted the former by making an impassioned speech in defence of his department on the Town Meeting floor. In this way, he used the full advantage his popularity in the town. He owrked with the Advisory Board to circumvent the policies of the selectmen and the Wage and Personnel Board.

The conflict between the Chief and the selectmen centered on the personnel issue. The 25-man department had one chief, one lietenant, four sergeants, and nineteen patrolmen. The selectmen thought there were too many administrators and complaint that the Chief and the Lieutenant were both on duty during the day. Chief Ferioli argued that he had just enough men to provide supervision for all shifts. He succeeded in preserving his administrative staff. The Selectmen also wanted to eliminate three positions in the department: one crime prevention officer and two patrolman positions. Chief Ferioli decided to fight the personnel losses. He especially wanted to fill the two uniformed positions. After dealing unsuccessfully with the Selectmen, he put his case before the Advisory Board. He agreed to make additional cuts in overtime, and the Advisory Board agreed to fund the two positions.

In a controversial move to save department funds, Chief Ferioli drastically reduced the woking hours of the trafic supervisors from 41 to 19.5. The new arrangement meant that some supervisors worked only one or two hours on certain days; they walked out over this issue. They stayed out for two weeks while town officials frantically sought replacements from other town departments to stand on corners and assist school children across streets. Finally, the Police Chief called the supervisors back at the old hours. However, his new budget eliminated 10 of the 16 supervisory positions.

## Impacts on the Fire Department

While the Fire Chief tends to agree with the Selectmen, the Fire Fighters Association acts independently, sometimes in opposition to the Chief, the Selectmen, and the Advisory Board. The union did not want Proposition 2 1/2 to diminish its power or negate its previously negotiated grants. It mobilized early to fight cutbacks. The union's first priority was to prevent layoffs; its second, to ensure that layoffs that could not be prevented would be made according to seniority.

Problems arose when the Chief instituted a new alarm system as a cost-saving measure. A unit needing help would radio for it at the scene of the fire instead of sounding the siren to bring all the firemen. The ambulance, which had previously gone out on all calls, would also wait until summoned to the scene. The Fire Chief estimated that the new system would save the town about $28,000 in overtime. The fire fighters mobilized immediately, arguing that the new system was unsafe. They launched a public battle with the Chief and filed a grievance. After a month-long conflict, the parties agreed to a compromise town alarm system. As a result of this conflict, the Selectmen asked representatives of the fire fighters union to meet with them along with the Advisory board and the Fire Chief to consider the Fire Department budget. But the meetings never took place. Acording to a spokesman for the union, "personality clashes" prevented informal negotiations.

The Fire Department's FY82 budget showed reductions in personnel, equipment, maintenance, and overtime. A fee for ambulamce service was adopted. (It was expected that most of the fees collected would be third-party payments.) Overtime funds were routinely cut every year, but the Chief routinely asked for more at Special Town Meetings. During FY81, the Chief asked for an additional $50,000 for overtime; the fire fighters expected him to do the same in FY82. The Chief and the Selectmen eliminated three department positions and would not allow the position of a retiring fire fighter to be filled. The fire fighters filed an unfair Labor practice suit with the state Labor Commission on the grounds that the men who were laid off were never officially notified. Although the board of Selectmen sent a letter to town departments warning of possible layoffs, the fire fighters argued that the letter was not sufficiently specific. The Town Meeting voted to rehire the men in exchange for discontinuing the suit.

Another grievance concerned the manner in which layoffs were made. As a matter of policy, the Chief decided to lay off only fire fighters, no Emergency Medical Technicians (EMT's). Because the EMT's were hired in the mid-1970's, they had less seniority than the fire fighters. But the union wanted layoffs to be made strictly according to seniority. Union leaders sent a letter to the Wage and Personnel Board asking them to negotiate the issue. This request was refused. The union threatened court action. Finally, the Chief agreed to use seniority as the basis for layoffs.

## Impacts on the School Department

The reductions made by the local and regional schools represented 45 percent of Bridgewater's budget cuts this year. The preliminary local schools budget, submitted by Superintendent Stephen Childs, presented a dilemma for the School Committee. The Committee, which began meeting in January 1981, had to reduce the previous year's budget by at least 15 percent. Yet Childs's preliminary budget called for an increase of $764,000, one-third of which ($217,961) represented a 6.8 increase in the salary account to cover contractually guaranteed raises. The remaining amount ($527,590) represented an increase in the fees of the Burnell School, a lab school run by Bridgewater State College for grades K-6. The fee for the Burnell School, which was pegged to the per pupil cost in the local schoo, had not been adjusted for several years. The marked increase in tuition prompted a decision to remove 225 of the 525-550 students enrolled there. This, in turn, necessitated a reorganization in the local system to accomodate the new students.

The School Committee encouraged as much community participation as possible by changing its meetings to Saturdays. (The School Superintendent estimated that 47 public meetings were held.) The committee also conducted a survey of parents concerning the provision of support services such as transportation and school meals. Although parents strongly favored these services, the Committee terminated the town's $90,000 school lunch subsidy and raised meal prices. It also stopped running three school buses; children living within a 1.5-mile radius of the schools (rather than a 1-mile radius) now have to walk.

However, the School Committee questioned the mandate to make a full 15 percent cut, and instead devised budgets with 3 percent, 7.5 percent, and 15 percent reductions. Even in making the 15 percent reduction, however, the Committee decided to cut things before people. Thus, expenditures for supplies, materials, and equipment replacement were either reduced or eliminated. The Committee terminated nonacademic programs before academic programs. Hence, art, music, home economics, industrial arts, and the summer recreation program were eliminated.

Approximately 83 percent of the school budget represented salaries. Unless all other budget items were eliminated (which was impossible given such necessary costs as energy), some cuts would have to be made in personnel. These included 18 teaching positions, a librarian, a library clerk, a secretary, 2 custodians, a van driver, 4 teacher aies, and an attendance officer. The dental hygienist was changed from full to part time.

The Superintendent sent notices to attend dismissal hearings to teachers with less than eight-years teaching experience. Of the 33 teachers who received such notices, 21 were tenured. However, the Superintendent made a commitment to the Teachers Association to cover the tenured teachers in the FY82 budget and rescind the dismissal notices when additional state aid was awarded.

Superintendent Childs presented a budget reduced by 15 percent to the School Committee, along with the less-reduced budgets. On a vote immediately before Town Meeting in early March, the School Committee members split over the 15 percent budget cut. A majority successfully backed a 13.2 percent cut, restoring three full-time teaching positions. Two weeks later, after meeting in executive session, the Committee publicly voted (five to one) to cut the same three teaching positions they had previously restored. The Committee finally decided that Town Meeting would not accept a mere 13.2 percent cut in the School budget.

Despite potential personnel losses, the local union of 130 members followed a Massachusetts Teachers Association directive not to get involved in budget making. No sharp conflicts developed between teachers and school oficials.

The budget for the regional school passed in an uneventful fashion. Superintendent Dr. Edwin Denton made a 15 percent budget cut without conflict. Again, the School Committee priorities -- cutting things before people and cutting nonacademic programs before academic ones -- affected the cuts. Several programs, including music, art, and athletics, were reduced. (In response, parents formed booster clubs to raise funds to restore some of these programs.) The regional school lost seven teachers as a result of resignations and retirements. With such losses, Denton wanted to ensure that the Town Meeting would make no further cuts. This goal was shared by his School Committee, the Teachers Association, and many town officials who had participated in School Committee work. Thus, a significant number of those in attendace at Town Meeting supported him.

## Town Meeting

The town meeting was postponed until June 23rd because of the complexity of the budget-cutting process. Town officials would not know how much additional state aid to expect until the state budget was passed. But the state budget did not pass until August; Town Meeting proceeded without a state aid figure.

Preparation for Town Meeting was hectic. The Advisory Board did not see the complete town budget until a week before Town Meeting, and it did not have an exact revenue projection because it was uncertain about the amount of free cash available. The Advisory Board was also reluctant to appropriate the $120,000 needed for revaluation. The board resented the state's imposition of revaluation without providing state funds to cover costs. After much deliberation, the Board finally agreed to revaluate, using the stabilization fund, to which the town makes yearly appropriations to pay for major capital expenditures. Another conflict developed over a $6,000 discrepancy between the wage packages presented by the Wage and Personnel Board and the Advisory Board's package, which was resolved in heated, frantic, last-minute deliberations.

Several departments came to Town Meeting prepared to do battle. The Police chief had filed a motion with the Wage and Personnel Board to rehire the crime prevention officer and had agreed with the Advisory Board to cut his overtime funds to hire two patrolmen. School officials wanted to avoid further cuts. The fire fighters intended to propose just that -- further cuts in the regional high school budget to rehire three of their own laid-off personnel.

About 700 people came to the Town Meeting, a normal attendance in Bridgewater. At the beginning of the meeting, John Heslin, Town Moderator, laid down an important procedural rule: no motion for reconsideration could be made until all articles in the Town Warrant were considered. This rule was designed to shorten the Town Meeting.

When the Police Department budget came up for consideration, the Police Chief made a long speech, defending his department, in an attempt to restore funds for men and overtime. However, when asked to identify another department which he would cut to provide these funds, he decided to withdraw the motion to increase Police Department funding. The Chief suffered another setback when the Selectmen discovered his deal with the Advisory Board. The two boards caucused on stage over this issue. The Selectmen prevailed upon the Board to cancel its deal, arguing that restoring Police Department funds would open the budget for numerous special exceptions. Thus, Chief Ferioli lost out on the men and the overtime.

The school budgets were passed as presented. At the end of the second night of Town Meeting, when consideration of the money articles was concluded, the regional school Superintendent, Dr. Edwin Denton, moved for reconsideration of budget items. He did this in the hope that reconsideration would be defeated, thereby preventing changes in any budgets. Many opponents contended that the motion violated the Town Moderator's procedural rule, since not all warrants had been presented. Dr. Denton defended his motion by arguing that changing the budget at this point would create conflicts among town departments. Since the meeting was packed with teachers, Denton's motion was defeated, and the budgets were made final. The Fire Fighters' union, which was going to ask for $81,000 from the regional school's budget to rehire its own men, was caught by surprise by Dr. Denton's tactic. Their plan of appealing to the electorate for more funding was thwarted.

Most of the articles in the Town Warrant, requesting appropriations for improvements or capital expenditures, were not considered at Town Meeting. A Special Town Meeting would be held to consider these after the state budget was passed. These articles requested considerable amounts of money for, among other things, a new elementary school, investment in the stabilization fund, investment in the Unemployment Compensation Fund, street resurfacing and construction, and water-main construction. No funds were appropriated for these types of articles this year, allowing the town to reduce expenditures considerably.

One week after Town Meeting, the Selectmen asked the Advisory Board to use $27,000 from the Reserve Fund to pay temporarily the wages of employees scheduled to be laid off. Since state representatives had predicted a large increase in state aid for Bridgewater, the Boards decided to use $6,000 to reinstate some of the laid-off employees on a temporary basis for July, with the understanding that they would be rehired permanently when state aid became official. The Advisory Board and the Board of Selectmen contacted all town departments to notify them of this decision. The Boards reinstated two highway employess, three EMT's, and the public health nurse, who decided not to return. The fire fighters decided to postpone their suit until the Fire Department men were permanently rehired.

Aside from the budget, the town dump issue received considerable attention at Town Meeting. Curbside collection had been instituted in Bridgewater several years before. But in March, the contractor increased the town's pick-up charge by $113,000, which enraged residents and encouraged town officials to look for another contractor. At Town Meeting, curbside collection was eliminated and a transfer station was approved for dumping. Residents now haul their own garbage to the dump for a $2 or $3 fee.

Two articles presented at Town Meeting represented two different responses to the budget process in Bridgewater. Both originated with the Advisory Board. Mr. Blackden, Chairman of the Board, proposed an article for reorganizing town government so that "less people would be involved in more government." Blackden hoped it would end the fragmention of Bridgewater's budget process and the proliferation of committee meetings. The article did not carry any specific recommendations. Although it was defeated, Mr. Blackden felt he had "planted a seed." The second article, proposed by John Noonan, the moving force on the Advisory Board, called for a state audit. The article reflected the Advisory Board's frustration in dealing with the Town Accountant. It was passed despite opposition from the Town Counsel, Robert Clark, who did not think the town needed a state audit.

## Distribution of State Aid

Bridgewater received $3.6 million in state aid, an increase of $1,447,000 over last year. At the October 1981 Town Meeting, state aid was allocated to reverse some of the cutbacks made in June. Appropriations were made to refund salaries in the Fire Department ($41,700); the Police Department ($25,000); the School Department ($18,000); the Highway Department ($11,309); the Library Department ($8,500); and the traffic supervisors program ($3,400). Matching funds for Chapter 329 repairs were allocated to the Highway Department ($42,688). The October Town Meeting placed $75,000 into a stabilization fund; allocated $5,000 for school transportation, $40,000 to pay legal expenses, and $120,000 to pay interest on short-term loans.

The distribution of state aid was accomplished without conflict. There was no disagreement between the Selectmen and the Advisory Board -- they agreed simply to restore what had been cut in June. No department request went unheeded: the Library Department hired a children's librarian; the School Department hired a guidance counsellor; the Highway Department rehired an employee; the Fire Department rehired three EMT's; and the Police Department added a new patrolman to the force.

## Labor Relations

Bridgewater's unions were loosely united in an effort to fight Proposition 2 1/2, but the informal coalition, which included fire fighters, teachers, and police, quickly broke down after Proposition 2 1/2 passed.

Union representatives thought Proposition 2 1/2 would greatly affect salaries. Except for the regional school teachers' contract, which was in mediation in FY82, contracts for town employees would not be negotiated until FY83 The main wassue facing the regional high school teachers was the raise/layoff dilemma. Negotiating for an acceptable increase might mean sacrificing teaching positions. The Teachers Association was ready to deal with this conflict. During 1982, in a survey conducted by the Association, teachers voted three to one to accept layoffs rather than forego salary increases. There is little doubt that other unions will be placed in a similar situation during FY83.

As a result of layoffs, the Teachers Association entered into impact bargaining with the School Committee. All teachers with less than eight years experience received letters notifying them of a dismissal hearing, although school officials expected to rehire many tenured teachers. As a result of impact bargaining, the dismissal hearings were postponed. Impact bargaining modified the reduction-in-force language in the teachers contract. To protect tenured teachers, the Association ratified the changes. After the School Committee approved, dismissal hearings proceeded. All except one of the 22 or 23 tenured teachers were reinstated. Twelve to fifteen non-tenured teachers were laid off.

The teachers face other issues. The house reorganization necessitated by the change in the Burnell School's financing arrangements, will cause many teachers to be moved around and, perhaps, back to their field of certification. According to the presidents of the two school assocations, the most devastating impacts of 2 1/2 have been psychological. Lay-offs have produced low morale. Many feel there is no future in education, that it is unsupported and unappreciated. According to Superintendent Denton, the six teachers who resigned this year, did so because they felt there was more of a future in the high tech industry than in teaching.

Town officials view the Fire Fighters union as the most significant source of labor opposition. The union struck a combative stance. It was willing to exercise its full statutory rights, including filing suits and grievances against he town. Members of the union participated actively in town politics. A member of the Advisory Board claimed that layoffs were made in the Fire Department mainly to let the fire fighters know who was in charge.

Despite the fact that the next round of budget cutting will necessarily affect personnel, there is no prospect for a wide coalition of labor groups. Events at the Town Meeting show that the fire fighters and the teachers have very little in common. The two teachers associations, however, have talked about working together on FY83 budget issues.

## Tax Savings

It is too soon to determine how 2 1/2 will affect the welfare of Bridgewater residents. Many homeowners will pay somewhat less in property taxes than they did last year. Many motor vehicle owners have already experienced substantial savings. It remains to be seen whether these gains will be offset by reduced services or increased fees. An immediate, visible consequence has been the loss of curbside trash collection, only tangentially related to the mandated budget cutbacks. Hardest. hit, however, will be parents with children in schools. They will now have to pay more for their children's lunches and may have to transport their children to school. Many children in grades K-8 will be moved around in the house reorganization. Classes in K-8 will be larger. At the high school. many athletic and cultural activities will be reduced.

## Summary

Budget making under Proposition 2 1/2 intensified already existing conflicts in Bridgewater. Differences between the Police Chief and the Selectmen flared. The fire fighters publicly fought their Chief, the Board of Selectmen, and the Advisory Board. Members of the Advisory Board publicly criticized the Town Accountant. Conflicts arose among town boards. John Noonan thought Bridgewater was the scene of a power struggle this year. He argued that the budget process was dominated by Selectmen Canepa and Buron, who influenced key individuals and departments, including the Highway Department, the Town Accountant, the Town Counsel, the Fire Chief, and members of the Wage and Personnel Board. Noonan suggested that people who disagreed with the policies of the Selectmen became victims of budget cuts. Selectmen Canepa and Buron thoroughly disagreed with this interpretation of budget events. They· argued that it represented Noonan's personal animosity toward them. The head of the Highway Department also disagreed vehemently with Noonan's evaluation. He argued that cutbacks were made without any attempt to victimize. However, the budget process in Bridgewater was clearly characterized by a great deal of controversy.

A further cut of 4.9 percent must be made in FY83 to bring the town to 2 1/2 percent of full value. Such a cut could prove devastating as town departments, which have made deep cuts in line items, attempt to deal with salary demands and escalating energy costs. At least one department head, Superintendent Denton, is not sure he will reduce his budget next year if asked. He feels he has cut as deeply as he can without damaging the system. The regional contract states that Town Meeting must accept whatever budget is approved by the regional School Committee. If asked to cut excessively next year, Denton may invoke the full legal authority of the contract. He explains that he did not do so this year in order "to share some of the sacrifices which had to be made."

It is important to consider that Bridgewater has been growing rapidly for the last 15 years. Growth is expected to accelerate when Interstate 495 is completed and will certainly increase the demand for services. If revenues can increase by only 2 1/2 percent each year, how is the town to fund an expansion of services? Small wonder that many townspeople are uncertain about what 2 1/2 means for the future of their community.

Chapter 12

# Burlington: A Worst Case Scenario

Andrew Laing

## Introduction

The completion of a section of Route 128 in 1951 ended Burlington's history as a small truck-farming center and began two decades of rapid development. Growth is only now beginning to slow down as the acreage of land available for development disappears. Burlington grew quickly. Between 1955 and 1965, its population increased from 5,225 to 19,743, or 278 percent. The town's population peaked in 1975 at 24,306, declining slightly to 23,687 by 1980. In 1970, the median income for families and unrelated individuals in Burlington was $12,897, compared with $8,742 in the Boston Metropolitan Area. As the population doubled between 1955 and 1960, 2,000 dwelling units were built. By 1950, 30 firms had located on or near Route 128 in Burlington; by 1965, 66 firms had moved there. School enrollment increased by 60 percent between 1960 and 1965, as 6,000 more people moved into town. By 1970, children between the ages of five and fourteen comprised 29.8 percent of Burlington's population, compared with 18.6 percent of Boston's residents.

Town officials continued to rezone land for industrial and commercial development, permitting large subdivisions of inexpensive housing to be built. By 1974, 559 firms employed 17,437 people in three main areas: the service industry, wholesale and retail trade, and manufacturing. Of those firms, 69 were manufacturing concerns, employing 5,043 people primarily in the electronics and computer fields. The massive wave of industrial and commercial development was topped off by the construction of the Burlington Shopping Mall in 1968.

The town's rapid growth led to massive increases in municipal expenditures and debts. It necessitated an enormous expansion of the school system and the town's infrastructure. By 1975, the town's net debt was 9.8 percent of its equalized valuation. Schools represented 49.8 percent; and other, 1.5 percent.

Consequently, a major budget issue in recent years has been the size of certain town departments and their appropriations. The School Department has decreased its staff 19 percent, from 691 in 1973 to 556 in 1981, but many have raised the possibility of closing schools as student enrollments continue to decline. (1) Police and Fire department budgets have also drawn criticism at recent Town Meetings.

By revaluing its property in 1968, Burlington became one of the first towns in the state to reach "full and fair" cash value. Since revaluation made the town appear wealthier than others, it received less state aid. Since then, town officials have not reassessed. Yet they were able to keep the tax rate under 2 1/2 percent of value. According to Town Assessor, Steve Gasparoni, and Henry Clifford, Chairman of the Ways and Means Committee (the town's Finance Committee), at least 40 percent of the town's property tax revenue in recent years has come from commercial and industrial properties at an effective rate of 3.2 percent of value. Residential properties have been taxed at roughly 2.1 percent of value.

Because of the continuous development, Burlington's assessed valuation has increased steadily. In 1973, it was $225,541,805. The state's 1981 equalized value for Burlington was $701 million. Town officials expect revaluation to yield an $860 million appraisal. The discrepancy between the two estimates of the town's valuation was at the heart of the controversy over Proposition 2 1/2 in Burlington.

Burlington has a representative, town meeting form of government, with 112 members elected from 12 districts. There is a five-member, elected Board of Selectmen which appoints the 15 members of the Ways and Means Committee. The town appointed its first Town Administrator in 1980.

## Views on Proposition 2 1/2

Burlington passed Proposition 2 1/2 by a margin of 39 percent (6,841 to 4,196). Most town officials thought the favorable vote for 2 1/2 was misinformed. They pointed out that since Burlington's tax rate was already below 2 1/2 percent, a vote for the tax limitation measure was unnecessary. Assessor Steve Gasparoni even suggested that a vote for 2 1/2 in Burlington implied a vote for higher taxes -- an encouragement to the town to increase the tax rate to 2 1/2 percent. Teachers and school administrators campaigned with the Fire Fighters union against Proposition 2 1/2. Arthur J. Ferreira, Chairman of the Board of Selectmen, was the only member of the Board to support Proposition 2 1/2. He thought it "would [ enable the town's managers] to take back power from the unions and force the School Department to be more economical."

## The Impact on Revenues

The first-year impact of Proposition 2 1/2 on Burlington depended on the town's assessed valuation. The FY81 property tax levy was $20,055,778.

Using the state's equalized valuation of $701,770,000, the town's property tax levy under Proposition 2 1/2 would be $17,544,250, a $2.5 million (13 percent) loss. In addition, the town lost about $1 million in auto excise tax revenue. At the beginning of the FY82 budget process, town officials thought they would have to use the state's equalized valuation. They did not expect to complete revaluation in time to send out tax bills based on the expected new valuation ($860 million), which would permit a property tax levy 15 percent greater than the FY81 levy. Burlington had joined with Newton and other towns in an unsuccessful suit to gain permission from the Department of Revenue to use their forthcoming higher value estimates in billing for taxes in FY82. (2)

## The Budget Process

Traditionally, the heads of departments prepare preliminary budgets based on target appropriations sent to them by the Ways and Means Committee in October or November. The Board of Selectmen then review the budgets of the Police, Fire, and Public Works departments; the Board of Health reviews the Department of Health budget; and the School Committee reviews the School Department budget. The supervisory bodies vote on the budgets by February and send them to the Ways and Means Committee which makes recommendations on the overall budget to the Town Meeting. Department heads work closely with administrative personnel in preparing their budgets. Last year, they worked on their budgets with the new Town Administrator as well.

The budget process for FY82 was affected significantly by Proposition 2 1/2. Just after the measure passed, a group of town officials began meeting informally to discuss its impacts and possible town responses. This group included the Town Accountant, the Superintendent of Schools, the Chairman of the Ways and Means Committee, and the Town Assessor. The group estimated Burlington's total FY82 revenue at $25,341,435; fixed costs (including trash collection and street lighting) at $7,763,226; and the net operating budget at $17,578,209. The School Department was allocated 63 percent of the net operating budget (department budget allocations were based on FY81 proportions).

It appeared that the town would have to cutback $3.5 million, or 15 percent. Meanwhile, the Town Accountant calculated a property tax levy of $21,500,000, a 15 percent increase over the FY81 levy, using the town's projected valuation of $860 million. To avoid speculation, however, the *ad hoc* group was committed to working only with the state's valuation figures and a conservative estimate of state aid. This strategy was viewed by Pat Mullin, the Town Accountant, as a means of deciding what budget items to refund later: "In effect what we culled out of the budget gave us a set of priorities on what to restore later." In November, the Ways and Means Committee sent guidelines to all department heads, asking them to prepare budgets with 15 percent reductions. The Committee argued that departments should be able to survive a one-year cut of 15 percent. The guidelines suggested that departments eliminate capital spending, reduce overtime, and materials and supplies wherever possible, but not personnel. The Committee did not want any department eliminated entirely.

However, the Selectmen decided not to make equivalent cuts in all departments, but to devise a total 15 percent cut in their portion of the operating budget (30 percent). Responses to the Ways and Means Committee's request had demonstrated the difficulty of making a 15 percent reduction in all departments. Small departments found a 15 percent cut especially difficult to implement. Therefore, the Selectmen prepared their own list of possible cutbacks and asked department heads to submit no-growth budgets, suggesting possible cuts. The Selectmen took other actions. They funded rubbish collection as a "fixed cost" item and decided to spend federal revenue sharing funds as soon as the check arrived (instead of waiting six months, as in the past). They instituted a hiring freeze and hoped to reduce departmental overtime expenses, although personnel reductions limited the amount of overtime they could cut.

The Chief of the Fire Department refused to reduce his budget, arguing that Proposition 2 1/2 was not intended to cut vital services. He maintained that he alone had the authority to draw up the department's budget. His refusal to submit a reduced budget forced the Selectmen to impose a reduction on the Fire Department. They used a statistical analysis of calls responded to by the Police and Fire departments to justify a larger cut in the Fire Department's budget than in the Police Department's. The Fire Chief disputed the results of the analysis on the grounds that they accounted only for the number of calls, not the time spent responding to them. In the end, the Selectmen prevailed, and the department's budget was cut 15 percent, resulting in 16 layoffs. The smaller departments faced varied reductions. The Town Hall Administrative staff lost three employees. The Library achieved a 15 percent cutback by severely reducing its book budget. The Burlington Council on Aging was scheduled to lose half the time of its van driver and its coordinator, both of whose salaries formed a major portion of its small budget; these cuts were restored by the Ways and Means Committee and the June Town Meeting.

The Selectmen also sought new revenue sources. They hoped to gain an additional $500,000 from doubling the water and sewage rates in FY81. (As a conservation measure, the rate was doubled for large consumers and increased 5 percent for residents.) The fee for the ambulance service was increased from $25 to $100 for FY82. In October 1981, Town Meeting approved increases in fees for building permits. The Recreation Department, financed on the basis of a revolving fund with seed money from the town, requested donations this year but did not increase its fees. The Selectmen devised no new managerial reforms this year. Major changes in management's rights to reassign jobs or reorganize work would require renegotiating contracts with unions. But the Selectmen thought the unions would refuse to cooperate on these issues.

## The School Department Budget Process

After the *ad hoc* committee allocated 63 percent of the budget to the School Department, the Superintendent, Tom Michael, met with administrators, principals, and union representatives to discuss reductions. The Superintendent wanted to minimize the impact of cutbacks on instruction. He made cuts in nonpersonnel and noninstructional items such as buildings, maintenance, and supplies. He devised fees for transportation and cafeteria services. He made personnel cutbacks among noninstructional employees first and then among teachers. Except for some high school electives and programs with less than 17 students enrolled, no programs were affected. The Superintendent achieved a major portion of his reductions by closing one of the middle schools.

Budget deliberations were complicated by ongoing negotiations over the teachers' contract. The teachers wanted seniority provisions to govern the potential layoffs they faced. But the School Committee, concerned about losing younger teachers, wanted to base layoffs on an evaluation of teachers' performances, with allowances for areas of specialization. A compromise was reached whereby layoffs were based on a combination of seniority and area of certification. Teachers also agreed to waive maximum class size provisions for two years. Salaries and benefits were not affected. The School Department had notified teachers of probable layoffs in May. The department had intended to lay off 20 teachers because of declining enrollment, but a total of 70 were eventually laid off.

Initially, the School Committee objected to closing the middle school. But after several weeks of discussion, it decided that closing the school was the only reasonable way to reduce the budget without harming the system. The School Committee also decided to fund only half of the school transportation budget. The Superintendent had propoed imposing fees for transportation, but the Parent-Teachers Organization voted to oppose such charges and complained about them at the School Committee's public hearings. Town Meeting later restored full funding for school transportation.

## The Ways and Means Committee

The Ways and Means Committee reviewed departmental budgets in April 1981. Its proposal for across-the-board cus had not been followed, but the Committee thought it should decide whether the reductions that had been made were sufficient and reasonable. The Committee recommended full funding of school transportation costs and the Council on Aging's van driver. It restored funding for two deputy chiefs in the Fire Department. Although the Committee made only small adjustments, it was developing plans for allocating the funds that the town could expect if its higher valuation were approved in time for the FY82 tax levy.

## Impacts on the Fire Department

The Selectmen presented a $1,208,621 budget for the Fire Department at Town Meeting, 22 percent less than its FY81 budget. The Fire Chief presented an increased budget of $1,714,639, which was defeated. The Selectmen's budget called for closing the Burlington Fire Substation, but the department refused to comply and the station stayed open. In all, 14 fire fighters were laid off. The Fire Fighters union mobilized the public against cutbacks in the department. It collected 6,200 signatures on a petition calling for Fire Department funding at the FY81 level. The union presented the petition at the June Town Meeting along with an amendment allocating any additional state aid received by Burlington to the Fire Department. Both were rejected, however the union began collecting signatures on a new petition calling for a referendum on the Fire Department budget.

Tom Corbett, President of the Fire Fighters union in Burlington, thought the statistical analysis used by the Selectmen in preparing the Fire Department's budget provided a justification for politically motivated cutbacks. He suggested that the "Selectmen had a vendetta against the union" because of its activities in the past. The Fire Fighters union has been involved in lengthy contract negotiations, including arbitration with the Joint Labor Commission, for the last 18 months. There was some question about whether to stop binding arbitration proceedings after Proposition 2 1/2 passed, but they have continued. The fire fighters maintain that the services they provide have not deteriorated despite layoffs. But they argue that they are now overworked and more susceptible to injuries. There have been four major injuries in the Department, which was recognized for its low injury rate in the past.

### Impacts on the Police Department

Although the Police Chief requested a budget of $2,038,859 for FY82, Town Meeting appropriated $1,576,136 for the department, down 7 percent from FY81. Seven positions were lost through attrition although there were no layoffs. The Chief expected the loss of these seven positions to reduce time spent on followup investigations and preventive programs, diminish clerical support, and eliminate control staff. Captain Ferguson speculated that a combination of reduced youth services and less police presence might cause increased vandalism.

The Police Officers union completed contract negotiations just as Proposition 2 1/2 passed, which speeded up negotiations. Although salaries and benefits were not affected this year, Captain Ferguson noticed low morale among police officers. He thought the loss of binding arbitration would increase the likelihood of labor disputes in the future.

### Impacts on the Department of Public Works

The Superintendent of the Department of Public Works expected his department to be cut 15 percent from its FY81 funding level of $1,008,232. He requested reduced budgets from the heads of the department's divisions -- water and sewer, highways, cemetery, engineering, and central maintenance. Some divisions required increased budgets because of rising fixed costs, but savings were made by transferring streetlighting and rubbish collection out of the Department of Public Works budget and into the town's fixed costs budget. The Superintendent cut back the capital improvements budget and eliminated 12 positions through attrition; the department now employs 41 people. It is now only doing "patch and paint" maintenance, according to the Superintendent, and the water and sewer division is doing more "in-house" maintenance than it has in the past. The positions of Superintendent of Highways and Superintendent of Water and Sewers may be combined, but a final decision on this has not been made yet. The final cutback for the department was 17 percent.

One of the DPW unions, the Burlington Municipal Employees Union, offered to forego a salary increase on the condition that other local unions follow suit. But other unions would not go along with the offer. The other DPW union, AFSCME, reported that working conditions were not affected by Proposition 2 1/2, despite personnel losses over the last two years and a reduced overtime budget. According to an AFSCME representative, however, union members thought their salary increases were indirectly affected this year by Proposition 2 1/2 because the Selectmen told the DPW negotiators that the town's pay package was a "take it or leave it" offer.

## Impacts on the School Department

The School Department budget was reduced $1.7 million from $12,832,291. Three administrators, 9 clerks, 13 custodians (out of 49), and 70 certified teachers (18 percent of the total) were laid off. Funding that had been cut from the school transportation budget was eventually restored. Class sizes in the middle school have increased slightly. The Superintendent reorganized personnel. He combined two coordinating positions to create an assistant superintendentship. He eliminated the post of assistant superintendent of business and a position in the central office. The Superintendent viewed maintenance as a major problem because of the reduced custodial staff and the capital expenditures budget. He thought continued cuts in these budgets would accelerate the deterioration of buildings. Special education, guidance, and alternative education have been affected by budget cuts more than general instruction. Representatives of the Burlington Teachers Association suggest that the major instructional impact of the cutbacks will be on art and social studies courses at the elementary school level.

## The October 1981 Town Meeting

By the fall of 1981, the Department of Revenue had decided to allow towns to use revaluation estimates in tax billing for FY82, as long as the new values could be certified by February 1982 or in time to send out corrected tax bills. (As of April 1982, the state had not certified Burlington's valuation or the tax rate.) This decision meant a substantial increase in revenue for Burlington. Its assessed valuation rose by $160 million. Representatives at the October Town Meeting chose a tax rate of $68 ($2 less than in FY81), increasing the town's tax levy $2.6 million over the earlier FY82 levy. In addition, state aid to Burlington was $581,000 more than in FY81. Of the $2.6 million in additional revenue, the October Town Meeting allocated only $718,000 for operating budgets. The rest was used to develop reserve funds, and $682,000 was deposited directly into a stabilization fund. The June Town Meeting had added $1.2 million in revenue sharing funds to the town's gross revenue. But in October, it decided that only $400,000 of it should be added to gross revenues. The stabilization fund will be used to pay for future capital expenditures.

The additional $718,000 for operating budgets modified some earlier reductions. The School Department was allocated $650,000 to refund transportation, athletic programs (no user fees will be charged), and school lunches (meal prices will be $.75 instead of $1). Four teachers, an aide, two librarians, a counselor, a special education teacher, three custodians, a typist, and two guards were rehired. The instructional supplies budget was also increased. The Police and Fire Departments were given the remaining additional operating funds. The Fire Department rehired four fire fighters and the Police Department hired seven new police officers.

## Summary

The use of funds made available through revaluation has minimized the impact of Proposition 2 1/2 on Burlington. Despite the prediction that more tax savings would be realized by owners of industrial and commercial property than owners of residential property, a combination of rapid increases in commercial and industrial property values and the introduction of classification makes this unlikely. With a residential factor of 65 percent, property taxes for Burlington's industrial and commercial sectors will stay about the same. Reductions in residential tax bills will average $200. Burlington is still a dynamic town -- a major new hotel and office complex are in the planning stages. Although land suitable for development is running out, it appears that for the next several years, Burlington's industrial and commercial property will cushion the effects of budget restraints

## Notes for Chapter 12

1. Student enrollments in Burlington Public Schools: 1973, 7,686; 1976, 7,033; 1979, 5,730; 1981, 5,052; 1982 estimate, 4,684.

2. The Supreme Judicial Court rejected Newton's case on the grounds that the Department of Revenue had the authority to administer regulations on the use of revaluation figures. The Court also found no evidence that the towns would suffer as a result of using the state's equalized valuation figures in calculating their tax levies.

Chapter 13

# Cambridge: A Search for New Revenues

Jan Lawrence

## Introduction

With approximately 96,000 residents in an area of six square miles, Cambridge is Massachusetts' fifth largest municipality and the fourth most densely populated city in the United States. Until the 1950's, Cambridge was a major manufacturing city with 120,000 residents. But when the manufacturing jobs left, so did many working–class residents.

Today, Cambridge's close proximity to Boston is attracting new office development. Harvard Square and Kendall Square (an area left largely undeveloped until the early 1970's) are less than 10 minutes from Boston by car or subway. More office and commercial expansion is being planned for 370 acres in the city's northwest corner where Route 2 crosses Alewife Brook Parkway. Industrial development is being considered for the 160 acre Cambridgeport Industrial District and East Cambridge Revitalization Area. Hopefully, these new developments will provide jobs for Cambridge's working–class population. Attracting industrial development is difficult because of Cambridge's relatively high land costs and reductions in federal industrial incentive programs.

Cambridge is best known, however, as the home of Harvard University and the Massachusetts Institute of Technology (M.I.T.). There has long been tension between the universities and the city. Education is a major business in Cambridge. Many businesses and residents locate in Cambridge primarily because of Harvard and M.I.T. But Kevin McDevitt, Chairman of the Cambridge Board of Assessors, estimated that properties owned by the two schools constitute one–fourth to one–third of the city's property and most of it is tax exempt. Together, Harvard and M.I.T.annually give $1 million in lieu of taxes to the city, a small percentage of the amount each would pay if taxed directly.

Cambridge is a city of diverse neighborhoods and people. Although city officials want to preserve this diversity, the population's composition has changed greatly in the last two decades. The city's minority population increased from 8.9 percent in 1970 to 17.7 percent in 1980; with Hispanic and Portuguese populations included, it is 20 percent. Since 1960, the proportion of residents between the ages of 18 and 34 grew to 52.5 percent by 1975, with the 25-34 age group growing the fastest. Only one population group -- the 65 and over group -- remained stable. All other age groups declined. Between 1960 and 1975, residents with less than a high school education decreased from 50.3 percent to 23.2 percent. High school educated residents remained relatively stable, 23.8 percent in 1960, 25.0 percent in 1975, while residents with more than a high school education doubled from 25.9 percent in 1960 to 51.1 percent in 1975. The city's median family income increased, in real dollars, from $9,800 in 1970 to $11,350 in 1975. Still, roughly 28 percent of Cambridge's families earned less than $7,000 a year in 1975. About 77.0 percent of Cambridge households were rented in 1975, and 75 percent of eligible voters in Cambridge were renters. (1)

## Cambridge Governmental Structure

In 1941, the City Council adopted a Plan E Charter -- vesting executive duties in the City Manager, and legislative duties in the Council. The nine members of the City Council are elected by a unique voting system called proportional representation (PR). (2) The Mayor, chosen by the Councillors from their number, has no special authority except to chair the Council and the School Committee, acting as its seventh member.

As Chief Administrative Officer, the City Manager is responsible for the management of all city departments (except the schools), for personnel policy, and for the budget. Except by a 2/3 vote, the City Council cannot increase the budget without the City Manager's approval; it can only reduce it. Specific laws restrict the City Council from interfering in the City Manager's business. The Council can only make inquiries of the City Manager.

Victors of the PR process are usually affiliated with the Cambridge Civic Association (CCA) or the Independents. The CCA was organized by progressives in 1945 to fight waste, patronage, corruption, and the city's political machine. Over the last three decades, the CCA has run slates of liberal candidates promoting rent control, school desegregation, affirmative action, merit personnel systems, alternative schools, and neighborhood preservation. Independents tend to represent the more conservative, the less educated, or the working-class constituencies in the city. Independents support unions and their seniority systems. Generally, Independents do not run a slate of candidates, although they broke this tradition in the Fall 1981 elections.

The six School Committee members are similarly elected and generally affiliated with the CCA or Independents. The School Committee appoints the School Superintendent, and maintains management authority, contract ratification, and budget-making authority. School Department and School Committee activities often overlap.

In the first year under Proposition 2 1/2, the CCA had a 5-2 majority on the School Committee, but only 4 of the 9 votes on the City Council. However, the Independents did not control the City Council because Al Vellucci, an Independent Councillor (recently elected Mayor), frequently voted with the CCA.

## Perceptions of City Government

Although noted for its liberal provision of services to a diverse constituency, Cambridge is generally viewed as a well-run city. Until July 1, 1981, the city was managed by James Sullivan. (Sullivan has since become the Director of the Boston Chamber of Commerce. The Deputy City Manager, Robert Healy, has been appointed the new City Manager.) During his eleven years with the city, Sullivan implemented a number of reforms. In 1974, with the support of CCA Councillors, he began using a performance budget, along with the traditional line-item budget. The performance budget lists each department's program costs and accompanying revenue sources. (Sullivan believes that Cambridge is the only city in the Commonwealth to account for revenue in such detail.) Sullivan also restricted city employment. In 1977, the city employed 2,587 full-time employees. In FY81, it employed 2,499 full-timers.

More important, Sullivan reduced the city's reliance on the property tax by increasing revenues from other sources. In FY77, 60.3 percent of the $97.1 million city/school budget was funded by the property tax; 20.5 percent from user charges; 15 percent from intergovernmental assistance; and 4 percent from miscellaneous sources. In FY80, property tax revenue accounted for 53.8 percent of the city's $121.9 million budget; 21 percent came from user charges; 22 percent came from intergovernmental assistance. Ex-City Manager Sullivan argued, "We put together a budget that enabled everybody to understand the system better. Understanding the system better means that it becomes more efficient. So there is a reduction in personnel without a reduction in services. We had an understanding of the need for making revenue sources acceptable and to raise them when they were inadequate. So we were doing some of the things that 2 1/2 proposed that we do before 2 1/2 came along."

Despite these efforts, the FY81 property tax increased from $188.40 to $230.40, the largest single-year increase since 1974. The *Cambridge Chronicle* attributed the rise to several factors: a pay increase of $1,000 for most employees; a doubling of the fuel bill; and a $12 million budget increase created by inflation. Sullivan might also have gambled that Proposition 2 1/2 would pass, and taken this last opportunity to raise taxes in FY81 to finance a mandatory, one-time $3.9 million school expense. (3) (The city could have paid the $3.9 million in two yearly installments, but the City Manager opted to pay the bill in FY81).

Not everyone agrees that the city is well managed. Although former Mayor Francis Duehay contended that waste or fraud would be uncovered if there were any, the CCA argued that management could be improved. The CCA advocates the use of performance evaluation and merit policies to increase productivity. CCA Councillor David Sullivan stated in his campaign literature that he would "press for eliminating the remaining patronage havens -- in Law, Building and Public Works Departments -- which waste money and frustrate citizens." Chamber of Commerce President, Joseph O'Connor, agreed the city was generally well-managed, but believes that its budget has gotten too "fat." While the Chamber's relations with the City Manager and many department heads have been good, the activities of the Chamber and the City Council (especially CCA Councillors) often conflict. O'Connor contended that Cambridge City Councillors ignore business needs: Business in Cambridge has no votes because business is largely owned by non-residents. The City Council believes that it can do anything to business and win votes.

## Pre-Proposition 2 1/2 Activity

By a vote of almost 2-1, Cambridge soundly rejected Proposition 2 1/2, making it the state's strongest opponent of the measure. Many Cambridge citizens, employees, and politicians publicly campaigned against Proposition 2 1/2 and no organization -- not even the Chamber of Commerce -- advocated it.

Manager Sullivan was not surprised by Proposition 2 1/2. He had been aware of it long before it became a referendum issue. In 1978, a similar bill was proposed by several state representatives. When they sought Sullivan's opinion, he agreed that the state's tax system was antiquated, but predicted that Proposition 2 1/2 would force cities and towns into bankruptcy because it eliminated revenues without providing alternatives. Sullivan warned against the easy transference of California's Proposition 13-type measures to Massachusetts.

In the fall of 1980, campaigning against Proposition 2 1/2 became a major activity of Cambridge city officials, politicians, teachers, parents, fire fighters, police officers, and residents. City Manager Sullivan -- often joined by Mayor Duehay -- spoke against the referendum at approximately 10 public functions and became somewhat of a state spokesman. He wrote editorials and articles that appeared in *The Boston Herald* and *The Real Paper* (Cambridge's now defunct alternative weekly). In October, the Mayor sent invitations on city stationery to 1,000 city leaders asking them to meet to discuss the potentially devastating impacts of Proposition 2 1/2. At the meeting, he requested interested citizens to join a political action committee, now the Coalition for Cambridge, to fight the referendum. (4) The fire fighters canvassed roughly two-thirds of the city before the primary and every single block before the November election. Teachers also canvassed the city and some teachers sent school children home with literature about the potential impacts of Proposition 2 1/2 on Cambridge schools.

Other City Councillors -- both CCA and Independents -- organized opposition. In a *Cambridge Chronicle* article Independent Councillor Walter Sullivan derided the measure as an ineffective and disastrous tool for dealing with cities' over-reliance on the property tax. In October, Chairman of the City Council's Finance Committee, David Wylie, staged a mock Proposition 2 1/2 budget hearing which received *Boston Globe* coverage. At the hearing, City Manager Sullivan predicted layoffs of 100 firemen, 100 police officers, and 175 public works employees. Assistant School Superintendent Oliver Brown projected 250 teacher layoffs (out of a staff of 900) and school closings. Public Works Commissioner Conrad Fagone warned that street cleaning would be eliminated and that sewer construction would be cut back.

The Chamber of Commerce leadership did not support Proposition 2 1/2, although they did not oppose it either. A good portion of the membership favored it not only to revalue property taxes, but also to force the city to adopt a more pro-business attitude. City Manager Sullivan thought the Chamber's refusal to take a position was selfish; City Councillor Saundra Graham argued that its silence indicated Chamber support.

## The Cambridge Vote on 2 1/2

Both City Manager Sullivan and Mayor Duehay claimed that their campaign against Proposition 2 1/2 successfully "educated" the voters on its potential impacts. Fire fighters and teachers claimed the same. But Assistant City Manager for Human Services, Jill Herold, thought that many liberals were unwilling to sacrifice hard-won gains in city and school services. She added that Cambridge residents employed by the city or the School Department feared losing their jobs.

Many Cambridge officials felt that Massachusetts' taxpayers viewed Proposition 2 1/2 as their only opportunity to vote for lower taxes. Others thought people supported the measure because they hoped tax reform would follow. Some officials claimed that taxpayers were influenced by the "false" impact information spread by the CLT campaign. But former City Manager Sullivan firmly believed, "the measure passed because some people were being murdered by inflation and jumped at the chance to cut an onerous expenditure."

## The Gap

Cambridge's Proposition 2 1/2 property tax levy limit remains uncertain but the estimated rollback is large. The city's current assessed valuation is $347 million. However, Cambridge kept its valuation low to receive greater state aid. A more accurate estimate is the state's FY81 equalized property value of $1.292 billion (yielding an assessment ratio of about 27 percent). Using the equalized value, Cambridge would have to reduce its property tax levy to $32.3 million to reach 2 1/2 percent of equalized value, a 60 percent reduction from its FY81 levy of $79.96 million.

Yet, the city may not have to cut this much. Like many other cities and towns, it is in the midst of revaluation. City estimates of full and fair value have ranged from $1.6 to $2.0 billion. A 2 1/2 percent levy limit would yield between $40 and $50 million. The city was scheduled to complete revaluation by September 1981, but the Department of Revenue rejected its new property values. The city is improving its data and accounting techniques to convince the Department that its results are not exaggerated.

In FY82, Cambridge had to operate with a property tax levy of $67.96 million (a 15 percent, $12 million reduction). FY83 will require a $56 million property tax levy. (The FY81 property tax levy represents an effective tax rate of 6.1 percent.) Once revaluation is completed, the tax rate will be determined. Taxes on business property currently provide 55.8 percent of the tax yield and taxes on residential property provide 44.2 percent. Valuation at 100 percent, without classification, (5) would reverse this ratio. (Except for condominiums which have been assessed at close to fair market value, residential properties have generally been assessed at 15 percent of their fair market values. Commercial and industrial properties have been assessed at 22 percent and 26–33 percent, respectively.) The City Council has already voted to implement classification once revaluation is certified.

Even with Proposition 2 1/2 and classification, the Board of Assessors predicted that many homeowners could expect the same or larger property tax bills with revaluation. Assessor McDevitt estimated that one-third of the homeowners will pay more taxes, one-third will pay less, and one-third will pay the same amount. A large burden may be placed on the elderly who comprise 29 percent of the owner-occupied households in Cambridge. City officials were worried that homeowners might not be as favorably inclined to override Propostion 2 1/2 once revaluation raises their taxes.

Cambridge officials were faced, therefore, with a $12 million loss of revenue from property taxes and an additional $2.7 million loss from auto excise tax reductions. A total of $14.7 million had to be cut or raised from other revenue sources.

## The Budget Process

Year one under Proposition 2 1/2 proceeded almost like any other, except that most departmental budgets had to be reduced. After the City Council's first meeting in January, the City Manager had ninety days to prepare the city's budget and submit it to the Council. The Council then had 45 days to revise it.

Immediately after Proposition 2 1/2 passed, City Manager Sullivan imposed a hiring freeze. In December, he informed department heads that they would have to cut their property tax revenues by 25 percent, 15 percent to comply with Proposition 2 1/2 and 10 percent to account for inflation. Department heads could increase their budgets only through non-property tax revenue sources. The City Manager asked for an across-the board cut because he believed all services were necessary or they would not have been funded in the first place. He also felt the reductions should be shared evenly. Sullivan wanted to know what effects cuts of this magnitude would have and how the city might minimize them. (Departments such as Hospital & Health Services, Traffic, and Community Development were not affected by the initial cutback because most of their revenue came from non-property tax sources. Departments that rely heavily on property tax revenue, such as Police, Fire, and Public Works, were decimated by the first round of 25 percent cuts.) Manager Sullivan asked the School Department to bear 41 percent or $6 million of the $14.7 million reduction, a loss proportional to its share of the FY81 property tax levy.

While department heads prepared budgets, City Councillors sought new revenue sources. Since Cambridge voters had overwhelmingly defeated Proposition 2 1/2, the Council's immediate reaction was to find a way to repeal it. (State law requires legislation to override Proposition 2 1/2 or adopt new taxes.) Two override bills were sent to the legislature -- one that could be adopted by a simple majority vote of the City Council and another that the Councillors felt would be more acceptable to legislators because it required a local referendum.

In case these override bills were rejected, the Council held a number of hearings in December, seeking proposals for alternative revenues. City Manager Sullivan worked with the Council. In mid-January, the Council approved a new tax package: a 1 percent payroll tax; a 1 percent tax on professional services; a 50 percent tax on the assessed value of currently tax-exempt institutions; and a head tax on dormitory residents. (Most of these measures would impose taxes on Cambridge's two largest employers -- Harvard and M.I.T.) Three other means of raising new revenues -- a local sales tax, a lottery, and vacancy decontrol -- were proposed and quickly defeated. The Independents vetoed the local sales tax; the lottery never had much support; and, vacancy decontrol was soundly defeated by the tenant lobby.

The business community, led by Clark Abt (of Abt Associates, a large Cambridge-based consulting firm), showed its strength at the next City Council meeting. Under fire, the Council rescinded its approval of payroll and professional services taxes. Chamber of Commerce representatives argued that a payroll tax would put Cambridge at a competitive disadvantage. Exasperated with the City Council's proposals, the Chamber, noticeably quiet until now, urged other approaches: the city should eliminate waste and unnecessary services, revalue its property at the highest possible level, encourage new development, analyze and modify the city's policies on condominium conversions and vacancy decontrol, and, most especially, promote business expansion. (6)

Administrators at Harvard and M.I.T. reacted to the city's tax package by lobbying the legislature to maintain their tax-exempt status and urging legislation for state compensation of municipalities with large amounts of tax-exempt property in their tax bases. During the summer of 1982 they were renegotiating their in lieu of tax payments. The city requested a doubling of the payments (from $.05 to $.10 per square foot). Harvard and M.I.T. are not legally obligated to meet this request. However, M.I.T. has already increased its payment from $382,000 in FY81 to $489,000 in FY82.

The City Council also created a Citizen's Task Force, composed of individuals of diverse political views, races, and occupations, to investigate strategies for coping with Proposition 2 1/2, especially to eliminate unnecessary expenditures, to improve management, and raise revenues. The Task Force began work in early February, and attended the City Manager's budget meetings with department heads.

Meanwhile, Sullivan was working to ease the budget cuts. Because of the $3.9 million, one-time expenditure for schools in FY81, he scaled down the budget reduction to $11 million. Of that $11 million, $6.4 million would be cut from the city budget and $4.4 million would be cut from the school budget.

Sullivan also continued to search for new revenues. New fees and user charges were to be evaluated in terms of their feasibility. Rates were to be kept low to prevent widespread non-payment or a denial of services to needy individuals. Sullivan decided that the Water and Sewer Departments could become self-supporting by increasing their charges. He raised water rates from $.46 to $.66 per 100 cubic feet, and sewer rates from $.31 to $.46 per cubic foot. These increases would burden Harvard and M.I.T. more than city residents. Sullivan also proposed making the Rent Control Department self-supporting by imposing a fee of $24 on each of the city's 20,000 rent controlled units. He suggested a $50 garbage collection fee per household to raise $1.7 million for the Public Works Department. User fees and charges were increased for services provided by general government, public safety, health, highways and streets, recreation, cemeteries, and day care. The total of revenues raised from fees and user charges increased from $23.6 million in FY81 to $30.7 million in FY82. Despite the size of the increase and the importance of such charges as a part of the budget, the $7.1 million increase in charges means only $3.3 million in property tax savings. Of the $7.1 million increase, $4.4 million were derived from hospital service charges and the hospital was already nearly independent of property taxes. (In FY81, $1.5 million of its $18.9 million budget came from property taxes. In FY82, property taxes will provide $800,000 of its budget.) Sewer charge increases, producing $1.2 million in additional revenues, made this department nearly self-supporting.

During budget preparation with department heads, Sullivan changed his budget strategy. Instead of implementing across-the-board cuts, he imposed greater property tax cuts on departments charging fees for service and on departments supported by intergovernmental funds. The City Manager also set some priorities. Public safety departments (police and fire) were given special consideration. Departments that had only one secretary and departments that helped raise or save revenue were spared the budget ax.

By mid-April, when the City Manager presented the budget to the City Council, the cuts and layoffs were not as severe as predicted. According to the

*Cambridge Chronicle*, the City Manager's budget eliminated 25 positions in the Fire Department, 10 positions in Health and Hospital Services, and 25 positions in the Police Department. The Manager proposed 63 layoffs in the Public Works Department if the City Council rejected the garbage collection fee.

Several new developments occurred in the 45-day period the Council had to review the budget: Manager Sullivan submitted the new revenue raising measures; the Chamber of Commerce advocated new rent control and condominium conversion policies; the Citizens' Task Force made its report; and, state aid became a more promising prospect.

The consequences of Sullivan's revenue raising measures concerned the Council. However, since a city ordinance states that the Council may only decrease the Manager's proposed water and sewer rates by cutting department budgets, and since Harvard and M.I.T. pay 55 percent of the city's water bill, the Council approved these fee increases. It rejected the garbage collection fee, arguing that it would be difficult to administer and difficult for low-income residents to pay. The Council's decision meant layoffs in the Public Works Department. A majority of the City Council members also voted against the $24 rent control fee.

The rent control issue prompted the involvement of the Chamber of Commerce. In a *Cambridge Chronicle* article, Charles Laverty, the Chamber's real estate committee chairman, claimed that rent control and the strict condominium conversion laws maintain an artificially low tax base in the city. Rent control has reduced rents in controlled units, thereby decreasing their market value, and, in turn, reducing taxes on controlled units. If 5 percent of the rental units were converted to condominiums, Laverty asserted, the city would receive an additional $1.1 million in revenue. If 20 percent were converted, $4.5 million in revenue would be generated. The Chamber of Commerce commissioned Harvard Professor Herman Leonard to conduct a study of who benefits from rent control. Chamber President O'Connor said the Chamber would proceed cautiously with the results of this study, analyzing all the possible impacts of rent decontrol responsibly. As might be expected, rent control proponents were skeptical. In his campaign literature, David Sullivan claimed that the lure of "potentially enormous real estate profits" is the real reason developers attack rent control laws.

On March 20, 1981, the Citizens' Task Force report was made public. By its accounting, Cambridge faced a $20 million, not a $14.7 million, shortfall. The Task Force estimated that in addition to the $14.7 million revenue loss, the city had to raise $5.3 million for wage and salary increases, county and city assessments health benefits, pensions, unemployment benefits, energy, and interest costs. Only part of the $20 million gap could be made up. The Task Force argued that aproximately $7 million could be saved through management efficiency and reorganization (e.g., consolidation of small departments, tightening of financial controls, elimination of unnecessary personnel, and duplication of functions.) The Task Force also believed that $5 million in user charges could be raised, yet they still found an $8 million shortfall. The Task Force report concluded, "[E]ither the state will have to provide additional revenues to the city or the city will have to achieve further economies by seriously slashing services and programs and inevitably laying off a large number of city personnel; by negotiating a freeze on wages and salaries and laying off a smaller number of employees; or by some combination thereof. . . . [T]he state, which historically has dictated so many programs and costs to cities and towns, has a responsibility to give this city and other cities and towns the proper resources and authority to serve their citizens well."

Finally, state aid prospects brightened. At the end of March, it seemed possible that Cambridge might receive $2.3 million less in state aid than it had received in FY81. But, by late May, as the City Council completed its review of the budget, the state legislature began debating substantial increases in state assistance. In a letter to Councillor Wylie, three days before the budget hearing, Sullivan estimated that the City Council could appropriate an additional $2.6 million -- $900,000 from a recalculation of the excise tax reduction and approximately $1.7 million in increased state aid.

Over the weekend, Wylie and the other City Councillors decided that the Council should prepare a package of funding restorations to avoid a public free-for-all. On Monday evening, the Council voted to make the following additional allocations: $1.6 million to the School Department; $263,000 to the Fire Department to avoid 15 layoffs; $99,000 to keep the Mt. Auburn library branch and the bookmobile open; $297,000 to the Rent Control Department [another $130,000 would be raised by a fee less than $24 per unit]; $45,000 to the Public Works Department; $15,000 to Human Services; $10,000 to the Hospital; and a few minor additions. By this time, budget cuts had been scaled down from $14.7 million to $5.4 million.

When state aid figures were made public in August, it became apparent that the City Manager's office had guessed well. The total amount of state aid to all cities and towns was more than Cambridge officials had anticipated. However, the distribution formula hurt Cambridge -- it received only 12.5 percent of its revenue loss from Proposition 2 1/2, $1.7 million. Councillor Graham, who is also a state representative, said that the state legislators had been misled on the distribution formula. Before the legislation was passed, Graham claimed to have been informed that Cambridge would recoup $6 million of its losses.

## Impacts on the Police Department

The Police Department's budget was increased one percent from $7.96 million in FY81 to $8.07 million in FY82. Yet, despite the increase, cuts still had to be made to accommodate the effects of inflation and mandatory wage increases.

First priority was given to maintaining the current patrol force. Lay-offs seemed imminent shortly after Proposition 2 1/2. In December, a letter posted at central headquarters listed 51 officers as potential candidates for layoffs. Morale plummeted. Not until the end of May were police officers assured that layoffs were going to be avoided. The department's authorized personnel level was 350; its force at the time was 278. Joseph Bellissimo, president of the Patrol Officers Association, claimed that the active force was only at 210 because of sickness and injuries. He believed thwas was too few to adequately police a city that has approximately one million people moving through it each day. Bellissimo claimed that Cambridge had been a "lucky" city so far in avoiding a high crime rate.

In order to maintain the 278 sworn personnel level, the Chief transferred 25 detectives to uniformed duty to fill vacancies. Therefore, the criminal investigations budget was halved to $274,770 in FY82. Although the department usually replaces 10–15 vehicles annually, it made no vehicle purchases in FY82. Three community relations staff positions were terminated. Youth crime prevention was virtually eliminated. The number of school crossing guards was reduced from 56 to 40.

The department began seeking ways to increase its revenues. Increased parking fines and ticketing were expected to generate $700,000 in FY82. But the increase would not yield the $859,072 required to fill 35 vacancies, fund civilian and traffic supervisors, or purchase new patrol vehicles.

The members of the Patrol Officers Association were very disturbed about Proposition 2 1/2. Bellissimo argued that, "Proposition 2 1/2 should respect home rule." Members of the Association predicted that another year of cutbacks would be impossible. They claimed that further cutbacks in an already undermanned police force would be publicly noticed and that Cambridge's "luck" against crime could run out.

## Impacts on the Fire Department

Although the Fire Department's budget increased from $6.85 million to $7.25 million, the fire fighting force was reduced from 300 to 280 men. No layoffs were necessary, but just after 2 1/2 passed, a list of 88 junior fire fighters was composed and rumors of layoffs began circulating. While these rumors were quickly dispelled, the fire fighters believed that their jobs were still uncertain. However, fire safety has always been a high priority with the City Council and the public, and it is likely to remain so.

The department receives 95 percent of its revenue from the property tax and it would be difficult to create charges for services that cannot be denied. But this year the Chief instituted a fee for emergency rescue service; the estimated $100,000 will be used to refurbish old equipment.

Since salaries account for 92 percent of the Fire Department's budget, any future cuts may mean layoffs. The fire fighters received an 8.2 percent salary increase in FY82 which may increase the likelihood of layoffs in the second round of city budget cutbacks in FY83. But the fire fighters believe their department was undermanned during FY82. They claim that a reduced force makes it difficult to serve an old, densely populated city like

Cambridgee, with its 10,000 laboratories and the Charles River to protect. On paper, the Fire Department appears to have escaped the budget ax, but its future is unclear.

## Impacts on the Public Works Department

The Public Works Department fared poorly in FY82. Its property tax funding decreased by 19.3 percent and its budget decreased by 4 percent (from $10.1 million in FY81 to $9.7 million in FY82). The department's staff was reduced from 380 positions to 303. Of the 77 positions lost, 30 lapsed because of early retirements and voluntary terminations, and the remaining 47 laid off were full-time, non-Civil Service laborers.

Personnel reductions have already resulted in decreased services. The budget for construction and street and sidewalk maintenance was nearly halved from $1 million to $580,000 and the number of employees was reduced from 60 to 32. Street, sidewalk, and driveway installation will no longer be provided. The schedule for street cleaning has been changed from once a month to once every two months. The number of rubbish collectors has been reduced. Normal replacement of rubbish trucks was not made in FY82. A grounds maintenance staff reduction from 37 to 26 will result in discontinuing the city's tree planting program. General maintenance was eliminated as a separate budget item and consolidated with the building maintenance budget. Only necessary repairs and painting will continue. Rehabilitation and new construction programs were eliminated.

Making substantial cuts was a difficult task for Public Works Commissioner Fagone. He prepared seven different budgets, ranging from a low of $8.2 million to a high of $10.4 million. He defined the services that could not be cut (e.g., garbage collection, snow removal, and services that met immediate needs). Capital expenditures for construction and preventive maintenance were sacrificed. Fagone believes that the consequences of not investing will become apparent in the long run. In fact, he views the FY82 budget as a stalling tactic, although a second round of similar cuts in FY83 will force him to cut into the "nuts and bolts" of the department.

Commissioner Fagone pointed out some other problems stemming from this year's budget. In the garbage collection division, a reduction in the number of collectors resulted in collectors being asked to do more work for the same pay, which created labor-management problems. The Commissioner said it was becoming more difficult to attract and retain good managers who are hard pressed to administer their programs with fewer and fewer resources.

## Impacts on Human Services

The new Human Services Department drew up its first budget in FY82. Previously, five departments delivered the city's human services (recreation, elderly services, youth resources, civic unity committee, and community schools).

(7) In 1978, the city hired Jill Herold, now the Assistant City Manager for Human Services, to plan the consolidation.

Although the new department budget is $300,000 less than the combined budgets of its five predecessors, Herold claims to have limited service reductions through management reorganization and efficiencies. Consolidating and centralizing fiscal, clerical, and support functions saved $45,000 and another $35,000 was saved by eliminating evening custodial service. By making departmental purchases with the city, Herold saved $16,000. She reduced the number of full-time employees from 61 to 52 (4 of these were early retirements, 2 were voluntary terminations, and 3 people were laid off) and the number of part-time employees from 37 to 19. She increased fees for sports league activities and use of the golf course, making both self-supporting. Total recreational fees have increased from $115,000 to $159,000.

Re-organization also gave Herold the opportunity to restructure the community schools program. In the past, an inequitable pay structure existed. People were earning between $11,000 and $21,500 for the same work. All positions were reopened; current employees were chosen first if they passed Herold's performance evaluation test. Comparable salaries, job descriptions, and promotional ladders were defined for all employees. To make salaries equitable, roughly half of the salaries were increased slightly, one-fourth remained the same, and one-fourth were decreased. The two directorships of the community school and the youth resources programs were merged into one position and a new director was hired at a reduced salary. Although most of these initiatives had been prepared before Proposition 2 1/2, the immediacy of budget cutbacks made it easier to implement the reforms.

## Impacts on Hospital and Health Services

After the School Department, Hospital and Health Services maintains the second largest city budget. The department's budget increased from $22,242,865 in FY81 to $25,052,675 in FY82, an increase made possible because only $804,260 of its budget is derived from property taxes. In fact, the health programs dependent on the property tax were actually cut. The school health service lost two of its seven public health nurses and one of its five doctors. Five code enforcement and sanitary inspectors were laid off and five receptionist positions were eliminated in the Hospital and Neighborhood Health Centers.

During FY83 the department may have more difficulty maintaining its budget. The city's officials believe that the city should provide health care at reasonable cost to its residents. Service charges for low-income patients may not keep up with costs. Federal budget cuts could also reduce program funding, especially from Medicare and Medicaid.

## Impacts on Other Departments

Other cuts were made throughout the city. A community relations specialist and a clerk in the City Manager's office were laid off, their supplies and travel expenses eliminated, saving $43,000. The City Council's Administrative Assistant position was eliminated and travel funds were decreased for a total reduction of $42,000. The Mayor's teenage employment program was reduced by $29,000. Personnel reductions were accomplished by leaving vacancies open in auditing, fund management, assessing and personnel administration which resulted in a savings of $272,300.

The Law Department's budget was reduced by $431,000. The department projected a decrease in litigation, laid off one individual and eliminated one vacant position.

The Historical Commission cut $24,000 by reducing its staff from four to two. This reduction will greatly curtail the Commission's ability to give advice on rehabilitation of historic properties.

General services reduced its printing and telephone bill by $35,000. A deputy sealer of weights and measures was laid off, a $17,000 cut. Two layoffs and the elimination of a vacant position in the Veteran's Benefits Department cut $94,000 from the budget. Two weekend standby signal maintainers were laid off, reducing the budget another $10,500.

Finally, the library budget was reduced from $1.3 million to $1.26 million. Seven librarian positions were eliminated, book and periodical purchases were reduced, building and equipment maintenance was deferred. Fines were increased to avoid further cutbacks. Another year of cutbacks will make it more difficult to save the bookmobile and keep the branch library open.

## Impacts on the School Department

Proposition 2 1/2's elimination of school committee fiscal autonomy meant that the Cambridge City Manager determined the amount of property tax revenues the school system would receive this year. The rest of the budget process was handled as usual -- the School Department prepared the first budget and the School Committee revised it.

By mid-January, the School Department had devised four budgets: a Proposition 2 1/2 budget of $33.3 million; a level-funded budget of $39.5 million; an educational budget of $39.9 million; and a departmental request budget of $43.8 million. These budgets were submitted to the School Committee. Shortly thereafter, City Manager Sullivan announced a savings of $3.9 million to the city from the one-time school expenditure. New calculations indicated that $1.6 million could be added to the school budget. Instead of a $6 million reduction, a $4.4 million reduction was required. The Proposition 2 1/2 budget was revised to $35 million. After considering these budgets for two months, the School Committee adopted the educational budget of $36.5 million.

The Committee gambled that state aid would be increased and that the school system would receive an additional $1.5 million.

City Manager Sullivan, Superintendent Lannon, and several City Councillors objected to this strategy. But the School Committee adopted the $36.5 million budget with a rider stating that if there were no additional state aid, a budget of $35 million would be adopted. At the end of May, City Manager Sullivan announced that an additional $2.6 million was available. The School Department received $1.6 million for a final budget of $36.7 million. The School Committee had gambled and won.

But the $36.7 million budget was almost $3 million less than in FY81. To maintain the same programs and personnel levels in FY82, $41.7 million was required to cover contracted salary increases and the effects of inflation. Therefore, an effective cut of $5 million had to be made to stay within the $36.7 million total.

In making cuts, school officials used several criteria: fulfillment of legal obligations, compliance with the voluntary racial balance plan, and maintenance of small class sizes. In addition, officials wanted to retain the support of a broad spectrum of parents in the public schools, especially those parents who could place their children in private or parochial schools. Toward this end, school officials tried to avoid making cuts in the alternative schools and open classrooms. They estimated that roughly 200 to 500 students might desert the Cambridge school system if such cuts were made. Losing these students, who are mostly white, would also jeopardize the system's racial balance plan.

A wide array of programs were cut. In kindergarten through grade 8, remedial reading, home economics, industrial arts, and guidance counselling were eliminated, as well as gym teachers for kindergarten through grade 3 and special instructors for science for kindergarten through grade 6. Reductions were made in art instruction, foreign language instruction, the number of librarians, individual help to students, instructional supervision of teachers,, teacher training and curriculum development, and materials for students. In secondary education, some elective courses were eliminated along with the occupational education academic unit. Reductions were made in instruction assistance, guidance counselling, instructional materials, and non-mandatory learning disabilities and psychological assistance programs. Half of the department heads returned to classroom teaching. Class sizes increased. All together, the cuts in elementary and secondary education amounted to $4.7 million.

Administrators eliminated 183 school department positions, including 19 administrators (12 of whom were returned to classroom teaching), 21 instructional aids, 19 custodians, 8 other staff positions, and 139 teachers. Of the 139 teaching positions eliminated, 29 were accomplished through early retirement and 110 through layoffs.

Teacher layoffs exacerbated the already strained relations between school officials and the Cambridge Teachers Association (CTA). During the contract negotiations for fiscal years 1981 and 1982, teachers had participated in a "work to rule" job action and gave their bargaining team the right to call a strike. (Teachers had fulfilled the requirements of their contract, but did not engage in extra activities.) CTA leaders believed that the reduction in force clause contained in their contract was clear: No tenured teacher shall be laid off as a result of a reduction in force if that tenured teacher is qualified for a position occupied by a teacher with less seniority in the Cambridge School System.

The CTA interpreted this clause to mean that layoffs would be conducted by strict seniority. But School Department and Committee officials wanted layoffs to be determined on the basis of the school system's needs and the teachers' qualifications for fulfilling them. For example, they argued that students should have the right of access to minority teachers. (The Cambridge system is 37 percent minority students, but only 11 percent minority teachers.) School officials could not lay off minority teachers without violating the voluntary racial balance plan. They argued further that all teachers were not equally qualified for all positions, notably, that alternative school teachers and traditional teachers did not have identical skills and experience. To ensure that teachers were qualified, School Department officials divided the system into 27 channels according to program areas, disciplines, and grade levels, and attached specific teaching requirements to each channel.

In late April, the department sent our 373 notifications of possible termination. At that time, CTA leaders realized that the channel system protected certain people, especially minority teachers and alternative school teachers. Approximately 230 tenured teachers received these notifications. Two-hundred teachers staged a mock funeral procession at the next School Committee meeting to protest the method of layoffs. Conflicts arose between minority and white teachers. The once unified union was splitting apart. The CTA filed a law suit against the School Committee claiming that its lay-off policy violated the reduction in force contract clause. Minority teachers, parents, and students filed a cross complaint charging past practices of intentional racial segregation and discrimination. Another group of Cambridge minority activists tried to file a counter suit in support of the minority position. The CTA protested third party involvement, claiming that the CTA suit involved a contractual issue between the CTA and the School Committee, not affirmative action. The CTA lost the first battle when a judge refused to rule on an injunction filed by the CTA to halt layoffs.

## City Savings through Management Efficiencies

While saving money through smarter purchasing was already practiced before Proposition 2 1/2, efforts were increased. Collective purchasing with other cities and towns was pursued further. Cambridge City Hospital changed its food contract from weekly contracts with various venders to an annual contract with one vender, saving $40,000. The city also began to purchase small, fuel efficient cars.

Cambridge also began a policy of listing all costs (e.g., clerical assistance, custodial services, energy costs, rent, and other overhead costs) in grant applications or outside contracts. Cambridge stopped subsidizing these costs of administering programs. Assistant City Manager O'Brien estimates that the city expended $500,000 to $600,000 annually to finance federal program costs in 1980.

City officials also implemented an integrated, computerized financial management system that records both revenues and expenditures. (The two functions were previously handled separately.) The Office of Fiscal Affairs had been planning the change even before the passage of Proposition 2 1/2 because of a change in the city's bank services. Assistant City Manager O'Brien says, "We are applying some of the private sector disciplines. Companies have to be competitive or they don't survive. Cities have to be competitive or they don't surv"ive either." Deputy City Manager Rossi adds, "You can get people to think more along your lines [ of efficiency] when resources are scarce."

## Effects on Fiscal Operations

A predicted $2.3 million loss in state aid, in addition to the property tax rollback mandated by Proposition 2 1/2, caused Moody's Investment Service to suspend Cambridge's AA bond rating between March 27 and July 7, 1981. In the interim, Cambridge used the more expensive bond anticipation notes. In July, Moody's lowered the city's rating to BAA, claiming that Proposition 2 1/2 threatened its future financial integrity because it depended heavily on the property tax. When the city borrows now, it costs 1.5–2.5 percent more. Assistant City Manager O'Brien estimates that the new rating may cost the city $180,000 annually and that if the city has to use bond anticipation notes more often, they will be issued at higher interest rates.

## Labor-Management Relations

Proposition 2 1/2 proponents contended that the measure would restore "sanity" to labor-management relations by giving management the upper hand. In Cambridge, relations were, in fact, good, except between school officials and the CTA.

Ray Clark, Chief Negotiator for the City of Cambridge, believed the unions were more willing to settle their contracts in FY82. Although FY82 negotiations continued until December 1981, no outside intervention was necessary to settle them. The previous year's negotiations resulted in two unions (Cambridge Police Officers Association [CPOA] and Cambridge International Association of Firefighters) employing mediation and fact-finding and another union (Local 195 of the Independent Public Employees Union [ laborers and clerical employee] ) staging a three-day strike to demand a re-vote of its contract. All city employee unions demonstrated to protest the city's allegedly intransigent collective bargaining position.

This year, the CPOA, the fire fighters union, and Local 195 initially requested almost the same increases they received at the end of long negotiations last year. They also waived discussion of working conditions, benefits, and vacations. City Manager Healy offered all unions either a $1,000 increase or an 6.2 percent raise, in order to maintain parity across unions. Local 195 chose a $1,000 increase, while police officers and fire fighters chose the 6.2 percent increase.

City negotiators argue that the current wage increases could result in future layoffs, but union members do not accept that argument. This year, the massive layoffs predicted did not occur. Union officials believe that relief will be found to avoid layoffs next year as well. City Manager Robert Healy argues that this supposition is inaccurate and short-sighted: "The concept of municipal finance is nebulous to most public employees. They think I have a bag of money in my drawer." Job vacancies and the increase in state aid allowed Healy to cover salary increases in FY82, but he contends that, unless the legislature reforms the entire tax structure or Cambridge votes to override Proposition 2 1/2, "there are no magic sources of revenue left out there."

Union officials present a different perspective of their unwillingness to sacrifice wage increases for jobs. Last year, fire fighters agreed to trade raises for jobs; then, a fact-finding investigation showed that funds were available and layoffs weren't necessary. As a result, the entire union supported wage increases this year. Young fire fighters reason that they may be laid off, but if recalled, they will return to a decent paying job. Members of the police officers union and Local 195 believe that raises are essential to keep pace with the cost of living. Both police officers and fire fighters believe they will be the last employees laid off since public safety employee reductions would jeopardize the city. Members of the CTA warn that management has not promised to save jobs if unions sacrifice wage increases.

Should layoffs become necessary, both police officers and fire fighters insist that Civil Service laws, mandating seniority as the sole criterion for layoffs, must be implemented. City officials seem to agree with this strategy.

Local 195 also operates under Civil Service regulations, but laying people off in their chief department, Public Works, will be difficult. Public Works has different divisions, employing people of varying seniority. Last year, an elaborate reduction-in-force bumping procedure was devised to structure layoffs. But only non-Civil Service employees were laid off. Should further layoffs become necessary, employees might be reassigned to different divisions and jobs, resulting in departmental disorganization, employee dissatisfaction, and labor-management problems.

The rift between the CTA and school officials over reduction-in-force procedures and the conflicts within the CTA may be lessened in the future. In recent School Committee elections, the Independents gained an elected seat. With Al Vellucci's election as Mayor, the Independents now have a 4-3 majority on the School Committee. The traditionally pro-union Independents may favor the CTA's seniority strategy for layoffs. Although the CTA now seems to favor protecting minority teachers from layoffs, it will not give alternative school teachers special consideration over more senior teachers. The CTA contends that senior teachers can be re-trained and will not accept a job assignment for which they are not qualified.

It is not yet clear what effects Proposition 2 1/2's elimination of binding arbitration will have. The fire fighters union has never used binding arbitration, although the CPOA has. CPOA President Bellissimo believes that binding arbitration is the only available option for settling disputes besides an illegal strike. If the CPOA were unable to reach an agreement with the city, Bellissimo considers recourse to the courts a possibility. This may not be necessary, however, since the appointment of City Manager Healy promises an improvement in the relations between the city and the CPOA. Years of poor relations with City Manager Sullivan prompted a letter from Bellissimo on behalf of the CPOA to the *Cambridge Chronicle*, lauding the appointment of Healy: "As Mr. Healy became manager things seemed to change as he displayed a willingness to discuss and remedy the problems that our organization faced. The alienation that persisted [between Manager Sullivan and the CPOA] began to dissipate as a renewed enthusiasm and hopeful outlook began to take form. Much of the credit is due Mr. Healy who demonstrated one all important quality, namely his honesty. His trademark has been a genuine concern for solving issues in a manner befitting a gentleman. This association realizes that our relationship with the manager will at times have inherent conflict but we realize that our counterpart is as dedicated to public safety as we are."

The change in city managers may improve labor relations in Cambridge more than a power shift caused by Proposition 2 1/2. Manager Sullivan had a reputation as a tough negotiator, whereas Manager Healy is viewed as a fair-minded, cooperative bargainer. Healy's stance may be responsible for the ease with which contracts were settled this year.

## Home Rule Legislation

Before Proposition 2 1/2 passed, Mayor Francis Duehay organized what is now known as the Coalition for Cambridge to defeat the referendum. Subsequently, the Coalition, comprised mostly of teachers, parents of school-age children, and city officials, became a state political action committee that lobbied the state legislature and the Governor to pass Cambridge's home rule or local override petitions. The coalition has formed alliances with citizens in other communities to pass override measures. Mayor Duehay, the Coalition's de facto chairman, explained his position, "While I agree that taxation changes are necessary, local officials should decide the number of teachers and police, not a state referendum."

The near-success of the Coalition's home rule efforts in the legislature prompted Representative Gerald Cohen to sponsor his own bill to amend Proposition 2 1/2. According to a *Boston Globe* article, Cohen hoped his bill would force the legislature to act on a comprehensive tax reform bill that had been lanquishing in the Senate for months. Both houses passed Cohen's override bill, amending it substantially before it was sent to the Governor. The changes made override much more difficult, i.e., voters, instead of the City Council, would have to repeal Proposition 2 1/2; a simple majority vote was needed to reduce the tax levy reductions from 15 to 7.5 percent, but a two–thirds vote was required to reduce levy reductions from 15 to 0 percent; and both reductions require annual votes. Governor King signed the bill into law in January 1982.

Already, the Cambridge Coalition is planning the campaign to override Proposition 2 1/2. An outpouring of support for the override measure is expected from politicians, city administrators, public employees, and parents of school–age children. Second year Proposition 2 1/2 budgets will be discussed in the City Council and other public forums, emphasizing the devastating effects of further cutbacks. Yet Coalition members expect a close vote. In essence, they will be asking citizens to increase their taxes since many anticipate higher property values because of revaluation.

## Conclusion

Most city officials thought Cambridge survived the first year of Proposition 2 1/2 fairly well. No major cuts or layoffs occurred except in the Public Works and School Departments. Ex–City Manager Sullivan claimed, "Cambridge handled 2 1/2 well and with a minimum amount of turmoil. It survived, to a large extent, because of education and interchange between management and the City Council." Several City Councillors, including Mayor Duehay, Graham, and Wylie thought Sullivan handled the budget process effectively.

The Citizens' Task Force members felt that their input into the budget process was shortchanged, that their recommendations were not considered thoroughly by the City Council. Manager Sullivan said all the Task Force's recommendations were already being worked on by the City Manager's office already. Sullivan explained the limitations of the Task Force's work, "The Task Force was very effective in the sense that it was an outside, objective view provided by citizens who had no stake in keeping the status quo or no stake in necessarily praising or criticizing what was going on. They were citizens who had a stake in the community. They were very diligent in the way they pursued it. The problem is, how do you take a $150 million budget and, in the space of two months, understand it and come up with recommendations that city government itself can't come up with. The answer is, you can't."

Cambridge survived year one of Proposition 2 1/2 by using a number of the recommendations the Task Force and the City Manager held in common: the $3.9 million one–time FY81 expenditure, $5 million in increased fees, a $1.2 million net gain in state aid, several management efficiencies, and the elimination of vacant positions. Next year, such savings will probably not be available. It will be difficult to realize a significant increase in revenue from user charges and fees next year. A garbage collection fee and a fee to make the Rent Control Department self-sufficient may have to be considered again.

City politicians, managers, and businessmen agree that another year of Proposition 2 1/2 is virtually impossible without massive cuts in services. Chamber of Commerce president O'Connor describes the possibility of the city surviving another year of 2 1/2 as an "Alice in Wonderland" dream.

Federal cutbacks may add further to Cambridge's revenue losses. In FY82, Cambridge received roughly $7.5 million of its $25 million intergovernmental revenues from the federal government -- $2.5 million in revenue sharing and $5 million in grants. Federal revenue sharing money is expected to decrease because funds are disbursed to local governments based on taxes collected and Proposition 2 1/2 will drastically decrease the city's tax collections. Revenue sharing monies have been partially funding a wide array of the city's programs and departments.

The Manpower and CETA programs, for which $3.27 million in federal grants is used, have been sharply curtailed by the Reagan Administration. Community Developmet Block Grant (CDBG), another program slated for cutbacks, totals $1 million in federal funds for Cambridge. David Vickery, Director of the Community Development Department, claims, "Proposition 2 1/2 will not dramatically affect this department. Ronald Reagan will dramatically affect this department."

Although Cambridge is in reasonable financial health heading into the second year of Proposition 2 1/2, the only way the city can avoid any devastating impacts next year is by passing some or all of the override measures. But override provisions are viewed only as an interim solution because the city would still have to depend on the property tax to support increased costs. Ending the dependence of municipalities on the property tax through comprehensive state tax reform seems unlikely because citizens may now have the local option to override Proposition 2 1/2 and because 1982 is a state election year.

## Notes for Chapter 13

1. Available housing at reasonable rates has been a controversial political issue due to the extremely tight housing market. In 1970, the Cambridge City Council barely passed (5-4 vote) a rent control law. Subsequent City Councils have maintained this delicate balance in favor of rent control, protecting residents of 20,000 housing units today. In 1981, the City Council also passed a moratorium on condominium conversions to preserve the city's rental stock.

2. Voters vote for as many candidates as they like, but rank each candidate in order of preference. After the vote, the number of votes a candidate must receive to be elected is determined by dividing the number of valid ballots cast

by one more than the seats to be filled and adding one to the result. Then, all ballots are distributed to each candidate's bin. If a candidate 'has enough No.1 votes to be elected, he or she is automatically declared a victor. Ballots beyond the needed number are randomly selected and redistributed to the No.2 candidate on the ballot. Candidates with few or no No.1 votes are eliminated and their ballots are also redistributed to the No.2 candidate. This process continues until nine candidates acquire the necessary votes. Approximately two-thirds of the ballots are used on the No.1 choice. Thus, there is great competition among candidates to get No.1 votes. A candidate cannot remain in the race without them.

3. The one-time $3.9 million expenditure consisted of $3 million for accrued payroll expenses to shift to a new state-mandated accounting procedure and $.9 million for the FY80 school deficit.

4. Barbara Anderson, CLT Director, charged Duehay with violating the campaign funding laws by using public monies to oppose Proposition 2 1/2. But Duehay claimed that he never engaged in political action committee activities during work hours or used public money for the Coalition's work. Anderson was unable to mount a credible court case.

5. Classification allows the City Council to tax business property and residential property at different rates. Cambridge voters approved the use of classification.

6. At this time, a 2 1/2 percent growth cap applied, allowing a municipality's tax base to increase at no more than 2 1/2 percent of the Proposition 2 1/2 levy limit per year. Thus, business expansion would not have increased Cambridge's tax base by more than 2 1/2 percent per year. However, the Cambridge Board of Assessors contended that as long as the city's levy was higher than 2 1/2 percent of the city's certified full and fair market value, the city had not established its Proposition 2 1/2 levy limit and the 2 1/2 percent growth gap did not apply. Any new increase in property value could be added to the city's property tax base. The 2 1/2 percent growth cap has since been repealed by the state legislature.

7. Cambridge's community schools provide classes for people of all ages and for every interest, from the recreational to the functional.

Chapter 14

# Chelsea: A Mayor Proposes

Jerome Rubin and Thomas Campbell

## Introduction

With an area of 1.8 square miles, Chelsea is the smallest city in the Commonwealth, and one of the poorest. Chelsea's population of 25,000 has fallen 40 percent since 1950, 17 percent since 1970. In 1977, per capita income was $4,741 compared with the state average of $5,826. According to the 1970 Census, 12.9 percent of Chelsea's residents had incomes below the poverty level. Median family income was $8,973, compared with $11,449 for the Boston Metropolitan area. Almost one-third, (30.5 percent) of Chelsea's population is older than sixty, and 14 percent is Spanish-speaking. Chelsea's unemployment rate has been consistently above the area average for several years. The city lost jobs steadily. Between 1967 and 1972, there was a 17 percent decline in retail and manufacturing employment. Low property values have been caused by the construction of the Tobin Bridge (1946) which cuts the city in half; the great fire of 1973 that destroyed over 20 percent of the city; and by an aging housing stock. Taken together, these characteristics render Chelsea acutely vulnerable to the restrictions of Proposition 2 1/2.

But a description of Chelsea's economic condition is incomplete without noting recent efforts to revitalize the city. Since 1975, city officials have aggressively sought federal redevelopment funds and three major projects are already underway. An abandoned Naval hospital and the surrounding 88 acres will be used to construct 1200–1400 housing units, a waterfront park, a marina, and light industry. Improvements will also be made in the adjacent neighborhood. To date, the city has used $8.7 million of $10.5 million in federal aid and $5 million in state aid. City planners hope to raise $80 million from private sources. They expect 900 jobs to be created by this development. An area devastated by the 1973 fire has been turned into Murray Industrial Park by the Chelsea Redevelopment Authority, which invested over $20 million to acquire and prepare the site. This investment should create 2,500 new jobs in Chelsea. Finally, to improve its housing stock, the city has initiated several programs. A $3.6 million Neighborhood Strategy Program will rehabilitate 74 units in the Central Business District. The Chelsea Neighborhood Housing Services Program (a private, non-profit partnership of residents, lenders, and city officials) administers high-risk revolving loans for improvements. EDA funds are being used to make public improvements in the Central Business District, to reconstruct parks and playgrounds, and to establish a local Industrial Development Finance Authority to obtain low-interest, tax-exempt revenue bonds to invest in physical plant and equipment.

Despite these vast plans and expenditures, city officials do not expect them to offset the impacts of Proposition 2 1/2. Although economic development in Chelsea is a long-term endeavor, federal aid cutbacks and Proposition 2 1/2 both threaten Chelsea's renaissance.

## Views on Proposition 2 1/2

Proposition 2 1/2 passed by nearly a two-to-one margin in Chelsea and city officials agree that it was the result of consistently high tax rates. In 1977, the tax rate in Chelsea was $242 per $1,000 assessed valuation, the second highest tax rate in Massachusetts. Although it dropped to $236 in 1978, it rose again the next year to $253. The FY81 tax rate was $245. But the editor of Chelsea's daily newspaper thought voters reacted as much to "government waste and the excesses of public employees" as much as they did to high tax rates. He argued, "People see city employees walking around at all hours of the day. They see teachers leaving at 2:15 and big salaries going to administrators. Chelsea is a very in-grown political system. Everyone knows everyone else, and they get things because they know everyone else. Now the rank and file have reacted against that way of doing things."

Some public employees viewed Proposition 2 1/2 favorably. The President of the Police Association thought "it was long overdue." Although the teachers association opposed Proposition 2 1/2, the School Superintendent, Vincent McGee, knew of many teachers who voted for it. Despite the fire fighters' campaign against it, union president, Bill Abramofsky, disparaged the anti-2 1/2 efforts: "Labor, as a whole, did not do its job. The school teachers and fire fighters were the only unions out there against Proposition 2 1/2 in Chelsea. It affected other city unions, but all their members could see were tax cuts and dollar signs. Some municipal unions even supported it."

Some city officials claimed that because Chelsea's residents approved the results of new development, they were not censuring the city government in voting for Proposition 2 1/2. They argued instead that voters were telling the legislature to do "something" about property taxes. Bill Abramofsky and Abe Morochnick, president of Chelsea Fair Share, thought voters wanted tax reform, but argued that they did not understand that the referendum might entail service reductions.

Although the city stood to lose a great deal from Proposition 2 1/2, Mayor Joel Pressman ardently supported it. Pressman, who was criticized for "gambling with the city's future," thought Proposition 2 1/2 was the only way to force the state to initiate tax reform and, like most mayors, he favored ending binding arbitration and school committee autonomy. He explained, "I have been going to the legislature for five years, explaining the problems with property taxes and my lack of control over the city's finances. It was like whistling in the dark. So the 2 1/2 people came along and I figured this was the last chance for us to get to tax reform. It passed and now people talk about reform and I think we'll get it."

## Previous Budget Issues

In the four years prior to 1981, several controversies developed over school spending. Administrators were criticized for earning more money than the Mayor and teachers were reproached for earning too much and for living outside the city. But School Superintendent McGee, hired to end patronage, viewed his past four years as a continual battle with School Board members and other city officials over his budget authority. Police and fire department budgets also provoked disagreements about the adequacy of protection, the elimination of vacant positions in the police department, and fire fighters' salaries. Abramofsky described the causes of some of the problems between the Fire Fighters Association and the city: "We went without pay raises from 1974 to 1978. We went through fruitless negotiation, then mediation, fact-finding, and finally binding arbitration. We got a $750,000 award over three years which cost us $60,000 in inflationary losses. If the Mayor had bargained in good faith, he would have saved the city money."

The Mayor tried to exempt Chelsea from binding arbitration in 1978 in order to spend more money on development and less on salary and wage increases. City Auditor Connor explained that when the legislature refused to exempt Chelsea from binding arbitration and school committee autonomy, the city had to pay out $860,000 in retroactive wage increases. She said, "Our taxes went up and it became more difficult to attract investors."

## Revenue Losses

Chelsea's potential revenue losses are severe under Proposition 2 1/2. Using the state's equalized valuation ($178.4 million), the 2.5 percent levy limit permits only $4.4 million in property tax revenue. The city's FY81 property tax levy was $14.5 million. Combined with a $415,197 loss of motor vehicle excise taxes, Chelsea's total revenue loss swells to $10.5 million, 60 percent of its FY81 revenue. Revaluation does not promise much relief. Reassessment will probably increase valuation to $300 million, allowing a property tax levy of $7.5 million, down 48 percent from FY81. Chelsea faces at least three years of 15 percent budget cuts. Local revenue reductions may be aggravated by federal cuts in development grants, housing subsidies, and social services. While officials are pessimistic, they could not predict federal funding policies in these areas.

In FY82, Chelsea reduced its property tax levy $2,176,161. Adding the $400,000 loss in motor vehicle excise taxes, the total first year revenue loss was $2,576,161, approximately 15 percent. Although there was some indication that state aid would be increased, city officials did not count on it when they prepared the FY82 budget.

## The Budget Process

In Chelsea, the Mayor's office develops the budget and presents it to the Board of Aldermen, which may cut, but not increase, the budget. The essence of the budget process is contained in the saying, "The Mayor proposes and the Board of Aldermen disposes." But some city officials thought Proposition 2 1/2 enhanced the Mayor's power "to dispose" . One School Board member argued, "Budget decisions were made solely in the Mayor's office. The Mayor looked for cuts this year. He had more power and took more initiative than ever before." Mayor Pressman, first elected in 1976, agreed that although he met with department heads and asked them to set their own budget priorities, his office exerted more control over Chelsea's FY82 budget than usual.

Soon after Proposition 2 1/2 passed, city officials (the Board of Aldermen, the Mayor, the Treasurer, and the Auditor) held a public meeting "to chart a course of action." The Aldermen wanted to open the budget process to the public to combat "wild rumors," but no plans to cope with cutbacks developed from the meeting. Shortly before Christmas 1980, Mayor Pressman presented a "worst case" budget, cut 28 percent. The budget was based on an estimated $2.65 million property and motor vehicle tax losses, additional costs in unemployment benefits caused by layoffs, and inflation. Initially, the Mayor proposed cutting all department budgets 15 percent. But since significant reductions made small departments inoperable, the Mayor proposed making greater reductions in the city's large departments: schools, streets and sewers, water, parks, libraries, engineering, police, and fire.
Aldermen Delorio and Nolan agreed with the Mayor that cuts should vary among all departments. But Alderman Mitchell wanted to protect public safety departments from any budget reductions or layoffs. He proposed making all necessary layoffs among City Hall employees.

At a February press conference, Mayor Pressman said he intended to lay off employees in City Hall and other departments before laying off police officers and fire fighters. He also announced that an accounting firm (Ernst & Whinney) had been retained to draw up budget priorities, determine where cuts could be made, help revise the city's fee schedule, calculate the rate of unpaid taxes and abatements, and analyze service delivery. The Mayor proposed that in the meantime, the city implement a hiring freeze, eliminate salaries for part-time Board members (such as those serving the Youth Commission), set up an outside contract for rubbish collection (at a savings of $150,000), and raise water rates and other user charges. He announced that layoffs had begun (four people at the library and three at the fire alarm station) and urged consideration of his proposals "to ease the burden."

Although the Mayor is required to submit a budget to the Board of Aldermen during the month of March, uncertainty over FY82 revenues and continuing negotiations with department heads delayed it until May. During March and April, layoff notices were sent to 75 nontenured school teachers and 14 fire fighters. The Aldermen urged the Mayor again to lay off City Hall employees, and reduce his own office expenses. But the Mayor refused to yield to pressure emmanating from "groups with vested interests," although he did withdraw his proposal to contract out for trash collection when he recognized that the Aldermen opposed it.

By the time the Aldermen reviewed the budget in late May, they thought there was very little left for them to do. Paul Casino, President of the Board of Aldermen, argued that the Board's work of reducing the budget had already been accomplished by the Mayor. But the Board made a total of $195,000 additional cuts -- $180,000 in unemployment compensation, $5,000 in college credit payments, and $5,000 in fire department overtime. Alderman Mitchell wanted to reduce the Mayor's expense account $11,352, but the other Aldermen did not approve. The Aldermen passed a budget (7-2 margin) on June 29, which reduced spending 9 percent, or $1.975 million. The budget reflected increases in fixed costs (25 percent of the total budget) -- in fuel costs ($100,000), pension costs ($284,000), Blue Cross payments (15 percent), unemployment, and debt and interest payments. While the entire budget was reduced from $21.870 million to $19.894 million, the city's spending was cutback from $14.782 million to $13.642 million (a 7 percent decrease) and the School Department's spending was reduced from $7.137 million to $6.252 million (a 12 percent reduction).

The Mayor's original cutback proposal ($2.576 million, 28 percent) was mitigated by increases in state aid and Chelsea's own-source (nonproperty tax) revenue. The city's user fees and charges, which had not been adjusted for over a decade, were increased to yield an additional $500,000. Water and sewer rates were raised, along with ticket fines and various fees for licenses. Payments in lieu of taxes, negotiated under Chapter 121A agreements (1) with new developers, were expected to increase revenue $125,000. The city also renegotiated the fee for oil storage licenses from $25,000 to $100,000. (The legislature must approve the new rate.) With court payments of $44,000 and a Massport easement payment of $55,000, city officials increased revenue from local sources $724,000. In addition, preliminary state aid estimates showed a net increase of $610,000 in state aid to Chelsea. These revenue increases, totalling $1.334 million, were factored into the budget passed by the Board of Aldermen. Although the overall budget reduction was 9 percent, some departments absorbed higher percentage reductions: the Streets and Sewers, Water, and Parks departments were each cut 30 percent; the Public Library, 29 percent; the Treasurer's department, 20 percent; the Police Department, 17 percent; Engineering, 16 percent; the Fire Department, 14 percent; and the Buildings Department, 8 percent.

## Impacts on the School Department

The School Department absorbed a 12 percent reduction in its budget ($885,000). Since 85 percent of the department's budget is earmarked for salaries, 33 teachers and 22 other school employees were scheduled for layoffs. The School Committee also approved (4–3) a 10 percent pay reduction for all school employees (a decision that was upheld by the Massachusetts Labor Relations Council, in a challenge by the teachers union.)

The Superintendent predicted increased class sizes. The special education program lost a speech therapist and its evaluation team. Fewer teachers in the bilingual program will have a serious impact on Chelsea's two largest elementary schools where nearly half of the students speak Spanish.

Superintendent McGee thought Proposition 2 1/2 would severely affect Chelsea's school system: "The cuts will be devastating. I think it will seriously impair the quality of education. We had a fairly good enrollment ratio, but now that's over. I believe the School Department took the brunt of the 2 1/2 cuts. In a way, we were used to get through the whole thing."

But Mayor Pressman disagreed with this analysis: "I don't think the quality of education will be impaired. The school people cried about budget cuts and then voted a 9 percent raise for administrators. Under the 4 percent cap, when the School Board overrode its budget, I had to go to court. Now the Board has to come to me. But Proposition 2 1/2 doesn't go far enough —— I'm given responsibility; I should have control. I should have line–item, as well as bottom–line control."

Deputy School Superintendent, Herbert Drew, hoped political decisions would not prevent a consideration of department improvements or obscure the future of education in Chelsea: "Look at it this way —— next year if we have to cut 15 percent, that will be another $900,000. Figuring that five people cost roughly $100,000, we will lose 45 teachers. At that point, and certainly with a third year of 15 percent cuts, I believe we should close the doors and go home. Morale will be too low. Students and parents in Chelsea want a quality education. They want a band. They want athletic teams to be bussed to the games. But they don't want to —— and often can't —— pay for it."

## Impacts on the Fire Department

In 1975, the Fire Department had 115 men. But attrition has resulted in a substantial loss of positions and the department now employs 92 men. The June budget called for a 14 percent reduction ($353,000), which might have resulted in 20 layoffs. But these were prevented when the Chelsea fire fighters agreed to open their union contract. The fire fighters traded $300,000 in overtime funds ("until such time as the city receives more local aid as projected") and their minimum manning provision for job security this year. (Overtime funds have remained constant over the past two years, but during heavy vacation periods and with normal rates of disability or sickness, the city may be short 21 or 22 men.) The department's maintenance and fire inspection budgets were decreased a third. Although layoffs were avoided, residents who recall the fire of 1973 remain edgy about any reductions in Chelsea's Fire Department.

Before Proposition 2 1/2 passed, the Fire Fighters union negotiated a pay raise (with the assistance of the Joint Labor-Management Committee) through binding arbitration. Union President, Bill Abramofsky, claimed that the settlement is binding, but Mayor Pressman did not agree: "My position is that Proposition 2 1/2 gets rid of binding arbitration. The union doesn't take that position. It has a decision from the Attorney General that the Joint Labor-Management Committee still exists and that the Board of Aldermen will have the final say over whether the pay raise stays in effect. The unions don't even think binding arbitration is abolished. We'll challenge the Attorney General's decision in court."

Abramofsky did not regret opening the contract to save jobs this year, but he argued that the Mayor should have bargained with the union in good faith: "He would have saved a lot of money. Once he realized he was in trouble with 2 1/2, he knew there had to be closer labor relations. He supported 2 1/2 and wanted to end binding arbitration. We felt that it was important to save the jobs and we knew the state aid was coming so we went along with opening our contract. We were the only labor group that cooperated. I hope some consideration will be given to us."

## Impacts on the Police Department

Despite early press reports of a 20 percent cut in FY82, layoffs in the Police Department were prevented by a large number of retirements. But the department lost 11 of 77 positions this way and the Police Chief considered the force "very thin on the streets." The President of the Police Officers union estimated that the department was now short 20 men.

## The Impacts on Smaller Departments

Directors of smaller city departments predicted that cutbacks would impair their operations. City Treasurer, Sidney Brown, was upset about the 40 percent reduction in his budget, which cost him four of the ten clerks on his staff. Although the four clerks were rehired in September (with additional state aid), Brown thought it ironic that his office -- responsible for tax collection -- would not even be able to function were Proposition 2 1/2 really put into effect in Chelsea. The loss of one employee in the Assessor's office caused one employee to predict a curtailment of services: "We won't do any research work for people anymore. Our books are open for people to use, but we can't do the property research for them. Next year's cuts will make it very difficult to reach and maintain 100 percent. It's silly to go to 100 percent and not maintain it."

City Auditor, Valerie Connor, planned to eliminate one of the four positions in her department in order to finance a computer system for accounting and record-keeping.

## The Impacts of Additional State Aid

State aid accounted for 33 percent of Chelsea's budget in FY81, one of the highest percentages in the Commonwealth. The statewide campaign to increase state aid encouraged city officials to believe that additional funds would be available in August. In July, Mayor Pressman announced his recommendations to distribute local aid: to restore the Fire Department's $300,000 in overtime (and reinstate the minimum manning provision) and to increase the School Department's allocation. However, the Mayor also asked department heads to set priorities for rehiring employees, because, he said, "not everyone will be rehired." (The School Department ended up losing 54 employees -- 32 teachers and 22 other employees. The city lost 9 employees.)

When the state legislature announced state aid allocations in late July, Chelsea ended up with $2,653,286, which covered all but $11,125 of its FY82 revenue losses. The Mayor wanted to hire 15 new police officers, restore all Fire Department reductions, allocate $350,000 to the School Department, rehire 25 city employees, purchase a new trash collection truck and two police cruisers, recall traffic supervisors, and refinance the bookmobile program. A 7 percent retroactive pay increase for police officers and fire fighters (from the Joint Labor-Management Commission award) commanded $575,000 of the state aid money. In addition, the Mayor set aside $540,000 to reduce the impacts of next year's 15 percent cut.

Other city officials agreed that Chelsea should take precautions against next year's cuts, but the city had $1.046 million in free cash in September 1981. The Mayor wanted to hold the full amount in reserve, but the Aldermen wanted to appropriate another $100,000 to the School Department and use the rest of the free cash to reduce the tax rate further.

The surplus from FY81 and whatever is carried over into FY83 from this year's state aid, are Chelsea's only buffers against a second round of cuts. City Auditor Connor estimated FY82 income "very conservatively," in the hope that a larger surplus will carry over into FY83. She thought the retroactive pay increases for police officers and fire fighters were unjustified expenditures during FY82 and warned, "We need to keep our belt tight to have funds for the future."

## Impacts on Government Waste and Efficiency

Although there were few efforts to improve efficiency during FY82, none of those interviewed thought Proposition 2 1/2 cut "fat" from the city government. City Auditor Connor argued, "2 1/2 was supposed to cut out the patronage and leave the services, but I'm not all that sure that's happening.

Starting out at the legislature, and all the way to the cities, the top people seem to be holding their jobs. Bill Abramofsky of the Fire Fighters union agreed: "It's all politics. What's being cut is not what has to be cut. "If Proposition 2 1/2 really cut waste, Barbara Anderson would be a hero.

### Impacts on the Future

In FY82, Moody's Investment Service lowered Chelsea's bond rating from B-aa to B-a, or "below investment grade," making it virtually impossible for the city to engage in long-term borrowing. Chelsea's relatively low credit rating has been unimportant in the past since most of its new capital investments have been funded through federal grants. The City Treasurer, Sidney Brown, thought the city might increase its short-term borrowing -- which depends more on interest rates than on credit rating.

The Director of Community Development, Michael Glavin, thought the consequences of Proposition 2 1/2 -- especially public service reductions that effect development -- would "have to be resolved to insure that the state remains attractive to investors." He thought Chelsea was in a good position to attract investors within the state, but as a competitor in New England, the state's level of corporate, sales, and income taxes could make more of a difference. Glavin thought federal cutbacks in local economic development funding would impede Chelsea's ability to increase its tax base to pay more of its own way.

The City Assessor saw no way to increase Chelsea's tax base in the near future, with or without revaluation or federal funding: "We may build or renovate a building here or there, but it won't add much. The city is less than 2 square miles. Almost 40 percent of it is tax exempt. We won't even be close to making up the difference with 100 percent revaluation. Let's say our valuation goes up to $200 million or even $250 million. 2 1/2 percent of that is nothing."

Few city officials believed Chelsea could survive a major budget cut without new sources of revenue, an override, or even more help from the state. Mayor Pressman still hoped the state would "cuts its own fat" and move toward tax reform: "There's no way we can continue cutting. We may be able to get through FY83, but it will be difficult. Maybe we can save some of this local aid for 1983, but there's no way 2 1/2 can be implemented in this city. I never thought it could, and I'll vote to override if I'm still here. It was just a means to get to property tax reform."

### Summary

Although the state "bailed out" Chelsea during FY82, most city officials thought budget-cutting would severely affect public services sooner or later. Abe Morochnick of Chelsea Fair Share thought this had already happened and with little tax benefit: "Proposition 2 1/2 will increase state taxes and add to the overall tax burden of middle- and low-income families. With the Reagan cuts, poor and working people will be hurt. People were hurt by Proposition 2 1/2 and tax relief will be minimal. But the editor of *The Chelsea Record* thought taxpayers in Chelsea would definitely benefit from Proposition 2 1/2: "The beneficiaries will be the taxpayers who were burdened by the public employees. The losers will be the public employees. There was a woman working in City Hall for 19 years who was let go. Teachers, who thought tenure set them up for life, and city employees don't have any security anymore. Their demands just can't be endless."

Both the City Treasurer and the City Assessor thought some residents would experience higher property taxes. They predicted that even with classification, taxes in older neighborhoods would increase 30 to 40 percent. They agree with Mayor Pressman, however, that without Proposition 2 1/2 residential taxes would have increased even more in the long run. Despite their differences, city officials argued that without some type of state fiscal reform, Chelsea would not survive the continual cutbacks mandated by Proposition 2 1/2. A higher and more extensive sales tax is supported by some businessmen and city politicians. But labor unions, particularly the fire fighters, strongly oppose the sales tax and support a graduated income tax. Fair Share supports a tax on corporations and legislative efforts "to close off loopholes."

## Notes for Chapter 14

1. Chapter 121A of the Massachusetts General Laws allows municipalities to negotiate with limited dividend corporations undertaking developments in blighted areas for specified payments in lieu of property taxes. The agreements are not subject to limitation by Proposition 2 1/2.

Chapter 15

# Framingham: Gambling on Revaluation

Thomas Campbell

## Introduction

Framingham has the largest population of any town in the state and is, in fact, the largest municipality in the country still using the town meeting form of government. While the town's population grew substantially from 1960 to 1970 (43 percent), the rate of growth slowed to 1.6 percent over the last decade. The 1980 Census reported a current population of 65,113, but local officials argue that it is closer to 70,000.

Framingham is situated on key transportation routes, making it a center of major industrial and commercial activity. Framingham has an unemployment rate (5.3 percent in 1978) consistently below the state and U.S. averages. Leading taxpayers and employers include the General Motors Corp., Dennison Manufacturing Corp., Zayres, Shoppers World, Bose Corporation, and Prime Computer. Town officials estimate that there are $40 to $50 million in construction projects underway in Framingham. However, residential construction has declined substantially. This slowdown is due, in part, to a ban on further construction of apartments (1972) and duplexes (1976), reflecting local sentiment against transients.

Framingham receives 52 percent of its property tax revenues from single-family dwellings, 25 percent from commercial and industrial property, 12 percent from multiple-family dwellings, and 8 percent from vacant personal property. From 1975 to 1979, the tax rate increased from $54 to $68. Since 1979, the tax rate has remained steady at $68. According to the State Department of Revenue, the town is currently assessed at 51 percent of full and fair cash value, although the Assessors thought the ratio was closer to 40 percent. Municipal expenditures from 1980 to 1981 rose 3.4 percent, staying within the 4 percent cap mandated by state law. Town officials have kept

Framingham well within its debt limit and expect to retire all current outstanding debt by 1993.

In 1981, Framingham received approximately $40.5 milion (66%) of its revenues from the property tax; $8.7 million (14%) from the state; $6.5 million (11%) from local receipts; $4.7 million (7%) from the motor vehicle excise tax; and $1.3 million (2%) from federal revenue sharing. Federal funds support some police and fire department salaries, the Visiting Nurses program, the Council on Aging, the Human Resources Board, and the Youth Commission. Town officials thought projected cutbacks in federal aid might eliminate these activities.

A major controversy in Framingham continues to be whether the town meeting form of government meets the increasing demands of a large population and a rapidly developing community. There have been three unsuccessful attempts to initiate a new form of government in the past decade. The last, in 1978, offered town residents three options: 1) to maintain the existing structure; 2) to adopt a system with a stronger Town Manager; or, 3) to change to a Mayor/City Council form of government. Although the third option received 38 percent of the vote, the inclusion of two alternatives for change split the vote, thus maintaining the status quo.

Framingham's local government is characterized by lack of direction and coordination in the executive branch. The executive departments consist of more than 20 independent boards, agencies, and commissions. A charter commission, set up in May 1979 to review town government, unanimously agreed that the goals of its deliberations should be: 1) to eliminate many autonomous boards; 2) to appoint an administrative officer with authority over budgeting, coordination, and implementation; and 3) to appoint a centralized policy-making body. In short, the Commission argued that the town needs a government that will direct its future and respond quickly to its needs. The criticisms that surfaced over the handling of the first Proposition 2 1/2 budget should be viewed against the backdrop of this controversy.

## Views on Proposition 2 1/2

While most local officials were opposed to Proposition 2 1/2, they agreed that it passed because of the increasing tax burden. But many protested that citizens wanted to retain the same level of public services. Some officials viewed the vote as the taxpayer's signal to the state legislature to reform the state tax structure. They claimed that voters were urging efficiency at all levels of government, not just at the local level. Lois Aronstein, Director of the Senior Center, noted the confusion among her clients: "The seniors couldn't really relate the cuts to the local level or see it as a local issue. In many cases, they associated the local cuts with the Reagan program of federal reductions. During informal discussions at the Center, influential people swayed opinion in favor of reduced taxes and efficiency in government. The threats about service cuts didn't work." Echoing this view, the Editor of the

*Middlesex News* said, "What the residents perceive is what counts, not what is."

A former state representative, currently District Court Clerk and Chairman of the Public Works Board, Tony Colonna, argued that the public is disgusted with high taxes and the creation of more and more public jobs. Taxpayers, he said, want the town to improve productivity and efficiency. Planning Director, Christy Maltus, argued that the public's dissatisfaction stemmed from government growth -- too fast and all at once -- as well as its perception that California avoided ruin with Proposition 13. But local officials thought voters would benefit little from 2 1/2. They claimed that revaluation and increased license fees and user charges would eliminate the anticipated tax savings.

Although in agreement with the thrust of Proposition 2 1/2, the Executive Administrator, Matthew Clark, opposed its specific provisions. He considered the first year's cutback unfair because it included the full loss of motor vehicle excise tax -- in Framingham a $2.5 million loss. (1) If this tax had been cut back a fraction at a time, its loss would have had a less severe impact in the first year. Clark argued that the 2 1/2 percent cap will limit expenditures even if local sentiment urges their increase.

## The Gap

The amount to be cut from the 1982 budget hinged on estimates of the new valuation. Using the Department of Revenue's FY81 equalized valuation of $1.2 billion, the town would have had to cut its property tax levy by more than $13 million. In FY82, it would have had to cut by 15 percent, from $40.5 million to $34.4 million. Combined with the $2.5 million loss of motor vehicle excise tax revenue, the total first-year revenue loss would have been $8.58 million, which would have resulted in numerous layoffs. Matthew Clark recalled that "the prospect of laying off up to 40 percent in some departments was enough to scare anyone."

Faced with dire predictions, the Finance Committee, the Board of Selectmen, the Board of Assessors, the Town Treasurer, and the Town Accountant, agreed that it would be reasonable to assume a valuation of $1.5 billion. The Department of Revenue judged this to be a fairly conservative estimate. Town officials began developing their budgets according to the new assessment, which yielded a revenue loss of $5.5 million, or 9 percent. It remained unclear, however, that the $1.5 billion assessment was an accurate projection. Over the summer, the Bureau of Accounts in the Department of Revenue calculated assessments at replacement, instead of market value, which resulted in lower assessments. To add to the uncertainty, the town's Board of Assessors would not report to the Finance Committee on the accuracy of the new assessments until revaluation was completed and certified by the Department of Revenue.

## The Budget Process

Budget responsibility and authority is scattered among numerous boards, committees, and elected officials in Framingham. Many departments and boards, including Public Works, Parks and Recreation, Libraries, Education, the Board of Health, the Planning Board, and the Redevelopment Authority are governed by elected boards. These boards review departmental budgets and make recommendations to the Finance Committee. The Finance Committee, a nine-member board appointed by the elected Town Moderator, reviews the budgets and proposes a consolidated budget to the Town Meeting. The Selectmen follow a similar procedure for the departments under their jurisdiction. In November, the Town Administrator submits recommendations on the department budgets under his jurisdiction to the Selectmen who then pass a budget on to the Finance Committee. At the Town Meeting, usually held in mid-April, 204 members elected by district, vote on the separate warrant articles that compose the final town budget.

The Finance Committee coordinates the various departments, investigates conflicts, and resolves disputes. If an impasse is reached, the Selectmen often hold a public hearing and vote on the problem. However, this year, the power of the Finance Committee appears to have increased. The Committee developed an effective revenue projection, established bottom-line figures for each budget, reviewed departmental spending plans, and participated in all department budget hearings. Because of the difficulty in projecting FY82 revenues and the extent of the cutback mandated by Proposition 2 1/2, department heads did not meet the November and December deadlines for submitting budgets. The smaller budgets, for departments such as Personnel and the Assessor's office, were finished on schedule. But the larger budgets, for Public Works, Schools, and the Fire Department, were not not submitted until March.

The Town Treasurer, Accountant, Finance Committee Chairman, and Executive Administrator developed and consolidated this year's budget in Framingham. These individuals made the crucial decisions about revenue estimates and the criteria to be used in making budget reductions. The Town Accountant, Robert Burke, reviewed the last five years' budgets and spending plans, and developed a set of proportional cuts for each department. He viewed past spending patterns as an implicit statement of priorities and thought reductions should equal a department's percentage of total allocations. The other members of the *ad hoc* committee agreed. The committee found that cuts could not always be made proportionally, especially in the smaller departments which could not function if one or two individuals were lost. After deducting fixed costs, level funding all maintenance and operation costs (except fuel), and figuring in increases necessitated by past collective bargaining agreements, the committee assigned each department a maximum budget total.

After a review of the town's miscellaneous income, the Selectmen decided that no license should be sold for less than $5, that the cost of liquor licenses should be raised, and that other fees should be evaluated for possible increases. The Executive Administrator believed, "users should pay for services; there should be no more free rides."

A survey developed by the Finance Committee in December was sent to each department head to identify possible cost-saving measures. The survey showed FY81 salaries and expenses, and requested an analysis of the consequences following 5, 10, 15, and 20 percent cuts. However, the survey indicated only which departments would comply with budget reductions. The Town Accountant, Robert Burke, said, "The survey was really of no value whatsoever. A few department heads said they weren't going to cut at all and were thinking of an increase. Some figured cuts after labor contracts, some didn't. We basically had to disregard the survey, do the budgets over again, and send the departments a bottom line."

During February and March, the Executive Administrator and Finance Committee held meetings with department heads to discuss the feasibility of 15 percent cuts and to negotiate a budget to recommend to Town Meeting. Although most department heads cooperated, the heads of the Public Works and Fire departments wanted budget increases. According to the Finance Committee Chairman, a reasonable budget was not drawn up until it was almost time to print it for Town Meeting. The Finance Committee held meetings two or three times a week in March to complete recommendations to Town Meeting. The Committee hoped to avoid layoffs by deferring certain "fixed cost" items which could be added back in once FY82 revenues became certain. The Committee allocated $1.95 million for health and life insurance, Workmen's Compensation, Unemployment Insurance, and street lighting, a shortfall of $1.363 million. It believed that it was politically easier to defer appropriations in "fixed costs," opening only a few budgets for reappropriation. The Finance Committee recommended the following departmental reductions to Town Meeting: Libraries, 17 percent; Public Works, 15 percent; Parks and Recreation, 13 percent; General Government, 11 percent; Schools, 10 percent; and Police, Fire, and Human Services, 7 percent each.

At Town Meeting, the Chairman of the Finance Committee usually outlines the rationale behind the budget, defending its major provisions. And usually, Town Meeting favors the Finance Committee's recommendations. But this year, Chairman Liz Harney announced that Town Meeting faced "a whole different ballgame." Because some budget items were underfunded and the revenue projection was uncertain, she urged the Town Meeting to wait until the fall before attempting to restore funds that had been cut. No one objected until the Fire Chief pleaded for full funding, threatening dire consequences for ambulance service and fire protection. Town Meeting then voted full funding for the Fire Department. This successful challenge opened the door to subsequent lobbying and debate by other department heads. Those who had accepted budget cutbacks decided that being competitive was the key to more funding.

The Chairman of the Public Works Board, Tony Colonna, was the most vocal opponent of the Finance Committee's recommendations. The Public Works Department was scheduled for a 15 percent reduction, and Colonna was angry. At the Town Meeting, he proposed restoring $144,000 to the department's budget, but was turned down. After threatening to stop garbage collection, Colonna urged the Board of Selectmen to hold a Special Town Meeting in July, which voted to increase his budget $144,000. The Special Town Meeting resolved other outstanding budget issues involving the libraries and school crossing guards. Contrary to the recommendation of the Library Trustees and Director, the town voted to increase funds to keep a branch of the library open in Framingham Center. And, whereas the Finance Committee recommended a reduction of school crossing guards from 57 to 14, the town voted to retain 38 guards and 3 spares.

Additional controversy surrounded the issue of revenue estimates. At Colonna's request, the Finance Committee had included in its revenue estimates income from the sale of a $500,000 piece of town land, even though the town would not receive these funds in FY82. Neither did town officials know whether projected fee hikes could be appropriated or whether fees had to be collected before they could be allocated. The confusion stemmed from a new statute, Chapter 339 of the Massachusetts General Laws, that allows (contrary to previous practice) increased user fees and charges to be allocated in the same year, as long as a logical reason for the increase is made at a Town Meeting and to the Department of Revenue. In general, town officials thought they did the best they could under difficult circumstances. Few had serious objections to the final budget. Nevertheless, people had criticisms, ranging from specific procedural objections to the more general issue of Framingham's form of government.

Framingham's Proposition 2 1/2 budget reflected a continuation of past budgets and organizational arrangements. A strong proponent of Proposition 2 1/2, Tony Colonna favored cutbacks, but argued that the town needed to rearrange its fiscal priorities. He thought the budget process should have involved more in-depth evaluation of town services and spending alternatives aimed at improving efficiency through a consolidation of efforts. The Finance Committee Chairman, Liz Harney, argued that Colonna needed to apply these recommendations to his own department. She added that merging departments, evaluating services, and developing a budget all at once was too much to expect.

The weaknesses of Framingham's form of government were revealed this year. The Board of Selectmen dealt ineffectively with budget-cutting disputes. John DelPrete, Chairman of the Selectmen, explained that the Board's primary role is to respond to crises. However, he argued, "We cannot plan for another board which answers to the electorate; when we've tried, some have been spiteful." But the Planning Director, Christy Maltus, who works under the Selectmen's jurisdication, argued that "the Selectmen are vague and don't want to antagonize anyone. . . . They don't want to be the political fall guys." Hence, they did not negotiate an acceptable budget cut with the Fire Chief and were unable to withstand pressure from the Chairman of the Board of Public Works when he threatened to end trash collection. Maltus thought these weaknesses were derived from the fragmentation of authority in Framingham, and commented, "When no one really has the power, things just keep dragging on."

Department heads are worried about the increasingly competitive and political nature of the budget process. Since both the Fire and Public Works departments increased their funding through a combination of effective lobbying and emotional pleading, other department heads now believe they too will have to fight for survival. The Director of the Senior Center, Lois Aronstein, said, "This year we took our cuts because we believed all departments would have to. The Finance Committee did an excellent job trying to be fair, but at Town Meeting, things changed politically and it was out of their control. . . . In the future, once some of these cuts are felt, we will have to become more political with a strong senior lobby, and I'm not sure if that will be fair." Emphasizing this point, the Personnel Director, Margie Smith, said, "No real consequences were attached to a refusal to accept the cuts. Other department heads should have realized that, but they missed the boat. They didn't demonstrate, but wanted to compromise and cooperate."

These criticisms call into question the capacity of Town Meeting to reconcile conflicts among departments. Teri Banoerjee, Co-Chairman of the League of Women Voters and Town Meeting member, objected that "no trade-offs or compromises were presented by the Finance Committee. . . . Some of us would have liked the cuts to be shared with Police and Fire, but this doesn't happen at Town Meeting." A critic of the Town Meeting form of government, and editor of the *Middlesex News,* Bob Moore, believes that "Town Meeting doesn't go after the information it should have. . . . With so many converging pressures, it's too lethargic. Homework hasn't been done by the majority, and the Finance Committee does not do the studies or propose ideas." But proponents of the Town Meeting form of government are attracted by the strong appeal of a democratic process that gives citizens direct authority over appropriations. State Representative Barbara Gray argued, "The mechanism exists to make adjustments; information is not the problem. We have to ensure that all departments get a fair hearing." The Town Moderator, Richard Allen, concurred, "204 people [Town Meeting members] cannot be controlled or manipulated; nothing can be hidden."

## Impacts on the School Department

The School Department requested a FY82 budget of $28,040,000, a 4 percent increase over the FY81 budget. (2) But the Town Meeting approved a final school budget of $24,375,000, 14 percent below the requested budget and 10 percent below the FY81 budget. The cutback resulted in the loss of 168 school positions: 78 teachers, 13 secretaries, 17 custodians, 19 teacher assistants, 14 bus drivers, and 27 other support personnel. Virtually all administrative positions were maintained this year, but school officials will eliminate the positions of 2 or 3 administrators who are expected to retire next year.

Deputy Superintendent Rigas Rigopoulos, said school officials tried to distribute cutbacks widely to preserve all programs and maintain direct student services. The School Committee eliminated the public information service and instituted fees for the intramural and regular school sports programs, as well as other student activities. The Committee increased school lunch fees from 40 to

75 cents. School Committee Chairman, Joyce Lundberg, feared that Proposition 2 1/2 cuts, combined with federal aid losses, would eventually curtail important school programs and erode the quality of education in Framingham. She intended to urge the other members of the School Committee to request more school aid from the state. In the meantime, she hoped that whatever benefits parents expected from Proposition 2 1/2 would not be offset by increased school fees.

## Impacts on the Police Department

The Police Department lost 14 positions this year, 12 through attrition. The department's staff consisted of 120 officers in 1970; it now has 95. The Police union president, Brent Laraby, thought the staff reductions would put a greater strain on the remaining officers, although they are willing to work harder to maintain service levels. But he thought the police force was at a disadvantage in protesting cuts this year because the Police Chief, not a strong public speaker, wanted to avoid the politics involved in restoring cutbacks as the Fire Department Chief had done. Laraby said that union members did not believe they could effectively circumvent the Police Chief, but he predicted that they would fight a second round of cutbacks.

## Impacts on the Libraries

The 17 percent cut in the Libraries budget (from $850,000 to $721,000), resulted in 6 full- and 10 part-time employee layoffs, a reduction in service hours, and a severe cutback in the book purchasing budget from $158,000 to $78,000. The Director of Libraries, Chuck Flarety, proposed closing the branch in Framingham Center. In terms of the number of books lent, it seemed most efficient to close the branch and retain full services at the new main library. However, the branch is located close to the wealthiest district in town, and its residents convinced the Town Meeting to keep the branch open three days a week. Flarety still advocates closing the branch.

## Impacts on Human Services

The directors of human service agencies agreed that the full impacts of Proposition 2 1/2 have not yet been felt. Since human service agencies rely on local, state, and federal funds, the squeeze caused by reductions at all three levels will not be experienced until January or February when cuts in food stamps, day care, fuel assistance, and other programs will exacerbate Proposition 2 1/2 cuts. The Director of South Middlesex Opportunity Council (SMOC), Paul Houlihan, said, "Historically, the town has not funded many human services. It's been conservative." When federal revenue sharing funds became available, the town used some of this money for essential services and some for human services not previously funded. Houlihan feared that with decreases in federal funds, those human service programs will be terminated because they have not been supported by town tax dollars in the past.

A perfect example is the Senior Center, which receives almost 90 percent of its funds from revenue sharing. This year, the Center cut back its outreach and leisure programs, its case manager staff, and eliminated its transportation services. With a 17 percent reduction in local funding, Director Aronstein predicted that cuts in federal aid would jeopardize the Center's existence. She argued that the combined effects of government cutbacks on human services could be devastating: "Human services are taking it on the chin; the problems have not been that evident, but they will become so. . . . The difficulty is that clients do not speak for themselves. Besides the competitive nature of obtaining scarce funds, as financial problems worsen -- housing shortages, fixed incomes not keeping up with inflation, and Medicare cuts -- there will be more demand and more aggravation which affect the health of seniors. And there will not be enough staff to meet their needs."

Both of the Human Service Directors have been resourceful in developing some innovative programs. To cope with the loss of bus transportation, the Senior Center is having an old school bus repaired by the Massachusetts Correctional Facility. Aronstein projects a 50 percent cost saving from this effort. SMOC is strongly emphasizing self-sufficiency in its programs, and the use of cooperatives in housing, food, and energy to reduce low-income individual's dependence on social programs.

## Long-Term Consequences - Development

Framingham has enjoyed substantial commercial and industrial growth in the past 15 years. The town is sometimes referred to as the "high tech capital of New England." Executive Administrator, Matthew Clark, thought cuts in local services would hamper the ability of local businesses to attract qualified people. Local amenities, good schools, transportation, and protective services are important considerations for business location and hiring. The Executive Vice President of the Chamber of Commerce, Michelle Cunya, hoped the legislature would amend the 2 1/2 percent cap on future expenditures so that communities could maintain quality services and fiscal flexibility.

## Labor Relations

The town bargains with seven unions -- libraries, public works, engineers, crossing guards, laborers, police, and fire. The town's negotiating team includes the Executive Administrator, the Personnel Director, and the Director of the department whose union is negotiating. All but the Fire Fighters union were in the second year of a three-year contract during FY82 which provides for a 7, 7.5, and 8 percent wage increase. Police officers also receive a 2 percent hazard pay increase. Relations between the fire fighters and police officers remain antagonistic. In the last contract negotiations, 1978-79, the Fire Department contract went into binding arbitration and the union lost (a rare event -- the Fire Department asked for greater wage increases than did the Police Department).

The town is trying to negotiate an end to the 9-year-old minimum manning provision in the fire fighters contract. But the union considers this unthinkable. The fire fighters argue that reducing the number of employees to the minimum per shift would cost the town more in overtime than it saves in wages. When there are not enough fire fighters to fill the minimum manning requirement, they must be hired from other shifts at overtime wages.

A major concern among unions was the choice between wage increases and job security that would be created by continued inflation and the 2 1/2 percent levy limit. Both police and fire fighters said they would consider scaling down pay raises to retain jobs. But without binding arbitration, union spokesmen thought some form of strike or job action would be necessary to fight further cuts.

## Future Fiscal Policy

Framingham's town officials are reviewing a variety of fiscal and organizational changes. A Town Committee has been set up to consider contracting out for trash collection services and increasing user charges on a yearly basis. And, although no one has taken the lead, there will probably be an effort to merge and consolidate some of the town departments. Most town officials supported a local override provision to raise the 2 1/2 percent tax limit and wanted the state legislature to cut back state services to produce more local aid. Almost everyone interviewed advocated some kind of state tax reform that would not increase the overall tax burden.

## Summary

Although revaluation confused FY82 budget-making in Framingham, it allowed the town to work with a $5.5 million revenue loss instead of one in excess of $8 million. Even so, the unwieldy relations among the town's many executive boards and departments made it difficult to plan the cutbacks. The Finance Committee's attempt to distribute cuts proportionately according to past expenditures was thwarted at Town Meeting by the Fire Chief, and later by the Chairman of the Public Works Board. Nearly everyone interviewed believes the local government needs to be streamlined and better coordinated. In some cases, this will mean consolidating departments and cutting administrative costs. In others, it will involve an evaluation of services, clearer management objectives, and public accountability. Although town officials feel constrained by Proposition 2 1/2, it may indirectly encourage and accelerate some of these developments.

## Notes for Chapter 15

1. In the past, Framingham has registered vehicles from other cities and towns to increase its motor vehicle excise tax revenues. Th town can do this because excise tax is levied and collected at the local level, and, as in the case of car rental firms, the town has made mass registration easier than in other localities. The result is that the town receives a large amount of revenue from the motor vehicle excise tax, $4.6 million.

2. School enrollment has declined from a high of 15,000 to 10,000.

Chapter 16

# Marshfield: Budget Cutting, A Joint Effort

Andrew Laing

## Introduction

Marshfield is a residential community thirty miles from Boston on the South Shore. The town's population has grown very rapidly since 1950. More than doubling in the 1960's, the population increased almost 40 percent since 1970, reaching 20,916 in 1980. In fact, Marshfield had the fastest rate of growth of any South Shore town due to the construction of Route 3, the availability of land for housing development, the town's recreational resources, and the quality of its schools. Marshfield is a prototypical suburb, with a predominantly white, young, and fairly affluent population.

The increasing population led town officials to expand Marshfield's services, especially the schools, and taxes began to rise. (1) From FY72 to FY81, the tax rate rose from $67.00 to $94.50. Several other factors contributed to the increasing tax burden. The Assistant Assessor, Joan Palsson, reported that Marshfield's property has been assessed at only 30 to 35 percent of full and fair market value. Last reassessed at $75 million in 1965, Marshfield's 1980 equalized valuation was $354 million, later changed to $400 million. The present revaluation of the town (to be completed by the end of 1981) has given rise to escalating estimates of the town's value. While the FY82 budget was being planned, the town's value was thought to be betweeen $450 and $470 million; by November 1981, the estimate had risen to $485 million, over $120 million above the state's 1980 equalized value for Marshfield. The FY82 levy limit agreed to by the Department of Revenue was based on the $450 million value.

Town officials believed the major cause of high property taxes was Marshfield's lack of industry, but they hope this situation will change. The Marshfield Industrial Development Commission succeeded in encouraging the first firm to locate in the town's industrial park. Town officials also blamed high taxes in Marshfield on the quality of town services, the effects of state mandated programs, the costs of maintaining beaches and the coastline, and the burden of the 4,600-person summer population. Former Town Administrator, Guy Lapriore, suggested that the lack of professional management during the period of the town's rapid growth resulted in higher than necessary taxation, along with the system of open Town Meeting at which "people just pass articles" that have a lasting effect on the town.

The larger budgets and higher taxes of the last two decades have led to increasing controversy in Marshfield. In 1977, a lower than expected level of state assistance led to a $10 increase in the tax rate (from $86.00 to $96.25), and for some residents that was the "straw which broke the camel's back." The Association of Concerned Taxpayers (ACT) organized to change the town's fiscal practices. The group was part of a "tax revolt" on the South Shore. ACT fought rising property taxes in Marshfield and prepared alternative budgets to those presented by town officials. ACT won support for elements of its budgets and for proposed cutbacks. It also managed to elect some of its members and supporters to town offices. ACT's Director, Robert Wetzel, became the Chairman of the Board of Selectmen in 1981.

In short, 1977 marked the beginning of fiscal restraint in Marshfield. Further reductions in state aid forced a budget cut of $400,000 in FY78 and the state later imposed its 4 percent "tax cap." Various town departments, such as the Department of Public Works, were being cut or level-funded. Also during the late 1970's, town officials thought the views of the School Committee shifted from "extremely liberal" to "conservative." Continued support for fiscal conservatism was reflected in the town's 58% vote in favor of Proposition 2 1/2

**The Budget Process**

Usually, department heads present "needs" budgets to the appointed nine-member Advisory Board, which makes budget recommendations to the open Town Meeting. The three Selectmen deal directly with heads of departments, and are sometimes under pressure from them to circumvent the recommendations of the Advisory Board. Judith Cooper, the present Chairman of the Advisory Board, described the "normal" situation as she sees it, "When I first came on the Advisory Board, the Selectmen were not interested in money issues; that was the last thing they wanted to deal with. Consistently, the Advisory Board and the Selectmen voted differently. We would say, "No more policemen!" The Police Chief would stand up and say, "Your children will rot in the streets!" And, lo and behold, the Selectmen would vote for the new policemen."

The Selectmen rarely dealt with the fiscal complexity of the town budget. Their elective status influenced them to represent particular local interest groups, such as the public safety workers. This "traditional" pattern was altered somewhat by the employment of a Town Administrator in 1975. The creation of the Town Administrator's post centralized budget-making. Most budget-related information passed through his office, and he prepared much of the town budget. However, the division of labor that remained among the Administrator, the Advisory Board, and the Board of Selectmen became increasingly problematic. At one point, the Advisory Board considered becoming a committee merely to investigate departmental budgets. Meanwhile, the Selectmen worked in the margins of the Town Administrator's authority. The Advisory Board became concerned that the Town Administrator's responsibilities had been inadequately formulated in the Town Charter. The former Town Administrator had a different view of the town's government: "Marshfield is like an octopus. . . . The diference between an octopus and Marshfield is that, at least an octopus has a central brain to control its tentacles. . . . We have too many autonomous situations. Department heads and town officials become lost in their little fiefdoms."

Conflicts simmered over differing responsibilities and authority. The resignation of the Town Administrator in the spring of 1981 and the decision not to rehire one for the time being has once more altered the budget process. The Advisory Board is more interventionist, and the Selectmen have more responsibility for the budget. The new relationship was reflected in Marshfield's budget preparations this year -- the first year under the provisions of Proposition 2 1/2.

Marshfield's total revenues were reduced from FY81's $20.3 million to $17.8 million, a reduction of about $2.5 million, or roughly 12 percent. Town officials expected to lose about $1.3 million in property tax revenue and about $700,000 in auto excise tax revenue. They expected an increase of $775,000 in state aid (over last year's $3.3 million), although the increase was actually $840,000. Town officials were uncertain how much federal aid Marshfield might lose, although the School Department identified some reductions in FY82.

In December 1980, the Town Administrator, Guy Lapriore, submitted revenue estimates for FY82 to the Board of Selectmen and the Advisory Board. He based his projections on a valuation of $450 million. At 2 1/2 percent, the property tax levy would be $11,250,000. The Selectmen asked town departments to reduce expenditures immediately. Since the decrease in the tax levy was less than 15 percent, the loss had to be absorbed in one year. The Administrator, the Selectmen, and School Committee members agreed to allocate 54.1 percent of the reduced tax levy to the school department.

At the beginning of 1981, the Advisory Board and the Selectmen thought they had a sound basis for deciding that a 12 percent budget reduction would be required for FY82. In preliminary discussions, they rejected across-the-board cuts in favor of ranking town services in order of importance and allocating funds accordingly. They asked department heads to categorize their services in the following way: 1) What are the legally mandated functions of your department? 2) What are the essential functions which must be provided by your department? 3) What other services does your department provide? The two boards requested an organizational chart of each department, showing how employees were distributed among the three categories. All mandated services constituted the first priority for funding, and all "essential services," the second. "Other services" formed the category liable for reductions. The two boards also requested a schedule of existing fees from each department.

The Advisory Board's subcommittees conducted lengthy reviews of departmental budgets. The Advisory Board jointly reviewed these budgets with the Selectmen -- a major change from past practice. One Advisory Board member explained: "Since so many cuts had to be made, we had to be sure, going into the Town Meeting, that everyone was in agreement with the budget we presented to the townspeople." Cooperation between the boards influenced the attitudes of department heads. The Chairman of the Advisory Board recalled: "We did get the information we requested from department heads; they were scared enough to do it, and do it right. . . . What was interesting was that no one even considered asking for more money, so the major cut was accomplished before anybody said, 'boo.' There were no opportunities to say, 'I only want 4 percent more.'

When the Advisory Board subcommittees met to negotiate budget reductions with department heads, Boards of Commissioners, and union leaders, the degree of responsiveness and cooperation varied. Conflicts were settled by the Selectmen. The process of negotiating cutbacks altered the role of the Advisory Board and its subcommittees. They became much more intensely involved in investigating departmental budgets. In the past, they had relied on the recommendations of the department heads.

Department heads made their cuts in different ways, with different results in each. Judith Cooper noted that the Department of Public Works "took massive cuts . . . mainly out of materials, whereas, the Board of Health reduced its budget 32 percent, almost all in personnel." Small, labor-intensive departments were unable to absorb substantial reductions without becoming inoperative. The Advisory Board also found union contracts a problem: "Union contracts set limitations on us. A lot of the kinds of flexibility that we wanted to have, we could not have. We could not recombine jobs. We could not hold off on step raises. We could eliminate a job or a whole department, but we couldn't eliminate half of the Recreation Director and half of something else. [These limitations] had more influence in building the budget than they should have."

Town officials reorganized staff and management positions to a limited extent. They postponed reappointment of a Town Administrator, combined the posts of Treasurer and Collector, appointed a full-time Town Clerk, and reopened a union contract in the Department of Public Works in order to conbine two divisions. Although they revised and increased the town's fee schedule, they decided that "contracting-out" was not suitable for most town services. Town officials are exploring the possibility of sharing services and purchasing with Marshfield's neighbor, Duxbury.

Although a "preTown Meeting" was held six weeks before the regular Town Meeting to allow the public to air its concerns fully, the Chairman of the Advisory Board thought the increased cooperation between the Advisory

Board and the Selectmen may have had adverse effects on "town democracy." She observed, "2 1/2 did, perhaps, irreparable damage to the Town Meeting form of government. . . . It took away the right of citizens to determine how much money would be spent, and where. By the time we limited the top and covered all the mandated stuff, we were left with very little to play with. . . . That was the damage of 2 1/2. It really changed the role of Town Meeting."

Selectman Wetzel disagreed. He thought the cutback process was "a wonderful experience in government, a rebirth of some of the old Yankee virtues." Limiting citizens' control over the budget at Town Meeting would eliminate some "nonsense." He argued that Town Meeting had become inadequate for dealing with complex budget issues. It is usually at Town Meeting, he said, the "all kinds of special interest groups are able to stuff things into the budget after they have been cut out." Wetzel thought "overstaffing" had been eliminated despite union opposition, which he said was "the biggest problem in government." Even with the pressure of 2 1/2, Wetzel argued that department heads failed to define productive goals clearly.

**Impacts on the Police Department**

Police Chief, Charles Chaplin, prepared a budget with a 15 percent cut. Negotiations over a new labor contract complicated the Chief's task, because covering salary increases implied cuts elsewhere in his budget. Inflation further limited his flexibility. By April, when the Chief met with the Advisory Board subcommittee, he had eliminated eight uniformed positions and one civilian position through attrition. Chaplin projected a termination of beach patrol service and winter cottage checks, and a reduction of man-hours allocated to investigations of auto theft, missing persons, and past larceny and breaking and entering complaints. He decreased man-hours for foot-patrols, finger-printing and photography services. The Advisory Board subcommittee made some minor changes, but approved most of the Chief's budget. The Advisory Board and the Selectmen also approved it.

The police labor contract was settled just before the June Town Meeting. It required an additional $68,000 in salary increases. To fund these increases, three men would have been laid off had not eight positions already been eliminated. The overtime budget was also cut $32,000. The force now maintains 45 officers and five civilians.

Captain William Sullivan, of the International Brotherhood of Police Officers in Marshfield, suggests that the town's budgetary process should have been a cooperative town effort. He supported the idea of community, union, and government cooperation to work out budget priorities. Elected officials could then make final decisions. He warned that reductions in community service programs would be harmful to Marshfield in the long run. Reductions in personnel such as juvenile officers will overburden those who remain, causing a high level of occupational "burn out."

## Impacts on the Fire Department

Acting Fire Chief Cipullo (the designated Chief resigned because of illness), found little to cut in the Fire Department's budget. He prepared a continuation budget, and actually increased two line items. The Advisory Board subcommittee reduced the department's budget by 15 percent. In close coordination with the President of the Fire Fighters union, Robert Donahue, Cipullo convinced the subcommittee to reduce the 15 percent reduction to between 11 and 13 percent. This saved the jobs of four of the eight fire fighters who would have been laid off. The increase also permitted one of the town's two substations to remain open. The final budget reduction for the Fire Department required four layoffs and four demotions. No positions were lost through attrition. Acting Chief Cipullo and the new Chief Gibson claimed that the department is now understaffed, which they cannot compensate for with overtime. This budget, too, was trimmed.

Robert Donahue, President of the Fire Fighters union described the FY82 budget process in Marshfield as a "battle." He felt that the Advisory Board subcommittee had usurped the Chief's budget-making prerogatives. The union, he said, was strongly opposed even to the lower budget reduction. It sponsored two amendments at Town Meeting, one to restore the budget to its FY81 level, the other to retain laid-off employees until Labor Day when additional state-aid monies might be allocated to the department. Neither amendment passed. Donahue argued that undermanned shifts would lead to an increased risk of injury. Instead of the eleven men previously on a shift, there are now eight or nine, divided among three fire stations. This situation might result in only two fire fighters being available to answer an alarm. Donahue thought it had become impossible to make changes in the budget at Town Meeting. He predicted that the "threat factor" -- having to find alternative sources for desired budget increases in other department budgets -- would lead to interdepartmental conflict.

## Impacts on the Department of Public Works

Budget reductions began in 1978 for the Department of Public Works. At that time, the department's staff was cut from 85 to 75; seasonal staff, from 18 to 12. Since then, the department eliminated one full- and one part-time position while accepting responsibility for the operation of a new sewage treatment plant requiring five people. Superintendent Gil Burns commented, "We had to meet the challenge of reducing appropriations for materials and personnel in a balance, so that we didn't have the materials and no one to work with them, or the people with no work they could reasonably perform."

Working out this "balance" caused friction with the Advisory Board and Selectmen who instructed the department to cut its budget by $350,000, roughly 15 percent, and to absorb a 6.5 percent negotiated pay increase. Burns first cut seasonal and temporary hirings and then reduced scheduled overtime. With a hiring freeze on even before 2 1/2, the department lost four positions through attrition. In addition, the DPW union contract was reopened to permit departmental reorganization. Equipment operators, whose job titles had previously described the specific types of equipment they were supposed to operate, were redesignated "heavy equipment operators." The Division of Trees and Greens was combined with Cemeteries, which cost the division a foreman and five tree workers. The elimination of positions occurred across all grades. A "bumping" system, based on seniority, was used. The budget reduction required five layoffs.

The department considered eliminating town-wide trash collection, but the Selectmen, the Advisory Board, and a number of citizens objected vehemently at the pre-Town Meeting. The Selectmen and the Advisory Board were also unhappy with the department's reduction of beach services, despite increased service charges. The department reduced its maintenance and expense budgets. The road maintenance budget was reduced by substituting $77,000 in state funds which enabled the town to reduce its usual appropriation by $50,000. Water and sewer services were not affected by cutbacks. The purchase of needed capital equipment, however, was deferred. The Superintendent was worried because the town needs drainage work, a new well site, and new landfill sites for which there is now no money available.

But the Advisory Board was dissatisfied with the way the department made its FY82 cuts. Judith Cooper complained, "We thought they made cuts in supplies in order to save people. We didn't even know whether they were going to have equipment and supplies to work with."

## Impacts on the School Department

According to the Assistant Superintendent of Schools, Paul McDonald, the key decision in preparing the FY82 school budget was whether the allocation of funds agreed upon in December 1980 (54 percent of the levy to support the school system) could still be obtained. McDonald recalled that school officials were reluctant to compete with other town departments, especially public safety: "If it came to closing a fire station versus closing a school, we felt we might come out second best." Elaine Ramsay, the President of the Marshfield Teachers Association, agreed.

In the past, McDonald prepared a "continuation" budget, including "option levels" for each budget area. This year, he prepared a budget with two major sets of options. The first assumed a reduction of $1.92 million, based on a $470 million assessed valuation for Marshfield. The second assumed a reduction of $2.19 million based on $450 million assessed valuation. The School Administrative Council, including principals, assistants, and superintendents, met to evaluate these two options by ranking school programs and services in order of importance.

The school budget was reduced 15 percent. School officials met their fundamental objective -- ensuring that no programs would be completely eliminated. All aspects of the school system were retained in the hope that reduced programs could be refunded in the future.

The teachers' FY82 contract required a 6.5 percent salary increase, which could not be met with a reduced school budget. The teachers agreed to reopen the contract and "cost barriers" were removed which permitted teachers to teach more classes. Benefits were reduced on items such as tuition assistance and faculty programs. By renegotiating the contract, Paul McDonald explains, "we eliminated most of the things which restricted us in the reorganization of personnel." But Elaine Ramsay noted how unnerving it was for teachers to reopen the contract: "There was so much fear about it -- the assumption is always that the School Committee wants to do you in, in terms of salary. This was not the case; salaries were not an item for discussion. I was in favor of reopening -- otherwise, we would have lost more teachers."

The teachers had a reduction-in-force clause in the contract that worked quite smoothly. However, school administrators, who left the teachers bargaining unit several years ago to form their own, want to be placed back on the teachers' seniority list. The teachers have refused and the issue is now in arbitration. Since the hiring freeze last January, eight teachers have retired. Several, in their late fifties, would probably have retired without the stimulus of Proposition 2 1/2.

The School Committee held a series of public hearings at which three main controversies emerged: 1) the subcommittee attempted to reinstate the teaching of French in the middle schools, but failed; 2) the public showed great concern over cuts in the schools' music programs; and 3) the "hockey parents" succeeded in restoring elements of sports programs which had been cut, much to the dismay of others -- notably the Advisory Board -- who were more concerned about the academic curriculum. Elaine Ramsay had hoped more people -- teachers and other citizens -- would be involved in the early stages of budget preparations. Union members opposed all cuts in the school budget. They thought the Advisory Board supported the school system in general, but still felt the school budget reduction was quite substantial.

Paul McDonald thought the schools would lose about 116 staff positions, of which 40 would be classroom teachers and the rest would be divided among administrators, special subject teachers, counsellors, librarians, secretaries, custodians, and teachers aides. He predicted that class sizes would increase and that programs such as elementary art, music, physical education, and remedial reading, would be reduced 50 percent. The budget for supplies was reduced 30 percent, the equipment budget was nearly eliminated, and a small reduction was made in the maintenance budget. The chief "uncontrollables" in the school budget -- energy, special needs expenses, and transportation -- were level-funded this year. No program was eliminated entirely, but McDonald warned, "I'm very concerned that we may lose our strongest constituents. . . . Although Marshfield is a middle class suburb, I'm concerned about the more affluent people in the town sending their children to private schools. These are the people we look to for support." But Advisory Board Chairman, Judith Cooper, thought "the damage to the school system was devastating, a mortal blow." Selectmen Sheila Gagnon agreed that "the school system was totally dismantled."

## Labor Relations

A growing population greatly changed the quality of labor relations in Marshfield. Before the enactment of the state collective bargaining statute in 1973 (which extended full bargaining rights to state and municipal employees, and introduced binding arbitration for police and fire employees disputes), only the DPW and the Police Department had union contracts. Now, town hall employees and fire fighters are unionized as well. A town labor negotiator has been employed since 1977. There has also been an informal coalition of union heads since 1977, that first arose over the issue of a town-wide insurance plan and was further solidified by the threat of layoffs caused by the activities of ACT in 1978.

The impact of Proposition 2 1/2 on labor relations in Marshfield is difficult to ascertain. Selectman Sheila Gagnon thought the tax limitation measure had weakened the unions. She suggested that the unions were using 2 1/2 as a "crutch:" "Every single problem is caused by 2 1/2; everything that can't be done is because of Prop 2 1/2. I really think they are using it to the hilt, and abusing it."

Gagnon thought direct negotiations between the Selectmen and the bargaining units was more productive than bargaining through a labor negotiator. Selectmen Hynes argued that the town's relations with its unions had improved because of Proposition 2 1/2. The unions, he said, now "recognize their inability to play games; management is back in the driver's seat." Selectman Wetzel shared this view: "Contract negotiation was easier because the unions knew what the stakes were and we had to deal more openly with the employees. Besides, the key people in the unions cooperated because they will pay lower taxes and know they aren't going to lose their jobs. The unions now understand the concept 'more fringe, less people'."

Police Captain William Sullivan thought labor relations were mainly affected in terms of salary increases and attempts to extend the working week of policemen. Police Chief Chaplin thought the "moral issue" -- how far each side should go to save jobs -- would influence wage negotiations. Robert Donahue, President of the Fire Fighters union, thought the direct negotiations with the Selectmen saved time by preventing the usual "negotiating rhetoric and idle talk." But he argued that the Selectmen only wanted to discuss the issue of wages while the union wanted to consider layoffs and manning. In all, Donahue thought 2 1/2 made labor relations worse. He predicted that the elimination of binding arbitration would result in strikes.

However, a member of the Advisory Board subcommittee on schools, Roberta Daneile, thought power had shifted away from the unions as a result of 2 1/2: "The union people are trying to save jobs, but they'll compromise on hours now. They will compromise on rate of pay. There are too many compromises they have to make now, so management has the upper hand.""

## Summary

Many people agree with Judith Cooper's opinion that Proposition 2 1/2 reduced the citizen's power over the local budget: "The taxpayers don't have too much voice at all. By the time the budget gets to them, it's done. . . . If you are a taxpayer at Town Meeting, you are presented with a *fait accompli.* You are aware that if you want to plug in $100,000 somewhere, it has to be taken from some other budget."

State Representative Philip Johnston noted the political irony of Proposition 2 1/2's association with "home rule" -- even as it effectively rules it out. The Town Accountant, Henry Adams, agreed: "I would think that the people that favored 2 1/2 would favor home rule, but it is working just the other way round. By cutting down what a town can spend, and hoping the state will subsidize, you are doing away with home rule."

By October 1981, reassessment had yielded a higher valuation than expected -- $485 million. State aid was increased $800,000 over FY81. A Special Town Meeting in October 1981, distributed roughly $520,000 among the town's departments. The School Department received 54 percent of the total, the same division used in the early budget process. The department rehired 13.5 teachers and an assistant principal. The Fire Department rehired four fire fighters and the Police Department hired a new policemen. Hence, the worst aspects of Proposition 2 1/2 budget-cutting in Marshfield, were mitigated by revaluation and increased state aid.

### Notes for Chapter 16

1. Marshfield's K-12 public school enrollments: 1961, 1,625; 1965, 2,651; 1971, 4,441; 1979, 6,827; 1980, 5,035; 1981 (est.), 4,872.

Chapter 17

# Quincy: Schools Take a Big Cut

Jerome Rubin

## Introduction

Located at the northern end of the South Shore, Quincy is a blue collar city with an urban character and a growing population. Quincy is the largest and most densely populated community on the South Shore. Its population remained stable in the 1960's, but began to rise in the next decade, as the MBTA red line was extended through Quincy, spurring commercial development and attracting new families. The 1980 U.S. Census reported a population of 84,000 for Quincy (almost all white.) City officials argue that it's closer to 87,000.

In 1970, median family income in Quincy was $11,094, compared with $11,449 for the Boston SMSA. At that time, 71 percent of Quincy families had moderate incomes and 5.3 percent had low incomes, compared with 66 percent and 4.6 percent in the Boston SMSA. However, between 1975 and 1977, the percentage of low- and moderate-income families declined by almost 50 percent.

Quincy is a South Shore center of industrial, wholesale, retail, and banking activity. Its largest employer, General Dynamics Shipyard, employs over 2,500 people. Although employment has declined 14.7 percent between 1970 and 1976, major new construction downtown has begun to reverse the trend. Quincy has attracted new employers (National Fire Protection Association and Stop and Shop) and its service sector has begun to grow, demonstrated by the fact that Quincy's State Street Bank branch, established in 1970, has become the city's third largest employer.

Quincy faces the same property valuation problem that most major cities face in Massachusetts -- a low tax base caused by aging housing stock. Until

203

recently, there has been no significant new construction. Quincy's property valuation in FY81 was $275,538,415 -- 50 percent residential and 50 percent commercial. (FY81's valuation was less than FY80's valuation of $278,077,477.) In order to cover its substantial service costs, the city increased its property tax rates. In FY80, the property tax rate was $224; in FY81, it rose to $242.60. Ex-City Auditor, Charles Shea, argued that Quincy's high property tax rate results from the variety of services the city provides to residents and non-residents: "Quincy is responsible for providing services that the surrounding towns don't provide. An example is the MBTA. Braintree residents used to use our station entrances -- we have three. Since the fee we are assessed is based on station count, we pay a couple million right there. Also, Quincy Hospital is the only major [publicly supported] South Shore hospital. Now people can't be turned away, but when they don't pay, the city has to pick up the tab."

## Views on Proposition 2 1/2

Everyone agreed that Quincy residents voted for Proposition 2 1/2 because of the city's "outrageous" property taxes. Beyond this observation, opinions varied. Ronald Fraser, a spokesman for the Quincy-based South Shore Chamber of Commerce, thought voters supported Proposition 2 1/2 because of the city's wasteful, inefficient service delivery system: "Agencies within municipalities tend to build empires. For years, residents have seen actions which they consider imprudent. Partially used schools were kept open and others were closed but maintained by the taxpayers; extravagant courses were being taught in the schools; programs projected to pay for themselves were not doing so; a half-dozen DPW workers were being assigned to projects that one person could handle. Proposition 2 1/2 forced a scaling-down, a tightening-up, and for the first time, administrators were looking at budgets and saying, "Where can we cut?" instead of "What are we going to add on?" It will ultimately force greater efficiency in municipal government."

Many city officials and citizens, including Mayor Arthur Tobin, noted a high degree of "blue collar" resentment toward "big government" and public employees. James Kelly, vice-president of the Fire Fighers union, described the angry reactions of workers at the shipyards when public employees distributed anti-2 1/2 leaflets. Although Kelly had support for the Fire Department, he thought Quincy residents believed the local government overstaffed and its employees underworked.

Social service providers and members of the teachers' union argued that Proposition 2 1/2 contained a multitude of "sweeteners," with adverse, but unanticipated consequences. Joanne Condon, a former Community Action Program employee, now a City Council member, explained that: "People are never satisfied with services. They complain that there are not enough police, fire, and library services. Now 2 1/2 had something in it for everyone, but that's not really fair. It didn't tell the whole story."

Joanne O'Malley, president of the teachers' union claimed that: "People did not realize what they were voting for. Even some teachers voted for it.

They thought they'd save taxes and didn't believe they'd lose their jobs. The amount saved in taxes is nothing compared to the job losses. We had couples who both lost their jobs. People directed their votes at public employees, no doubt, but they wanted tax reform."

## The Gap

In FY81, Quincy imposed a tax levy of $66,845,636. In FY82, the 15 percent reduction mandated by Proposition 2 1/2, amounted to $10,026,845. In FY83, the city must cut an additional $8.5 million. By then, the tax levy will be down to $47.5 million. But the city will have to cut again to reach the level ($37.5 million) allowed by Proposition 2 1/2 (i.e., 2.5 percent of $1.5 billion). Despite Quincy's development boom, city officials do not expect revaluation to greatly increase property values. They hope to reach a value of $1.5 billion, $200 million more than the 1981 equalized value.

According to Charles Shea, former City Auditor, the actual FY82 cutback was $17 million, accounting for excise tax losses, retirement cost increases, and temporary borrowing costs. The loss from motor vehicle excise tax revenue for FY82 was $1.6 million (city officials over-estimated the excise tax receipts expected for FY81 by over $2 million). Quincy's operating budget was cut 17 percent in FY82. Moody's Investment Service lowered the city's bond rating from A to Ba which raised its short-term interest rate one full percentage point. (1) It also appeared that Quincy's fixed costs (i.e., unemployment compensation, retirement benefits, Blue Cross-Blue Shield) would increase several million dollars. Pension payments alone rose $500,000 in FY81.

City officials found it difficult to predict what effect federal cuts would have on Quincy's budget. Former Auditor Shea did not anticipate a great impact, except on the Public Works and School departments. The city would continue to receive about $2 million in revenue sharing funds. Community Development Block Grant funds, the catalyst for much of Quincy's recent development, were expected to remain constant this year. But school officials expected a 25 percent reduction in federal funds for Quincy schools in FY82. The School Department lost a Title III grant ($130,000), representing 10 percent of the junior college budget. The head of the Public Works Department, James J. Richoetti, expected the share of CDBG funds made available to the Public Works Department to be reduced.

City officials expected Quincy to receive about $3.7 million in state aid (which it did). The city budget was approved at $6 million over the 2 1/2 limit. City officials expected $3 million of the deficit to be covered by increased receipts at Quincy City Hospital. They expected the remaining $3 million to be made up by state aid, leaving about $500,000 for distribution among operating budgets.

## Prior Budget Issues

The 1979, state-imposed tax cap ushered in the era of budget-cutting in Quincy before Proposition 2 1/2 became law. In September 1979, city officials instituted a "no hire, no fire" policy which helped the city avoid a worse situation with layoffs this year, according to former Auditor Shea. For example, the Public Works Department lost 30 to 35 positions prior to Proposition 2 1/2.

The School Department has been the primary focus of past budget controversy in Quincy. School Department. School Superintendent Dr. Lawrence Creedon argued: "We've always had controversy over the schools. . . . The constituency in support of schools is next to nothing. We have an aging population, and people criticize the quality of our schools even though our achievement scores have risen for eight years now." Last year, the School Department had to cut $3 million from its budget. Much of this year's controversy over the school budget was a continuation of last year's debates.

## The Budget Process

Quincy's budget process is carried out in three steps. First, department heads submit proposed budgets to, and then meet individually with, the Mayor. The Mayor then submits a budget to the City Council which holds several weeks of public hearings and reviews portions of the budget with department heads. A final budget is returned to the Mayor for approval. However, most of this year's budget work was actually handled by the City Auditor's office instead of the Mayor's. Once the City Assessors determined the property valuation, and calculated the 2 1/2 levy limit, a budget total was more or less fixed -- a reversal of the normal procedure. Former Auditor Shea described the process: "We set out the deficits we had to cover, what our levy limit would be, and then we calculated our fixed costs (40%). We then tried to apportion the remainder among the departments. We called in the department heads, explained the cuts, and, because they know their own needs best, left it to them to make the specific line-item cuts. "

Shea thought this year's negotiations with department heads were very difficult. Some department heads refused to make reductions in their budgets and were forced to accept those imposed by the auditors. Both the Fire and Police Chiefs requested level-funding and complained vociferously when the auditors imposed reductions.

The strongest protest came from School Superintendent Creedon who felt that his department had suffered enough as the city's "historic whipping boy." Relations between the School Committee and the Mayor's office have long been antagonistic. By ending school autonomy, Proposition 2 1/2 heightened this antagonism. Some even questioned the purpose of a school committee without budget powers.

On December 10, 1980, the School Department submitted its "Financial Plans in Response to Proposition 2 1/2" to the city. The Superintendent's office had prepared seven alternative budgets as well as a detailed budget defense, including a statistical comparison of school and city expenses, evidence of the department's efficiency efforts, and illustrations of the potential damage likely to result from less funding. The School Department also filed suit against the city, contesting its share of the municipal budget. The department finally submitted a budget that was $1.6 million over the FY82 budget limit set by the Mayor's office.

Although the Auditor's office tried to distribute cuts evenly among departments, the Mayor explained why this was not possible: "There's not really much to cut in some departments. We had to cut over $10 million. That has to affect the five big budgets: fire, police, schools, public works, and the hospital. But my priority was definitely public safety."

In late May, Mayor Tobin submitted the budget to the City Council. But the Council had very little work to do on this year's budget. Councillor Joanne Condon explained: "Quincy's type of government is "strong Mayor, weak Council." The Mayor created the budget in consultation with department heads. Although the Council met at least 12 times with department heads, we could only reduce the budget, not add to it. Last year, we cut $11 million from the budget. This year, we voted for it as it was because it had been cut so much already. We have no real control, but we have to answer complaints about the cuts."

The City Council clashed with Mayor Tobin over one major issue. In his final budget, the Mayor had deleted funding for water and sewer services to create support for an independent water and sewer commission with its own revolving account. Council members objected to joining budget issues with the structure of financing services and voted down the Mayor's proposal even though they actually supported an independent commission. The Council's rejection created a budget deficit that had to be made up with state aid.

The School Department absorbed 45 percent of the total city-wide reductions. Its budget was cut 22 percent, proportional to its share of the city budget. The budgets for the Police and Fire Departments were each cut 12.5 percent. Departments believed to be critical to maintaining fiscal solvency (such as the Treasurer's Department) avoided substantial cuts. Programs providing services for youth and the elderly lost all city funding, but were covered for the year with federal Community Development Block Grants funds.

The Auditor claimed that "less essential" services, such as recreation, were eliminated to save "essential services." But Council member Condon complained that no cuts were made in the Mayor's budget. And Superintendent Creedon thought the Mayor's priorities protected city departments at the expense of the School Department.

Quincy citizens became involved in the budget process in a number of ways. Both the Superintendent's office and the teachers association worked closely with parents through the PTA's. Representatives from all PTA's came to a City Hall meeting to discuss school closings and the proposed school budget cuts. Competing neighborhood interests, however, made it difficult to unite effectively against these cuts.

City Council members received an unusually large number of calls about proposed cuts in Police and Fire, and elderly services, and about school closings, and budget cuts for the rent grievance board. But both city officials and community leaders agreed that the level of citizen participation was low. Former Auditor Shea argued that while the Mayor invited people to meetings to discuss budget issues, "they didn't come; they never do." The Director of the Community Action Project, Rosemary Wahlberg, agreed: "People don't really go to the budget hearings. They don't follow the issues. They only attend meetings if their services or jobs will be cut. Not even the elderly came out in large numbers. In spite of Proposition 2 1/2, it was business as usual."

Despite citizens' concern, the five schools finally closed were not those with the smallest enrollments. Nor did tenant protests prevent the firing of the Rent Grievance Board Director. City Councillors and interested residents were unable to maintain funding for the Conservation Commission and the Council on Aging.

A coalition of four major unions and representatives of the Community Action Program worked against Proposition 2 1/2, but collapsed after the election. Conflicting interests and pro-2 1/2 sentiment among union members contributed to the collapse. Members of the Fire Fighters union believed the teachers just wanted "to save their own skins," while CAP representatives thought each faction was concerned only with its own agenda.

## Impacts of Proposition 2 1/2

City officials noted that despite a 17 percent budget cut, Quincy did not suffer severe layoffs. This was due to the no-hire policy adopted under the 4 percent cap, incentives for early retirement, and efforts to raise new revenues this year. However, there are now 550 fewer city employees than there were in FY81 -- one-third less in the School Department and more than 50 percent less in the library system.

## Impacts on the School Department

In FY82, the School Department cut its school budget by $6,746,410, a 22 percent reduction. Approximately $4.5 million in salaries was cut, resulting in the elimination of 500 school positions, of which 294 were layoffs. (School enrollments had declined from about 17,000 students in 1971 to about 10,000 in 1981.)

The Superintendent claimed that his department was the hardest hit of any in the state. Some impacts were immediately apparent. Nearly half of the high school teachers were laid off. Non-academic courses such as gym and shop were reduced. The school system's individualized curriculum was abandoned and high school drama and grades 7-9 athletics were eliminated. According to the president of the teachers association, low morale is a major problem: "The morale of teachers is quite low. We haven't been paid our 1979-80 raise, an issue still in the courts. We did get a raise for 1980-81 and 1981-82. No matter what anyone says, a teacher's morale will affect classes. Our curriculum had been individualized, but that's gone. We won't have as many special courses like music and shop. And in science, my area, we won't have the same levels and variety."

School officials clearly thought the School Department was treated unfairly in relation to other city departments. The School Department absorbed nearly half of the total city cuts while the Police and Fire departments avoided substantial cuts. The Superintendent argued that the department was not in a position to absorb a 22 percent cut without impairing services severely. The department had already lost 100 positions and had closed three elementary schools before Proposition 2 1/2 passed.

## Impacts on the Fire Department

From a FY81 budget of $5,968,053, the Fire Department was cut back 12 percent, or $700,000. Because 80 percent of the department's budget consists of salaries, most of the cuts were made in personnel: 29 positions were eliminated at first, resulting in 10 layoffs. The other 19 men retired. Although the ten men laid off were later rehired with state aid funds, this year's loss of 19 positions followed the elimination of seven positions last year.

The Fire Chief and union representatives believe that a continual loss of positions is impairing the department's ability to fight fires. In the past, the Chief has relied on the overtime budget to fill in the gaps in his force, but this year's overtime budget was cut $60,000 and the Chief claimed that it would not last beyond the fall of 1982.

The Chief made no allocation this year for the purchase of trucks or new equipment. In FY79, he allocated only $18,000 for capital expenditures and the rest was raised by city borrowing. But Quincy's lower bond rating makes borrowing for new equipment unlikely in the near future. The department's equipment is quite old and fire fighters complained that it is neither repaired nor replaced. They argued that equipment that is constantly falling apart constitutes a danger to the men.

Neither the Chief nor the union representative thought Proposition 2 1/2 promoted efficiency in the Fire Department. Both felt there was little waste to begin with. The department is salary-intensive and nearly all positions are active. The Chief observed: "I felt that for what people paid, we were providing a high level of service. We have a class 2 rating, as high as it can be. There isn't much slack at all. So when we cut personnel from providing a service, it's simple -- we provide less service."

## Impacts on the Police Department

The Police Department's budget was cut almost 8 percent in FY82, from $6,041,486 to $5,568,749. Although no police officers were laid off, the department had eliminated a total of 35 positions over the past three years. The budget officer said the department's desired number of patrolmen is 188, but that only 153 positions were currently filled. The unfilled positions have not been eliminated, but they remain unfilled because of budget shortages.

The most serious losses for the department were reductions in the number of back-up cars available and in beat coverage. The department also began ranking calls and the Chief thought some might go unanswered.

## Impacts on the Public Works Department

The cutback in the Department of Public Works translated into the elimination of 57 positions. Before Proposition 2 1/2 went into effect, the department had eliminated 30-35 positions. Department officials believe the department is now "short" over 90 people.

The City Engineer thought no serious reductions in services had resulted from the loss of personnel. However, road resurfacing was curtailed when the state reduced funding from the gasoline tax. The city's sewer system needs about $2.5 million in repairs and construction, but since the city raises no sewer-use revenue, it cannot qualify for categorical federal aid for sewer construction. A service for people who want to widen their driveways was eliminated.

The City Engineer began a series of cutback measures two years ago when he thought a Proposition 2 1/2-type law likely to pass. He laid off some people, transferred others, and increased fees and outside contracting. The Engineer thought Proposition 2 1/2 helped him to implement cuts in a department that had an excess of personnel.

## Efficiency and Innovation

Budget constraints imposed by the tax cap and Proposition 2 1/2 prompted Quincy city officials to consolidate some departments, rely more on user fees and charges, increase outside contracting, and create new revolving accounts for self-supporting services.

At the Mayor's request, the City Council revised the city's fee schedule. Increased fees for licenses raised $44,000 and the new revenue prevented layoffs in the clerk's office. The Public Works Department raised its fees for electrical and plumbing inspection. The Police Department raised its fees for gun and parking permits. The City Hospital increased its charges 11 percent and the city raised its water rates 12.5 percent.

Public Works Department expenditures have decreased 47 percent in the last two years. The department ended its landfill operation last year and contracted with a private firm, requiring fee payments for commercial dumping. The fees covered the costs of landfill and saved the city about $400,000. A private contract for street cleaning also added greatly to savings on equipment costs.

The Police Department, which ran the ambulance service, began contracting privately for this service. Former Auditor Shea reported that this change eliminated 12 positions in the department and saved $400,000.

Proposition 2 1/2 encouraged the consolidation of services provided by the Council on Aging and the Youth Commission under the administration of the Planning Department. Because the Community Development Block Grant funds controlled by the Planning Department can only be used in certain areas, some services for the elderly, such as recreation, will no longer be offered. Only help for immediate needs -- food, medical care, and transportation -- will be provided. Fortunately, most of the children previously served by the Youth Commission live in Community Development areas and will continue to be served by the Planning Department.

This year, city officials established free standing accounts for the hospital and the junior college. Both must now generate sufficient revenues to support themselves. Although both changes were initiated before Proposition 2 1/2 took effect, former Auditor Shea said they were considered in anticipation of it.

Despite these innovations, not everyone believed "waste" had been reduced in Quincy. Some observers claimed that layoffs by seniority allowed older, less efficient employees to stay on, while younger, more qualified employees were released. But City Council member Joanne Condon thought the patronage system in Quincy prevailed: "Proposition 2 1/2 didn't guarantee that 'fat' would be cut. Some important people were laid off, but you'll still find "fat." There's nothing in the law that says the Mayor has to lay off his political appointees. Go down to the treasurer's office and you'll see less people there than in the Mayor's office."

## Labor Relations

Although the Quincy Education Association actively worked with parents before and after Proposition 2 1/2 passed, it was unable to forestall cuts in the school budget. No new contract needed to be negotiated (the union already had a contract that contained reduction-in-force language by seniority), but the union president explained the union's inability to be effective on budget issues this year: "The Association was not actually involved in the budget-making. The Superintendent did invite me to sit in on budget discussions, but we didn't have overtime or anything to trade for jobs. We prepared a list of cuts we thought could save jobs. We submitted the list to the Superintendent, but it was rejected."

The Association lost about one-third of its members as a result of layoffs. Union president O'Malley thought the school year would be made difficult by multiple transfers (some buildings lost 50 percent of their staff members), grade re-assignments, increased class sizes, and doubled teaching loads. She expected these changes to alter working conditions in Quincy's public schools severely. The union president said teachers were pessimistic about future negotiations with the city: "Unfortunately, we have to negotiate a new contract next June. It will be difficult to negotiate a new contract given the constraints of Proposition 2 1/2 on public employees and Reagan's treatment of PATCO."

During the budget process, Quincy's fire fighters (who were also active in the anti-2 1/2 campaign) were the most visible union. At one point, they led a picket line in front of City Hall. The fire fighters argued that Proposition 2 1/2 worsened labor relations and the department's operations. The union's primary complaint was that Proposition 2 1/2 created a shortage of men, violating minimum manning agreements, and endangering firemen. City officials have not closed any sub-stations, which aggravates the problem. For example, a West Quincy ladder truck which previously ran with three men now runs with two. The union filed a grievance last November, claiming that at times one West Quincy station is manned by only four fire fighters. Thus, manning has been reduced from 40 men to 35 men for ten trucks. The union has requested arbitration over the alleged contract violation.

The fire fighters proposed that the city rehire the 10 men who were laid off this year. The city proposed that the union drop its manpower grievance and accept vacation schedule changes, but no agreement was reached. The city eventually rehired the 10 men with state aid funds. When the fire fighters contract expired in June, they were unsure what trade-offs they would make in bargaining with the city. A union spokesman said that "a pay increase just doesn't seem feasible with layoffs going on," even though their last pay raise occurred over a year ago. According to the union's vice-president, Jim Kelley, "Proposition 2 1/2 weakened us. If the city dragged its feet before, we pushed it. We have no strength now and that will hurt negotiations. But the public supports fire protection in Quincy and that will keep us in good shape."

The president of an independent union representing 1,000 city employees (Hospital, Library, and Public Employees Union), John Keefe, claimed that Quincy laid off more employees than the other 21 communities the union represents. But this union's problems in Quincy predate the enactment of Proposition 2 1/2. Under the 4 percent cap, the city laid off 40 union members in June 1980. Keefe contended that "phony bookkeeping" and "continual overestimation of receipts" causes Quincy's perennial deficits and complicates its current budget crisis. He argued futher that many layoffs were unnecessary this year and could be attributed more to "politics" than to budgetary constraints.

The union has accused city officials of hiring new city employees while firing others. It has filed over 35 reinstatements cases since 1980, winning 25 of them so far. The union challenged the city when it laid off all employees of the engineering department over a contract dispute. All nine were rehired with full back pay and 10 percent compensation.

Because the police and fire unions no longer have binding arbitration, Keefe thought "bargaining would be fairer" for non-uniformed employees. While he believed that all public employee unions should have binding arbitration, he thought it allowed police and fire employees a disproportionately large slice of the municipal pie.

Keefe has ready his union's challenge for next year's negotiations: "We won't entertain the notion of going without a pay raise. The cities will just have to come up with the money somehow."

## Impacts on Development

Quincy is in the middle of a development boom. Officials in the Planning Department attribute much of the city's growth to its proximity to Boston. If federal Urban Development Action Grants are eliminated, some development projects will suffer. However, one planner argued that lower property tax rates might encourage development in Quincy in the long-run.

The Chamber of Commerce in Quincy strongly supported Proposition 2 1/2 (except for the now amended section limiting the addition of new construction value to the tax base). Chamber members take the position that lower taxes and "streamlined government" will encourage business development in Quincy.

## "Winners and Losers" Under Proposition 2 1/2

Not surprisingly, those who strongly supported Proposition 2 1/2 thought "everyone would benefit" from the cap on property taxes. Mayor Tobin thought the results would be mixed -- that some groups would suffer. Representatives of public employees' unions contended that ultimately everyone would lose because service reductions would end up costing more than the savings in taxes. Former City Auditor Shea argued that "winners" and "losers" cannot be identified without reference to the tax structure: "If Quincy had been at 100 percent valuation, everyone would have benefitted. Take me -- I have an old house. My tax bill will double under revaluation. Since commercial property has always been assessed higher than residential property, the tax load will shift from commercial to residential. Therefore, commercial property will benefit most."

The Director of the Community Action Program thought low-income residents would be hurt most directly, with the harshest effects coming from reductions in federal and state services. Federal support for family planning and health services will be reduced and Community Development Block Grants, already supporting a health center in Hough's Neck, several "well-baby" clinics, and the Kennedy Health Center, will be spread thinly as more services (e.g., elderly and youth services) are covered with CDBG funds. The Director of the Community Action Program observed:

The immediate effect of Proposition 2 1/2 was to eliminate small departments without constituencies, such as the Rent Grievance Board. The Board's director helped tenants and found them apartments after condominium conversions. Quincy has one of the largest elderly populations in the state, but the coordinator for the Council on Aging was lost in consolidation. Schools are really the number one poverty program though. Middle class kids go to private schools. Those most hurt are the poorest kids."

## State Fiscal Reform

Nearly everyone agreed that the state should help the cities, but there were differences of opinion about how best to do this. The fire fighters union supported a graduated income tax; the municipal union president supported a broader sales tax; and the teachers union president supported tax reform, but no specific proposal. The Chamber of Commerce spokesman supported increased state aid to the cities and towns. The City Assessor supported a graduated income tax, but thought it was politically unrealistic. politically. The Mayor, too, supported reform efforted, but no specific proposal. As a short-term solution, the City Auditor suggested that the state exempt the principal and interest on long-term debt issued before June 30, 1981 from Proposition 2 1/2 constraints, which would guarantee Quincy's solvency, and be helpful to the state's older cities.

## The Future

Nearly everyone interviewed believed that Quincy faced hard times ahead. The Chamber of Commerce spokesman thought revaluation, new construction, the announced intent of the administration to classify, and increased state aid to the cities and towns would mitigate the effects of 2 1/2 over the next few years. Nor did he think the average citizen would notice a substantial difference in the services he or she receives. But Mayor Tobin argued that another $10 million cut in FY83 would certainly affect public safety. The Fire Chief contended that another cut would force the closing of certain fire stations. The City Engineer argued that "all the extras" have been eliminated in the Public Works Department and that a second round of cuts will affect services. The teachers association president maintained that the School Department "cannot survive another year of cuts like this year's. We'll have to lay-off another one-third of our teachers." Summing up the fears of most of Quincy's city officials, the City Assessor said, "We had 17 vacancies in the Police Department this year, but we won't have them to cut next year. We cut $15 million this year, but we do have fixed costs to cover as well. We already took the junior college and the hospital out of the city's budget and cut the library by 50 percent. So where is there room to cut next year? This year, we coped, but I really fear next year."

## Notes for Chapter 17

1. In anticipation of Proposition 2 1/2's effect on Quincy's bond rating, the City Auditor and Treasurer sold $7 million in unsold bonds before election day.

Chapter 18

# Salem: Controversy over Cuts

Jerome Rubin

## Introduction

Salem is located 16 miles northeast of Boston. During the China Trade, the city of Salem was a more important port than the city of Boston. However, following a naval blockade by the British during the War of 1812, Salem's merchants moved to Boston. They never returned and Salem's port declined as an employer and revenue source. In the 1860's, a number of French Canadians moved to Salem to be followed by other Catholic immigrants later in the 1800's. These people were attracted by jobs in Salem's textile, apparel, leather, and leather products industries. When these industries declined or moved south, Salem remained a regional center of manufacturing until Route 128 by-passed the city. Although some Salem residents work for the "high tech" firms, located along Route 128 and the absolute number of jobs in Salem has slowly increased, unemployment continues to rise. Between 1970 and 1976, the unemployment rate rose from 4.6 percent to 10.3 percent.

As manufacturing jobs decreased, the relative importance of other sectors of the city's economy increased. Today, the largest employer is the health industry. With three hospitals and numerous clinics, Salem serves as a regional medical center. Government, including city, state, county, and federal offices, is the second largest employer, followed by the city's largest manufacturing firm, a Sylvania light bulb plant. (The largest employers are Salem Hospital, a non-profit private institution, the City of Salem, and Sylvania, in that order.) Other important sources of employment include utilities, tourism, insurance, and banking.

Between 1965 and 1978, the city's population fell from 40,112 to 37,855. Salem has a higher proportion of elderly, low- and moderate-income people than its neighbors on the North Shore. (Beverly, Swampscott, Danvers, and

Peabody are all either closer to Boston or more accessible to Route 128.) There has been very little new development in Salem and the city's housing stock is aging.

Despite these handicaps, Salem has upgraded its facilities over the last decade, rebuilt its harbor area, increased tourism (witches and harbor), and encouraged the rehabilitation of its older homes. These efforts have attracted some younger people. Tourism is up, bringing in revenues at a rate of almost $1 million a year since the late 1970's. The tourist industry now accounts for almost 9 percent of all retail jobs. Downtown redevelopment is credited with halting the slide of wholesale and retail jobs in the city. Despite declining school enrollments, the city built a new high school and three new elementary schools. It also built a new fire station, water treatment facilities, a Chronic Disease and Rehabilitation Hospital and a parking garage. These projects have increased the city's debt. Between 1965 and 1978, debt retirement increased 342 percent, the largest increase of any single item in the city's budget. In 1974, it was 16 percent of the city budget. City officials do not expect debt expenditures to decrease until the late 1980's. Salem's renewal projects were financed mostly through borrowing and state, rather than federal, funding.

Between 1965 and 1978, municipal expenditures increased about 11.5 percent each year. Education expenditures, which account for over one-third of the city budget, increased 300 percent during that period. In the same period, public safety (fire and police) expenditures, which accounted for 12 percent of city expenditures, rose by 5.8 percent a year. In 1967, the city spent $9,378,000 from revenues of $10,717,000. In 1972, it spent $18,205,000 with revenues of $16,672,000, and in 1977, $35,459,000 of $37,036,000. During this same period, the number of city employees increased from 1,175 to 1,568.

About 41 percent of the city's revenues come from real estate taxes (43 percent of the city's land area is tax exempt). The city's assessed valuation increased from $96,650,400 in 1968 to $119,600,500 in 1978, to $121,922,800 in FY81. (New England Power Company accounts for 35 percent of the city's total assessed valuation.) In FY81, Salem collected $24,934,174 (with a tax rate of $205.00) on an assessment of $121,922,800. The state's 1980 equalized valuation was $609.5 million, suggesting an assessment ratio of 20 percent. Revaluation will be completed in July 1982 and some officials, including Mayor Jean Levesque, thought revaluation would preclude further budget reductions.

## Past Budget Issues

In the past, the Mayor's office dominated the budget process. There were some mild conflicts over increasing funding for the Fire and Police departments, but as one observer noted, "There was always a sense that there was enough to go around." This year, that sense was lacking and the budget process turned out to be very controversial.

According to the City Assessor, a perennial problem around budget time is whether to increase the tax rate. The Mayor has opposed tax increases and put off revaluation yearly to avoid the political repercussions of imposing higher taxes. The fact that New England Power has paid as much as 40 percent of the city's property tax in recent years, allows city officials to avoid tax increases.

## Views on Proposition 2 1/2

Proposition 2 1/2 passed by an overwhelming margin in Salem (60–40). Most of those interviewed thought voters were caught up in the statewide campaign against high property taxes. Others suggested that Salem residents were influenced by the support for Proposition 2 1/2 in surrounding communities where property taxes have risen steadily in recent years.

Mayor Levesque argued that Proposition 2 1/2 held enough "goodies" to attract broad support from the electorate: a voter might have wanted to lower property or excise taxes, to end binding arbitration or school committee autonomy. Superintendent of Schools, Henry O'Donnell, attributed the vote to Salem's disproportionately older population (55 percent of the population is over age 50), arguing that cuts in education seemed less critical to this group than tax reductions. He thought that parents of children who attend parochial schools (10 percent of school-age children now) probably shared this view and voted accordingly. The Chief of Police and the Fire Marshall thought that, although voters were fed up with high property taxes, they would not have voted for Proposition 2 1/2 had they realized it would result in public safety reductions.

## The Gap

Using the state's 1980 equalized valuation ($609.5 million), Salem will have to reduce its FY81 property tax levy by 39 percent, or $9 million, to comply with Proposition 2 1/2. In FY82, the city cut $3,790,000 (15 percent). The city also lost $800,000 in excise taxes and about $200,000 in federal revenue sharing funds. Thus, Salem will lose $5.6 million in revenue in one year.

Beyond the loss of federal revenue sharing funds ($200,000), city officials could not predict how much state and federal revenues would eventually be cutback or how it would affect Salem. They hoped these cuts could be absorbed by departments.

The Department of Public Services must operate with reduced state funding and a reduced allocation from the city (22 percent less) this year. Until four years ago, the state gave Salem $200,000 a year from gasoline tax revenues and Chapter 81 Publicworks funds to repair streets and sidewalks. But last year the city received only $40,000. The Director of Public Services, Tony Fletcher, explained that the department should be able to make up the difference between what the state provides and what the work requires. But it cannot afford to do that. Fletcher argued that his department will be held responsible for other state reductions in road maintenance (plowing, sanding, painting stripes) -- work that he will be unable to finance.

Spokesmen for the Hispanic community in Salem believe that state cuts in AFDC, Medicaid, bilingual education, housing, and emergency relief will severely affect lower income residents. Salem's small Hispanic community fears that in addition to these cuts, "2 1/2 will totally destabilize this community." Community spokesman, Romera Knutsen, added, "We were having a hard enough time already."

By August 1981, Salem's list of cuts in federal aid was already long. Salem was the prime sponsor of the CETA job training program for 17 North Shore communities. This $12 million program was cut to $4 million. As competition for shrinking federal funds continues, the Director of the North Shore Community Action Program thought services for low-income groups would lose out to more "essential" services.

Salem's Planning Director, who heads a department heavily dependent on federal aid, anticipated a reduction in Section 8 housing funds and UDAG and EDA grants. Although the Director was uncertain what city departments or services would be affected by reductions in these funds, he knew of at least one EDA grant, earmarked for library rehabilitation, that will be cancelled.

Severe cutbacks in federal aid for water treatment have already slowed Salem's schedule for water treatment maintenance and sewer improvements. EPA 92-500 funds were cut from $6 billion to $3 billion under President Carter and President Reagan has reduced it further (to $1.4 billion). According to the Public Service Director, Tony Fletcher, Salem has "a real water problem." But the city is still using money borrowed four years ago for water treatment. The City Engineer thought a combination of federal fund cutbacks and diminished borrowing potential would make it difficult to carry out the city's much needed sewer improvements. (Moody's Investment Service lowered Salem's bond rating from AA to Ab.)

Services for the elderly in Salem have suffered federal cutbacks: a 25 percent reduction in the Title I program and a 20 percent reduction in funds providing full support for the Congregate Lunch and Home Delivery Meals programs, half of the support for the Council on Aging staff, half of the health clinic staff, and half of the special bus system expenditures.

Like other Massachusetts cities, Salem counted on the state for help in dealing with the effects of Proposition 2 1/2. Salem officials expected a $1.1 million increase in state aid, which covered 27 percent of the city's revenue losses. The first $500,000 in state aid was already earmarked to cover a deficit in the Mayor's budget. Other priorities for state aid money included funding school transportation ($200,000); honoring a collective bargaining agreement with municipal employees ($300,000); funding for street lights; purchasing police cruisers ($45,000); and purchasing public works equipment ($175,000). The Fire Department wanted to reopen a station ($290,000) and the Director of the

Council on Aging hoped to receive $1 million of the state aid money. The City Council supported both of these requests.

In the end, Salem's FY82 "cherry sheet" contained $6,816,372, an increase of approximately $1.2 million over the previous year. By November 1981, $96,000 was appropriated for police salaries, $260,000 for school bus transportation, $85,000 for street lighting, and smaller amounts between $5,000 and $8,000 were appropriated for various purposes. The city is considering about $300,000 for employee raises.

## The Budget Process

Salem has a Plan B government -- strong Mayor/weak City Council. The official budget process begins when department heads submit their requests to the Mayor. The Mayor then meets with them to develop department budgets. The Mayor's overall budget goes to the City Council which can reduce, but not increase, it. The Mayor can veto the Council's reductions, but this power is rarely used. The City Council wanted a more active role in the budget process this year, but Council President, Joe Centarino, said the Mayor continued to consider the budget his job. A tight budget means the Council has less responsibility. The Council cut only $85,000 from the FY82 budget and Centarino remarked, "We barely trimmed around the edges."

The primary budget controversy this year (as distinct from the actual cuts) involved relations between the Council and the Mayor. In February 1981, the Council complained that it was being excluded in this important budget-making year. But the Mayor argued that the Council need not be doing anything special or different. When the budget finally came before the Council, it made cuts in the Planning, Legal, and Engineering departments -- departments close to the Mayor's office.

The Mayor did not develop the budget alone, however. The Director of the Planning Department and the City Solicitor worked with him. The Mayor also retained the Chairman of the Economics Department of Salem State College as a budget advisor. This group determined what would be cut. In January, the group requested a 17 percent cut in all departments. Despite differences in the size of department budgets, the Mayor thought there was very little slack in any of them. He hoped to distribute the cuts evenly.

But some department heads argued that a 17 percent reduction would incapacitate their departments. The Fire and Police Chiefs, under pressure from their unions and Salem residents, argued for smaller cuts. By March, the Mayor's group had established priorities and recommended differential cuts. Public safety had first priority. The public's resistance to police and fire cuts made these clearly the most sensitive budget areas. Accordingly, the Mayor's group shifted reductions away from the Police and Fire department budgets to the "non-essential" areas. As a result, thirteen departments or programs no longer receive city funding: Christmas decorations, parade events, concerts, the Cultural Arts Commission, Fireman's Memorial, Heritage Day Celebration,

Historic Commission, Human Rights Commission, Tourist Commission, Waterways Commission, and Weights and Measures. The Director of Public Services, Tony Fletcher, explained how the Mayor's group arrived at these cuts: "First, the Mayor established what had to be done to insure reasonableness of public safety and services. That includes, for instance, water treatment. Then he went back and saw what departments could live with. Then we looked at what might be called more "peripheral" items. The Planning Department was cut. We lost a marketing agent and people associated with tourist promotion."

Other departmental cuts ranged from 6 percent for police and fire, to over 50 percent for the Parks Commission. The city imposed a cut of less than 7 percent on the Fire Department. (The Fire Fighters union spokesman claimed that it really amounted to a 17 percent cut because the city did not include a recently negotiated pay raise in the new budget.) City Planner, Gary Senko, said the budget group sought to make reductions in departments that had vacancies or where early retirements were possible, so that positions could be eliminated.

Both the Mayor and the City Council claimed credit for consolidating departments in order to save money. City officials estimate that consolidating the Council on Aging, the Department of Health, Veterans Servies, and the Human Rights Commission (sharing clerical and secretarial support) will save the city $150,000 a year without impairing services. But the Director of the Council on Aging doubted the savings and thought the appropriations for the new department were insufficient. City Council President, Joe Centarino, proposed merging the Parks and Recreation departments. Although the Parks Director objected vehemently to the merger, Centarino said the overlap between the two departments "had reached the point of absurdity."

The Mayor and department heads close to him thought the budget cuts were made with an eye to greater efficiency. However, other department heads thought increasing efficiency was impossible and argued that budget reductions were made arbitrarily. Dennis Flynn, President of the Fire Fighters union, argued: "The cuts in fire and police were purely vindictive. In no other city were so many men cut from those departments. But we've opposed the Mayor in every election and we're one of the strongest unions in the state."

Few department heads or personnel organized to oppose budget cuts. Rene Lewis, Director of the Council on Aging, (which faced a 14 percent reduction) explained: "Everyone was fighting the consolidation of five departments into one Human Services Department. People said, "I'm not against you, but I spent $1,200 on phones last year and I need it again this year." That's the worst thing about 2 1/2 and the Reagan cuts -- they pit the poor against the poor." The Superintendent of Schools agreed that people felt backed against the wall. Within the School Department, he recalled teachers fighting guidance counsellors for jobs.

Closing a fire station in the Salem Willows neighborhood led to the occupation of the fire house by local residents and the establishment of "People's Fire House No. 6." But re-opening the station seems unlikely.

Cuts in school bus transportation also elicited substantial public dissent. More residents attended this hearing than any other, except the one on Fire Department cuts. Citizens organized for the meeting and presented testimony on the dangers and hardships imposed on children walking more than two miles to school. Numerous Hispanic residents attended the hearing because their neighborhood is far from the new Salem High School. Despite protests, the School Superintendent and the School Committee let the transportation cuts stand. The Superintendent said he supported a bill to give localities autonomy on transportation decisions, but the Mayor kept school transportation high on his list of items to be funded with state aid.

The School Department absorbed the largest budget reduction among departments, resulting in cuts in school sports, guidance counselling, and elective classes. The cuts aroused serious protest from students. A walk-out of 250 high school students in late winter led to a rock-throwing incident, and ultimately, to negotiations with the Superintendent.

Both the business community and the Mayor's office objected strongly to the City Council's reduction in the Planning Department budget. The reduction cost the department an assistant planner who had brought in over $18 million in grants over a two-year period. (His was one of two city-funded positions of the 22-member staff.) Critics argued that the Council's action was designed to punish the department for working closely with the Mayor. The Director of the department hoped to obtain outside funding for the position.

Representatives of the Hispanic community complained about their relations with the city. The Point neighborhood, home for most of Salem's Hispanics, is represented by a French Canadian councilor who speaks for the "French" in the neighborhood, the Hispanics claim, but not for them. A spokesman argued that the city did not consider the needs of the Hispanic community during the budget process. He thought the city's neglect was particularly evident on the school busing issue.

## Impacts on the School Department

The School Department reduced its budget 17 percent, or $3.1 million. (Negotiated pay increases had to be absorbed, which means the reduction was actually a 22 percent cut.) School sports and extra-curricular activities were eliminated entirely. The transportation budget was reduced. School department layoffs totalled 100, including 70 teachers, 7 principals, and assistant principals, 10 clerical employees, 11 custodians, and 2 nurses. Although no academic program was eliminated entirely, class sizes will increase.

The Superintendent argued that Salem's schools came through the first year of Proposition 2 1/2 in "good shape: We were in a period of consolidation already. We had anticipated closing one administration building and four elementary schools. It was a combination of declining enrollment and consolidation. Proposition 2 1/2, which came after our planning, ended up being a tool to implement our planned consolidation. We cut deeper than we wanted to, but those cuts would have come anyway." Union officials disagreed. They thought the quality of education would be severely affected this year. However, the Superintendent believed that the next round of cuts -- when there would be no more fuel, no more "frills," and no more buses to cut -- would destroy "the heart of eduction."

## Impacts on the Public Services Department

Salem's second largest department, Public Services, handles engineering, cemetery, motor vehicles, streets, solid waste disposal, and water. In FY82, its budget was reduced 17 percent, or $3.1 million. Because $700,000 is fixed in contractual agreements for solid waste disposal, the effective budget cut was closer to 24 percent.

The City Engineer thought too many cuts were made in the technical side of his department's budget (i.e., meter reading, engineering work, etc.). He felt he could "make this budget work with closer cooperation among staff, but found other impacts difficult to predict. For example, the Engineer does not know how much snow will fall or how many water mains will break in any given year. Last year, the department ended up with a huge deficit in street maintenance and small surpluses in other areas.

Proposition 2 1/2 accelerated the Public Services Department's plans to cut back. Except for additional water treatment facilities, no capital expenditures had been planned. However, Proposition 2 1/2 cutbacks reached into areas that were not targeted for reductions. According to the Chief Engineer: "Prior to 2 1/2, I cut 52 people from the department. I haven't missed them. One reason I'm here is to tighten up the department. At the same time, I look at the Parks Department with 34 people. Absolutely unnecessary. These are politically protected positions, but Proposition 2 1/2 forced the cuts. Unfortunately, we end up losing some of the best people."

The Public Service Director predicted that another 15 percent reduction next year would decimate his staff. He thought the sewer, water, and refuse divisions would have to increase their fees.

## Impacts on the Fire Department

Salem's Fire Department was trimmed 19 percent, or $471,988. Thirteen of the department's 112 positions were eliminated. The city closed one fire station so that it could comply with contract clauses covering overtime and minimum manning. Residents of the neighborhood that lost the station believe they are endangered as a result of greatly reduced response time.

The President of the Fire Fighters union claimed that no other Massachusetts city has laid off as many fire personnel. He considered the budget cut an effort to break the union. He rejected the notion that the cuts would promote efficiency within the department. "In fire and police departments," he said, "97 percent of our budgets go for salaries. We have only three administrators. Everyone rides the trucks. Where can we cut?" He warned that the union would not give up its benefits and would support the reopening of the Salem Willows station. Money for the latter, he proposed, should come from state aid and a reduction of "patronage jobs" in the Mayor's office. But members of the Planning Department argued that because Salem has had "more than adequate" fire protection in the past, the cut was justified.

Salem's Fire Marshall thought further cuts in FY83 would require the complete elimination of preventive inspections (already reduced this year), along with such services as lockout assistance, rescues, and fire prevention programs. He also predicted the loss of at least one more company, which he considered very dangerous.

The President of the Fire Fighters union was angered at the prospect of two years without pay raises. He predicted difficult bargaining ahead with union walkouts a possibility.

## Impacts on the Police Department

Salem's Police Department faced a reduction of $349,000 (13 percent) from its FY81 budget and a loss of 14 of its 91 police officers and one clerk. The department cancelled 14 positions that had been open because of vacancies or early retirement.

According to the Police Chief, a smaller police force seriously hampers the department. Although its work load has increased 60 percent in the last 12 years, the Chief argued the force then had 91 officers in addition to a 25-man reserve force which it does not have now. The Chief thought the department still offered the city adequate protection, but he has had to take some consolidation measures that made him uncomfortable. Police officers cover more geographic area than before, which means, according to the Chief, that "people are doing more."

Before Proposition 2 1/2, the Police Department answered emergency calls with equal attention; now calls are weighted according to a newly established priority system. The Chief predicted increased response times, especially on weekends -- perhaps up to two or three hours for low-ranking calls. Two years ago, the city began contracting with a private ambulance firm, thus freeing 9 men and 2 replacements from the Police Department who covered ambulance protection. With that "cushion," the Chief felt that Proposition 2 1/2 was workable this year, but the ambulance service will again be made the department's responsibility.

Like other department heads, the Chief feared next year's round of budget cuts for which he had already targeted the elimination of the foot patrolmen who cover the downtown business area. "This year, there was some room to maneuver," the Chief said, "but if I have to go further, it would jeopardize the city's safety." He counts on the state "to turn this 2 1/2 around."

## Impacts on the Council on Aging

With one of the highest proportions of elderly residents in the state, (22 percent of the city's population), Salem has an active Council on Aging. Five years ago, the city gave the Council its own building to house a variety of services. But this year, the city reduced the Council's budget 14 percent, which may be critical because the Council's federal funds may be cut 20 percent. The Council will lose federal funding for its lunch and transportation programs. Although the reductions in municipal funding did not affect the Council's "life support" activities, it forced a cutback in recreational activities (e.g., field trips and craft classes). The Director of the Council was concerned about the effects of reducing these activities, arguing that they encourage sound health. When asked about the possibility of increasing efficiency, the Director insisted that the Council's "potential for waste is minimal." He also questioned the amount of money the city will save by merging the Council on Aging with four other departments into a Human Services Department.

## Impacts on Other Departments

Other, smaller departments faced cuts which are likely to hamper their operations. Ironically, the Assessor's office, mandated by law to carry out 100 percent revaluation, possibly adding thousands of dollars to Salem's tax base, lost one clerk and one assessor. The Chief Assessor complained that his re-assessment schedule "has been completely ruined." He indicated that the delay might cause the city to use state equalized valuation again, resulting in more cutbacks. The City Clerk's Department, cut back 17 percent, was, according to the *Salem Evening News,* "caught between a 17 percent reduction and breaking state election laws mandating street and water lists."

All together, Proposition 2 1/2 cost the city of Salem 105.5 jobs through layoffs or attrition, in addition to 100 jobs similarly lost in the School Department. The city's FY82 work force, approximately 1,383 equivalent full-time employees, equals its 1972 employment level.

## Municipal Innovation

Proposition 2 1/2 forced Salem officials to consider innovative ways to fund and deliver services. Most of these steps were in the embryonic stage, but it is likely that future budget cuts will encourage further innovation.

Ten years ago, Salem used a Police Reserve Force which the Police Department drew on whenever it was short of men. The force saved the city money by allowing the department to cover peak periods without hiring additional men. Under the current budget constraints, the Police Chief viewed reinstatement of the Reserve Force as an absolute necessity. A majority of the City Council members wanted it back, but it must be negotiated back with the union, which is apprehensive. Union members thought reservists might deprive full-time men of off-hour private jobs such as directing supermarket, parking lot traffic. They also feared that reservists might encourage further layoffs. But the Reserve Force remained the Chief's top priority for next year's contract negotiations.

The Clerk's office and the Department of Public Services increased fees for marriage licenses, city permits, and some other services, but the City Council President said "these fees would have been increased anyway. Proposition 2 1/2 just moved them along." The City Engineer said that the fee increase for water had nothing to do with Proposition 2 1/2 either. But he indicated that another 15 percent budget cut next year would force his department to create new charges and fees for trash collection and other services. While there was considerable speculation over the summer about the need for user fees, few were imposed. Some user fees were established by the Planning (subdivision permits) and Conservation (wetlands permits) departments, and the Zoning Board of Appeals, which now finances its operations with hearings charges.

Salem has relied increasingly on revolving accounts to finance departmental budgets over the past few years. Instead of funding a departmental activity only with the property tax, a department generates revenue for a specific service and uses that revenue to finance that service. Salem's Shaughnessy Hospital, the city's largest department, and the Off-Street Parking Commission are funded in this manner. City officials are currently considering establishing a similar account for the Harbor Department.

The City Council President, Joe Centarino, initiated a pilot program to share the cost of purchasing equipment with Salem's neighbor city, Beverly. Centarino indicated that both cities get better prices for equipment purchased jointly. He thought the program could save Salem a substantial sum of money. He was also interested in sharing services with other cities. He said, "Much of what we do locally, we can do regionally more efficiently."

Salem contracts with private firms to provide some city services. The practice is opposed by municipal unions, but outside contracting remains popular among city administrators. Salem's Mayor explained why: "Government is costing too much money. I found in my eight-and-a-half years in this office, that we can accomplish more through outside contracting. The fringe benefits the city pays are oustripping our ability to hire the right people for the right jobs. The pension benefits we pay are outrageous."

## Private Sector Initiative

The Mayor, the City Planner, the Police Chief, the City Assessor, and other department heads hoped the private sector would fund some of the "extras" that the city will no longer be able to afford. Salem's business sector appeared willing to cooperate. A new merchants association, initiated by the manager of the East India Mall, planned to discuss coordinated efforts for promotional and celebratory activity. Some have also proposed that merchants take greater responsibility for lighting and security. Merchants located on

Pickering Wharf, a major retail/tourist area, already provide their own security. The Director of the Chamber of Commerce predicted that, in the future, the city might write service provision into its terms of agreement with new business developments.

## Long-Term Impacts

Both the Mayor and the Chief Assessor maintain that 100 percent revaluation would provide the city with sufficient revenue to avoid further budget cutting next year. According to the Mayor, Salem's actual assessed valuation is $850 million (an increase of almost 40 percent over the state's equalized valuation). This figure would yield a levy about equal to the FY82 property tax levy. The state granted Salem an extension to revalue at 100 percent.

Opinions on the various impacts of Proposition 2 1/2 differed, but people agreed that deep school cutbacks would hurt young people. The Council President added: "The dust hasn't settled yet. But I think the young people are the losers. Parks and Recreation got the most devastating cuts. Youth services were badly hurt, and, of course, education. Youth, who don't vote, will be hurt the most."

Low-income and elderly constituents thought they would become victims of Proposition 2 1/2. The feared federal and state reductions in the services they use.

Few people interviewed felt that Proposition 2 1/2 would have many beneficiaries. The City Assessor thought "everyone would benefit" as the city moved away from property taxation as a primary source of revenue. The Director of the Chamber of Commerce had some misgivings about the ability of Salem's citizens to adjust to the new austerity. The Director pointed out that "the corporate and commercial communities could adjust their books to meet their needs, while the residential community could not." She thought the beneficiaries of 2 1/2 would be those who adopted a "sense of self-sufficiency," and that adverse effects on low-income residents would be mitigated by federally funded development projects such as UDAG and CETA job training.

A number of those interviewed doubted that Salem homeowners would realize any tax saving from Proposition 2 1/2. Moving to 100 percent valuation (even with classification) will increase taxes on the city's older houses which have not been re-assessed in over 20 years. This is particularly acute in Salem's case because New England Power has been paying 30-40 percent of the city's property taxes. New charges and increased fees might also offset possible tax savings. The School Superintendent estimated that an average family with two children to bus, who each participated in one after-school activity, might have to pay over $300 a year.

The Council President offered still another perspective: "2 1/2 took away binding arbitration from police and fire unions. In the long-run that has to take away their power. That will give the Mayor more power vis a vis the unions, but 2 1/2 also diminishes his power in that he can't just spend as he likes. He can't just do capital projects. . . . Overall, 2 1/2 lessens the power of the city."

## Labor Relations

For many years, the Mayor's office and the Fire Fighters and Police unions have had antagonistic relations, which were exacerbated by Proposition 2 1/2. The Mayor welcomed the elimination of binding arbitration (as well as the end of School Committee autonomy): "Ending binding arbitration was one of the carrots. Binding arbitration was one of the worst pieces of legislation in recent years. Binding arbitration gave a particular group of people superior advantage over everyone else. But the President of the Fire Fighters union argued that the union never took advantage of the city, never negotiated a contract that surpassed cost-of-living increases of 7-8 percent. He is certain that when they negotiate salary increases next year, the city will cry, "We have no money!" He predicted that "without binding arbitration, there will be strikes."

The Mayor's office wanted to re-open the fire fighters' contract this year, in order to keep a fire station open. The new terms involved sacrificing overtime, pay raises, and other benefits. But the union was intransigent. According to the President of the Fire Fighters union: "We said 'no chance'. We're not taking a step backward for the labor movement with 11 percent inflation. Once you start going backwards -- open that contract -- you never stop. Overtime is the real stickler. We have an agreement guaranteeing so many jobs for so many men each year. But we can't run a department without full coverage." The union unsuccessfully demanded that the city use the increased state aid to re-open the fire station.

While the police union opposed cuts of any kind in the Police Department, it did not respond as militantly as the Fire Fighters. Unlike the Fire Department, the Police Department faced no direct layoffs. The major issue facing the Police union will be the Police Chief's attempt to revive the Police Reserve Force next year.

## Financial Stability and Borrowing

Both the Mayor and the Planning Director are concerned that high interest rates and a suspension of the city's long-term bond rating will complicate their effort to function in a "fiscally sound" manner. The Treasurer estimated that Proposition 2 1/2 will cost the city $200,000-$300,000 more per bond issue, if the city is able to borrow. Because Salem has relied on public money to leverage private money, and that source is drying up, borrowing may become crucial for future development. The Treasurer thought short-term borrowing would remain unaffected by Proposition 2 1/2. Last year, the city borrowed $9 million in short-term notes and the Treasurer expected that it would borrow more this year.

## Impact on Future Growth

Representatives from both the business community and the city government are guardedly optimistic about Salem's future development. The city has limited undeveloped land, and few observers expect much new construction. However, they do not expect cuts in services, attributable to Proposition 2 1/2, to discourage further housing renovation and downtown redevelopment. Federal cutbacks might have a discouraging effect, but the City Planner hoped private development would replace federal funds. Salem planners continue to seek public money, and Salem still has a three-year "Small Cities" grant, a major UDAG grant, and applications for two new UDAG grants.

## Summary

The extent to which revaluation will increase the tax base and allow the city to avoid further budget cutbacks remains uncertain. Despite the Mayor's optimism, most city officials look to the state to "bail out" municipalities in some way over the next few years. Over half of those interviewed (including the Superintendent of Schools, the President of the Fire Fighters union, the City Council President, and the Director of the Council on Aging), supported a graduated income tax, a progressive extension of the sales tax, and a relaxation of the limits of local bonded indebtedness.

Chapter 19

# Sandwich: Selectmen Take the Lead

Melvyn Colon

## Introduction

Sandwich voters rejected Proposition 2 1/2. The majority of town residents saw little need for a tax reduction since the tax rate in Sandwich was already low. The possibility of reduced services certainly did not increase Proposition 2 1/2's appeal. Selectman Eugene Carr believes that residents voted "no" because they felt they already controlled town government. Sandwich, he argues, is and has been well-managed and its residents appreciate this.

For FY81, the tax rate in Sandwich was $18.40 per $1,000 of assessed value. The low tax rate, common among towns on Cape Cod, was due to the high total valuation of town property. The total value of real estate in Sandwich in FY81 was $382,891,550, very high compared to communities of similar size. Because of this, the per capita tax levy is also quite high. In FY81, the average per capita property tax levy for Massachusetts towns with 10,000 to 25,000 people was $518; in Sandwich it was $807. FY81 property taxes equalled $7,045,204.52.

Several factors account for the high value of land in Sandwich, chief among them, the town's maintenance of 100 percent valuation. (In FY81, Sandwich was at 94 percent of full valuation.) According to the town accountant, Sandwich revalues every 10 years. The Canal Electric power plant also boosts the total property value and provides 38 percent of Sandwich's tax revenue. In addition, Sandwich is a desirable place to live, and its beach property appreciates very fast. Finally, good town management has contributed to the low tax rate.

Although Sandwich's FY81 tax rate was well below the Proposition 2 1/2 limit, the town might have suffered significant revenue losses. Proposition 2

1/2 requires towns with a tax rate lower than 2 1/2 percent to use their FY79 tax rates. Sandwich's FY79 rate was $14.50, almost $4.00 less than the FY81 tax rate. ($1.50 of the increase resulted from a change in the formula used by the state to determine reimbursement for state-owned land.) Using FY81 property valuation, this would have meant a loss of $1.5 million in tax revenue. However, the State Department of Revenue's across-the-board, 13 percent, state-wide increase in property values allowed Sandwich to compute its tax levy on a higher valuation than town officials originally anticipated. For FY82, the town was allowed to raise $6,667,057, a loss of 5.4 percent. (Sandwich raised $7,045,204.52 in FY81.) In addition, the motor vehicle excise tax was reduced from $615,000 to $349,000. In effect, Sandwich faced a total revenue loss of $644,000.

Sandwich officials anticipate federal budget reductions as well. In FY80, Sandwich's school system received $44,226 in Title I funds, which will be reduced. The federal government may also eliminate Public Law 874 which gives municipalities tuition payments for children whose parents are connected to Otis Air Force Base -- Sandwich would lose $32,000. The town may also lose as much as $250,000 if Revenue Sharing is reduced or eliminated.

## Budget-Making in Sandwich

In the past, the Selectmen usually began the budget process by negotiating funding needs with department heads. The Selectmen then forwarded a set of budget proposals to the Finance Committee, which reviewed and made recommendations to the Town Meeting. The Board of Selectmen traditionally control the budget process in Sandwich. They also serve as the Board of Assessors, which probably encourages fiscal restraint since they are responsible for raising the funds they spend. The immediate result of the Selectmen's strength is that the Finance Committee has remained weak.

After Proposition 2 1/2 passed in November 1980, the Selectmen took immediate action to improve the town's fiscal position. They asked town departments to return 5 percent of their FY81 budgets in the hope that the expected $355,000 would help offset the motor vehicle excise tax loss. The Selectmen actually collected about $200,000. They also laid off four town employees that November: two workmen from the Parks Department, a Conservation Commissioner, and a custodian at the library.

In order to determine each department's funding level, the Selectmen then decided which departments provided the most crucial services. The school system was deemed most important; its budget was to be increased by 1 percent. Town government, including the cost of running Town Hall, collecting fees, salaries for town officials and support staff, also received high priority. The Police and Fire Departments were level funded. "Less critical" departments, such as the Parks Department and the Council on Aging, were cut. The Council on Aging was deemed "less critical" only because it appeared that the Council was not likely to spend all of its FY81 appropriation. In that light, a FY82 cutback seemed reasonable. In previous years, the Town of Sandwich has purchased land for conservation. No money was committed for this purpose this year.

The Selectmen prepared a budget significantly different from previous years. In January, the Selectmen and the Finance Committee issued maximum budget targets to department heads. Selectman Carr suggested that these disrupted the usual pattern of negotiations: "It took away all the arguing, all the "Well, look at him, he should be cut, not me!" If department heads had been allowed to come in and argue, they would never have agreed to the cuts. They did come in and argue special circumstances, but we made only one exception, which is a tremendous change from before."

The Selectmen thought this change in procedure made relations with the Finance Committee "easier and simpler." But they did not set priorities for department heads since they do not consider themselves managers of town departments. Department heads formulated their own budgets and determined cuts within the limits set by the Selectmen. Most department heads wanted to preserve essential services and avoid layoffs. They proposed reductions in secondary services, such as the Crime Prevention Program in the Police Department.

## Impacts on the Police Department

The Police Department's budget was increased by more than $8,000 to $634,000. However, Police Chief, Robert D. Whearty, Jr. faced a contractual pay raise of 9 percent plus a step increase. The total increase came to 13.9 percent. In a budget in which all but $84,000 represents manpower costs for the 26-man force, meeting the 13.9 percent raise meant significant reductions elsewhere in the budget. Although there were no layoffs and the Chief managed to level-fund essential services, he reduced the hours of police coverage by 23 percent which, in manhours, amounted to losing seven men. Funds for overtime were reduced from $73,000 to $18,000. Chief Whearty cut the Summer Police Program, the Court Program, the gasoline budget, and the in-service program. The Crime Prevention Officer, the Safety Officer, and a detective were put back in uniform. One officer retired and his position was not filled. Instead of purchasing four cruisers, the department will buy only two. Routine services, such as house and business checks will be reduced. Chief Whearty predicts the cuts will result in higher winter crime rates.

## Impacts on the Fire Department

The Fire Department's budget was reduced by $374 to $435,778. Chief Ferdinand L. Alvezi also faced a negotiated pay raise this year, and five of his men were due for a step increase. The bulk of the Fire Department's budget (approximately 84 percent) consists of salaries, but only the night dispatcher was laid off. Of the 18 fire fighters, one retired and his position was not filled. The overtime budget was not affected. Chief Alvezi cut back on the purchase of new equipment and hoses. A physical exam, required every two years, did not have to be budgeted this year, which saved the department $1,000.

## Impacts on the Highway Department

The Selectmen and the Finance Committee decided that the Highway Department's budget should be reduced by 7 percent. The head of the Highway Department, James L. Crocker, and his assistant, Patricia Grady, submitted a budget with a smaller reduction. The Boards reviewed Crocker's budget and suggested that he eliminate two more positions. Crocker met with the Finance Committee to argue in favor of retaining the men. The Finance Committee agreed with him and the Highway Department was level funded at $203,000.

Crocker was also faced with meeting a contractual salary increase of 7.5 percent. There were no layoffs, but one man left the department, reducing the work force to eight. Crocker made no equipment purchases this year.

Crocker was the only department head to challenge his proposed budget allocation. The Highway Department suffered the largest cut of any department in absolute terms, because its ratio of manpower to non-manpower cuts was the smallest of the town's large departments. As it turned out, it was fortunate that the Highway Department was level-funded because there were more than 50 requests to take over private roads at Town Meeting this year.

## Impacts on the Council on Aging

Although a small department, the Council on Aging assumes great importance in Sandwich because over one-fourth of its residents are elderly. The Council Director, Herb Nelson, estimates that his agency provides meals and/or transportation to about half of Sandwich's elderly residents. The Council's budget was reduced from $25,000 to $20,000 this year. Nelson did not oppose the cut because he believes high taxes hurt the elderly even more than other residents. He is more concerned about federal cuts, especially since he was just refused a grant. (So far, he has not lost any staff. Many of the Council's services are provided by volunteers. The major Council expense is travel -- many elderly residents need transportation to and from Council activities.

## Impacts on the School Department

The Sandwich school system serves about 2,000 students. Its budget, increased in FY82 by $100,000 to $4.2 million, is, by far, the town's largest.

The School Department budget process was complicated. Even before Proposition 2 1/2 passed, department heads submitted budgets to their school principals. The principals drew up their budgets and submitted them to the

School Committee in January. The Assistant Superintendent, James Sibson, compiled another budget which dealt with such system-wide items as energy and transportation. The Superintendent and the School Committee then negotiated a final budget during a number of public meetings held during January and February.

The School Committee faced two problems this year: contractual raises and energy costs. The 130 teachers in Sandwich's chapter of the Massachusetts Teachers Association had negotiated a contract that would give them an 8 percent raise in FY82. This alone substantially exceeded the $100,000 increase. In addition, the recently constructed high school uses an electric heating system and school officials projected an increase of $124,850 in heating costs. In all -- increases in salaries, heating costs, and transportation costs -- the School Committee faced an 11 percent ($458,236) increase in costs in FY82.

Sandwich residents were reluctant to reduce the school budget. When it appeared certain that there would be substantial reductions in athletics, music, and art, parents organized to voice their objections at public hearings. Accepting the need for spending limits, parents organized "booster clubs" to raise funds for athletics. They believed that the schools on the Cape should retain some sports programs.

The teachers were particularly active, attending School Committee hearings to oppose reductions that would affect the quality of programs. But two other issues loomed large for the teachers. They still had no "reduction-in-force" language in their contract. Both before and after Proposition 2 1/2 passed, the teachers association negotiated with the School Committee to insert RIF language in the contract. They were unsuccessful both times. However, the School Committee did follow seniority in their layoff procedure. The second issue provoked even more emotion. Some members of the School Committee urged the teachers to forego 1 or 2 percent of their salary increases in order to prevent layoffs. The teachers objected, arguing that their contract should be honored. They argued that their status as professionals entitled them to raises. They contended that even teachers who would be laid off supported this position.

In the end, there were some reductions: 12 teachers were laid off, 11 of whom were nontenured. All 30 nontenured teachers were notified that they would not be rehired as a precautionary (and legal) measure. At least a couple of elementary school teachers would have been laid off because of lower enrollment this year. Eight teacher aides and four custodians were laid off. One administrator, one instructor in the restaurant training program, and a coordinator of instructional services lost their jobs. There were reductions in the guidance, secretarial, and coaching staffs. The number of library aides, crossing guards, and summer helpers was reduced. Department salaries were cut. The fee for school lunches was increased and a fee was introduced for participation in athletics.

## Impacts on the Community School

Sandwich has a full-functioning community school program, offering instruction in athletic and nonathletic activities. Classes are available to all Sandwich residents and nonresidents. The Community School uses the high school as its headquarters. Participants pay to attend classes and these fees offset a substantial portion of the school's costs.

Every year the town appropriates funds to be used as seed money by the Communiy School. From the seed money, the School generates its own revenue which is placed in a deposit income account. For FY81, the town appropriated $52,000, from which the School generated $75,000 in revenue. The Director of the Community School, Craig Eldredge, thought he would need $35,000 to meet his budget target of $115,000 for FY82. The Finance Committee gave him $20,000, which, added to last year's $75,000 income, gave the Community School a total budget of $95,000. Director Eldredge plans to make the Community School self-sufficient. In order to do this, he needs to obtain state approval to open a revolving account which would allow payment of costs to be made as revenue comes in.

## Town Meeting

Eight hundred people -- a average attendance in Sandwich -- came to the Town Meeting on May 4, 1981. To this point, the budget process had been orderly, well-managed, and relatively frictionless. Town meeting was no different. The Finance Committee made a full set of recommendations to the Town Meeting, all of which were passed without discussion.

## Looking Ahead

The Selectmen were planning for the next fiscal year, even as they hammered out their FY82 budget. Assuming a 10 percent rate of inflation, and a permissible increase in the tax levy of only 2 1/2 percent, the Selectmen concluded that Sandwich will experience a shortfall of about 7 1/2 percent in FY83. Therefore, they decided to save as much as possible. Approximately $200,000 in Sandwich's own-source revenue will be set aside this year.

Another source of income which will be saved for next year is additional state aid. Sandwich received about $166,000 in net state aid which was 24 percent of its FY82 revenue loss. The Selectmen have earmarked this income for particular expenditures: to buy a roof for a school building ($30,000), to cover increased energy costs, and to rehire some employees. But they plan to keep most of the aid -- $100,000 -- in reserve. In all, the Selectmen have established a cushion of 8 percent to cover the expected 10 percent increase in town costs -- an example of why Sandwich is considered to be a well-managed town.

.Another example of good management is the county purchasing system of which Sandwich is a part. Cape towns pooled some funds and hired a purchasing agent. Department heads in each town are asked to go through the purchasing agent when buying supplies, equipment, or services. This system works well for participating towns. For example, the agent was able to buy large quantities of road salt for participating towns at a substantial discount.

## Labor Relations

No contracts were negotiated this year so it is difficult to determine what impact Proposition 2 1/2 will have on labor relations in Sandwich. Current dealings between teachers and the School Committee suggest that salaries will be the main issue. Unions may be asked to accept scaled down raises in return for retaining personnel. Although union personnel seem to sympathize with town officials' efforts to comply with Proposition 2 1/2, they do not want to forego salary increases.

The teachers are entering the second year of a three-year contract. Reduction-in-force language remains an issue. The quality of relations between the teachers' union and the School Committee still seems to be good. However, teacher morale is low. Disagreements surfaced among union members over what position to adopt with the School Committee. Some members felt that the union was too militant; others felt that it was not militant enough. Another source of anxiety for the teachers was not knowing what procedure would be used to make personnel cuts. Thus, they want RIF language in their next contract.

The Police and Fire unions are entering the final year of a three-year contract. The elimination of binding arbitration may change their upcoming negotiations with the Selectmen. Although labor relations in Sandwich have been good, the previous contract in the Fire Department was settled by binding arbitration. Its elimination will remove bargaining leverage from the unions and may create lengthy labor disputes.

The unions in Sandwich get along well. They formed a coalition to fight Proposition 2 1/2. Although the coalition disbanded, the teachers expect to revive it to minimize the effects of Proposition 2 1/2 on public employees. By themselves, the teachers lobbied the state legislature to repeal the "no-growth" provision of the law this year.

## Summary

How has Proposition 2 1/2 affected the welfare of Sandwich residents? The tax levy was not significantly reduced by 2 1/2. The effective tax rate, based on last year's valuation, is about $17.00, a reduction of a little more than a dollar. The greatest savings will probably come from the reduction in motor vehicle excise taxes. On the other hand, these tax savings may be offset by increased fees for school lunches, ambulance services, and school athletics, among others. The small reduction in the budget of the Council on Aging may have a disproportionate effect on the elderly community, especially if transportation services are drastically reduced. Parents of school-age children, teachers, and the elderly are most likely to suffer from the cutbacks.

Already well below 2 1/2 when the tax limitation measure passed, Sandwich did not suffer a crippling loss of revenues. This, plus a history of good management and good relations among town departments, unions, and the Selectmen, enabled the town to deal with 2 1/2 with a minimum of disruption. The past centralization of budgetary authority in the hands of the Selectmen facilitated the budgetmaking process and kept potential interdepartmental conflicts to a minimum.

Despite successful handling of a difficult situation, town officials still fear what is to come. They especially resent being forced to make spending reductions at a time when their town is experiencing rapid growth.

Chapter 20

# Springfield: Cut First, Restore Later

Stephen Amberg

## Introduction

Ten years ago, Springfield would have seemed an unlikely candidate to survive easily the first year of Proposition 2 1/2. However, major changes in Springfield have not only begun to revitalize the city, but have also strengthened its fiscal foundations. Springfield had a budget surplus in FY81. Nevertheless, even this well-managed city government may suffer a real decline in service quality if another year of tax and spending cuts occurs along with further inflation. The city's surplus has already been spent.

For years, Springfield was considered a failing city of the old industrial Northeast. By the early 1970's, the city had suffered visibly from suburban growth, downtown commercial decline, industrial stagnation, and a deteriorating tax base. Early private and federal renewal programs funded the city's efforts to tear down old buildings, build a Civic Center, run a highway into the downtown area, and construct a downtown mall-office tower. But basic trends were slow to turn around. In the mid-1970's, the Springfield Armory, a major in-town industrial employer, closed, along with the city's largest department store.

In 1976, a new private effort to redevelop the downtown was organized. The new effort was marked by exceptionally close, public-private cooperation and a below-prime-rate mortgage pool established by the city's leading financial institutions. Spearheaded by the publisher of Springfield's two daily newspapers, David Starr, and James Martin, president of Massachusetts Mutual Life Insurance, Co. (the second largest employer in the metropolitan area), the staff and board members of Springfield Central, Inc., included former and current public officials. Many downtown businesses also joined. Mayor Theodore Dimauro pledged public support. City planners and members of Springfield

239

Central jointly drew up a new master plan for the downtown, featuring retail, office, and market rate housing development. The efforts of Springfield's planning staff were supplemented by private architects and planners. Renewed emphasis was placed on seeking public monies and securing property tax abatements to leverage private investment.

Careful public management has been an important element of Springfield's revitalization effort. The property tax rate has been cut three of the last four years. The city is comfortably below its debt ceiling and, until Proposition 2 1/2, had an AA bond rating.

Proposition 2 1/2 had few local promoters. The revitalization coalition, including the newspapers, politicians, and the Chamber of Commerce opposed it. The high technology firms, located in Springfield's suburbs, supported it. The labor union leadership largely opposed it and joined the state-wide, anti-Proposition 2 1/2 coalition. Yet, the measure passed in Springfield by 1,500 of the 46,000 votes cast. Although Proposition 2 1/2 had a majority of voter support, the Election Department reports that only three of eight wards -- the middle and upper class districts -- passed it.

## Budget Overview

Springfield's general fund budget for FY82, including state aid, totalled $124,811,051, $3 million more than in FY81. (1) Items budgeted separately from the general fund (including water, parking facilities, and waste water funds) absorbed approximately $1 million in cuts, about 10 percent of their FY81 allocations. Cuts in general funds were replaced with increased fee revenue.

The city's budget has grown substantially since 1976 (from $88,413,698 to $124,811,051, or 41 percent). Many new public expenditures have resulted from increases in federal monies, which are not included in the budget totals. According to the City Assessor, Robert Shea, property tax receipts covered just over 50 percent of FY81's expenditures. The tax rate has been lowered in three of the past four years, from a high of $97.50 to $91.00 in FY78, and to $76.50 in FY82. In FY82, state aid provided $6.9 million; property taxes, $53 million; motor vehicle excise taxes, $11.7 million; water and sewer charges, $10 million; other fees, $11.5 million; and revenue sharing, $3.6 million. In FY82, property tax receipts provided just 42 percent of the city's expenditures. User charges covered about 9 percent. Last winter, Springfield's officials forecast a need to reduce expenditures $8.9 million. Subsequent collections of fees and taxes, plus improved cash management, brought the "budget gap" down several million dollars. State aid ($8.4 million) resulted in a small increase in the FY82 budget.

## The Budget Process

Despite the small increase in Springfield's budget, the city was forced to go through a budget-cutting process. State aid was in doubt throughout the spring and summer and was not announced until a supplementary state budget passed in mid-August.

Springfield has a Plan A -- strong Mayor-Council -- form of government. The Mayor prepares the budget and sends it to the Council, which may reduce, but not increase, expenditures. The Council has authority to create and abolish positions.

Immediately following passage of Proposition 2 1/2, Mayor Dimauro ordered a hiring freeze. This policy eliminated 327 city positions (excluding the School Department), saving $4 million. In December 1980, Mayor Dimauro began the official budget process by requesting each department head to submit an impact statement estimating the effects of an 11.5 percent across-the-board cut. (The statements are not available to the public.) These reductions were imposed to meet a budget ceiling of $117 million. The Mayor's also received budget advice from representatives of Massachusetts Mutual Life Insurance Co., Monsanto, and the Chamber of Commerce.

At this stage, department heads had to make decisions about their services. Once mayoral budget hearings began in February, however, only department heads working closely with the Mayor actually prepared budgets reduced 11.5 percent. Among these departments were the Mayor's office, the Auditor's Department, Planning Department, the Public Works Department, and the Civic Center. Some departments had cut their budgets less than 11.5 percent, while others either deferred to the Mayor or hoped to bargain for higher appropriations. Total initial requests were $8 million over the Mayor ceiling. During the sparsely attended hearings, Mayor Dimauro, Budget Director Henry Piechota, and Budget Analyst Jay Pyles, pared requests further. Budget officials hoped the required impact statements would serve as program-budget statements.

The School Department's budget process ran parallel to the city's during this early stage. The department attempted to involve parents, teachers, and administrators in the process of deterining priorities. Some people believed that the department's first year without fiscal autonomy would be difficult. The department initially requested a 6 percent increase in its budget, although it proposed a reduction in its personnel account of 7.2 percent.

Frustrated with the Department's perpetual overspending and alleged administrative overstaffing, Mayor Dimauro was determined to cut the school budget. With the cooperation of School Department administrators, the Mayor presented a budget to the City Council in May that included 541 layoffs and a total cut of about 11 percent. The Springfield Education Association called the new budget the result of "dirty politics," a vindictive reaction to the previous year's teachers' strike.

In late April, the City Council abolished 327 vacant positions created by the hiring freeze. This action accounted for about four-fifths of the cuts in the city budget. The Mayor's May budget recommendation to the Council totalled $120 million; $5 million less than department heads requested, but $3 million more than his earlier budget ceiling. (Late tax and fee collections made up most of this difference.) According to press accounts, the Mayor was determined to maintain essential services. In early May, the press reported that he had earmarked $1.6 million of the city's expected state aid for public safety -- police and fire services -- and the Municipal Hospital. The Council passed the budget in mid-June, virtually unchanged. There was, in fact, little the Council could do.

The Council tried to take action in at least three significant areas: preserving some jobs, encouraging increased citizen participation, and studying user charges. First, after intensive lobbying by fire fighters, the Council refused to abolish one entire fire company as recommended by the Mayor and the Fire Commissioners. It also provided "back door" raises for an unknown number of employees by abolishing positions and creating new ones at higher pay scales for the same individuals. Following strong public outcry, the Council protested the 10 percent reduction in the number of street lights turned on at night.

Before Proposition 2 1/2 passed, the Council President, Vincent DiMonaco, appointed a citizens budget committee to review department budgets and study user charges. The committee included Council members, prominent private citizens, and staff advisors from Massachusetts Mutual Life Insurance, Co. By involving citizens in budget details and in discussions with department heads, the committee enhanced the efforts of the Council and the city government. Several members of the Council have adopted more active roles by seeking ways to increase revenues and maintain services within the budget framework presented by the Mayor.

The final step in the budget process was the enactment of a Supplemental Budget based on an $8.4 million increase in state aid. Mayor Dimauro announced his priorities for state aid on July 1st, including restoring cuts in the Fire Department, rehiring school personnel, and raising salaries. In August, the City Council approved $3 million to rehire 151 teachers and 74 nonteaching school personnel. It also voted $2.2 million for salary increases negotiated in collective bargaining, funds to turn on most city street lights, and extra money for police, fire, and the Municipal Hospital.

There were also major efforts at management innovation. In the spring of 1980, Mayor Dimauro commissioned a management study from Main, Hurdman & Cranstoun. The study was presented privately in July 1981. It recommended new management methods that would increase revenues $3.9 million. In a late July newspaper story, Mayor Dimauro said that half of the recommendations had already been implemented, saving from $1 to $2 million. The Mayor also created a Cash Management Committee, composed of private and public members, and staffed by Massachusetts Mutual Life Insurance, Co. auditor, Richard Leveille.

After the receipt of state aid, department cuts ranged from a low of 4.2 percent for the Waste Water Department to a high of 13.2 percent for the Parks and Recreation Department. Other departments with reduced budgets included the School Department (5 percent); the Water Department (9.5 percent); and Libraries and Museums (6.7 percent). The Municipal Hospital budget was increased 5 percent; Public Works was increased 5.9 percent; Public Buildings, 2.3 percent; Police, 2.2 percent; and the Fire Department, .9 percent.

## Impacts on Libraries and Museums

The Libraries and Museums Association is a private organization which receives about two-thirds of its budget from the city to run Springfield's libraries and museums. In FY81, the budget was $3,390,578; in FY82, it was $3,161,389, a 6.7 percent reduction. The cuts have not yet been decided. In fact, a City Council task force is now studying the city's relationship with the Association. The task force was prompted by librarians who charge that city funds, budgeted to the Library, are being misallocated to the museums and the Association's administration. In addition, they charge the Association's trustees (mostly suburban residents and prominent business people) with discriminating against city residents who patronize libraries, in favor of suburbanites who patronize the museums.

A private oganization, the Association has refused to open its books to the Council. But the Council has hired an independent private auditor to review the Association's expenditures. Normally, Mayor Dimauro could be expected to defend expenditures for libraries and museums, but he has stated that they "are not in the same high priority category as police and fire." Moreover, the Mayor was angered by the Association's 10 percent salary increases, more than twice the city's own collective bargaining proposals. (Already, the fire fighters have demanded comparable raises.)

## Impacts on the Parks and Recreation Department

The Parks and Recreation Department has been undergoing reform for over a year as a consequence of a 1977 Dimauro campaign promise to clean up some well-publicized corruption. Superintendent William Foley called Proposition 2 1/2 a "boon," an opportunity to help carry through further reorganization in FY82. But he warns that a second round of cuts would "very badly hurt" the department's ability to maintain facilities and services.

Parks and Recreation absorbed the largest cut -- a 13.2 percent reduction ($3,007,532 to $2,609,220) -- of all city departments. Foley's initial "budget adjustment" strategy was to make reductions in materials and supplies. But he was only able to focus about 10 percent of the cuts in these items, because so much of the department's budget is comprise of personnel salaries. Foley then tried to protect as many of department's 149 permanent employees as possible. Seventeen positions left vacant by the city-wide hiring freeze accounted for about 45 percent of the reduction. The elimination of 68 seasonal positions, such as life guards and recreational leaders, saved another 30 percent. The remaining cuts were made by hiring fewer sundry laborers and by reducing the overtime budget. Although recreational facilities such as the ice-rink and golf course, are prime candidates for increased fees, Foley did not raise them because he thought the intent of Proposition 2 1/2 was to reduce costs, not pass them on. Recreation operating costs were halved while park maintenance costs increased slightly.

The purpose of reform was to increase managerial accountability and Proposition 2 1/2 furthered this objective. The principal reform was decentralization of programs and divisions around the city districts. The central administration, therefore, has greater monitoring and communications capacity. Each district manager is held accountable for parks and programs in his neighborhood. Foley said the department is now more productive, with clear goals and a basis for long-range planning. Reorganization has also asserted the central administration's right to reassign personnel, over objections based on seniority rights claimed by AFSCME Local No. 1596.

## Impacts on the School Department

The cuts in public school programs were among the largest budget cuts. People disagreed on the reasonableness of these cuts and on their educational impacts. It appears that City Hall blamed the tax cutting fervor in Springfield on school expenditures, and, despite some public opposition, made certain that the schools would absorb a good share of the cuts. Many people believed that declining enrollment should have resulted in fewer administrative personnel. A bitter teachers' strike at the beginning of the 1980 school year contributed to the ill-will. On the other hand, according to Superintendent John Deady, Springfield's per pupil costs are below the state's average and the school system has a good record of sending its students to colleges.

The School Department originally requested a 6 percent increase which included a 7 percent cut in personnel. The Superintendent, with his cabinet of senior aides, conducted the department's internal budget process. The teachers' union, the Springfield Education Association, submitted its own proposal to the Superintendent which reduced the school budget by about $2 million by making cuts in supplies, programs, and school bus transportation. (The SEA's proposal for cutting busing costs involved redistricting schools to allow shorter rides; such a plan may be considered in the future.) The Parent-Teacher Organization was only somewhat involved in setting budget priorities. Superintendent Deady noted that parents and students were "amazingly quiet."

The Mayor cut the School Department's budget 11.5 percent ($6 million). State aid restored $3 million, two-thirds of which was used to rehire 151 of the 350 teachers laid-off in June. Almost all teachers who wanted to return did. The remainder of the state aid was used to rehire bus monitors, and clerical and custodial workers. In the final reckoning, four schools were closed, the alternative junior and senior high schools were consolidated, the department reduced part of the pregnant teenagers program, 60 percent of all athletic programs, all new text book purchases, a third of all teaching specialists, and school supplies. It raised the cost of school lunches 25 percent and increased adult education fees.

Superintendent Deady believed the final first year cuts were moderate, although he will not predict what effects they might have on the school system. SEA President Charles Alvanos is less sanguine. He emphasized the disruptive and demoralizing impact of sending lay-off notices to 500 employees. Dr. Deady thought more reductions in the next two years would fundamentally undermine the public schools and teacher morale. He predicted that the goals of public schools would have to be entirely redefined if Proposition 2 1/2's mandate remains unchanged.

All agreed that needy students, for whom special services are crucial, are the most vulnerable. SEA President Alvanos thought that class and race changes in the student population were being reflected in the public's attitude toward public schools. Moreover, parental involvement is minimal, he said. He wanted to see the kind of leadership spurring downtown development organized to revive the public schools.

## Impacts on the Public Works Department

Like the Parks and Recreation Department, the Department of Public Works had a reputation for patronage and corruption in the mid-1970's. The current Director, a successful contractor, was appointed by Mayor Dimauro to "clean up" the department's operations. According to press reports, Director Lyons has successfully brought his private sector experience to bear on public management. In constant dollars, DPW expenditures were cut in fiscal years 1979 and 1980, although the FY81 budget was increased by 10 percent (mostly to cover snow removal). The Director reorganized the department and instituted new billing and purchasing practices. According to the press, he has attempted to boost productivity by increasing employees' responsibilities (rather than hiring to fill vacant positions) and splitting salary savings among them. Proposition 2 1/2 may halt this practice because of the union's sensitivity to job losses and the department's inability to continue buying increased productivity in this way.

In the first year of Proposition 2 1/2, the department's budget was increased 5.9 percent to $8,101,435. However, the department initially requested a decrease of 11.7 percent, in compliance with the Mayor's request. According to newspaper accounts, cuts were made in maintenance and services, not capital projects, including disconnecting 1,236 street lights, which accounted for three-fourths of the cuts; slower and more selective snow removal; less frequent trash pick-ups in all major commercial areas; no "Spring clean-up;" the elimination of 108 positions, 71 of which were laborers and tradesmen, at a savings of about $1.1 million; a 75 percent cut in street resurfacing and sidewalk construction; elimination of maintenance of private streets; and, no covering of the city's land-fill. Fees for residential services were increased.

Disconnecting the street lights provoked over 200 protests in two weeks. Many of the protests came from elderly residents. The Council scheduled a meeting in early July and went on record against turning off lights. Mayor Dimauro responded by turning on about 10 percent of the lights and state aid restored most of the rest in August at a cost of $700,000. The remainder of the state aid was used to rehire employees.

## Impacts on the Planning and Community Development Department

Every person interviewed is certain that budget reductions in these two department will impair the city's extensive development efforts. After expenditure increases of almost 9 percent from FY78 to FY81, the Planning Department's FY81 budget of $317,739 was decreased 11.3 percent to $281,817 for FY82. The Planning budget does not reveal the significance of the department which seeks and directs the use of millions of dollars of federal aid and borrowed funds to continue its work. Mayor Dimauro apparently assured the Planning Department that it will not suffer a reduced budget next year.

Yet, besides slower project implementation and delayed borrowing (until the bond rating is clarified), no one is certain how departmental expenditures will be affected. Much depends on the new federal budget as well as competition among local applicants for funds. Total federal monies coming into Springfield in FY81 amounted to $65 million, $4.2 million of which was CDBG money. FY81 federal funds represented a $40 million increase over FY80, largely because a new federal office building was being constructed and the Section 8 program was doubled.

Already, as a result of Economic Development Assistance (EDA) and Urban Development Action Grants (UDAG) cuts, the Assistant Director for Community Development, Raymond Warren, observed that the conflict over Community Development funds between downtown business interests and neighborhood interests is "getting very intense." EDA cutbacks have slowed, and, in one case, halted industrial projects. With little vacant land, the city requires such funds for clearing and assembling development sites. Planning Director, David Moriarty, is cautiously optimistic that the city will be able to go ahead with its plans to attract high technology firms.

Community development is also affected by CDBG funds for home improvement loans, Section 8 rent subsidies and rehabilitation, and energy conservation. "Housing preservation" in the inner-city has been, and will continue to be, a Springfield priority. Yet, city planners forecast an enormous budget crunch if federal funds are reduced when demands from advocates of underfunded social services increase and compete with those of commercial and industrial developers. An immediate example is a city-owned building used rent-free by a neighborhood health center that will be charged rent in FY82, even though it is unable to pay. In short, crucial decisions will have to be made soon.

## Impacts on the Human Service Department

According to Assistant Director, Stephen O'Malley, Human Services funding has "taken it on the chin" since the state imposed a 4 percent spending cap. O'Malley perceived Proposition 2 1/2, which reduced the department's budget 25 percent to $100,377 in FY82, as the "ultimate insult." However, the largest contributor to the Human Services budget -- the CDBG public service account, which provides nearly two-thirds of its budget -- remained in doubt. Federal budget cuts will hurt the department far more than Proposition 2 1/2.

The Director of Human Services, Jean Bass, thought that, despite President Reagan's predictions, private contributions are not likely to make up for the loss of public funding. United Way of Springfield announced that it will not attempt to replace funds lost as a result of state or federal reductions. An immediate result is that the department decided not to fund a health center that was going to lose federal money.

## Impacts on the Fire and Police Departments

Public safety was Mayor Dimauro's announced budget priority and the Police Department came through virtually unscathed. The Fire Department did comparatively well, too. The main public safety casualty was free ambulance service, operated by the Fire Department.

The Fire Department's General Fund budget was increased .9 percent in FY82 to $7,882,493. With federal revenue sharing funds included, the department's budget total increased from $9,381,121 in FY81 to $9,552,493 in FY82, an increase of .2 percent. Fire Chief Raymond Soudet and the Fire Commissioners proposed a large cut in the early stages of the budget process, abolishing 42 positions: 24 ambulance personnel, one fire prevention officer, one alarm maintenance man, 10 ladder company men, 3 lieutenants, 2 captains, and one deputy fire chief. After lobbying by the fire fighters, the City Council voted not to abolish the company. State aid prevented the other scheduled layoffs and the 24 ambulance employees were assigned to Fire Department duty.

Although the department's budget was increased slightly, the Fire Chief considered his fire companies too lean already. Each ladder company lost a man, which may cause undermanning from time to time. The Chief predicted that limits on capital outlays would eventually prevent him from purchasing needed equipment. Some vehicles are thirty-years old. The Chief thought investments in new equipment such as hydraulic ladders and a computer support system would be cost-effective in the long run. But the costs of borrowing prevent such long-range planning. The Chief argued that the Mayor has continually slighted the department on pay raises and equipment replacement. The Chief said that fire fighters felt unappreciated by the public. He predicted that declining morale might result in work slow-downs or declining service quality.

The Police Department's General Fund budget rose from $9,264,591 in FY81 to $9,468,991 in FY82. With federal revenue sharing funds creating new positions, the department's budget rose from $10,689,591 in FY81 to $11,468,991 in FY82, an increase of 7.2 percent. The budget includes 29 new officer positions, approved before Proposition 2 1/2, but funded in September 1981.

## Impacts on Other Departments

According to the Director of Personnel, Joseph Dougherty, Springfield's affirmative action efforts have not suffered as a result of vacancies or layoffs. However, the City Solicitor disagreed. Currently, minorities comprise 19 percent of the city's workforce, while making-up 21 percent of its population. Both the Police and Fire departments remain well below these percentage proportions and are experiencing difficulties in fulfilling court-ordered hiring goals. Also, 16 minority School Department employes have taken their layoffs to the Massachusetts Commission Against Discrimination.

The city's Personnel Department is a center for management innovation. For example, the department has achieved "large savings" in workman's compensation through closer monitoring of claims from employees and doctors. Director Dourgherty hopes to decentralize fiscal accountability for workman's compensation to department heads to create further savings. The department has developed an Employee Assistance Program to counsel employees on ways to improve their job performances. To continue its development of such reforms, the Personnel Department staff was increased 50 percent to 15 employees.

Not surprisingly, revaluation caused a 19% increase in the Assessor's Department budget from $650,801 to $776,825. However, the department abolished the positions of four clerks, and significantly increased the amount of work it contracts out to private firms.

In the Municipal Water Department, 25 positions which were vacant when the hiring freeze was instituted, were abolished by the City Council. The department's budget was reduced from $5.4 million to $4,933,358, a 8.6 percent decrease. Personnel and equipment were the main budget items affected. Manager George Sweeney said that services such as water line repair might be slower.

The city's local Waste Water facilities absorbed a $189,637, or 14 percent, reduction. Its FY82 budget was $1,357,000.

Springfield's Municipal Hospital supplements its budget with Medicare and Medicaid reimbursements. After hospital officials claimed that the city's initial plans to cut the hospital budget would make the hospital "unprofitable," the Council restored the proposed cuts. After public safety, the hospital had priority for about $700,000 of the state aid funds. Thus, the hospital budget was increased 5 percent ($370,833) to $7,767,911 for FY82. The personnel budget was decreased, but the budgets for contracted services and supplies were increased.

The Health Department's budget was increased $12,457 to $917,566, a 1.4 percent increase.

## Impacts on Labor Relations

There was some speculation that when the city began collective bargaining with all 17 units in late 1981, Proposition 2 1/2 would have altered the balance of power in favor of the city. Loss of binding arbitration combined with the city's limited ability to raise revenues, will seriously undermine the efficacy of the collective bargaining process, according to one union spokesman. The city now has a fixed figure for departments in advance of negotiations, he argued, while union leaders, also under pressure, attempt to secure wage increases that will offset inflation. Union spokesmen said public employees might consider work slowdowns and strikes in the absence of binding arbitration, as they did before it was enacted in 1974.

The city's May budget permitted no raises for its 3,000 employees. But, upon receipt of state aid, Mayor Dimauro allocated $2.1 million for a 4 percent, across-the-board wage increase. It was unlikely that increases would be distributed equally among employees -- some unions are in stronger bargaining positions than others. Because 1981 was an election year in Springfield, AFSCME and the Fire Fighters union hoped to take advantage of the Mayor's need for votes. Members of public employee unions were, therefore, irritated when the city's AFL-CIO Council endorsed the Mayor.

Union spokesmen already negotiating with the city, suggested that Proposition 2 1/2 has given the city a strong argument in limiting the costs of any agreement. The city is seeking productivity agreements and some mild give-backs in benefits and rights. Among the latter are tighter restrictions on sick leave, pay received for time spent in court, and longevity bonuses. Solicitor James Dowd thought increasing productivity through collective bargaining agreements would be difficult. The city hoped to trade layoffs for a union waiver of seniority rights and job assignments so that management could retain its most productive employees and reassign them more efficiently. But the Police and Fire Fighters unions hoped to win on this point because the public opposes layoffs in public safety departments.

Other unions, such as AFSCME Local No. 910 will accept layoffs to obtain better wage agreements. All unions sought 8-10 percent wage increases and none intended to receive less than the others.

The president of AFSCME Local No. 1596, Thomas Sullivan, thought three main labor relations problems have resulted from Proposition 2 1/2. First, reductions in the number of city employees means more work for those remaining, resulting in morale and job classification problems. Second, if people are not promoted for doing more work, they will demand wage increases. Third, city employees now depend on state aid for funds to provide wage increases. This makes the state's allocation an all-important issue and undercuts local bargaining. It puts AFSCME in the uncomfortable position of representing both city and state employees, who will then be competing for state funds. Within the union, Proposition 2 1/2 has created conflicts between older and younger employees, between those better and less well paid, between those with more and less seniority. In general, AFSCME members are demanding higher wages and a two-year contract to avoid next year's pressure for a trade-off between layoffs and wage increases.

Kevin Coyle, counsel for the International Brotherhood of Police Officers, considered the loss of binding arbitration the main problem for the police union. Its loss puts extra pressure on the bargaining sessions. The union's bargaining package will be as demanding as those in past years and union members are willing to sacrifice positions to obtain wage increases. They did not favor hiring 29 new officers this year, because they thought it would diminish their ability to negotiate a pay raise. Apparently, they will not protect the new officers from layoffs. Coyle thought the voters wanted service cuts when they endorsed Proposition 2 1/2, not the institution of substandard wages. Productivity will not be an issue for the Police Department since management already has considerable flexibility in assigning jobs.

In general, the unions seek wage and benefit increases rather than job security. A common bargaining front did not develop out of their anti-2 1/2 coalition activities, although unions marched together on Solidarity Day. Still, they have not devised a common strategy beyond lobbying the state legislature for more local aid.

## Impacts on Development

Two businessmen deeply involved in Springfield's commercial and industrial development, David Starr (publisher of the city's newspapers and president of Springfield Central) and Donald Binns (director of two industrial development corporations and vice-president of the Chamber of Commerce), thought Proposition 2 1/2 would not hamper the city's economic growth. Starr said the city's downtown commercial revitalization plan, well underway, "can't be touched" by Proposition 2 1/2. The city won a crucial federal grant (UDAG) in September 1981, suggesting that such funds are still available. Moreover, the city, allied with Springfield Central and the Chamber of Commerce, has become extremely adept at securing state and federal money. Starr was confident that the city could compete even if funds were reduced.

On the other hand, Proposition 2 1/2 has brought the city's involvement in industrial development to a halt -- at least temporarily. One major project is stymied by the city's inability to increase its tax revenues and official wariness about the public's reaction to borrowing for public improvements related to the project.

Although Donald Binns was confident of the continuing cooperation of Mayor Dimauro and the City Councillors, he thought Proposition 2 1/2 had encouraged developers to look for new ways of doing things. The Chamber of Commerce has urged city officials to consider themselves entrepreneurs, investing public revenues in private development projects with the prospect of earning returns greater than projected tax revenues over a five-year period.

In general, the idea of the city as entrepreneur was enthusiastically supported by a number of officials. Mayor Dimauro delivered an address favoring public sector entrepreneurship. Other city officials, including several City Councillors, support this approach, although they are uncertain how extensively the city can or should risk public revenues. Councillor Richard Neal, who co-sponsored a city resolution with Councillor Mary Hurley to establish tax incentive zones in Springfield, thought the city "should get away from the idea of federal programs. We can do some of this stuff on our own. It has to be self-help." Coming to grips with the implications of 2 1/2 for the city's long term economic development will be the main concern in FY83.

## Notes for Chapter 20

1. During the research for this study, Springfield held elections for Mayor, City Council, and School Committee. Because of the elections, the Budget Director, the Police Chief, and the Director of the Department of Public Works did not make themselves available for interviews, making it difficult to report the city's complete fiscal strategy in the first year of Proposition 2 1/2.

Chapter 21

# Wayland: Dealing with Uncertainty

Andrew Laing

## Introduction

Wayland is an affluent suburban community located 17 miles from Boston. From a population of 4,407 in 1950, the town grew to 13,461 in 1970 and declined to 12,633 by 1980. People were attracted by the town's quiet rural character (zoning laws have prevented tract development), the high quality of its school system, and its lack of industry. Many residents work for high technology firms along the western edge of greater metropolitan Boston. The town's population growth resulted in an expansion of the school system and other public services. (School enrollments peaked in 1971 at 4,000 students and declined to 2,603 by 1980.) Tax rates increased, stabilizing only in the late 1970's. But Wayland's citizens have supported a large town debt in the past to pay for a school system of renowned quality and a high level of other services. The lack of industry and commerce means the town's tax base is mainly residential.

The tax levy in Wayland rose from $5,389,379 in 1970 to $9,973,000 in 1980. In 1974, the town was reassessed to reach full and fair cash value. By 1981, however, the Finance Committee reported that Wayland's assessment ratio had fallen to 50 percent. The town was scheduled to reassess its property once more in 1982. Town officials expect reassessment to double the town's value from $230,705,328 to an estimated $456,500,000, substantially greater than the state's equalized valuation of $345,700,000.

Over the last five years, Wayland has operated on a tight budget. In 1978, the Finance Committee attempted to stabilize the tax rate and prevent further escalation of the town's budget. Members of the Finance Committee were concerned that Wayland's taxes were higher than those of other comparable towns. They discovered that, compared with similar towns, Wayland had fewer children in private schools, resulting in high public school spending. The comparison also showed that because the average cost of housing in Wayland was lower, its tax base was smaller. In addition, state aid to Wayland had declined, partly because the state allocated less for local aid (as it attempted to balance its own budget), and partly bacause the state's school aid formula penalized Wayland for its growing assessed value. Since 1978, the town has practiced fiscal restraint, reducing its personnel level from 204 employees to 130 in 1981, and stabilizing its tax rate. At 50 percent of full value, the tax rate was $44.60 per thousand in FY80; it was $45.00 in FY81; at 100 percent of full value, town officials expect it to be $23.30.

Wayland's tax rate has been close to 2 1/2 percent of value. Using the town's current estimate of its value ($230,705,328), the overall loss of property and excise taxes mandated by Proposition 2 1/2 would be about $557,000 for FY82, or 5 percent. The Finance Committee was pessimistic about state aid, based on previous years' experience, and projected a reduction of $200,000. The Committee expected a 6 percent reduction in total revenues. But the town was able to calculate its FY82 tax levy with a higher valuation. The actual loss of revenue was 3 percent.

Several groups in Wayland actively opposed Proposition 2 1/2 before November 1980, notably school teachers and the League of Women Voters. They were supported by many parents of school-age children and some public employees. Just before the vote, the Finance Committee issued a statement condemning the tax limitation measure.

### The Budget Process

Wayland has an open town meeting form of government, with a traditionally powerful Finance Committee whose members are appointed by the Selectmen. The Finance Committee usually begins its budget work by setting financial targets for each department. Department heads then prepare budgets based on these figures and present them either directly to the Finance Committee or, if under its authority, to the Board of Selectmen. The Selectmen's departments work closely with the Executive Secretary before presenting their budgets. The Selectmen forward department budgets to the Finance Committee, which makes recommendations on them to the Town Meeting.

Most town officers agreed that this year's procedures differed from those of the past only in the uncertainty inherent in projecting total revenues, which created problems in setting financial targets for the departments. The town's assessed value was continually negotiated with the state right up until Town Meeting. The uncertainty over revenues was compounded by an indefinite state aid estimate.

Soon after the vote on Proposition 2 1/2, the Finance Committee requested all town departments including the School Department to prepare budgets reduced 10 percent from FY81. These budgets were supposed to reflect inflation, contractual wage increases, and mandated costs. The 10 percent cutback was based on conservative estimates of excise tax revenue losses, state aid, and increased fixed costs. These preliminary budgets were intended to provide the Finance Committee with an understanding of how services would be affected by such a cut and to indicate sources of alternative financial support such as fees.

The Finance Committee did not tell department heads how to rank services in reducing their budgets. However, Committee members believed that health, education, and public safety were the town's priority services, but they wanted budget reductions to be "reflected appropriately" throughout all town departments. Members of the Finance Committee thought their responsibility was to decide overall policy and avoid getting bogged down in the financial minutiae of each town department. They wanted department heads to prepare budgets that could be sustained in the long-run. The Finance Committee discouraged departmental cutbacks that could only be implemented or effective one time.

The Finance Committee notified the Selectmen of its request for reduced departmental budgets. The members of both boards had agreed, early on, to present a united front at the Town Meeting. Although the Finance Committee had requested 10 percent budget reductions, town officials assumed they would be able to use a higher assessment value to set the tax rate for FY82. In short, they expected a total budget reduction of less than 5 percent.

Initially, town officials thought a full-fledged reassessment of the town's property would be unnecessary. From November 1980 to January 1981, the Finance Committee hoped to "factor up" the town's 50 percent level of assessed value to 100 percent and halve the tax rate to achieve the equivalent of "full and fair" value. Town officials met twice with representatives of the Department of Revenue. State officials agreed that it should be possible for Wayland to use this procedure since property values had not increased greatly since the last reassessment.

By February, Wayland's financial situation appeared to be improving. The Finance Committee had better information on cherry sheet charges, pension costs, and motor vehicle excise tax revenues. Department heads had discussed their informal budgets with, and submitted them to, the Finance Committee. The Finance Committee was more optimistic about being able to "factor up" the town's assessment value, and state aid looked better than anticipated. The Committee asked department heads to revise their budgets, assuming a 5 percent cut.

By this time, the Finance Committee and the Selectmen agreed that reductions should vary among departments. In consultation with the public safety department heads, the Selectmen decided not to cut their departments as much as others and scheduled a 4 percent increase in public safety expenditures.

Although Wayland's total town budget was reduced 3 percent, its overall operating budget was cut 5.4 percent. Departmental budget reductions varied greatly. For instance, the Highway Department's budget was eventually reduced 23 percent; Health, 7 percent; Parks and Recreation, 10.3 percent; the Regional Vocational School, 8.8 percent; General Government, 5.6 percent; School Department, 5 percent; and Libraries, 10.13 percent. These differences arose because the average 5 percent reduction was predicated on "normal" budget figures for FY81, which excluded one-time capital expenditures or unique and extraordinary items. Thus, the Highway Department's cutback was based on a FY81 budget figure, reduced by $146,000 in capital expenditures; Parks and Recreation's "extra" 5 percent cut resulted from the transfer of many of its programs to a fee-supported structure. Another major exception to the prescribed pattern was the 38 percent increase in "Unclassified" budget expenditures, attributable to the rising costs of health and building insurance.

The Finance Committee was prepared for the Town Meeting in April, when the Department of Revenue decided not to allow Wayland to "factor up" its assessments to 100 percent. The Department would only permit the town to use its equalized valuation of $345,700,000. A major crisis ensued when the Selectmen and the Finance Committee concluded that the state's equalized valuation would entail further budget reductions of $800,000. The budget process came to an abrupt halt; the Town Meeting was postponed as the Finance Committee and the Selectmen pondered a solution to this reversal of their budget plans.

The Finance Committee and the Selectmen called a Special Town Meeting to vote on a warrant providing for the immediate reassessment of the town's property. The warrant passed, enabling the budget Town Meeting to commence on the assumption that revaluation would double the current assessed value, again, yielding a tax rate reduced by half. (Had the Special Town Meeting voted not to reassess, the Finance Committee would have further delayed the budget Town Meeting until department heads could revise their budgets to absorb the $800,000 reduction.) The Department of Revenue approved Wayland's decision to reassess and allowed estimated tax bills, based on an estimate of reassessed value, to be sent out prior to the completion of revaluation. Hearings on the results of the reassessment were scheduled for November 1981.

The Town Meeting was held in May. No major changes were made in the budgets -- $30,000 was restored to one of the school's language programs and $29,000 was added to the police budget to fund a youth officer and another patrolman.

On the whole, Wayland's FY82 budget process was not unusual. The Selectmen were more involved than usual in financial considerations, especially in assisting the Finance Committee in its negotiations with the state. A more detailed understanding of the budget reductions may be gained by a closer look at some departmental budgets.

## Impacts on the Police Department

In FY79, the Police Department lost an officer and in FY80, eliminated school crossing guards. The department was level-funded in FY81 and received a 4 percent increase in FY82. Despite the increase, the Chief proposed eliminating a youth officer position and transferring $68,000 to a separate budget set up by the Selectmen for funding the new Joint Communications Center, to be shared with the Fire Department. The Selectmen approved this budget, but at Town Meeting, citizens voted to re-fund the youth officer position and hire a new patrolman.

## Impacts on the Fire Department

The Fire Department has also experienced budget reductions, resulting in fewer fire fighters responding to alarms and less money allocated for overtime. There are presently 24 fire fighters in the department.

Although the Joint Communications Center was planned before Proposition 2 1/2 passed, members of the fire fighters union associated it with the anti-union sentiment they perceive in connection with Proposition 2 1/2. Because the Center employs civilian staff, a fire fighter will be released from the dispatcher's position and the department's overtime allocation for this position will be eliminated. The union attempted to prevent the implementation of the Center by court injunction. This was later overturned by the State Appeals Court following the town's petition.

## Impacts on the School Department

When Proposition 2 1/2 passed, a draft school budget had already been prepared. For a few weeks, the School Committee was unsure what the new law entailed. In December, the School Committee met with the Finance Committee to discuss Proposition 2 1/2's implications and then began to prepare a budget reduced by 10 percent.

The Superintendent of Schools, William Zimmerman, urged the School Committee to prepare a budget only slightly reduced, because he thought it would be best to await amendments to, or an override of, Proposition 2 1/2. Zimmerman feared that radical changes in school programs would cause a flight of children to private schools. Overruling Zimmerman, the School Committee insisted that Proposition 2 1/2 be dealt with as a long-term mandate.

The School Committee agreed that the first cuts in the school budget should be made in areas such as transportation, cafeteria service, and maintenance. Second-order cuts would be made in services such as guidance counselling, library services, and administration. If further cuts were needed, they would be made in classroom activities. The Committee tried to avoid layoffs and maintain instructional programs. It was unable to substitute any federal or state funds for local funds, or close buildings to cut back (which had been done previously in response to declining enrollments).

Meetings of the School and Finance Committees generated some friction over the School Committee's lost fiscal autonomy. The Chairman of the Finance Committee reported: "We wanted to meet in the Finance Committee room. The School Committee wouldn't do it. They would not come to the Finance Committee room to discuss their budget. We would not go to their room. . . . We wanted them to understand that we were going to tell them how much money they could spend, and we were going to make it stick from the very beginning. So we asked them for a 5 percent reduction and they said they could live with it."

Despite the problems of adjusting to new relationships, the school budget process was not characterized by conflict. The teachers' contract, signed in June 1981, was not affected by the cutback. School officials emphasized that the groups involved, including the parents' organizations, supported the school's strategy for cutting back.

## Impacts of 2 1/2 on Wayland

Wayland's overall 3 percent reduction placed it among those towns least affected by Proposition 2 1/2. The town's personnel loss was limited to 40: 35 from the School Department (5 of whom would have been dropped because of declining enrollment), one from the Highway Department, one from the library system, one from General Government. Four-and-a-half nursing positions were transferred from the town's payroll to the local Parmenter Health Center, and services needed by the town will be purchased from the Center. Twenty part-time and seasonal positions in the Parks and Recreation Department will either be phased out or sustained by fees. Town officials feared that fewer public employees would result in slower handling of public business.

The Board of Health will no longer collect garbage for the town, since this service was used by few residents. (A motion to restore this service was defeated at Town Meeting.) Use of the Town Building is being restricted to two evenings a week.

Wayland's fees were last changed by state statute in 1959. The general upgrading of Town Clerk's fees will result in an additional $4,000 for the town, while other fees are expected to raise another $10,000, exclusive of fee supported programs. The Park and Recreation Department's extension of user fees is expected to raise $42,164. The Highway Department proposed charging a fee to residents using its dump, but the Finance Committee refused the proposal because using the dump is compulsory.

Library officials eliminated some special services and will purchase far fewer books than in previous years. The funds previously available to the Planning Board and the Conservation Commission to retain the services of professional consultants have been reduced severely. The Highway Department deferred the purchase of equipment this year and eliminated services such as oiling roads and clearing up culverts and streams. Road maintenance, while never a high priority in Wayland, was forced further down the list.

The Police and Fire Chiefs both thought their departmental services were unaffected by Proposition 2 1/2. The Police Chief reduced his overtime budget which might make it difficult to maintain minimum-manning. Members of the Fire Fighters union thought Proposition 2 1/2 was being used against the Fire Department to reduce its responsibility and overtime allocation for the new Joint Communications Center. They also claimed that Proposition 2 1/2 would lower their wage settlement in contract negotiations this year.

The impacts of Proposition 2 1/2 have probably been felt most in Wayland's school system. The Superintendent said that the maintenance accounts were "decimated," that there is no money for new books or equipment, and very little for general supplies. Class sizes have increased slightly at the junior and senior high levels. Of 157 teachers for general instruction, 16 have been lost. Of 23 special education instructors, 2 have been lost. The library and guidance staffs each lost a half position. Of 90 noncertified positions (custodial, secretarial, etc.), 14 were lost. Meal prices at the school cafeteria have increased. Curriculum development over the summer months was eliminated.

More subtle impacts on the town were cited in the Report of the Finance Committee: "The unremitting pressure of tightening budgets and decreased flexibility in services available in the town is creating an effect which cannot be seen in budget projections and cannot be defined in terms of effect on the tax rate. That is the declining level of support services available to volunteer town government participants. As they find it more and more difficult to fulfill their tasks because of a lack of assisting personnel, volunteers are less and less willing to remain involved."

Wayland's officials did not respond to Proposition 2 1/2 with managerial reform. (The town's offices were reorganized as recently as 1979). The Joint Communications Center is the forerunner of a Public Safety Department, and there is discussion of combining Highways and Park and Recreation to form a Department of Public Works. However, neither of these reorganizations is directly associated with Proposition 2 1/2.

Town officials thought the town's reserve funds would become more difficult to manage, with less margin for error. They predicted more departmental budget overruns. The School Department had already run into financial trouble, citing a budget error that will require $44,000 in additional funding. (It assumed that the state would fund the transportation of handicapped adults to sheltered workshops. However, the state cancelled this funding. In addition, an arbitration award against the School Committee required another $18,000.) The Chairman of the Finance Committee viewed the School Department's problems as symptomatic of what happens when departments try to administer tight budgets: "The School Department is telling us that they made an error in their budgeting. They wouldn't have told us that in the past; they just would have coped with it."

By far, the largest number of complaints about the new town budget, received by the Executive Secretary, concerns the additional day per week that the town dump is closed.

The impact of Proposition 2 1/2 on labor relations does not seem to have been significant. The troubles in the Fire Department cannot be associated directly with the new law. None of the town's labor contracts were re-opened for negotiation. The loss of binding arbitration was not considered a major issue -- except by the Fire Fighters union -- because this mode of dispute was rarely used in Wayland. Some observers suggested that the attitudes and assumptions the negotiating parties have about Proposition 2 1/2 might affect contract settlements in the future.

The budgetary power of groups in the town does not seem to have been affected either. Members of the Fire Fighters union thought Proposition 2 1/2 gave management more confidence and power in departmental negotiations. The Superintendent of Schools considered the School Committee's loss of fiscal autonomy the result of fiscal constraint more than a legal change, in the sense that effective autonomy is destroyed by budget reductions. But others noted that the School Committee still maintained control over the details of the school budget and town officials agreed that Wayland's residents will continue to support a high quality school system. Finally, the working relationship between the Finance Committee and the Board of Selectmen was strengthened by the budget activities of both this year.

## The Future

Town officials expected the legislature to modify Proposition 2 1/2 before the next fiscal year, so that no further cuts would be necessary. Otherwise, Wayland faces another budget reduction of $200,000, which will almost certainly mean layoffs in the School, Police, and Fire departments.

Unless enrollments continue to decline, the Superintendent of Schools argued that the school system cannot survive another cutback. Restoring the maintenance account, purchasing new text books and supplies, and meeting salary increases would cost about $600,000, he estimated. The Superintendent hoped no radical changes would have to be made in the school budget to avoid layoffs next year.

Revaluation allowed Wayland to avoid the debilitating effects of Proposition 2 1/2 in FY82. The state certified Wayland's assessed valuation at $474 million, and the town chose a tax rate of $22.40, providing a tax levy of $10,617,000 (slightly less than the FY81 levy). Local officials rejected classification. The most remarkable aspect of the budget process in Wayland was how awkward and disruptive even a "small" reduction of 3 percent was for a town that is relatively well-endowed.

# Part Four

## Analysis and Interpretation

Chapter 22

# Understanding How and Why the Most Drastic
# Cuts Were Avoided

Lawrence Susskind and Cynthia Horan

## Introduction

"In what may be a transcendant political development of the 1980's Massachusetts now rivals California as a laboratory for supply-side economic theory..." wrote Rowland Evans and Robert Novack in their column on July 21, 1981. (1) But the catalyst for this alleged "political transformation," Proposition 2 1/2, prompted predictions of disaster as frequently as words of praise. In July 1981, the Massachusetts Department of Revenue estimated that the law's mandated cuts in property and automobile excise taxes would cost cities and towns $482 million in FY82 alone. (2) It also projected that the distribution of tax losses would be very uneven. Forty-three of the state's 351 municipalities -- including its largest cities and the state capital, Boston -- faced property tax reductions of 45 percent. Others faced no losses at all. Moreover, unlike California when Proposition 13 was passed, Massachusetts had no state budget surplus. Walter V. Robinson, a reporter for the *Boston Globe*, dubbed Proposition 2 1/2 "shock therapy for politicians who are comfortable adding programs and increasing spending but uncomfortable eliminating programs and slashing spending." (3)

More than a year after voters approved Proposition 2 1/2 by a three-to-two margin, evaluations of its consequences are just becoming available. However, this paper offers a different perspective. In June 1981, the IMPACT: 2 1/2 Project staff initiated case studies of the budget processes in thirteen cities and towns. We were interested in the ways that communities facing large tax rollbacks went about the task of deciding where and how to cut. We set out to learn how Proposition 2 1/2 constrained budget-making in various municipalities; how local officials attempted to preserve or cut particular programs and personnel; whether and how power shifted in budget-making;

and, finally, how officials, employees, and citizens viewed Proposition 2 1/2s immediate consequences. From June to December 1981, seven M.I.T. graduate students interviewed local officials, employees, representatives of the poor and minorities, neighborhood activists, service providers, the press, and business spokesmen. They also reviewed secondary sources such as newspapers budgets, and planning documents. Thirteen case studies emerged -- they contain the most detailed accounts of Proposition 2 1/2 yet published.

This paper summarizes our major findings. Its initial section explains the methods used to select our study sites and structure our interviews. In the second section we summarize how the severe budget cuts feared initially were prevented. The third and fourth sections characterize the process of budget-making and the apparent consequences of the first year's budget cuts. The final section speculates on the key factors shaping the longer term effects of Proposition 2 1/2 -- federal budget cuts, changes in the state aid formula, and the shifting business climate.

## Selecting Study Sites

For the purposes of our monitoring effort, we did not choose a representative sample of cities and towns but selected municipalities facing large revenue losses. Municipalities with the largest revenue cuts, we reasoned, would face the greatest problems, and would have to make the greatest adjustments in budgeting practices.

Several other concerns shaped our selection procedures. It seemed crucial to analyze the state's largest cities: all eight faced large revenue losses. Springfield and Cambridge were chosen to represent this group. The former is the state's third largest city and its location in the western part of the state provides representation of cities outside the Boston SMSA. Cambridge is a racially diverse, politically active, and reputedly well-managed city.

In choosing the remaining sites, we used a set of "hardship" indicators: percentage property tax reduction mandated by Proposition 2 1/2; per capita income, 1970; per capita expenditure, 1980; population growth, 1970-1980; and residential share of the tax levy. We applied these indicators to all municipalities in the state with populations over 2,000. Next, scales were developed for each indicator. For example, in scaling the residential share indicator, municipalities receiving 50 percent or less of their property tax levy from residential uses were classed as low; those receiving between 51-80 percent, as moderate; those receiving greater than 80 percent, as high. Municipalities were then categorized for all five indicators.

Our next step was to select combinations of categories and then municipalities which represented those combinations. One set included high tax loss, low income, and high per capita expenditure municipalities: municipalities that we assumed would be hurt severely. Quincy, Salem, and Chelsea were chosen from this group. A second set included high tax loss, high income, high per capita expenditure municipalities: rich localities with high levels of services.

Wayland, Burlington, and Marshfield represented this group. (While similar in tax loss, income, and service levels, these towns have varying growth rates and property tax base characteristics.) A third set of municipalities includes fast-growing towns with varying tax losses, incomes, and expenditure levels: Amesbury, Sandwich, and Bridgewater. Finally, since this selection process yielded mostly suburban sites, we decided to add places that were neither suburbs nor big cities -- i.e., Arlington and Framingham. In sum, the case study sites represent high revenue loss communities and of those, municipalities with low per capita incomes and high per capita expenditures.

## Case Study Design

Our primary objective was to analyze the FY82 budget process. We were interested in how people thought about what they were doing as well as what they did. We relied extensively on interviews, newspaper accounts, and analyses of budget documents.

The overall study design consists of several components. First, in order to place the FY82 decision process in context, we collected information about influential groups, economic changes, spending and taxing patterns, and assessment practices. Past budget controversies were investigated. Key actors were identified.

Each case study, then, includes a reconstruction of the FY82 budget process. Since most of our case study communities faced FY82 property tax levy limits below their FY81 property tax levies, we assumed we would be studying "cutback" budgeting. We asked several broad questions to analyze this component. Did local officials attempt to reduce expenditures without cutting services, for example, by enhancing productivity through management reforms? Or did they look for new revenues to replace property tax and motor vehicle excise tax losses? If forced to cut, what criteria did they use for making cuts? Did they cut capital expenditures rather than operating expenditures? Did they utilize across-the-board cuts or attempt to assess the relative benefits and costs of different programs? Who defined these alternatives? Were there conflicts or disagreements over the choice of strategies? How successful were the tactics employed in meeting the locality's budget problem?

Tied to our analysis of decision-making was an effort to understand shifting power relations. Who made the key decisions? Who opposed them? Did local officials encourage broad public participation in budget-making?

We also attempted to assess Proposition 2 1/2s short- and long-term impacts. We assumed that spokesmen for competing interests in the same municipality would disagree in their predictions of impacts. Nevertheless, it seemed important to understand how these decision-makers viewed the consequences of their choices. Thus, we probed for views on two potentially negative outcomes: the service losses of those most reliant on the public sector (the poor, minorities, the young, and the elderly) and job losses. We also asked about tax savings, improvements in government efficiency, and changes in the climate for private investment.


## Preventing the Worst

In the end, local officials did not have to make the deep cuts that had been predicted. In the next section we will describe how efficiency measures and the imposition of new fees and charges helped prevent a portion of the cuts. Revaluation, state aid increases, and hiring freezes, however, were the major elements in avoiding deep cuts.

At the outset of the FY82 budget process, most of the case study communities faced significant immediate, as well as long-run, revenue losses. Eight faced several years of property tax reductions; four others faced a one-year property tax reduction plus substantial losses in excise taxes, as indicated in Table 22.1. Even Sandwich, with a tax rate below 2.5 percent, expected a significant rollback since Proposition 2 1/2 originally required it to utilize its 1979 tax rate of $14.50, almost $4.00 less than its 1981 tax rate of $18.40. The rate would have produced a property tax loss of $1.5 million, about one-sixth of the FY81 levy in addition to an excise tax loss of $200,000. Given these restrictions local officials began the budget process requesting significant cuts. Arlington's Town Manager asked for 30 percent cuts; Cambridge's Manager, for 25 percent cuts; Chelsea's Mayor, 28 percent cuts. Burlington, Bridgewater, and Framingham officials asked for 15 percent cuts. But no budget was actually reduced by these percentages.

Revaluation permitted higher than expected levy limits. None of the case study towns had been certified at full and fair value. On January 1, 1980, the Department of Revenue calculated assessment ratios (6) for the case study communities as shown in Table 22.2. Seven of the localities were scheduled to revalue in FY82. Five communities increased the value of their tax bases substantially as shown in Table 22.3 (Quincy and Cambridge have not finished their reassessments as of this writing). These higher values resulted in substantially higher levy limits. Burlington will now probably have a limit higher than its FY81 property tax levy. Marshfield, Wayland, Framingham and Amesbury lost almost no property taxes. (The Department of Revenue's decision to increase 1980 equalized values by an inflation factor or 13 percent, meant that Sandwich faced a tax loss of about $340,000 instead of $1.5 million). (Wayland chose a tax rate lower than 2.5 percent.) In all five towns, local officials remained uncertain about their levy limits while finalizing their budgets. Not until fall 1981 did the Department of Revenue decide that municipalities in the process of revaluation could send out estimated tax bills as long as revaluation was completed by February 1982. Thus, all five towns went through a process of cutting, although the cuts were gradually scaled down. In Burlington, for instance, officials used a very conservative assessment figure and scheduled severe cuts, despite the ultimate hike in property values.

Case study communities slated to revalue in FY83 count on revaluation to soften future cutbacks. Arlington officials predict that the town will be

### Table 22.1
### Property and Excise Tax Losses

|  | Property tax Rollback (millions) | % of FY81 Property tax levy | Excise tax loss (millions) |
|---|---|---|---|
| Cambridge | 47.60 | 60.0 | 2.70 |
| Chelsea | 10.00 | 69.0 | 0.40 |
| Quincy | 34.00 | 51.0 | 1.60 |
| Salem | 9.20 | 37.0 | 1.00 |
| Springfield | 31.00 | 50.0 | 3.17 |
| Amesbury | 1.65 | 28.0 | 0.30 |
| Arlington | 9.40 | 30.0 | 1.50 |
| Bridgewater | 1.32 | 19.0 | 0.45 |
| Marshfield | 1.50 | 12.5 | 0.70 |
| Framingham | 8.50 | 15.0 | 2.50 |
| Burlington | 0.30 | 15.0 | 1.00 |
| Wayland | 0.26 | 2.5 | 0.30 |

### Table 22.2
### Assessment Ratios

| Cities |  | Towns |  |
|---|---|---|---|
| Cambridge | 26% | Arlington | 46% |
| Chelsea | 37 | Bridgewater | 29 |
| Quincy | 24 | Burlington | 49 |
| Salem | 20 | Framingham | 51 |
| Springfield | 52 | Marshfield | 37 |
|  |  | Sandwich | 94 |
|  |  | Wayland | 66 |

## Table 22.3
## FY82 Certified Reassessments

|  | 1980 State EQV (millions) | FY82 full valuation (millions) |
|---|---|---|
| Amesbury | 151 | 226 |
| Framingham | 1,300 | 1,600 |
| Burlington | 701 | 860 |
| Marshfield | 354 | 520 |
| Wayland | 349 | 474 |

certified at $1.2 billion, a 30 percent increase over its equalized value of $887 million. This valuation would permit a FY83 levy limit higher than the FY82 levy. Some Cambridge officials hope to add one billion dollars to their $1.3 billion valuation. The four other cities expect fewer gains from reassessment. Chelsea's tax rate is so high that despite an expected 67 percent increase in valuation, it will still have to cut its levy by 48 percent. Officials in Quincy, Salem, and Springfield do not project substantial increases over the state's equalized value, but they do worry that revaluation will shift tax burdens and raise residential property tax bills. The Department of Revenue has slated all five cities for 15 percent cuts.

State aid yielded a second unexpected source of revenue. Since Governor Edward King initially proposed only $37.5 million in new financial assistance to local governments (one-tenth of their projected revenue loss), local officials were quite pessimistic. Legislative wrangling added to their uncertainty. Budgets were drawn up assuming that there would be no additional state aid; some municipalities actually predicted decreases. Arlington officials factored in a projected state aid figure, but then prepared a second budget without that amount. Not until July 1981 did the legislature agree to add $265 million in local assistance. Thus, it was not until fall that local officials decided how to distribute these additional aid funds.

Table 22.4 shows the differences between FY81 and FY82 state aid allocations, as well as the percentages of the total Proposition 2 1/2 revenue loss replaced by net cherry sheet aid (i.e., the difference between 1982 aid and 1982 charges for state, county, and other purposes). While Table 22.4 demonstrates that all the case study localities obtained more aid this year, it also shows the wide range of aid increases. More interestingly, the table indicates the great differences in the replacement of lost revenue. While Wayland received 117 percent of its revenue loss, Cambridge and Burlington received only 12 percent. A similar range exists statewide. While 156 localities received more than their Proposition 2 1/2 revenue losses, 53 others received less than 25 percent. (7) (In February 1982, the Massachusetts Taxpayers

Foundation reported that in the 222 localities that had set their tax rates by December 31, 1981, additional state aid replaced 64 percent of their property tax reductions.) (8) This pattern exists because, unlike the California legislature, the Massachusetts legislature did not replace a specific fraction of each community's revenue loss, but rather distributed assistance using a pre-existing local aid formula. (9)

Not all localities had allocated their state aid by the end of 1981. In most places, officials restored funding for the least popular cuts -- layoffs of policemen and fire fighters. Arlington officials rescinded a wage freeze; Salem officials decided to refund school transportation; Springfield officials turned on more of the city's street lights. Not all localities funded operating budgets. Burlington and Sandwich officials retained layoffs and established stabilization funds as a cushion against future cuts.

**Table 22.4**
**State Aid**

| | FY81 State Aid Receipts (millions) | FY82 State Aid Receipts (millions) | Percentage Difference | % Revenue Loss Replaced by Net State Aid |
|---|---|---|---|---|
| Cambridge | 14.888 | 17.220 | 16 | 13 |
| Chelsea | 6.963 | 9.616 | 38 | 98 |
| Quincy | 12.734 | 16.499 | 30 | 31 |
| Salem | 5.646 | 6.816 | 21 | 28 |
| Springfield | 52.964 | 60.962 | 15 | 56 |
| Amesbury | 3.668 | 4.245 | 16 | 46 |
| Arlington | 5.997 | 7.696 | 28 | 24 |
| Bridgewater | 2.196 | 3.667 | 70 | 99 |
| Burlington | 3.690 | 0.951 | 16 | 12 |
| Framingham | 9.108 | 10.972 | 20 | 23 |
| Marshfield | 3.368 | 4.200 | 27 | 32 |
| Sandwich | 1.863 | 1.975 | 6 | 25 |
| Wayland | 2.452 | 2.728 | 11 | 117 |

Sources: Masachusetts DOR; Massachusetts Taxpayers Foundation, Municipal Financial Data, 1982.

Finally, local officials used hiring freezes to make reductions in the work force. All case study municipalities, except Marshfield, imposed a hiring freeze soon after Proposition 2 1/2 passed. Marshfield, along with Wayland, Bridgewater, and Quincy, had instituted departmental hiring freezes after the state's 4 percent tax cap was enacted in 1979. Table 22.5 indicates the impact of hiring freezes in our case study communities. While attrition thinned the ranks of policemen and fire fighters, school officials had to fire substantial

Table 22.5
Comparison of Employee Losses

|            | Police | Fire | Schools |
|------------|--------|------|---------|
| Attrition  | 37     | 45   | 243     |
| Layoffs    | 2      | 40   | 1390    |

numbers of teachers, administrators, and supporting staff workers. Of the 85 fire fighting positions lost, 45 were the result of attrition. Of the 39 police positions lost, 37 resulted from attrition. Only 243 of 1,663 school positions eliminated were voluntary leaves. Of the total number of layoffs in the thirteen case study communities (1,767), only 18 percent resulted from attrition. Teacher layoffs accounted for 88 percent of all job losses. Citing the Massachusetts Division of Employment Security, the Massachusetts Municipal Association reported that of the 30,400 person reduction in municipal work forces across the state, from November 1980 to November 1981, 56 percent were the result of layoffs. (10)

Local officials cannot count on revaluation, state aid, and attrition to ease future cuts. While the amended law now permits a small levy increase as new property is added to the tax rolls, the windfall of revaluation cannot be repeated. (The levy limit can only increase at 2.5 percent annually, even though property values may increase more rapidly. Thus, higher property values will result in lower effective tax rates.) State aid is largely beyond the control of municipal decision-makers who must hope that the state will be generous with aid again next year. They are skeptical about the prospects of a major overhaul for the state-local fiscal structure. Attrition may continue to shrink the work force; it permits the loss of younger and minority workers and clearly ignores performance. Thus, it may have to be supplanted by more explicit personnel policies.

## Priority-Setting

*The Process*

In all case study communities, observers noted that fewer people than usual participated in the annual budget process Typically, a small group centered on the estimated revenue losses, determined a set of priorities and imposed budget targets on department heads. One city official aptly described the general pattern:

> We set out to cover our deficits, decide what our
> levy limit would be, and calculate our fixed costs.
> We tried to apportion our remaining funds among

> departments. We met with all department heads to
> explain the cuts, and then left it to them to
> decide what specific cuts to make. We thought
> they knew their own departmental needs.

Officials argued that uncertainty over revenue losses and state aid levels
precluded widespread consultation. Also, they feared that greater participation
would exacerbate controversy and conflict. While differences exist between
cities and towns, neither the formal assignment of budget authority, nor the
size of expected revenue losses seemed to shape the actual process. There was,
in fact, remarkable similarity among all case study sites in how their officials
managed budget-making.

In the case study cities, the mayor (or manager, in the case of
Cambridge) has legal responsibility for the budget. Legislative bodies can only
decrease the budget; they cannot increase it. In Springfield and Quincy, both
Plan A cities, city councils can abolish or create positions. However, formal
structures did not dictate the specifics of the FY82 process. In Springfield
(Plan A) and Salem (Plan B), the mayor, the budget director, one or two
department heads politically allied with the mayor, and sometimes "outside"
advisors, put the budget together. In Quincy (Plan A), Mayor Arthur Tobin
actually delegated the task to his auditors. Chelsea Mayor Joel Pressman
apparently made the most important decisions himself.

Although their budgetary authority is limited, City Councillors felt
especially excluded. More than one insisted that budget hearings were pointless
since all the cuts had been made and since the Councils cannot add to
expenditures. Many argued that a more open process would have prevented
resentment and speculation -- particularly about layoffs. (Only in Cambridge
did the normal working relationship continue as the manager drew up the
budget and negotiated with departments while the City Council focused on
finding new revenue sources.)

Town budget processes legally involve many more independent actors:
Town Manager/Administrator, Advisory Board/Finance Committee, Board of
Selectmen, Town Meeting, as well as elected and appointed boards of
semi-independent commissions. With so many actors, town officials sought to
coordinate budget information and prevent endless negotiation. As one local
official worried, "Marshfield is like an octopus. . . . The difference between
an octopus and Marshfield is that at least an octopus has a central brain to
control its tentacles.. . ." In three case study towns -- Arlington,
Framingham, and Burlington -- officials organized ad hoc groups to run the
budget process. (Two of these towns, Arlington and Burlington, have town
managers.) Such groups included the Town Manager, Chairman of the Finance
Committee, a Selectman, School Superintendent, and Town Accountant. In three
other towns, such coordination was not necessary: Wayland has a traditionally
strong Finance Committee; Sandwich, a legally powerful Board of Selectmen
(they are also the Board of Assessors and each oversees several departments);
Bridgewater, a personally dominant Board of Selectmen, with many years of

experience. In Marshfield and Amesbury, the Finance Committee and the Selectmen worked more or less harmoniously.

Agency influence over budgets declined. While maintaining their line item budget authority, few department heads established their budget limits. In very few situations did a department head convince the budget-makers to raise an appropriation. In protest over this loss of authority, many department heads refused to meet mandated cuts, forcing mayors or Advisory Boards to draw up revised line item budgets. Long-standing hostilities, particularly between mayors and school superintendents, also soured working relations.

Equally absent from budget-making were unions, service clients, and the general public. Although in almost every case study locality, unions had organized to fight the passage of Proposition 2 1/2, such coalitions collapsed after the election. None was mobilized during the budget process. Competition for funding replaced coalition-building. What public pressure there was focused most often on city councils, but even councillors remarked on the lack of general interest. The strongest public protests ocurred in Salem where high school students walked out over school cuts and residents occupied a closed fire station. Neither action prevented the projected cuts. Dissatisfied citizens were most successful when their views were shared by town officials. Library branch closings were halted in Framingham and Arlington because some Advisory Board members or Selectmen supported the public.

In fact, it is in their relation to the public (through town meetings) that town officials demonstrated the degree of control they had gained over the budget process. Whether open (Bridgewater, Sandwich, Marshfield, Wayland), or representative (Arlington, Burlington, Framingham, Amesbury), town meetings influenced expenditures and reductions surprisingly little. Officials preparing budgets worked hard to limit town meeting input. In some towns, local officials required that anyone proposing an expenditure increase at town meeting had to propose an equivalent decrease elsewhere in the budget. Town meetings were not without controversy, however. As in the past, disgruntled department heads appealed for higher aproprations. With one exception, they were refused. (In Framingham, the Public Works Commissioner threatened to halt garbage collection unless funds were restored. After his plea proved successful, several other department heads also managed to obtain increases.)

The weakened role of town meetings disturbed some participants. Even in contentious Framingham, one town meeting representative contended,

> No trade-offs or compromises were presented by
> the Finance Committee. . . . Some of us would
> like to see the cuts shared with Police and Fire,
> but this doesn't happen at town meetings.

In Marshfield, where the Selectmen and Advisory Board actually held a pre-town meeting" to hear public concerns, one official worried that Proposition 2 1/2 had done "irreparable harm" to town meetings by eliminating the "right of citizens to determine how much money would be spent and where."

*Major Budget Issues*

While the revenue losses differed, all localities went through a process of budget-cutting and secondarily sought to raise new revenues, improve efficiency, or pursue other reforms.

*Cutting.* With the exceptions of Quincy and Marshfield, local officials initiated the budget process by proposing across-the-board cuts. They claimed that such an approach maintained well-known service priorities. In some communities, officials also wanted to determine how a similar percentage cut would affect different departments. And, of course, across-the-board cutting, like attrition, postponed difficult choices.

This approach was quickly abandoned. It became evident that small departments could not absorb the cuts that larger departments could. Since departments differed in their labor-intensiveness, the meaning of across-the-board cuts differed in terms of people lost. Marshfield's attempt to set priorities foundered for the same reason. In Springfield and Cambridge, officials decided that some departments could institute new or higher user fees and could therefore lose more property tax revenues than other departments.

Abandoning across-the-board cuts did not result in careful attempts to set priorities. Budget officials often attempted to force department heads to rank programs and utilize zero-based budgeting. Such efforts, however, had little influence over budget allocations. Some department heads refused to cooperate. Others resented the allegedly competitive aspects of such procedures. Only Salem, in fact, terminated funding for 13 departments identified as "nonessential." Arlington and Salem, two municipalities that had recently conducted surveys of citizens' service preferences, did not utilize these surveys. One city budget advisor agreed with his critics that much priority-setting was nothing more than political bargaining (in part, because of the well-known difficulties of measuring and comparing the benefits of public programs.) His thoughts are echoed throughout the other cases:

> In a sense, there were no cost effective criteria. The cuts were more politically determined -- which areas were most sensitive and what you could get away with. We had certain constraints. We knew people wanted police and fire. We were also aware of declining enrollments so schools were cut fairly deeply.

> At one point, we attempted to measure the effectiveness of the fire and other departments but it was held up by politics. Performance criteria are difficult to do and take a long time. . . . It's nearly impossible. So we went through each budget, compared median salaries, the number of personnel, salaries as a percentage of the budget total, and then we made a subjective guess.

The models are nice, but the data just aren't there.

In the end, public safety was given top priority everywhere. Several towns utilized proportional cuts by imposing on the schools a share of the FY82 revenue loss equivalent to their share of the FY81 budget. School budgets were a popular target in the cities. Public Works departments were hard hit, largely because personnel costs made up a smaller portion of their budgets (and fewer layoffs were involved in cuts). Beyond these, it is difficult to generalize about priorities. "Essential" programs were defined very differently even in municipalities with seemingly similar needs. For example, while the revaluation process protected the Assessor's budget in Quincy, it did not do so in Salem or Chelsea. Libraries were a mayoral priority in Chelsea, but not in Springfield. Human service agencies fared badly; no consideration was given to likely future cutbacks in federal and state support. In fact, in cities many human services lost all their local support and were shifted to federal funds.

Within departments, attempts were made to minimize personnel cuts and to preserve basic services and functions. Such priorities were most visible in school departments which suffered the largest budget reductions. Without exception, superintendents focused cuts on non-academic programs and services. Fees were established for athletics and other extracurricular activities. Next, nonpersonnel items such as books, supplies, and maintenance was reduced. Noninstructional personnel were cut before teachers. Where academic cuts were unavoidable, they were made in electives and courses with small enrollments. Departments of public works showed similar priorities: materials budgets were reduced before personnel and seasonal personnel were laid off before permanent employees.

This selective cutting process, based on vague criteria developed by a few people, provoked dissatisfaction and resentment despite the fact that cuts were scaled down as the process continued. In four of the five cities, councillors, department heads, and union leaders quite consistently viewed the final budget as an arbitrary creation of the mayor, designed to protect patronage jobs while "desimating" basic services. In all localities, human service department heads worried that the budget process was becoming increasingly politicized and competitive and that their neediest clients would never be able to compete. In fact, they predict that the poor will compete among themselves.

*Deferring Capital Expenditures.*    Since Proposition 2 1/2 weakened municipal credit ratings in the state, deferring capital expenditures was hardly a local choice. In March 1981, four months after the law's passage, Moody's Investment Services suspended the bond ratings of 37 cities and towns in Massachusetts (including two case study sites, Cambridge and Chelsea). A survey by the Massachusetts Municipal Association reported that the number of municipal bond issues dropped from 64 in 1980 to 10 in 1981. The value of bond issues dropped from $263 million to $10 million. (11) The report called this decrease "alarming" and warned of threats to public safety and health.

The case study towns reflect this situation. While none reported a capital spending freeze most officials did not even contemplate capital expenditures this year. Two immediate problems have already emerged. Fire chiefs in several localities reported delays in purchasing new fire trucks, ladders, and other equipment. They warned of increased hazards to firemen and the public, particularly since the number of firemen had declined. Three of the five case study cities have postponed crucial water and sewer improvements as well.

Prospects for future borrowing are mixed. Two amendments to Proposition 2 1/2 attempt to improve access to the municipal bond market. One permits localities to exempt debt and interest from the levy limit. However, the Department of Revenue has issued regulations that penalize communities below the 2.5 limit if they vote to exclude pre-Proposition 2 1/2 debt. (Their levy limit is calculated on a lower tax base.) The other amendment authorizes the state treasurer to pay bond-holders should a municipality be unable to meet its obligations. Since state action must be requested by local officials (the procedure is not automatic), this provision may have little effect on buyer attitudes. In addition, the amendment specifically states that it is not pledging "the full faith and credit of the Commonwealth." General municipal bond trends will also make borrowing costly. Municipal bond rates have risen dramatically: from less than 6 percent in 1977, to 11 percent in February 1980, to 14 percent today. (12) Reagan tax reductions, the creation of new tax-exempt savings certificates and a record supply of new municipal issues suggest high rates will continue.

*Searching for New Revenues.*   Raising nonproperty tax revenues presented an alternative to budget-cutting. Although the dollar impact of such revenues on this year's budgets is limited, their importance may grow, especially in municipalities with slow growing property tax bases. Local officials were often uncertain as to the legality of new charges. (13) In addition, many were wary of levying new charges given the public's support for tax limitations.

Table 22.6 indicates the changes case study towns made in fees. All communities raised at least one fee. With the exception of water and sewer fee hikes, significant revenue increases were not predicted. Schools were another target of fee increases as localities sought to end subsidization of lunches.

## Table 22.6
## Changes in User Fees and Charges

| Community | Increase Existing Fees | New Fees |
|---|---|---|
| Springfield | School lunches<br>Adult education fees<br>Public works services | |
| Framingham | School lunches<br>Sewer service<br>Town licenses<br>Liquor licenses | Athletic activities |
| Arlington | Water and sewer service | |
| Chelsea | Oil storage fees<br>Water and sewer service | |
| Bridgewater | School lunches | Ambulance service<br>Landfill stickers |
| Sandwich | School lunches<br>Ambulance service | Athletic activities |
| Quincy | Public works services<br>City services fees<br>City licenses<br>Police permits<br>Parking fines<br>Hospital services<br>Water services | Athletic activities |
| Salem | City permits<br>City licenses<br>Water service | Subdivision permits<br>Wetland permits<br>Zoning hearing charges |
| Wayland | Town clerk fees<br>Parks & recreation services<br>School lunches | |
| Marshfield | | Beach parking fees |
| Cambridge | Water and sewer service<br>Parking fines<br>Sports fees<br>Golf course fees | Emergency rescue |
| Amesbury | School lunches | |

Few new fees were added. Those adopted did not involve charges on broad segments of the population. Proposals to levy fees for the use of the town dump and school transportation were rejected in several communities after public protest. Instead, towns adopted charges for occasional or noncompulsory services: the ambulance, beach parking, zoning hearings.

Cities rely on user charges more than towns and it was in cities that fee increases added most to projected revenues. With the City Council and a Citizen Task Force both studying the issue, Cambridge officials made the most determined and successful efforts to utilize new fees. Through numerous fee increases the city was able to add $6.2 million in new revevues, about one-half of its projected FY82 property tax loss. A brief analysis of its decisions illustrates the potential and limitations of charges as revenue sources. In the first place, the future revenue potential of existing city charges appears very limited. The city has two categories of charges: "Licenses and Permits" and "Charges for Services." Revenues from the former rose by over 35 percent, but still added only 0.8 percent ($1.1 million) to the city's $126 million general fund. (The net addition to revenues was $288,000.) The other group of charges increased by 25 percent or $5.9 million. Despite the size of these increases city calculations indicate that this $5.9 million increase in charges means only $1.7 million in property tax savings. $4.4 million of the increased revenues derive from hospital service charges and the hospital was almost entirely independent of the property tax levy already. (In FY81, $1.5 million of its $18.9 million budget came from property taxes. In FY82, property taxes will provide $800,000.) Sewer charge increases, producing $1.2 million in additional revenues, made this department nearly self-supporting. (The water department is also self-supporting.) Whether other property tax-financed services can shift to fee financing seems unclear. Could a charge be levied for street cleaning or snow removal? The City Manager advocated a garbage collection fee to pay for the $1.5 million budget for rubbish removal. He also urged imposing a charge on all rent controlled units to make the Rent Control Board self-supporting. After months of study, the Citizen Task Force did not identify any further sources of new fees. Finally, designing equitable fees which are sufficiently broad-based to provide significant revenues is not easy in a city with a sizeable poor population. The City Council rejected the Manager's proposals for garbage collection fees and rent control charges primarily on the grounds that they would hurt low-income residents. (14)

Cambridge officials also considered other nonproperty tax revenue sources. First, they sought to renegotiate the amounts paid in lieu of taxes by tax-exempt institutions, notably Harvard and M.I.T. The City Council considered -- and ultimately rejected -- the imposition of nonproperty taxes including a city sales tax, a 1 percent tax on professional services, and a payroll tax.

Two other actions suggest possible future trends. Three towns raised their revenues by selling town property. (Arlington, Burlington and Framingham sold schools; Bridgewater, a house and a fire engine.) Three communities modified traditional financial practices to provide additional revenues: Arlington utilized its free cash, Burlington considered using its stabilization fund (increased state aid forestalled this), and Framingham deliberately underfunded fixed costs hoping (correctly) that state aid would permit full funding later on.

*Improving Efficiency.*    Lowering the cost of services was a frequently espoused goal. Table 22.7 displays the productivity measures mentioned by local officials. While many of these were planned prior to Proposition 2 1/2, local officials agree that the new law accelerated such efforts. In Cambridge, for example, officials were able to implement a computerized financial management

**Table 22.7**
**Reorganization and Finance Charges**

| Reorganization | Finance Changes |
| --- | --- |
| Consolidation and/or centralization of human services programs or public work services | New purchasing practices, i.e., joint purchasing with neighbor communities |
| Consolidation of schools | New integrated financial management computer systems |
| School and fire station closings | |
| Job reassignment, i.e., jobs redefined, reclassified, or combined | Services made self-supporting, i.e., hospital services, school lunches, recreational services |
| Increased private contracting for service, i.e., nursing, ambulance, public works services | |

system which had long been resisted by agency heads.

Some efforts are continuations of existing practices (increased contracting out) while others represent significant attempts to redefine institutional and financial arrangements. Most notable, perhaps, is Quincy's establishment of revolving accounts for its city hospital and junior college in order to make both independent of the city's general fund.

Local officials agree that the vote for Proposition 2 1/2 was a call for more efficient government. However, the case studies raise several issues. First, most local officials seem uncertain about what future measures they can take. Efficiency measures are not obvious. Second, implementing such measures will be as difficult as identifying them in the first place. Groups with power over programs may resist many proposed reforms, particularly in an environment of cutbacks. There is already a widespread feeling among many department heads and workers that efficiency measures will be imposed on unpopular groups and weak programs rather than on truly wasteful programs. (For example, mayors rarely reduce their own staffs, but reorganize and cut the budgets of human service agencies.) Third, many efficiency measures involve the reorganization of job structures, and, hence, will involve lengthy and difficult negotiations with unions representing teachers, policemen, and fire fighters. Innovation will require time.

*Eliminating Services.*    Perhaps because most localities did not suffer large revenue losses, the elimination of programs was the least used budget strategy.   Table 22.8 exhibits the programs eliminated in our case study communities.   Only Salem, which faced significant tax rollbacks, actually terminated city funding for several city departments. Even the school systems, consistently cut more than other departments, attempted to maintain "a skeleton" of programs in the hope that more funds would be available next year.

*Labor Relations*

A striking feature of almost all the case study communities is the contentious quality of labor-management relations. With the exception of Sandwich, local officials and union representatives routinely described labor relations as difficult. Local officials, particularly elected officials, blame unions for government problems, including the passage of Proposition 2 1/2. In return, union representatives view their employers with skepticism and mistrust.

In several places, the F82 budget process began in the midst of on-going labor disputes. Burlington, Arlington, Bridgewater, and Quincy were involved in lengthy and often bitter contract negotiations. In Chelsea, the city and fire fighters disagreed over whether a salary increase negotiated in binding arbitration (before Proposition 2 1/2 became law) still held. Quincy teachers are suing over a wage hike the city denied because of the 4 percent tax cap. Wayland police and fire unions recently attempted to obtain an injunction against the new Joint Communications Center which they view as threatening their jobs.

As noted earlier, unions had little influence over this year's budget. Their main power lay in contractual language stipulating benefit increases, minimum manning and layoffs, as well as Civil Service regulations. This year, the impact of such regulations was mixed. Minimum manning provisions appear to be most at issue. Chelsea fire fighters relinquished minimum manning provisions to prevent layoffs on the promise that such provisions would be restored with increased state aid. In several places, union spokesmenn charged that layoffs were causing a violation of minimum manning provisions. In Amesbury, minimum manning provisions prevented layoffs. In Salem, they did not. Although Civil Service generally governs police and fire layoffs, only in Springfield have such regulations become an issue. As the city begins new contract negotiations, it is attempting to persuade the unions to waive Civil Service regulations on seniority and job assignments. The unions plan to

**Table 22.8**
**Services Eliminated**

| Community | Services Eliminated |
| --- | --- |
| Springfield | New school textbook purchases, private street maintenance, city landfill service, spring clean-up, ambulance service |
| Chelsea | Evaluation program for special education |
| Cambridge | Community relations service |
| Salem | Christmas decorating, funding for parades, concerts, the Cultural Arts Commission, Firemens Memorial, Heritage Celebration, Historical Commission, Waterways Commission, and Dept. of Weights and Measures |
| Quincy | High school drama and junior high athletics |
| Burlington | Some high school electives, courses with small enrollments |
| Framingham | School public information service |
| Marshfield | Police beach patrols and winter cottage checks |
| Bridgewater | School music, art, home economics, industrial arts, athletics, and summer recreation programs |
| Wayland | Trash pickup, road oiling, culvert and stream clearing |
| Amesbury | School library book purchases, junior high athletics, busing for students living within two miles of the school |

mobilize public support for public safety in an effort to fight "give-backs." While not covered by Civil Service regulations, teachers have protection through reduction-in-force (RIF) language in their contracts. With the exception of Burlington and Bridgewater, where teachers negotiated over such clauses, reduction-in-force means layoffs on the basis of seniority.

Local officials often asserted that contractual rights prevented rational budgeting and greater efficiencies. One Selectmen complained,

> Union contracts set limitations on us. The kinds of flexibility that we wanted to have, we could not have. We could not recombine jobs. We

> could not hold off on steep raises. We could
> eliminate a job or a whole department, but we
> could not eliminate half of the Recreation Director
> and half of something else. These kinds of
> limitations had more influence in budget-making
> than they should have.

Several unions did allow their contracts to be renegotiated when wages were not at issue. Marshfield teachers agreed to eliminate restrictions on personnel reorganization in an effort to help cut school department costs. Burlington teachers compromised on their RIF clause to include provisions on creditation as well as seniority. They also waived provisions regarding class size. Burlington DPW workers opened their contract to permit job reclassification. As noted, the Chelsea fire fighters also reopened their contract. However, both Salem fire fighters and Sandwich teachers refused requests for wage reductions in order to save jobs. One union leader insisted:

> We said no. We did not want to take a step
> backward for the labor movement. Not with 11
> percent inflation! Once you start going backwards
> -- open that contract -- you never stop.

Perhaps because layoffs were so few and, because of contractual protection, formal grievances were kept to a minimum. Bridgewater fire fighters filed an unfair labor practice suit with the Massachusetts Labor Relations Commission over improper termination procedures. Department of Public Works employees in Burlington have challenged the "bumping" procedure used to reorganize their jobs. Amesbury DPW workers filed a grievance over the town's decision to postpone wage increases.

Nevertheless, Proposition 2 1/2 has clearly aggravated labor relations. First, in many places, activist union members believe their departments were political targets for budget cuts, a belief confirmed by the statements of local officials. Second, they predict that Proposition 2 1/2s elimination of binding arbitration combined with a cap on property tax levies will weaken their future bargaining power. Union leaders assume that local government officials will present them with fixed contract offers on the grounds that "they have no more money." Slowdowns and strikes will probably result.

Finally, union spokesmen claim that Proposition 2 1/2 demonstrates that they have lost public support. (A view shared, to some extent, by public officials.) Public unions led the fight against Proposition 2 1/2 and see its passage as a sign of dissatisfaction with local services. This view is more prevalent among teachers than public safety employees, many of whom hope to mobilize public concern over "crime" and "protection" to prevent future budget cuts. On the other hand, several fire fighters unions lost bids for higher appropriations at this year's town meetings and fear that even they may have lost the public's respect.

## Impacts

In this section, we will consider more quantitative measures of budget cuts as well as some possible benefits of Proposition 2 1/2. (15)

### Changes in Municipal Appropriations

Not surprisingly, the most obvious consequence of Proposition 2 1/2 is a reduction in municipal appropriations. Table 22.9 presents FY81 and FY82 appropriations for ten of the thirteen case study communities. The table shows that even though we selected localities facing high revenue losses, actual changes in appropriations vary. No municipality cut appropriations by 15 percent, even though eight lowered property taxes by that percentage. There is considerable variation: while three municipalities lowered appropriations by approximately 10

### Table 22.9
### Percent Change in Local Appropriations FY81-82

| Community | Schools | Police | Fire | Streets | Parks | Garbage | Library | Debt | Total |
|---|---|---|---|---|---|---|---|---|---|
| Amesbury | -7.7 | 10.5 | 9.0 | n.a. | n.a. | 10.6 | -8.2 | -2.8 | 3.5 |
| Arlington | -5.2 | n.a. | 3.6 | n.a. | n.a. | n.a. | n.a. | n.a. | -6.3 |
| Burlington | -8.5 | 0 | 9.4 | n.a. | -8.0 | 10.1 | -3.6 | -1.3 | -2.0 |
| Chelsea | -4.8 | 4.0 | 7.4 | -15.9 | -1.0 | 21.9 | -19.5 | -1.9 | -1.5 |
| Framingham | -9.7 | 1.7 | -1.8 | 14.8 | -6.7 | -6.2 | -15.0 | -13.0 | -9.5 |
| Marshfield | -9.0 | -10.4 | 0.7 | n.a. | -49.9 | 12.3 | -6.6 | 39.0 | -8.0 |
| Quincy | -19.6 | -8.2 | -6.8 | -67.7 | -23.7 | -17.0 | -23.1 | -1.5 | -35.2 |
| Salem | -15.7 | -1.6 | -8.2 | -37.1 | -34.6 | 1.7 | -16.0 | -4.6 | -9.1 |
| Springfield | -10.1 | 2.2 | -5.5 | -12.5 | -12.0 | 50.8 | -6.8 | 5.9 | 1.6 |
| Wayland | -5.0 | -2.9 | -1.9 | -22.9 | -2.1 | -100.0 | -0.6 | -4.0 | -6.1 |

percent, two increased appropriations.

There is no apparent pattern to these changes. Two cities in our category of high impact communities (high revenue loss, high expenditures, low income), Salem and Quincy, suffered among the largest reductions in appropriations (9 and 11.5 percent, respectively). But a third city, Chelsea, had to cut appropriations only 1.5 percent because state aid restored 98 percent of its revenue loss. (The fact that Chelsea still decreased appropriations suggests that without state aid, Chelsea would have been forced to make quite substantial cuts.) Our second category (high revenue loss, high expenditure, high income) demonstrated a range of cuts: Marshfield, a drop of 8.5 percent; Wayland, of 6 percent; Burlington, of 2 percent. These differences suggest the importance of revaluation: Burlington's property levy limit is 7 percent greater than its

FY81 property tax levy. In our third category ("neither city nor suburb"), Arlington had a 6 percent decline, while Framingham made a 9 percent cut.

Other indicators are no more successful. Rank-orderings of per capita income and per capita equalized valuation 1980 are not interesting. Of the two poorest places (on both indicators), Springfield increased its appropriations slightly, and Chelsea made the lowest reduction. Wayland, the wealthiest community (on both indicators), suffered a 6 percent drop. The localities with the greatest percentage reductions demonstrate great differences in wealth and per capita expenditures. Quincy and Salem are both high spending towns with low per capita incomes and low per capita equalized valuation. But Framingham ranks high on both income and valuation.

The lack of strong relationships between the attributes of places and FY82 appropriations is perhaps not unexpected. We have already discussed the differential, but very significant, impact of state aid. Chelsea, Springfield, and Amesbury received more than 40 percent of their revenue losses in state aid. State aid clearly prevented Chelsea from making the appropriations reductions forced on Quincy and Salem. It is more difficult to trace the effects of revaluation. While the case studies indicate that revaluation permitted local officials to scale down revenue losses, the figures show a mixed pattern. Of the five municipalities revaluing this year, Amesbury and Burlington avoided large decreases in appropriations. However, neither has yet set their tax rates and levy limits. Wayland, which chose a tax rate of $22.40, could have avoided cuts had it chosen a higher tax rate.

*Changes in Functional Appropriations*

There are distinctive patterns to changes in functional appropriations. Education, libraries, and parks were reduced in all municipalities for which information is available. The other services show declines in some municipalities, increases in others. A comparison of the range of appropriations changes for education, police, and fire demonstrate the drastic cuts imposed on schools (Table 22.10).

Although this pattern is not surprising, given education's large share of local budgets, schools, in general, bore a disproportionate share of total cuts. Table 22.11 compares education's share of total cuts to its share of FY81 appropriations for the nine towns which reduced total appropriations. In Arlington, Framingham, and Marshfield the educational reduction was proportional. In Wayland, education was spared. In Burlington, Cambridge, and Chelsea, the decrease in educational appropriations was significantly larger than the total appropriations cut. The two communities increasing total appropriations, cut educational appropriations. The two other functions showing consistent decreases, libraries, and parks, also suffered decreases larger than their budget percentages, but here the dollar cuts were small.

## Table 22.10
## Appropriations Changes for Selected Departments

| Range | Education | Police | Fire |
|---|---|---|---|
| 15% decrease | Quincy<br>Salem | | |
| 10-15% decrease | Springfield | Marshfield | |
| 5-10% decrease | Framingham<br>Marshfield<br>Amesbury<br>Arlington | Quincy | Quincy<br>Salem<br>Springfield |
| 0-5% decrease | Wayland<br>Cambridge<br>Chelsea | Salem<br>Wayland | Framingham<br>Wayland |
| 0-5% increase | | Springfield<br>Chelsea<br>Framingham<br>Cambridge | Arlington<br>Marshfield<br>Cambridge |
| 5% increase | | Amesbury | Amesbury<br>Burlington<br>Chelsea |

## Table 22.11
## Appropriations Changes for Selected Departments

|  | % of FY81 Appropriations | % Total Municipal FY82 Appropriations Reductions |
|---|---|---|
| **Schools** | | |
| Arlington | 41.0 | 34.0 |
| Burlington | 51.0 | 214.0 |
| Cambridge | 30.0 | 75.0 |
| Chelsea | 51.0 | 161.0 |
| Framingham | 46.0 | 47.0 |
| Marshfield | 52.0 | 56.0 |
| Quincy | 43.0 | 62.0 |
| Salem | 33.0 | 57.0 |
| Wayland | 57.0 | 45.0 |
| **Libraries** | | |
| Burlington | 0.7 | 0.8 |
| Cambridge | 0.1 | 0.4 |
| Chelsea | 0.2 | 25.0 |
| Framingham | 1.0 | 2.0 |
| Marshfield | 0.9 | 0.7 |
| Quincy | 0.1 | 2.3 |
| Wayland | 1.9 | 0.1 |
| **Parks & Recreation** | | |
| Burlington | 1.6 | 4.2 |
| Chelsea | 2.0 | 1.3 |
| Framingham | 0.8 | 0.6 |
| Marshfield | 0.3 | 2.0 |
| Quincy | 1.0 | 2.4 |
| Salem | 2.0 | 9.0 |
| Wayland | 2.9 | 1.0 |

*Per Capita Changes in Appropriations*

Per capita changes in appropriations best suggest the actual dollar losses to individuals across places and among services as well as the varying impact of Proposition 2 1/2 on different communities. (16) Per capita changes range from a $43 increase in Amesbury to a $103 decline in Quincy. (The average drop in appropriations was about $47.)

The relatively deep cuts in education are very clear again. In communities making deep cuts, per capita drops in education were great. While Quincy's total per capita appropriations declined by $103, its education appropriations declined by $78, police appropriations declined by $7, and fire appropriations, by $6. In Salem, total per capita appropriations dropped by $102; education, by $58; police, by $1.00; and fire, by $5.00. In Springfield, while total appropriations rose by $15., police appropriations rose by $1.00, fire appropriations per capita fell by $3.00. Per capita school appropriations, however, fell by $37.00.

How will these changes in appropriations affect service quality and the quality of life in Massachusetts communities? In many communities, police and fire chiefs maintained that public safety is already threatened. One suburban fire chief contended that his department could not cope with a major fire if his budget were lowered next year. Many of his city counterparts agreed. Police and fire response time has risen. Local officials differ in their assessments. For example, the effects of education budget cuts are disputed even in localities making the largest reductions. In Salem, the School Superintendent maintained that Proposition 2 1/2 accelerated necessary consolidations already in progress. Quincy school officials saw their school system as "the historic whipping boy," suffering politically motivated and disastrous cuts. Given the overall drop in education appropriations, it seems inescapable that children have suffered the burden of Proposition 2 1/2. And, in cities, the burden has fallen on poor children who are mostly likely to attend public schools.

Local officials all worry about 1983. They assume that fixed costs (anywhere from 10 to 40 percent of case study budgets) will increase at rates faster than inflation and certainly at rates higher than 2.5 percent. Since department heads typically cut supplies and maintenance before personnel, many foresee severe equipment problems. Human service directors, facing federal cuts, assume that local funding will not be available.

Looking ahead, there can be little doubt, however, that city officials foresee a much bleaker future than their counterparts in towns. Even in Framingham and Arlington, which suffered above average reductions in appropriations, local officials seemed to believe that the worst is over; that revaluation, coupled with management reforms and some state tax reform guaranteed to provide local assistance, would prevent long-term damage. Perhaps, because all the cities face another year of property tax levy reductions, as well as federal budget cuts, their officials feared the worst. As one related,

> I fear next year. This year, we had seventeen vacancies in the police department -- next year, we won't. This year, we cut $15 million, but we have fixed costs as well. We already transferred the junior college and the hospital out of the general fund budget. We already cut the library by 50 percent. So, where's the room?

Another official claimed,

> After the second cut, the city would no longer be operational. You're not an existing community after something like that. You might as well dissolve as a corporate entity.

## Tax Savings

Everyone interviewed agreed that people supported Proposition 2 1/2 to lower their property taxes. In the ten towns that have set their FY82 tax rates, tax rates have declined (Table 22.12). Almost all declined by the full 15 percent.

**Table 22.12**
**Tax Rate Changes, FY81-81**

| Community | FY81 tax rate | FY82 tax rate | % decrease |
|-----------|---------------|---------------|------------|
| Arlington | 87.00 | 73.50 | 15.5 |
| Bridgewater | 44.00 | 35.90 | 18.4 |
| Cambridge | 230.40 | 199.80 | 13.2 |
| Chelsea | 245.40 | 206.00 | 16.0 |
| Framingham | 58.00 | 22.90 | 57.0 |
| Marshfield | 94.50 | 25.00 | 74.0 |
| Salem | 205.00 | 173.00 | 15.6 |
| Sandwich | 18.40 | 17.08 | 7.0 |
| Wayland | 91.00 | 76.50 | 15.9 |
| | 45.00 | 22.40 | 50.0 |

Sources: Massachusetts Taxpayers Association, op cit., Impact: 2 1/2 Case Studies, The Boston Globe, March 6, 1982.

It is impossible at this time to determine which categories of property owners will ultimately benefit from lower tax rates. Marshfield and Wayland remind us that revaluation will accompany falling tax rates. (Marshfield's final certified full and fair cash value was 47 percent higher than its 1980 EQV; Wayland's was 36 percent higher.) Individual tax bills may rise despite falling rates. Overall, the nonresidential share of taxes will probably decline since residential property was underassessed relative to commercial property. In several cities, the assessors predict that even with the 2.5 percent levy limit, revaluation will raise many residential tax bills. They hope classification will ease this shift. One city assessor anticipated that some residential tax bills will increase by 40 percent even if the city adopts classification. Shifts in the tax burden obviously depend on many factors, notably the prior variation in assessment ratios and the size of the nonresidential property tax base. In Burlington, where revaluation raised assessed values by 23 percent, officials first feared that residential property owners would pay higher taxes. But now, with classification and continued growth in commercial and industrial sectors, they believe that residential bills will drop an average of $200, while commercial and industrial bills remain constant. Moreover, court-mandated revaluation would have hiked tax bills even higher with Proposition 2 1/2's levy limit.

## Another Year of Proposition 2 1/2

On March 3, 1982, the Department of Revenue announced that forty communities with 40 percent of the state's population would again have to lower property tax levies in FY83. Twenty-four of these municipalities are cities. Of the eighteen places scheduled to reduce the full 15 percent, fifteen are cities. Seven of the thirteen case-study communities are slated for decreases; Cambridge, Chelsea, Quincy, and Springfield face 15 percent reductions. The department estimated statewide tax-levy reductions at $175 million, about one-half of the FY82 drop. Although the first year of Proposition 2 1/2 did not exact the toll predicted, FY83 may bring new problems. While some of these problems are sure to result from mandated cuts in tax levies, others may well result from delaying strategies used in the first year.

In FY82, the state played the critical role in mitigating levy reductions. By cutting funds for state-agency operations, direct payments to individuals, and debt -- as well as laying off 6,000 public employees -- the state was able to provide $265 million in additional local aid. In FY83 it will provide $153 million more than it did in FY82. (Because of a $410 million increase in state tax revenues, the state will apparently not have to cut its own spending as much as in FY82.) Yet, with unemployment rising and the recession hurting the state's high technology sector, can state revenues continue to restore the $660 million in local revenues lost in FY82 and FY83? Will state taxes have to be raised to help cities and towns cope with inflation (which is sure to exceed the 2.5 percent increment in taxes to which communities are limited)? On the other hand, to what extent should the state recoup Proposition 2 1/2 tax cuts?

The formula for allocating local aid is as controversial as the amount allocated. Criticism of the FY82 distribution formula prompted design of a new formula related to FY82 revenue losses caused by Proposition 2 1/2. But this formula must be renegotiated every year. Some observers feel that state aid should be a regular allocation (tied to the growth in specific state tax revenue) rather than a varying amount fixed every year by the legislature. This issue, however, has not been decided. Nor is there any agreement on the primary purpose of state aid. Should the priority be to maintain services, to equalize spending, or to ensure that the needs of the state's poorer residents are met?

Instead of furnishing more local aid, the state could empower municipalities to use local-option taxes. Such a policy might permit more local control over fiscal decisions. It would also permit taxing of nonresidents. Yet it is not clear how local-option taxes would minimize the fiscal disparities among communities. In Massachusetts, it has not been obvious that local-option taxes are less progressive than state aid raised through the commonwealth's relatively regressive tax structure.

Municipalities have already begun to tap existing nonproperty-tax revenues and, to a lesser extent, to levy charges. Since Massachusetts localities make less use of charges than municipalities nationwide, raising fees seems a promising revenue-raising strategy. Like local taxes, fees can be levied on nonresidents. Ideally, fees tie service financing to actual service cost, promoting greater efficiency. However, fees do not consider a user's ability to pay. They may thus burden low-income people, particularly if municipalities institute charges for locally mandated services, such as garbage collection and school bus transportation.

New local-revenue sources cannot be considered apart from revaluation. Proposition 2 1/2 lowered total property taxes in FY82. Yet if tax burdens are shifted to owners of older residential properties, tax saving will be realized by commercial and industrial interests. This is sure to trigger another round of public outcry about the "unfair" property tax. While the state consitution requires uniform valuation (within similar land-use categories) it does not dictate how the tax burden should be apportioned. If revaluation shifts the tax burden onto poorer households, the state could adjust its own tax structure to compensate.

Throughout the state, there is a shared assumption that new state aid of new local nonproperty taxes should restore property taxes cut by Proposition 2 1/2. Such an assumption is shared by state and local politicians, many lobbying groups, and even the sponsor of Proposition 2 1/2, Citizens for Limited Taxation. Yet the restoration of even 50 to 60 percent of the property taxes lost will not forestall the need for substantial cuts, particularly in cities that face continued levy reductions and further reductions in federal aid. The case studies suggest that local officials have great difficulty establishing explicit, effectiveness-based criteria for making budget cuts. There is no apparent political reward for reducing expenditure levels. Nonexplicit policies -- notably, deferring capital expenditures and hiring freezes -- are politically easier to enact. Yet such policies invariably cause other problems. Local officials are well aware that deferring capital expenditures will impose costs in the future. The failure to make necessary improvements may even endanger health or safety in the near future. But such deferrals obviate more troublesome layoffs or service cuts. Attrition may decimate the ranks of younger and minority workers, but it avoids battles with the unions. Given the apparent aversion to hard decisions in FY82, there is little reason to believe that officials will devise "innovative, efficient" management or financing strategies.

In the end, while reducing taxes, Proposition 2 1/2 may well institutionalize fiscal disparities even greater than those attributed to the burdensome property tax. By mandating a uniform local property-tax rate, local spending is tied to local valuation. High-valuation towns are permitted to raise more money per capita than low-valuation towns, although a community cannot choose to tax itself at a rate greater than 2.5 percent to provide more services. Even municipalities with growing tax bases will realize lower and lower effective tax rates, since levy limits can only increase by 2.5 percent annually. Nor is there any relationship between "need" and levy limits imposed by Proposition 2 1/2. The four case-study municipalities scheduled for full 15 percent reductions in FY82 include the three communities lowest in per capita valuation. All four have 1980 per capita valuation, less than half that of the two wealthiest towns. Not surprisingly, all four are central cities. For many communities, Proposition 2 1/2 can hardly be considered an equitable solution to the state's persistent fiscal problems.

## Notes for Chapter 22

The assistance of John Brouder and Tom Hammond of Senator John Olver's office in the Massachusetts State Legislature and Karl Kim of the IMPACT: 2 1/2 Project are gratefully acknowledged.

Prepared for the Workshop on Budgeting Under Fiscal Stress and Financial Retrenchment at the American Society of Public Administration Conference in Honolulu, Hawaii, March 1982.

1. "Taxachusetts into Battle," *The Boston Globe*, July 21, 1981.

2. *The Boston Globe*, March 25, 1981.

3. *The Boston Globe*, May 12, 1981.

4. The assessment ratio is determined by dividing the valuation as determined by the local assessors by the state's estimate of full and fair cash value.

5. Commonwealth of Massachusetts Department of Revenue, Division of Local Services, "Preliminary Impact of 2 1/2 and Estimated Impact of 2 1/2 on Fiscal 1982 Property Tax Levies," as of July 1, 1981.

6. Massachusetts Taxpayers Foundation, "1982 Property Taxes: An Interim Report," Boston, February 4, 1982.

7. The legislature chose the lottery formula to allocate these funds. This formula attempts to equalize revenue sources since it disperses funds in inverse ratio to per capita equalized valuation.

8. Massachusetts Municipal Assocation, Report on the Impact of Proposition 2 1/2, January 1982.

9. Massachusetts Municipal Association, op. cit.

10. *The Boston Globe,* February 2, 1982; *Business Week,* October 26, 1981.

11. Massachusetts laws do not include specific prohibitions against imposing fees and charges. Proposition 2 1/2 states that "no government entity shall make any charge or impose any fee for goods provided or services rendered in excess of the cost of furnishing such goods or providing such services."

12. This concern for the poor may also constrain hospital officials since reductions of Medicare and Medicaid budgets will reduce the ability of low-income people to pay for health care.

13. The numbers here are not drawn from the case studies but from a later Impact: 2 1/2 survey of municipal appropriations. Thus, our figures here may differ from those reported in the case studies. 14. FY81 and FY82 per capita appropriations for the sample are included in Chapter 26, Table 26.3 -- ED.

14. This concern for the poor may also constrain hospital officials since reductions of Medicare and Medicaid budgets will reduce the ability of low-income people to pay for health care.

15. The numbers here are not drawn from the case studies but from a later Impact: 2 1/2 survey of municipal appropriations. Thus, our figures here may differ from those reported in the case studies.

16. FY81 and FY82 per capita appropriations for the sample are included in Chapter 26, Tables 26.3 and 26.3 -- ED.

Chapter 23

# The Initial Impacts on State and Local
Finances

Katharine L. Bradbury and Helen F. Ladd, with Claire Christopherson

## Introduction

The first section of this paper puts Proposition 2 1/2 into the Massachusetts fiscal context and relates it to the level and growth of the state's property taxes and spending. Because a major goal of Proposition 2 1/2 was to reduce property tax burdens, the second section examines why Massachusetts property taxes are so high relative to those of other states and briefly describes previous unsuccessful attempts to lower them. The third section looks at the first year aggregate effects of Proposition 2 1/2, including its effect on property tax assessment. The fourth section of this paper analyzes on the combined effects of Proposition 2 1/2 and new state aid on the distribution of taxes and total spending across local governments. The fifth section examines Proposition 2 1/2s impact on school budgets. The paper concludes with a summary of findings and policy recommendations.

## Proposition 2 1/2 and the Local Fiscal Context

The 351 cities and towns in Massachusetts levy all the property taxes in the state. These municipalities include large urban centers, wealthy bedroom communities, and small poor communities in rural areas. In contrast to many other states, especially those outside New England, county governments and special districts in Massachusetts have few responsibilities, and finance their budgets by assessing cities and towns. The property tax is the only broad-based tax that Massachusetts cities and towns can use. Small amounts of motor vehicle excise revenue account for their only other tax revenues.

Local schools are also financed largely through property taxes levied by cities and towns. Most school district boundaries are the same as those of cities and towns. Before Proposition 2 1/2, school committees enjoyed fiscal autonomy in the sense that each city or town legislative body was required to accept the school budget as proposed by the school committee and to raise the necessary property taxes as part of the municipal tax levy. The budgets of regional school districts were financed by assessments on the member cities and towns in accordance with agreements made at the time of school district formation.

Two characteristics of local government in Massachusetts are noteworthy. First, local property tax burdens are high compared to those in other states. Second, local spending -- especially school spending -- has recently grown more rapidly than the U.S. average. Massachusetts has been among the four states with the highest property taxes per capita and among the 12 states with the highest property taxes as a percent of income for at least 20 years. In FY80, Massachusetts communities collected an average of $555 per capita through property taxes, as compared to $290 for local governments in the country as a whole. Property taxes averaged 6.2 percent of personal income in Massachusetts, and 3.4 percent for the nation.

During the 1970s, local government expenditures in Massachusetts increased faster than the United States average both per capita and as a percent of local personal icome. From FY71 to FY80, per capita direct general expenditures of Massachusetts local governments increased at an annual rate of 9.9 percent, a percentage point faster than the nation. Expenditures as a percent of personal income grew 2.0 percent in Massachusetts, while they rose less than 1 percent for the United States as a whole.

Local expenditures for education comprised 47 percent of total local expenditures in Massachusetts in FY80. Their growth, in particular, exceeded national growth averages: the annual growth in local school expenditures in Massachusetts, both per capita and as a percent of income, exceeded the corresponding national growth rates by over 3 percentage points during the FY71 to FY79 period. In *per pupil* terms, Massachusetts expenditures were 5th highest among the states in FY78 and 23 percent above the U.S. average. They reached this level from a position below the national average as recently as 1971. (1)

## Why Property Taxes are So High in Massachusetts

Governmental inefficiency and waste were commonly cited at the time of the vote on Proposition 2 1/2 as the cause of Massachusetts' high property taxes. Unfortunately, public sector expenditures cannot easily be separated into their productive and nonproductive components. However, it is possible to identify the extent to which above-average property taxes reflect above-average expenditures or above-average local reliance on property taxes.

Table 23.1 analyzes three possible explanations for the difference between per capita property tax burdens in Massachusetts and those in the United States as a whole in FY80: differences in total state and local spending per capita, in local spending as a share of state and local spending, and in property taxes as a fraction of local expenditures. (2) The first column shows the $555 per capita property tax burden in Massachusetts, the $290 U.S. average burden, and the percentage by which the Massachusetts burden exceeds the U.S. average. Columns 2, 3, and 4 show the multiplicative components of the following identity:

$$\frac{\text{local property taxes}}{\text{population}} = \frac{\substack{\text{state and local} \\ \text{direct general} \\ \text{expenditures}}}{\text{population}} \times$$

$$\frac{\substack{\text{local} \\ \text{direct general} \\ \text{expenditures}}}{\substack{\text{state and local} \\ \text{direct general} \\ \text{expenditures}}} \times \frac{\substack{\text{local} \\ \text{property taxes}}}{\substack{\text{local} \\ \text{direct general} \\ \text{expenditures}}}$$

The differences between Massachusetts and the national average for each component show the percentages by which Massachusetts property taxes per capita exceed or fall short of the U.S. average solely as a result of variation in each component. For example, the 10.7 percent above-average state and local per capita spending in Massachusetts raises property taxes 10.7 percent above the U.S. average. Similarly the 9.1 percent below-average local share lowers Massachusetts property taxes 9.1 percent below the U.S. average.

The clearcut conclusion emerges that most of the above-average property tax burden in Massachusetts can be accounted for by above-average reliance on local property taxes to finance local spending. Property taxes as a fraction of local direct general expenditures are 56 percent in Massachusetts in contrast to 29 percent in the United States as a whole. The importance of this 90 percent difference can be seen as follows: if Massachusetts had derived the same proportion of its local revenues from property taxes as other states in 1980, but had its own 1980 total spending level and local spending share, Masachusetts property taxes would have been $292 per capita, or essentially the same as the U.S. average.

The contribution of above-average per capita state and local spending should also be noted, but its contribution to the difference in property tax burdens is only one-eighth as great as that of the sources of local revenues variable. This finding indicates that above-average spending is not the major cause of the state's high property taxes. Hence it follows that while wasteful spending may play some role, it can not be the major culprit.

## Table 23.1
### Why Are Massachusetts Local Property Taxes Above Average?
### Component Parts of Differences in Per Capita Property Taxes, FY80

| | Local property taxes ──────── Population | State & local direct general expenditures ──────── Population | Local direct general expenditures ──────── State & local direct general expenditures | Local property taxes ──────── Local direct general expenditures |
|---|---|---|---|---|
| Massachusetts | $555. = | $1796. × | 0.554 × | 0.558 |
| United States | 290. = | 1622. × | 0.609 × | 0.293 |
| Difference between Mass. and U.S. as percentage of U.S. | +91.5% | +10.7%* | −9.1%* | +90.2%* |

Source: U.S. Bureau of the Census, Governmental Finances in 1979-80, TAbles 5, 12 and 17.

*These percentages can be interpreted as the percentages by which property taxes in Massachusetts differ from the U.S. average solely as a result of deviation of the component from the U.S. average.

Local governments in Massachusetts account for a slightly smaller share of state and local spending than local governments nationally. This reflects the limited role of Massachusetts county governments and high state spending on redistributive functions such as welfare and Medicaid. Because of the offsetting effects of above-average state and local spending and below-average local share, local direct general expenditures per capita in Massachusetts are less than 1 percent above the U.S. average ($994 vs. $987).

Table 23.2 takes the analysis one step further by showing the specific components of local revenue in Massachusetts and in the United States as a whole. Column 1 shows that property taxes account for about 49 percent of local government general revenues in Massachusetts and about 28 percent in the United States. (These percentages differ from those in the last column of Table 23.1 because local general revenues are not precisely equal to local direct general expenditures.) The key finding is that in Massachusetts "other" (i.e., neither aid nor property tax) revenue sources account for only 10 percent of local general revenues, a percentage well below the 28 percent U.S. average. Thus, we conclude that a major explanation for high property taxes in Massachusetts is that local governments are not empowered to use other taxes such as income or sales taxes and that they rely less than other states on fees and charges.(3)

**Table 23.2**

**Specific Revenue Sources as Fractions of Local General Revenue, FY80**

|  | Property Taxes | State Aid | Federal Aid | Other |
|---|---|---|---|---|
| Massachusetts | 0.495 | 0.278 | 0.127 | 0.100 |
| United States | 0.282 | 0.350 | 0.091 | 0.277 |
| Difference be-<br>tween Mass.<br>and U.S. | +0.213 | -0.072 | +0.036 | -0.177 |

Source: Governmental Finances in 1979-80, Table 5.

Another small factor contributing to the high property tax proportion is the below-average aid, expressed as a fraction of local general revenues, provided by the Massachusetts state government. If Massachusetts had given the average proportion of state aid in 1980, property taxes as a fraction of local general revenue would have been reduced by 7.2 percentage points to 42.3 percent of local revenues. According to the equation in Table 23.1, this reduction would have decreased per capita property taxes by about 14 percent.

Concern about high property taxes in Massachusetts is not a recent phenomenon. Many studies have documented its adverse effect. (4) And during the past 15 years, the state legislature has tried to alleviate property tax burdens by increasing the amount of state aid distributed to local governments and by taking responsibility for certain local expenditure functions. None of these state actions can be considered successful if the criterion for success is how high property taxes were after their enactment. Even in the years in which state aid increased substantially, local property taxes continued to rise. However, in the absence of such policies, property taxes would be even higher than they now are. Moreover, many of these state actions were oriented toward the equalization of resources across communities as well as alleviation of local property tax burdens.

Only with the state's imposition of a 4 percent tax cap was the growth of property taxes temporarily halted. The 4 percent limit applied to both local taxes and appropriations for fiscal years 1980 and 1981. Partly because of the cap and partly because of increased state aid and the use of local cash reserves, property taxes in Massachusetts actually declined in FY80 for the first time in several decades. The following year, however, property taxes increased by the largest amount in four years. Expenditures included in the cap increased by 6.3 percent, as communities routinely took advantage of the law's override provision. Virtually no new state aid, increased assessments on cities and towns to support county and regional authorities, and depleted cash reserves all contributed to communities' decisions to override the cap.

Thus, state policies, including the 1979 state tax cap law, have not been sufficient to reduce Massachusetts' property tax burdens. As pointed out above, the state government should not be faulted on the expenditure side: the local share of state and local spending is lower in Massachusetts than elsewhere. With respect to the revenue side, however, we restate our earlier conclusion that property taxes are high in Massachusetts because property taxes account for a substantially higher proportion of local revenues in Massachusetts than elsewhere.

## Aggregate Effects of Proposition 2 1/2

The correct way to measure the revenue impact of Proposition 2 1/2 is to use the difference between revenues allowed with the law and those that would have been raised without the law. In most of this paper, however, we measure losses as the difference between the revenues in the year before Proposition 2 1/2 and those allowed after Proposition 2 1/2. This appproach is flawed in two ways. Even as a measure of the required change from one year to the next, it understates the magnitude of the required adjustment because of inflation. Second, it understates the impact unless no revenue growth would have occurred in the absence of the Proposition 2 1/2. The advantage of this method is that it requires no arbitrary assumption about how fast revenues would have grown in the absence of the limitation measure. At the same time, the direction of the bias is clear; in all cases our reported results understate revenue losses. This downward bias can be dramatic under reasonable assumptions. (5)

### First Year Losses in Local Tax Revenues

The estimate of the first year revenue losses (or gains) from Proposition 2 1/2 used here is the difference between FY81 actual tax revenues and those permitted in FY82. (6) The property tax increases allowed in low tax rate communities are treated as revenue gains even though the permitted 2 1/2 percent growth is likely to be less that the growth that would have occurred without Proposition 2 1/2. However, the loss of motor vehicle excise (MVE) revenues means that all cities and towns face absolute reductions in tax revenues in FY82.

As of the beginning of FY82 (July 1, 1981), the Masschusetts Department of Revenue (DOR) estimated that Proposition 2 1/2 would reduce FY82 local tax revenue by a total of $486 million compared to FY81. This represents about a 14 percent reduction in total tax revenues. The total net reduction is divided between changes in property tax and MVE revenues as follows:

| | |
|---|---:|
| Property tax levies | |
|   Allowable increases | |
|     (169 communities) | $16,292,732 |
|   Required decreases | |
|     (182 communities) | −357,260,189 |
|   Net change in property tax levies | −340,967,457 |
| | |
| Motor vehicle excise revenues | −145,249,603 |
| Total change in tax revenues | −486,217,060 |

Although MVE revenues represent only a small portion of local tax revenues (about 6.5 percent in 1981), the size of the decrease in the MVE rate -- 62 percent -- makes the reduction of MVE revenues an important component of the first year revenue losses caused by Proposition 2 1/2. The estimated net property tax loss of $341 million is about 10 percent of the $3,346 million total property taxes levied in FY81.

The greatest uncertainty in estimating revenue losses and gains arises from Proposition 2 1/2s use of "full and fair cash value" of taxable property to define the maximum allowable tax rate. This creates uncertainty because in 1981 only 98 of Massachusetts' 351 cities and towns were in compliance with the ruling of a 1974 court case requiring assessment at 100 percent of market value. The other 253 cities and towns were scheduled to complete revaluation during 1982 and 1983.

For purposes of Proposition 2 1/2, DOR defined full and fair cash value for FY82 as a city's or town's state-determined 1980 equalized valuation adjusted upward by a uniform 13 percent for inflation and by additional amounts for demonstrated growth in a community's tax base. In addition, the DOR gave communities that had revalued in 1981 the option of updating their 1981 assessments to bring them in line with 1982 values, and gave communities that were in the process of revaluing the option of using their 1982 revaluation figures if they could complete the revaluation and have it certified by February 1982.

Because the state's equalized valuation figures, even after the 13 percent inflation adjustment, typically understate a community's true valuation, many communities that fought revaluation in the past now have an incentive to revalue and to update valuations to minimize the revenue losses mandated by the tax limitation measure. (7) This impact on property tax administration -- though not fully anticipated -- may be one of the most important effects of Proposition 2 1/2. At the same time, we note that the 2 1/2 percent limit on the annual growth of tax levies that applies once the tax rate is at 2 1/2 percent means that Proposition 2 1/2 provides little incentive for low tax rate communities to update their assessments the first year or for others to update their assessments in the future.

The July estimates reported above incorporate reasonable assumptions about the effects of these options, but probably overstate the required first year revenue losses in some communities, especially those implementing 1982 revaluations. (8)

*State Government Response*

Proposition 2 1/2 says very little about state government spending and taxes. (9) In particular, it did not require the state to offset local tax losses with new state aid. In response to pressure from local government officials and after six-and-one-half months of bitter debate, however, the legislature increased the amount of aid distributed to local governments in 1982 by $265 million over its 1981 level.

Unlike California when Proposition 13 passed, Massachusetts essentially had no state surplus. This fact, combined with the reluctance of legislators to raise state taxes in the aftermath of an overwhelming vote for local tax reduction, left cuts in state spending as the only source of revenue for new local aid. Thus, the legislative debate on new state aid was a debate over how the revenue reductions mandated by Proposition 2 1/2 should be allocated between the state and local governments. The key short-run issues were: (1) how much new local aid to provide; (2) how to finance it; and (3) how to distribute it. (10)

At one extreme, the "Share the Pain Bill" was based on the view that the state had an obligation to help cities and towns. This bill called for $360 million in new state aid, distributed in proportion to the first year loss in tax revenues caused by Proposition 2 1/2. At the other extreme was Governor King's initial budget proposal for only $37.6 million in new aid. This proposal was explicitly based on the view that the vote for Proposition 2 1/2 was a reaction to the problems of local government and did not obligate the state government in any way. The final local aid increase of $265 million represented a compromise between the Governor, the House, and the Senate, and required substantial cuts in state government agencies and employees. With the focus of the debate on the amount of new aid and the source of funds the problem of distributing the new state aid was virtually ignored. The implications of the last-minute decision to distribute most of the new aid using an equalizing formula with none distributed in line with first year revenue losses is discussed later in this paper.

*State and Local Government Shares*

The immediate effect of Proposition 2 1/2 is to reduce the share of state and local taxes collected at the local level. Based on the DOR July estimates of FY82 local tax reductions and on state taxes as shown in the 1982 state budget, we calculate that local taxes in Massachusetts will be reduced to 40.7 percent of total state and local tax revenues in FY82.

Table 23.3 compares this percentage to previous Massachusetts experience and to the experiences in the United States as a whole and in California. In all three areas the local share of taxes has been falling over time, although, especially in Massachusetts, the decline has been erratic. The first year impact of Proposition 2 1/2 is to reduce the local percentage by over 5 percentage points, bringing it closer to the U.S. average. This is a large drop in relation to previous yearly changes but small in relation to the dramatic first year reduction experienced in California in 1979, the first year after Proposition 13 rolled back local property taxes to 1 percent of 1975 market values. This difference between Massachusetts and California largely reflects the phasing-in of Proposition 2 1/2. Additional reductions are likely in future years as state income and sales tax revenues grow with inflation and local property taxes are reduced furthur in some communities and rise at a maximum rate of 2 1/2 percent per year in others.

**Table 23.3**
**Local Taxes as Percentage of State and Local Taxes**

|      | Massachusetts | California | United States |
|------|---------------|-----------|---------------|
| 1965 | 58.2          | 53.4      | 49.0          |
| 1970 | 50.7          | 50.7      | 44.7          |
| 1975 | 53.2          | 48.0      | 43.3          |
| 1976 | 48.0          | 48.1      | 43.1          |
| 1977 | 49.3          | 47.2      | 42.5          |
| 1978 | 49.1          | 45.1      | 41.5          |
| 1979 | 46.7          | 31.9      | 39.3          |
| 1980 | 44.9          | 30.2      | 38.7          |
| 1981 | 46.0          | n.a.      | n.a.          |
| 1982 | 40.7          | n.a.      | n.a.          |

n.a. = not available. Source: Governmental Finances, annual issues. Massachusetts data for 1981 from Massachusetts Taxpayers Foundation, State Budget Trends 1973-82, p.6. Massachusetts share for 1982 estimated by the authors with data from the Massachusetts DOR and 1982 State Budget.

Without new state aid and ignoring all other nontax revenue changes between FY81 and FY82, Propositon 2 1/2 would have lowered the absolute level of local spending by approximately 8 percent. The effects of this spending reduction on the local *share* of total state and local spending are estimated by altering the FY80 ratio of local to state and local direct general expenditures to reflect what would have happened if the proportional local revenue reductions required by Proposition 2 1/2 had taken place in 1980 with no other changes (including no changes in federal aid and no growth in user charges and fees). As shown in Table 23.4, the local share of expenditures was 55.4 percent in FY80, the latest year for which census data are available. Our estimates indicate the revenue provisions of Proposition 2 1/2 reduce the local share of spending to 53.4 percent.

## Table 23.4
### Simulations of Effects of Proposition 2 1/2 on
### Massachusetts State-Local Spending Shares and Revenue Shares

| Spending and Revenue Shares* | 1980 Value | Adjusted for local tax effects of Prop. 2 1/2 | Adjusted for local tax effects and new state aid** |
|---|---|---|---|
| Local direct general expenditures as percentage of state and local direct general expenditure | 55.4 | 53.4 | 55.5 |
| Property taxes as percentage of local general revenues | 49.5 | 45.8 | 39.5 |
| State aid as percentage of local general revenues | 27.8 | 29.8 | 32.1 |

*Comparable shares for the U.S. as a whole in 1980 are shown in Tables 23.1 and 23.2.

**New state aid refers to the aid induced by Prop. 2 1/2. In 1982, this is the additional aid of $265 million minus the $38 million initially proposed by Governor King.

To incorporate the effects on the local spending share of the new state aid induced by the pressures of Proposition 2 1/2, we define new aid as the total $265 million increase minus the $38 million proposed by the Governor in his initial budget. That is, we view the $38 million as aid that would have been provided even in the absence of Proposition 2 1/2. With this $227 million in new state aid, Proposition 2 1/2 *raises* the local spending share slightly to 55.5 percent. The share rises with the new state aid because the state absorbs a slightly larger portion of the revenue reduction ($227 million divided by $486 million = 47 percent) than its share of total spending before Proposition 2 1/2 (45 percent).

Although it may be tempting to conclude from this that the state absorbed *more than* its share of the required spending reduction, we believe this conclusion is unwarranted. As shown in Table 23.2 and repeated in Table 23.4, property taxes (including MVE revenues) accounted for 49.5 percent of local general revenue in FY80. Table 23.4 shows that the tax effects of Proposition 2 1/2 reduce this percentage to 45.8 percent. By augmenting local revenues state aid reduced this ratio further but only to 39.5 percent, a percentage still well above U.S. average of 28.2 percent. An alternative strategy for reducing this imbalance in the mix of local revenues would have been to enable Massachusetts communities to levy other broad-based local taxess such as income and sales taxes. However, since municipal governments in Massachusetts are, in general, too small and fragmented to avoid the most adverse effects of local sales or income taxes, not only was new state aid an appropriate response to the first year pressures of Proposition 2 1/2, but even more state aid might have been desirable. (11)

## Impacts of Proposition 2 1/2 across Cities and Towns

The 351 cities and towns in Massachusetts vary widely in revenue-raising ability, spending levels, and tax rates. For example, taxable property per capita ranged from $6,000 to $126,000 in 1981; total spending (including that for schools) by municipal government ranged from a low of $300 per capita to a high of $1900; and effective property tax rates ranged from 0.6 percent to 10 percent. (12) This diversity means that Proposition 2 1/2 had widely varying first-year effects on individual cities and towns. Proposition 2 1/2 required communities with effective tax rates above 2 1/2 percent to reduce property tax levies enough to reach the 2 1/2 percent limit or by 15 percent; low tax rate communities could raise levies by only 2 1/2 percent. (13) This section, which examines the magnitudes across communities of these first-year tax reductions, begins with an examination of the sources of the wide variation in pre-Proposition 2 1/2 tax rates.

Table 23.5 groups Massachusetts cities and towns into population size categories, after eliminating the 15 towns with population under 500. The data show that larger cities and towns had higher tax rates, on average, than smaller ones. The range between the group average tax rates shown in Table 23.5 is quite wide: with an average tax rate of 2.35 percent, the 110 towns with population under 5000 were 21 percent below the typical community, while the largest cities' and towns' average rate of 5.09 percent was 70 percent above that of the typical community and more than twice that of the small towns. The average municipality has a 3 percent property tax rate, but because so many more people live in the larger (higher tax rate) communities than in the smaller towns, the average resident in the state faced a property tax rate of 4.4 percent. (14)

The table includes two measures of per capita spending, gross expenditures and nonfixed local expenditures. The former includes all financial commitments of the city or town for FY81 including local school spending and/or each municipality's share of a regional school district's spending. Any of these commitments not financed out of fees and charges, intergovernmental aid, or motor vehicle excise revenues must be financed out of the property tax levy. Nonfixed local expenditures exclude state and county assessments (for example, for the regional transit authority in the Boston area), pension payments, and debt service expenditures, and hence provide a better measure of the spending that can be cut by the community in the short run.

It is apparent from Table 23.5 that small tax bases contribute more than high spending levels to the high tax rates of the largest cities and towns. The smallest towns taxed themselves on average at a rate below 2 1/2 percent in FY81, and raised $508 per capita. The largest cities and towns taxed themselves at an average rate more than twice as high to raise only 14 percent more property tax revenue per capita, on average. Their revenue-raising disadvantage was partially offset by higher state aid and other nontax revenues. Thus, in order to spend about 27 percent more than the smallest cities and towns, the largest communities taxed themselves about twice as heavily. This seems to run counter to the popular impression and the arguments made during the debate prior to the 2 1/2 vote, that excessive spending was the basic cause of high property tax rates. The data imply that while higher spending in large communities may play some role, it is not the major contributor to the high average tax rates in these communities.

*Patterns of First-Year Revenue Losses before New Aid*

About 182 of the 351 cities and towns were required to reduce property taxes to bring them down toward their tax rate limit. Communities with tax rates below the limit were allowed to raise tax levies but only by 2 1/2 percent. In addition, all communities lost revenue from the statewide reduction of the motor vehicle excise (MVE) rate from 6.6 to 2.5 percent. When these changes are combined, all the cities and towns faced absolute tax revenue reductions in FY82.

Table 23.6 shows these first-year revenue losses for the five population groups of cities and towns, where losses are defined as the difference between tax revenues permitted under Proposition 2 1/2 in FY82 and actual tax revenues in FY81. As shown in column 1, the average required property tax reductions range from 1.5 percent in the smallest towns, which typically had low rates, to 14.9 percent in the largest communities, all of which had FY81 tax rates well above 2 1/2 percent. Because MVE revenues were reduced by 62 percent statewide, the per capita changes shown in column 2 vary only slightly over the groups and reflect variations in the ratio of auto registrations to population. Smaller towns' losses resulted mostly from motor vehicle excise cuts while the losses of the biggest cities and towns were largely attributable to property tax rate reductions. (15)

Two qualifications should be noted. First, and most important, the losses reported here simply represent reductions in the tax revenues from one year to the next, rather than the difference between FY82 permitted tax revenues and what tax revenues would have been in FY82 in the absence of Proposition 2 1/2. Thus, the reported losses understate the full effects of the limitation in any municipality to the extent that property tax levies would have increased without the tax limitation measure. Second, the reported losses are only estimates; they are based on assumptions about 1982 property valuations made by the DOR in July 1981. Because some communities are still in the process of determining their 1982 valuations, actual revenue losses are still unknown.

Taken by themselves, the tax reductions shown in columns 1 and 2 of Table 23.6 benefit local taxpayers, with taxpayers in large communities benefiting more on average than those in small communities. At the same time, however, local tax reductions may lead to cuts in local public services. Column 3, which shows the combined property tax and motor vehicle excise reductions as a fraction of FY81 gross expenditures, indicates percentages by which communities would have had to cut spending in the absence of any new state aid or other revenue changes. The spending impacts are large: the average percentage reductions range from almost 5 percent to over 10 percent across groups and the average resident lives in a community facing revenue losses equal to 8.4 percent of gross expenditures. Because not all expenditures can be cut in the short run, revenue losses as a fraction of nonfixed expenditures (shown in column 4) provide a better indication of the cuts in operating expenditures required by the revenue provisions of Proposition 2 1/2. The group average reductions range from 5 to 13 percent, and individual town or city losses range from under 1 to 19 percent. Notably, all but one of the population groups show virtually this full range. The exception is the group of largest cities and towns, none of which have revenue losses that are less than 10 percent of FY81 expenditures.

Table 23.7 groups the cities and towns by the size of the Proposition 2 1/2 revenue losses as a fraction of FY81 budgets (before new state aid). Because some small and medium-sized as well as large communities faced large revenue losses, the patterns shown in Table 23.7 run counter to the popular view that most of the communities hit hardest by Proposition 2 1/2 were large cities with low incomes, high tax rates and high spending. The cities and towns with the greatest first-year revenue losses -- 12 percent and over -- had moderately high incomes, property values, tax rates and spending; Proposition 2 1/2 hit these communities the hardest because they were most dependent of all the groups on property taxes and the motor vehicle excise for revenue, as shown in column 7. The two groups with the smallest revenue losses (0-3 and 3-7 percent) were also heavily dependent on property tax and motor vehicle excise revenues but because they had higher property valuations, their tax rates were lower, leaving them less constrained by the 2 1/2 percent limitation. At the extreme, the communities in the group least hard hit by Proposition 2 1/2 were the richest (in terms of equalized valuation or income per capita), on average, which allowed them to finance average FY81 spending levels higher than any other group, with average tax rates below 2 1/2 percent.

Somewhat surprisingly, it is the municipalities with revenue losses between 7 and 12 percent of 1981 expenditures rather than those with losses over 12 percent that have the lowest incomes and property values and the highest property tax rates. This reflects the fact that a greater share of the expenditures of these communities was financed with nontax revenues than was the case for the highest loss communities.

One of the most striking characterstics of all these groupings, however, is the wide range of income levels, per capita valuations, and spending levels around the group averages shown in the table. In particular, high and low spending communities are scattered throughout the range of losses.

Determining whether the net effects of large tax savings and large impacts on local budgets are harmful or beneficial to the residents of a particular community raises complex and difficult questions beyond the scope of this paper. The evaluation depends in part on the extent to which spending reductions lead to efficiency gains rather than service reductions, how much people value tax cuts relative to service cuts, and who is affected by service cuts. Because large expenditure reductions are likely to be more disruptive than small reductions, however, it seems appropriate that they be partially offset by new state aid.

## Effects of New State Aid on Revenue Losses

New state aid partially offsets the effects of the first-year tax losses on local spending. Most of the new aid was distributed using the Equalizing Municipal Grant (EMG) formula, which allocates aid in direct proportion to population and in inverse proportion to per capita equalized valuation. (16) Columns 5 and 6 of Table 23.6 show the effects of this new state aid on average revenue losses expressed as percentages of the two spending measures for each group of communities. The new aid substantially alleviated the first-year spending impacts of Proposition 2 1/2 in all cities and towns, but more so in smaller than in larger communities. Thus, after new state aid, average revenue losses range from 1.7 percent to 7.8 percent of FY81 nonfixed spending across population groups in contrast to the 5.3 to 13.4 percent range of losses before the new aid.

The EMG has been criticized for not meeting one major goal of new state aid for FY82, that of "cushioning" the impact of Proposition 2 1/2 on local budgets. An earlier proposal would have directly addressed the "cushioning" goal by replacing approximately half the revenue loss of each community. As a one-year program, this "half-gap" aid would have given cities and towns more time to adjust to Proposition 2 1/2s limits. This form of aid -- i.e., aid to offset a determinate fraction of each local government's revenue loss -- was also the approach taken by the California legislature in response to Proposition 13.

Column 1 of Table 23.8 shows the pattern of aid that results from offsetting exactly half the first-year revenue loss of all communities. Because large communities on average faced larger tax losses as a fraction of spending than small communities, half-gap aid as a fraction of spending increases with community size. This approach is flawed, however, because it fails to address the possibility that the vote for Proposition 2 1/2 was a vote against "business as usual." By offsetting a constant proportion of first-year revenue losses, half-gap aid maintains pre-Proposition 2 1/2 spending disparities. To the extent that some of the spending differences reflect governmental inefficiency and waste, an aid program that allows such differences to continue -- after a public vote that to many was a vote for more efficient government -- seems undesirable. (17)

By distributing per capita aid inversely with per capita equalized valuation, the EMG formula favors communities with small per capita tax bases. As shown in column 2 of Table 23.8, the $205 million of new aid distributed under this formula is a higher proportion of gross expenditures in large communities than in small, although the differences across groups are not as great as they are with half-gap aid. The distribution, however, ignores the "cushioning" goal; column 5 shows that, on average, small communities received more state aid than they lost in revenue while the largest cities and towns received state aid equal, on average, to 45 percent of their revenue losses. These averages conceal even greater variations across individual communities. Some communities, for example, received new aid that was five times larger than their first-year revenue losses while other received less than 15 percent of their first-year revenue losses. On average, the biggest losers (those with tax revenue losses greater than 12 percent of gross expenditures) received aid equal to only 26 percent of their losses, while those with the smallest losses (0-3 percent) received more aid than the revenues they lost, resulting in a 144 percent average replacement rate (see final column of Table 23.7).

A third aid formula incorporates elements of both these two types of new state aid. It starts with the EMG formula, but then takes account of the size of the revenue loss by setting the minimum amount of aid at 30 percent and the minimum amount at 100 percent of a city's or town's first-year revenue loss under Proposition 2 1/2. We refer to this as 30-100 aid. The $222 million that would have been distributed according to this formula under an amendment passed by the House in the fall of 1981 (but not enacted) has the characteristics shown in columns 3 and 6 of Table 23.8. (18) It offsets the most undesirable effects of the EMG distribution and at the same time preserves the EMG formula's basic equalizing feature. For example, it would raise to one-third the average replacement for cities and towns with losses over 12 percent, and reduce the aid provided to cities and towns with losses under 3 percent to 91 percent of their losses, on average. It would also increase the average aid going to cities and towns with losses of 7 to 12 percent. Because it would have cushioned the first to year budget adjustments more evenly across communities, this 30-100 aid would have been preferable to the EMG distribution that was actually used.

*Long-Run Effects and the Need for a New State Aid Formula*

About 40 of the larger cities and towns will be required to reduce property tax levies up to 15 percent more in the second year of Proposition 2 1/2 and some may be required to make additional cuts in the following year. (19) Even those communities facing no further reductions, however, will continue to be affected by the tax limitation measure. In an inflationary period, the 2 1/2 percent limit on the annual growth of levies assures that the gap between actual revenues and what revenues would have been without

Proposition 2 1/2 will continue to widen. Moreover, this growth limit provision implies that once effective tax rates are reduced to 2 1/2 percent, they will *continue to fall* -- provided only that taxable property values grow at more than 2 1/2 percent per year. Aside from possible overrides (discussed below) the only exceptions to the 2 1/2 percent growth limit are new development or property renovation or rehabilitation adding more than 50 percent to a property's value. With such development, the municipality can exempt from the limit revenues equal to the previous year's tax rate multiplied by the incremental value of the property.

Proposition 2 1/2 has major implications for the long-run pattern of spending across communities. Before Proposition 2 1/2, differences in discretionary spending across jurisdictions reflected differences in service costs or needs, preferences for public services, and efficiency. Importantly, resource-poor communities were allowed to tax themselves more heavily than others to support desired expenditures. Proposition 2 1/2 changes this by equalizing tax rates across jurisdictions. In the absence of overrides, the reduction of high tax rates to 2 1/2 percent would result in local tax revenues that vary across communities directly in line with local tax bases. (20) The wide divergence in tax bases shown in Table 23.5 illustrates the significance of this outcome: large, low-base communities will end up with per capita property tax revenues half the size of those in small, high-base communities. The current distribution of state and federal aid alleviates the harshness of this outcome somewhat, since it is equalizing in the aggregate; that is, communities with less abiliy to raise their own revenues receive more intergovernmental transfers. But the costs of providing basic local government services (e.g., police, fire, schools) do not vary in proportion to local tax resources, even as augmented with intergovernmental transfers. Thus, cities and towns with smaller per capita tax bases would be forced to provide fewer or lower quality services to their residents.

Needs for local government services and the costs of providing them vary across cities and towns for a number of reasons. (21) For example, some places have more school age children or more miles of locally maintained and locally policed roads or more properties to protect from fire than others; some areas have commuters as well as local residents using their services; some areas have more densely developed or older residential and commercial structures that make fire prevention and fire protection more costly per acre or per capita than in newer spread-out residential towns. Some of these cost differences imply that low-base areas not only are less able to raise any given revenue amount per capita, but also are likely to be high-need areas, that is, areas that face higher costs per capita to provide any given level of services.

Legislative amendments enacted at the end of the 1981 session changed the override provisions of Proposition 2 1/2 to allow individual places to ease the tax rate restriction on a year-by-year basis. (22) This brings relief on the service provision side: low-base/high-needs areas can again tax themselves more heavily to provide needed services. But the underlying problem will remain: just as before Proposition 2 1/2, it is the most fiscally strained places that will end up with the highest tax rates. Significantly, most of the 40 cities and towns facing possible second-year cuts had FY81 per capita property valuations well below the overall average.

Proposition 2 1/2 attacks but does not directly remedy the fundamental problem of Massachusetts local government finances identified in the first sections of this paper: excessive reliance on one revenue source -- property taxes. To minimize the adverse long-run effects of the Proposition, the state should set up a guaranteed revenue-sharing program for future years with the funds distributed to local communities inversely to local resources and directly with service "needs." (23) The EMG formula, used for first-year aid, is a start in this direction but not complete; it equalizes across tax base differences but implicitly assumes that "needs" are proportional to population. A revenue-sharing plan that balanced needs and resources would allow local governments to retain some discretion in choosing levels of individual services to reflect local preferences (24) and would maintain the incentive for all cities and towns to spend as efficiently as possible. At the same time, it could give all communities access to resources sufficient to provide their residents a reasonable level of local public sector services.

**Impacts on School Budgets**

Proposition 2 1/2 has potentially important implications for spending on elementary and secondary education. Because school spending accounts for over half the budget in many Massachusetts communities, it is difficult for cities and towns to make substantial reductions in overall budgets without making comparable reductions in school budgets. In addition, because Proposition 2 1/2 ended the fiscal autonomy of school committees by making their budgets subject to the will of the town or city legislative body, supporters of education spending feared that school spending might bear more than its share of the burden of local revenue reductions.

In order to examine the effect of Proposition 2 1/2 on school budgets, we use responses by school committees in 132 cities and towns to a survey conducted by the Massachusetts Department of Education in June 1981. These 132 cities and towns comprise 44 percent of the state's 297 cities and towns with operating school systems and appear to be representative of the state's nonregional school systems except for the biggest cities. (25) The June 1981 survey date means that in some cases the FY82 budgets reported by the school committees had not yet been approved by the local legislative body (26) and there was uncertainty about the amount and distribution of new state aid.

*Size of School Budget Cuts*

Table 23.9 presents 1982 school budget data for the 132 communities for which we have survey responses. Columns 1 and 2 show how the sample is distributed among the same five population size categories used in earlier tables and reports the average number of pupils in the sample communities by category. Column 3 shows that the percentage by which preliminary 1982 school committee budgets fall below 1981 budgets varies from 3.7 percent in the smallest communities to 9.6 percent in cities and towns with populations between 25,000 and 50,000.

A comparison of column 3 with column 4 indicates that for all population groups the average percentage reduction in school budgets is substantially larger than the average percentage reduction in nonfixed municipal expenditures (including schools) resulting from the Proposition 2 1/2 loss in revenues after new state aid. (27) Thus, unless the preliminary school budgets were changed dramatically in response to the new state aid, school spending was apparently disproportionately affected by Proposition 2 1/2.

This outcome is partially explained by the trends shown in columns 5-8. During the five-year period 1975-80, per pupil education expenditures in our typical sample community grew by 58.4 percent, or about 14 percent after correcting for inflation. (28) For the state as a whole, local school expenditures per public school enrollee increased in nominal terms by 64 percent while local government expenditures per capita for all nonschool purposes grew by 50 percent between 1975 and 1980. (29)

This more rapid growth in school spending provides some support for the view that larger proportionate cutbacks could be made in school spending than in other categories. Rapid growth, however, need not imply excessive service levels. In Table 23.9 service levels are measured by school expenditures per weighted pupil, where the pupil weights are Department of Education estimates of costs used in the current school aid formula. (30) For example, the six largest communities in the sample had below-average school expenditures per weighted pupil in 1980 (i.e., low service levels) in spite of the fact that they had the largest per pupil expenditure increase between 1975 and 1980. The real question is the extent to which the recent growth in school spending accurately reflects local preferences for education services and changing views about the education of special needs students.

In addition, if the trends shown in columns 7 and 8 for the historical period continue into the present, the number of public school pupils is falling relative to the overall population in all population size categories. With this change in relative needs, a change in the mix of the total budget package away from education spending may be appropriate. However, even if such an adjustment is called for in the long run, large cuts in a single year are likely to be disruptive.

*Impact on Service Level Disparities*

With many small school districts and relatively low state small school aid, Massachusetts is characterized by wide variation in per pupil school spending across districts. (31) The impact of Proposition 2 1/2 on these interdistrict spending disparities can be seen in Table 23.10, which shows the percentage changes between 1981 and 1982 in total school budgets and instructional spending in the 132 sample communities grouped by 1980 service level. The groupings are quintiles of communities based on expenditures per weighted pupil. (32) Column 2 illustrates the wide variations in education service levels across jurisdictions. Average spending per weighted pupil in the high-service communities is about twice that in the low-service communities.

Based on the average percentage changes in school budgets shown in column 3, we conclude that Proposition 2 1/2s initial impact is to increase somewhat the disparities in education service levels across cities and towns, especially at the upper end. In particular, communities spending the most per weighted pupil before Proposition 2 1/2 made the smallest cuts and communities in the middle service level quintile made the largest cuts in 1982 school budgets.

Columns 4 and 5 present estimates of changes in instructional spending and in number of teachers from the same Department of Education survey. The patterns are basically the same as those for changes in total school committee budget, and strengthen the earlier conclusions that education cuts are substantial and that Proposition 2 1/2 makes the distribution of education services across jurisdictions more unequal than it was before the tax limitation measure was passed; on average, instructional expenditure and teacher reductions in low-service communities exceed those in high-service communities.

## Conclusions

This paper has examined the size and distribution of local government revenue reductions required by Proposition 2 1/2. Measurements of impact were based on the limited data available one year after the Proposition's passage and halfway through its first fiscal year of implementation. Although the estimated revenue losses may differ from actual losses, especially as a result of revaluations recently or soon-to-be completed in some municipalities, they provide a useful description of the current situation and a starting point for policy debate.

The tax rate and levy growth limitation provisions of Proposition 2 1/2 reduced tax revenues available to every city and town in the Commonwealth in FY82, but the impacts varied tremendously across cities and towns. After the first year, the highest tax rate cities and towns will have further required levy reductions, and all other communities will be constrained by Proposition 2 1/2s restriction of levy growth to 2 1/2 percent per year. In addition, currently planned cutbacks in federal aid will reduce the revenues of local governments, especially those of the larger cities and towns now most dependent on federal aid and also hardest hit by Proposition 2 1/2.

This paper has developed the argument that enactment of substantial new state aid is an appropriate response to the revenue losses of local governments because Massachusetts' high property taxes before Proposition 2 1/2 were mostly attributable to excessive reliance on property taxes as a local revenue source. The question of how that aid should be financed has not been addressed, but even as local revenue growth is constrained by Proposition 2 1/2, state revenue sources, most importantly income and sales taxes, will continue to increase with growth in the economy. Depending on the distribution formula used, new state aid may ease the short-term adjustment problems of hard-hit city and town governments, and may also offset the inherent long-run tendency of a tax rate limitation to widen spending disparities that result from unequal revenue-raising ability. The first-year aid program enacted by the legislature, which uses the Equalizing Municipal Grant formula to distribute most of the aid, chooses the latter goal. A variant of that aid program (which we call 30-100 aid) would have balanced these two goals somewhat better for the first year.

In later years, some of the most undesirable long-run effects of Proposition 2 1/2 could be reduced by eliminating the 2 1/2 percent limitation on annual levy growth, substituting instead a permanent rate limit of 2 1/2 percent. This continuation of a tax rate limit rather than a levy growth limit would also maintain the incentive for cities and towns to update their assessments, one of the most favorable first-year effects of Proposition 2 1/2. A rate limit would also be more neutral than a levy growth limit with respect to changes in the overall inflation rate.

Additional state aid to local government is also needed in future years. Ideally, the distribution of such aid across cities and towns would be responsive to interlocal variation in both service needs and taxable resources. Such equalizing aid would reduce the spending disparities caused by disparities in needs and revenue-raising capacity that existed before Proposition 2 1/2, and would also offset the worsening of spending disparities based on resource disparities that would otherwise occur under Proposition 2 1/2s uniform rate limitation.

TABLE 23.5
TAX AND SPENDING CHARACTERISTICS OF CITIES AND TOWNS

| Population Group | Number of cities and towns | 1980 popula- tion | Percent of state total 1980 population | Effective tax rate | EQV per capita* | Per capita gross expendi- tures | Nonfixed local expendi- tures per capita | Prop. tax levy per capita | Property taxes as % of gross expen- ditures | State aid per capita** |
|---|---|---|---|---|---|---|---|---|---|---|
| 5,000 or less | 110 | 2,222 | 4.3 | 2.35 | $24,892 | $802 | $709 | $508 | 63.2 | $125 |
| 5,001-10,000 | 75 | 6,930 | 9.1 | 2.80 | 20,366 | 815 | 715 | 504 | 61.3 | 139 |
| 10,001-25,000 | 91 | 16,001 | 25.5 | 3.17 | 17,744 | 884 | 759 | 539 | 60.3 | 164 |
| 25,001-50,000 | 39 | 33,625 | 22.9 | 3.63 | 17,206 | 949 | 771 | 577 | 61.0 | 159 |
| 50,001 or more | 21 | 104,138 | 38.2 | 5.09 | 11,865 | 1,019 | 803 | 578 | 56.1 | 229 |
| Statewide total | 336 | 5,718,720 | 100.0 | --- | --- | --- | --- | --- | --- | --- |
| Average city or town | --- | 17,020 | --- | 2.99 | 20,239 | 858 | 737 | 528 | 61.3 | 149 |
| Average resident | --- | 94,563 | --- | 4.42 | 15,352 | 992 | 805 | 584 | 58.7 | 199 |

Notes: The 15 towns with population under 500 were excluded. The total 1980 population in these towns is 4,582, which is .08 percent of the state population.
        All table entries except column 1 and "Average resident" row are simple unweighted averages for all cities and towns in the group.
        *Massachusetts DOR estimate of market value of taxable property.
        **Total amount estimated to be paid to city or town in state distributions and reimbursements (shown on "cherry sheets"). These amounts do not include aid paid directly to regional school districts.

TABLE 23.6

REVENUE CHANGES MANDATED BY PROPOSITION 2 1/2

| Population Group | % change in property tax levy | Change in motor vehicle excise revenues per capita | Total change in tax revenue (before new aid) as % of nonfixed expenditures | | Change in revenue net of new EMG* as % of nonfixed expenditures | |
|---|---|---|---|---|---|---|
| | | | gross expenditures | nonfixed expenditures | gross expenditures | nonfixed expenditures |
| 5,000 or less | - 1.5 | -$28.4 | - 4.7 | - 5.3 | -1.5 | -1.7 |
| 5,001-10,000 | - 2.5 | - 28.7 | - 5.2 | - 5.9 | -1.5 | -1.7 |
| 10,001-25,000 | - 5.9 | - 29.1 | - 6.9 | - 8.1 | -3.4 | -4.0 |
| 25,001-50,000 | - 9.0 | - 27.6 | - 8.4 | -10.5 | -5.0 | -6.3 |
| 50,001 or more | -14.9 | - 21.9 | -10.5 | -13.4 | -6.1 | -7.8 |
| Average city or town | - 4.6 | - 28.2 | - 6.2 | - 7.3 | -2.7 | -3.3 |
| Average resident | - 9.9 | - 25.4 | - 8.4 | -10.5 | -4.5 | -5.7 |

Notes: change is measured as difference between allowed FY82 revenues and actual FY81 revenues.
*EMG is the equalizing municipal grant formula.

TABLE 23.7

FISCAL CHARACTERISTICS OF CITIES AND TOWNS BY REVENUE LOSS

| Revenue Loss Group* | Number of cities and towns (cities) | % of state total 1980 population | FY81 effective tax rate | FY81 equalized valuation per capita | 1975 per capita income | FY81 gross expenditures per capita | FY81 property tax and motor vehicle excise as % of gross expenditures | New state aid as % of tax revenue loss |
|---|---|---|---|---|---|---|---|---|
| 0-3% loss | 131 (1) | 18.3 | 2.39 | $26,415 | $5140 | $891 | 68.1 | 144 |
| 3-7% loss | 70 (2) | 11.3 | 2.63 | 19,478 | 4830 | 778 | 67.1 | 94 |
| 7-10% loss | 34(13) | 22.5 | 3.75 | 13,054 | 4598 | 866 | 59.9 | 53 |
| 10-12% loss | 51(14) | 29.5 | 4.00 | 13,681 | 4635 | 863 | 63.9 | 39 |
| 12% or greater loss | 50 (9) | 18.4 | 3.53 | 16,700 | 4898 | 871 | 71.4 | 26 |

*The measure of revenue loss is the difference between allowed FY82 revenues and actual FY81 revenues as a percent of gross expenditures, before new state aid.

TABLE 23.8

ACTUAL AND PROPOSED NEW STATE AID TO LOCAL GOVERNMENT

| Population Group | New aid as percent of FY81 gross expenditures | | | New aid as a fraction of tax revenue loss | | |
|---|---|---|---|---|---|---|
| | Half-gap | EMG | 30-100 | Half-gap | EMG (range) | 30-100 (range) |
| 5,000 or less | 2.3 | 3.2 | 2.8 | 0.50 | 1.04 (0.07-4.8) | 0.77 (0.30-1.0) |
| 5,000-10,000 | 2.6 | 3.7 | 3.2 | 0.50 | 1.03 (0.12-3.8) | 0.78 (0.30-1.0) |
| 10,001-25,000 | 3.5 | 3.5 | 3.4 | 0.50 | 0.87 (0.11-5.4) | 0.64 (0.30-1.0) |
| 25,001-50,000 | 4.2 | 3.4 | 3.7 | 0.50 | 0.57 (0.13-2.1) | 0.57 (0.30-1.0) |
| 50,001 or more | 5.3 | 4.4 | 5.0 | 0.50 | 0.45 (0.13-1.1) | 0.51 (0.30-1.0) |
| Average city or town | 3.1 | 3.5 | 3.3 | 0.50 | 0.90 (0.07-5.4) | 0.70 (0.30-1.0) |
| Average resident | 4.2 | 3.9 | 4.0 | 0.50 | 0.65 (0.07-5.4) | 0.58 (0.30-1.0) |
| State total aid (millions of dollars) | 243 | 205 | 222 | 243 | 205 | 222 |

Note: See text for definitions. EMG is the equalizing municipal grant formula used to distribute the actual new state aid.

## TABLE 23.9
### IMPACTS ON PRELIMINARY SCHOOL BUDGETS

| Population Group | Sample size | District pupils(a) 1980 | % change in school committee budget FY81-FY82 | Municipal revenue loss after new state aid as % of nonfixed expenditures | 5-year % change in per pupil expenditures(b) 1975-80 | Expenditures per weighted pupil(c) 1980 | 5-year percent change in students 1975-80(d) | 10-year percent change in population 1970-80(e) |
|---|---|---|---|---|---|---|---|---|
| 5000 or less | 38 | 308 | -3.7 | -0.8 | 61.4 | 2154 | -3.7 | 33.5 |
| 5001-10,000 | 30 | 1269 | -4.7 | -1.5 | 54.2 | 1731 | -8.1 | 15.9 |
| 10,001-25,000 | 42 | 2959 | -6.8 | -3.0 | 56.0 | 1900 | -9.3 | 11.0 |
| 25,001-50,000 | 16 | 6135 | -9.6 | -5.9 | 61.3 | 1971 | -15.7 | -1.4 |
| 50,001 or more | 6 | 11325 | -9.2 | -6.0 | 69.3 | 1791 | -15.2 | -5.5 |
| Average sample community | | 2577 | -5.9 | -2.5 | 58.4 | 1938 | -8.5 | 16.3 |

Notes: The table is based on the 132 cities and towns for which we have data from the June 1981 survey of school committees by the Massachusetts Department of Education.
(a) Net average membership of students in the local school district excluding local students attending regional schools.
(b) The expenditure concept used for this calculation is average integrated cost. This includes expenditures made on behalf of all students in the city or town, including those attending regional schools. Source: Massachusetts Department of Education.
(c) See text for definition of weighted pupils. Expenditures exclude those made for students attending regional schools.
(d) Students are defined as net average membership and include local pupils attending regional schools. Source: Massachusetts Department of Education.
(e) Based on 1970 and 1980 Census of Population.

TABLE 23.10

EFFECTS ON SCHOOL COMMITTEE BUDGETS

132 CITIES AND TOWNS BY SERVICE LEVEL CATEGORIES

| Service Level Group* | Communities in Sample/Total Communities | FY80 Expenditures per weighted pupil sample/total | Percent change in School budget FY81-FY82 | Percent change in instructional spending FY81-FY82 | Percent change in teachers FY81-FY82 |
|---|---|---|---|---|---|
| 1 (low) | 29/56 | 1412/1411 | -5.6 | -4.2 | - 9.7 |
| 2 | 27/56 | 1652/1645 | -5.8 | -6.5 | -10.9 |
| 3 (middle) | 22/56 | 1865/1864 | -7.2 | -6.3 | -12.2 |
| 4 | 29/56 | 2080/2085 | -5.9 | -6.1 | - 8.9 |
| 5 (high) | 25/56 | 2755/2709 | -4.9 | -4.2 | - 9.5 |
| Average | | 1938/1943 | -5.9 | -5.5 | -10.2 |
| Number of observations | 132/280 | 132/280 | 132 | 131 | 123 |

*Service levels are measured by FY80 expenditures per weighted pupil, where the weights are those used in the current school aid formula. The groups are quintiles of the 280 communities for which data were available on expenditures per weighted pupil.

## Notes for Chapter 23

Reprinted from the *New England Economic Review,* January/February 1982 (part one), March/April 1982 (part two), by permission of the authors.

Helen F. Ladd would like to thank the Institute for Research on Educational Finance and Governance for research support for this paper.

1. U.S. Department of Education, *Digest of Educational Statistics (year),* annual issues. Data refer to expenditure per pupil in average daily attendance in public elementary and secondary schools.

2. The motor vehicle excise in Massachusetts is included in the Census Bureau's definition of property taxes.

3. Before concluding that the solution to Massachusetts' property tax problems is to enable local communities to use other local tax sources, Massachusetts' fragmented governmental structure should be considered. Unlike other states which have successfully used local income or sales taxes at the county level, Massachusetts has no governmental jurisdictions with taxing powers sufficiently large to be suitable for local nonproperty taxes.

4. For example, see Robert W. Eisenmenger, Alicia H. Munnell, Joan T. Poskanzer, Richard F. Syron,, and Steven J. Weiss, "Needed: A New Tax Structure for Massachusetts," *New England Economic Review,* May/June 1975, pp. 3-24, for a careful description of the problems resulting from Massachusetts' heavy reliance on the local property tax.

5. For example, suppose a specific community is required to reduce property taxes by 15 percent in the first year of Proposition 2 1/2 and thereafter may increase the levy by 2 1/2 percent annually. Suppose further that in the absence of Proposition 2 1/2, this community would have increased its property tax levy by 5 percent each year. Proposition 2 1/2 therefore reduces local property tax revenues by 19 percent the first year, 21 percent the second, and 23 percent the third. The measure used in this paper, however, shows smaller losses -- decreasing rather than increasing over time -- of 15, 13, and 11 for the first three years.

6. We modify this procedure slightly for the motor vehicle excise reduction which went into effect on January 1, 1961, halfway through FY61. Here the FY82 revenue loss is defined in relation to 1980 calendar year revenues. Note that these estimates assume that the taxable base is the same after Proposition 2 1/2 as before. If people respond to the lower tax rate, however, by upgrading their automobiles, the taxable base will grow and our estimates of the before-after difference will be too high.

7. Public officials were previously reluctant to revalue because they had little to gain from doing so. Revaluation would bring dramatic shifts in property tax burdens, particularly away from business property onto residential property, but also across and within neighborhoods. In addition, revaluation could result in a loss of state aid. This occurred because the DOR typically underestimates true

market valuation for communities assessing below 80 percent and consequently gives them more than their share of state aid distributions that vary inversely with estimated valuation.

8. The estimates assume that (1) communities wishing to update their 1982 valuations do so with a minimum increase of 13 percent over the 1981 valuations and (2) those communities scheduled to implement new revaluations in 1982 do so with a minimum additional increase of 10 percent over the preliminary inflation-adjusted estimate of full and fair cash value. The estimates are weakest for the 120 communities with populations over 500 that were scheduled to implement revaluation during FY82. Of the 120, 37 were scheduled for tax reductions between 0 and 15 percent; these reductions will be moderated if the certified valuation figures exceed the DOR estimates. Also among the cities and towns scheduled to revalue in FY82, 53 were scheduled for tax increases and 30 for cuts of the maximum 15 percent. Although revaluation could alter either of these groups' first year revenue changes, the impacts are likely to be small.

9. The only provisions affecting state spending and taxes are the rental deduction which reduces state income tax revenues and the requirement that the state finance any local programs it mandates that are not accepted by the cities and towns.

10. The debate on how much aid to provide took place at a time of uncertainty about the first year revenue losses under Proposition 2 1/2. Early estimates suggested that losses would be over $600 million, but part of this reflected the loss of MVE revenues over an 18-month period. Preliminary estimates by the DOR showed a $390 million net loss in property tax revenues and an 18-month loss in MVE revenues of $225 million. As noted in the text, on July 1, 1981 the DOR estimated a 10-month loss of $490 million.

11. We make this statement based on our analysis of the causes of high property taxes in the state. To the extent that the electorate believes that high property taxes are the result of inefficiency and waste, however, additional state aid may create problems; by giving aid to cities and towns, the state makes it possible for local officials to avoid the hard choices that many supporters of Proposition 2 1/2 wanted them to be forced to make. For an analysis of what voters wanted, see Helen F. Ladd and Julie Boatwright Wilson, "Proposition 2 1/2: Explaining the Vote," John F. Kennedy School of Government, Research R81-1, April 1981.

12. Taxable property values (called "equalized valuations") are estimated by the Massachusetts DOR for cities and towns that do not assess property at 100 percent of market value. The equalized values are likely to be underestimates of actual 1981 full market values because they are based on 1980 valuations. In addition, the DOR tends to underestimate the property values in cities and urbanized towns by a greater amount than those in homogeneous residential communities. Effective tax rates are calculated as the ratio of a city's or town's property tax levy to its equalized valuation. Hence, the effective tax rate is overstated where the equalized valuation is underestimated. The 10 percent maximum figure cited in the text is for Boston, and is likely to be an overestimate for these reasons.

The analysis throughout the text is based on the 336 Massachusetts cities and towns with population over 500. Because the 15 towns with 1980 population less than 500 contain less than one tenth of 1 percent (.08 percent) of the state's population, results for the remaining 336 cities and towns are representative of the entire state.

13. Some low tax rate communities were exceptions. Those with 1979 tax rates below 2 1/2 percent were assigned that lesser percentage as their limit. If their current tax rate is above that limit, they are required to reduce their property tax levy to the limit or by 13 percent annually until the limit is reached.

14. The figures reported in the "average resident" row of Table 23.5 are weighted averages of the individual community data, where the weights are community population. Hence, for each column they represent the community characteristic (tax rate, valuation, expenditures) faced by the average resident in the state. All other rows (except "statewide total") weight all cities and towns equally.

15. Some of the smaller towns also experienced large property tax reductions because of the provision setting the limit equal to the 1979 effective property tax rate for towns in which that rate was below 2 1/2 percent.

16. The EMG is also known as the lottery formula because it has been used to distribute revenues from the state lottery. The formula defines an individual municipality's share as follows:

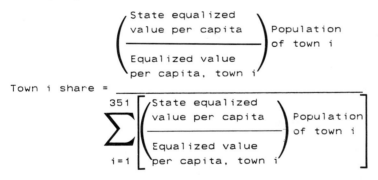

17. See Helen F. Ladd and Julie Boatwright Wilson, "Proposition 2 1/2: Explaining the Vote," John F. Kennedy School of Government, Research Report R81-1, April 1981 for evidence that the desire for and expectation of more efficient government was a major factor motivating support for Proposition 2 1/2.

18. The amounts of aid provided under the three plans shown in Table 23.8 are not exactly comparable because the state totals (as shown in the final row) are not equal. However, the patterns across city and town types are the focus here.

19. Massachusetts DOR estimates.

20. Over the longer run, the limitation of levy growth to 2 1/2 percent is likely to result in tax rate disparities widening again after the high rate areas have reached 2 1/2 percent. That provision states that a city's or town's property tax levy may grow at a maximum of 2 1/2 percent annually regardless of growth in the taxable property base. Communities with rates below 2 1/2 percent in 1979 have that lower rate as their limit; with a 2 1/2 percent annual levy growth limit, their rates are likely to remain well below 2 1/2 percent. At the same time, effective tax rates will fall more rapidly in fast growth areas than in areas with base growth only slightly above 2 1/2 percent per year. These two factors will combine to widen disparities if history is any indication: areas with low effective property tax rates in FY81 showed greater growth (in population) during the 1970s than areas with higher tax rates.

21. The latter are notoriously difficult to measure, but are illustrated by high costs of fire protection in areas with rundown buildings, high traffic control costs where many nonresident commuters use the roads, and high per pupil school costs where substantial fractions of students need bilingual or remedial education. At a simpler level, school needs can be measured by the number of students.

22. As originally passed, Proposition 2 1/2 allowed local overrides only in biennial statewide November elections, and required a two-thirds favorable vote with the participation of at least 30 percent of a municipality's eligible voters. Because the timing of the possible override election was unrelated to the budget process, overrides were not a viable option for FY82. The amendments now permit two-thirds of the board of selectmen or city council (with the mayor's approval) to put a referendum question up for a vote at any time. A majority vote on the referendum may allow up to a 5 percent increase in the levy or a lessening of the required reduction to 7 1/2 percent. Approval by two-thirds of the voters allows a levy increase over 5 percnt or lessening of the reduction to below 7 1/2 percent. In no case, however, may a community vote to increase its tax rate beyond 2 1/2 percent.

23. An equalizing aid formula would also (somewhat inaccurately) cushion required second-year revenue losses because those cities and towns that are facing second-year cuts on average have low revenue-raising capacity. However, since there are low-base communities with no second-year cuts, a more target-efficient approach would be to allocate part of the new aid in proportion to FY83 losses and part on an equalizing basis.

24. If the 2 1/2 percent rate limit or 2 1/2 percent annual levy growth limit are binding constraints on all communities, then local decision makers have no discretion in setting the budget total. They retain the power, however, to allocate available revenues among uses.

25. The two qualifications on the sample's representativeness are as follows: First, the sample excludes the 52 regional academic and the 27 regional vocational school districts. (Similar data are available for about 40 regional districts, but we have not analyzed them.) Second, only 6 of the 21 towns and cities with population over 50,000 are included in the sample, and none of the three largest cities -- Boston, Springfield, and Worcester -- is included. Hence,

the results reported here underrepresent both the state's smallest communities, many of which are members of regional school districts, and its largest cities.

26. We do not view this as a major limitaion of the data, however, since in most towns the general magnitude of the cuts was negotiatied between the school commitee and the finance commmittee in advance of the town meeting.

27. Note that if these municipal revenue losses were expressed as a fraction of gross expenditures, the percentage changes would be closer to zero, and the contrast with school reductions even greater.

28. Correction for inflation uses the U.S. state and local public sector price deflator.

29. Sources: Expenditure and population data from *Governmental Finances,* 1974-75 and 1979-80 editions; enrollment data from *Digest of Education Statistics,* 1975 and 1980 editions.

30. The pupil weights are those used in the current school aid formula and represent the approximate relative costs of educating different types of students. The weights (which refer to full-time equivalent students) are as follows: regular day program, 1.0; transitional bilingual program, 1.4; special education program, 6.3; vocational education day program, 2.0; low income pupils, an additional weight of 0.2. Because the Department of Education does not calculate expenditure per weighted pupil, we estimated it for each city and town as follows: We first adjusted total expenditures and total full-time equivalent students from the end-of-year reports for students attending regional schools and for students "tuitioned-in" from other districts. We then divided this per pupil expenditure by a cost index calculated as the ratio of net average membership minus our estimate of regional school pupils to weighted pupils as reported by the Department of Education. The adjustments reflect the fact that weighted pupils as reported by the Department of Education for any city or town exclude students attending schools outside their district of residence on a tuition basis as pupils of their city or town of residence.

Ideally, one should deflate the expenditure numbers by an index of the costs of educational inputs across districts. Such an index is difficult to construct even if one bases it solely on teacher salaries. The difficulty is that high teacher salaries (even for a given education and experience level) may reflect high costs in one jurisdiction and high quality in another.

31. According to estimates by the National Center for Education Statistics, Massachusetts' disparity index of 2.22 was the highest of any state in 1977. The disparity index is the ratio of expenditures at the 95th percentile of students to expenditures at the 5th percentile of students. As a result of the 1979 school aid package, Massachusetts' index is now probably somewhat lower than it was in 1977. But in the aggregate, state school aid to local governments in Massachusetts still covered only 30 percent of local education expenditures in FY80, far less than the U.S. average (53.6 percent).

32. Because of data limitations, our quintiles are based on only 280 of the 297 school districts operated by cities and towns. This should have no effect on the conclusions.

Chapter 24

# Impacts on Public Sector Labor Relations

Rebecca R. W. Black

## Introduction

Proposition 2 1/2 has altered the climate and structure of public sector labor relations in Massachusetts. The collective bargaining law (1) covering public employees in Massachusetts was amended by the passage of Proposition 2 1/2, eliminating binding arbitration, a dispute resolution mechanism that had been in existence for police and fire fighter units since 1974. School committees are no longer autonomous units within municipal government, a change that redefines the "employers" of school personnel. Towns can now revoke their previous acceptance of various statutes, such as Civil Service regulations and incentive pay programs, affecting the terms and conditions of employment. Most important, Proposition 2 1/2 has limited municipal revenues that can be raised from property and auto excise taxes, and thus, has constrained expenditures. Given these new financial limitations, the number of public sector jobs and/or wage and benefit levels must be cut. Indeed, the choice of either reducing the number of jobs or reducing wages has become the major decision facing public unions and municipal managers.

The passage of Proposition 2 1/2 has changed power relationships, both through an alleged shift in the desires of the electorate and the new demands generated by fiscal constraints on municipal budgets. Although the vote for Proposition 2 1/2 has yet to be understood, many municipal officials have interpreted its passage as a loss of support for public employee unions and as a mandate for management to reduce the size of local government. Union leadership has also been challenged as new issues have arisen and conflicts emerged among union factions. The new environment for collective bargaining has created pressure for clarification of legal rules as well as the creation of new ones. All of these changes may affect the ability of unions and management to negotiate effectively.

The contractual and legal rights of unions and their members limit the choices open to municipal managers in coping with fiscal stress. Public managers are not free to cut budgets when and as they like. In many cases, they are bound by law to negotiate with unions before implementing decisions. Some of the changes brought about by Proposition 2 1/2 will alter the length of time it takes to complete contract or other negotiations and will influence the willingness of the parties involved to reach compromises or generate acceptable agreements. Delays will impose their own costs. Disagreements and stalemates will affect the ability of management to implement decisions effectively. This is particularly important now that enhancing productivity has become essential.

The magnitude of the impacts of Proposition 2 1/2 on labor relations is still not known, since the major requirement of the law (i.e., the property tax limitation) only took effect on July 1, 1981. Continued uncertainty over the level of state aid to localities and disagreements over projected levels of tax revenue (caused by disputes over revaluation) confounded the municipal budget process. The state budget (with its local aid component) was not passed until August, 1981. Some revaluation problems were not resolved until December 1981. Proposition 2 1/2 is an ongoing tax limitation. In many localities, its full impacts will not be felt until FY83. Further, suggested changes in the law itself, or in the state tax structure, or in levels of state aid, complicate any effort to predict the impacts on labor relations in the Commonwealth.

Even if all these unknowns were clarified, the full impact of Proposition 2 1/2 would not be known for some time. The loss of binding arbitration, for example, is relevant only after several successive contract or grievance negotiations. The impact of Proposition 2 1/2 on wage settlements, and on the choice between higher wages and the number of public sector jobs, will also take several years to materialize.

The process by which the first round of municipal budget decisions was reached and union response to the implementation of those decisions do suggest, however, some of the trends in labor relations likely to emerge over the next few years. This is especially true of personnel reductions, which emerged as an immediate issue in a number of cities and towns where personnel budgets had to be cut. The initial fiscal constraints imposed by Proposition 2 1/2 brought to the forefront the link between the size of the work force and the level of wages being paid. As unions and management were confronted with potential layoffs, the trade-off between wages and jobs emerged in stark relief. The issue of layoffs, therefore, provided an early opportunity to observe union/management relations under Proposition 2 1/2.

The level of wages and employment carries a different significance for management and labor. For management, the need to make layoffs suggests that service levels may be reduced. Because contractual or legal provisions limit management's ability to determine who is laid off, personnel cuts often mean that the overall character of the work force must change. The loss of younger or more productive workers can further magnify cuts in service levels, as can low morale induced by job insecurity. The short-term costs of layoffs (i.e., severance pay or unemployment compensation) can also throw a budget out of balance. (Because layoffs have not been common in the public sector, especially in smaller towns, many municipalities have not created unemployment insurance programs and, therefore, must now face the full cost of such compensation.) Layoffs can also be used as a political weapon to "break" unions.

For labor, layoffs represent a loss of union members, an undermining of morale, and a potentially increased work load for remaining members. Wage reductions, however, not only decrease the value of remaining jobs, but incur political costs to unions, as wage gains frequently symbolize a union's power. A willingness to discuss wage reductions while a contract is in force may require the contract to be opened, which has its own real and symbolic importance.

Wages and the size of the workforce are not the only items that can be traded in order to limit layoffs. Personnel and work rules also incur costs to employers. A provision for minimum manning -- a rule requiring a certain number of people working per shift or vehicle -- incurs overtime costs if insufficient personnel are employed regularly. Stipulations or provisions that limit management's flexibility in organizing work hours, job assignments, or the movement of employees within or across departments, can be changed through negotiations to limit the effects of budget reductions on wages or the size of the workforce.

To summarize, the threat or reality of layoffs became the focus of the labor-management system during the first round of budget adjustments in Massachusetts municipalities. The process by which personnel and budget reductions were made exposed many of the legal and political aspects of the relationships between management and labor. The goals and strategies of each became more visible. And, as new issues were addressed, the relationships, themselves, were changing.

## Review of Past Public-Sector Labor-Management Relations in Massachusetts

The legal framework for public-sector labor relations in Massachusetts is Chapter 150E of the General Laws. Chapter 150E was enacted in 1973, following an upsurge in public-sector unionizing in the state. The legislation expanded a 1965 statute that first gave municipal employees the right to organize and bargain. Under 150E, employers are obligated to bargain with public employees over wages, hours, the terms and conditions of work, and the standards of productiviy and performance. Employers and employee representatives are required to negotiate in good faith until an agreement or an impasse is reached. The statute prohibits strikes by public employees. Continuing disputes may be resolved through mediation and other procedures administered by a state agency. Between 1974 and 1980, binding arbitration could be used to resolve police and fire disputes, but was eliminated by Proposition 2 1/2.

The watch-dog of the collective bargaining law is the Massachusetts Labor Relations Commission (MLRC), created in 1937, but endowed with substantially greater powers through the 1973 legislation. The Commission certifies bargaining units and hears complaints about prohibited practices filed by either unions or management. The Commission's powers to order relief include issuing cease and desist orders, reinstating employees with back pay, and awarding other compensation. Through its hearings, the Commission has played a strong role not only in enforcing the rights of public employees to organize and bargain, but in developing case law precedents governing the legal relationship between management and unions.

Chapter 150E, as interpreted by the MLRC, affects the content of collective bargaining, and, therefore, the extent to which a union can protect its members through negotiations and contract provisions. The law distinguishes between mandatory and nonmandatory subjects of bargaining; only with regard to the former can formal impasse be reached and a charge of unfair labor practice be sustained. Only a few subjects relating to job security have so far been ruled to be mandatory subjects of bargaining. The minimum number of personnel per shift is a permissible subject, although the number of employees on a fire fighting apparatus, or in a police vehicle, to the extent that a question of safety is raised, is mandatory. (2) Contracting out work that is usually done by bargaining unit employees is also a mandatory subject. (3)

Since determining the level of service falls within management's domain, there is no obligation to bargain over a decision to reduce the personnel level. However, there is a legal obligation to bargain over the impact of such a decision on employees' terms and conditions of work. The impact of such decisions can be interpreted to cover the means by which a reduction is reached -- i.e., through attrition, layoffs, work-sharing -- and in which order -- i.e., strict seniority -- as well as the affect of a reduction on work load distribution, or other terms and conditions of employment for the remaining workforce. (4)

If contracts contain a reduction-in-force (RIF) clause, the obligation to "impact bargain" over a decision to reduce the force may have been satisfied already, but management must comply with the contract language. If such matters are not already covered in the contract, management must give notice to the union of proposed changes with sufficient specificity to permit an appropriate response. Such notice must be served far enough in advance of implementing changes to enable effective bargaining. (5)

If impasse is reached, and it is proven that management has bargained in "good faith," a reduction in force may be implemented. The penalty to management for failure to bargain (or for implementing layoffs without having reached a good faith impasse) may be reinstatement of employees with full back pay. This is usually the case if layoffs could have been avoided through bargaining or if the identity of the employees is unknown. (6) Thus, Chapter 150E affects the process and timing by which layoffs can be made. It also determines the degree of union involvement in such decisions, through its dominion over the collective bargaining process.

The Civil Service Statute, Chapter 31, is another law relevant to job security and reductions in force for a segment of public employees. Civil

Service has been in effect much longer than the collective bargaining law. The statute was enacted in 1884 to protect public employees and the public at large (as consumers of services) from the caprices of political pressure and patronage. Under its centralized system, various exams, rules, and reviews regulate the hiring, promotion, transfer, and discharge of employees, screening them on the basis of merit rather than political attributes. Although cities must hire and layoff through the Civil Service system, towns have the option (not the obligation) of adopting Civil Service regulation of their employees. Hence, Civil Service coverage is not uniform within or across municipalities. According to the Public Relations Bureau of the Department of Personnel Administration, 134 cities and towns in Massachusetts have no Civil Service coverage, 56 have all employees covered, and 16 have partial coverage (mostly of police officers and fire fighters).

Under the terms of the Civil Service Code, layoffs must be made by reverse seniority with various bumping and recall rights. Employees slated to be laid off have the right to a hearing, locally, and may appeal to the Civil Service Commission (equivalent to the MLRC). In an appeal, the employer must demonstrate to the Commission that layoffs or abolition of positions were made necessary by "lack of work or lack of funds," and that the employer acted in "good faith," i.e., followed the appropriate procedures. The automatic right to a hearing, plus the necessity of proving lack of funds or work incurs management costs (especially in terms of time and legal representation), while insulating the employee from arbitrary or political actions.

The State Board of Conciliation and Arbitration administers mediation, fact-finding, and voluntary interest arbitration for resolving collective bargaining disputes. Cases are brought before the Board by petition of one or both parties. (7) A similar agency, the Joint Labor Management Committee (or Dunlop Committee, as it is commonly called, after its Chairman, John Dunlop) oversees all police officer and fire fighter negotiations, and is responsible for dispute resolution procedures, including binding arbitration (prior to Proposition 2 1/2). (8) Although the Board and JLMC are not necessarily involved in mid-contract issues of layoffs, their responsibilities in collective bargaining influence the contractual and procedural constraints on reduction-in-force decisions.

The state courts are also active members of the labor relations environment as enforcers of collective bargaining agreements. While the MLRC ensures the right and duty of collective bargaining, the courts uphold the viability of the contract. Should a layoff decisions appear to violate contractual provisions, the union or management may file in court. The courts are also used to gain immediate relief, especially for temporary injunctions against layoffs.

### The Immediate Impacts of Proposition 2 1/2 on the Legal Framework of Public Sector Bargaining

The immediate effect of Proposition 2 1/2 on the law governing public sector collective bargaining was to repeal Section 4 of the outside sections of Chapter 150E, which permitted last-best-offer arbitration for municipal police and fire disputes. The authority of the JLMC became uncertain. Attorney General Bellotti delivered an opinion to the JLMC on February 10, 1981, establishing that it could not bind the legislative branch of municipal governments, but leaving some ambiguity regarding its powers over the executive branch. A decision by the Supreme Judicial Court in August 1981, cast further doubt over the power of the Committee to bind either branch. The JLMC is still in existence, however, and continues to oversee all collective bargaining negotiations involving municipal police officers and fire fighters. It continues to administer dispute resolution procedures. (9) The Committee's case load was small over the summer of 1981, but it has grown larger since then.

The law continues to prohibit public employee strikes, but the elimination of binding arbitration creates a vacuum regarding the final resolution of collective bargaining disputes after fact-finding. It is too early to predict the effect of the loss of binding arbitration on negotiations, and opinions vary widely. (It should be remembered that the new fiscal constraint of Proposition 2 1/2 coincides with the elimination of binding arbitration and complicates assessment of "pure" impacts.) Some observers foresee protracted negotiations with the possibility of strikes. The JLMC's Senior Labor representative predicts increased hostility, but not necessarily strikes. Union representatives, in general, predict more difficulties throughout negotiations. At the local level, the majority of union spokesmen believe that police and fire unions have lost power to management -- although Joseph Bonavito (AFSCME) adds that power is now more equitably balanced between public safety unions and other municipal employee unions. Managers, too, perceive a shift of power away from unions. One town official believes managers feel "a new emboldment" with the loss of binding arbitration.

The Labor Relations Commission, the Civil Service Commission, and the courts all experienced an increased case load because of Proposition 2 1/2. The Chief Counsel for the MLRC reported that 40 percent more cases were filed between April and June of 1981 than were filed during the same period in 1980. (10) Between mid-February and the first of September, the MLRC classified 82 of the cases filed as cases related to Proposition 2 1/2. Twenty-one of these 82 cases have been related to layoffs or are requests to "impact bargain." Twenty-five involved charges of bad-faith bargaining for failure or refusal to execute contracts. Fourteen are listed as miscellaneous, including one charge filed over the right of a public employee to wear a "Save our Services" button on the job. Thirteen were related to duty to bargain over the revocation of optional laws, primarily Civil Service regulations and incentive pay programs. Four complaints involving duty of fair representation were filed by employees against their unions, and one was filed by an employer against a union. Between January and September 1981, 17 strike-prevention petitions were filed, wherein the employer notified the MLRC that a union intended to strike.

A number of these cases represented new issues, compelling decisions for which there are no clear precedents in the MLRC case law. The Commission was forced to create new rules through interpretation of ambiguities in the existing law. Because charges were not filed until the summer, decisions were not made on many of the major issues until late fall (1981). As of this date, some issues continue to go unresolved. Actions in the courts remained undecided or on appeal throughout the fall. Thus, the rules governing the implementation of layoffs and other personnel issues were evolving as the first cutbacks were being made.

The Commission made several decisions in November 1981 clarifying the duty to bargain over the impact of decisions to layoff. In one decision, it was reaffirmed that the obligation to impact bargain includes bargaining over alternatives to layoffs, including work sharing, early retirement, or attrition. (11) The decision further distinguished management's right to determine the level of service from how a personnel reduction is to be made. In another decision, the Commission defined more clearly the conditions under which management might utilize a previously established exception to the general requirement of reaching impasse prior to implementing layoffs. (12) (The Commission rejected management's use of exception in this case because management had not given sufficient notice to the union that it was bargaining against a deadline and it had not introduced evidence to show "that layoff had to occur on the date that it did and could not have been delayed pending bargaining without jeopardizing [ management's] legitimate desire to achieve fiscal year 1981 savings.")

A case of discriminatory motivation in a layoff decision was heard in the City of Quincy. (13) The City laid off 73 percent of the employees in the Engineering Department, in contrast to 5-29 percent of the employees in eight other departments. The union representing the engineering employees alleged that the disproportionate layoffs were in retaliation for a long history of protected (union) activity in that department. In general, the City relied only on Proposition 2 1/2 financial impacts for its defense. The Commission found a violation of the law and ordered reinstatement with full back pay.

The range of subjects that must be covered in mandatory "impact bargaining" following a reduction-in-force decision remains unresolved -- especially where RIF clauses are included in contracts. Under law, there is no duty to bargain what is covered by a contract, but several MLRC attorneys argue that there is considerable latitude given to define the comprehensiveness of such clauses, and, therefore, the issues left to be bargained. The bargaining obligation for impacts on the remaining force (i.e., safety, opportunities for overtime, workload, and productivity) is especially in need of further interpretation, mostly because few cases have arisen. MLRC and JLMC staff members have noted that most impact bargaining so far has focused only on the means of force reduction, not on the impacts on the remaining force. (14) One staff member found the lack of interest in issues involving remaining personnel "surprising." It is not clear, then, that conditions of work (or productivity) will become an issue of more concern to union members should further personnel cuts become necessary.

A question arose concerning the duty of employers to bargain with unions over the revocation of Civil Service regulation or the by-laws adopted for incenve pay (such as police education or longevity pay.) In a number of towns, managers proposed revocation, inspiring unions to file prohibitive practice charges over the failure to bargain. In most cases, such proposals were rejected by town meetings, rendering the issue moot. (15) The South Hadley Town Meeting voted to rescind Civil Service regulation of some of the town's employees, and the local police union filed a complaint. A hearing officer heard the case in November and found the town to have "unlawfully and unilaterally" placed the Civil Service revocation article on the town warrant. (16) The finding has been appealed to to the full Commission which has not yet issued a decision on this question.

Only a few cases concerning failure to fund contract provisions have arisen recently before the MLRC. (17) In one case, a county employer ran out of money and did not pay employees for a week. The MLRC found a violation of the law because the employer, at the time of the execution of the contract, failed to request supplemental appropriations. The employer, thereby, made a de facto commitment to the union that sufficient funds were available, and was responsible for all contractual provisions. (18) In a case involving state employees, a charge was filed by a union when the Governor vetoed an appropriation bill from the legislature that would have paid employees' salaries. The MLRC dismissed the charge without issuing a complaint because the Governor stated that he intended to fund the contractual provisions through layoffs (the determination of level of service is management's right). (19) The same union filed another charge for failure to pay a negotiated wage increase. In this case, the MLRC issued a charge on the grounds that no action had been taken to fulfill the contractual provisions, either through appropriation or layoffs. (20)

In one well-known case that went through the courts and is now under appeal to the Supreme Judicial Court, the ruling allowed the Boston School Committee to layoff teachers despite contractual provisions against such reductions because of financial circumstances. The teachers' contract covered FY81-83; a no layoff clause was in effect through FY82. A critical component in the union's appeal is an argument for the viability of multi-year contracts. The School Committee is required by law to request appropriation sufficient to cover only the first year of a contract. The union is arguing that once the initial appropriation is granted, a commitment is made to provide sufficient funds to cover provisions for the remaining years of the contract. Otherwise, the teachers' argue, "c.150E, sec.7a which permits three-year collective bargaining agreements for public employees will be rendered ineffective and superfluous." (21)

A potential difficulty arises in determining a union's duty of fair representation in cases involving reductions in force and minority employees. According to MLRC's Chief Counsel, however, close to two-thirds of minority municipal employees have been hired pursuant to court orders. The forum for hearing complaints of discriminatory layoffs is, therefore, likely to be the federal courts, rather than the MLRC. U.S. District Court orders have recently been issued for affirmative action considerations in the order of layoffs –– for example, Judge Garrity's order in December 1981 to maintain a 20 percent minority representation among school personnel despite layoffs, and similar order from Judge Mazzone concerning Boston police officers and fire fighters.

The right of supervisors to bump into the rank-and-file is an issue on which the MLRC has made a number of decisions –– especially in the case of schools. The Commission has ruled that "the decision of whether to appoint displaced administrators as teachers is within the sole discretion of management." (22) In another opinion, the Commission found that once an administrator enters the teachers unit, seniority and other terms and conditions of employment are governed by the teachers', not the administrators', contract. (23) The Commission reaffirmed that decision in a recent case, making it clear that "the supervisory union cannot insist on bargaining over terms and conditions of employment of administrators after they leave the unit and become teachers." (24)

The Civil Service Commission experienced a four-fold increase in its case load because of Proposition 2 1/2, according to its General Counsel. The majority of the Commission's decisions have favored the employer and permitted the implementation of layoffs. An exception occurred in the spring of 1981. An issue arose over the definition of "lack of funds" in a case brought before the Commission by the Belmont fire fighters union. The town had reserve funds sufficient to cover the salaries of five tenured fire fighters who had been laid off for budgetary reasons. On appeal by the union, the Commission ruled that because of the monetary reserves, the condition for layoff because of lack of funds was not satisfied and ordered reinstatement of the employees. (25) Management appealed the decision to Superior Court and won, primarily on the right of management to determine the basic allocation of funds among governmental functions. (26) The Commission's Legal Counsel argues that the circumstances and rulings in the Belmont case were aberrant.

Alterations have been made in the institutional arrangements affecting public sector labor relations through amendments to several statutes in the "outside sections" of the new state budget. (27) The Board of Conciliation and Arbitration (BCA) has been removed from the control of the Department of Labor and Industries and is now an independent agency. The Chairman has powers of appointment over mediators, arbitrators, and the management and labor members of the board, and can promulgate rules and regulations for the board. The JLMC has become part of the BCA under a single budget, but continues to function autonomously. Although its budget has not been affected by the change so far, the JLMC has lost some of its independence and access to direct legislative support.

Decisions made by the Labor Relations Commission are now reviewed by the Appeals Court, bypassing the Superior Court. One result, according to an MLRC Commissioner, is a reduction in the number of appeals, partly because procedures for review by the Appeals Courts are more stringent and require more legal preparation than those of the Superior Court. The Labor Relations Commission has been empowered to refer refusal-to-bargain cases to the BCA and the JLMC for mediation. (Prior to this amendment, cases were brought to the agencies through petition by one or both parties.)

These changes primarily reflect efforts to promote efficiency and consistency among the various branches of the labor relations system. They also appear to signify increased state legislative support for formal dispute resolution procedures as an alternative to the adversarial and sometimes lengthy procedures of litigation. Whether inspired by the passage of Proposition 2 1/2 or not, the strengthening of mediation services is a progressive step towards easing a potentially hostile climate of labor-management relations.

The legal framework for public sector labor relations was not immediately or dramatically altered during the first year of Proposition 2 1/2. Instead, a number of points in the case law evolved as they were redefined and clarified. As conditions changed, municipal managers and employees faced new issues as well as variations of old ones. In some instances, gaps in the case law were filled as new issues were heard. In other cases, the inexperience of unions and management in handling the procedures and obligations involved in making reductions in force -- especially through layoffs -- increased the case loads of dispute resolution agencies. The second round of such decisions will hold fewer surprises, although there are still some issues under litigation or awaiting review that may affect the next round of budget adjustments.

Although the changes in the legal system are important and may influence specific aspects of personnel reductions, they are not fundamental to the actual decision to layoff employees. Legally mandated procedures and restrictions may impose time and money costs, but are otherwise irrelevant. Similarly, the quality of relationships between unions and management and the extent to which they cooperate under fiscal constraints, lie mostly outside the legal framework.

## Preliminary Case Study Findings

This preliminary review of the impacts of Proposition 2 1/2 is based on the series of thirteen case studies which comprise Part III of this volume. They are based on extensive interviews with public officials, union leaders, and special interest groups. Most of the cities and towns studied experienced, at least at the outset, a large gap between available revenues and previous expenditures. Therefore, they had to plan for considerable cutbacks in established programs and services. Although the researcher's primary focus was the budget process (and not labor relations), the role of organized labor emerged in most of the cases. In addition to these case studies, the author conducted interviews with public employee union leaders and with key personnel in the state labor relations system to help place the case study findings into a broader context.

Major issues and actions highlighted by the case studies can be summarized under three headings: 1) layoffs and the budget process under Proposition 2 1/2; 2) union demands; and 3) the effects of union action. The discussion will be limited to unions for police officers, fire fighters, and teachers. The focus is specifically on those unions that faced potential layoffs.

*Layoffs and the Budget Process under Proposition 2 1/2*

Although a number of cities and towns were forced by Proposition 2 1/2 to make deep budget cuts, the actual reductions in service personnel were less severe than had initially been predicted. This was true for a variety of reasons, not the least of which was the buffering effect of the additional state aid allocated by the legislature. Also, revaluation allowed many communities to increase their tax "take" despite the tax limit imposed by Proposition 2 1/2. A number of localities generated more revenue by adopting new fees and user charges, or made the decision to use reserve funds to cover initial gaps.

A great many communities avoided dismissing public employees by offering attractive early retirement packages and by allowing attrition to thin the ranks of municipal employees. Cuts in overtime budgets were also widely used as were cuts in non-personnel items in lieu of reductions in force. Finally, many communities chose to put off needed capital improvements, thereby reducing capital budgets and avoiding reductions in operating funds.

Most municipal managers chose to protect public safety allocations at the expense of schools. Police and fire departments generally fared better than schools, public works, parks and recreation, and libraries, in terms of total budget cuts and layoffs. The rationale commonly given was that the libraries, and parks and recreation offered "less essential" services. Declining enrollments and the loss of school committee budget autonomy were most often used to justify educational budget reductions, suggesting that school committees had failed in the past to eliminate wasteful spending and unnecessary personnel. Most layoffs, therefore, occurred among teachers and non-public safety personnel. Fire fighters did share some of the layoffs. Almost no police officers were laid off in the case study communities, despite the fact that the police and fire departments often had similar cutbacks. Personnel reductions were made through attrition.

In many communities, the Selectmen or City Manager gained new control over the budget process. In others, traditionally acquiescent bodies, such as town meeting, asserted themselves more forcefully. Numerous conflicts arose over who would have primary control over the budget. In some instances, unions took advantage of the fragmented nature of budget decision-making. In some, they appealed their cases directly to town meeting. A great many department heads felt that they had lost some of their budget autonomy because of the care with which official committees went through each and every budget item, searching for ways of cutting back. Some union leaders believe this process diluted their influence as well.

The role of labor in the cutback planning process did not stand out dramatically by way of increased activity or impact on management policies. There were no strikes or notable job actions prior to or after layoffs were announced. (Indeed, the lack of strikes across the state surprised many knowledgeable observers.) This does not imply that labor's impact on the budget process or on layoff decisions was absent, but was perhaps, indirect or less visible. The most visible unions were the fire fighters unions.

Overall, perceptions of a reduction in the power of public employees unions were consistent throughout the case study communities. There are no outstanding instances that exemplify such a shift, but the perceptions are there, nonetheless.

## Union Demands

Union involvement with Proposition 2 1/2 began before municipalities started their budget cutbacks. Statewide union organizations opposed Proposition 2 1/2. The Massachusetts Teachers Association proposed an alternative to Proposition 2 1/2 which garnered sufficient support to be put on the November 1980 ballot, but it did not pass. Local public employees were active in campaigns against Proposition 2 1/2, but to degrees varying by union and locality. There was considerable support for the bill among union members as well. The few union coalitions that emerged arose in opposition to the passage of Proposition 2 1/2.

After Proposition 2 1/2 passed, a number of statewide union organizations lobbied the legislature for increased local aid and for various amendments to the bill. The Professional Fire Fighters of Massachusetts, representing a majority of organized fire fighters in the state, and the Massachusetts Teachers Association were particularly active in lobbying for additional state aid as were the largest unions (AFSCME and NAGE), representing state and local employees. AFSCME and NAGE had to balance requests for increased state aid with assurances that state employees would not be laid off. Union involvement was aimed at avoiding layoffs by eliminating the fiscal constraints necessitating cutbacks. Whether or not the unions were primarily responsible, the large increase in state aid substantially reduced the impact of 2 1/2 and helped to prevent significant numbers of layoffs.

The state-level activities of the unions affected union policy at the local level. It was the stated policy of the fire fighters, for instance, not to agree to any wage reduction or other avoidance of layoffs in order that the "full impact of 2 1/2 be felt."

At the local level, unions expressed their demands concerning layoffs at various stages of the budget process, as outlined below:

1. Pre-existing action, primarily through contractual provisions that limit management's ability to layoff (e.g., minimum manning, class size, or outright prohibitions against layoffs) or that stipulate the means of layoff (e.g., seniority, RIF clauses). Such provisions, normally negotiated into contracts prior to the current budget process, shape union involvement at the time of the budget process.

2. Involvement in budget allocations, influencing the level of reductions expected from each department. Such involvement depends on the ability of unions to put political pressure on key officials or to agitate for public support.

3. Involvement in actual layoff decisions once particular departments have been targetted for specific reductions. It is here that legally-mandated impact bargaining occurs. This is the most likely point to suggest alternative sources of revenues, trade-offs of jobs for lower wages, or new contract provisions. This is also the point at which efforts are usually made to force reductions-in-force on non-union personnel.

4. Reactions to layoff decisions or policy implementations. Such activities include job actions, legal action, or organizing political support to gain reinstatement.

The prevalence of contractual provisions that limit management's ability to affect layoffs or dictate the order of layoffs varied more by union type than among communities in the case studies. Teachers had greater contractual provisions, both in number of contracts in which they were included and in the depth of those provisions. Not only were RIF's explicitly included in most contracts, but also provisions for work load and, in one case (Burlington), for class size. Amesbury teachers had also negotiated an attachment to their contract that prohibited laying-off tenured teachers. Previous experience with declining enrollments, school closings, and the decline in teaching jobs explains, in part, the prevalence of such contractual provisions. Teachers are not covered by Civil Service, although they do have rights to notice and hearing before the appointing authority under Chapter 71. Therefore, contract stipulations play a larger role in governing layoff procedures.

In fire fighter and police union contracts, RIF provisions were less prevalent because Civil Service regulations cover most public safety employees. In contrast to teachers, public safety employees' experience with layoffs was rare. In towns where reductions had been made in previous years, personnel losses had been made through attrition. Six fire fighter locals had previously negotiated minimum manning clauses which affected overtime costs and, to some extent, layoffs. In general, RIF procedures for police, fire fighters, and teachers dictated layoffs by reverse seniority.

There was little direct union activity during the allocation of funds among departments. In only one case did union representatives actively participate in the initial budget allocation process. In Marshfield, the president of the fire fighters union negotiated alongside the fire chief with the advisory board for increased funding. A joint committee comprised of union members, the fire chief, and the mayor was created in Burlington in response to the considerable conflict that had arisen over the budget. However, the committee dissolved prior to any decision-making. Police and fire fighter unions did attend informational meetings in Arlington, but felt they had no real influence on decisions.

Three fire fighter locals lobbied for full or partial refunding of departmental budgets at town meeting after official layoffs had been proposed and, in some cases, implemented. One union in Burlington collected signatures for a petition to restore funding to the fire department. The petition was rejected at town meeting, but the union continues to gather petitions to hold a public vote on the issue. The Marshfield local sponsored two amendments to the warrant to prevent or delay fire fighter layoffs, but neither passed. In Bridgewater, the fire fighters prepared a proposal for town meeting calling for increased cuts in the regional school budgets to cover fire fighter positions, but town meeting procedures blocked their effort. Fire fighters in Springfield also lobbied the City Council to prevent the closing of a fire company.

In many communities, unions (mostly fire fighter, but sometimes police) carried out public campaigns for maintenance of services and against cuts. This included picketing City Hall in Quincy and using media in Burlington, Bridgewater, and Framingham. Public safety personnel continued to receive public support which they exploited at public meetings. In a number of cases, unions exerted pressure on their department heads who then bargained directly with the key officials involved in budget allocations. Union influence through indirect channels is difficult to detect, but potentially effective. The Salem fire fighters were especially noted by the researcher to have exerted influence indirectly through the fire department chief.

Teachers unions were noticeably inactive in influencing budget allocations to school departments. Two teachers unions obeyed the MTA directive to avoid involvement. Teachers feared that in any open competition with public safety, they would lose. They felt the schools had no public or official support for such a contest, mostly because of declining enrollments, demographic shifts, and the high visibility of school costs on tax bills. Teachers felt at a disadvantage relative to other departmental personnel because school committee autonomy was lost. Past channels of budget influence became irrelevant with the end of school committee budget autonomy.

Once departmental budgets were determined and choices between personnel and other budget items were being made, specific demands concerning layoffs emerged. During this third stage -- the decision to lay off -- formal structures for negotiation between unions and management existed through legally mandated impact bargaining. There was heightened awareness that layoffs were a real, not a threatened, possibility. Three types of union actions were evident in the case studies: union proposals for alternative cuts; trade-offs between contractual provisions and jobs; and bargaining over the order of laying-off.

In Quincy, Burlington, and Springfield, teachers proposed alternatives to layoffs to their school committees. Burlington teachers proposed imposing charges for school bus transportation to fill funding gaps. Springfield teachers proposed further cuts in supplies and programs, and a reorganization of school districts to save on transportation costs. The school committees, in all cases, rejected these union proposals. In several cases, police and fire fighter unions publicly opposed layoffs, but did not offer specific alternative proposals. (The president of the fire fighters union in Salem publicly suggested that layoffs be made in the mayor's office, rather than in the fire department.)

Town officials proposed trade-offs involving contractual provisions to three teachers and two fire fighters unions. Sandwich teachers were asked to forego a negotiated wage increase in return for fewer teacher layoffs. The union rejected this proposal. The Marshfield teachers union agreed to open its contract with the result that restrictions on personnel reorganization and provisions for teachers' aides (non-union personnel), were eliminated, along with some benefits. (Wages were not an issue.) Savings from these concessions reduced the number of layoffs. The Burlington teachers were in the middle of contract negotiations during the budget process. They compromised with management over the RIF clause, tempering strict seniority with allowances for certification by area. The union also waived contract provisions for class size restrictions. The congruency of new contract negotiation with the budget process forced the union to consider trade-offs to hold jobs.

The Salem fire fighters refused to open their contract to reduce wages and benefits in return for keeping a fire station open in retaining jobs. Chelsea fire fighters, however, did open their contract to eliminate a minimum manning clause to save overtime costs. The union did this with the provision that the clause be reinstated upon receipt of a stipulated amount of state aid. The Chelsea fire fighters, unique among the public safety unions in opening their contract, indicated that they were seeking more cooperative relations with the mayor to reverse a history of hostile negotiations. In return for concessions on minimum manning, they expected "consideration" at a later point. The president of the PFFM, Dusty Alward stressed that the union knew that relations between Chelsea's mayor and the state legislature were good and that considerable state aid to Chelsea was certain. With this knowledge, the fire fighters did not give anything up, but merely delayed a benefit. (The city did receive state aid above the stipulated amount needed to reactivate the clause.)

None of the case study unions agreed to open contracts to trade jobs for a wage cut. Representatives of three major statewide union organizations (MTA, PFFM, and IBPO) indicated that their members had been advised against such action. According to the general counsel, the general policy of the MTA is not to "fund the status quo by 2 1/2." PFFM came out strongly against opening contracts to take wage cuts for three reasons: 1) opening contracts is bad "unionism;" 2) taking lower wages is "subsidization of Commonwealth citizens;" and 3) lobbying against public safety layoffs is an effective means of encouraging more state aid. Union spokesmen also feared that once wages were lowered, they would never be increased. In general, there was a distinct unwillingness on the part of unions to open contracts for any reason -- the collective bargaining contract reflecting the real and symbolic power of a union. A number of fire fighters contended that if contracts were opened and wages or other concessions made to save jobs, the jobs would not be worth having.

Because teachers contracts usually included extensive provisions for reductions in force, teachers were limited in negotiating or influencing layoff decisions.

The teachers union president of Quincy argued that the the union had nothing to trade—off and could not influence the layoff decision. Because impact bargaining may not be required where RIF's are included in contracts, a forum for negotiation is eliminated. The more terms and conditions of work are stipulated, the more likely it is that concessions to save jobs will require opening a contract. For the Marshfield teachers, opening their contract may have been the only way to create alternatives to layoffs. In contrast, layoffs in police and fire departments may have been avoided by savings achieved in personnel reorganizations that were allowed because contract provisions were not so restrictive. Hence, contract openings were avoided.

Impact bargaining over the order of layoffs, prior to their implementation, was only noted in one case. Bridgewater teachers bargained with the school committee to protect tenured teachers from layoffs. When the Cambridge school committee proposed that teacher layoffs be made by procedures other than strict seniority, teachers staged a mock funeral procession to protest.

Once the decision to implement layoffs was made, a number of teacher and fire fighter unions used political and legal tactics to challenge layoffs. The Salem fire fighters were informally involved in a citizen's take—over of a fire station to protest its closing (many fire fighters' wives were among the citizens). The union also publicly demanded its reopening, suggesting that cuts be made in the mayor's "patronage" staff. The only mention of public protest by teachers unions at this stage, was a statement made to the press by the president of the Chelsea teachers association. Three legal actions by fire fighters unions were noted in the cases. Quincy and Bridgewater fire fighters petitioned for arbitration, the former alleging that layoffs violated its minimum manning clause, the latter that the manner of layoffs violated proper notification and order procedures. The Wayland fire fighters filed a grievance over the establishment of a Joint Police and Fire Communication Center, which required a civilian dispatcher who would replace a fire fighter. The union obtained a temporary injunction preventing implementation, but the injunction was overturned.

The teachers unions also sought legal recourse over the order of layoffs. In Marshfield, a grievance petition was filed by teachers to prevent administrators who had been bumped into the teachers union from regaining seniority rights. The administrators had separated from the teachers unit several years before, but desired to maintain their old seniority status when working in a teaching capacity. In Cambridge, the order of layoffs caused conflict involving factions of the teachers union. The union sued the school committee for violating its seniority RIF clause; teachers had been laid off in a manner which gave priority to minorities and those who taught at the alternative schools.

To summarize, the case studies indicate that union demands took a variety of forms and actually took form at different points in the budget process. The unions, in general, demanded the prevention of layoffs. Where layoffs occurred, they sought to control who would be laid off. The majority of teachers, firemen, and police officers were covered by provisions stipulating the order of layoffs, although only in the case of teachers was this primarily a demand which had been expressed previously (Civil Service status is not the choice of the employee). Unions actually used the pre-existing provisions to exert control. Th greatest involvement in budget allocations appeared to be through public campaigns waged against cuts. In very few instances did unions lobby directly for greater funding. Even fewer unions accompanied their demands for more financial support with proposals for alternative savings or ways of compensating for their department's increased funding.

The case studies show that explicit trade-offs between contract provisions and jobs were unusual and proposed only by management. Wage reductions were not accepted to prevent layoffs. Once layoffs had occurred, almost all protests took the legal form. (The increased case load at the MLRC, in the courts, and the Civil Service Commission indicate that this trend was statewide.) No strikes occurred.

The extent to which unions expressed their demands differed by union type. The fire fighters were, by far, the most vocal and active in all stages of the layoff process. The fire fighters unions were perceived, in most cases, to be stronger and better organized than other unions. The state organization is also powerful. As was the case for policemen, fire fighters had substantial public support against public safety cutbacks, which they were able to exploit to their benefit.

The police officers were the least visible among public employees in the case study communities. Although they worked with fire fighters in public campaigns and continued in their opposition to layoffs, the lack of specific activity can be attributed, in part, to the fact that few police departments faced layoffs. Personnel reductions were achieved through attrition. Police unions tend to be less well-organized and less powerful than fire fighters unions, however, which is partly due to the lack of a single representative of unionized police at the state-level.

Teachers unions were unexpectedly quiet. In most cases, their involvement centered on restricting the order of layoffs, with little direct action or input in the other "stages" of the budget process. In a few instances, teachers made concessions on contractual provisions to save jobs, but their lack of action is primarily due to the perceived lack of public support.

*Effect of Union Demands*

Union contracts had a clear effect on management decisions. Contracts successfully limited management by prescribing the order of layoffs, and the extent of work reorganization and job reassignment that might be done. Where RIF provisions were in effect, layoffs were made by reverse seniority, making the impact of force reductions fall on younger, less experienced employees. Management's opposition to strict seniority was evident in a number of cases -- e.g., the preference given to minority and alternative school teachers in Cambridge (leading to the continuing legal battle with the union) and the concession made by the Burlington teachers union to include certification allowances in the criteria for ordering layoffs. The Bridgewater fire chief wanted to lay off three more senior fire fighters in order to retain three Emergency Medical Technicians (EMT's). He was forced to abide by strict seniority, however, when fire fighters threatened to file a grievance over violation of the contract RIF.

Few contracts contained provisions that successfully prohibited or limited layoffs. The Amesbury teachers contract was a rare exception. Management was prevented, in that case, from laying off tenured teachers and was forced to seek other ways of cutting back the school budget. But in no instance did minimum manning provisions prevent layoffs for fire fighters. On the contrary, in Salem, a mimimum manning provision provided management with a justification for closing a fire station.

Contractual provisions provided unions with a base from which to initiate grievances or other legal proceedings. If these did not actually prevent layoffs they delayed their implementation and imposed costs on management. The case of the Bridgewater fire fighters is the only one in which recourse to the legal system resulted in a reversal of management's decision: the town meeting voted to rehire the laid off fire fighters as long as the union dropped its grievance. Unions frequently used their ability to file charges to force management to negotiate.

In many instances, contracts served to increase the number of layoffs rather than to prevent them. It is clear from a number of cases that, had management been able to reduce wages and benefits and eliminate provisions that impose costs, it would have done so to prevent force reductions. The number of layoffs resulting from contractual provisions can not be ascertained. However, jobs were saved in those communities where unions agreed to open contracts to eliminate specific clauses for defined outcomes. Chelsea's fire fighters saved 20 jobs by removing the minimum manning clause (although the jobs might have been saved by increased state aid anyway). Fewer jobs were lost in Marshfield when teachers removed a number of non-wage contract provisions. Sandwich teachers and Salem fire fighters might have avoided all or a portion of layoffs had they accepted management's proposal to cut wages.

In a few cases, the effect of union actions during budget allocations is relatively clear. The Springfield fire fighters prevented the elimination of a fire company by lobbying the City Council. Negotiation between the Springfield Advisory Board, the union president, and fire chief reduced the fire department's budget cut by 4 percent and prevented four layoffs. The case writer in Quincy concluded that union campaigns against cuts in the fire department were partly responsible for a smaller budget reduction and fewer layoffs. The failure of unions to increase funding for their departments or to prevent layoffs was the clear result in several cases. All union appeals at town meetings were rejected. All union proposals to budget committees or department heads for alternative cuts or savings were rejected.

However, in most cases, the effect of union demands is difficult to determine. We have no record of how involved unions were in decisions to avoid layoffs by reducing overtime, encouraging early retirements, or eliminating vacant positions. If these were trade-offs made by unions, they were not as visible as those restricted by contract provisions. It is especially unclear what effect public campaigns had on minimizing budget cuts and layoffs. Police and fire unions were the most vocal in opposition to cuts; teachers, the least. The figures indicate that public safety suffered much smaller reductions in force than school departments: fewer than 50 fire fighters and only 2 police officers were laid off in the case study communities, while close to 1,500 teachers and school personnel were dismissed. (28)

The numbers are not a reliable indicator of the effect of union involvement. Many other factors came into play in distributing allocations among departments. In all cases, public safety was a high priority for public officials and residents. Schools, generally, had a lower priority. (The only exception was Sandwich -- the school department was a top priority among residents and officials alike.) Teaching positions were threatened by declining enrollments, as well as by waning public support. One-third of Wayland's teachers would have been dismissed even without Proposition 2 1/2 cutbacks. In Burlington, 30 percent would have been dismissed. In some cases, teachers became victims of old hostilities between school committees and mayors or selectmen. When budget authority was terminated for school committees, the old conflicts resulted in school department budget cuts. This was the case in Burlington, Chelsea, and Bridgewater. These kinds of factors affected union strategies, and placed teachers unions at a disadvantage from the beginning.

Police and fire unions had substantial public backing, which they exploited to achieve their own ends. To what extent union action had an independent effect is unclear, but many officials at the state and local level believe that it played an important role. Union activity increased public demand for maintaining a high level of public safety service.

The historical opposition of unions to management appeared to have a negative effect on the number of layoffs. Union leaders representing fire fighters believe that the strength of their unions inspired discriminatory layoffs. This was the case in Salem, Bridgewater, and Burlington where union leaders contended that 2 1/2 was being used to "break the union" and claimed that layoffs were vindictive. An Advisory Board member in Bridgewater substantiated their charge: "The main reason for fire fighter layoffs was to let them know who was in charge." Wayland's fire fighters claimed that staffing the new Joint Communication Center with a civilian rather than a fire fighter constituted a "vendetta" against the union. Hostilities between executives and school committees which resulted in more teacher layoffs may have been the result of the activities of teachers unions in the past. Vindictive motives may explain why fire fighters suffered more layoffs than policemen.

The case studies show that unions were clearly the most successful in exerting their demands through their negotiated contracts. This is not surprising, since the contract is accepted as the most legitimate protector of union interests. Much of unions' strength, therefore, depended on the history of their negotiating power, tempered with foresight and a willingness to enforce bargained provisions. The importance of the collective bargaining contract heightens the affect any changes in the balance of power between management and unions will have in the future. Changes in the scope of bargaining brought about through legal rulings will affect the degree to which unions can demand to bargain over job security provisions. (If many communities succeed in removing police and fire personnel from civil service regulation, the law may be important in determining union ability to replace these job security regulations with contractual provisions.)

The degree of public support was critical in determining union strategies and their success. Public safety personnel campaigned actively, drawing on public interest, and were successful in limiting the impact of Proposition 2 1/2 on their departments. Teachers, in contrast, feared open competition, lacking public support, and suffered for it. The ability of unions to influence management decisions, therefore, was determined as much by the environment, as by any characteristics intrinsic to the unions.

The impact of union involvement in the politics of budget adjustment is less clear. Unions clearly failed in a number of attempts, while in others, lobbying in conjunction with department heads succeeded in increasing funds. The quality of relations developed in the past among unions, department heads, and municipal executives may have been critical to those outcomes.

## The Likely Long-Term Effects of Proposition 2 1/2 on Public Sector Labor Relations

Changes in the public sector labor relations system are still tentative. The layoff issue did not touch a major portion of the formal collective bargaining system in the first year of Proposition 2 1/2. Both union and management strategies were based on uncertainty about the future fiscal status of municipalities in Massachusetts. They do not necessarily reflect choices that will continue to be made on the basis of ongoing fiscal limitations.

Formal relationships between management and unions have not yet been altered to any great degree. No real coalitions of public employee unions have yet emerged. Although most unions were united in opposition to any budget cuts, actual bargaining typically involved single unions, often in competition with other unions. Management was under pressure to make rapid budget adjustments during a period of continued uncertainty about the level of state aid (and thus, the revenues available for FY82). The normal budget process was disrupted in some instances, introducing new political actors or creating shifts in the location of power. Unions sometimes used the fragmented nature of the budget process and attempted to generate political pressure on behalf of their respective departments. The case studies suggest that labor and management may form temporary coalitions in particular departments, at least for the purpose of convincing public officials and residents that cutbacks would be harmful.

The legal system was called on to resolve more labor issues than in previous years, as evidenced by the increased case loads of the Labor Relations Commission, the Civil Service Commission, and the courts. However, some observers suggest that with the experience gained from the first round and the clarifications in the law that have occurred, case loads will not be as heavy in round two, but will reflect more profound or difficult legal issues.

The scope of bargaining was not expanded. There was no indication of sincere union interest in becoming directly involved in budget-making decisions (which would mean taking responsibility for generating alternatives or setting priorities among municipal functions). Management's right to make service level decisions was not challenged, although unions maintained their right to oppose decisions once they had been made. In only three instances were alternative means of cutting department budgets suggested by unions (all three were teachers unions). All other proposals made by unions entailed shifting the full burden of cuts to other municipal departments. One union attorney argued that unions had never been asked to become involved with decision-making when times were good, and that they are unwilling to assume responsibility now that cutbacks must be made.

Impact bargaining was kept to its narrow definition -- who and how to lay off. Lack of concern for the impact of layoffs on the remaining work force was quite noticeable and was confirmed by personnel in various state agencies. Staff members at JLMC and MLRC were "surprised" at the lack of bargaining over impacts on the remaining force, or noted that alleged impacts (i.e., safety risk or increased work load) were used more as a strategy to delay implementation of layoffs than from a desire to negotiate. The only exceptions involved teachers, who had previously negotiated their concerns about work load and work organization into their contracts. Their previous experience with force reductions may have had a bearing at this point, and indicate that other unions may expand their concerns as layoffs become more familiar.

Unions were unwilling to prevent or limit layoffs by taking wage reductions. This reluctance was part of the unions strategy to heighten public opposition to cuts and increase state aid allocations. Whether the reluctance to accept alternatives to layoffs will continue once it becomes clear that deeper budget cuts cannot be avoided, is uncertain. The case studies suggest a general unwillingness to open negotiated contracts. Changes in nonwage provisions (e.g., personnel organization) are more acceptable, especially where contracts already permit such adjustments.

Local officials perceive a loss of power for unions, especially because of the elimination of binding abitration and school committee fiscal autonomy. The restrictions on municipal revenues are also believed to have enhanced management's bargaining position. A Marshfield Selectman contends that "unions now recognize their inability to play games . . . management is in the driver's seat." Clearly, management expects compromises on wages and work organization restrictions to be forthcoming when jobs are threatened. Union leaders at the local level expect it to be more difficult to increase wages in the future.

The general counsels for the MTA and IBPO do not perceive a real shift in power from unions to management. They argue that relationships have become more complex, but that unions have not lost anything. A spokesman for the IBPO stressed the importance of public reactions to police and fire cuts. The MTA expects teachers to gain increasing public support as the impact of cuts in education becomes visible in the coming year. The head of the PFFM did perceive a changed political context for unions, but attributed it to actions at the federal level (e.g., the Reagan Administration's stand in the PATCO strike), as much as to the constraints imposed by Proposition 2 1/2.

Union leaders feel they must develop more sophisticated methods of tapping political support from more varied sources. (AFSCME leaders pointed to a new strategy that will link their efforts with public interest groups.) Some observers fear heightened hostilities and more drawn out negotiations. Some predict strikes in the second round of cuts. Others predict a higher quality of bargaining, with less posturing, more willingness to compromise, and quicker settlements.

New contract negotiations will emphasize provisions for reductions in force. It is unlikely that unions that do not already have provisions for strict seniority reductions in force or minimum manning will be able to win them because of management's equally heightened interest in such issues. It is not clear whether wage increases will actually decrease compared to previous years. In cases that have reached the state agencies (through petitions for dispute resolution) there is some evidence that the pattern of wage settlement is not substantially different from previous years (perhaps only a percentage point or two lower).

Uncertainty reigns. Major decisions are still being awaited in the courts and from the Labor Relations Commission. Contract negotiations, delayed until more information about long-term financial conditions was available, are now beginning. Year two of Proposition 2 1/2 will bring greater experience to the bargaining table, but also deeper cuts. Changes in the nature of labor relations are just beginning to emerge, and with them, the need for further study.

## Notes for Chapter 24

1. Chapter 150E of the General Laws.

2. City of Newton, 2 MLC 1192 (H.O., 1975), aff'd. 4 MLC 1282 (1977).

3. City of Boston, 4 MLC 1202 (1977).

4. Newton School Committee, 5 MLC, 1016 (1978).

5. Boston School Committee and Administrative Guild, 4 MLC 1912 (1978).

6. Newton School Committee, op. cit.

7. Section 9, 150E.

8. Section 4 of Chapter 1078 of the Acts of 1973, as amended. The JLMC was created in 1978 as a compromise solution to intense conflict which arose between unions and municipal managers over the renewal of binding arbitration and Chapter 150E. The Joint Committee is comprised of management and police and fire union representatives, and a neutral chairman. Through its intervention in dispute resolution for local police and fire disagreements, it was intended to provide a "balanced" state perspective on local collective bargaining agreements, and to enhance meaningful negotiation leading to settlements without need of arbitration.

9. The Committee's Senior Management representative noted that the majority of JLMC cases, before Proposition 2 1/2, reached settlement prior to any formal award; less than 5 percent of the cases went to last-best-offer arbitration. The on-going case load (26 petitions were filed between October and December 1981) suggests that the Joint Committee remains a viable dispute resolution institution, even without its final arbitration powers.

10. Although it remained above 1980 levels, the MLRC's case load declined in the fall and winter months of 1981, compared with the summer's activity. One Commissioner explained that the height of the controversy over new contract negotiations and personnel reductions coincided with municipal budget-making near the conclusion of the fiscal year. The Commissioner expects increased activity at the MLRC as municipalities begin round two of their Proposition 2 1/2 budget-making.

11. City of Malden and Malden Firefighters (MUP-4357, Nov. 25, 1981).

12. New Bedford School Committee (MUP-4210, Nov. 6, 1981). A 1978 decision established that where circumstances beyond the control of the employer require immediate action, bargaining after the imposition of change may satisfy the employer's bargaining obligation. (The Boston School Committee - Administrative Guild, 4 MLRC 1912 (1978).)

13. City of Quincy (MUP-4232, Nov. 13, 1981).

14. Safety and workload issues did arise in two cases decided in the fall, one heard by the Commission (City of Boston, MUP-3821, Nov. 2, 1981), concerning fire fighters and the closing of three fire stations, and one heard in Superior Court, concerning a new round of Boston police officer layoffs. The MLRC found that only if safety and work load impacts of management decisions exceed "pre-existing parameters," are they bargainable; in this case, the union failed to prove that they did. The court ruled against the police union in its complaint of safety risk through more layoffs, but skirted the issue of safety impact by finding that the city had offered to bargain, but the union failed to respond. A similar situation occurred in the fire fighter case. Only the city had relented and offered to bargain over impacts but the union's response was "far less than vigorous." The Commission concluded that the intent of the union in raising safety issues was to prevent implementation of management's decision rather than to negotiate a resolution to the dispute.

15. Under a new law (Chapter 767 of the Acts of 1981), towns may rescind all Civil Service coverage, with certain exceptions, through town meeting or referendum, or, in cities, by a vote of the City Council. Partial revocation requires a petition to the state legislature. According to a staff person at the Massachusetts Municipal Association, some motivations for revoking Civil Service regulation of public employees include problems with filling positions due to delays in obtaining examination results, dissatisfaction with the pool of applicants for municipal positions (possibly because of the Commission's affirmative action policies), and the time and money spent following Civil Service procedures and regulations. However, the public may still vote to retain coverage to avoid a return to political patronage and the cost of maintaining a local personnel system.

16. South Hadley (MUP-4410, Nov. 24, 1981).

17. Under the law, it is the obligation of the employer to request from the legislative body an appropriation necessary to fund items of contract, within 30 days of executing that contract. If the request is refused, the parties return to the bargaining table. Chapter 150E, Section 7B.

18. County of Suffolk (MUP-4466, Nov. 17, 1981).

19. Commonwealth of Massachusetts, (SUP-2598, Nov. 4, 1981).

20. Commonwealth of Massachusetts, (SUP-2599, Nov. 4, 1981).

21. Brief for the Plaintiffs-Appellants, Appeal from a judgment of the Superior Court in Kathleen Kelley, et al v. School Committee of Boston, 1981.

22. Canton School Committee (MUP-2425, 1981).

23. Saugus School Committee (7 MLC 1849, May, 1981).

24. Chelmsford School Committee, AO-4, Nov. 13, 1981.

25. Docket D-964, March 26, 1981.

26. Town of Belmont v. Civil Service Commission, C.A. No. 81-18-26, June 12,1981. The union has appealed the court's reversal of the Commission's ruling to the Supreme Judicial Court (No. 2707).

27. According to the Counsel staff for the Senate, "outside sections" are those sections passed with the budget but are not appropriations of funds. Through their inclusion with an appropriations bill, they avoid the normal procedures of analysis required of bills introduced independently. As such, they are not meant to alter the intent of a law, but rather refine it.

28. Similar trends are evident across the state. The MTA estimates that 14,000 teachers received layoff notices out of a membership of about 60,000 (25 percent). Even if most were not eventually laid off, the proportion is larger than for police or fire. The PFFM estimates that less than 350 or 2-3 percent of the 11,700 unionized fire fighters were laid off statewide, and an even lower percentage has been estimated for police officers.

Chapter 25

# Increasing Reliance on User Fees and Charges

Patricia L. McCarney

## Introduction

Historically, Massachusetts' cities and towns have under-used fees and charges compared with the average national use. However, the property tax limitations imposed by the passage of Proposition 2 1/2 are causing a number of cities and towns in Massachusetts to seek alternative revenue sources. The FY82 case study findings of the Impact: 2 1/2 Project indicate that a number of services formerly financed through the property tax are being funded with user fees and charges revenue. The case study findings on user fees and charges in Massachusetts are presented here to show one aspect of the outcomes experienced under Proposition 2 1/2 and to inform municipal officials who are currently considering implementing or expanding a fee-for-service system.

Eleven of the thirteen case study communities showed serious interest in user fees and charges as revenue alternatives to the property tax. Most of the cities and towns in the case study sample already had a fee schedule and a number of programs were supported by user charges. However, in response to Proposition 2 1/2, municipal officials evinced a new interest in increasing fees which had remained unchanged for years and in seeking new services for user charge implementation.

## Summary of Findings

The case study communities shared a number of actions in relation to user charges. For example, most communities charge for school lunches, but have not signficantly increased meal prices since their institution. With the passage of Proposition 2 1/2, however, a number of such increases have been

351

implemented. In Springfield, the School Department raised the school lunch charges 25 percent; in Burlington, the elimination of a $100,000 subsidy to the school lunch program meant an increase in charges to a level which allowed the program to be self-supporting (a partial refund was allowed at a later date); in Bridgewater, the School Committee retained the meals program when parents showed a strong preference for this service, but eliminated the town's subsidy of $90,000 and raised the charges accordingly; in Framingham, school lunch fees increased from $.40 in 1980 to $.75 in 1981 and possibly to $1.25 in 1982; and, Sandwich and Wayland both increased their charges for school lunches.

Charges in other education-related activities were common in a number of case study communities. Salem and Sandwich, for example, introduced a new set of fees for student participation in school athletics; in Framingham, this new fee was set at $20 per student per year. The town of Arlington conducted a brief survey of other cities and towns in the Commonwealth to determine which were considering, and which already had, a system of user fees and charges for athletic programs. Of the 31 cities and towns surveyed, six stated that they already had a system of athletic fees in effect, nine stated that they were considering athletic fees, and sixteen stated that they were not. Fees for athletic programs have been uncommon in the past, but nearly half the towns surveyed might be using such fees within the year. School transportation charges were increased in some of the cities and towns that already charged. Burlington decided against charging either for athletics or transportation to school. In Bridgewater, a survey of parents ndicated strong interest in maintaining transportation to school (the School Committee had considered eliminating it) and as a result, only service within a 1 1/2 mile radius of the schools was terminated.

It was argued, in a few of the surveyed cities and towns, that the education-related charges might offset the property and excise tax savings from Proposition 2 1/2. For example, the Salem School Superintendent estimated that an average family with two children to bus, who each participated in one after-school activity, might have to spend over $300 a year. These concerns were shared in Bridgewater, Sandwich, and Framingham. The Town Manager of Arlington added argued that because user charges cannot be deducted from federal income taxes, it would be cheaper to pay for many services through municipal taxes. Parents of school-age children appear to be affected most by the new and increased education-related user fees and charges -- particularly athletic fees, school lunch charges, and transportation fees.

Charges for ambulance services were imposed for revenue purposes in a number of case study communities. Fees were introduced in Sandwich and Springfield. In Burlington, the fee for ambulance services, already in effect, was increased from $25 to $100 in FY82. Health and hospital services in Cambridge, largely funded by service charges, imposed the largest increase in fees and charges of any city department (totalling $4.4 million). Salem's Shaughnessy Hospital bases its system of charges on a revolving account, which allows some flexibility in financing its own service costs with the related revenues raised.

A number of fees and charges related to Public Works departments are described in the case studies. In nearly all the cases, increases -- and often substantial increases -- occurred in charges for water and sewer services. For example, in Springfield, officials expected FY82 water and sewage charges to provide $10 million in revenue. In Burlington, the Selectmen hoped to gain an additional $500,000 by doubling the water and sewer rates for large commercial consumers (the residential rate was increased only 5 percent). In Arlington, water and sewage fees are being reviewed separately from the town's table of fees and charges. Arlington continues to charge for water as a member of the Metropolitan District Commission (MDC). The MDC's charges are mandatory and its new charges will be instituted in FY83. Arlington officials expect these and the town's new sewer charges to add $750,000 in revenue. In Cambridge, the City Manager decided to make the Water and Sewer Department self-supporting by increasing its charges. He raised water rates from $.46 to $.66 per 1,000 cubic feet, and sewer rates from $.31 to $.46 per cubic foot. The burden of these increases, he argued, would devolve on the major users of these services, (namely, Harvard and M.I.T.), rather than on city residents. Marshfield also raised its fees and charges for public works services; Salem increased its water fees (although city officials argued that these would have been raised regardless of Proposition 2 1/2); and both water and sewer rates were increased in Chelsea. In Quincy, the Mayor made no allocation for water and sewer services in the final budget, in an effort to create support for a self-supporting water and sewer commission with its own revolving account. Others opposed the Mayor on this issue. However, the city raised its water rate 12.5 percent anyway. The Public Works Department also increased its fees for electrical and plumbing inspection.

Trash collection fees were a common issue in a number of case study communities. Budget cutbacks prompted Marshfield's officials to consider eliminating trash collection, but this was not done. It was done in Bridgewater, however, when the private conractor increased his curb-side trash collection charge by $113,000. Town officials approved an alternative scheme at a cost of $61,500, whereby residents disposed of their own trash at a transfer station for a yearly fee of $2 or $3. In Wayland, the Highway Department's proposal to charge residents for using the town dump was rejected by the Finance Committee because residents have no alternative. In Salem, athough no trash collection fee was yet in place, the City Engineer argued that another 15 percent budget cut in FY83 would force him to create new charges and fees for trash collection and other services. In Framingham, the option of contracting out is being reviewed for trash collection services. Cambridge's City Manager suggested a trash collection fee of $50 per household to raise $1.7 million for the Public Works Department, which was subsequently rejected by the City Council. In Chelsea, the Mayor suggested setting up a private contract for trash collection (at a projected savings of $150,000), but the Board of Aldermen did not support this proposal.

Parks and Recreation departments in many of the case study communities also instituted or increased user fees and charges. These departments were most often faced with the largest percentage cuts in budget allocations since Proposition 2 1/2 passed. Their responses have varied. For example, in

Springfield, recreation fees were increased, whereas in Burlington, the Recreation Department kept its fees at the FY81 level and requested donations for revenue support. In Wayland, many of the Parks and Recreation programs were transferred to a fee supported structure, and the revenue expected was to form the greater part of all the FY82 appropriations. For the town as a whole, in FY80 and FY81, appropriations for fee-supported programs were nil; the proposed FY82 appropriations, however, were set at $48,764, and $42,164 of this was expected from the Parks and Recreation Department's extension of user fees. In Cambridge, the Human Services Department increased the sports league and golf course fees, making both self-supporting. Total recreational fees have increased from $115,000 to $159,700.

Extensive examinations of user charges were undertaken in Chelsea, Cambridge, and Arlington. In Chelsea, the Mayor retained an accounting firm (Ernst & Whinney) to help revise the city's fee schedule. The city's fees and charges had not been changed for over a decade, and with Proposition 2 1/2, were increased to yield $500,000 in additional revenues. Cambridge officials wanted new fees and charges to be considered in terms of their practicability to administer and collect. They hoped to keep rates low enough to prevent non-payment or denial of services to needy individuals. Overall, revenue raised from all fees and charges in Cambridge increased from $23.6 million in FY81 to $30.7 million in FY82. The Town Manager of Arlington studied the pros and cons of a user fee system. A user charge system would allow revenue to be collected from non-residents and non-taxpayers for use of town services; avoid subsidization of specialized services, not available to the general public; and, help measure the demand for services. But the Town Manager warned against setting a fee so high that needy citizens are deprived of important services. Although Arlington raised its fees for licenses and inspections in 1981, many of its fees had not been changed since 1975. A new table of fees and charges was approved in September 1981, which in most cases followed the state's maximum rates.

## Conclusions

From this summary of case study findings, it is clear that various systems of user fees and charges were in effect in most of the cities and towns studied. However, the heightened level of municipal interest in fees and charges is a direct result of the pressure, since the passage of Proposition 2 1/2, to find alternative revenue sources. Municipal officials have done some research to understand the principles of a user charges system; they have instituted new fees and charges; and increased others that had been unchanged for years.

From this summary of findings, two main issues emerge. First, it is generally agreed that a charge should cover the costs of operating a service, or some specific portion of it. In most of the cities and towns studied, fee increases were sought to cover costs, but there is an increasing sentiment among municipal officials that more systematic knowledge of service provision costs is needed. In many ways, Proposition 2 1/2 has encouraged municipal officials to go about cost accounting more rigorously than before to determine a reasonable schedule of user charges.

A second issue is, who is being affected most by new or increased user fees and charges? The elderly are believed to one such group, as well as parents of school-age children because of increases in school lunches and newly established fees for transportation and athletic programs. An number of municipal officials argued that tax savings might be offset by such increases, and this might be more true for some groups than for others.

Since Proposition 2 1/2 passed, the need to produce new revenue has generated a rapid increase in the growth of new and increased user charges throughout communities in Massachusetts. However, preliminary indications from the case studies suggests that haste can produce problems in developing a reliable system of charges. A sound understanding of costs is a basic requirement in determining fees. Thus, cost accounts have become increasingly important in budget-making under Proposition 2 1/2 and in establishing a sound user fee schedule. Periodic review of costs is also needed to increase fees in response to higher costs. Methods to determine whether particular groups of residents are unduly burdened by new or increased user charges are also needed.

In addition to its revenue raising potential, a system of user charges, as a financing mechanism, has other, non-revenue potential. For example, user charges are a more equitable way of financing certain specialized services that are not offered to, or funded by, the general public. Costs are covered directly by those benefiting from the service. Although Massachusetts municipalities have pursued expanded user charges for revenue purposes, it is likely that much more will be done with this underutilized revenue source in the future. of user charges.

Chapter 26

# Impacts on Municipal Appropriation Levels

## Karl E. Kim

This study depicts the immediate impacts of Proposition 2 1/2 on local budgets by analyzing municipal appropriations in Massachusetts. Since communities sometimes spend more and sometimes less than the amount they appropriate for each purpose, this analysis provides only a preliminary estimate of spending changes immediately following the adoption of Proposition 2 1/2. Appropriation levels reflect the attitudes and feelings of budget-makers at the beginning of each budget cycle; in this case, immediately after Proposition 2 1/2 took effect.

Prior to the passage of Proposition 2 1/2, communities in Massachusetts set tax rates in the conventional manner. First, they determined total planned expenditures. Then, they estimated the nonproperty tax revenue (state and federal aid, income from user fees and charges, and other local sources), that they could expect. The amount of property tax revenue needed was the difference between planned expenditures and nonproperty tax revenues. Before passage of Proposition 2 1/2, governments merely set their tax rates at a level that would yield the amount of property tax revenue needed. Now, communities must not exceed an effective tax rate of 2 1/2 percent of assessed valuation. This means that communities must adjust their revenue requirements to live within the tax rate limitation imposed by state law.

The governing body in each Massachusetts community must adopt an ordinance or resolution each year providing an authorization to spend. This ordinance must be adopted either during town meeting or by the city council. In most local governments, the chief executive officer prepares the proposed budget. Usually a budget staff or finance committee works closely with the chief executive and department heads to pull together the annual budget. Once a proposed budget is prepared, legislative and public consideration must be completed before a final budget can be approved. This process often takes the better part of a year.

Once proposed budgets are adopted by governing bodies, planned expenditures become law and communities are legally authorized to spend the amounts appropriated. Usually this cycle is completed in the spring just prior to the start of the new fiscal year, which in Massachusetts begins on July first.

## Sample Communities

A sample of 61 communities was chosen to represent the 256 largest cities and towns in Massachusetts. We wanted a mix of communities that reflected differing levels of population size, population growth, income, residential property and estimated revenue losses due to Proposition 2 1/2. Of the 61 communities initially selected, 44 responded to the survey -- 9 cities and 35 towns.

## Data Analysis

FY81 appropriations were compared with FY82 appropriations. This was not a simple task since large year-to-year variations in allocations for particular government services exist. This has always been the case (it is not due to Proposition 2 1/2). From time to time, communities decide to reprivatize ("contract out") certain services. Sometimes, department reorganization can cause major shifts in the way allocation levels are recorded. At best, this analysis suggests only how spending may have changed (but not why) which services suffered the greatest cutbacks in appropriations, and how appropriations were altered in different types of communities.

## Preliminary Findings

A general decline in the level of local government spending has taken place in Massachusetts since 1977. In this report, per capita appropriations are compared because they are not sensitive to variations in the cost of providing services due to economies of scale, geographical attributes, and other variations likely to affect operations.

Appropriations declined from FY81 to FY82 for almost all categories of local government spending in Massachusetts. The mean appropriations for most services were lower in FY82 than in FY81. Average appropriations increased in two areas -- debt and garbage removal -- as indicated in Table 26.1. Table 26.1 also indicates that parks and recreation, roads and streets, and libraries suffered the greatest reduction in appropriations. Reductions in school and fire department appropriations were also large. Based on the aggregate figures, reductions in police department appropriations were relatively low.

The large reductions in street and park appropriations, relative to other government activities is probably due to the special nature of these services.

**Table 26.1**
**Percent Change in Municipal Appropriations**
**FY81-FY82**

| Appropriations | Percent Change |
|---|---|
| Schools | - 6.5 |
| Police | - .5 |
| Fire | - 4.2 |
| Streets | -10.6 |
| Parks & Recreation | -22.9 |
| Libraries | -10.5 |
| Garbage Removal | 1.6 |
| Debt | 4.0 |

They are material-intensive rather than labor-intensive. Since many communities in Massachusetts follow a practice of cutting "things" before people, services such as street maintenance and parks are cut first. In addition, recreation programs run by parks departments typically employ large numbers of part-time and teenage workers. These employees rarely benefit from union protection against layoffs.

Reductions in library appropriations tend to occur for similar reasons. In addition to requiring large allocations for materials, libraries differ from other services in that much of their funding comes from endowments and other nongovernment sources. For example, public libraries in Springfield receive 25 percent of their funding from nongovernment sources. Also, libraries are often considered a "nonessential" public service, a view that led to large cuts in library services in the first year after passage of Proposition 2 1/2,

Reductions in school and fire department appropriations, while not as large in percentage terms as the reductions in streets and parks, involve substantial cutbacks in absolute dollar terms. This is all the more obvious when we consider that many communities spend upwards of 60 percent of their total annual budgets on public education and well over 6 percent on fire protecation.

Increased appropriations to cover debt repayment are not surprising. While many communities have deferred new capital improvements, a few have been forced to increase short-term borrowing to make up the gap between the cost of planned expenditures and available property tax revenues. In some cases, communities had no choice but to increase short-term borrowing to live up to previous financial obligations, even if they chose to cut back overall.

Increases in garbage removal aappropriations appear to reflect a belief that garbage removal is an absolutely essential government service. Nevertheless, the overall increase in this area is small.

## Appropriations by Service Area

Eight local services were examined in detail: schools, police, fire, streets, parks and recreation, garbage removal, libraries and debt. Of the 44 communities in the sample, only 4 increased school appropriations in FY82. The majority cut between 3 and 10 percent of their FY81 appropriations. Six communities lost less than 3 percent. There were 27 communities that lost more than 5 percent. The cities of Salem, Quincy, and Everett each cut in excess of 15 percent.

With regard to police budgets, 15 communities reduced FY82 appropriations and 29 increased police allocations following the passage of Proposition 2 1/2. Most of these increases were in the 5 percent range; only 3 communities increased appropriations more than 10 percent.

Although the aggregate mean figures show a decrease in fire appropriations, 21 communities increased fire department appropriations. About one-half of these increases were less than 5 percent. There were 18 communities that decreased fire department appropriations. Most of these decreases were in the 5 to 10 percent range.

Only 9 communities increased appropriations for streets. Of the remaining communities, 5 decreased appropriations by less than 3 percent, 8 decreased appropriations by 5–10 percent, and 16 decreased appropriations by more than 10 percent.

Only one city in the sample, Gloucester, increased its appropriations for parks and recreation. Two communities, Pelham and Lynnfield, appropriated the same amount in FY82 as they had in FY81. The remaining communities cut parks and recreation appropriations. Fourteen cut appropriations by more than 25 percent, 23 communities cut appropriations by more than 10 percent. These data suggest that parks and recreational services were hard hit by Proposition 2 1/2.

Communities varied widely in terms of changes in their appropriations for garbage removal. Of the 33 communities from which information was received, 17 increased FY82 appropriations, one remained the same, and 15 decreased their FY82 appropriations. The distribution of percentage changes for garbage removal appropriations was more evenly distributed than for any other services.

Very few communities increased appropriations for libraries during FY82. Only 6 communities made increases, and these all amounted to less than 5 percent. Fourteen communities cut more than 15 percent, and 25 communities cut more than 10 percent. Library appropriations were cut substantially throughout the state.

The final category of government activity studied was debt service. Sixteen communities increased their debt service appropriations and 23 showed decreases between FY81 and FY82. There were 15 communities with a 5 percent increase or decrease in debt appropriations.

Examining total appropriation levels (i.e., adding together appropriations for the eight activity areas), we find that only 4 of the 44 communities in our sample increased appropriation levels over FY81. The majority cut appropriations 3–10 percent. Seven communities showed decreases of 10–15 percent; two communities, Quincy and Everett, had decreases in excess of 15 percent.

Recapping: appropriations for parks and recreation, streets, libraries and schools tended to decrease in most communities. For these services, the percentage decrease in appropriations between FY81 and FY82 was larger than for police, fire, garbage removal and debt service. The range of percentage changes in appropriations was quite large for most of the services studied. This is clear evidence that communities responded in different ways to the mandate of Proposition 2 1/2. This may also reflect differences among communities in the level of services they were providing prior to Proposition 2 1/2. No community increased its total eight-service appropriations level by a substantial margin. Most communities decreased total appropriations by 3 to 10 percent.

## Differences among Communities

Communities in the Commonwealth differ in size, growth rate, income, percent residential property and many other ways. In order to take account of these differences and the potential impact that they might have on appropriations, we grouped communities along six dimensions: 1980 population, population growth 1970–80, 1970 median family income, percent residential property, population density, and the estimated revenue loss/gain during the first year of Proposition 2 1/2. For each of these attributes three categories were formed. (The categories are described in Chapter 3 of this volume). Table 26.2 shows the number of sample communities in each attribute category.

For each attribute the following were calculated: (1) the percentage change in appropriations for all eight government activities and the percentage change in the total of the eight activities from FY81 to FY82; (2) the number of communities in each service area with cuts greater than 5 percent, cuts less than 5 percent, and increased in FY82 appropriation levels; (3) the percentage distribution of communities with cuts greater than 5 percent, less than 5 percent, and increases; and, (4) the mean percentage change in appropriations for each activity area.

*Population Size.* For the largest communities (population greater than 27,000) reductions in appropriations were concentrated on schools, streets, parks and recreation, and libraries. One-half of these communities had increases in police appropriations and 40 percent had increases for garbage removal. Almost 80 percent of the largest communities had cuts greater than 5 percent in school appropriations compared to about 60 percent of the communities in either the

**Table 26.2**
**Attribute Categories**

| Attribute | Number of Communities |
|---|---|
| Population size | |
| Small | 8 |
| Medium | 19 |
| Large | 14 |
| Population growth | |
| Declining | 20 |
| Low growth | 13 |
| Moderate growth | 8 |
| Income | |
| Low | 11 |
| Moderate | 18 |
| High | 10 |
| Residential property | |
| Low | 11 |
| Moderate | 15 |
| High | 13 |
| Density | |
| Low (<387 people/sq. mile) | 10 |
| Moderate (387-2549 people/sq. mile) | 20 |
| High (>2549 people/sq. mile | 11 |
| Proposition 2 1/2 Revenue Gap | |
| High | 10 |
| Low | 22 |
| No-gap | 9 |

small or medium categories. While the largest communities had the highest proportion of cuts greater than 5 percent, all communities regardless of size appear to have reduced, more or less, the same activities. When the eight service areas are totalled, a few communities in the small and moderate population groups had modest increases in appropriations. None of the largest communities experienced an increase in the eight-appropriation total.

*Population Growth.*   Communities with declining population were less likely than growing communities to increase appropriations. While about 70 percent of those communities with population growth (low and moderate) increased fire department appropriations, only 33 percent of the declining communities did so. Although a larger proportion of the low and moderate growth communities increased police budgets, 55 percent of the declining communities had increases in police appropriations. There was also a noticeably large proportion (80 percent) of the moderate growth communities that increased garbage removal appropriations compared to the declining communities (47 percent had increases in garbage removal appropriations). In general, declining communities tended to have larger cutbacks in more service areas. While there are differences between declining and growing communities, there is little difference between low and moderate growth areas.

*Income.* When communities were grouped according to household income, there were noticeable differences between the high income communities and other communities. High income communities had the fewest cuts greater than 5 percent for almost all service areas. In these communities, it was also more likely for there to have been increases in appropriation levels.

Although cutbacks in school budgets occurred in all communities, cuts were least severe in high income communities. Fifty percent of the high income communities in our sample had school budget cuts in excess of 5 percent; over 80 percent of the low and moderate income communities had cuts in this range. Fewer of the high income communities also cut as deeply into library budgets as did the low and moderate income communities. In general, high income communities cut their budgets less than the low and moderate income communities. While 70 percent of the high income communities and 27 percent of the moderate income communities had cuts in this range.

*Residential Property.* The percent change in appropriations did not differ widely when communities were grouped according to percent residential property. In all three groups, a similar proportion of communities with increases in fire department budgets, however, was higher in the high residential property communities than in either the low or moderate residential property municipalities. In general, high residential communities had low mean percentage changes in appropriations relative to the other communities.

*Population Density.* Low density communities had fewer cutbacks (greater than 5 percent) than high density communities. Eighty percent of these communities increased police budgets, while only 36 percent of the high density communities increased police budgets in FY82. Similarly, 86 percent of the low density communities in our sample increased garbage removal appropriations, compared to about 45 percent in either the medium or low density categories. The mean percent change in street maintenance appropriations for low density communities was less than one percent; for medium density communities, the average street budget reduction was about 9 percent; for high density areas, the reduction was much larger, 23 percent.

*Revenue Gap.* Ninety percent of the high gap communities (those having to cut the full 15 percent from FY82 levies) had school budget cuts in excess of 5 percent. Seventy percent of the low gap towns and 27 percent of the no-gap towns had school budget cuts in this range. One-hundred percent of the high gap communities cut parks and recreation appropriations by more than 5 percent; 71 percent of the low gap communities and 62 percent of the no-gap communities had park and recreation cutbacks of this magnitude. In general, the largest and most frequent cuts occurred in those communities requiring the full 15 percent levy reduction. While 67 percent of the no-gap communities increased police budgets, 60 percent of the high gap communities increased police appropriations in FY82. A similar proportion of both high gap and low gap communities increased appropriations for garbag removal.

## Summary and Conclusions

In the first year following enactment of Proposition 2 1/2, allocations for most government activities declined. A number of communities increased spending for garbage removal, debt service and police. Reductions in appropriations for parks and recreation, streets, libraries, and schools, tended to be larger and more frequent than those for other services. There were almost no communities that increased their eight-service total appropriations. Most communities decreased their total appropriation by 3-10 percent.

Large population communities tended to experience the largest and most frequent cuts. This was also true for communities with declining populations and high population density. In general, communities with large residential areas suffered fewer cutbacks than those with less residential area. There was a strong relationship between cutbacks and revenue losses due to Proposition 2 1/2. While it is not surprising to find that communities that had to cut the full 15 percent from their levies had the largest reductions in appropriations, it was surprising to find that many of these communities increased spending on police and garbage removal.

Although our data indicate a general decline in government spending and that "nonessential" services were most likely to be cut, there is substantial variation in how communities responded to Proposition 2 1/2. Even after communities were grouped according to various attributes, there was tremendous variation in mean percentage change. While Chelsea cut its parks and recreation budgets by less than one percent, Salem cut its parks and recreation spending in this area by 35 percent. While Concord increased its police budget by 7 percent, Marshfield decreased police spending by 10 percent. Cambridge increased its fire department appropriations, while Worcester decreased fire expenditures by over 9 percent. While Watertown decreased debt service appropriations by 13 percent, Norwood increased by 5 percent.

This analysis has suggested some patterns in municipal appropriation levels in the first year following the passage of Proposition 2 1/2. While Proposition 2 1/2 affects all communities, it is apparent that the budgetary respose to the new law if neither uniform nor clearcut. The second year of Proposition 2 1/2 raises additional questions. Will the patterns identified so far continue? How will services that received large cutbacks in the first year fare in the second year? Will the same services be cut, or will municipalities restore funding to those services that were cut immediately following enactment of Proposition 2 1/2?

## Table 26.3
## Per Capita Appropriations, FY81
## 44 Community Sample

| Community | School | Police | Fire | Streets | Parks | Garbage | Library | Total |
|-----------|--------|--------|------|---------|-------|---------|---------|-------|
| Amesbury | 383.30 | 42.00 | 39.78 | n.a. | n.a. | 8.09 | 11.64 | 1232.21 |
| Arlington | 280.55 | 53.29 | 52.85 | 27.65 | 11.47 | 16.10 | 16.89 | 506.20 |
| Burlington | 570.48 | 80.08 | 64.85 | n.a. | 18.72 | 14.70 | 8.60 | 1113.60 |
| Cambridge | 399.75 | 83.30 | 74.99 | 105.08 | n.a. | n.a. | 14.10 | 1345.65 |
| Chelmsford | 491.78 | 48.52 | 52.05 | 47.36 | 7.07 | n.a. | 10.12 | 712.86 |
| Chelsea | 01.44 | 85.53 | 99.80 | 43.71 | 12.08 | 19.63 | 11.73 | 590.45 |
| Clinton | 306.75 | 36.92 | 33.10 | 45.17 | 6.64 | 11.03 | 5.64 | 485.97 |
| Concord | 679.88 | 54.70 | 47.69 | 20.81 | 6.63 | 4.60 | 22.49 | 1089.98 |
| Dalton | 355.53 | 33.94 | 11.11 | 39.63 | 13.31 | 15.45 | 8.23 | 483.55 |
| Dartmouth | 357.18 | 45.21 | n.a. | 30.04 | 4.74 | 4.04 | 9.04 | 699.80 |
| Dennis | 286.09 | 67.48 | 43.32 | 53.21 | 3.75 | n.a. | 2.52 | 491.25 |
| Dover | 585.77 | 78.53 | 14.27 | 72.51 | 17.22 | 2.66 | 11.79 | 974.57 |
| Dracut | 373.98 | 36.47 | 27.15 | 17.36 | 2.25 | 7.61 | 5.01 | n.a. |
| Everett | 368.39 | 72.92 | 90.67 | 47.92 | 18.25 | 11.86 | 11.00 | 907.25 |
| Foxborough | 522.91 | 43.66 | 34.00 | 46.42 | 5.23 | 6.71 | 12.55 | 884.54 |
| Framingham | 414.41 | 39.66 | 60.90 | 19.06 | 7.93 | 21.50 | 13.05 | 892.94 |
| Georgetown | 523.70 | 29.12 | 6.37 | 41.33 | 4.13 | 8.89 | 8.40 | 931.03 |
| Gloucester | 392.78 | 52.96 | 65.73 | 36.43 | 21.94 | 12.26 | 10.34 | 895.15 |
| Hatfield | 357.08 | 10.36 | 5.75 | 32.64 | 1.95 | 5.37 | 6.13 | 741.59 |
| Ipswich | 389.76 | 45.16 | 32.67 | 26.20 | 19.24 | 19.09 | 11.27 | 821.26 |
| Leicester | 367.50 | 37.16 | 7.89 | 53.21 | 5.65 | 1.69 | 4.02 | 606.15 |
| Longmeadow | 562.98 | 47.69 | 24.02 | 37.76 | 28.75 | 15.21 | 10.64 | 931.50 |
| Lynnfield | 527.64 | 57.32 | 17.70 | 22.87 | 3.55 | 14.77 | 14.20 | 870.64 |
| Marshfield | 465.14 | 66.02 | 49.29 | 106.57 | 3.24 | 7.79 | 8.28 | 895.67 |
| Norwood | 383.71 | 57.31 | 49.78 | 8.33 | 10.07 | 9.83 | 12.21 | 1313.50 |
| Palmer | 375.18 | 30.67 | n.a. | 37.98 | 10.67 | 2.05 | 10.18 | 519.43 |
| Pelham | 459.35 | 9.26 | 4.50 | 70.91 | 0.35 | 3.78 | 1.80 | 682.83 |
| Pittsfield | 367.33 | 44.77 | 60.89 | 97.46 | 11.87 | n.a. | 9.81 | n.a. |
| Quincy | 394.82 | 81.28 | 80.62 | 77.81 | 2.71 | 2.70 | 12.61 | 213.08 |
| Salem | 367.91 | 54.71 | 69.32 | 25.93 | 26.75 | 20.36 | 12.86 | 1121.63 |
| Seekonk | 472.44 | 52.96 | 27.43 | 38.44 | 1.58 | 11.41 | 6.74 | 714.96 |
| Southwick | 460.50 | 34.34 | 4.10 | 31.34 | 1.43 | 8.89 | 4.13 | 573.58 |
| Springfield | 336.12 | 60.82 | 51.28 | 1.68 | 19.47 | 1.36 | 22.26 | 873.33 |
| Sturbridge | 498.61 | 30.02 | 27.01 | 67.44 | 4.59 | n.a. | 5.10 | 823.90 |
| Watertown | 331.62 | 66.16 | 78.64 | 74.29 | 8.99 | 14.98 | 18.81 | 853.82 |
| Wayland | 628.51 | 53.00 | 47.20 | 65.01 | 26.91 | 3.10 | 18.07 | 921.44 |
| Wellesley | 522.38 | 65.07 | 68.42 | 46.70 | 33.33 | 2.68 | 29.00 | 797.72 |
| Wenham | 304.05 | 54.41 | 29.70 | 48.53 | 6.92 | 14.75 | 12.51 | 588.95 |
| Whitman | 345.72 | 43.31 | 35.16 | 59.38 | 2.77 | 7.06 | 2.58 | 692.73 |
| Worcester | 377.60 | 57.54 | 55.00 | 18.99 | 13.36 | 11.08 | 17.34 | 611.85 |

## Table 26.4
## Per Capita Appropriations, FY82
## 44 Community Sample

| Community | School | Police | Fire | Streets | Parks | Garbage | Library | Total |
|---|---|---|---|---|---|---|---|---|
| Amesbury | 353.68 | 46.39 | 43.37 | n.a. | n.a. | 8.95 | 10.69 | 1275.85 |
| Arlington | 263.07 | 50.62 | 54.41 | 23.63 | 10.27 | 15.56 | 13.52 | 478.37 |
| Burlington | 522.05 | 80.10 | 70.97 | n.a. | 17.22 | 16.18 | 8.29 | 1090.98 |
| Cambridge | 384.07 | 84.69 | 76.08 | 97.58 | n.a. | n.a. | 13.24 | 1324.53 |
| Chelmford | 462.89 | 48.72 | 54.31 | 38.97 | 1.40 | n.a. | 9.40 | 682.26 |
| Chelsea | 287.11 | 88.97 | 107.17 | 36.76 | 11.96 | 23.93 | 9.44 | 581.56 |
| Clinton | 283.45 | 39.55 | 31.34 | 45.54 | 5.85 | 7.24 | 5.83 | 451.29 |
| Concord | 661.09 | 58.35 | 51.50 | 20.75 | 4.14 | 3.81 | 22.21 | 1067.04 |
| Dalton | 306.10 | 36.79 | 11.01 | 38.45 | 9.86 | 16.92 | 6.28 | 431.58 |
| Dartmouth | 358.70 | 45.64 | n.a. | 30.26 | 3.05 | 4.03 | 8.53 | 709.11 |
| Dennis | 263.90 | 71.49 | 44.16 | 47.18 | 2.14 | n.a. | 2.04 | 471.10 |
| Dover | 569.51 | 82.11 | 14.37 | 72.08 | 15.73 | 2.83 | 11.18 | 967.52 |
| Dracut | 375.79 | 1.94 | 27.71 | 17.23 | 2.17 | 12.85 | 5.11 | n.a. |
| Everett | 293.52 | 57.81 | 71.88 | 39.06 | 15.09 | 8.33 | 8.72 | 776.63 |
| Foxborough | 469.78 | 43.43 | 31.65 | 44.49 | 4.95 | 6.71 | 10.60 | 831.29 |
| Framingham | 374.35 | 40.34 | 59.80 | 21.73 | 7.40 | 20.16 | 11.09 | 808.54 |
| Georgetown | 493.41 | 31.16 | 6.79 | 21.59 | 0.56 | 5.72 | 7.36 | 717.68 |
| Gloucester | 348.04 | 55.57 | 62.25 | 29.65 | 22.68 | 11.83 | 9.46 | 822.82 |
| Hatfield | 336.65 | 9.38 | 5.29 | 30.03 | 1.76 | 8.10 | 6.09 | 616.54 |
| Ipswich | 409.41 | 49.50 | 34.80 | 24.68 | 17.92 | 20.43 | 11.30 | 829.48 |
| Leicester | 383.43 | 37.71 | 7.18 | 52.20 | 4.19 | 1.85 | 3.96 | 607.11 |
| Longmeadow | 522.88 | 51.53 | 25.18 | 34.34 | 26.39 | 18.43 | 10.36 | 899.49 |
| Lynnfield | 522.48 | 62.19 | 18.90 | 21.48 | 3.55 | 14.64 | 14.47 | 870.17 |
| Marshfield | 423.40 | 59.18 | 49.63 | 96.86 | 1.62 | 8.75 | 7.73 | 822.52 |
| Norwood | 381.62 | 57.42 | 54.59 | 1.21 | 7.12 | 10.43 | 12.72 | 1375.71 |
| Palmer | 354.20 | 37.98 | n.a. | 35.09 | 10.60 | n.a. | 10.16 | 503.56 |
| Pelham | 480.97 | 13.05 | 4.95 | 85.09 | 0.35 | 5.40 | 1.80 | 727.28 |
| Pittsfield | 336.78 | 45.14 | 63.47 | 85.14 | 8.42 | n.a. | 7.92 | n.a. |
| Quincy | 317.46 | 74.48 | 75.10 | 25.13 | 9.73 | 10.53 | 9.72 | 786 09 |
| Salem | 310.21 | 53.83 | 63.64 | 16.31 | 17.51 | 20.71 | 10.80 | 1019.62 |
| Seekonk | 451.73 | 54.19 | 28.25 | 35.31 | 0.41 | 9.37 | 6.47 | 712.70 |
| Southwick | 407.52 | 36.60 | 4.31 | 24.71 | n.a. | 8.17 | 2.93 | 507.93 |
| Springfield | 299.44 | 62.17 | 48.47 | 1.47 | 17.13 | 2.05 | 20.76 | 887.62 |
| Sturbridge | 468.59 | 32.10 | 17.94 | 71.16 | 3.93 | n.a. | 5.02 | 812.11 |
| Watertown | 288.99 | 56.13 | 61.64 | 63.83 | 7.10 | 15.85 | 15.88 | 744.14 |
| Wayland | 596.90 | 51.49 | 46.31 | 50.11 | 26.35 | n.a. | 17.96 | 865.51 |
| Wellesley | 515.13 | 64.79 | 55.59 | 50.94 | 31.44 | n.a. | 28.08 | 777.31 |
| Wenham | 284.45 | 53.37 | 9.50 | 51.66 | 6.42 | 16.01 | 11.96 | 574.65 |
| Whitman | 300.42 | 42.01 | 35.63 | 67.86 | 2.10 | 6.83 | 2.15 | 630.90 |
| Worcester | 348.61 | 52.93 | 49.94 | 16.22 | 11.99 | 9.67 | 16.23 | 580.75 |

TABLE 26.5

DISTRIBUTION OF PERCENTAGE CHANGES IN APPROPRIATIONS
FY81-FY82

### SCHOOLS

| >25% decrease | 15-25% decrease | 10-15% decrease | 5-10% decrease | 5% decrease-5% increase | 5-10% increase | 10-15% increase | 15-25% increase | >25% increase |
|---|---|---|---|---|---|---|---|---|
| | Everett | Dalton | Amesbury | Cambridge | Ipswich | | | |
| | Quincy | Foxborough | Arlington | Chelsea | | | | |
| | Salem | Gloucester | Burlington | Concord | | | | |
| | | Springfield | Chelmsford | Dartmouth | | | | |
| | | Southwick | Clinton | Dracut | | | | |
| | | Watertown | Dennis | Kingston | | | | |
| | | Whitman | Framingham | Leicester | | | | |
| | | | Georgetown | Lynnfield | | | | |
| | | | Hatfield | Norwood | | | | |
| | | | Longmeadow | Pelham | | | | |
| | | | Marshfield | Seekonk | | | | |
| | | | Palmer | Wellesley | | | | |
| | | | Pittsfield | | | | | |
| | | | Sturbridge | | | | | |
| | | | Wayland | | | | | |

### POLICE

| >25% decrease | 15-25% decrease | 10-15% decrease | 5-10% decrease | 5% decrease-5% increase | 5-10% increase | 10-15% increase | 15-25% increase | >25% increase |
|---|---|---|---|---|---|---|---|---|
| Dracut | Everett | Kingston | Arlington | Burlington | | Clinton | Amesbury | Palmer |
| | Watertown | Marshfield | Hatfield | Cambridge | | Concord | | Pelham |
| | | | Quincy | Chelmsford | | Dalton | | |
| | | | Worcester | Chelsea | | Dennis | | |
| | | | | Dartmouth | | Georgetown | | |
| | | | | Dover | | Ipswich | | |
| | | | | Foxborough | | Longmeadow | | |
| | | | | Framingham | | Lynnfield | | |
| | | | | Gloucester | | Southwick | | |
| | | | | Leicester | | Sturbridge | | |
| | | | | Norwood | | | | |
| | | | | Pittsfield | | | | |
| | | | | Salem | | | | |
| | | | | Seekonk | | | | |
| | | | | Springfield | | | | |
| | | | | Wayland | | | | |
| | | | | Wellesley | | | | |
| | | | | Wenham | | | | |
| | | | | Whitman | | | | |

| >25% decrease | 15-25% decrease | 10-15% decrease | 5-10% decrease | 5% decrease-5% increase | 5-10% increase | 10-15% increase | 15-25% increase | >25% increase |
|---|---|---|---|---|---|---|---|---|
| **FIRE** | | | | | | | | |
| Framingham | Everett | | | Clinton | Arlington | Amesbury | | |
| Kingston | Watertown | | | Foxborough | Cambridge | Burlington | | |
| Sturbricge | Wellesley | | | Gloucester | Chelmsford | Chelsea | | |
| | | | | Hatfield | Dalton | Concord | | |
| | | | | Leicester | Dennis | Georgetown | | |
| | | | | Quincy | Dracut | Ipswich | | |
| | | | | Salem | Dover | Lynnfield | | |
| | | | | Springfield | Framingham | Norwood | | |
| | | | | Worcester | Longmeadow | Pelham | | |
| | | | | | Marshfield | Southwick | | |
| | | | | | Pittsfield | | | |
| | | | | | Seekonk | | | |
| | | | | | Wayland | | | |
| | | | | | Whitman | | | |
| **STREETS** | | | | | | | | |
| Georgetown | Chelmsford | | Arlington | Cambridge | Clinton | Sturbridge | Framingham | Kingston |
| Norwood | Chelsea | | Dennis | Hatfield | Concord | Wellesley | Whitman | Pelham |
| Quincy | Everett | | Pittsfield | Ipswich | Dalton | Wenham | | |
| Salem | Gloucester | | Springfield | Longmeadow | Dartmouth | | | |
| | Wouthwick | | Watertown | Lynnfield | Dracut | | | |
| | Wayland | | Worcester | Marshfield | Foxborough | | | |
| | | | | Palmer | Leicester | | | |
| | | | | Seekonk | | | | |

## PARKS

| >25% decrease | 15-25% decrease | 10-15% decrease | 5-10% decrease | 5% decrease-5% increase | 5-10% increase | 10-15% increase | 15-25% increase | >25% increase |
|---|---|---|---|---|---|---|---|---|
| Chelmsford | Everett | Arlington | Burlington | Chelsea | | | | |
| Concord | Quincy | Clinton | Dover | Dracut | | | | |
| Dalton | Watertown | Springfield | Foxborough | Gloucester | | | | |
| Dartmouth | Whitman | Sturbridge | Framingham | Lynnfield | | | | |
| Dennis | | | Hatfield | Palmer | | | | |
| Georgetown | | | Ipswich | Pelham | | | | |
| Kingston | | | Longmeadow | Wayland | | | | |
| Marshfield | | | Wellesley | | | | | |
| Norwood | | | Wenham | | | | | |
| Pittsfield | | | | | | | | |
| Salem | | | | | | | | |
| Seekonk | | | | | | | | |
| Southwick | | | | | | | | |
| Worcester | | | | | | | | |

## GARBAGE

| >25% decrease | 15-25% decrease | 10-15% decrease | 5-10% decrease | 5% decrease-5% increase | 5-10% increase | 10-15% increase | 15-25% increase | >25% increase |
|---|---|---|---|---|---|---|---|---|
| Clinton | Concord | Worcester | Framingham | Arlington | Dalton | Amesbury | Chelsea | Dracut |
| Everett | Quincy | | Southwick | Dartmouth | Dover | Burlington | Longmeadow | Hatfield |
| Georgetown | Seekonk | | | Foxborough | Ipswich | Marshfield | | Pelham |
| Wayland | | | | Gloucester | Leicester | | | Springfield |
| | | | | Lynnfield | Norwood | | | |
| | | | | Salem | Watertown | | | |
| | | | | Whitman | Wenham | | | |

## LIBRARIES

| >25% decrease | 15-25% decrease | 10-15% decrease | 5-10% decrease | 5% decrease- 5% increase | 5-10% increase | 10-15% increase | 15-25% increase | >25% increase |
|---|---|---|---|---|---|---|---|---|
| Kingston | Arlington | | Georgetown | Amesbury | Burlington | | | |
| Southwick | Chelsea | | | Cambridge | Clinton | | | |
| | Dalton | | | Chelmsford | Concord | | | |
| | Dennis | | | Dartmouth | Dracut | | | |
| | Everett | | | Dover | Hatfield | | | |
| | Framingham | | | Gloucester | Ipswich | | | |
| | Foxborough | | | Marshfield | Leicester | | | |
| | Pittsfield | | | Springfield | Longmeadow | | | |
| | Quincy | | | Worcester | Lynnfield | | | |
| | Salem | | | | Norwood | | | |
| | Watertown | | | | Palmer | | | |
| | Whitman | | | | Pelham | | | |
| | | | | | Seekonk | | | |
| | | | | | Sturbridge | | | |
| | | | | | Wayland | | | |
| | | | | | Wellesley | | | |
| | | | | | Wenham | | | |

## DEBT

| >25% decrease | 15-25% decrease | 10-15% decrease | 5-10% decrease | 5% decrease- 5% increase | 5-10% increase | 10-15% increase | 15-25% increase | >25% increase |
|---|---|---|---|---|---|---|---|---|
| Dracut | Clinton | Framingham | Everett | Amesbury | Cambridge | Dover | Chelmsford | Marshfield |
| Ipswich | Georgetown | | Gloucester | Arlington | Dartmouth | Longmeadow | Dennis | Wenham |
| | Kingston | | | Burlington | Foxborough | Seekonk | Leicester | |
| | Southwick | | | Chelsea | Palmer | | Worceser | |
| | Whitman | | | Concord | Sturbridge | | | |
| | | | | Dalton | | | | |
| | | | | Hatfield | | | | |
| | | | | Lynnfield | | | | |
| | | | | Norwood | | | | |
| | | | | Pelham | | | | |
| | | | | Quincy | | | | |
| | | | | Salem | | | | |
| | | | | Watertown | | | | |
| | | | | Wayland | | | | |
| | | | | Wellesley | | | | |

TOTAL PERCENTAGE CHANGE FOR EIGHT SERVICE AREAS

| >25% decrease | 15-25% decrease | 10-15% decrease | 5-10% decrease | 5% decrease- 5% increase | 5-10% increase | 10-15% increase | 15-25% increase | >25% increase |
|---|---|---|---|---|---|---|---|---|
|  | Everett | Dalton | Arlington | Amesbury | Pelham |  |  |  |
|  | Quincy | Georgetown | Clinton | Burlington |  |  |  |  |
|  |  | Salem | Dracut | Cambridge |  |  |  |  |
|  |  | Southwick | Foxborough | Chelmsford |  |  |  |  |
|  |  | Watertown | Framingham | Chelsea |  |  |  |  |
|  |  |  | Gloucester | Concord |  |  |  |  |
|  |  |  | Kingston | Dartmouth |  |  |  |  |
|  |  |  | Maarshfield | Dennis |  |  |  |  |
|  |  |  | Pittsfield | Dover |  |  |  |  |
|  |  |  | Springfield | Hatfield |  |  |  |  |
|  |  |  | Wayland | Ipswich |  |  |  |  |
|  |  |  | Wenham | Leicester |  |  |  |  |
|  |  |  | Whitman | Longmeadow |  |  |  |  |
|  |  |  | Worcester | Lynnfield |  |  |  |  |
|  |  |  |  | Norwood |  |  |  |  |
|  |  |  |  | Palmer |  |  |  |  |
|  |  |  |  | Seekonk |  |  |  |  |
|  |  |  |  | Sturbridge |  |  |  |  |
|  |  |  |  | Wellesley |  |  |  |  |

Chapter 27

# Coping with Cutbacks: Responses in 17 Local Governments

John M. Greiner and Harry P. Hatry

## INTRODUCTION

Voter approval of Proposition 2 1/2 has meant that many cities and towns in Massachusetts have had to plan on experiencing large reductions in revenue over the next several years. These revenue reductions come on top of the general worsening of the fiscal condition of many cities in recent years and reductions in federal assistance for a number of programs important to local governments (e.g., CETA). (1) As a consequence, it has been expected that local governments in Massachusetts will experiment with a variety of strategies for coping with the changing revenue picture, including cutbacks in staff and services, contracting out, increased use of volunteers, greater public/private sector cooperation, the introduction of user fees and charges, etc. We here catalogue initial efforts to cope with Proposition 2 1/2 by agencies in 17 Massachusetts cities and towns. The 17 sites of interest were selected jointly by the Urban Institute research team and IMPACT: 2 1/2 project staff. Twelve of the seventeen governments had already been targeted by the IMPACT: 2 1/2 research team for in-depth case studies. An additional five jurisdictions were included on the basis of early information developed by project staff and recommendations by knowledgeable municipal officials in the State of Massachusetts concerning governments likely to exhibit innovative responses to Proposition 2 1/2. Table 27.1 lists the 17 sites in our sample along with pertinent demographic and fiscal characteristics.

This report summarizes our information on actions taken in response to Proposition 2 1/2 by agencies in each of the 17 sites. The data were drawn from the following sources:

- Interviews by MIT project staff with city and agency officials in each of the 17 sites (this was the primary source of information).
- Agency records and reports provided in connection with those interviews.
- Case study reports on twelve of the 17 sites prepared by the IMPACT: 2 1/2 staff on the basis of independent interviews undertaken as part of another phase of the IMPACT: 2 1/2 research project.
- Detailed responses by seven sites to an August 1981 Massachusetts Municipal Association questionnaire on municipal responses to Proposition 2 1/2.

The present report focuses primarily on *agency-level* responses to Proposition 2 1/2 in five service areas: police, fire, libraries, parks and recreation, and public works. Responses by other agencies (with the exception of school departments, which were not included in this study) and by the government as a whole (e.g., responses developed by the city manager's office) are summarized in Section 7. The report concludes with a summary of overall findings and conclusions drawn from the results for the individual services.

## Effects of Proposition 2 1/2 on FY82 Agency Appropriation Levels

Table 27.2 summarizes post-Proposition 2 1/2 changes in appropriation levels for services in 15 of the 17 sites. (Comparable before and after data on appropriation levels were not available for Bridgewater and New Bedford.) These figures include appropriations for both capital and operating expenses. They also incorporate the offsetting effects of any state aid distributed to the given service.

The six services covered by Table 27.2 can be grouped into three broad categories:

1.    *Services experiencing generally small budget cuts:*    Police, fire, sanitation.

2.    *Services sustaining moderate cuts:*    Libraries.

3.    *Services experiencing large cuts:*    Parks and recreation, street maintenance.

The agencies falling into the first group reflect the high priority assigned by public administrators and political leaders to preservation of the public health and safety. Note, however, that there was considerable variation between governments in the cutbacks sustained in a given service area. Thus, even though the average percentage change in appropriations for sanitation services was relatively small, the actual post-Proposition 2 1/2 percentage changes in appropriations for sanitation departments in the various sites ranged from 100 percent decrease to a 51 percent increase.

Variations between agencies and service areas in the cutbacks sustained in the wake of Proposition 2 1/2 reflect a number of influences in addition to the priorities placed on those services by municipal officials. For instance, there were marked differences between agencies and between governments in the amounts that had to be appropriated to provide contractually–mandated wage increases for agency personnel. In several cases, the impacts of Proposition 2 1/2 in a given agency were moderated by actions the agency had taken prior to Proposition 2 1/2, for instance, in response to the state's 4 percent cap on spending increases (which took effect in FY80). Such agencies often had made significant personnel reductions and other economies in the years preceding Proposition 2 1/2, with the result that further spending cuts were sometimes not as great as one might have expected.

There were, however, other forces that tended to exacerbate the effects of Proposition 2 1/2. Examples include continuing pressures from inflation and wage increases required under contracts with municipal employee unions, cutbacks in and restrictions on certain classes of state aid (e.g., for libraries and highways), and reductions in various federally–funded programs. (The sharp curtailment of CETA positions in FY81 was especially painful for many municipal agencies.) Thus, while general state aid and other factors helped moderate the impacts of 2 1/2, their effects were diluted, to some extent, by other developments.

## Classification of Actions Taken by the Agencies

We classified the responses to Proposition 2 1/2 by agenies in the 17 sites according to the categories summarized in Table 27.3. Most of these categories are self–explanatory. However, in a few cases some further elaboration might be helpful.

● The distinguishing feature of the class of responses titled "cost cutting/reduced service levels" is that no direct effort was made by the local government to ameliorate or offset the effects of the reductions in costs and service levels. For example, if an agency attempted to offset a reduction in staff by encouraging service delivery by the private sector, we would classify it as "increased reliance on or assistance from the private sector," not as "cost cutting."

● The subcategory entitled "transfer charges to other funds or agencies" includes efforts by a department to bill accounts or agencies that are better able to bear the given expense (perhaps because of the presence of a revolving fund.)

● In "contracting" services, a government enters into a contract with a private firm or non–profit agency for the provision of services. "Franchising" of a service, on the other hand, involves the awarding of an exclusive or non–exclusive contract to a private firm or other group authorizing the provision of a service within a certain geographical area. Under a franchise agreement, the citizen pays the private firm directly for the service.

- "Encouragement of private delivery of services" and "increasing the burden on private organization" can reflect contrasting approaches to dealing with the private sector as a government cuts back on service delivery. In the first instance, the government simultaneously encourages private deliverers to assume more responsibility for services. Such encouragement can take the form of subsidies, grants, changes in tax regulations, and other measures. The second category (increase the burden on private organizations) refers to efforts by local governments to leave the provision of services up to the private sector without actively encouraging or assisting the private sector in the assumption of those responsibilities. Examples of the latter class of responses include the elimination of subsidies for private recreational organizations, the (unilateral) closing of public clinics and other social delivery centers, etc.

- "Increased citizen co-production of services" refers to efforts to increase the role of--or burden on--the citizen in those cases where service delivery involves (or could involve) a joint effort by a government agency and the citizen receiving the service. (2) Examples of actions falling into this category include increased citizen self-help and efforts to avoid the need for service (e.g., by prevention, conservation, etc.).

The response classification given in Table 27.3 is not perfect. Many of the categories overlap, and some responses could just as well have been classified under other headings. For instance, the contracting out of services could also be viewed as an improvement in productivity and management, and the elimination of subsidies (e.g., lighting for private athletic leagues) could often be classified both as increasing the burden on private organization and as raising fees and charges.

Each of the next five sections focuses on a single major service area. the seventh section summarizes results for a number of other agencies. In each section, the various actions taken by the local agencies in an effort to cope with Proposition 2 1/2 are organized according to the classification given in Table 27.3. In those cases where an action appears to fall into more than one category, we have included it in each category.

**Table 27.1**
**Selected Characteristics of the 17 Jurisdictions**

| | 1980 Population | Prop. 2 1/2 Revenue Gap* | Income Level(1) | Percent Residential(2) | Growth Rate(3) |
|---|---|---|---|---|---|
| Amesbury | 13,961 | 50 | 1 | 1 | 3 |
| Arlington | 48,219 | 48 | 2 | 2 | 1 |
| Bridgewater | 17,202 | 41 | 2 | 2 | 3 |
| Burlington | 23,486 | 39 | 3 | 1 | 2 |
| Cambridge | 95,322 | 64 | 1 | 1 | 1 |
| Chelsea | 25,431 | 76 | 1 | 1 | 1 |
| Everett | 37,195 | 41 | 2 | 1 | 1 |
| Framingham | 65,113 | 42 | 2 | 1 | 2 |
| Marshfield | 20,916 | 35 | 3 | 2 | 3 |
| New Bedford | 98,478 | 54 | 1 | 1 | 1 |
| Pittsfield | 51,974 | 41 | 1 | 1 | 1 |
| Quincy | 84,743 | 60 | 2 | 1 | 1 |
| Salem | 38,220 | 50 | 1 | 1 | 1 |
| Springfield | 152,319 | 56 | 1 | 1 | 1 |
| Watertown | 34,384 | 51 | 2 | 1 | 1 |
| Wayland | 12,170 | 35 | 3 | 2 | 1 |
| Worcester | 161,799 | 62 | 1 | 1 | 1 |

* Percentage reduction in 1980 property tax receipts under Proposition 2 1/2. Source: "Municipal Financial Data Including 1980 Tax Rates," Massachusetts Taxpayers Foundation.

(1) Key: 1 = <$9,073; 2 = $9,073-11,951; 3 = >$11,951.
(2) Key: 1 = <73%; 2 = > or equal to 73%.
(3) Key: 1 = < or equal to 0%; 2 = >0%-<15%; 3 = > or equal to 15%.

**Table 27.2**
**Percentage Changes in Appropriation Levels for Selected**
**Municipal Services after the Introduction of Proposition 2 1/2**

| Community | Police | Fire | Streets | Sanitation | P&R | Libraries |
|-----------|--------|------|---------|------------|-----|-----------|
| Amesbury | 10.5 | 9.0 | -- | 10.6 | -- | -8.2 |
| Arlington | -5.0 | 3.0 | -14.5 | -3.4 | -10.5 | -20.0 |
| Burlington | 0.0 | 9.4 | -- | 10.1 | -8.0 | -3.6 |
| Cambridge | 1.7 | 1.5 | -7.1 | -- | -- | -6.1 |
| Chelsea | 4.0 | 7.4 | -15.9 | 21.9 | -1.0 | -19.5 |
| Everett | -20.7 | -20.7 | -18.5 | -29.7 | -17.3 | -20.7 |
| Framingham | 1.7 | -1.8 | 14.0 | -6.2 | -6.7 | -15.0 |
| Marshfield | -10.4 | 0.7 | -9.1 | 12.3 | -49.9 | -6.6 |
| Pittsfield | 0.8 | 4.2 | -12.6 | -- | -29.0 | -19.2 |
| Quincy | -8.4 | -6.8 | -67.7 | -17.0 | -23.7 | -23.1 |
| Salem | -1.6 | -8.2 | -37.1 | 1.7 | -34.6 | -16.0 |
| Springfield | 2.2 | -5.5 | -12.5 | 50.8 | -12.0 | -6.8 |
| Watertown | -15.2 | -21.6 | -14.1 | 5.8 | -21.0 | -15.6 |
| Wayland | -2.9 | -1.9 | -22.9 | -100.0 | -2.1 | -0.6 |
| Worcester | -8.1 | -9.2 | -14.6 | -12.7 | -10.2 | -6.4 |
| Mean | -3.4 | -2.7 | -17.9 | -4.3 | -17.4 | -12.5 |

Notes:   1.   Capital  and  operating  appropriations plus  state  aid  are
included.   The data were prepared by Karl Kim of the IMPACT:   2 1/2 Project
on the  basis of local warrant  articles and were verified in  each case by
the town accountants.

        2.   A dash (--) means that separate appropriations were not made for
the service, the service is not provided by the town, or that adequate data
were not otherwise available.

## Table 27.3 Response Classification

---

Cost-Cutting/Reduced Service Levels
 Reduce services to the public
 Reduce internal (administrative/support) services
 Reduce or delay purchases, replacements or other expenditures

Improvements in Productivity and Management
 Work harder
 Introduce employee incentives
 Provide additional training
 Introduce new or additional technology
 Alter operational procedures
 Alter organizational structures
 Miscellaneous productivity improvement efforts
 (e.g., civilianization, cash management, etc.)

Acquisition of Additional Revenues/Financial Assistance
 Introduce or raise fees and charges
 Introduce or raise taxes
 Solicit funds and contributions
 -From the public sector (grants, subsidies, aid, etc.)
 -From the private sector (donations, contributions of funds
 or equipment, etc.)
 Establish revolving funds
 Transfer charges to other funds or agencies

Increased  Reliance on/Assistance from  other Public Agencies  (for Service
Delivery)
 Intragovernmental assistance, transfer, or sharing of service delivery
 Intergovernmental assistance, transfer, or sharing of service delivery

Increased Reliance on/Assistance from Private Sector for Service Delivery
 Contract out services
 Franchise service
 Encourage private delivery of services (subsidies, grants, altered
 regulations, etc.)
 Solicit/receive free assistance from the private sector
 Increase the burden on private organizations (e.g., eliminate subsidies,
 close government facilities, etc.)

Increased Reliance on/Assistance from Individual Citizens
 Increase use of volunteers
 Increase citizen coproduction of services (self-help, prevention, etc.)

Reduction of Demand for Service Without Affecting Need
 Introduce/raise fees and charges to adjust demand
 Alter regulations or eligibility requirements
 Otherwise discourage use of service (red tape, etc.)

---

## POLICE

Police departments in the 17 sites generally experienced relatively small reductions in appropriations as compared to other city agencies. The mean change in police appropriation levels subsequent to the introduction of Proposition 2 1/2 was −3.4 percent for the 15 sites for which comparable before and after data were available. Only fire services experienced a smaller average reduction. The relatively limited cuts experienced by most of the 17 police departments apparently reflected the strong emphasis of city management and elected officials on preserving public safety.

Nevertheless, there was considerable variation among the 17 sites with regard to the impact of Proposition 2 1/2 on police department funding levels. Police departments in a number of cities experienced major reductions in appropriations. (See Table 27.2.) On the other hand, post−Proposition 2 1/2 funding levels increased for several other police departments. (The largest occurred in Amesbury, where police appropriations increased by 10.5 percent in FY82.) Note, however, that many of these departments had to absorb contractually−required wage increases of as much as 10 percent. Amesbury, for example, was required to provide police officers with an 8 percent pay increase in FY82 under the first year of a three−year contract. Several other sites were already in the process of negotiating with police unions over contracts for coming years, and their FY82 appropriations included funds for possible negotiated wage increases. In order to absorb such wage increases, even police departments that exhibited an increase in post−Proposition 2 1/2 appropriations sometimes had to make some cuts. (1)

Because 70−95 percent of police department expenses in the 17 sites consisted of wages and salaries, the departments generally had very little flexibility in avoiding staff cuts when reductions in expenditures had to be made. Nearly every police agency cut back non−personnel expenditures (such as equipment replacement) as much as possible. Nevertheless, most of the 17 agencies still had to reduce staff levels and staff hours. The losses in funded positions ranged from 29 in Everett and 21 in Watertown to none in either Amesbury or Springfield.

In most sites, staff cuts were spread broadly. Reductions were made in patrol personnel, detectives, and crime prevention staff; in civilian as well as sworn personnel; and in supervisory as well as non−supervisory staff. While most of the staff reduction occurred through attrition and the elimination of vacant positions, some layoffs did occur. For instance, Arlington laid off one clerk; Everett laid off six police officers; and Watertown laid off eight police personnel. Some of these individuals, however, were rehired within a few months as vacancies occurred or additional state aid was received.

Most departments also made major reductions in their budgeted overtime. However, it was not clear whether these reductions would last. Some police officials felt that in the face of the other staff reductions that had been sustained, additional overtime would be needed to fill in for absent personnel. Others pointed out that there are frequently special unforeseen circumstances (such as a series of violent crimes) that necessitate the expenditure of considerable overtime. Several police officials suggested that they were likely to return to the town meeting later in the year to seek additional overtime funds.

Police department responses to Proposition 2 1/2 and the ensuing staff reduction were quite varied. The most common response consisted of straightforward cost cutting and the reduction of services without compensatory actions. The second most common response was to attempt to improve department productivity especially through the use of operational changes and improved resource management. The following responses were identified among the 17 police departments.

## Cost-Cutting/Reduced Service Levels

### Reduction of Services to the Public

In most cases, staff cuts were translated into reduced services for the public. The entire spectrum of police services was affected.

*Police Patrols.* Many departments reduced police patrol activities, with the result that fewer officers were on the street at any given time. The use of foot patrols was especially hard hit.

NEW BEDFORD: Foot patrols in New Bedford cut back considerably.

QUINCY: Walking patrols were reduced, and the canine corps was eliminated. (In the words of one police official, "The dogs were laid off.") Patrols of outlying areas were also reduced, and fewer backup units were available for officers in the field. However, efforts have been made to compensate for some of these cutbacks by prioritizing calls and improving patrol strategies for outlying districts (as described later under "Improvement of Operational Procedures").

ARLINGTON: Evening foot patrols were reduced from three units to one unit. However, the number of daytime foot patrols remained at three.

EVERETT: Provision of walking patrols now depends on manpower availability with priority being given to patrols in the city's two main squares. Contract stipulations (for instance, on minimum manning levels) reportedly prevented major changes in patrol assignments.

WORCESTER: Worcester moved from a mix of one- and two-man patrol cars to two-man cars only. These units were assigned responsibility for larger areas than had previously been the case. Provisions for backup units were drastically reduced: such units are now provided only in emergency situations. Unlike the sites described above, Worcester introduced foot patrols in its downtown area in the first year of Proposition 2 1/2. Officers were, however, instructed to cut back on some services (such as checking on the licenses of various establishments).

Other jurisdictions which reported the reduction or elimination of residential and/or foot patrols included Marshfield, Burlington, and Watertown.

*Investigations.*   Investigative units experienced staff cuts in a number of the sites. In some cases as many as 75 percent of the detectives were eliminated. (In a few jurisdictions, efforts were made to compensate for these cuts by prioritizing cases in terms of solvability—see "Improvements in Productivity.")

WATERTOWN: The detective unit was reduced by seven persons (almost 50 percent), with a corresponding decrease in followup investigations.

BURLINGTON: The time spent on followup investigations has been reduced.

QUINCY: This city reduced its investigative force by five detectives.

NEW BEDFORD: The number of plain-clothes units was reduced.

CHELSEA: Some detectives were reassigned to patrol duty.

MARSHFIELD: The number of detectives has been reduced from four to one. The workload on the remaining detective is so great that minor crimes—and even some major crimes—are no longer investigated.

ARLINGTON: The criminal investigation staff was reduced from 11 to 9.

*Traffic Enforcement.*   Five sites reported reductions in traffic enforcment activities.

EVERETT: Traffic enforcement staff and related activities were reduced by almost 50 percent.

NEW BEDFORD: The traffic divi28192sion was eliminated and traffic enforcement efforts were cut back. To reduce paperwork, officers were instructed not to make out reports for accidents involving less then $200 in damages.

ARLINGTON: With the reduction in foot patrols, it became necessary to use traffic and parking enforcement officers to fill in when cruiser patrolmen were absent. (Foot patrol personnel had previously been used to take up the slack.) The new policy has resulted in a decrease in traffic and parking enforcement services in order to maintain the number of cruisers on patrol at any given time (which, according to police officials, is the department's highest priority).

WORCESTER: Traffic enforcement and related school safety activities have been reduced.

BRIGEWATER: The number of traffic supervisors (school crossing guards) was reduced 50 percent (from 16 to 8). However, traffic enforcement continues to receive heavy emphasis from regular patrol officers as a general way to discourage crime.

*Juvenile and Community Services.* The effects of Proposition 2 1/2 were also felt in police-juvenile and police-community relations. Juvenile services were especially hard hit in many of the smaller towns.

EVERETT: The number of juvenile officers was reduced from three to one.

MARSHFIELD: The juvenile officer was eliminated.

BURLINGTON: The juvenile relations effort in this town was eliminated.

FRAMINGHAM: Community and juvenile relations services were sharply reduced. These services ranged from talks on rape and crime prevention before community groups to the high school drug program.

QUINCY: Plans to expand the Juvenile Unit were scrapped.

*Other Service Reductions.* Although most departments reported that crime prevention activities had not been curtailed, Bridgewater eliminated its crime prevention officer, and Burlington reduced the amount of time devoted to crime prevention. In Everett, police responsiveness to calls to the department's emergency number was initially curtailed in the wake of bitterness over staff reductions. Police officers reportedly sometimes responded to such calls by telling the caller to phone the Mayor for action. Such practices ceased after equipment for taping all emergency calls became operational.

*Reductions in Internal (Administrative/Support) Services*

While most of the cost cutting undertaken by police departments in the 17 sites focused on the reduction of personnel, other budgets and staff services were also reduced.

*Reduced Training.* New Bedford eliminated its program of cadet volunteers in January, 1981, because of the high cost of training cadets. Three other sites--Wayland, Quincy and Burlington--reported reductions in their budgets for officer training. The police chief in Quincy observed that "this may in the final analysis be one of the most disastrous effects of Proposition 2 1/2."

*Reduced Maintenance.* Quincy and New Bedford reported reduced maintenance services for police vehicles. In New Bedford, the police garage was closed from midnight until 8:00 a.m. due to the loss of garage staff, and officers were asked to perform more of their own maintenance.

*Reductions in Records and Data Collection Services.* Cutbacks in clerical staff support forced several departments to reduce the number of statistics and other records they prepared. Other departments reported a general slow-down in record services.

EVERETT: Records staff were reduced 50 percent (from 8 to 4), with a corresponding reduction in the amount of data collection and records preparation.

WATERTOWN: Staff reductions have reportedly led to a slowdown in the preparation of police records.

MARSHFIELD: Photographic services have decreased.

QUINCY: To help cut costs, this department is trying to reduce the number of records it keeps.

FRAMINGHAM: This town eliminated its crime analysis officer.

*Reductions or Delays in Purchases, Replacements and Other Expenditures*

Six of the seventeen sites reported cutbacks in purchases of police vehicles and other equipment.

CAMBRIDGE: Instead of replacing police cars on a three-year schedule, replacements dropped to zero in the year following the introduction of Proposition 2 1/2.

WORCESTER: Worcester reported that normally it replaced about 40 police cars per year. In the year preceding Proposition 2 1/2, vehicle replacements fell to 17. Proposition 2 1/2 then brought all vehicle replacements to a halt.

WAYLAND: This town used to have an annual replacement policy. But with the advent of Proposition 2 1/2, purchases of virtually all new equipment ceased.

BRIDGEWATER: The scheduled replacement of a police cruiser in this town was eliminated in the wake of Proposition 2 1/2.

QUINCY: This city cut back on capital purchases for the police department in the year following the introduction of Proposition 2 1/2.

FRAMINGHAM: In the first year of Proposition 2 1/2, this town switched from a policy of trading in all of its police cars on an annual basis to a policy of trading in only half of the cars each year. The result, however, was a large increase in vehicle repairs, and the town switched back to its policy of replacing cars on an annual basis.

Three of the sites also undertook some rather specialized cost-cutting activities.

WORCESTER and QUINCY: To reduce telephone bills for the police department, a number of telephones and extensions were eliminated. This reportedly led to a saving of $1,300 per month in Worcester.

ARLINGTON: With the introduction of a new communications system, this town will be able to eliminate its police call boxes and associated maintenance costs.

## Improvement of Productivity and Management

Productivity improvements and other management innovations constituted the second most common response to Proposition 2 1/2 among the 17 police departments. The examples encompass many important productivity improvement strategies. The following productivity improvement efforts were reported.

### Working Harder

Police officials from many of the sites in our sample reported that their employees were working harder to compensate for reductions in staff. Indeed, police chiefs in several cities asserted that the quality and quantity of police services had been maintained despite cuts in staff levels. They attributed this to greater efforts by the remaining personnel. Seven sites also noted that police personnel had assumed additional responsibilities.

WAYLAND: The loss of one officer has forced a number of police personnel to assume additional duties. For instance, the officer responsible for prosecuting cases now undertakes detective work as well.

PITTSFIELD: Staff cutbacks have meant additional assignments for police personnel. The police captain is now responsible for two divisions, and lieutenants work overlapping shifts. The crime prevention officer is now also responsible for investigative duties.

CHELSEA: Many officers are now working double shifts. And the elimination of the dog officer and the position of janitor has meant that the remaining personnel have had to assume the responsibilities of those individuals.

NEW BEDFORD: With the elimination of the traffic division, regular patrolmen have had to increase their involvement in traffic control and enforcement strategies.

QUINCY: This city has begun to make greater use of superior officers (lieutenants) for "street" assignments and investigative work. This has allowed some detectives to return to street patrol duties.

SALEM: Reductions in staff have meant that the remaining officers must patrol a larger geographic area and that all staff must work harder.

SPRINGFIELD: Even in this city, where the police department has been virtually untouched by Proposition 2 1/2, higher level officers are reportedly undertaking additional duties in order to maintain and improve productivity.

Union officials in Marshfield warned that staff cuts in the police department will overburden those who remain. The result, they fear, will be high levels of occupational "burnout" among police officers.

## Introduction of Employee Incentives

Only one example of "positive" employee incentives was reported among the 17 sites.

ARLINGTON: The newly negotiated contract covering police and fire personnel in Arlington includes an incentive provision that allows employees to earn additional personal days for every month that they are not absent on sick leave.

## Introduction of New or Additional Technology

Police Departments in four sites have introduced or begun to look into the use of improved technology to enhance agency productivity.

QUINCY: With the help of federal funds, this city installed equipment to permit the microfilming of records. New telephone equipment has allowed the department to keep tighter control over long distance calls. Department officials also report the introduction of a new computer system designed to be compatible with other city data processing facilities and needs. In addition, police officers were issued individual walkie-talkies for use even when off duty. It was expected that the availabiltiy of this equipment would improve crime prevention and crime reporting. The change was made possible by the introduction of a new central radio communications console.

WORCESTER: The police department reduced its $250,000 electric bill by $40,000 per year through the introduction of various energy saving techniques. A $67,000 project is currently underway to redesign department lighting and air conditioning. It is expected that this effort will save an additional $80,000 per year. Further reductions in costs are expected to be achieved by conversion from electric heating to other energy sources.

SPRINGFIELD: Police officials report that major economies have been achieved through the use of gas additives and the lowering of thermostats in buildings.

NEW BEDFORD: Police officials are investigating the possibility of introducing additional traffic lights to help alleviate the need for police officers to control traffic during rush hours.

*Improvement of Operational Procedures*

In several of the sites, alterations were made in patrol and enforcement strategies in response to the changes brought on by Proposition 2 1/2.

BURLINGTON: This town introduced a neighborhood policing concept under which officers are given complete responsibiliy for providing services in a particular area.

WATERTOWN: In this town, the use of localized beats was eliminated, and officers now patrol "at large."

PITTSFIELD: Overlapping shifts were introduced in this city to help handle peak crime periods while reducing overall staff levels.

ARLINGTON: To help compensate for the loss of criminal investigation staff, the department has begun to prioritize cases by solvability. And while cutting back overall traffic enforcement activities, this department introduced a program known as "quality traffic enforcement." Under this program traffic enforcement efforts are focused primarily on locations which have had the greateat number of accidents over the past several months. Police officials report that since the introduction of the program, there have been reductions in the number of accidents and in the number of injury accidents.

NEW BEDFORD: Responses to calls for service have been prioritized. For example, an officer is sent to the site of a reported stolen vehicle only if the offense occurred within the last half-hour.

QUINCY: With the introduction of a new (federally funded) communications console, calls for service are now screened and assigned a priority for response. The department has also developed new case reporting forms which incorporate solvability factors. And a combination of two-man cars and one-man "satellite" cars is now used for patrolling outlying districts. Police officials report that these innovations have made patrols and investigations more efficient.

CAMBRIDGE: This city has introduced a new computerized dispatch system which prioritizes calls and can assign patrol vehicles to the areas of greatest need. (This is the culmination of an effort that had been in the planning and development stages for many years.)

SALEM: Calls for service are now prioritized. The department is proposing a change from two-person to one-person cruiser patrols during the evening hours. Police officials feel that they will be able to provide increased visibility with somewhat fewer people under this strategy. They also believe that the units will then be close enough to back each other up. (Note that Salem is a relatively compact city of eight square miles.)

*Alteration of Organizational Structures*

Several organizational changes at the patrol or "beat" level were described above (see examples for Burlington, Watertown, etc.). Several other efforts to alter and enhance organizational structures were also reported.

NEW BEDFORD: This city eliminated its traffic division and assigned reponsibility for traffic enforcement to the individual patrol districts. Motorcycle patrolmen who had been assigned to the traffic division were reassigned to police stations.

QUINCY: After the loss of five detectives, the drug, organized crime, and detective units were combined.

SPRINGFIELD: This city reorganized its police districts.

WAYLAND and ARLINGTON: Both towns introduced joint communications centers designed to consolidate police and fire dispatching. (Note that both joint communications centers had been planned for a long time and are not directly related to the introduction of Proposition 2 1/2.)

*Miscellaneous Productivity Efforts*

Several police agencies initiated or increased the civilianization of police department functions. By replacing officers with lower cost civilians the agencies are able to make more trained police personnel available to street duty.

MARSHFIELD and CAMBRIDGE: These two sites are using civilians to replace police officers who had been doing clerical work. Cambridge also uses civilians as dispatchers. The substitution has allowed the relevant police officers to return to patrol duties.

QUINCY: The introduction of civilian "Teleserve Operators" (under a federal grant) made it possible for 12 uniformed officers to return to patrol.

FRAMINGHAM: This town has replaced some uniformed dispatchers with civilians.

WAYLAND: As part of the introduction of this town's joint police/fire communications center, all uniformed dispatchers were returned to patrol duty, and dispatching operations were taken over entirely by civilians.

One department—Arlington—is trying to establish the new position of "community safety officer." These personnel would be trained to handle both police and firefighting responsibilities as needed. Salem is seeking to establish a force of (paid) reserve officers:

SALEM: Police officials in Salem are trying to reinstate the Police Reserve Force. This unit (which was eliminated a number of years ago) would be utilized to cover peak periods and to fill in for regular officers during temporary staff shortages without making it necessary to hire additional full-time police personnel. Re-activation of the reserves is, however, a sensitive issue that must be negotiated with the union, which fears that the reserves will deprive officers of off-dut28192y security jobs, and possibly encourage further staff reductions.

## Acquisition of Additional Revenues/Financial Assistance

Relatively few of the 17 police departments made efforts to acquire additional resources from non-city sources.

### *Introduction or Increasing of Fees and Charges*

In at least four of the sites, police departments increased or initiated fees and charges.

WORCESTER: This police department eliminated the provision of "free" protection for parades. The cost of police protection now must be borne by the organizations involved. The police department also introduced a fee of $10 for out-of-town attendees at its weapons responsibility training class. (An ordinance was needed to allow such a fee.) These classes must be attended by anyone seeking a license to carry firearms in the City of Worcester.

QUINCY: Quincy's police department raised fees and charges wherever possible, including fees for gun permits and parking permits.

CAMBRIDGE: Additional revenues are being obtained under a new ordinance that makes false alarms from private security systems subject to a fee. This ordinance was also designed to cut down on the number of falso alarms from such systems.

SALEM: This city contracted out its ambulance service (previously operated by the police department). A citizen calling for an ambulance (or the citizen's medical insurance company) must now pay a fee for that service.

### *Solicitation of Funds and Contributions*

Many of the sites used federal revenue sharing funds and state aid to underwrite police salaries after the introduction of Proposition 2 1/2. As noted previously, Springfield utilized general revenue sharing receipts to fund an additional 29 police positions. Springfield also receved a federal grant that provided assistance to the city's crime prevention efforts.

One department made an effort to tap resources from the private sector.

QUINCY: This city is actively seeking private resources to help underwrite police operations. For instance, the city has tried to secure community funding of police motor vehicles. Charitable organizations such as the Sons of Italy as well as a number of private yacht clubs have provided funds for the City's waterfront patrols (including two new outboard motors) and related lifesaving equipment.

### Increased Reliance on/Assistance from Other Public Agencies

Police departments in the 17 sites made virtually no effort to transfer responsibility for their services to other government agencies. (2) In fact, in three jurisdictions (Burlington, Pittsfield, and New Bedford) police departments had to take on additional responsibilities because of funding cuts in other municipal agencies. In these three instances, it was up to the police to provide for park patrols when the department of parks and recreation cut back or eliminated its park security forces.

### Increased Reliance on/Assistance from the Private Sector for Service Delivery

A few efforts have been undertaken by police departments to obtain greater private sector involvement in the direct delivery of service (as contrasted with private provision of financial resources). None of these efforts have been extensive. No examples were reported of the use of franchising or of securing donated (in-kind) services from the private sector.

#### Contracting Out of Services

The two examples of contracting out both involved emergency medical (ambulance) services that had been handled by the police department. (See the section on fire services for cases where emergency medical services that had been the responsibility of the fire department were contracted out.)

SALEM: Salem contracted out its ambulance services and put the police officers who had been involved in the service back on patrol. The contracting out of ambulance services was combined with the introduction of a user fee for persons requesting such services.

QUINCY: This city transferred responsibility for providing emergency medical services from the police department to the city hospital. The latter then contracted the service to private ambulance companies. City officials report the elimination of 12 police department positions and a savings of $400,000 per year by contracting out this service.

#### Encouragement of Private Delivery of Services

Only one example of this type was reported among the 17 police agencies.

EVERETT: As of January 1, 1982, Everett eliminated the emergency ambulance services previously provided by the police department. Now when the department gets a request for medical assistance, it sends a police car to the scene and calls a private ambulance. The department reports that no complaints have been received about this arrangement so far. Benefits have included savings in overtime and training costs, in addition to allowing ambulance officers to return to the beat.

## Increased Reliance on/Assistance From Individual Citizens

The 17 police departments made few efforts to obtain more assistance from the publc in the delivery of police services.

### Increased Use of Volunteers

Three sites reported greater use of their (volunteer) police auxiliaries.

ARLINGTON: Arlington's police auxiliary currently consists of about 30 persons and has grown steadily over the last five years. Prior to the introduction of Proposition 2 1/2, the police auxiliary was used primarily for crowd control. Crime prevention was handled by CETA employees. With the phasing out of CETA personnel and the introduction of Proposition 2 1/2, the department has expanded the role of the police auxiliary, expecially in the area of crime prevention. For instance, members have begun to conduct additional patrols designed to prevent vandalism and break-ins. Town officials note that the police union had to be assured that the volunteers would not be used to replace regular police personnel or to reduce opportunities for overtime.

QUINCY: At a time of reduced resources, police officials in Quincy report that the Police Auxiliary has assumed greter importance in assisting with crime prevention and related programs. The Auxiliary sets up all Neighborhood Watch programs and works closely with the regular Crime Prevention Unit in connection with programs to promote the safety of senior citizens, school children, and others.

WAYLAND: Wayland's 30-member police auxilary has become more active over the past few years. Although originally used primarily in supportive roles such as flood control, the department has begun to emphasize the inclusion of a member of the auxiliary as a ride-along during regular police patrols. This serves as training for the volunteer while providing, in effect, two-man patrol units.

One department, however, was forced to reduce its use of volunteers in the wake of Proposition 2 1/2.

NEW BEDFORD: New Bedford dropped its police cadet program (which involved 10-11 cadets) because of the high cost of providing them with training. The cadets had helped the department in the areas of records and communications.

*Increased Citizen Co-Production of Services*

Responses by three departments tended to put a greater burden on the public for the provision of police services.

CAMBRIDGE: The false alarm ordinance passed by the City Council was designed to reduce the number of unnecessary calls to the police from private security systems. This ordinance is expected to stimulate security users to make their equipment less susceptible to false alarms.

NEW BEDFORD: This city now requires citizens to come to the police station to file a minor complaint. In the past, police officers were sent directly to the complainant to take such reports.

QUINCY: Quincy has organized a number of crime prevention programs seeking to stimulate property owners to take greater precautions in the protection of the city's waterfront area.

# FIRE

Fire departments in the 17 sites experienced relatively small overall reductions in funding levels. The mean change in total appropriations after the introduction of Proposition 2 1/2 was −2.7% for the 15 jurisdictions in our sample for which comparable before vs. after data were available. This represented the smallest average decrease in funding levels of any of the major services we examined. As with police services, the relatively small reductions reflect the high priority that city administrators and political leaders placed on preserving public safety.

The relatively small size of the mean reduction in fire department budgets in the wake of Proposition 2 1/2 is, however, somewhat misleading. There was considerable variation among the departments with regard to pre- vs. post-Proposition 2 1/2 budget levels. (See Table 27.2.) A number of departments experienced major cuts in appropriations: Watertown (down 21.6%), Everett (down 20.7%), Worcester (down 9.2%), Salem (down 8.2%), and Quincy (down 6.8%). On the other hand, funding levels in six departments rose subsequent to Proposition 2 1/2. The increases ranged from 1.5% (Cambridge) to as much as 9.0% (Amesbury) and 9.4% (Burlington). However, since most departments had to deal with or anticipate the impacts of contractually mandated wage increases for fire department personnel, even agencies with higher budget levels usually had to make some cuts in staff levels or equipment.

Expenses for personnel constitute a large proportion of a fire department's budget. While most of the departments in our sample pared back expenditures for overtime, maintenance, and equipment purchases, such cuts were usually not in themselves adequate to achieve the necessary budget reductions. Thus, most of the departments (at least initially) undertook some staff reductions in the wake of Proposition 2 1/2. Often these reductions were quite large. For instance, Springfield eliminated 42 positions; Worcester, 36; Everett, 33; Quincy, 30; and Watertown, 29. Even the smaller jurisdictions were often faced with the prospect of relatively large reductions in firefighting personnel. Examples included Burlington (initially down 16), Chelsea (down 5), and Marshfield and Bridgewater (each of which initially eliminated 4 positions). On the other hand, Amesbury, Framingham, and Wayland avoided any reductions in the number of fire department employees.

The staff reductions affected firefighters as well as civilians, management as well as non-management. Most of the reductions were achieved through attrition. However, in a number of sites, there were substantial layoffs of fire department personnel. (1) The largest occurred in Everett and Watertown (each of which laid off 21 persons), followed by Burlington (15 layoffs), New Bedford (11 persons laid off), and Quincy (10 layoffs). The arrival of state aid in the fall of 1981 allowed a number of governments to rehire at least some of the fire department personnel who had been eliminated. (For instance, in December, 1981, Quincy was able to rehire all of the ten firefighters that had been laid off.) But although the net staff reductions were sometimes less than those indicated above, they were, nevertheless, quite severe in many cases.

In three sites, additional cost reductions were realzed through the demotion of existing personnel. Thus, in Everett, eight lieutenants were demoted to privates after the loss of two fire companies. In Salem, six fire department employees were temporarily demoted. Marshfield demoted four employees.

Most of the fire departments in the 17 cities responded to Proposition 2 1/2 by cutting costs and reducing services. There were a few scattered examples of efforts to ameliorate the service reductions, ranging from productivity improvements to the initiation of fees and the contracting out of peripheral activities, but generally there was little innovation among the 17 fire departments. We found the following responses.

## Cost-Cutting/Reduced Service Levels

### Reduction of Services to the Public

In most cases, the staff cuts described above were translated into reduced levels of service to the publc. Both fire suppression and fire prevention activities were affected. In the case of fire suppression activities, fire departments tended to choose from four major response strategies.

*Reduction of Fire Companies.*   Four of the departments reduced the number of fire companies in operation. (A fire company usually corresponds to a single piece of fire suppression equipment--e.g., a ladder truck or a pumper--and the staff necessary to operate it.)

BURLINGTON: This town eliminated one engine company.

EVERETT: One engine company and one ladder company were eliminated. However, no fire stations were closed.

NEW BEDFORD: This city eliminated one ladder company. The number of fire stations, however, remained unchanged. The company chosen for elimination was housed in the part of town that had the fewest number of high buildings potentially requiring fast response by a ladder unit.

SALEM: One engine company was eliminated.

SPRINGFIELD: Fire officials proposed eliminating one fire company and redistributing the staff among the remaining units. However, firefighters lobbied vigorously against such a move, and the reduction was not implemented.

*Reduction of Fire Stations.*   Elimination of a fire station is potentially more serious than elimination of a fire company, since it is likely to increase the average time for the first unit to arrive at the scene of a fire. One site completely eliminated a fire station; two others reduced staff levels to the point that some stations had to be closed for short periods of time. Two other jurisdictions are considering future reductions in the number of stations maintained.

SALEM: This city took one fire station out of service to comply with contractually-mandated minimum manning and overtime requirements. Because the municipality is quite compact, the closing was not expected to cause significant increases in response times. For a time, the station was occupied by protesting local residents who re-named it "People's Fire House No. 6." The union refused an offer by the city to negotiate the re-opening of the station in return for concessions on overtime requirements, scheduled wage increases, and other benefits covered by the current contract.

PITTSFIELD: Although the number of fire stations in this city has remained the same, staffing levels have been reduced to the point at which the city is sometimes unable to man a station when firefighters are out sick or on vacation. At these times, the fire station in question is temporarily closed.

WAYLAND: One station is now closed on occasion.

BRIDGEWATER: In the wake of Proposition 2 1/2, this town scrapped plans for building a new fire station in a high growth area.

WATERTOWN: Department officials in this town considered closing one fire station. The proposal, however, stimulated a strong reaction by firefighters and the public, and the idea was abandoned.

*Reduced Response Levels.*   Fire departments in 4 of the 17 sites reduced their standard responses for various types of fire alarms in an effort to cope with reduced manpower.

CHELSEA: This city used to respond with three engine companies and a ladder truck. Now it sends two engine companies and a ladder truck.

EVERETT: After eliminating one ladder company, this city decided to send one fewer ladder company as part of its standard response.

NEW BEDFORD: Prior to Proposition 2 1/2, the standard response to an alarm was three engine companies and two ladder companies (three engine companies and one ladder company for a box call). However, after eliminating a ladder company in the wake of Proposition 2 1/2, New Bedford altered its standard response to two engine companies and one ladder company for all box calls and one engine company plus one ladder company for fires reported by telephone.

BRIDGEWATER: Before Proposition 2 1/2, an ambulance was sent as part of the standard response to a fire alarm. In the wake of the cutbacks induced by Proposition 2 1/2, an ambulance is now sent only when summoned.

*Reduced Manning.*   Fire departments in 8 of the 17 sites decided to reduce manning levels.

ARLINGTON: This town went from a complement of 25 firefighting personnel per shift to 24 persons per shift. This was still, however, well above the contractually stipulated minimum of 19 persons per shift. For those occasions when the staff level for a given company fell below the minimum manning level (e.g. due to heavy absenteeism), the relevant piece of apparatus was put out of service and the remaining firefighters were temporarily assigned to other units. Under this policy, up to two pieces of fire apparatus could be put out of service in a given shift. Thus, the department was usually able to meet minimum manning requirements without having to bring in staff to work overtime.

CAMBRIDGE: Staff reductions have necessitated the frequent movement of personnel between companies and fire stations to keep the companies evenly staffed.

CHELSEA: The minimum manning requirement has been reduced from 22 to 20 persons per shift. The change was negotiated with the union after the latter re-opened its contract to avoid an impending layoff of up to 20 firefighters.

MARSHFIELD: Manning levels have been reduced from 11 to 8 or 9 per shift. These staff are spread among three fire stations, with the result that only two firefighters may be available to answer an alarm.

QUINCY: Manning levels were generally reduced (for instance, the manning level for a ladder company was reduced from three to two). This meant that fewer firefighting personnel would be present at a fire. The union argued that this reduction violated minimum manning agreements and filed a grievance over the city's acion. The grievance has since gone to arbitration (as of October 1982, no decision had been reached).

SPRINGFIELD: Staff cutbacks have forced this city to reduce manning levels. Ladder companies, for instance, now operate with one less firefighter. The chief noted that it was likely to take longer to put out a fire with the reduced manpower and that the chances for injuries were correspondingly increased.

WATERTOWN: Manning levels were reduced by one person per vehicle. This has meant that some vehicles have had to be removed from service when firefighters are out sick or on vacation. The department uses a priority system for determining which pieces of apparatus will go out of service (these designations are made on a rotating basis).

WAYLAND: Manning levels for fire alarms and semi-emergencies have been reduced.

WORCESTER: The fire chief reported that during the summer of 1981, "department staffing was as much as 37 percent below authorized strength. As much as 27 percent of the time, apparatus operated without officer supervision, and as much as 60 percent of the time, apparatus was operating two or more men short."

Efforts to change manning levels were sometimes affected by contractual stipulations and labor disputes. In addition to the experiences of Salem, Chelsea, and Quincy (reported above), two other departments had to face this issue.

AMESBURY: The contract for firefighters stipulates a minimum manning level of five persons per shift. This prevented the chief from proposing layoffs of firefighting personnel during the first year of Proposition 2 1/2.

FRAMINGHAM: This town is currently trying to negotiate an end to the nine-year-old minimum manning provision in its contract with the firefighter's union.

Fire suppression services were not, however, the only fire department services to be reduced in the wake of Proposition 2 1/2. Thus, fire prevention, inspection, and other efforts were also sometimes affected.

*Reduction in Inspection/Fire Prevention Efforts.* Ten of the seventeen fire departments reported cutbacks in fire inspections and other fire prevention activities.

BURLINGTON: Inspections of mercantile buildings are now performed only when complaints are received.

CHELSEA: This city's five fire prevention staff were returned to active duty as firefighters. The chief, however, claims that this has resulted in little loss of service because few inspections were previously being performed.

EVERETT: Inspections of stores and apartments were curtailed during the temporary loss of one inspector. Inspections of gas stations and garages are now made on a priority basis.

FRAMINGHAM: Inspections of existing commercial buildings have been reduced by 10 percent. (However, inspections of new buildings have been unaffected.)

NEW BEDFORD: Firefighters in this city used to conduct inspections of private homes. Because of the high cost of the fuel needed for driving fire department vehicles to these inspections, the inspections were eliminated after the introduction of Proposition 2 1/2. Currently the department performs only the legally required fire inspections.

PITTSFIELD: This city reports a sharp cutback in its fire prevention program.

QUINCY: The city's fire prevention bureau was cut from eight to five persons. This has resulted in fewer inspections of gasoline storage facilities, businesses, and commercial buildings.

SALEM: Inspection schedules have been lengthened from once every eight months to once every twelve months as part of a general reduction in the number of fire inspections.

SPRINGFIELD: Inspections have been cut back, in part because of the high cost of gasoline. Before Proposition 2 1/2, the city inspected all houses on a prescribed annual schedule; these inspections (which were conducted by firefighters) have been eliminated. Currently, no firefighters are used for inspections. The latter are performed only by the fire prevention bureau and are limited to those mandated by law.

WATERTOWN: The town's inspection staff was cut from two to one. Inspections of homes by fire company personnel have been eliminated to reduce expenditures for gasoline. Business inspections have also been reduced.

*Other Service Reductions.*   Two sites reported other cost-cutting efforts which directly affected the services delivered to the public.

MARSHFIELD: This town's rescue vehicle was removed from service. A regular fire truck is now sent on rescue calls.

NEW BEDFORD: A number of non-emergency services to the public have been eliminated by this city's fire department. For instance, fire trucks will no longer respond to a request to pump out a flooded cellar (except where the danger of fire exists). Services such as getting cats out of trees have also been eliminated.

*Reductions in Internal (Administrative/Support) Services*

Many of the fire departments in our sample reported efforts to reduce or eliminate expenditures for services which only have an indirect effect on the public. Most of these cutbacks involved the training of fire department staff and the maintenance of fire apparatus.

*Reduced Training.*   Two departments reported cutbacks in the training of fire personnel.

ARLINGTON: With fewer staff available to fill in for vacancies and less money for sending firefighters to the Massachusetts Fire Academy, the fire department has been forced to curtail training efforts.

WORCESTER: Training of firefighting personnel has been "drastically reduced" in this city.

*Reduced Maintenance.*   Four sites -- Bridgewater, Cambridge, Chelsea, and Pittsfield -- reported reductions in the maintenance of fire department apparatus. Pittsfield indicated that its preventive maintenance program had been cut back. On the other hand, the New Bedford fire department reported that it has sustained its maintenance activities even while losing one mechanic.

*Reductions or Delays in Purchases, Replacements, and Other Expenditures*

Three governments--Bridgewater, Quincy, and Worcester--have suspended their purchases of new equipment since the introduction of Proposition 2 1/2. In the case of Quincy, officials noted that because of the city's reduced bond rating (partly attributable to Proposition 2 1/2), interest rates on any funds borrowed for replacement of fire apparatus would be prohibitively high.

Three other cities -- Chelsea, New Bedford, and Springfield -- had not purchased any new fire apparatus for several years prior to Proposition 2 1/2. Under the Proposition, they have had to continue this policy.

## Improvement of Productivity and Management

Only scattered efforts were made by the 17 fire departments in our sample towards improving productivity and introducing related management innovations. Most of the major productivity improvement strategies were, however, represented by one or more examples.

*Working Harder*

Fire chiefs in three governments -- Arlington, Everett, and Watertown -- reported that staff reductions were forcing the remaining fire department personnel to work harder. For instance, in Everett the workload of the one remaining fire inspector doubled after the loss of the other inspector.

In some cases, fire department personnel have had to take on additional responsibilities and assignments.

ARLINGTON: The responsibilities of the chief fire prevention officer have been shifted to the fire chief and other management personnel. In addition, firefighters are now responsible for conducting various fire and building code inspections.

Fire chiefs and union officials in several sites voiced concerns that firefighters may become overworked, with a resulting increase in susceptibility to injuries.

*Introduction of Employee Incentives*

While many departments reported reductions in the morale of their employees, only one had made any effort to introduce employee incentives.

ARLINGTON: Although the new contract for firefighters provided for considerable sick leave, firefighters were also given the opportunity to earn additional time off for good attendance. Thus, firefighters now earn one day of personal leave for every quarter during which they charge no sick leave.

*Improvement of Operational Procedures/Introduction of New Technology*

Revised operating procedures adopted by Bridgewater and Cambridge had the effect of selectively altering responses to fire alarms. In the case of Bridgewater, the change in procedures was coupled with the introduction of new technology. Two other sites--Wayland and Everett--also reported operational changes.

BRIDGEWATER: By providing firefighters with personal pagers, the department was able to selectively call staff when the need arose. The introduction of the pagers was part of a compromise worked out between the union and department management in a dispute over reductions in staff and manning levels. Previously, the town's fire whistle was sounded when additional firefighting help was required. This meant that all reserves were called to the scene. Under the new system, the recall can be matched to the need. The town reported a savings of over $26,000 in overtime during the first year in which this policy was used.

CAMBRIDGE: This city is now sending a small "task force" of firefighters and equipment in response to box alarms. The task force determines whether more equipment is needed and radios for help accordingly. Because over half of the city's calls are false alarms, large savings are expected.

WAYLAND: Fewer people are called for semi-emergencies (such as pumping), and those who are called are not kept at the scene as long.

EVERETT: As noted previously, inspections of gas stations and garages are now handled on a priority basis.

*Alteration of Organizational Structures*

Two departments reported the introduction of organizational changes in an attempt to streamline operations.

PITTSFIELD: This city's fire department was reorganized by placing its two operating divisions under the single remaining deputy fire chief.

WAYLAND: This town has been investigating and moving towards the implementation of a consolidated police/fire public safety department for the last several years. The joint communications center which began operation in 1981 is a forerunner of this consolidation. The firefighters union tried to block the implementation of the joint center in the courts. However, its injunction was overturned by the state appeals court.

*Miscellaneous Productivity Improvement Efforts*

WAYLAND: With the startup of this town's joint communications center serving both the police and fire departments, firefighters working as dispatchers were replaced by civilian personnel and returned to active duty. A civilian also replaced a firefighter serving at the reception desk.

ARLINGTON: This town is attempting to establish the new position of "community safety officer." These personnel would be trained to handle both police and firefighting responsibilities, as needed.

## Acquisition of Additional Revenues/Financial Assistance

The 17 fire departments reported few efforts to acquire additional financial resources. Most involved increases in fees and charges. No specific efforts to solicit additional federal grants or contributions from the private sector were reported. (Note, however, that federal revenue sharing funds were used to underwrite fire department salaries in some cities.)

### *Introduction or Increasing of Fees and Charges*

Fire departments in four sites increased fees and charges to the public.

BRIDGEWATER and CAMBRIDGE: These two governments implemented user charges for ambulance services. In the case of Bridgewater, 95 was charged for each ambulance call plus $4 per loaded mile of patient transport. An additional $15 was charged for the administration of oxygen. The tab was usually picked up by the patient's medical insurance. (Department officials report that if a patient was uninsured, the service was usually provided free.) The department reportedly earned over $10,000 in the first six months after the fees were introduced.

SPRINGFIELD: The fire department has increased the fee for oil burner permits. A fee is also charged for ambulance services.

FRAMINGHAM: This town increased its fee for oil burner permits from 50 cents to 5 dollars.

NEW BEDFORD: A $5 fee was introduced for smoke detector inspections. The department also initiated a $100 annual fee for "master boxes" (central fire alarms in hospitals or commercial buildings that are tied directly to the fire department). The $100 fee includes five service calls; additional calls (e.g. to reset the alarm) are billed at a rate of $25 each.

### *Other Fund-Raising Efforts*

Two sites -- Bridgewater and Salem -- supplemented fire department resources by selling surplus fire trucks. Bridgewater sold two fire trucks, bringing in a total of $30,000. Salem sold one ladder truck and put a pumper up for sale. (The closing of a fire station in Salem meant that the city no longer had space for storing the surplus ladder truck.)

Worcester reported efforts to identify private resources to offset fire department expenditures.

## Increased Reliance on/Assistance from Other Public Agencies

Mutual assistance agreements between fire departments in Massachusetts have provided some unique opportunities for increasing interdepartmental assistance in the wake of Proposition 2 1/2. The responses, however, have been mixed. While several departments have reported increased reliance upon mutual aid, others have been concerned about the costs which mutual aid agreements impose on their own services.

BURLINGTON, CAMBRIDGE, and EVERETT: All of these sites reported increased reliance on mutual aid from neighboring departments when the town's own fire department resources were stretched thin.

SALEM: This governmet altered its mutual aid agreement with three nearby towns. Prior to Proposition 2 1/2, if a piece of fire apparatus in one of the towns was called to a fire, one of the other towns would send a piece to cover until the original unit returned from the fire. Now mutual aid is not supplied unless requested. The new policy proved disastrous for Salem in February 1982, when the city had two large fires half an hour apart and insufficient equipment to fight the second blaze.

WATERTOWN: This town is considering whether it should abandon its commitment to mutual aid. Department officials note that one engine is committed to go out one or two times per week on mutual assistance runs. This has meant increased costs due to the logistics of moving men and machines between fire stations in different towns. On the other hand, a fire official observed that the high proportion of elderly residents in Watertown increases the likelihood of emergencies that would require assistance from departments in neighboring jurisdictions.

Note that mutual aid agreements between governments are not always feasible. For instance, the fire chief in Worcester noted that the city is an "island" and that no effective mutual aid is immediately available. Hence, the department must be prepared to depend on its own firefighting resources.

## Increased Reliance on/Assistance from the Private Sector for Service Delivery

We found only one instance where a fire department sought additional assistance from the private sector in the provision of services. This example involved the contracting out of ambulance services. No other efforts to encourage increased private provision of fire services were reported among the 17 departments.

SPRINGFIELD: Before Proposition 2 1/2, this city's fire department provided free ambulance services. These services required the presence of three vehicles and 24 emergency medical personnel. In the wake of Proposition 2 1/2, the city contracted such ambulance services to private carriers. The latter have been able to provide the necessary service with only two vehicles. Citizens are, however, charged a small fee. The cost of ambulance services has been completely removed from the fire department's budget, and the 24 men involved have been reassigned to other fire department duties.

## Increased Reliance on/Assistance From Individual Citizens

The 17 fire departments made virtually no effort to increase the involvement of the public in the provision of department services. In particular, the departments reported no efforts to increase the use of volunteers or to encourage greater citizen co-production of services.

However, a law passed by the State of Massachusetts just prior to the introduction of Proposition 2 1/2 has had the effect of increasing citizen co-production of fire prevention services. The law requires the installation of smoke detectors under certain circumstances. (Such detectors can reduce the amount of fire suppression effort needed.) Detectors must be installed in new single family homes and when a house is sold. Hard-wired detectors are now required in apartment buildings. Fire departments are required to inspect buildings to ensure that these regulations have been met.

## LIBRARIES

The average decrease in library appropriations after the implementation of Proposition 2 1/2 was 12.5 percent for the 15 sites for which comparable before and after data were available. The average reduction in library appropriations was therefore greater than that for police and fire but less than the reductions typically experienced by public works and parks and recreation. In a few cases, the losses in funding experienced by library departments were moderated by factors unique to public library systems. In particular, the presence of endowment funds and extensive prior reliance upon volunteers reduced the impacts of Proposition 2 1/2 on some libraries.

In general, libraries in the 17 sites received considerably less state aid to help offset their deficits than did police and fire services. The Quincy library, which was the hardest hit library system of those in our sample, found itself in a Catch-22 situation. In order to qualify for state aid in Massachusetts, 12 percent or more of a library's budget must be allocated to the purchase of books. However, under the pressure of Proposition 2 1/2 (and the spending cap that preceded it), Quincy had to reduce its book purchases below the level needed to be eligible for state aid.

The budget reductions experienced by libraries in the 17 sites varied considerably. Cutbacks in the year after the introduction of Proposition 2 1/2 ranged from 23 percent (Quincy) and 21 percent (Everett) to virtually nothing at all (e.g., Wayland and New Bedford), at least after the offsetting effects of state aid are taken into account. (See Table 27.2.) (1) However, as in the case of other services, library budgets often had to absorb large contractual wage increases. Thus, even level-funded agencies had to make cutbacks and economies in some instances.

All of the sites except New Bedford made reductions in library staff and staff hours. The largest cutbacks occurred in Quincy where over 50 percent of all library staff (including part-time personnel) were eliminated. Other sites losing a large number of library personnel included Framingham, Watertown, and Pittsfield (which lost 30 percent of its employees). In smaller sites such as Burlington, Bridgewater, Chelsea, and Wayland, library departments experienced a net loss of one or two persons each.

For the most part, staff reductions in the 17 sites were focused on non-professional full-time and part-time staff. For instance, Quincy eliminated four janitors and all part-time library help. In Marshfield, all five part-time staff (primarily shelvers and sorters) were released. Professional library staff, however, were not immune to cutbacks. Thus, Wayland eliminated the position of assistant library director, and the children's librarian was eliminated in Bridgewater.

Most of the reductions in library staff were achieved through attrition, but layoffs did occur in some cities (e.g., Cambridge, Chelsea, Everett, and Quincy). While a few governments (e.g., Bridgewater and Chelsea) were able to rehire a few library personnel after the distribution of state aid, in most cases library departments received little supplemental assistance of that type. An exception was New Bedford, where a relatively large infusion of state aid allowed the department to retain two branch libraries that would have otherwise been closed.

Another strategy sometimes used to reduce personnel expenditures was to cut back the hours of library staff. Libraries in three jurisdictions--Amesbury, Everett, and Wayland--took this approach. (In Everett, staff hours were reduced in only one of the city's two major libraries.) Most of the reductions in hours involved part-time library staff. However, in Everett all staff in one library, including professionals, agreed to go on a four-day work week to avoid layoffs (library hours were not affected).

One town--Wayland--partly compensated for the loss of high-level staff by increasing the hours of lower-paid personnel. Thus, in the re-shuffling of responsibilities that followed Wayland's elimination of the assistant director position, the hours of a part-time library assistant were increased. On the other hand, Salem replaced some low-paid part-time staff with full-time workers, a change that reportedly yielded savings in supervision and improved work quality.

Most of the responses to Proposition 2 1/2 by library departments in the 17 sites involved cost-cutting and reductions in services, without compensatory actions. The second most common reaction was to attempt to acquire additional revenues or financial assistance, either through increases in fees and charges or the solicitation of funds from outside sources. Although productivity improvements appeared to be the third most common response to Proposition 2 1/2 by library departments in the 17 sites, most of the activity focused on long-range improvements such as the introduction of automated check-out facilities . Cost savings from most of these innovations are still several years away from being realized. Overall, the 17 libraries exhibited little innovation in the first year of Proposition 2 1/2. The following examples were reported.

## Cost Cutting/Reduced Service Levels

*Reduction of Services to the Public*

For the most part, the staff reductions described above were translated into reduced services for the publc. The following cutbacks and service reductions were identified.

*Closing of Branch Libraries.* While several departments considered closing branch libraries at one time or another, branches were actually eliminated in only two jurisdictions. (2)

> EVERETT: Two of this city's three branch libraries were closed. One of them, however, was a store-front facility that probably would have been closed anyway, according to city officials, because of recent increases in rent. Note also that Everett is a relatively compact city and

thus has potentially less need for branch libraries (as pointed out by one city official). The city is also unique in operating two organizationally independent central libraries.

FRAMINGHAM: One branch, near the main library, was closed after an examination of circulation patterns indicated that it was reasonable to expect patrons to make use of other library facilities.

Five other jurisdictions considered the possibilty of eliminating branch libraries but subsequently abandoned the idea.

NEW BEDFORD: The library department's initial plans in the wake of Proposition 2 1/2 called for the closing of two branch libraries. This evoked a heavy protest from the public. When state aid was received, much of it was used to restore funds for these two branches.

WATERTOWN: This town attempted to close down one of its two branch libraries. Public opposition, however, prevented such a move. As a compromise, the town sharply cut back branch library hours, and only one branch is open at any given time. The two branches are staffed by a single group of employees who shuttle between the two installations, spending two days per week at one branch and three days per week at the other.

WAYLAND: The Board of Trustees decided to close the Cochituate branch in FY83 (the second year of Proposition 2 1/2) if voters did not override the fiscal limitations imposed by Proposition 2 1/2. The potential closure of this branch proved to be very unpopular, and as part of the override passed in the spring of 1982, the public voted specifically to authorize the $10,000 needed to keep the Cochituate branch open.

Other sites that investigated and rejected the closing of branch libraries included Arlington and Pittsfield.

*Reduction of Library Hours.* Eleven of the seventeen library departments chose to reduce the hours of central and/or branch libraries. The largest reductions occurred in Watertown (where the main library cut service by 11 hours per week and the two branches each lost 49 hors per week) and Quincy (where central library hours were reduced 15 percent and branch library hours were reduced 50 percent). Other sites experiencing significant cutbacks in library hours included Bridgewater, Chelsea, and Pittsfield. Many jurisdictions eliminated weekend and/or Monday hours.

*Reductions in Services and Special Programs.* A wide variety of library programs were affected by the budget reductions, including children's services, adult programs, services for senior citizens, and outreach services such as bookmobiles. The following two examples illustrate the range of cutbacks in services and programs made in two departments.

QUINCY: This city has limited its library program to the provision of only the basic services. Among the programs which have been eliminated are the monthly book discussion group, the weekly film group, and outreach services to nursing homes and senior citizen housing projects. The library department has closed its book deposits at senior citizens' projects, and department staff have cut back on speaking engagements to community groups. Only the children's program and a single film series have been left intact.

WAYLAND: The library department has eliminated nearly all adult programs except those "one shot" offerings that require little preparation and publicity. Among the programs that have been dropped are the department's financial series, its career workshop, a series on writing resumes, and workshops on the use of reference materials. Library staff have eliminated all outside speaking engagements.

Many of the library directors interviewed noted that library services are generally slower in the wake of Proposition 2 1/2. Here is how individual areas fared.

1. Children's services. Children's services were reduced in four sites: Amesbury, Arlington, Bridgewater, and Watertown. The cutbacks ranged from reductions in the hours of the children's department to the complete elimination of children's services at branch libraries (Arlington). Two jurisdictions, however--Quincy and Wayland--made a point of preserving their children's programs while reducing most other services.

2. Adult programs. In several jurisdictions, adult library programs sustained serious cuts. Quincy and Wayland eliminated virtually all adult programming, as described above. Springfield and Watertown also reduced their services for adults.

3. Senior citizens programs. Programs for seniors were reduced in Arlington, Bridgewater, Pittsfield, and Quincy. Bridgewater made, perhaps, the most serious cutbacks in programs for the elderly. (However, as noted later, many of those programs were subsequently carried on by volunteers.) Note also that the reductions in outreach services described below often had their greatest effect on elderly library users who otherwise lacked transportation to library facilities.

4. Outreach services. Bookmobile services were reduced or eliminated in Chelsea, Worcester, and Framingham. Quincy cut back outreach services to nursing homes and housing projects for senior citizens. And as indicated above, library staff in both Quincy and Wayland drastically reduced outside speaking engagements and other community relations efforts.

5. Other specialized services. In Amesbury, the reserve list was eliminated; books are now available only on a first-come, first-served basis. Reference services were reduced in Arlington, Framingham, and Wayland. In Worcester, library officials reported that most specialized services had been eliminated.

*Reductions in Internal (Administrative/Support) Services*

Libraries in four jurisdictions reported cutbacks in internal operations and housekeeping services. Specific examples included delays in the sorting and reshelving of books (Bridgewater and Springfield) and delays in overdue book notifications (Watertown). In Wayland, preparation of various library usage statistics has been eliminated as a cost-saving measure. In Cambridge, air conditioning levels have been reduced in order to cut costs.

Two governments reported reductions in maintenance services as a cost-cutting measure. The Bridgewater library is mending and repairing fewer damaged books than in the past. And in Quincy, repairs and maintenance of library facilities have been drastically cut back.

*Reductions or Delays in Purchases, Replacements, and Other Expenditures*

All but one of the 17 sites reduced their purchases of books and other materials. The following examples are typical.

AMESBURY: Purchases of books have been reduced by 33 percent, periodicals by 20 percent, and reference materials by 10 percent.

BURLINGTON: Book purchases have been reduced by 40 percent, and purchases of audiovisual material have been completely eliminated.

QUINCY: Quincy's budget for the purchase of books and other library materials has gone from $129,000 in FY80 to $80,000 in FY82 (the first year of Proposition 2 1/2) to 0 for FY83.

WORCESTER: Cutbacks in this city's book budget have resulted in the purchase of 9,000 fewer books and the cancellation of 114 (of 1,200) subscriptions. Purchases of other materials have also been reduced.

SALEM: The book budget was cut by 30 percent. In an effort to ameliorate the effects of the ensuing reduction in the number of available volumes, the library has limited the number of books that may be borrowed at one time by a single user.

BRIDGEWATER and WAYLAND: Both of these governments kept their book budgets at the previous year's level in the wake of Proposition 2 1/2. However, because of inflation, fewer books will be purchased.

The only library among the 17 that did not experience reductions in its book budget was New Bedford. All purchases of books and other library materials in this city are made from funds provided by a substantial endowment given to the library many years ago. As a result, purchases of library materials were unaffected by Proposition 2 1/2. On the other hand, worn out and obsolete library equipment--needed to maintain services--was not replaced in New Bedford.

## Improvement of Productivity and Management

The 17 libraries exhibited few innovations that might be characterized as productivity improvements. Many of the responses which were identified focused more on long-term improvements than on short-term savings.

### Working Harder

Officials from several of the 17 library departments reported that their remaining staff are working harder to maintain library services. In a few cases, library staff have had to assume additional responibilities.

BRIDGEWATER: Staff cutbacks made it necessary for the reference librarian to help out with circulation and for the person in charge of circulation to also handle children's services, including everything from planning children's programs to running the story hour and reshelving books.

QUINCY: Everyone on the library staff, including professionals, now spends at least one day per week on clerical tasks.

WAYLAND: Staff cutbacks have made it necessary to expand the responsibilities of the part–time cataloger to include assisting with reference services. The library no longer has a separate night staff. Instead, three library professionals now share responsibility for staying late.

### Improvements of Operational Procedures

Libraries in three sites reported operational changes that potentially improved productivity.

ARLINGTON: Inventory control and circulation management have been improved.

BRIDGEWATER: Cataloging procedures have been streamlined, and a new "pre–processing" technique has saved staff time in connection with library purchases. The process involves getting the (private) book seller to handle some of the paperwork needed.

PITTSFIELD: This city's library department has revamped its procedures for purchasing supplies and books. The changes have included switching to a new book vendor, tightening controls on purchases by imposing new requirements for purchase orders, redesigning purchase order forms to reduce typing, and making greater use of joint ordering arrangements with the state that allow the library to take advantage of sharply reduced prices for certain types of office supplies.

### Introduction of New or Additional Technology

Four governments reported the introduction of technological innovations for their library facilities. Several others were planning similar efforts.

NEW BEDFORD and QUINCY: Libraries in these cities are currently in the process of automating their cataloging services.

BRIDGEWATER and SALEM: Libraries in both jurisdictions undertook changes in lighting to reduce costs. Bridgewater introduced a high-intensity lighting system which reportedly costs less to operate. Salem changed to the use of smaller, independent lights in its book stacks, resulting in lower lighting bills and flexibility to turn on only those lights that are needed.

Arlington, New Bedford, Wayland, and Worcester have all begun to investigate the introduction of automated check-out procedures. Arlington anticipates that such a system will be operational by 1984; New Bedford, by 1986. Worcester has already begun intensive planning and training for such technology.

WORCESTER: Library officials joined with other librarians in the area in submitting two proposals for federal grants to facilitate the automation of library services. Both proposals were funded: a $5,000 grant to provide workshops for librarians on developments in library automation, and a $25,000 grant for the study of an automated system that would serve libraries in central and western Massachusetts. In the year prior to Proposition 2 1/2, the library was given a microcomputer, and library staff were trained to use the computer in providing library service.

In two other cities--Pittsfield and Springfield--library officials stressed the importance of introducing new library technologies to maintain service delivery levels.

## Acquisition of Additional Revenues/Financial Assistance

The acquisition of additional financial resources represented a relatively important post-Proposition 2 1/2 strategy for the libraries examined. In many cases, the libraries were able to build upon pre-existing sources of revenue and assistance.

### *Introduction or Increasing of Fees and Charges*

Four jurisdictions made efforts to increase revenues by raising fees and charges. Library fines were increased in Cambridge, Pittsfield, and Salem. Pittsfield, which lies close to the New York border, also introduced a $15 per year charge for out-of-state library users. Arlington introduced a charge for the use of its meeting rooms.

Officials of Springfield's library system report that the introduction of library fees was discussed but rejected. Springfield's libraries are operated by a non-profit organization--the Library and Museums Association--to which the city makes an annual contribution. The provision of branch libraries was viewed by city officials as an especially important product of the city's contribution to what would otherwise have been a private, highly centralized library system. Library officials feared that the introduction of library fees would jeopardize the city's objective by discouraging people from using the branch libraries.

*Solicitation of Funds and Contributions*

Libraries in Bridgewater and Worcester were the beneficiaries of increased financial help on the part of private support organizations.

BRIDGEWATER: The Friends of the Bridgewater Library are underwriting most of the specialized programs now offered by the library. Note that a directory of local services, compiled by library staff with the help of the Friends of the Library, has been funded by local banks for several years.

WORCESTER: The Friends of the Worcester Public Library joined with the library's Board of Directors to buy a microcomputer for use by library staff. The Friends of the Library also paid for training library personnel in the use of microcomputer technology. (While these contributions occurred in the year prior to Proposition 2 1/2, library officials expect their benefits to be felt during the current period of service cutbacks.)

Library officials in Marshfield, Quincy, and Salem reported intensified efforts to solicit private funds and contributions. The Salem library has publicized the need for contributions from the public in its informational bulletins. Quincy library officials report that more individuals from the community have come forward to help with funding.

In a few cases, libraries have benefitted from additional state and/or federal funding in the wake of Proposition 2 1/2. As noted previously, New Bedford's public library system was allocated considerable state aid in order to avoid the closing of two branches. Quincy, however, has found itself ineligible for state library funds because, in the wake of funding cutbacks, it cannot meet the requirement that at least 12 percent of its budget be spent for the purchase of books.

Two libraries have benefited from or anticipate additional federal support. As noted previously, the Worcester library joined others in the area in a succesful effort to obtain federal grants totaling $30,000 for training and feasibilty studies related to the automation of library services in the central and western Massachusetts area. Wayland is currently working with other nearby libraries to try to secure outside funding for automated checkout facilities. The Wayland library is also seeking the assignment of a (federally-funded) Jobs Corps trainee to the library department.

*Other Fundraising Efforts*

Officials of Cambridge's library system reported that they have begun to hold book sales to help raise funds.

## Increased Reliance on/Assistance From Other Publc Agencies

Three library systems have begun to work with other nearby libraries to improve service delivery.

ARLINGTON: This library system is cooperating with surrounding towns in the development of a system for automated cataloging and resource control. Library officials in Arlington also report more sharing of material and on-line data bases with neighboring libraries.

WAYLAND: Officials of this library are working with staff from nearby libraries to obtain external fundng for the installation of automated checkout facilities.

WORCESTER: Library officials in Worcester have begun to work with other librarians in exploring ways to utilize automation to facilitate multi-library cooperation and planning, as well as greater access to information. As noted previously, librarians from the Worcester area joined in submitting two successful proposals for federal funds that could ultimately lead to an automated library system serving the entire central and western Massachusetts region.

## Increased Reliance on/Assistance from the Private Sector for Service Delivery

Two of the seventeen library systems--those in Springfield and Pittsfield--are already partly or completely operated by private, non-profit organizations. In each case, the city makes a contribution towards the operation of the library. Efforts by other libraries to increase private sector delivery of library services have been very limited.

### Contracting Out of Services

No examples were found of increased contracting out of public library services. One of the libraries in our sample terminated a contract with a private firm.

WAYLAND: When a CETA worker who had been assigned to the library lost his federal funding, the library cancelled its contract with a private cleaning service and hired the ex-CETA employee as a custodiam.

### Solicitation/Receipt of Free Assistance from the Private Sector

Officials of one library have been able to persuade a private company to take on, without charge, certain operations that otherwise would have to be conducted by library personnel.

BRIDGEWATER: Under the library's new "pre-processing" system, the book seller handles some of the order processing and related paperwork that would otherwise have to be done by library staff. Library officials report that this saves on staff time and allows them to make more book purchases.

## Increased Reliance on/Assistance from Individual Citizens

### *Increased Use of Volunteers*

Libraries in four sites reported increased reliance on services from volunteers.

ARLINGTON: The number of volunteers used for clerical work in this town's library system more than doubled in the first year of Proposition 2 1/2. The department has also revitalized the Friends of the Arlington Library, which will take over the operation of the entire volunteer program. It is expected that the Friends of the Library will also undertake an effort to generate greater community support for the town's library system.

BRIDGEWATER: This town is making greater use of volunteers, especially through its Friends of the Library organization. The latter group currently plans, sponsors, and publicizes all special adult library programs. It also provides travelogues for the elderly and has helped the library compile a directory of local services.

Other governments that reported increased reliance upon volunteers include Amesbury and Quincy. New Bedford is exploring the use of volunteers as supplementary assistants, although library officials noted that care must be taken to ensure that the volunteers do not usurp regular staff duties.

On the other hand, one site reported that it was unable to make greater use of volunteer help.

WATERTOWN: The number of volunteers used by this library system has remained at 22. Volunteers are used to handle historical prints, vertical files, overdue notices, and the library's darkroom. However, library officials report that union contract provisions prohibit them from using volunteers for any activity covered by a paid employee's job description.

### *Increased Citizen Co-Production of Services*

One government -- Bridgewater -- has reported that the public is assuming greater responsibility for providing some of the services usually supplied by library staff.

BRIDGEWATER: Library officials report that in the wake of the cutbacks induced by Proposition 2 1/2, the public has spontaneously begun to help the remaining library staff. Library patrons ask fewer questions, are patient in the face of delays in services, and are taking it upon themselves to learn their own way around the library.

## PARKS AND RECREATION

Parks and recreation agencies in the 17 sites experienced some of the largest post–Proposition 2 1/2 budget reductions of any of the services we examined. The average reduction in parks and recreation appropriations in the wake of Proposition 2 1/2 was 17.4 percent for the 13 sites for which comparable before and after data were available. (See Table 27.2.) Only street maintenance services experienced greater reductions, on the average.

All 17 sites reported decreases in parks and recreation budgets subsequent to the implementation of Proposition 2 1/2. The decreases in appropriations ranged from a low of 1.0 percent in Chelsea to as much as 29.0 percent in Pittfield, 34.6 percent in Salem, and 49.9 percent in Marshfield. In Burlington, Marshfield, and Pittsfield, the parks and recreation agencies experienced a larger proportional cutback in appropriations than any other major service. On top of these cutbacks, most parks and recreation agencies also often had to absorb the effects of substantial contractually mandated wage increases. Moreover, parks and recreation generally received little of the supplemental state aid that was used to help cushion the impacts of Proposition 2 1/2 in other agencies.

These reductions reflect the relatively low priority placed on parks and recreation programs by city administrators and political leaders. They may also reflect, in part, the long–term decline in the school age population and the correspondingly reduced need for certain types of parks and recreation programs and facilities.

The organization of park and recreation services varied considerably among the 17 sites. Most of the 17 governments provided these services by means of separate park and recreation agencies. A few combined the two services organizationally. In some cases, the park and/or recreation division was part of another organizational unit, making parks and recreation impacts difficult to isolate from other effects. For instance, parks was a unit of the Department of Public Works in Marshfield and Watertown. In Amesbury, park and recreation services were both provided by the Department of Public Works. And in Cambridge, parks was a division of Public Works while recreation was a division of the Human Services Department.

In addition to the foregoing complexities, park services were often fragmented among several divisions, including park maintenance, playgrounds, forestry, the shade tree commission, and cemeteries. A few park departments maintained park police units; most, however, did not.

The organizational differences described above made it difficult to isolate and compare parks and recreation responses to Proposition 2 1/2 in some of the 17 sites. In general, however, we have tried wherever possible to include all potentially park–related services (e.g., forestry, cemeteries, playgrounds, etc.).

In most cases, the budget cuts sustained by parks and recreation agencies were translated into losses of personnel, although purchases of equipment and materials were usually also sharply cut back. Only Amesbury and Bridgewater, both of which had very small park and recreation activities to start with, avoided any cutbacks in full-time or part-time staff.

In general, full-time staff experienced the fewest reductions. Two governments--Burlington and Chelsea--lost no full-time parks and recreation personnel (although both sites reduced the number of part-time staff). On the other hand, Pittsfield lost 10 of 24 full-time parks and recreation staff; Quincy, 17 of 37 full-time staff; and Cambridge, about 15 of 42 full-time staff. In most cases, parks appeared to absorb the majority of the losses in full-time personnel. For example, 36 full-time parks positions were eliminated in Salem; 17 in Springfield; and 12 in Cambridge. The losses in full-time recreation personnel were considerably less: three in Cambridge; three in Quincy; and zero in most of the other sites examined. (However, in several cases the proportion of full-time recreation staff lost exceeded that for parks.)

The loss of full-time staff was minimized, especially in the case of recreation personnel, by the elimination of a large number of seasonal and part-time positions in the 17 parks and recreation departments. These included summer laborers, park security guards, and a variety of summer and winter recreation staff (sports instructorss, coaches, lifeguards, recreation leaders, and playground supervisors). Pittsfield lost 74 out of 164 part-time staff positions in the first year of Proposition 2 1/2; Chelsea lost 24 out of 43 part-time staff; and Everett lost all part-time recreation staff as well as half of its seasonal (summer) park employees. Part-time park security officers were cut back or eliminated in Burlington, New Bedford, and Pittsfield.

Most of the losses in full-time and part-time staff were achieved through attrition. A few layoffs did occur, however, in New Bedford, Pittsfield, Quincy, and Salem.

Parks and recreation agencies in the 17 sites reduced personnel expenses in several other ways besides direct cuts in staff levels. Overtime expenditures were cut back drastically in many of the jurisdictions. In Everett, some parks and recreation personnel went on a four-day work week. The city also saved money by replacing one employee who left the agency with a person who was considerably less expensive. Some parks and recreation staff in Pittsfield took demotions and pay cuts to retain their jobs. And in Quincy, staff expenses were reduced by shortening the hours of part-time personnel.

The responses to these cutbacks by parks and recreation departments in the 17 sites were varied. The most popular strategy involved simple cost cutting and reduction of service levels without compensatory actions. The second most popular approach was the acquisition of additional resources. Here, parks and recreation departments tried everything from introducing (or increasing) fees and charges to establishing enterprise funds and soliciting contributions from the private sector. Other popular strategies for dealing with the impacts of Proposition 2 1/2 included increased reliance on the private sector and greater use of volunteers. Indeed, parks and recreation departments appeared to make greater use of the private sector than any other service we examined. On the other hand, parks and recreation agencies placed very little emphasis on productivity improvement as a strategy for responding to Proposition 2 1/2. We found the following responses.

## Cost-Cutting/Reduced Service Levels

### Reduction of Recreation Services

A recreation official from Quincy summarized many of the responses by recreation departments in the 17 sites by observing that he had moved from asking for more dollars to cutting programs in the wake of Proposition 2 1/2. (1) Every site except Wayland reported major cutbacks in recreation programs and services. The following three examples illustrate the range of the cuts in recreation services made by given jurisdictions:

BRIDGEWATER: This town no longer provides six weeks of supervised play during the summer, one of its two pre-Proposition 2 1/2 recreation programs. All that now remains is a summer swimming program.

PITTSFIELD: Reductions in recreation programs included the elimination of supervised play in 15 of the city's 24 playgrounds (and the corresponding reduction of playground staff from 59 to 24); a 50 percent reduction in the number of lifeguards for city pools; and the elimination of ski instruction, tennis instruction, and all but one session of swimming instruction.

WORCESTER: This city made massive across-the-board reductions in recreation programs. Ten recreation programs were completely eliminated (out of a total of 132). These included the municipal golf course, four youth baseball leagues, a winter basketball league, and the handicapped children's camp. The number of staffed playgrounds and neighborhood parks suffered a drastic reduction. The season for the city's pools was reduced by one week during the first year of Proposition 2 1/2; for the second year, the pool/beach program was cut by another week, and pool schedules were cut by two hours per day. The summer playground schedule was reduced by two weeks, and outreach programs such as the traveling zoo were also cut back. Other cutbacks included the elimination of concerts (including three concerts for the elderly) and special holiday programs.

While most sites were forced to make massive across-the-board reductions in recreation programs, a number of different strategies emerged to guide these decisions. For instance, in Arlington the emphasis was on weeding out the weaker, marginal programs such as family fun night and baton twirling. In Springfield, the emphasis was on preserving the programs for children and senior citizens and on consolidating, to the extent possible, all recreation programs in the city's major park areas.

A number of approaches were used in reducing the level of recreation services. These ranged from the outright elimination of a program to reduction of the program's size (e.g., enrollment) or curtailment of the program's season and/or daily schedule. (The City of Quincy reportedly made a major effort to reduce program hours rather than shutting down programs completely.)

Tables 27.4a and 27.4b indicate the types of recreational programs cut back in each of the 17 sites. The following paragraphs summarize some of the highlights of those cutbacks and the detailed strategies used.

*Supervised Recreation Programs in Parks and Playgrounds.*   Nine of the seventeen sites reported that they had eliminated supervised play and recreation program in one or more parks or playground facilities. For example, Arlington eliminated supervised recreation in four of the sixteen parks that had previously provided supervised summer recreation programs; Framingham did the same for 12 of its 24 playgrounds. Two sites reduced playground hours, and four others shortened the season during which supervised play was offered. Springfield, for example, now staffs some of its playgrounds for only half a day; Amesbury and Springfield both reduced their playground season by one week.

*Operation of Pools and Beaches.*   Seven of the seventeen sites cut back on the operation of municipal pools and beaches to reduce, among other things, the costs of providing lifeguards. For instance, New Bedford closed two beaches, and Springfield closed six of its nineteen pools (primarily those in high income areas where residents can afford to travel to the beach or to other pools). Other departments elected to reduce the length of the pool (or beach) season or to reduce the hours the pool was open each day. (The season was initially cut by one week in Amesbury and Worcester; Quincy eliminated Saturday operations.)

*Operation of Summer Camps and Day Care Facilities.*   Arlington and Burlington both reduced summer day camp enrollments. Four other jurisdictions reduced camp and day care programs for retarded and handicapped children. For instance, Watertown and Bridgewater eliminated transportation of mentally retarded children to special needs facilities.

*Reduction of Organized and Informal Sports Activities.*   Six of the seventeen sites reported cutbacks in programs such as basketball, hockey, baseball, ice skating, and boxing. The experiences of Burlington and Watertown are typical:

BURLINGTON: This town cut back adult programs for skiing and boxing; family swimming was eliminated. All were targeted because of low participation levels.

WATERTOWN: The department eliminated a "drop-in" center for informal recreation. Informal basketball sessions were also eliminated. Instead, the department established formal summer and winter basketball leagues to help encourage more regular attendance. Nighttime tennis has been eliminated, and fewer courts are being flooded to provide winter ice skating.

*Reduction or Elimination of Instructional Programs.*   Instructional programs ranging from baton twirling to ski lessons, swimming to ceramics, have been eliminated in eight of the seventeen sites. Many of these programs (e.g., tennis, sailing, ballet, and physical fitness) were oriented towards adults. In the case of Burlington, all of the programs eliminated had been suffering from poor attendance.

*Curtailment of Other Youth Programs and Services.*   Five jurisdictions reported other cutbacks in youth programs and activities. Burlington, for example, reduced the hours of its youth center, and Springfield reported that its youth services had fallen 15 percent.

*Miscellaneous Programs Reduced or Eliminated.*   Outreach programs (for instance, vans to transport children from housing projects to park programs) have been eliminated in New Bedford and Worcester. Quincy and Worcester have closed the municipal ski tow. (Quincy reported receiving more complaints about the latter action than any other service reduction.) Other programs that were cut back included concerts, the stocking of fish in local ponds, and the hours of community centers. Six sites reported the curtailment or elimination of lighting for night activities.

EVERETT: Security lighting of basketball courts has been eliminated, and the lights have been turned off at 11 playgrounds. Night games are currently being held at only one playground.

QUINCY: This city now closes its basketball and tennis courts at night.

Note, however, that one of the 17 jurisdictions -- Wayland -- did not have to reduce recreation services during the first year of Proposition 2 1/2. A long-standing effort to introduce user fees and make recreation programs self-supporting has meant more recreation programs in FY82 than in previous years, according to department officials.

*Reductions in Park Services.*   Park programs also experienced widespread cutbacks in many of the 17 sites. (Wayland again was an exception.) The following examples illustrate the range and mix of park maintenance cutbacks for given jurisdictions.

EVERETT: Park maintenance personnel in this city now spend less time per park on maintenance. Resodding and removal of tree stumps have been eliminated, tree spraying and removal continue but at reduced levels. The city's twice-a-year tree survey has been eliminated, and the practice of having park maintenance personnel monitor sidewalk contractors to prevent them from damaging trees has been dropped. There have been sharp cutbacks in the maintenance of playgrounds--cleaning, painting, repairs to benches, etc. And to reduce overtime, maintenance personnel no longer help at playgrounds on holidays.

NEW BEDFORD: Prior to Proposition 2 1/2, park maintenance crews regularly visited the city's small and outlying parks. In the wake of Proposition 2 1/2, such parks receive only irregular, unscheduled maintenance (primarily after complaints have been received). Most park maintenance activities are now focused on the city's four large parks. Park security patrols have been eliminated, and to reduce overtime, maintenance personnel now prepare for concerts, festivals, and other weekend events during the preceding week.

WORCESTER: Reductions in park maintenance efforts included longer periods between mowing, less litter control, the elimination of regular grooming of the balll fields, and the elimination of all major repair work. Lighting for nighttime events was reduced. To help limit the impact of the cutbacks on park facilities, the park department made its greatest reductions in the maintenance of median strips, traffic islands, and small neighborhood parks. Park personnel also cut back sharply on overtime work by eliminating weekend cleaning and staffing of the community house and the golf course club house, and setups for league games and other weekend events.

Table 27.5 summarizes the reported cutbacks in park maintenance services for each of the 17 sites. The following paragraphs provide further details.

*Reduced Care and Maintenance of Parks, Playgrounds, Pools, and Sports Fields.* Twelve of the seventeen sites reported cutbacks in their general maintenance of parks, playgrounds, and other facilities. The services affected ranged from the liming and upkeep of courts and ballfields to mowing and control of litter. The following examples illustrate some of the cutbacks that have been made in general park maintenance.

ARLINGTON: Park maintenance personnel currently do only necessary maintenance. The marking of ballfields has been reduced from five times a week to twice a week, and basketball courts are painted less often. Fertilization, drainage repairs, and weed control have all been reduced. No new picnic tables are being provided, and preventive maintenance has been sharply cut back. Parks personnel report that the turf is beginning to show deterioration.

SALEM: This city closed its greenhouse and reduced the maintenance of beaches, ballfields, swimming pools, and cemeteries.

SPRINGFIELD: Maintenance schedules have been stretched out. Thus, cleaning and mowing now occur once a month rather than once a week; trees are cut back less often; and ball fields are not relined as frequently. (Park department officials note that even though six pools have been closed, they must still be maintained.)

WATERTOWN: This town no longer assigns one man per park per day for maintenance activities. Parks are only cleaned once a week, and the grass is cut much less frequently. To reduce the need for weekend overtime, the department no longer floods courts to make ice skating rinks. And the lights are no longer turned on in the evening.

*Reduction or Elimination of Park Security Forces.* Three departments -- Burlington, Pittsfield, and New Bedford -- reduced or eliminated park police units. New Bedford, which completely eliminated its park security officers, now depends on the city police to protect the parks.

*Reductions in the Planting, Care, and Removal of Trees.*   Four sites have had to sharply curtail their efforts to plant, preserve, and prune trees. Arlington is typical.

ARLINGTON: This town has eliminated its annual survey of shade trees, an effort that had been billed as preventive maintenance for trees. Trees are trimmed less often, and complaints are handled more slowly. The only tree-related activity that has continued undiminished is the removal of dead trees, which is legally necessary to avoid liabilty to the town.

*Reductions in Overtime and Weekend Services.*   Five of the seventeen sites reported cutbacks in weekend and other overtime activities by park maintenance pesonnel. The following are illustrative:

QUINCY: Weekend overtime has been abolished, thus eliminating the collection of litter, the cleaning of restrooms, and the chalking of ballfields over the weekend.

WORCESTER: To reduce overtime, the use of community houses on an overtime basis has been eliminated, as has after hours staffing of the golf course club house. Overtime park cleanups, setups for athletic leagues, and staff coverage at weekend programs have all been eliminated.

Note that no reductions in the maintenance of park and recreation vehicles were reported. Indeed park officials in Quincy were careful to point out that preventive maintenance schedules for parks vehicles were being adhered to.

Many of the sites reported that the services remaining in the wake of the cutbacks induced by Proposition 2 1/2 were often slower than in the past. Arlington, Everett, Springfield, and Worcester all commented on the delays associated with many of the remaining park maintenance services.

Finally, it should be noted that even as park maintenance services were being cut back, demands for those services were often increasing. Prior efforts to rehabilitate park and recreation facilities, often with state and federal funds, continued to proceed oblivious to the costs that they would be imposing upon park maintenance services in the future. Many park maintenance officials complained about the continuation of such projects at a time when the park department was having to cut back dramatically. As one park official pointed out, the effectiveness of the federal investment in recreation and park facilities was being jeopardized by this department's inabilty to provide maintenance after the facilities were completed. The following examples illustrate the pressures on park maintenance services that have continued unabated.

ARLINGTON: Although the department has eliminated virtually all of its capital outlay, the town in still building and enlarging parks. Department officials expect these new facilities to make major additional demands on the department for lighting, recreation programs, and the maintenance of swimming facilities.

QUINCY: Even as the parks department was sharply reducing staff and programs, major renovations were made to some playgrounds with Community Development funds. According to park department officials, reductions in department funding were curtailing the required maintenance of these playgrounds.

SPRINGFIELD: After having built a new hockey arena, the city found that it was too expensive to equip the hockey teams. The city is also experiencing increasing pressure for the provision of soccer fieldss. Current facilities and maintenance funds, however, are already stretched to the limit.

*Reductions or Delays in Purchases, Replacements, and Other Expenditures*

*Purchases of Supplies and Expendables.* Four of the seventeen governments ordered reductions in purchases of baseballs, basepads, and other supplies and materials. For example, Arlington is no longer replacing picnic tables. Cambridge has cut back on purchases of baseballs, swings, etc. and is not replacing them as often or as fully as requested by staff. Springfield has made similar reductions in purchases: baseballs, basepads, etc. are only supplied for major sites, and baseball teams are encouraged to bring their own bases. Everett has also made major reductions in purchases of equipment and supplies.

*Replacement of Vehicles and Other Equipment.* Six sites -- Arlington, Bridgewater, Chelsea, New Bedford, Quincy, and Watertown -- reported cutbacks in replacements of vehicles, recreational equipment, and park maintenance machinery. The following examples are illustrative.

ARLINGTON: The budget for replacement of parks vehicles, previously funded at a level of $35,000 per year, has fallen to zero.

NEW BEDFORD and BRIDGEWATER: Parks departments in both of these jurisdictions have received no new equipment for a number of years. This policy is continuing under Proposition 2 1/2.

*Reductions in Capital Outlay.* Four sites -- Arlington, Quincy, Salem, and Worcester -- reported the elimination of all major capital outlays for parks and recreation following the introduction of Proposition 2 1/2. Quincy has noted that with the cessation of capital improvements, repair needs are beginning to mount.

*Miscellaneous Cost Cutting.* Quincy's recreation department has reduced its use of school gym facilities because cutbacks in school budgets have made it necessary for the school to charge the recreation department for providing custodial services for those gymnasiums.

A number of governments, including Everett, New Bedford, Watertown, and Springfield, have eliminated subsidies for private recreation leagues (such as the Babe Ruth League), drill teams, and other non-profit organizations. Some of these cutbacks are described later in the section entitled "Increased Burden on Private Organizations."

## Improvement of Productivity and Management

Parks and recreation departments in the 17 sites have made very limited use of productivity and management innovations in dealing with the impacts of Proposition 2 1/2. They did not report undertaking any increased training or the introduction of new technology to help improve productivity. The primary productivity improvement strategies by parks and recreation departments in the 17 sites involved operational improvements and planned reorganizations.

### Working Harder

Despite the many reported cutbacks in staff and programs, only one of the affected sites indicated that staff were working harder or assuming additional responsibilities. (In some other cases, however, one can presume that this was occurring. For instance, where there were one three full-time recreation professionals to run the recreation department in Quincy, there is now only a director.)

The one site which reported that its staff were working harder was Wayland. This was also the only site whose recreation programs were not cut in the wake of Proposition 2 1/2. The harder work was attributed to improved management procedures and increasing efforts to make programs self-supporting. (Under such conditions, according to department officials in Wayland, park and recreation personnel are working directly for the users.)

### Improvement of Operational Procedures

Scattered examples of improved operational procedures, often involving better planning and prioritization, were reported by four of the seventeen departments.

ARLINGTON: Recreation department officials are reportedly weeding out "weaker" and marginal programs and focusing on those with the greatest interest. The parks department has begun to use "floating" crews that can be sent where they are needed most. In the past, crews had been assigned to particular playgrounds.

SPRINGFIELD: Recreation officials in this city have intensified efforts to determine the demand for various types of sports and to provide those activities for which demand is highest. In a sense, this has introduced a certain amount of competition between various sports for agency dollars. The department is consolidating its programs into fewer playgrounds to assure better, more predictable, attendance. To the extent possible, activities have been concentrated in the main park areas. And despite objections by union representatives, parks management has asserted its right to reassign park personnel regardless of seniority.

PITTSFIELD: This city redesigned a municipal dock facility to permit its operation by fewer staff.

WAYLAND: This town also reports the introduction of improved management procedures, in part as an outgrowth of its emphasis on fee-supported programs.

Note that the introduction of revolving funds (described below) by a number of jurisdictions can also potentially lead to the improvement of management and operating procedures.

*Alteration of Organizational Structures*

Although five governments were reported to be investigating new organizational arrangements for the parks and recreation area, only two--Quincy and Salem--have implemented such changes.

QUINCY: This year the city combined the cementery department and the forestry department with the parks department. The city reportedly saved $3,000 in heating bills by closing the forestry building.

SALEM: This city consolidated its parks and recreation departments into a single organizational unit. (However, the two directors were retained.)

WORCESTER: The recreation department in this city is being reorganized in FY83 to serve as a resource center and coordinator for leisure service activities in the city. A division focusing on fund-raising for special recreation programs and events will be established as part of the organizational changes.

WAYLAND: Park responsibilities in this town are assigned to the highway department, while recreation services are provided through a separate recreation division. The town is considering the creation of a consolidated department of public works that would include all parks and recreation activities.

NEW BEDFORD: Although the city council has suggested that the parks and recreation departments be consolidated, such a change has not been implemented, in part because of opposition from the mayor.

## Acquisition of Additional Revenues/Financial Assistance

This represented the second most popular strategy for coping with Proposition 2 1/2 among parks and recreation departments in the 17 sites. A number of initiatives were reported.

*Introduction or Increasing of Fees and Charges*

All but 3 of the 17 sites -- Amesbury, Bridgewater, and Chelsea -- reported introducing and/or increasing fees and charges for park and recreation services. Philosophies towards these increases differed, however, especially among te recreation departments.

ARLINGTON: Recreation officials noted that their philosophy of recreation has been changing over time. Currently, there is greater emphasis on packaged programs which generate fees. It was noted, however, that this has led to a loss of casual leisure activities conducted on an informal basis.

BURLINGTON and CAMBRIDGE: These two governments have followed a policy of no or only small fees for youths, and large fees for adults. Recreation officials in Cambridge believe that the quality of service is better when services are not provided free: they note that people are likely to expect more when they have to pay for it.

WAYLAND: Since 1979, the department has tried to make more and more park and recreation programs fee-supported. By doing this, town officials point out, some recreation specialists are now, in effect, employed directly by the users. The steady increase in fee-supported programs has reportedly made it possible for Wayland to provide more recreation programs in 1982 than it did in 1979.

SPRINGFIELD: Recreation officials in this city do not believe in the widespread use of fees and charges for recreation services. It is the recreation director's belief that the intent of Proposition 2 1/2 was to cut costs, not to pass them on. Recreation officials believe that the greatest need for their service lies with poor people, persons who cannot afford 50 cents a day for swimming. Consequently, recreation staff have avoided the introduction of fees for services widely utilized by poorer residents. Those fees which were introduced (for aerobic dancing, figure skating, and ice time) focused on programs that were expected to appeal more to the affluent user.

NEW BEDFORD: Although some fees have been increased in this city, parks and recreation officials have been trying to keep the increases to a minimum. They note that with the city's rising unemployment rate, the need for low-cost recreation facilities is increasingly urgent.

The following examples illustrate the diversity and ingenuity of the various parks and recreation departments in raising fees and charges.

ARLINGTON: Over the past decade, receipts from fees and charges have increased from $5,000 (1973) to $61,000 (1982). The department tries to keep programs self-supporting. In the wake of Proposition 2 1/2, camp fees were increased from $15 to $30 to cover all costs, fees for instructional elemetary basketball were raised from $3 to $10 (this now includes the cost of overhead and supplies), and soccer fees rose from $3 to $5. Three new self-supporting programs were introduced: aerobic dancing, T-ball, and soccer. Adult softball leagues must now pay for lighting the fields at night.

FRAMINGHAM: Fees and charges have been introduced for adult tennis lessons and for swimming lessons. A fee of $300 per team for men's slow-pitch softball has also been initiated.

QUINCY: Adult recreation programs are now generally funded from fees rather than the general fund. For instance, a $1 per use fee has been instituted for men's basketball; a fee of $2 has been initiated for participation in women's fitness programs. There have also been increases in pool fees: from $12 to $20 for adults, $8 to $10 for children, and $22 to $35 for family membership. Permits for athletic leagues, which used to be free, now must be paid for. And the cost of lighting the ballfields at night has been totally shifted to the using leagues.

WATERTOWN: Fees and charges have been introduced in most areas. The summer camps and most adult programs are currently self-supporting. Summer camp fees were raised from $20 to $30 to cover transportation costs, and a new summer basketball team fee of $100 was introduced. Increases also occurred in the fees charged for golf, aerobic dancing, and baton twirling lessons. The town has moved away from informal basketball programs towards the establishment of more formal league sports. Such an approach provides more predictable attendance and the possibility of charging team or league fees (the latter range from $100 to $125). Private organizations such as adult softball leagues must now pay for lighting playing fields at night.

WAYLAND: In the first year of Proposition 2 1/2, this town made the following programs self-supporting: the provision of lifeguards and beach police, swimming instruction, beach registration, alpine field maintenance, and playground leaders. For example, beach user fees were raised from $1 per person to $5 per person, with family membership going from $5 to $15 per family. Park and recreation officials currently expect fees and charges to bring in about $42,000.

WORCESTER: Before the introduction of Proposition 2 1/2, fees were charged for only four recreation programs (including the golf course). Proposition 2 1/2 has stimulated recreation department management to institute small fees and charges whenever possible for registration and for reservation of facilities. Use of facilities is free unless reserved for special dates and times. Two of the pre-existing fees (those for basketball leagues and golf) were raised in the wake of Proposition 2 1/2. Among the new fees which were instituted were charges for softball permits, tennis permits, winter and summer women's basketball leagues, the boy's winter basketball tournament, youth soccer, picnic permits, and swimming lessons. Each of the above fees includes an assessment for lighting costs, when appropriate. For FY83 (the second year of Proposition 2 1/2), the fee schedule has been broadened considerably with new fees for tennis tournaments, the rental of rooms in community houses, wood cutting permits, special park use permits, etc.

Note that the elimination of municipal subsidies for private recreational organizations (e.g., the provision of free lining and lighting for baseball leagues) may indirectly increase fees for the public as the leagues in question raise their own membership fees.

## Establishment of Revolving Funds

The movement towards more fees and charges for park and recreation services was often associated with greater use of revolving funds. Such funds tend to emphasize (or even ensure) that a given function is handled on a self-supporting basis. Other advantages include the removal of the corresponding dollars from the department's budget and the potential encouragement of better management techniques. Five of the seventeen governments reported the introduction or increased use of revolving funds.

BURLINGTON: This town established a new revolving fund for its recreation programs in 1980.

FRAMINGHAM: A revolving fund for use by parks and recreation was established in the wake of Proposition 2 1/2. The funds deposited in the account can, however, only be spent for contracts and materials, not salaries.

SPRINGFIELD: This city's new recreation revolving fund has a $5,000 maximum. Any excess goes to the general fund. (Note that department officials have expressed some concern over the maintenance of the golf course at a time when most golf fees go into the general fund.)

WATERTOWN: This town has re-established a revolving fund for its recreational programs. The department's adult programs are self-supporting, and the summer camp and aerobic dancing take in more than they cost. The recreation department has been able to cover other programs from the income produced by the latter efforts. Department officials report that the use of a revolving fund in conjunction with the more "profitable" recreation programs has forestalled the elimination of much of the town's adult recreation programming and has even allowed them to introduce new programs from time to time.

WORCESTER: This city is taking advantage of a new state law (adopted in July 1981) that broadened the use of enterprise funds by local governments. The new law provides greater flexibility in the use of such funds. Worcester converted its golf course to an enterprise fund during the first year of Proposition 2 1/2, thereby eliminating $140,000 from its tax levy. The golf course is now operated as a business, covering all expenses from receipts; the excess goes to the general fund.

## Solicitation of Funds and Contributions

One government in our sample--Worcester--has been successful in acquiring additional state and federal funds to help with its recreation programs. The receipt of matching state funds for that city's handicapped camp has allowed the department to sharply cut back its salary requests for this program. Furthermore, community development funds have been able to cover park maintenance and park facilities in some cases. (The reimbursements for the federal funds go directly into a park facilities fund.)

There have, however, been widespread efforts to identify sources of funding and contributions from the private sector. Parks and recreation departments in 8 of the 17 sites reported efforts of this type. Some examples:

ARLINGTON: The recreation department is currently doing some fund raising. For instance, the department has induced local banks to pay for publicity brochures (previously, the brochures were funded out of the department's supplies budget).

BURLINGTON: Both the park and the recreation agencies are seeking additional donations from private sources. The parks department completed a playing field with the help of donations.

EVERETT: The Council on Aging has helped out with the replacement of equipment used in programs for senior citizens. The Council has donated vans, tables, and chairs to the city for these purposes. City officials report that these contributions have helped the department avoid cutbacks in services to the elderly.

NEW BEDFORD: The recreation department of this city is actively pursuing private donations. The Polaroid Foundation (Polaroid has a large plant in New Bedford) purchased gym equipment for the city and donated $1,500 to send children to the city's summer camp.

QUINCY: The recreation department received financial assistance from private athletic leagues to improve lighting and field conditions. The leagues have also absorbed the cost of providing electricity for the lighted facilities they use.

SPRINGFIELD: Springfield's recreation department has approached numerous business and service organizations for financial assistance. Businesses have provided $5,000 to open a neighborhood pool and have financed trips to basketball games and amusement parks. Contributions have also been received from the Elks and Lions Clubs. And the city was successful in soliciting contributions from downtown businesses to help underwrite the rehabilitation and maintenance of a downtown park. (Businesses abutting the park were targeted for contributions since the improvements to the park would enhance their own properties.)

WORCESTER: The parks and recreation department in this city has begun a fundraising drive.

*Other Fundraising Efforts*

Parks and recreation departments in three jurisdictions have turned to renting out their own facilities in an effort to generate increased funds.

FRAMINGHAM: This department received custody of a gymnasium located in a school that was no longer being used. The department is currently renting out the use of the gym and putting the proceeds into a revolving fund.

NEW BEDFORD: This city also rents its gymnasiums when they are not otherwise being used. Rental fees were increased from $15 for the first two hours and $6 for every succeeding hour to a flat rate of $10 to $12 per hour.

WORCESTER: In September 1981, the parks and recreation department sought bids for leasing the municipal golf course to a private organization. No bids, however, were received. The city subsequently decided to operate the golf course as an enterprise fund.

In Arlington, payments received from insurance policies covering motorists who have damaged or knocked down trees have become the primary source of funds for tree replacements. This is part of a government-wide effort to recover such "third-party" reimbursements whenever possible.

*Transfers of Charges to Other Funds or Agencies*

Parks and recreation officials in one of the 17 sites reported changes in the accounts to which they were charging activities.

ARLINGTON: The costs of tennis, roller skating, and summer camp programs have been removed from the recreation account and transferred to the account for the town's ice skating rink. Funding for the latter has grown steadily in recent years.

## Increased Reliance on/Assistance From Other Public Agencies

*Intra-Governmental Assistance, Transfer, or Sharing of Service Delivery Responsibilities*

Park and recreation departments in several governments transferred responsibility for certain aspects of their services to other departments. Thus, reduction or elimination of park police patrols in New Bedford, Pittsfield, and Burlington had the effect of transferring responsibility for park security to the regular municipal police. And the park department in Chelsea was successful in transfering responsibility for a children's lunch program to the school department.

In a few instances, however, park and recreation departments have had to assume additional responsibilities for programs and services provided by other agencies feeling the pressure of Proposition 2 1/2. Thus in Springfield, cutbacks in the number of school custodians meant that the parks department had to assume responsibilty for maintaining some school grounds. And in Watertown, shrinking school department budgets meant that the latter department could no longer pay for custodial services when school facilities were used for recreational programs. The recreation department must now pay for such custodial help.

## Increased Reliance on/Assistance from the Private Sector for Service Delivery

Efforts by parks and recreation departments in the 17 sites to increase their involvement with and reliance on the private sector were more diverse than those exhibited by any of the other services examined.

### Contracting Out of Services

Departments in three jurisdictions have moved towards contracting out some park maintenance responsibilities.

CAMBRIDGE: This city has contracted out the maintenance (clean-up and mowing) of three parks.

WATERTOWN: The parks department in this town has contracted out landscaping and other maintenance services for four high-visibility parks comprising 35 percent of the town's park lands.

EVERETT: Because the city garage is understaffed, playground department staff have often been unable to have vehicles repaired in a timely way. To overcome these problems, the department has begun to use the services of private garages from time to time.

### Franchising of Service Delivery

Worcester's park and recreation officials have reported efforts to expand the use of franchises for park concessions. Minimum bids have been established for the concessions at each park, and fee schedules have been established to allow franchised vendors to serve additional parks. Park and recreation officials note that a number of athletic leagues have been franchised to sell refreshments at their games.

### Encouragement of Private Delivery of Services

Three of the seventeen departments emphasized their continuing reliance upon and encouragement of recreation services provided by private organizations such as the Babe Ruth Leagues, the Little League, and youth hockey. Thus, recreation officials in Everett noted that non-profit recreation groups such as the Pop Warner League have handled much of the non-school recreation needs of the community and have helped limit the adverse impacts of Proposition 2 1/2. Cambridge's recreation department is continuing to provide grants to several private groups (such as the Little League) to assist them with their programs. Bridgewater continues to rely on six privately-operated soccer fields for the provision of league soccer.

*Increased Burden on Private Organizations*

Park departments in several sites have had to take actions increasing the financial burden on private recreational groups. Usually these actions have involved the elimination of subsidies from the department for the recreation activities provided by the private organizations. In some cases, the loss of these subsidies has meant that the fees these organizations charge the public have had to be increased. Although the loss of such subsidies might potentially discourage a private organization from providing the service in question, in this case it generally has not. These organizations have reportedly been very understanding of the position of the park and recreation departments, and they have willingly assumed the additional burdens needed to maintain services.

NEW BEDFORD: Although the parks department used to cater to the softball leagues by maintaining the fields and providing free lighting, the leagues are now asked to help maintain the fields themselves. They must also pay the cost of lighting the fields at night.

SPRINGFIELD: This city used to pay for the officials needed by private athletic leagues. The officials are now provided by the leagues (which have raised fees). Baseball teams must now supply their own bases, where once they were provided by the parks department.

WATERTOWN: Although the recreation department used to pay for umpires at Little League games, the leagues must now pay for their own umpires. Organizations using the playing fields at night must now pay for lighting, a change which has led to an increase in the fees for the independent adult softball leagues.

## Increased Reliance on/Assistance from Individual Citizens

*Increased Use of Volunteers*

The utilization of volunteers has long been a tradition in parks and recreation agencies. Seven of the seventeen sites in our sample reported greater utilization of volunteer help in the wake of Proposition 2 1/2. Some examples:

ARLINGTON: As this town's recreation department has had to cut down on the use of part-time help, greater emphasis has been made on utilizing volunteers. The department has stopped paying coaches, transforming them in effect to volunteer status.

BURLINGTON: The recreation department31822 in this town is also making greater use of volunteers. Some of that help is coming from private youth sports organizations which are assisting with the maintenance of parks.

PITTSFIELD: Parks and recreation officials in Pittsfield are relying on increased volunteerism to maintain and strengthen services. A consultant has been hired to stir up interest in volunteerism. In addition, the city has established a new Citizen Volunteer Alliance Project which will work with neighborhood organizations and attempt to get them to provide volunteer help to supplement parks and recreation services.

QUINCY: The parks department has benefited from the help of 200–300 girl scouts and boy scouts as cleanup crews. During the first year of Proposition 2 1/2, the Citizens for a Cleaner Commonwealth organized a group of retarded adults to help clean up the parks. Unfortunately, the organization ran out of funds and has not been able to provide further assistance.

SPRINGFIELD: Groups of individuals have volunteered to help the recreation department maintain baseball dianonds, and downtown businesses have helped with park maintenance. Neighborhood cooperation in the maintenance of sports fields is also being developed.

WORCESTER: The department coordinates and works with a volunteer organization known as P.A.R.T.N.E.R.S., a group of 51 agencies providing recreation services. Together, they work to improve coordination, efficiency, communication, and utilization of recreation resources. The group serves as a bridge between the department and the city's neighborhoods.

On the other hand, New Bedford has shied away from seeking greater use of volunteers. Recreation officials claim that they have had little success in attracting or utilizing volunteers in the past.

TABLE 27.4A

REPORTED REDUCTIONS IN RECREATION PROGRAMS AND SERVICES

| | Supervised Recreation in Parks and Playgrounds | | | Operation of Pools and Beaches | | | Reduction of Summer Camps and Day Care Facilities | |
|---|---|---|---|---|---|---|---|---|
| | Closed Facilities | Reduced Hours | Shortened Season | Closed Facilities | Reduced Hours | Reduced Season | Regular Day Camps | Facilities for Handicapped and Retarded |
| Amesbury | | | x | | | x | | |
| Arlington | x | | | | | | x | |
| Bridgewater | x | | | | | | | x |
| Burlington | x | | | | | | x | |
| Cambridge | | x | | x | | | | |
| Chelsea | | | | | | | | |
| Everett | | | | | | | | |
| Framingham | x | | | | | | | |
| Marshfield | | | | | | | | |
| New Bedford | x | | | x | x | | | x |
| Pittsfield | | | | x | | | | |
| Quincy | x | x | | | x | | | |
| Salem | x | | | | | | | |
| Springfield | x | | x | x | | x | | |
| Watertown | | | x | | | | | x |
| Wayland | | | | | | | | |
| Worcester | x | | x | | x | x | | x |

TABLE 27.4B

REPORTED REDUCTIONS IN RECREATION PROGRAMS AND SERVICES

| | Reduction of Organized or Informal Sports Activities | Reduction/Elimination of Instructional Programs | Curtailment of Other Youth Programs and Services | Miscellaneous Programs Reduced or Eliminated |
|---|---|---|---|---|
| Amesbury | | | | |
| Arlington | | | | Lighting of parks |
| Bridgewater | X | X | | |
| Burlington | | X | X | |
| Cambridge | | | | |
| Chelsea | | | | |
| Everett | X | X | X | Lighting of parks/playgrounds |
| Framingham | | | | |
| Marshfield | | | | |
| New Bedford | X | | X | Community Center hours, outreach programs, lighting |
| Pittsfield | | X | | Ski tows, lighting of courts |
| Quincy | | X | | |
| Salem | | X | | |
| Springfield | | | X | |
| Watertown | X | X | | Lighting of tennis courts |
| Wayland | X | | | |
| Worcester | X | | X | Ski tows, concerts, outreach programs, lighting, stocking of fish ponds, etc. |

**Table 27.5**
**Reported Reductions in Park Maintenance Services**

| | Facilities | Security | Tree Care | O.T./Weekends |
|---|---|---|---|---|
| Amesbury | | | | |
| Arlington | × | | × | |
| Bridgewater | × | | | |
| Burlington | | × | | |
| Cambridge | × | | | |
| Chelsea | × | | | |
| Everett | × | | × | × |
| Framingham | | | | |
| Marshfield | | | | |
| New Bedford | × | × | | × |
| Pittsfield | × | × | | |
| Quincy | × | | × | × |
| Salem | × | | × | |
| Springfield | × | | | × |
| Watertown | × | | | |
| Wayland | | | | |
| Worcester | × | | | × |

Notes:   "Facilities" refers to reduced care and maintenance of parks, pools, playgrounds, and sports fields.

"Security" refers to reduction or elimination of park security forces.

"Tree Care" refers to reductions in planting, care and removal of trees.

"O.T./Weekend" refers to reductions in overtime and weekend services.

# PUBLIC WORKS

In this section, we focus on street and sidewalk maintenance, solid waste collection and disposal, snow removal, street sweeping, sewer maintenance, wastewater treatment, traffic engineering, street lighting, and vehicle maintenance. These services are often grouped organizationally within a single public works department. However, certain services--such as sanitation, traffic, and wastewater--may be provided by organizationally independent units (particularly in the larger cities).

The various public works services in the 17 sites were affected in different ways by the introduction of Proposition 2 1/2. Sanitation and street maintenance services illustrate the contrast. For sanitation, the mean change in appropriations associated with the introduction of Proposition 2 1/2 was -4.3% for the 13 jurisdictions for which we have comparable before and after data. This represents one of the smallest average reductions in appropriations of any of the service areas we examined. In part, it reflects the priority placed by public administrators and political leaders on preserving health and safety.

On the other hand, the corresponding mean change in appropriations levels for street maintenance services was -17.9% for the 13 jurisdictions. This was the largest average budget reduction experienced by any of the major services.

There was considerable variation between the sites in the actual cutbacks made in public works budgets. The variation is higher than for any of the other major services examined (see Table 27.2). Thus, changes in appropriations levels for sanitation services after the introduction of Proposition 2 1/2 ranged from a 29.7% decrease in Everett and a 100% decrease in Wayland (which eliminated all municipally-supported garbage collection efforts) to a 50% increase in appropriations in the city of Springfield. Appropriations for sanitation services rose in seven sites after the introduction of Proposition 2 1/2. In five of those seven sites, waste collection was privately contracted in six of the seventeen sites. In two additional sites, no refuse collection services were provided at municipal expense.)

It appears that contracted waste collection costs were less controllable than those of municipal sanitation agencies. Where service was provided by public employees, public works officials generally exercised the option of making some cutbacks in sanitation staffing and other expenditures. Apparently this could not be done as readily where service was privately contracted.

Street maintenance appropriations decreased in the first year of Proposition 2 1/2 for all but one site (Framingham) among the thirteen for which we have comparable before vs. after appropriations data. The decreases ranged from 7.1% in Cambridge to 37.1% in Salem and 67.7% for Quincy. In five of the thirteen governments, the reductions in street maintenance were larger than the reductions experienced by any of the other services we examined. (1)

Public works budgets also had to provide for negotiated wage increases (Worcester eliminated eight staff positions in order to absorb such increases) and substantial increases in the prices of services purchases from outside (e.g., street lighting). These added to the pressure on public works budgets.

Many of the 17 public works departments experienced staff reductions of as much as 20–35%. Examples included Worcester (which lost 110 positions), Springfield (which eliminated 108 positions from the city payroll), Cambridge (which lost 84 positions), and New Bedford (down 67 positions). Only Wayland--the smallest government in our sample--experienced no staff losses.

Street and highway maintenance generally experienced the largest cutbacks (as high as 20–35%). Most governments preserved sanitation staff levels. There were some exceptions, however. For instance, Pittsfield contracted out its sanitation services and eliminated 31 of its 34 sanitation workers. Pittsfield was unable to make reductions in wastewater treatment staff, however, reportedly because of EPA regulations.

Layoffs of public works employees occurred in 8 of the 17 governments. (In Worcester, 54 public works personnel were laid off.) In most sites, the layoffs were focused primarily on laborers, although some supervisory and part-time personnel were released. Very few public works personnel were rehired after the distribution of supplementary state aid in the fall of 1981. In fact, most public works departments received little supplementary state aid. Springfield and Salem were exceptions; here additional state aid was used to rescind cutbacks in street lighting and (in the case of Salem) to purchase needed equipment.

The responses by public works agencies in the 17 sites to the first year of Proposition 2 1/2 exhibited greater diversity than any other service area examined. As with other services, by far the most common response was cost-cutting/service reduction. However, there were numerous examples of other innovative responses. These included acquisition of additional financial resources (the second most popular response), improvement of productivity and management (the third most popular response), and greater use of the private sector (the fourth most common response). The following examples were found.

## Cost Cutting/Reduced Service Levels

All 17 sites cut costs and/or services in the public works area. A great variety of public works activities were affected. These included services to the public, internal (administrative and support) services, purchases of materials, and capital expenditures. The areas affected in each of the 17 sites are summarized in Tables 27.6 and 27.7.

The cutbacks in expenditures and service levels reported by the various public works departments are too diverse to describe in detail. However, the following four examples illustrate the range of reductions in public works services undertaken by specific sites.

BRIDGEWATER: This town eliminated its program of sidewalk rehabilitation and reduced work on curbs. Crack sealing and certain types of patching were also cut back. A program to inspect utility cuts one year later to identify and, if necessary, repair any settling was also eliminated. Maintenance of secondary roads has been drastically cut back in favor of work on main roads for which state aid is available. Resurfacing activities have been cut in half. The town anticipates future cutbacks in snow plowing budgets. (Streetsweeping activities, however, have not been cut back.) Installation of new sewers has been eliminated, drainage work has been sharply cut back, and sewer maintenance has been reduced. The painting of centerlines has been eliminated, and only crosswalks and parking areas are currently being lined. A program to install new guardrails has been dropped, and the replacement of traffic signs has been sharply reduced. Cemetery landscaping has also been curtailed. Purchases of new vehicles have been eliminated. However, the department has continued preventive maintenance efforts for the city's vehicles.

EVERETT: The city's street and sidewalk maintenance program has been reduced. Two of the three street and sidewalk crews were eliminated, and no "cosmetic" fix-ups are being undertaken. The city no longer hauls away snow after plowing operations nor clears snow from funeral homes, but an effort is still made to clear school areas, depending on the staff available. Cleaning in front of churches has been given a lower priority but is also done, when possible. Storm drain and catchbasin repairs and cleaning have been reduced. The sign department has been reduced from three men to one full-time employee, with additional help provided by other units as available. Staff in the city's vehicle maintenance shop have been reduced by half, with the result that preventive maintenance has been curtailed.

ARLINGTON: This town has attempted to sustain maintenance activities while reducing capital expenditures. Potholes continue to be filled, although there have been cutbacks in chip sealing efforts. The department no longer hauls away snow after it has been plowed. Fall leaf pickups have been eliminated. Street sweeping activities have been drastically cut back, and underground maintenance of water and sewer facilities is taking longer. Preventive maintenance of traffic signals and pavement marking activities have been sharply reduced (only crosswalks and school zones are being marked regularly). Replacements of new equipment have been eliminated, as has the town's $250,000 capital expenditure program. This has led to sharp cutbacks in highway construction and water main replacement. A program under which 51 percent of the citizens in an area could petition to have a street built was temporarily eliminated until funds from increased sewer fees permitted it to be re-established.

SPRINGFIELD: This city reports a 3-4 week backlog in pothole repairs and the elimination of free maintenance of privately-owned streets. Use of infrared street patching, however, has been expanded. Snow plowing activities now focus primarily on the main roads, and no overtime is allowed. Cutbacks in sanitation services have included less frequent commercial pickups, slower pickups of bulk items, and the elimination of the city's spring cleanup effort. Elimination of two of the city's sewer maintenance crews has led to slower responses on sewer backups. The schedule for cleaning storm drains has, in effect, gone from once every two years to once every six years. There have also been slowdowns in traffic engineering services, including street line painting and emergency repairs (repairs which used to be completed overnight now require up to one week). The city attempted to cut street lighting by 10 percent; however, an outcry by the press and the public plus a resolution by the City Council ultimately resulted in the restoration of most street lights after the receipt of supplementary state funding. The city has made a point of not reducing vehicle maintenance, preferring instead to stretch out purchases. Thus, packers are being kept for 8–10 years instead of being replaced on the usual 5–year cycle. However, even replacements of 8–10 year old packers have been sharply reduced. The city has also experienced a 75 percent reduction in capital expenditures such as street resurfacing and sidewalk construction.

Public works officials in most of the sites reported that they were providing fewer services. (Two exceptions should be noted. New Bedford has reportedly been able to maintain the provision of pothole patching and other street maintenance services because they are underwritten almost entirely by federal funds. And Wayland is increasing the number of traffic lights, the only jurisdiction to report an increase in traffic services.) Most public works directors indicated that their main priority was to preserve public safety, e.g., to emphasize pothole repairs, snow and ice removal, and responses to emergencies. In many cases, public works activities were reportedly reduced to the point where personnel were only responding to emergencies and complaints. Another common strategy was to reallocate effort to activities where outside funding was available--e.g., maintenance of roads for which federal or state aid could be used. Where possible, the emphasis has been on increasing maintenance and extending the life of existing facilities rather than reconstruction or the purchasing of new facilities.

In most of the 17 sites, the results have been slower service, mounting backlogs, and drastic reductions in vehicle replacements and capital expenditures (e.g., street and sidewalk construction, street resurfacing). Many of the departments eliminated the little "extra" services they had provided, such as the widening of private driveways, repairs to private roads, "cosmetic" fixups, the removal of plowed snow, and the plowing of funeral, church, and school facilities.

Three governments--New Bedford, Bridgewater, and Wayland--made major reductions in the provision of refuse and garbage collection services. New Bedford reduced collections from twice to once a week, while both Bridgewater and Wayland completely eliminated municipally-supported collections. (The latter two examples are described at the end of this section.) Some other observations:

Street and sidewalk maintenance, especially sidewalk and curb repairs, were especially hard hit by Proposition 2 1/2. Thus, cutbacks were reported by many departments in crack sealing and other preventive maintenance activities. However, the repair of potholes, although sometimes slower, has continued unabated in most cases.

The primary strategy used to control snow plowing costs was the elimination of snow removal (after plowing). The plowed snow will now be left to melt!

Reduction of street lighting costs has been a difficult issue for several sites in the face of sharply escalating electric bills. Five governments turned off some of their street lights. (Several others reported that public protests had prevented cutbacks in street lighting.) Some reductions were as high as 50 percent (e.g., in Bridgewater). However, most reductions in lighting tended to hover around the 10 percent level, apparently because of limitations imposed by the State Department of Utilities on the amount by which street lighting could be reduced.

## Improvement of Productivity and Management

One director of public works noted that "Proposition 2 1/2 forces you to be more efficient." Thus it is significant that productivity improvement was the second most popular response to the introduction of Proposition 2 1/2 by public works agencies in the 17 sites. All of the major productivity improvement strategies, with the exception of additional training, were tried in at least one site.

### Working Harder

Public works directors in four jurisdictions--Arlington, New Bedford, Pittsfield, and Worcester--reported that their employees were working harder.

NEW BEDFORD: Sanitation crews, which used to complete their routes around 1:00 p.m., are now coming in about 3:30 because of the increased loads (collections having been cut from twice to once a week). Sharply increased efforts by public works department clerical staff have also been reported.

ARLINGTON: This town's vehicle maintenance agency continues to handle the same number of vehicles and repairs, alsong with an extensive preventive maintenance program, with three fewer mechanics.

PITTSFIELD: Staff cutbacks have reduced this city's sewer and drain division to three people. Since the division continues to be on 24-hour call, the remaining staff are stretched very thinly, with frequent requirements for overtime. Department officials fear that the continuing intrusions of overtime responsibilities on the private lives of these workers will lead to refusals by the employees to work the additional overtime needed.

### Introduction of Employee Incentives

One city -- Quincy -- introduced a number of programs to motivate employees to achieve higher productivity. However, Springfield found that the cutbacks associated with Proposition 2 1/2 forced it to cancel a pre-existing incentive system. (2)

QUINCY: This city has implemented quality circles to encourage participation and productivity improvements by public works employees. The department's Specification Review Committee, designed to standardize specifications for equipment purchased by the agency, also utilizes extensive inputs from line workers. In addition, the department is strengthening its safety committee in an effort to reduce the costs of injuries and illnesses through tighter administration of safety rules.

SPRINGFIELD: Before the introduction of Proposition 2 1/2, this department refrained from filling vacant positions. Instead, employee responsibilities were increased, and the saving in salaries was split between the department and the employees affected. With the introduction of Proposition 2 1/2, however, the vacant positions that had served as the source of the funds for this shared savings system were eliminated.

*Introduction of New or Additional Technology*

Five jurisdictions reported the use of new technology to help improve productivity. Three cases involved greater use of computers, although the role of Proposition 2 1/2 in stimulating the changes is uncertain.

AMESBURY: Water and sewer bills are now being processed by computer. As part of this change, the town is issuing a single bill for water and sewer expenses rather than billing them separately as had been done in the past.

SPRINGFIELD: Public works officials in this city are investing in computers to handle the department's accounting, inventory, and ordering functions. Although this will initially involve a slight increase in staff, the department expects savings over the long run.

QUINCY: This city's public works department is moving towards computerization of many of its functions.

CAMBRIDGE: This city has begun to purchase more fuel efficient automobiles.

WORCESTER: The traffic division has increased efforts to conserve energy, including the use of lower wattage bulbs, more efficient switches, and greater utilization of flashing traffic lights.

*Improvement of Operational Procedures*

A variety of operational improvements were reported by 7 of the 17 sites. Most involved the reorganization and/or reassignment of public works crews.

AMESBURY: The public works department eliminated a winter night shift and reassigned the four men to daytime work. Public works officials felt that these people could be used more productively during the day. (Previously, their primary responsibility was to wait for and respond to emergencies.)

BRIDGEWATER: This town has gone from two-man sanding and plowing crews to one-man crews. And by sending out supervisors to check on nighttime calls for service, the department has saved on overtime costs while being better able to tailor crew size to the job at hand in those instances where further work is needed.

WATERTOWN: This town consolidated its three street maintenance crews into a single unit.

MARSHFIELD: Government officials negotiated a change in the job descriptions of equipment operators in discussions with the public works union (which re-opened its contract). All equipment operator job titles had specified the type of equipment. However, these detailed specifications have been dropped in favor of a single "heavy equipment operator" title. This allows more flexible utilization of staff.

EVERETT: This city has reduced the number of specialized street maintenance crews in favor of crews with more generalized responsibilities. The repair of sidewalks is now handled by one multi-specialty crew where once three separate specialized crews performed the job. The city's hot tar crew is now assigned a wide variety of other functions. Based on the number of men available each day, the department puts together a "pick-up" crew of about ten persons which is responsible for performing any work that is needed.

SPRINGFIELD: Public works management has asserted its right to move employees between divisions according to need. Although these changes met some resistance, the department was able to overcome them. (Department officials report that without the stimulus of Proposition 2 1/2, the city council would probably have bent to pressure from the unions and prohibited such flexible assignments.) Department officials also report that once the flexible assignments were established, workers like the cross training and skills development that these assignments provided.

QUINCY: A Specification Review Committee was established by the director of public works to re-assess equipment procurement. By coordinating equipment specifications, the committee has been able to move from having as many as nine varieties of a given piece of equipment to the use of two or three types.

*Alteration of Organizational Structures*

Although organizational changes to public works departments were reported by five governments, all but one were in the planning stage.

MARSHFIELD: This town's contract with the public works union was re-opened for negotiations that addressed changes in the organization of the public works department. As a result, the Division of Trees and Greens was combined with Cemeteries, and the positions of a foreman and five tree workers were eliminated.

ARLINGTON: Pavement marking and street sign work, currently spread between the public works and traffic engineering divisions, will be combined within the Department of Public Works in 1983. The town is also planning to establish a separate water and sewer division that would be self–supporting through user fees.

FRAMINGHAM: Water and sewer operations have been consolidated at one pumping station, saving $10,000. There has not, as yet, been an overall consolidation of water and sewer operations.

WAYLAND: This town is considering combining its highways and parks and recreation departments into a single department of public works. Planning for such an effort, however, preceded the introduction of Proposition 2 1/2.

BURLINGTON: Government officials are considering combining the positions of Superintendent of Highways and Superintendent of Water and Sewers.

*Miscellaneous Productivity Improvement Efforts*

Public works agencies in four sites were implementing a variety of other productivity improvement efforts.

SPRINGFIELD: The department has found that by substituting fly ash purchased from a local utility company for its existing landfill cover material, it could reduce the cost of landfill cover material by 2/3.

BRIDGEWATER: Municipal vehicles that are used only seasonally are now registered and insured only seasonally.

WORCESTER: This city's traffic department is making an intensive effort to recycle old signs rather than purchasing new ones.

QUINCY: This city's new public works commissioner is stressing the improvement of department management.

## Acquisition of Additional Revenues or Financial Assistance

Acquisition of additional financial resources constituted the third most widely used strategy in responding to Proposition 2 1/2.

*Introduction or Increasing of Fees and Charges*

Public works agencies in the 17 sites exhibited widespread interest in introducing or increasing fees and charges. Most of the increases focused on two areas: water and/or sewer fees, and landfill/disposal fees. However, several other interesting efforts to increase fees and charges were also reported.

*Water and/or Sewer Use Fees.*    Burlington, Cambridge, Framingham, Quincy, Watertown, and Worcester, reported introducing or increasing fees for water and/or sewer usage. In Framingham, sewer rates increased by 50 percent. Both Salem and Pittsfield were seeking increases in water and/or sewer rates.

*Landfill/Incinerator Fees.* Fees for using the municipal landfill or incinerator were raised in Bridgewater, Framingham, Quincy, Wayland, and Worcester. For instance, Quincy introduced a fee for commercial users of the landfill; the fees paid by those users completely cover the cost of the city's landfill contract. In Wayland, fees were established for the disposal of construction materials. Springfield is looking into the introduction of a landfill fee; such a fee has not, however, been introduced as of yet.

*Waste Collection Fees.* Chelsea was the only community that raised the fees charged to homeowners for waste collection services. Two sites considered changes in waste collection fees but decided against it. Public works officials in Springfield discussed the introduction of a refuse collection fee that would make the service pay for itself; it was decided, however, that such a fee would be politically unfeasible. While Arlington was able to increase rubbish collection fees for some businesses, a court ruled that the town could not increase collection fees for apartments without making all commercial users absorb similar increases.

*Fees for Additional Street Lighting Services.* In Bridgewater and Marshfield citizens were reportedly paying directly for some street lighting services. Thus in the case of Bridgewater, which cut back street lights by 50 percent, it has been reported that some subdivisions have been paying the extra costs necessary to retain street lighting at the prior level.

Other examples of increases in fees and charges implemented by public works departments include a rise in the minimum parking ticket fee in Arlington, increased building inspection fees in Quincy, a rise in the fees charged for cemetery lots and burials in Salem, and increased charges for beach services in Marshfield.

Public works interest in the establishment or raising of fees and charges appeared to be growing. Many of the sites reported that additional fees or fee increases were planned for the second year of Proposition 2 1/2. The public works director of one large city noted that most of the department's fees had historically been pegged at levels below the cost of service in order to stimulate citizens to sign up for the necessary work. As a result, the city has had many fees but little income from those fees. Another public works official, however, pointed to a potential problem with the fee system. He noted that although the collection of most fees depended upon the efforts and conscientiousness of his department, the fruits of those activities went into the general fund. He felt that the department would have much more incentive for conscientiously collecting fees and reimbursals if the department could be given at least a percentage of the receipts collected.

*Solicitation of Funds and Contributions*

Four sites reported increased efforts to utilize state and federal funding sources for supporting public works activities. The efforts by Springfield, which involved having the public works department bid against private contractors for federally funded community development work, represented an especially innovative approach.

BRIDGEWATER: Street construction activities have been focused only upon those roads for which state or federal reimbursements are available. Because of federal restrictions, secondary roads in Bridgewater are not eligible for federal reimbursements (federal regulations require right-of-ways to be wider than many of the town's older streets, which are quite narrow). The town has also been unable to use state funds to upgrade its traffic signals because it wants to maintain angle parking in the town center, contrary to state highway regulations.

PITTSFIELD: This city's public works department is relying heavily upon state and federal aid.

QUINCY: By introducing a sewer use tax, this city is much closer to qualifying for federal categorical aid for sewer construction.

SPRINGFIELD: To avoid having to eliminate 80-100 public works employees whom the department felt would be needed in the future (e.g. to re-start various maintenance activities after added revenues are received from the city's reassessment of property values), the public works department successfully bid against private contractors for state and federal community development and UDAG projects. The department was able to win contracts totaling $1.5 million in FY82 and $2 million in FY83 to keep public works employees working. Thus, a large number of public works employees are working on park construction and other work that normally would have been undertaken by private contractors. Public works officials reported that the city underbid private firms by 30-35 percent. In order to avoid unfair competition with small contractors, the city has hired union workers at union scale for specialty work. City costs are kept low by not charging administrative overhead and otherwise doing the work at cost. Department officials report that while there was some initial resistance from public works employees and employee unions to working on regular construction projects, the effort has had the unexpected effect of giving city employees greater confidence in themselves and their capabilities. They see that they are able to handle the same work as private contractors and do it for less.

Two public works departments reported greater efforts to solicit funds and contributions from the private sector.

BRIDGEWATER: The Bridgewater Improvement Association has helped out with several general services that the department has been unable to handle in the face of budget reductions, such as planting flowers and landscaping the town common. The Association has also donated money for tree planting.

NEW BEDFORD: A shopping center in this city paid for the installation of a traffic light serving access roads to the center.

*Other Fundraising Efforts*

The following additional approaches to raising funds from external sources were reported by public works departments from the 17 sites.

PITTSFIELD: This city's public works department has reportedly recouped approximately $56,000 in claims and charges that had not been collected in previous years.

SPRINGFIELD: Public works officials are looking into the possibility of renting out city equipment to private users.

WAYLAND: Increased contracting out of services has allowed this town to begin to sell some of its existing public works equipment.

*Establishment of Revolving Funds*

Three jurisdictions reported increased efforts to utilize revolving funds in connection with public works activities.

SPRINGFIELD: The public works department of this city is making an extensive effort to identify opportunities for utilization of revolving funds, e.g. for wastewater treatment. One idea that is being examined is the initiation of a revolving fund for repairs of the many privately-owned streets in the city.

ARLINGTON: The traffic department in this town has established a separate signal repair account using payments received from automobile insurance policies. This account is used to pay for repairs of traffic signal knockdowns without having to go through the red tape of using the town's normal accounting procedures. It is reported that knockdowns are now fixed within one day.

WORCESTER: This city is looking into the possibility of introducing enterprise funds for water, sewer and landfill services.

*Transfers of Charges to Other Funds or Agencies*

Proposition 2 1/2 has induced public works administrators to give greater attention to where they charge particular activities.

ARLINGTON: Charges for catchbasin cleaning have been moved from the drainage account to the snow and ice account. (The rationale for this change was that most of the catchbasin cleaning work was done to remove sand which had been spread on the town's streets during the winter.) However, it was also likely that funds would be more readily available in the snow and ice account than the drainage account.

CAMBRIDGE: The public works department now bills the water department, which has its own source of revenue, for the repair of utility cuts. The city's traffic department, which is funded entirely from various parking revenues, must now pay for expenses such as telephone and electricity that were previously paid by other government agencies.

BRIDGEWATER: As noted previously, street repair activities have been shifted from secondary roads to main streets where state and federal assistance is available.

EVERETT: Public works officials are relying on the fact that on the average, four employees are out on workmen's compensation at any given time. This means that on the average there are four public works positions that can be maintained at no cost to the city. This expectation has allowed the department to keep four additional men on the public works rolls but off the budget.

## Increased Reliance on/Assistance from Other Public Agencies

*Intragovernmental Assistance, Transfer, or Sharing of Service Delivery Responsibilities*

In New Bedford, a public works crew which had been responsible for handling traffic signs was transferred to the traffic commission. Unlike the department of public works, the traffic commission was self sufficient through parking and traffic revenues; it had adequate funds to underwrite the costs of the traffic sign crew.

There is a possibility, however, that some additional responsibilities will be imposed on public works agencies as other departments adjust to Proposition 2 1/2. Thus, the police department in New Bedford is urging the signalization of more intersections to help that department cope with cutbacks in its traffic enforcement division.

*Intergovernmental Assistance, Transfer, or Sharing of Service Delivery Responsibilities*

No examples of this type were reported by public works departments in the 17 sites. Public works officials in Springfield noted that one potential area for intergovernmental cooperation--cooperative purchases--generally benefitted the small towns more than the larger cities.

## Increased Reliance on/Assistance from the Private Sector

Public works departments in the 17 sites reported a number of initiatives addressed towards securing greater involvement by the private sector in the delivery of public works services. The emphasis on this strategy may reflect the historically high usage of private contractors by public works agencies (e.g., for street resurfacing, sewer construction, and similar major projects).

*Contracting Out of Services*

Public works agencies in numerous sites reported increased usage, experimentation with, and planning of private contracts for the delivery of public works services. As noted previously, sanitation services were delivered under private contracts in six of the seventeen sites in the year prior to the introduction of Proposition 2 1/2. Implementation of Proposition 2 1/2 encouraged one site to contract out waste collection services and another to begin experimenting with such contracts. Other services were also contracted.

PITTSFIELD: Solid waste collection was privately contracted for the first time in FY82. The changeover involved the release of 31 of the city's 34 sanitation personnel. The three remaining people--all supervisors--joined the administrative office of the public works department. They oversaw the operation of the solid waste contract and provided backdoor collection for those citizens eligible to receive it (the latter was not provided under the contract). Waste collection operations cost $657,301 in the year prior to the contract; the contracted cost for the first year was $494,495.

AMESBURY: A 20 percent cutback in public works staff has forced the department to look towards private contractors for help with any construction projects. Street sweeping and catchbasin cleaning have also been contracted out. Government officials believe that the town is realizing additional savings by not having to repair or replace its aging equipment since the establishment of the contracts.

ARLINGTON: An exclusive contract has been arranged with a private firm for the pickup of bulk items. (Previously, the sanitation department had picked up bulk items on demand.) The private contractor receives no fee for this service. However, the firm is allowed to keep all of the refrigerators, washers, and other items it picks up and to dispose of them as it sees fit.

BRIDGEWATER: This town contracted with a private landfill for the establishment of a transfer station to be used by citizens for the disposal of their rubbish. A separate contract for rubbish collection was terminated at the same time, leaving it up to individual citizens to dispose of their own solid waste.

CAMBRIDGE: The public works department has begun to contract out window washing and custodial services, the pickup and removal of plowed snow, snow plowing for large storms, street sweeping, and street and sidewalk repairs.

PITTSFIELD: The elimination of one equipment operator position has meant that the public works department must now hire private equipment and operators to provide emergency services. The city closed its dump and contracted waste disposal to a private firm which converts the waste to steam and sells it to other firms.

QUINCY: Private contractors are now used for snow plowing and street cleaning to supplement city workers.

WATERTOWN: The town is now contracting out a variety of public works activities. Plans for FY83 include the contracting of street sweeping, line painting, and sign painting services.

WAYLAND: This town contracted with a private firm for the provision of landfill services. Contracts for catchbasin cleaning, street sweeping, and pavement marking are anticipated in the near future.

Two sites have been reluctant to increase their use of private contractors.

BRIDGEWATER: Although a few contracts already exist, public works officials in this town have expressed the feeling that, since they have the equipment and the expertise, it is cheaper for them to do most of their work in-house than for them to contract it out.

EVERETT: Everett's mayor has expressed reluctance towards contracting out public works services. One of his concerns is that even if such contracts are initially cheaper, contractors would raise the fees once the city no longer had the machines or mechanics available for providing the service itself. He also expressed concern that the public works employees released would be unable to find other jobs.

*Encouragement of Private Delivery of Services*

Two sites reported efforts that could encourage increased private sector delivery of public works services currently provided by the city.

QUINCY: Prior to the introduction of Proposition 2 1/2, the department of public works would widen driveways for private citizens. The department now merely issues a permit for such work and leaves the contracting and payment for the effort up to the individual citizens.

SPRINGFIELD: Public works officials have expressed the opinion that the agency should not be in the business of clearing sewer backups. They feel that this service, which generates no income but considerable liability for the city, should be handled by "rotorooter" firms.

## Increased Reliance on/Assistance from Individual Citizens

Public works departments in the 17 sites reported no efforts to increase the use of volunteers. However, two governments made major efforts towards increasing the burden on citizens for waste collection services.

*Increased Citizen Co-Production of Services*

Bridgewater and Wayland both completely eliminated the provision of waste collection services at government expense. It was left to citizens to either hire a private contractor or bring their own refuse to the town dump.

BRIDGEWATER: For several years prior to the introduction of Proposition 2 1/2, this town had a contract with a private firm for curbside collection of refuse. However, just prior to the implementation of Proposition 2 1/2, a dispute developed between the contractor and the town over the price for those services. The contractor demanded that its $125,000 fee be increased by $113,000 in the middle of a contract. The town refused, in part because of widespread complaints with the quality of refuse collection services and the increasing pressures brought on by Proposition 2 1/2. (Service complaints included missed pickups, frequent breakdowns, etc.) Board of Health officials ruled that the contractor had violated the terms of the contract, and they secured the services of another private refuse collection firm to provide services through the end of FY81. When the lowest bid received from private firms for the provision of refuse collection services in FY82 came to $250,000, an aroused town meeting voted to terminate all municipally funded refuse collection services for the next year. Instead, the town contracted with a private landfill for the provision of a transfer station to be open to the public four days a week. It would then be up to the individual citizen to take his own trash to the transfer station for disposal. The cost of the transfer station, including disposal in the landfill, came to $61,000. There had been some concern by municipal officials that citizens would not take their refuse to the landfill but would instead dump it on local streets. To discourage such actions, members of the town's highway department have made an extra effort to track down litterers, including going through illegally dumped trash to identify the responsible individuals from mail and other items included with the trash. These persons have subsequently been taken to court. The highway department does, however, feel that there has been more littering along the route to the landfill since the town discontinued curbside pickups.

WAYLAND: Town officials decided to discontinue provision of garbage collection, a service that had been provided by the municipal Board of Health. At the time that the garbage collection service was discontinued, it was reportedly utilized by only a small number of citizens. The decision to discontinue was ratified by the public at the town meeting.

An ordinance has been proposed in one site that would put increased burdens on property owners for making sidewalk repairs.

CAMBRIDGE: This city has recommended that property owners undertaking extensive renovation or construction efforts be required to repair, replace, or construct new sidewalks in conjunction with those renovations if the sidewalks are substandard. (In the past, many buildings had been reconstructed while leaving the sidewalks in poor condition for the city to repair or replace.)

*Reduction of the Demand for Service*

Among all the service areas, there has been only one reported instance in which a government agency has sought to reduce demand without correspondingly reducing need.

SPRINGFIELD: Landfill fees in this city have been raised to discourage use by private citizens and hence extend the life of the landfill. The city also reports adjusting the price charged for use of the landfill to help match the volume of rubbish brought to the landfill with the "spot market" demand for sludge.

TABLE 27.6

AREAS OF REPORTED REDUCTIONS IN PUBLIC WORKS SERVICES TO THE PUBLIC

| | Street and Sidewalk Maintenance | Snow Plowing and Removal | Street Sweeping | Refuse Collection* | Solid Waste Disposal Services | Water and Sewer Services | Traffic Control/ Engineering Services | Street Lighting** |
|---|---|---|---|---|---|---|---|---|
| Amesbury | | | | | | | | |
| Arlington | X | X | | | | | | X |
| Bridgewater | X | | X | X | | X | X | |
| Burlington | X | | | | | X | X | X |
| Cambridge | X | | X | | | | | |
| Chelsea | X | | X | | | | | |
| Everett | X | X | X | | | X | X | |
| Framingham | | | | | | | X | |
| Marshfield | X | X | | | X | | | |
| New Bedford | X | | X | X. | | | X | |
| Pittsfield | X | | X | X | | X | X | |
| Quincy | X | | | | | | | X |
| Salem | X | | | | | X | X | |
| Springfield | X | X | | X | | X | X | X |
| Watertown | X | X | | | | X | | X |
| Wayland | X | | | | X | | | |
| Worcester | | | | | | | X | |

* Note that two sites -- Bridgewater and Wayland -- eliminated all garbage and refuse collection services at government expense. Citizens must now either bring their own refuse to the town dump or purchase the services of a private collector. These examples are described under "Increased citizen Co-Production of Services."
** Some of these reductions were temporary.

**Table 27.7**
**Other Cost-Cutting Efforts Reported by Public Works Agencies**

|  | Vehicle Maintenance Reductions | Equipment Purchase/Replacement Reductions | Purchase of Materials Reductions | Capital Expenditures Reductions* |
|---|---|---|---|---|
| Amesbury |  |  |  |  |
| Arlington |  | × |  | × |
| Bridgewater |  | × | × | × |
| Burlington |  | × | × | × |
| Cambridge |  |  |  |  |
| Chelsea |  |  |  |  |
| Everett | × |  |  |  |
| Framingham |  | × |  | × |
| Marshfield |  | × | × | × |
| New Bedford |  | × |  |  |
| Pittsfield | × | × |  | × |
| Quincy |  |  |  | × |
| Salem |  |  |  | × |
| Springfield |  | × | × |  |
| Watertown | × | × |  |  |
| Wayland | × | × |  |  |
| Worcester | × | × | × | × |

* Most of these involved cutbacks in street resurfacing and street and sidewalk construction.

## OTHER AGENCIES

The previous five services were not alone in absorbing -- and responding to -- the fiscal pressures created by Proposition 2 1/2. Other municipal agencies -- Finance, Buildings, Personnel, Social Services, etc. -- also frequently sustained cuts or made changes to help offset revenue losses arising from Proposition 2 1/2. Responses were also formulated by the city manager's, mayor's, or selectmen's office. The responses generated at these levels tended to be broader in scope, affecting all or most municipal services. Examples included changes in tax policies (e.g. re-valuation), modifications of labor agreements and employee benefits, and implementation of broadbased studies of ways to improve government management.

In this section, we describe some of the ways in which these other agencies and levels of government responded to Proposition 2 1/2. This is not a comprehensive accounting of such responses--no systematic effort was made to identify initiatives in these areas. However, the examples which were encountered help to round out the picture of municipal reactions to Proposition 2 1/2. Some, as noted above, involve approaches not addressed in prior sections.

### Cost-Cutting/Reduced Service Levels

*Reduction of Services to the Public*

The following examples illustrate the service reductions made in other local government services.

WAYLAND: Use of municipal buildings for public meetings has been restricted to two evenings per week in an effort to hold down costs.

CHELSEA: Staff losses by the assessors office have meant the elimination of property research services for citizens (persons needing such information must now do the research themselves). The cutbacks have also reportedly jeopardized the agency's ability to update and maintain the property re-assessments due to be completed in FY82.

SPRINGFIELD: Sharp reductions were made in water department staff, resulting in delays for water line repairs and slower delivery of other water supply services.

SALEM: In determining budget priorities, government officials cut back a variety of "non-essential" areas. City funding for the following programs and agencies was eliminated: the Christmas decoration program, parade events, concerts, the Cultural Arts Commission, the Fireman's Memorial, the Heritage Day celebration, the Historic Commission, the Human Rights Commission, the Tourist Commission, the Waterways Commission, and Weights and Measures. Cuts in city funding for the Council on Aging forced a reduction in recreational activities for seniors. And staff losses in the assessor's office have meant slowdowns in the city's re-assessment schedule and potential revenue losses.

QUINCY: Because it shifted the funding of elderly services to federal Community Development Block Grant (CDBG) funds, this community has had to reduce the scope of the services provided. CDBG funds are restricted both as to the neighborhoods in which they can be used and the services that can be provided with them. This has meant cutbacks in the neighborhoods where elderly services are provided and greater emphasis on satisfaction of immediate needs—food, medical care, and transportation. Secondary services such as recreation have been eliminated.

Quincy officials noted that cutbacks have often been especially serious for those departments without large constituencies. As an example, they pointed to the elimination of the city's Rent Grievance Board in the wake of Proposition 2 1/2.

*Reductions in Internal (Administrative/Support) Services*

Several sites reported reductions in internal services, ranging from building maintenance to electronic data processing.

ARLINGTON: As a cost-cutting measure, Arlington terminated its contract with a private firm for cleaning municipal buildings. Instead, the responsibilities of two municipal custodians were expanded to include the maintenance of four more buildings. While there may be a net reduction in building maintenance services because staff are spread more thinly, government officials feel that the quality of service has improved with the substitution of municipal personnel.

PITTSFIELD: This city reports reductions in roof replacement and other repairs of municipal buildings.

BRIDGEWATER: To reduce costs, this government delayed a planned computer needs study aimed at improving its electronic data processing capabilities.

*Reductions or Delays in Expenditures*

Several governments reported jurisdiction-wide efforts to reduce expenditures on personnel, equipment, and capital investment.

*Wages, Salaries and Benefits.* Staff reductions were not the only way in which governments tried to cut back personnel expenditures.

AMESBURY: As a cost-cutting measure, this government attempted to delay for several months the implementation of a wage increase scheduled to take effect at the same time as Proposition 2 1/2. After 15 nurses in the town's hospital quit in protest over the postponement, a special town meeting granted hospital employees an increase. Contract negotiations for other municipal employees were finally completed in October, 1981; they incorporated substantial wage increases funded from additional state aid.

ARLINGTON: Less money was appropriated for pay increases in the first year of Proposition 2 1/2. Arlington officials also report plans for future reductions of employee benefits.

SPRINGFIELD: Cost savings have been realized by delaying the filling of vacant positions. Tighter controls over sick leave usage, worker's compensation, and longevity bonuses have also been reported as a cost saving measure. And city officials have been seeking to negotiate productivity agreements with municipal employee unions that would include givebacks of certain rights and benefits.

Despite these and other citywide efforts to control personnel expenditures, many of the 17 sites had to absorb the costs of substantial pay increases in connection with contracts negotiated with public employees.

*Equipment Purchases and Replacement.* Many agencies in the 17 sites reported efforts to reduce or eliminate expenditures on new equipment. For instance, Arlington and New Bedford reported a government-wide emphasis, emerging from top-level officials, on deferring or eliminating equipment purchases wherever possible.

*Capital Expenditures.* The following two sites illustrate the high-level efforts that were made to curtail capital spending in the wake of Proposition 2 1/2.

BRIDGEWATER: Implementation of Bridgewater's long-range capital plan was delayed.

ARLINGTON: Town officials report the temporary elimination of capital improvements for municipal buildings and delays in other major capital expenditures after Proposition 2 1/2.

## Improvement of Productivity and Management

A number of other productivity improvement efforts were reported by the 17 sites at the agency and citywide levels. The examples encompass nearly every type of productivity improvement strategy, with the exception of employee incentives and the provision of additional training.

*Working Harder*

Two governments reported additional instances of increased burdens for municipal employees.

BRIDGEWATER: With the loss of this town's public health nurse, the latter's duties have been shared by the Board of Health agent and his secretary.

MARSHFIELD: Government officials report the consolidation and re-alignment of jobs at the town hall. Examples include the elimination of a mail room clerk (departments now handle their own mail) and the re-organization of switchboard responsibilities.

*Introduction of New or Additional Technology*

Several governments reported citywide efforts to increase the use of computers and conserve energy. (The role of Proposition 2 1/2 in these programs is, however, uncertain.)

QUINCY: Legislation has been introduced to establish a data processing department for the entire city as part of a general effort by the city to make greater use of computers.

WORCESTER: This city is working with the Honeywell Corporation to develop a new management information system.

WATERTOWN: Town officials are reviewing a proposal to automate tax billings.

PITTSFIELD: This city reports increased use of computers in several agencies -- including the offices of the tax collector, retirement board, city tax assessor, and city treasurer -- to help maintain service levels with fewer employees. Several projects to winterize municipal buildings have also been undertaken to save dollars and energy.

FRAMINGHAM: To reduce energy costs, this town dropped ceilings from 14 feet to 10 feet and upgraded valves and controls on radiators in municipal buildings.

*Improvement of Operational Procedures*

A number of operational improvements were reported.

ARLINGTON: Government officials report that Proposition 2 1/2 forced them to take a "good hard look at operations." The result has been the introduction of several operating and organizational improvements (some involved the implementation of earlier recommendations by consultants). Examples included efforts to improve the efficiency of mail-room, personnel, and municipal business operations, and the use of "floating" custodial crews for the town's schools (a change necessitated by the elimination of 12 custodial positions).

FRAMINGHAM: To reduce energy costs, evening meetings are now held in only one section of the town hall. A secretarial pool has been set up in the selectmen's office as a way to improve staff utilization.

SALEM: This city's electric division reports greater prioritization of inspections. Highest priority is given to inspections of buildings still under construction.

SPRINGFIELD: The personnel department in this city has begun to monitor worker's compensation claims more closely. Responsibility for the intensified oversight effort will ultimately be decentralized and delegated to the various departments.

## Alteration of Organizational Structures

Many of the governments reported organizational changes that coincided with the introduction of Proposition 2 1/2. Often, these had been planned or begun before the introduction of 2 1/2. But while the role of Proposition 2 1/2 in connection with these organizational changes is somewhat uncertain, 2 1/2 probably put further pressure on governments to initiate or speed up these organizational re-alignments.

ARLINGTON: Building, plumbing, and code enforcement inspections were consolidated after the introduction of Proposition 2 1/2. Electronic data processing facilities for the school system and the municipal government were also combined. The police and fire departments are moving into a single administration building, and the town is considering consolidation of the two agencies.

SALEM: The Council on Aging, the Department of Health, Veterans Services, and the Human Rights Commission were consolidated into a single department. City officials report a saving of $150,000 per year, largely from the sharing of clerical and secretarial support staff.

QUINCY: City officials report the consolidation of some departments. For instance, the Council on Aging and the Youth Commision have been subsumed under the city's Planning Department.

MARSHFIELD: Town officials report a number of efforts to reorganize staff and management positions subsequent to Proposition 2 1/2. For instance, the positions of treasurer and tax collector were combined, and two divisions of the department of public works were consolidated (the department's union contract had to be re-opened in order to implement the latter change).

WAYLAND: This town is considering the consolidation of its police and fire departments into a single public safety agency (a joint communications center serving the two departments has already been established). There are also plans for establishing a department of public works by consolidating highways with parks and recreation. None of these changes, however, was a direct result of Proposition 2 1/2.

AMESBURY: This town moved to a town manager form of government during the first year of Proposition 2 1/2. Although the role of 2 1/2 in stimulating the change is unclear, the changeover was formally adopted in April, 1981--three months before Proposition 2 1/2 took effect. The new town manager has implemented several reorganizations and consolidations. Examples include the establishment of a central purchasing agency and the assumption of responsibility for school and grounds maintenance by the municipal government.

WATERTOWN: This town also converted to a town manager form of government as Proposition 2 1/2 took effect. The necessary revisions to the town charter were adopted in July, 1981--the first month under Proposition 2 1/2. Government officials report plans for future reorganizations, including the possible consolidation of the police and fire departments and substitution of civilians for uniformed dispatchers.

FRAMINGHAM: Town officials report that Proposition 2 1/2 has been pushing this government from a highly decentralized organization to a more "streamlined and better coordinated" arrangement. But while some consideration has been given to consolidating certain departments, no organizational changes have been approved as yet.

*Miscellaneous Productivity Improvement Efforts*

Three other general strategies for improving productivity were reported by the various sites: productivity bargaining, improved financial management, and comprehensive management studies.

*Productivity Bargaining.*

SPRINGFIELD: This city is seeking to negotiate productivity agreements with municipal employee unions. These agreements would reportedly incorporate selective givebacks of rights and benefits, including a waiver of seniority rights. This effort is being coupled with tighter controls on sick leave usage and on the awarding of longevity bonuses.

*Improved Financial Management.*

ARLINGTON: Zero base budgeting has been used as a way to come up with the budget cuts necessitated by Proposition 2 1/2.

CAMBRIDGE: This city plans to start recovering full indirect (e.g. administrative) costs in connection with federal grants.

WATERTOWN: This town introduced its first capital improvement program during the initial year of 2 1/2.

WORCESTER: A new financial management system went into effect in this city in January, 1982. The system included cash management to maximize investment returns, increased computer followup of outstanding receivables, and procedures to shorten the turn-around time for billing the federal or state government. The city is investigating the costs and benefits of contracting out for services.

SPRINGFIELD: This city has also made a major effort to improve cash management. The city is now investing its funds in short-term, interest-bearing accounts. A Cash Management Committee has been established, and it is reported to have identified up to $2 million worth of savings. And $5.7 million worth of savings are reported to have come from greater frugality, more intensive pursuit of delinquent taxes, and careful monitoring of department expenditures.

*General Management Improvement Studies.*

ARLINGTON: A Government Reorganization Committee has been formed, and a task force has been established to investigate possible management improvements and reorganizations in areas such as electronic data processing and police and fire services. In addition, an external group is studying library operations. The town also contracted with a private management consulting firm for a study of alternatives for responding to Proposition 2 1/2.

CHELSEA: A management consulting firm was hired by city officials to help them respond to Proposition 2 1/2. The firm assisted in drawing up budget priorities, determining where cuts could be made, revising the city's fee structure, reviewing unpaid taxes and abatements, and analyzing service delivery.

PITTSFIELD: City officials have hired a management consulting firm to undertake a general review of city departments.

SPRINGFIELD: This city also has had a management consulting firm review possible management improvements. The study was completed in July 1981, the first month of Proposition 2 1/2. A number of changes in management methods were recommended, including better ways to invest municipal revenues. These recommendations were reportedly implemented.

## Acquisition of Additional Revenues/Financial Assistance

Efforts to obtain additional financial resources represented one of the major responses from a citywide perspective in the 17 sites. A great variety of efforts were reported.

*Introduction or Increasing of Fees and Charges*

Nearly all of the sites reported widespread efforts to increase fees and charges. In some cases, these were said to have made significant contributions to municipal revenues (Springfield was reported to cover 9 percent of its costs from user charges). Other governments -- such as Everett -- viewed fees and charges as a relatively minor source of revenue.

ARLINGTON: Government officials reported giving careful consideration to the pros and cons of instituting or increasing municipal fees and charges. They note that because fees for service cannot be deducted from federal income taxes, it is often cheaper for citizens to pay for a service through taxes rather than a fee. The town has, however, established new rates for numerous services.

BRIDGEWATER: Since the state no longer provides free flu vaccine for senior citizens, Bridgewater has begun to charge seniors for flu shots. The visiting nurse service has also instituted a $3.00 fee for TB tests (although the town expects to pay this fee for seniors in future years).

BURLINGTON: Ambulance fees were raised from $25 to $100 for FY82, and the fee for a building permit was increased.

CAMBRIDGE: This city reports widespread increases in license fees.

CHELSEA: Implementation of Proposition 2 1/2 led this city to adjust its fees and user charges for the first time in over a decade, resulting in an additional $500,000 in municipal revenues. The increases included water and sewer rates, fines, and license fees.

FRAMINGHAM: A minimum of $5.00 is now charged for any license. Liquor license fees were raised from $1,000 to $1,500, and town clerk fees were increased.

MARSHFIELD: The Board of Selectmen requested that each department provide it with a schedule of all existing fees and charges. Widespread revisions were subsequently made in the town's fee schedule.

NEW BEDFORD: City officials raised all fees and charges that could be increased without authorization by the city council, including fees for parking, inspections, ambulance services, and zoning appeals (the latter went from $100 to $1,000). The city explored the possibility of greatly increasing oil storage fees (a charge imposed for the inspection of oil tanks). However, the large increase contemplated did not prove to be feasible.

QUINCY: In the wake of Proposition 2 1/2, this city reports greater reliance on fees and charges for service. The mayor asked the city council to review all fee schedules, and widespread increases were implemented. The city reports earning an additional $44,000 per year from increases in license fees. Other fee hikes included an 11 percent increase in city hospital charges and a 12.5 percent increase in water rates.

SALEM: Proposition 2 1/2 was reportedly responsible for speeding up increases in marriage license fees, fees for city permits, and other charges. Fees were introduced for subdivision permits, wetlands permits, and zoning hearings. (The latter fees now finance all operations of the Zoning Board of Appeals.)

WATERTOWN: Fees were instituted or increased for ambulance services and liquor licenses. Town clerk fees and commercial refuse collection fees were also raised.

WAYLAND: Increases in town clerk fees were reported to have brought in an additional $4,000, while increases in other charges (exclusive of fee-supported programs) added another $10,000 to municipal revenues. Town officials report that these were the first general increases in municipal fees since 1959.

WORCESTER: Prior to the implementation of Proposition 2 1/2, Worcester's city manager sent a memo to all department heads requesting that they review fees and charges and increase or initiate fees where appropriate. A wide variety of suggestions was received, including the initiation or increasing of airport landing fees, charges for copies of tax maps, electrical and code inspection fees, fees for building permits and related licenses, health permits, cemetery fees, and vocational school tuition. Many of these suggestions were followed up. However, in several cases, the service in question was under the jurisdiction of an independent board or commission, limiting the city's flexibility to increase fees and charges.

SPRINGFIELD: A subcommittee of the city council was established to look into the use of fees and charges. Wherever possible, efforts were made to replace cuts in the general fund with increased fee revenue. A wide variety of license and other fees were increased during the first year of Proposition 2 1/2. City officials report that user charges now cover as much as 9 percent of municipal costs.

EVERETT: While this city also increased fees and charges, the changes were reportedly small. City officials felt that fees and charges were relatively unimportant as a source of city revenue.

Another site reported that major increases in fees and charges were planned for FY83, the second year of Proposition 2 1/2.

PITTSFIELD: This city expects to introduce sewer usage and ambulance charges in FY83. Widespread increases in fees and fines are also contemplated.

*Introduction or Increasing of Taxes*

Probably the most common response to Proposition 2 1/2 at the citywide level was to re-assess private property at 100 percent of full and fair value. Most of the sites completed or initiated such re-valuations. By bringing property tax assessments up-to-date, many governments significantly increased their tax base, allowing them to greatly limit or even avoid revenue losses under Proposition 2 1/2.

In two of the seventeen sites, voters approved overrides of some of the provisions of Proposition 2 1/2.

WAYLAND: Citizens voted to override a stipulation of Proposition 2 1/2 that limited growth in the town's property tax levy to 2 1/2 percent per year. For FY83, the tax levy was allowed to grow by 5 percent. Citizens also voted to exclude future municipal debt (and the associated interest) from the cap on property tax levies.

CAMBRIDGE: By the required 2/3 majority, voters approved an override of all of the second year tax levy reductions required under Proposition 2 1/2. Cambridge was the only government in the state to pass such an override. The primary force behind its passage was reported to be the parents of public school children. (It should also be noted that Cambridge originally rejected Proposition 2 1/2 by a vote of almost 2 to 1, the widest margin against the Proposition of any city in the state.)

Several other efforts to increase revenues through the collection of additional taxes were reported.

SPRINGFIELD: As noted previously, this city intensified its pursuit of delinquent taxes as part of its overall cash management program. City officials report that the effort has netted an additional $3 million.

CAMBRIDGE: City officials have decided to pursue a back taxes suit against the Boston and Maine Railroad, rather than settling out of court. They believe that the effort and risk involved in pursuing the suit are outweighed by the likelihood of a higher return.

EVERETT: In the wake of serious losses of revenue under Proposition 2 1/2, city officials have begun to press the General Electric Company and the U.S. Air Force to make payments in lieu of taxes for a plant located in Everett that GE operates for the Air Force.

*State Aid*

One of the most important factors in alleviating the effects of Proposition 2 1/2 was the distribution of additional aid to local governments by the State of Massachusetts. As noted in the first section, the $248 million in additional state aid was critical to the ability of many sites to limit budget reductions and pay wage increases during the first year of 2 1/2. For some sites, the extra state aid was enough to offset virtually all of the revenue lost under Proposition 2 1/2. For instance, the extra state aid received by Chelsea covered all but $11,000 of that city's first-year revenue losses under Proposition 2 1/2 (state aid accounted for 1/3 of Chelsea's budget in FY81, one of the highest such proportions in the state). Other governments--for instance, Everett--were less successful in receiving additional state aid and consequently were forced to undertake large-scale layoffs and other cutbacks in major services.

*Other Fundraising Efforts*

No general citywide efforts to solicit additional funds and contributions from the private sector were reported by any of the 17 sites. However, Arlington has made an effort to seek third-party support for some of its services:

ARLINGTON: This town is trying to secure third-party payments (e.g. from insurance companies) whenever possible. For instance, third-party payments are being used to help underwrite the expenses of the Youth Center. The Center actively pursues reimbursements from private health insurance companies for psychological counseling and other treatments provided to youths who are covered for such services under existing family health insurance policies. The town has introduced legislation in the State Legislature that would allow it to collect from Blue Cross and Blue Shield for similar youth counseling services (currently state law prohibits such payments). Third-party payments (from automobile insurance policies) are also being used to pay for tree replacement and traffic signal repairs (as described elsewhere in this chapter).

Two sites reported other potentially interesting fundraising ideas.

WATERTOWN: This government developed a lease agreement for renting unused municipal space. The town has also sold the Watertown Arsenal property to developers (it took over the arsenal from the U.S. government 19 years ago). Municipal officials estimate that the town will earn $1 million per year in taxes after development of the old arsenal property.

SPRINGFIELD: Members of this city's Chamber of Commerce have urged city officials to see themselves as entrepreneurs and to invest public revenues in private development projects. Although some municipal officials have expressed interest in the idea, no efforts to follow it up have been reported.

*Establishment of Revolving Funds*

As noted in earlier sections, the 17 sites have shown considerable interest in moving, where possible, from property taxes to user fees and charges as the basis for supporting municipal services. This movement has often been facilitated by the establishment of revolving funds or enterprise accounts.

QUINCY: Increasingly, city officials are establishing revolving funds for self-supporting services. These actions are linked to widespread increases in municipal fees and charges. (In anticipation of Proposition 2 1/2, revolving funds were established for the city's hospitals and junior college, with the stipulation that these organizations be self-supporting.)

SALEM: This city's hospital and Off-Street Parking Commission were already financed through revolving funds going into Proposition 2 1/2. The city is now considering the establishment of a revolving fund for its Harbor Commission.

Arlington has joined other local governments in supporting legislation designed to modify state laws that restrict the use of enterprise funds. Of particular interest is the elimination or relaxation of rules that limit the size of an enterprise fund to $5,000 and that prohibit a government from carrying over such funds from one year to the next. (At present, any surpluses at the end of a fiscal year revert to the general fund.)

*Transfers of Charges to Other Funds or Agencies*

Two sites reported that funding for some services has been transfered to non-traditional (e.g., federal) sources.

QUINCY: As noted previously, elderly and youth services are now funded primarily from federal Community Development Block Grants rather than city sources.

ARLINGTON: This town's Planning and Community Development Department sustained a 25 percent cut. Salaries for department staff are now paid from federal Community Development Block Grant funds.

Under pressure from Proposition 2 1/2, some governments have been requiring that departments with their own revenue sources do more to carry their share of the financial burden. Cambridge is illustrative:

CAMBRIDGE: This city's hospital and water departments (both of which have their own revenue sources) are being required to pay for other city services. For instance, the city now bills the water department for holes in the street that result from water projects, and the city bills the hospital for printing services.

## Increased Reliance on/Assistance from Other Public Agencies

Few additional examples were reported of increased intra- or inter-governmental assistance. The following cases illustrate the two major types of mutual assistance: increased intra-agency assistance (Amesbury) and increased inter-governmental assistance (Cambridge, Salem, and Marshfield).

AMESBURY: Responsibility for maintaining public schools and school grounds has been transferred from the school system to the town government.

CAMBRIDGE: City officials report that they are discussing collective purchasing arrangements with other cities and towns in the area. No final agreements, however, have been reached.

SALEM: A joint purchasing agreement has been worked out with the nearby town of Beverly. This agreement, which covers equipment purchases, has reportedly resulted in better prices. Municipal officials have also begun to explore opportunities for sharing services with other towns on a regional basis.

MARSHFIELD: Government officials are investigating the possibility of establishing a joint purchasing agreement and sharing common services with the neighboring town of Duxbury.

## Increased Reliance on/Assistance from Private Sector for Service Delivery

*Contracting Out of Services*

Widespread interest was expressed by the 17 sites in incresed contracting out of services. However, few examples of contracts (beyond those described in contracting efforts were noted, they were not always clearly related to Proposition 2 1/2.

QUINCY: City officials reported greatly increased use of outside contracting.

SPRINGFIELD: The assessor's department eliminated four clerical positions while significantly increasing the amount of work contracted out.

WAYLAND: This town transfered 4-1/2 nursing positions from the Board of Health to a local non-profit health center. The town now purchases all its public health nursing services from the center. (Municipal officials note, however, that the primary reason for the transfer was to solve some problems associated with certifying the nurses, rather than to save money. Some cost savings are expected, however, over the long run.)

WATERTOWN: City officials reportedly have contracted or are considering contracting for numerous services. They note, however, that in some cases the changeover from municipal provision of the service has been motivated by a desire to improve on the low quality of municipally provided services rather than to reduce costs.

WORCESTER: City officials have begun to investigate the costs and benefits of contracting out more municipal services.

Note, however, that Arlington decided to eliminate a private contract for the cleaning of public buildings in favor of using municipal custodians.

*Encouragement of Private Delivery of Services*

One city reported some initial efforts to work more closely with the private sector regarding service delivery.

SALEM: City officials are looking to the private sector to provide some of the "extras" that the city no longer pays for. Thus a new merchant's association is considering sponsoring certain promotional and celebratory activities in Salem, and the Chamber of Commerce notes that the provision of certain services may be required in future agreements with developers of business sites. (Merchants in one waterfront area already provide their own security.)

*Solicitation/Receipt of Free Assistance from the Private Sector*

Only one site reported receiving free "in-kind" assistance (as contrasted to financial aid) from the private sector after Proposition 2 1/2.

QUINCY: The Quincy Chamber of Commerce offered help from private enterprise in improving the efficiency of city government. The result has been an examination of the city's personnel department, retirement board, and treasurer's office with the help of expertise provided free from the private sector.

Note also that the city of Springfield has received free assistance from private business executives (see below). However, these people were acting as private individuals; their assistance did not represent a corporate decision to provide help.

## Increased Reliance on/Assistance from Individual Citizens For Service Delivery

### Increased Use of Volunteers

Two governments reported innovative top-level efforts to encourage the use of volunteers.

SPRINGFIELD: This city has made a number of efforts to secure the advice of private citizens on budgetary matters. A Citizen's Budget Committee was established to review department budgets and study user fees. High level officials from the Massachusetts Mutual Life Insurance Company, Monsanto, and the Chamber of Commerce have also provided advice on budgetary matters. And the city has established a Cash Management Committee consisting of both private and public sector members and staffed by the auditor of Massachusetts Mutual Life.

ARLINGTON: This town is endeavoring to establish a coordinated volunteer program designed to centralize its intake of volunteers. Government officials note, however, that the volunteers will not replace municipal workers.

## FINDINGS AND CONCLUSIONS

1. In general, the initial efforts by agencies in the 17 sites to cope with the budgetary cutbacks induced by Proposition 2 1/2 exhibited relatively little innovation. By far the greatest number of responses involved straight-forward cost-cutting and reductions in service levels without compensatory efforts. This type of reaction is perhaps to be expected in the first year of a change such as Proposition 2 1/2. The natural reaction is to cut first and seek new resources or new service delivery arrangements later. The continuing uncertainties associated with the size of the budget reductions that would be necessary probably also discouraged efforts to make major changes or innovations in service delivery arrangements during the first year of Proposition 2 1/2. Thus, a number of agencies counted on receiving at least some supplementary state aid to reduce or eliminate the need for major budgetary cutbacks. It is to be expected that agencies will hesitate to embark upon groundbreaking innovations in service delivery arrangements while budget levels, budget-making procedures, and the need for further cutbacks remain uncertain.

2. Nevertheless, various agencies went beyond simple cost cutting and reduction of service levels in responding to Proposition 2 1/2. The second most common response to 2 1/2 by both police and fire departments was to try to improve productivity. For the other three services—libraries, parks and recreation, and public works—the acquisition of additional revenues and financial assistance tended to be the second most popular strategy for coping with 2 1/2.

Even greater diversity was exhibited among the third and fourth most popular responses. In the case of police and fire, the responses were so diverse as to prevent any one from standing out as the third (or fourth) most popular. Libraries and public works departments tended to emphasize productivity improvement as their third most likely response to Proposition 2 1/2. In contrast, the third most likely response for parks and recreation departments was incresed use of the private sector. While a fourth most popular response could not be distinguished for library services, for parks and recreation the fourth most popular response was greater use of volunteers. For public works, greater use of the private sector ranked fourth.

3. Several factors served to cushion the impact of Proposition 2 1/2 at the agency level. These tended to differ by agency and by local government. The following moderating influences were identified:

- Pre-Proposition 2 1/2 efforts to improve efficiency and reduce expenditures often affected the magnitude of the impact of Proposition 2 1/2 on agency budgets. Some governments and some agencies, acting under the influence of the state's four percent cap on annual spending increases and other directives, implemented major staff reductions and other efficiencies in the years prior to Proposition 2 1/2. Such actions reduced agency budgets even before Proposition 2 1/2, sometimes apparently facilitating the achievement of the reductions required under 2 1/2, sometimes making additional cuts even more painful. (For instance, the director of one agency felt that he had been unjustly penalized for prior management improvements when asked to absorb the same or larger cutbacks in the wake of Proposition 2 1/2 as other municipal agencies.)

● Federal revenue sharing funds and the provision of additional state aid reduced the impacts of Proposition 2 1/2 for some agencies. Most such aid apparently was channelled towards maintaining police and fire services. In governments receiving little state aid (such as Everett), the latter services experienced major budget reductions.

● In some cases (e.g. libraries and parks and recreation), extensive pre-Proposition 2 1/2 utilization of volunteers appeared to help mitigate the effects of the cutbacks.

● A few municipal library departments were protected to some extent by the existence of substantial endowment funds that helped them maintain purchases and other aspects of service delivery.

4. On the other hand, some circumstances have tended to exacerbate the effects of Proposition 2 1/2. Federal reductions in CETA and other programs, cutbacks and restrictions associated with certain types of state aid (e.g. for libraries and highways), and regulations imposed by state agencies (e.g. on allowable reductions in street lighting) have contributed to greater fiscal stress and, in some cases, limited a government's flexibility in responding to 2 1/2.

A special problem arose in the maintenance of parks and recreation facilities. Even as park maintenance services were being cut back, prior efforts to build and rehabilitate parks and recreation facilities (often with state and federal funds) proceeded oblivious to the costs they would be imposing on park maintenance in the future. This is putting added strain on efforts by park and recreation departments to cut back expenses.

Contracts with municipal employee unions have also sometimes added to the burden of 2 1/2. Many governments had to absorb large contractually-mandated wage increases along with the cuts occasioned by Proposition 2 1/2, and officials of several jurisdictions reported being hampered by labor agreements in consolidating jobs, delaying step increases, and similar responses. (On the other hand, unions in a few sites responded to Proposition 2 1/2 by reopening contracts to permit these and other changes designed to improve productivity and save jobs.)

5. If nothing else, Proposition 2 1/2 tended to make some agencies more conscious of where personnel and services were charged. Indeed, the pressures of Proposition 2 1/2 may in some cases have distorted accounting practices by encouraging agencies to charge services to those accounts that were in the best financial shape (e.g., revolving funds, emergency snow and ice accounts, etc.) Such "creative accounting" appeared to be especially prominent among public works agencies, for which there existed a number of alternate accounts and revolving funds.

6. Several agencies reported increased use of revolving or enterprise funds for activities that had their own revenue sources (e.g., fees from self-supporting recreation programs, traffic and parking fines, sewer usage levies). These funds were usually expected to pay for services provided to them by other agencies, for instance utilities, printing services, inspections of water utility cuts by street maintenance staff, etc. In one case, an entire maintenance crew was transferred from a hard-pressed public works department to a financially self-sufficient traffic and parking agency that had its own revolving fund.

The net effect of such funds is not clear. They have the advantage of keeping expenditures for those activities out of the agency's budget. They are also potential sources of cash for covering other department activities and of seed money for introducing new programs and stimulating change. Over the long run, these funds are likely to make the managers of the relevant activities more cost conscious since they are billed for all the costs that they incur. And having such funds is also likely to partly insulate the activity in question from budgetary and political pressures, making it easier to raise future fees and charges to cover the full costs incurred.

It is not clear, however, whether the use of revolving or enterprise funds in any way reduced expenditures or increased total government revenues, at least over the short run. And a potential drawback associated with the use of revolving or enterprise funds is that they limit the flexibility of public officials; the associated revenues are dedicated to one specific purposes or agency and are not readily available for supporting other activities.

7. Although many agencies raised fees and charges in the wake of Proposition 2 1/2, there were a number of important dissenters who questioned the overall value and equitability of such a strategy. For instance, it is often cheaper for the taxpayer to pay for a given public service through local taxes (which can be deducted from federal income taxes) than to pay for them through fees and charges. Recreation departments in several jurisdictions did not raise some user fees because of the potentially harmful effect of such fees on the poor. Other recreation departments made an effort to hold down fees for youth programs while greatly increasing them for adult activities. The fore-going considerations raise major equity questions which have not as yet been adequately addressed. Given the greatly increased utilization of fees and user charges by local government agencies in the wake of fiscal cutbacks such as Proposition 2 1/2, careful study of the equity issues associated with government fees and charges--and how to handle them--should have high priority.

8. All six sites that contracted for waste collection prior to Proposition 2 1/2 experienced increased costs during this first year under 2 1/2. (In the case of Bridgewater, the increase was viewed by the townspeople as so exhorbitant that they voted to discontinue all municipally-funded refuse collection.) On the other hand, most sites where waste collection was provided by municipal employees reduced waste collection costs in FY82. The contracting sites were apparently less able to reduce collection costs because of multi-year contracts

and/or the difficulties of getting private firms to reduce prices, especially during inflationary periods. This placed greater burden on other public works services to absorb the cutbacks needed.

9. The initial responses by agencies in the 17 sites to Proposition 2 1/2 indicated that central coordination of agency responses is likely to be desirable. We saw little evidence of such coordination. A number of examples occurred in which the reaction of one agency to Proposition 2 1/2 affected (1) other agencies in the same government, or (2) other local governments.

(1) Interactions between agencies. In several casses, the decisions taken by one agency in response to Proposition 2 1/2 have increased or decreased the workload of other agencies. Examples of reductions included reduced need for park maintenance and after school recreation programs in the wake of school closings, and reductions in the need for public works to service lighting fixtures as night lighting of parks was reduced. Examples of increases include unilateral decisions by park departments to reduce or eliminate park security forces (placing greater burden on police patrols), reductions in organized recreation programs and supervised parks and playgrounds (potentially leading to increased vandalism and youth crime with a corresponding strain on police services), cutbacks in the maintenance of park facilities (potentially giving rise to grass fires and related demands on fire services), reductions in the public school custodial forces (sometimes making it necessary for park and recreation departments to maintain school grounds and to pay custodial costs for the use of school facilities in connection with after-hour recreation programs), and efforts by one police department to increase the number of traffic lights as a way to help reduce the need for traffic control officers (thus increasing the workload of the city's signal maintenance division).

(2) Effects on agencies in other local governments. The director of the public library system at one site felt that his libraries were experiencing greater usage by out-of-town residents in the wake of cutbacks in library hours in the surrounding towns.

While the above interactions are not especially common or serious, they suggest that greater central oversight and coordination between agencies and even between governments are warranted.

10. An issue that is just beginning to emerge is the extent to which budget and service reductions leave a government liable for damages when citizens--or employees--are harmed because of the rollback in service levels. For instance, Pittsfield's Director of Public Works noted that although the city forester still certified trees in need of removal, there is no money for removing those trees. The question posed by city officials--if a tree listed for removal should cause damage or injuries, would not the city be liable (since it had already committed itself to the dangerous condition of the tree)? Similar issues have arisen in connection with citizens--or firefighters--who suffer

injuries or other losses in fires after cutbacks in fire stations, fire companies, and manning levels because of Proposition 2 1/2.

11. Proposition 2 1/2 has had a number of impacts on local government staff which may have important long-run implications for productivity improvement. Officials in many of the agencies we examined reported that staff morale was very low. Decreased morale, coupled with the frequent need to assume additional responsibilities and -- in effect -- work harder for the same pay, are likely to result in increased accidents, turnover, and absenteeism over the long run. Government and union officials in several municipalities expressed fears that increasing numbers of employees would suffer from occupational "burnout." All of these may have a counterproductive effect on agency productivity. Thus, even while agencies are experiencing fiscal and staff cutbacks, there appears to be a need for some type of incentive -- monetary or otherwise -- to help maintain employee morale and productivity in the face of these changes. (Yet in Springfield, a productivity incentive for public works employees had to be dropped when budget cuts induced by Proposition 2 1/2 eliminated the vacant positions used to fund the program.)

Several other reported effects on agency staff may hamper productivity over the long run. These include:

● The loss of younger, more skilled, and more efficient employees through the application of seniority rules. This has reportedly created situations such as a tree division where the employees are too old to climb trees and a department with an 84 year old employee who cannot be retired. Several fire chiefs expressed concern that the rising average age of firefighters was contributing to increased injuries. In addition, the high losses of low-tenure minority workers reported by some departments may damage community relations over the long-run.

● Loss of management and supervisory staff. The effects of the loss of supervisory staff are difficult to assess at this point. Some agency directors (especially fire chiefs) caution that the remaining crews will be less effective without adequate supervision. On the other hand, it is not clear at this time whether the loss of management staff was out of proportion to the loss of non-management personnel.

Taken together, the changes in local government staff wrought by Proposition 2 1/2 may make it more difficult for the agencies to improve productivity over the long run, unless some remedial actions are taken.

12. There were several other instances where responses to Proposition 2 1/2 have had a potentially harmful effect on long-term productivity improvement. This was especially evident in the case of police departments: a number of police chiefs reported that the budget austerity brought on by Proposition 2 1/2 had forced them to slow down or eliminate productivity improvement programs that had been introduced before 2 1/2. Other officials have reported that this austerity has stifled innovation and shut off the seed money necessary for stimulating change and renewal.

The need for cutting costs has sometimes meant the termination of other potentially productive efforts. Thus, the widely-reported slowdowns and terminations of maintenance and replacement programs for vehicles and other equipment may, in fact, represent a mortgaging of the future in order to realize short-term savings in the present. Other examples include the elimination of volunteers (because of high training costs) and the termination of several private contracts in favor of performing the work in-house.

However, agency officials in a few governments -- for instance, Springfield and Quincy -- have made an effort to retain programs that maintain or improve productivity in the face of other cutbacks. The differences in management motivations and rationales as regards the preservation vs. the elimination of productivity improvement programs during a time of fiscal stress need to be evaluated further.

13. Officials in several jurisdictions reported that public tolerance and expectations in the wake of Proposition 2 1/2 have adjusted to the reduced availability of government resources and programs. For example, public works officials in New Bedford noted that the change from twice-a-week to once-a-week refuse collection elicited few complaints. This they attributed to a lowering of expectations in connection with Proposition 2 1/2. Similar observations were made by library and parks and recreation directors in a number of sites. This may be an early indication that the public is willing to tolerate some reductions in service delivery in exchange for reduced taxes.

14. A major response to cutbacks, one that affected everyone from line employees to the mayor or city manager, was to be more selective in choosing which particular activities or programs to handle with the dwindling resources. Increased competition appears to be emerging in the wake of this need for selectivity -- between groups, between agencies, perhaps ultimately between jurisdictions. (Some initial signs of increased, explicit interdepartmental competition were reported by agency officials in several sites.)

Competition can be a creative or a destructive force. It is not yet clear how it will develop in the 17 governments examined here.

On the whole, first-year responses to Proposition 2 1/2 have tended to focus on cost cutting and reductions in service levels. It is, perhaps, natural for administrators to be reactive rather than pro-active during a period of fiscal retrenchment. The emphasis is more on cutting back -- and cutting one's losses -- than taking the initiative and planning for the future.

Yet it need not be so. The preceding pages testify to the fact that there are alternatives to mere cost cutting-strategies that can be used to help maintain services even as resources fall. These techniques -- productivity improvement, acquisition of additional financial assistance, and greater reliance on other public agencies, the private sector, and individual citizens for service delivery -- hold promise for alleviating the squeeze on services.

True, the effectiveness of many of these approaches has not yet been carefully evaluated. And the initial experiences of the governments in our sample have given some early indications that several of these strategies may be mixed blessings.

Despite such uncertainties, many agencies did not hesitate to experiment with alternate service delivery arrangements while cutting back expenditures. In the years ahead, the need for broadening agency responses beyond mere cost cutting, and for developing strategies for creatively *managing* -- rather than reacting to -- impending cutbacks, is likely to grow increasingly urgent. Coping need not -- and should not -- be synonymous with cutting!

## Notes for Chapter 27

The work that provided the basis for this publication was supported by funding under a grant from the U.S. Department of Housing and Urban Development, Office of Policy Development and Research. The substance and findings of that work are dedicated to the public. The author and publisher are solely responsible for the accuracy of the statements and interpretations contained in this publication. Such interpretations do not necessarily reflect the views of the Government, the Urban Institute, or its sponsors.

The authors gratefully acknowledge the assistance of Karl Kim, Larry Segel, Gary Barnes, John Gafni, Jeanette Grunwald, Andrew Laing, Patricia McCarney, Lisa Menelly, Elizabeth O'Donnell, Valerie Phillips, Saul Rubin, Phil Sabella, and Lora Silverman of the IMPACT: 2 1/2 Project.

Introduction

1. See, for instance, Harvey Garn, Michael J. Flax, Michael Springer, and Jeremy Taylor, "Models for Indicator Development," The Urban Institute (Wasington D.C., 1976), and Gordon P. Whitaker, "Co-Production: Citizen Participation in Service Delivery," *Public Administration Review* (May/June, 1980), pp. 240-246.

Police

1. Springfield, however, was an exception. Prior efficiencies plus federal revenue sharing funds made it possible for Springfield to add 29 positions to its police force in the first year of Proposition 2 1/2. It should be noted that the police union in Springfield opposed the increase in positions. Union officials believed that it was inappropriate to increase police staff levels at a time when other departments were experiencing major cuts, and the union indicated that it would not protect officers filling the new positions from layoffs in subsequent years.

2. However, as noted previously, New Bedford's police department is looking into the possibility of getting additional traffic control lights to reduce the need for police traffic control activities during rush hours. The addition of traffic lights would mean extra responsibilities for the city's signal maintenance division.

Fire

1. To avoid layoffs, firefighters in Chelsea reopened their contract and negotiated changes in overtime and minimum manning provisions in return for job security. The only staff reductions that occurred in Chelsea involved normal attrition.

Libraries

1. Note, however, that New Bedford's library had to initiate layoffs and reductions in branch hours prior to Proposition 2 1/2 in order to meet the level-funding requirement imposed on it under the 4 percent spending cap.

2. Quincy, however, closed four branch libraries a year before Proposition 2 1/2 took effect. The closings were made following a reduction in library appropriations after the 4 percent spending cap and -- to some extent -- in anticipation of 2 1/2.

Parks and Recreation

1. In this section, we have tried to distinguish between reductions in services to the public vs. reductions in internal services. Instead, we have grouped all cost cutting/reduced service level responses by whether they primarily involved parks or recreation services.

Public Works

1. In a fourteenth site -- Bridgewater (for which comparable appropriations data were not available) -- the public works director reported that public works had been cut proportionally more than any other service in the city.

2. Worcester reports that it is more dependent than ever upon the benefits accruing from an incentive system that was first established in 1979. At that time, the sanitation department introduced a system under which employees could leave work with a full day's pay when their assigned routes were completed. This innovation allowed the city to reduce the number of sanitation crews. The task system has also reportedly eliminated any temptation to work overtime.

Chapter 28

# The Pattern of Differential Impacts

Jerome Rothenberg and Paul Smoke

## Introduction

This study explores the early effects of Proposition 2 1/2 on a sample of 41 local governments in Massachusetts. Table 28.1 presents selected characteristics of the cities and towns included in the sample. This paper is divided into five sections. The first section explores how different types of communities have been differentially impacted by revenue cuts mandated by Proposition 2 1/2. The second section examines the pattern of appropriations cuts implemented by communities in the first year of Proposition 2 1/2. The third section discusses available evidence concerning revenue diversification in response to Proposition 2 1/2. The fourth section looks at the change in municipal bond ratings between 1980 and 1982. Finally, the fifth section attempts to synthesize the evidence presented.

## Revenue Losses

Total revenue losses for localities come from decreased yield of both the real property tax and the motor vehicle excise tax. Two essentially exogenous sources serve as offsets to these losses: statute-mandated revaluation of real property assessments and State aid given to local governments. The revenue loss (or gain) to which localities must adjust is that net of State aid and the change in revenues produced by revaluation. This paper examines the impact of all four of these ingredients on net total revenue losses. It is important to note that a failure to account for inflation suggests that the data discussed in this section understate the real revenue loss suffered by communities due to Proposition 2 1/2. The failure to account for revenue growth that would have occurred in the absence of the limit also biases the revenue loss figures downward. On the other hand, no attempt has been made to account for capitalization of lower property tax rates into property values. The effects of capitalization would tend to work in the opposite direction, suggesting that these revenue loss figures overstate the actual loss.

Table 28.2 summarizes the four ingredients related to revenue loss: real property tax cuts, motor vehicle tax cuts, revenue change via revaluation, and state aid. All revenue loss items are discussed in terms both of the total mandated cut and that cut required to be accomplished within the first year. No more than 15 percent of the total 1981 base period revenue are required to be cut in any year. Mandated cuts in excess of this must be extended over subsequent years, with the same 15 percent ceiling operating. All figures are expressed as percentages of total base period 1981 property tax revenues. Note that the definition of total cut used in this study is the reduction in the property tax levy required to reach 2.5 percent of full and fair valuation immediately. In other words, total revenue loss is measured as the difference between property tax revenues raised in the year before Proposition 2 1/2 and those allowed after Proposition 2 1/2. The correct way to measure the revenue impact of the limit is to determine the difference between revenues allowed under the law and those that would have been raised in the absence of the law. (See Chapter 23 of this volume). Unfortunately, to measure this difference would require some assumption about how fast revenues would have grown in the absence of the limit. Thus, using a proxy measure of the revenue impact has some advantages. The measure used in this paper, however, is a fairly arbitrary way to determine the longer-term impact of Proposition 2 1/2, and other measures of "total cut" might yield very different results. For example, instead of comparing the pre-Proposition 2 1/2 levy with a levy of 2.5 percent of full and fair valuation, the latter could be compared with the tax levy required to maintain real expenditures at the 1981 (pre-Proposition 2 1/2) level. No more than 15 percent of the total 1981 base period revenue are required to be cut in any year. Mandated cuts in excess of this must be extended over subsequent years, with the same 15 percent ceiling operating. All figures are expressed as percentages of total base period 1981 property tax revenues.

It is clear from Table 28.1 that property tax revenue cuts differ widely across localities. The mean pre-state aid total revenue loss (column (6)), including property tax and motor vehicle excise, was 21 percent. The median loss is only half of this – 10 percent – indicating that some communities experienced very large cuts. The diversity of experience is borne out by the standard deviation, also 21 percent. So the standard deviation is as great as the mean cut, testifying to a very large spread of experience. Thus, at the high end Chelsea sustained a cut of 75 percent, Worcester 60 percent, Cambridge 58 percent, Quincy 59 percent, and Springfield 54 percent. At the low end, Wellesley and Wayland had 2 percent, and Sturbridge, Seekonk, Ipswich and Dover had 3 percent. Indeed, as column (1) shows, with regard to the property tax alone, ten of the forty-one localities are permitted *increased* revenues! These are for the most part communities that had effective tax rates at or lower than 2 1/2 percent and are therefore allowed to increase property tax revenues by as much as 2 1/2 percent. Revenue losses on property taxes show an even greater dispersion than total revenue loss (mean 15.6 percent, median

3.6 percent, standard deviation 22.2 percent, standard deviation/mean 1.42). All communities, however, sustained losses in motor vehicle excise revenues. These are on the average much smaller in absolute terms than the real property tax losses (mean 5.2 percent, median 5.4 percent) and far less varied in absolute terms (standard deviation 1.2 percent) and in relative terms (standard deviation/mean=.278).

The above figures refer to total revenue losses. For some communities, 17 in our sample, these exceed the amount that is required to be sustained in any one year (15 percent). In the distribution of revenue cuts that had to be sustained in the first year (1981-1982), (column (7)), the numbers are smaller for these 17. So the mean first-year losses must be both smaller and less dispersed than total losses. The mean first-year loss is 11 percent, median 10 percent (as before), and the standard deviation 7 percent.

The figures in columns (6) and (7) include the effect of one of the offsets mentioned above, mandated revaluation of real property assessments. While all communities must ultimately move to a current full market value assessment basis, only 18 in this sample availed themselves of this option during the observation period (Column (3)) -- "availed" because revaluation had the effect of raising total permissible real property tax revenues in 17 of these 18. Moreover, these increased permissible revenues are very substantial, offsetting approximately 55 percent of the mandated cuts in real property revenues for those communities where cuts were required. Interestingly, almost all the revaluating localities had mandated cuts considerably below the one-year ceiling.

The other offset to mandated cuts is the state aid devised partially as a means of mitigating hardship resulting from Proposition 2 1/2. Regression analysis has been used to explain the distribution of this aid. Columns (13) and (14) show post-aid and (post-revaluation) revenue cuts, on both a total and first year basis, respectively. The mean total cut is 14.5 percent (compared with 21 percent before aid), the median is 4 percent (compared with 10 percent), the standard deviation is 21 percent (compared with 21 percent). Thus, State aid has decreased average required cuts, but has not decreased the dispersion of these cuts (hence, an unchanged standard deviation and a median that decreased more than mean). This alone suggests that big losers were not proportionately aided but that aid went disproportionately to smaller losers. This will be examined below.

Communities differ substantially in the size of the before-and-after offset revenue impacts. The sample is grouped in terms of three criteria - size, wealth and recent decade growth - to examine the distribution of revenue impacts further. Tables 28.3 A, B, C show these distributions.

Consider the grouping by population size in Table 28.3A. The total before-aid revenue cut rises dramatically from 8 percent for the smallest localities to 15, 16, 38, and 58 percent for the largest. First year loss is, as expected, less radical but also rises from 6 percent to 19 percent. State aid as a percentage of the total revenue cut, quite the contrary, is highest for the smallest localities (139 percent) and descends precipitously as size increases (94,

77, 12, and 9 percent). As a result, the post-aid total revenue cut is even more radically biased in favor of small communities and against larger ones: one percent for the smallest, rising to 7, 10, 34, and 53 percent for the largest.

These means hide the substantial variation in smaller communities (standard deviations between one and 1 1/2 times the size of the mean for the 2 smallest size groups, declining as a percentage of the mean for groups 3 and 4, and falling to the lowest absolute value of all for the largest communities (where the mean is by far the highest). This is also suggested by medians that are small percentages of their respective means for the smallest three groups but actually greater than the mean for the two largest groups. *Thus, revenue cut burdens grow larger with city size and become increasingly more uniform.*

Table 28.3B shows the distribution of impacts based on wealth (measured as per capita equalized property valuation in 1980). Once again there is a clear pattern. Revenue loss before aid varies strongly and inversely to wealth: percentage loss is greatest for the poorest localities and falls considerably as wealth rises (37, 25, 13, 9 percent). This pattern is displayed even more dramatically by the respective medians: 41, 15, 4, 4 percent. Once again, there is a distinct pattern in the dispersion of burdens. For the two poorest groups the standard deviation is high in absolute terms, and is nearly as great as the mean burden. The dispersion declines appreciably for the two richest groups in absolute terms, but falls slower than the mean burden, so that the relative dispersion is slightly higher than for the poorest group. *In sum, therefore, the initial revenue losses are highly regressive, falling much more heavily on poorer than on richer jurisdictions.*

State aid is intended, partially, to offset Proposition 2 1/2 revenue burdens. Such aid did not, however, decrease the regressivity of such burdens. Aid as a percentage of revenue loss is lower for the two poorest groups than for the richest two (73 and 65 percent, as against 121 and 81 percent). The dispersion of aid is fairly high for all groups, and especially in relative terms. Median impacts therefore show an even more striking version of this pattern: 32 and 27 percent for the two poorest groups, as against 115 and 81 percent. The result of this is an exacerbated relative regressivity of impact on post-aid burdens: 25, 19, 7, and 6 percent for poorest to richest group.

Revenue burdens in terms of jurisdiction growth presented in Table 28.3C, are also important. Growth is a potentially important characteristic of jurisdictions with respect to fiscal strength and public service needs. On the one hand, high growth may signify a strong, attractive resource base for economic activity; on the other it may reflect growing -- possibly as yet unmet -- needs for public infrastructure. Absolute decline may well bring special adjustment problems for local government because of adverse demographic, business selection and fixed cost constraints.

A distinct pattern emerges along this dimension as well. Burdens are inverse with growth; but the more striking pattern is that the group of localities experiencing absolute decline in population has a much higher revenue loss (38 percent) than all other groups (hovering between 13 and 9 percent). The difference in burdens between decline and no-growth is much greater than that between no-growth and growth, or slight growth and heavy growth. If population decline does not significantly free public resources because of fixed capacity constraints, as has often been argued, then this pattern of revenue losses would represent an additional difficulty for declining jurisdictions.

Once again the dispersion of impacts is greater for the high burden groups than for low burden groups. Taking some account of this by looking at medians, the pattern is somewhat different. The decline group now shows an even greater burden (44 percent) and all of the growth groups a much lower burden (4 percent for all). But now the zero growth group shows a much higher burden than all the growth groups (10 percent).

State aid once again does not moderate the perverse pattern. Much larger percentages of revenue loss occur for low-loss groups than for high: 49 and 66 percent for decline and zero-growth groups, as against 101, 72, and 142 percent for the growth groups. Again, adjusting somewhat for the extreme values characteristic of substantial variance in aid, the pattern of median impacts is even more decisive: 17 and 49 percent for decline and no-growth groups, as against 67, 104, 101 percent for the increasingly growing groups. The result is to exacerbate relative post-aid burden mean (median) differentials (31 (38), 8 (5), 6 (1), 7 (0), 1 (0) percent). *Thus, growing communities essentially avoid any revenue loss, no growth communities bear a modest loss, but declining communities sustain losses massive in absolute terms and enormous in relative terms.*

To summarize these grouped impacts, Proposition 2 1/2 imposed widely differing revenue losses, but was enormously more severe on localities generally presumed to be less able to cope with such losses: larger, poorer, declining. Smaller, wealthier, and high-growth communities generally experienced insignificant losses. It should not be thought that the three axes along which the impacts have been traced are in reality one, or even two -- so that large jurisdictions are poor *and* declining or no growth. In fact, the three dimensions are only slightly related for this sample of communities -- the correlation coefficients are: *0.334 percent* for size and wealth *0.236 percent* for size and growth *0.150 percent* for wealth and growth.

Since the three dimensions are insignificantly related to one another, it is appropriate to examine the separate influence each has on revenue loss burdens. Regression analysis was used for this purpose. Revenue losses (as a percentage of the 1981 levy) before aid (both for total and first year magnitudes) are regressed linearly on 1980 population (S), per capita 1980 equalized property valuation (W), and population growth, 1979-80 (G). The results are:

(1) TRC = 26.451 + 0.313S - 0.776W - 0.049 G
            (3.791) (4.310) (2.600) (0.621)
        $R^2$ = 0.521 $\overline{R}^2$ = 0.482 F = 13.417

(2) YRC = 14.708 + 0.081 S − 0.346 W + 0.040 G
$\quad\quad\quad\quad$ (5.547) (2.926) (3.055) (1.298)
$\quad\quad\quad\quad$ $R^2$ = .412 $\overline{R}^2$ = 0.365 F = 8.651
$\quad\quad$ where TRC is total pre−aid revenue loss as a percentage of 1981 levy and
$\quad\quad\quad\quad$ YRC is first−year, pre−aid revenue loss as a percentage of 1981 levy.


$\quad\quad$ Total revenue cuts were more related to the three classifying variables than to first−year revenue cuts, but the differences were not important. One−half of the variance of total cuts can be "explained" by the three−way classification, slightly more than one−third of first−year cuts. In both regressions size and wealth are significant influences, size increasing burdens and wealth, the more significant variable, decreasing them. The apparent effects of growth are actually due to the relationship with size and wealth.

$\quad\quad$ To what extent is State aid related to the size of the revenue losses and to our classifying variables? Equations (3) − (8) show the appropriate regressions.


(3) A = 445,861.137 + 0.185 YR
$\quad\quad\quad\quad$ (2.174) (4.411)
$\quad\quad\quad\quad$ $R^2$ = 0.313 $\overline{R}^2$ = 0.316 F = 19.461
$\quad\quad$ where A is total dollar value of state aid and
$\quad\quad\quad\quad$ YR is the dollar value of first−year revenue loss

(4) A = 853,150.672 + 23.204 S − 38.468 W + 13,992.538 G
$\quad\quad\quad\quad$ (2.032) (5.308) (2.141) (2.864)
$\quad\quad\quad\quad$ $R^2$ = 0.552 $\overline{R}^2$ = 0.516 F = 15.222

(5) A = 569,659.094 + 0.307 YR + 49,336.259 S
$\quad\quad\quad\quad$ (1.600) (4.170) (6.808)
$\quad\quad\quad$ −34,017.574 W + 13,506.757 F
$\quad\quad\quad\quad$ (2.269) (3.320)
$\quad\quad\quad\quad$ $R^2$ = 0.698 $\overline{R}^2$ = 0.665 F = 20.820


$\quad\quad$ These regressions show that State aid does have an absolute responsiveness to size of revenue loss. In a single correlation (3), about one−third of the variance of aid represents a response to the size of the first year revenue loss (see Chapter 8 of this volume). Aid is also related to the three classifying variables. Contrary to the impression gained from the grouped data patterns, aid is *positively* associated with size and *negatively* with wealth. Consistent with the grouped data impressions, it is positively associated with growth. This means that the aid formula does have an equalizing impact, but it is weak.

$\quad\quad$ Equations (6) − (8) analyze normalized measures of aid.


(6) ATR = 131.748 − 1.050 S − 1.091 W + 0.068 G

$$(3.745) \ (2.865) \ (0.725) \ (0.167)$$
$$R^2 = 0.193 \ \overline{R}^2 = 0.128 \ F = 2.955$$

(7) $AYR = 149.741 - 1.007 \ S - 1.713 \ W - 0.020 \ G$
$$(4.469) \ (2.885) \ (1.195) \ (0.055)$$
$$R^2 = 0.190 \ \overline{R}^2 = 0.124 \ F = 2.889$$

(8) $AP = 14.372 - 0.046 \ S - 0.368 \ W + 0.012 \ G$
$$(7.923) \ (2.410) \ (4.736) \ (0.566)$$
$$R^2 = 0.389 \ \overline{R}^2 = 0.340 \ F = 7.866$$

where ATR is aid as a percentage of total revenue cut,
AYR is aid as a percentage of first-year revenue cut, and
AP is aid as a percentage of 1981 property tax revenues.

Aid as a percentage of the total revenue cut is related only – and quite weakly overall – to size, where larger size leads to a *decrease* in the percentage of both total and first-year loss made up by aid. So, in relative terms, aid is biased against size, contrary to the positive gross responsiveness of aid to size (equation (4)).

The story is different for aid as a percentage of base period property tax revenues. Here, the classifying variables explain one third of the variance and both size and wealth have explanatory power. Again, size has a negative influence, but so too does wealth. Thus, as a percentage of initial revenues, aid is biased against both size *and* wealth. It is thus less explicitly regressive than heretofore suggested.

In sum, therefore, aid is modestly responsive to revenue losses and modestly progressive with respect to wealth. The consequences of this offset are shown in equations (11) and (12), where post-aid revenue losses (both total and first year) are regressed on the classifying variables.

(9) $TLA = 12.078 \div 0.358 \ S - 0.409 \ W - 0.061 \ G$
$$(1.717) \ (4.888) \ (1.357) \ (0.746)$$
$$R^2 = 0.507 \ \overline{R}^2 = 0.467 \ F = 12,686$$

(10) $YLA = 0.336 + 0.126 \ S + 0.021 \ W + 0.28 \ G$
$$(0.105) \ (3.786) \ (0.155) \ (0.754)$$
$$R^2 = 0.293 \ \overline{R}^2 = 0.238 \ F = 5.172$$

where TLA is post-aid total revenue cut as a percentage of property tax revenues, and
YLA is post-aid, first-year revenue cut as a percentage of 1981 property tax revenues.

Total percentage post-aid revenue loss is more closely related to the classifying variables than first-year percentage post-aid loss. Only size is a significant variable here, positively related to the percentage loss.

The pre-aid with post-aid results are compared (equations (1) – (2) versus (9) – (10). For both, total cuts are better explained than first year cuts; the overall fit for the former is about the same in pre-aid and post-aid regressions. For first-year cuts the overall fit is better for pre-aid than post-aid. All variables have the same sign in the four regressions, but while the pre-aid regressions showed both size and wealth significant, the significance of wealth is wiped out in the post-aid regressions. This is due to the fact that the mild progressivity of aid offsets the initial strong bias against poorer jurisdictions in terms of revenue loss. Size retains about the same magnitude (as well as sign) of impact in pre-aid and post-aid situations. In terms of size of remaininng revenue loss, the earlier descriptive analysis from Tables 28.1 and 28.2 showed that aid decreased absolute losses and loss differences but widened relative loss differences.

## Expenditures  Appropriations  Adjustments

Faced with post-aid revenue cuts, localities can cope in a number of ways: (1) seek additional revenues from other sources, (2) reduce expenditures, (3) increase borrowing. Expenditure adjustments are discussed first.

Table 28.4 shows changes in appropriations between 1981 and 1982 expressed as a percentage of 1981 appropriations, for the 41 town and city sample. Changes in seven component expenditure categories are listed, as well as total appropriations. While these seven do not completely exhaust local spending, they are close to being comprehensive. For each category, including "Total," AC designates the percentage change in that category between 1981 and 1982, and TR designates the *average* annual percentage change in that category for the period 1976–80. To help make sense of the distribution of these changes, columns for mean, standard deviation, median, maximum and minimum are included. Note that the appropriations and expenditure figures presented are totals, including capital outlays. Thus, they might be expected to demonstrate greater fluctuation than would be the case if operating expenses alone were examined.

Distribution is important here. The variety in the distribution of revenue losses was emphasized earlier. Those losses were in large measure imposed on the localities. Appropriations changes, on the other hand, represent voluntary decisions by the local government, where there are a number of options for adjusting to revenue losses. Their voluntary responses may reflect public perceptions about the relative importance of present versus future needs, or they may only reflect the relative power of particular officials or interest groups.

Total appropriations fell 5.6 percent, a clear turnaround from the average annual 10.8 percent increase in the period 1976–80. Appropriations in the aggregate certainly responded to the Proposition 2 1/2-generated revenue decreases. The dispersion of responses, however, is quite high, 7.7 percent, exceeding the mean decline by some 40 percent. The dispersion is *relatively* greater than the dispersion of earlier growth, although smaller in absolute terms. The median decline is less than the mean (4.1 percent), but this supports a range from a 35 percent cut (misleadingly high, since this case represents the withdrawal of a hospital and junior college from the municipal budget) to a 6.5 percent increase. In all these measures there is a clear turning point discontinuity between the preceding trend and the 1981–82 appropriation change.

To test the responsiveness of appropriations to mandated revenue cuts on an individual locality basis the percentage change in total appropriations was regressed on both the total and first–year, post–aid revenue losses as a percentage of 1981 property tax levies. losses. Equations (11) and (12) show the results.

$$(11)\ XC = -3.986 - 0.111\ TLA$$
$$(2.757)\ (1.952)$$
$$R^2 = 0.093\ \bar{R}^2 = 0.069\ F = 3.809$$

$$(12)\ XC = -4.076 - 0.323\ YLA$$
$$(2.019)\ (2.204)$$
$$R^2 = 0.116\ \bar{R}^2 = 0.092$$

where XC is percentage appropriations change;
        TLA, YLA are total and first–year post–aid revenue cuts as percentage of 1981 property tax levies.

The results were surprising and potentially important. While the revenue loss percentage was a significant explanatory variable for appropriation change, its overall explanatory power was trivial. This was true for both total and first–year revenue loss. An attendant implication stems from the slightly stronger influence of first–year revenue loss over total revenue loss. The reverse of this would imply that jurisdictions paid attention to future needs for additional expenditure restraint by cutting today beyond today's immediate constraints. Instead, the greater explanatory force of first year revenue cuts suggests that jurisdictions delayed adjusting to the future, adjust *at best* to immediate felt needs. Indeed, the weak appropriations response suggests lagged responses even to immediate needs.

The relationship might be masked by the systematic variation of revenue loss with the locality attributes – size, wealth, growth. This was tested by regressing appropriations change on these variables. This resulted in an even smaller total explanatory power, and no attribute was close to significance.

Finally, regressing appropriations change on all the variables, as expected, did no better. Equations (13) and (14) show this.

$$(13)\ XC = -5.451 + 15.422\ TLA + 0.50\ S + 0.014\ W$$
$$(1.479)\ (1.876)\ (1.086)\ (0.089)$$
$$+0.040\ G$$

$$(0.998)$$
$$R^2 = 0.144 \ \overline{R}^2 = 0.043 \ F = 1.426$$

(14) $XC = -7.226 + 42.285 \ YLA + 0.048 \ S + 0.087 \ W$
$$(2.109) \ (2.438) \ (1.181) \ (0.601)$$
$$+0.061 \ G$$
$$(1.556)$$
$$R^2 = 0.196 \ \overline{R}^2 = 0.101 \ F = 2.068$$

Revenue loss was the only significant explanatory variable, but its overall power was meager. As in the previous regressions, first year revenue cuts had a stronger expl, and here thatnatory power than total, and here that difference is marked.

An examination of the sectoral pattern of appropriation cuts was also considered. All categories showed a mean decline in appropriations, and these represented a dramatic reversal of the previous five-year strong growth trend. Four expenditures categories were cut by a greater percentage than total appropriations (5.6 percent): schools 6.5 percent, streets 10.6 percent, parks 22.9 percent, libraries 10.0 percent. Three categories were cut less: police 0.5 percent, fire 4.2 percent and sanitation 4.2 percent. But these figures tell only one part of the story.

The dispersion of total appropriation's cut was large relatively, but not very much so absolutely. Only the schools category was similar in magnitude. The other six categories had extremely high dispersion in absolute terms and, for police, fire and sanitation, enormous in relative terms. Indeed, high dispersion seems to be a consistent aspect of expenditure change over time. The stereotypical picture of local expenditures rising smoothly and uniformly over time -- a supposed sign of their being out of control -- is belied by the high dispersion among sectoral growth rates in 1976 to 1980, and by the exceptionally high but differing standard deviations within each sector during that period. Localities clearly differed greatly among one another, and their sectoral growth patterns differed.

The outcome of this diversity of experience is shown by the median figures. While mean police appropriations fell by 0.5 percent, median appropriations actually rose by 1.5 percent. Possibly even more striking, a 4.2 percent decline in mean fire appropriations was accompanied by a median increase of 0.7 percent. The 4.2 percent mean decrease in sanitation appropriations accompanied an essentially zero median change. Clearly, some jurisdictions made very large negative adjustments in these categories, considerably deviating from the adjustments in other jurisdictions not only in magnitude but in direction as well. The medians in the other categories show cuts, but much less than the means.

This emphasis on diversity of response -- in magnitude and even direction -- is borne out by the range of responses, from minimum to maximum. In every category huge negative responses existed side by side with non-trivial, even very large positive responses. Yet this was not unique to the post-Proposition 2 1/2 period. As indicated above, the dispersion of the 1976-1980 trend is every bit as great as the dispersions of 1981-82 appropriation changes; moreover, while the median trends are highly bunched across categories, the ranges for the different categories are enormous, higher than 1981-82, and similarly embrace negative and positive growth.

The foregoing implies that adjustment to Proposition 2 1/2 has not consisted of a uniform, rule-of-thumb decrease across expenditures categories. Categories clearly differ in vulnerability to cuts, and different communities adopted different strategies of adjustment mix across categories.

Three categories seem sheltered -- police, fire, and sanitation -- and of these police seems most favored, receiving non-trivial increases against the retrenchment tide. At the other extreme, parks, streets, and possibly libraries appear most expendable -- but they display high dispersion and their ranges show widely divergent treatment by different jurisdictions. The schools category seems to have experienced only moderately greater cuts than total appropriations, and to have one of the smallest ranges of diversity. This hides the extraordinary salience of this category, however.

If we examine not the percentage change of each category but for how much of the total appropriations cut its change was responsible, an entirely different picture emerges. Cuts in the especially vulnerable categories -- parks, streets, and libraries -- together accounted for only 15 percent of total appropriations cuts. One category – schools – alone accounted for 161 percent of total mean appropriations cuts! This category comprises the largest single expenditure category (about 1/2), so its greater than average cut represented the overwhelming source of appropriations adjustment. Indeed,the savings made on school cuts permitted communities to raise their appropriations, on the average, for police and fire, and permitted many individual communities to raise appropriations in any of the other categories. The dependence on school cuts was not uniform, though. Quite the contrary: the standard deviation of share of overall cuts is huge in absolute terms, although the smallest among categories in relative terms.

What accounts for these diverse expenditure adjustments? Are they specific to the inherent character of the sectors, or did they stem from different degrees of balance and adjustment to past circumstances? In the former case they reveal something about long-standing social preferences, in the latter they reveal something about the process of adjustment in the public sector to changing situations: lags, uncertainties, capacity inflexibilities, and lumpiness.

An attempt has been made to test these issues in equations (15) to (18). The first two regressions examine percentage change in each category, the second two the share of total appropriation change by category. The seven appropriation categories are pooled for the 41 localities in these regressions.

The first regression considers whether the cut in a given category is influenced by the quantitative importance of the category in overall appropriations, or by some temporal adjustment imbalance (lags, capacity constraints, etc.), as reflected by the strength of recent growth in the sector. Accordingly, percentage sector cut for 1981–82 is regressed on the size of that sector as a percenage of total appropriations in 1981, and in the mean annual percentage change in expenditures for that category in 1976–80.

(15) $ACC = -9.839 - 0.001 \, T + 0.097 \, M$
$\phantom{(15) ACC = -9.839} (2.453) \, (0.148) \, (1.149)$
$\phantom{(15) ACC = } \overline{R}^2 = 0.044$

where ACC is category appropriation change, 1981–82,
$\phantom{where}$ T is trend (mean annual percentage change in category expenditures, 1976–80)
$\phantom{where}$ M is importance (category appropriation 1981/total appropriation 1981).

It is obvious that percentage cuts in categories are not influenced by either growth or the importance of the sector.

The second regression examines whether sector cuts reflect social preferences, where such preferences are influenced by community characteristics. ACC is regressed on the two familiar classifying attributes: size and wealth.

(16) $ACC = -6.925 - 0.011 \, S - 0.044 \, W$
$\phantom{(16) ACC = -6.925} (1.871) \, (0.300) \, (0.274)$
$\phantom{(16) ACC = } \overline{R}^2 = 0.007$

It is apparent that preference factors as reflected by community size and wealth do not affect sector cuts.

While the adjustment process and community size/wealth characteristics do not influence the percentage change in sector appropriations, it is possible that they may affect the share of each sector change in total appropriations. Sector appropriation change 1981–82 as a percentage of total 1981–82 · appropriation change is regressed on the first pair of factors and then on the second.

(17) $CST = -16.803 + 0.031 \, T + 3.459 \, M$
$\phantom{(17) CST = -16.803} (1.257) \, (0.437) \, (2.689)$
$\phantom{(17) CST = } \overline{R}^2 = 0.178,$

where CST is sector share of total appropriations change, 1981–82.

The overall explanatory power is still very low in absolute terms, but much larger than in the ACC regressions. The reason for this is the strong significance of the importance variable. To put the result into perspective, consider the following regression.

(18)  $CST = 34.673 - 0.296\ S - 0.309\ W$
$$\quad\quad\quad\quad\quad (1.335)\ (1.110)\ (0.277)$$
$$\bar{R}^2 = 0.003$$

Community size and wealth do not influence the category share of total appropriations change.

Politicians who believe that Proposition 2 1/2 cannot be reversed soon will attempt to make budget cuts for which little disturbance in service levels will be noticed by voters. This can be achieved in three ways.

1) Cut actual waste.

2) Cut programs which are large and diverse enough so that minimum efficiency levels will not be approached by the cuts, and/or where cuts can take the form of decreasing variety or specialized forms of the basic services instead of decreasing aggregate service levels.

3) Cut programs where changing circumstances – e.g., migration or demographic changes – have left excess capacity, an excess which would be politically difficult to remove in "normal" times, but is excusable in periods of acknowledged stringency.

In effect, Proposition 2 1/2 can serve as an excuse or trigger to make downward adjustments that were previously desired but were politically too dangerous to undertake except under special circumstances.

These three considerations are in fact versions of a scale factor: they suggest that large programs may skim off large absolute amounts of expenditures and disguise the effect so that little basic service level decline is obvious to voters. The relative unmanageability of large, intricate programs suggests that waste is greater in such programs.

All three considerations point to education as an obvious source of potentially large absolute savings. In addition to scale considerations, decreases in the school age population have created significant redundancies in the school establishment. This, together with only a loosely perceived relationship between the volume of school inputs and size of the "outputs" of schooling, facilitate considerable budget cuts in this category, when politically-protected by a universally perceived period of sharp stringency (see Chapter 22 of this volume). It should be noted that Proposition 2 1/2 also eliminated the fiscal autonomy of local school committees, permitting local budget officials to attack school spending in ways they could not before.

The inherent social importance of a service can protect an expenditure category against cuts, even in an emergency. Thus, median police budgets actually increased, given the perceived need due to a sharply rising crime rate.

The rise in median fire protection budgets also probably stems from higher risks due to the growing arson-for-profit industry. In sanitation, too, with its relative homogeneity of services, it is not possible to disguise easily the impact of budget cuts on service levels. Park and library programs are small enough for cuts to have serious impacts on service levels, but these are partially hidden because of the variety and subtle quality variations possible within the programs. In addition, social priorities may well establish these as "fringe" or elite benefits, quite appropriate to trimming in times of emergency. The category that does not easily fit into this scheme is streets. Cuts here are hard to disguise, and the intense, widespread American concern with auto transportation would suggest a protected status for that category. Yet it is subject to a percentage cut roughly twice as great as for total appropriations, and this results in being 15 percent of total appropriations cuts attributable to this category, the second largest in the group. A possible explanation is the importance of capital outlays relative to current expenses; cuts may take the form of postponing capital outlays while holding current maintenance outlays. This would "disguise" budget cuts.

The education category is so central to both the overall size of the appropriations cut and its mix that it is useful to examine it more closely. The possibility that educational outlays were largely responsive to important internal changes rather than to the external pressure of Proposition 2 1/2 has been tested. It is well known that school-age population has been declining in the State, and many communities have excess capacity in both buildings and personnel. Regressing the percentage change in school appropriations on the 1976-80 trend did not reveal a relationship. On the other hand, a moderately direct relationship was discovered between the percentage change in school appropriations and the size of the Proposition 2 1/2-inspired revenue losses. Equations (19) and (20) show this:

(19) ECP = −4.373 + 0.147 TLA
$$\qquad (4.640)\ (3.962)$$
$$R^2 = 0.287\ \overline{R}^2 = 0.269\ F = 15.695$$

(20) ECP = −4.455 + 0.437 YLA
$$\qquad (5.267)\ (4.765)$$
$$R^2 = 0.368\ \overline{R}^2 = 0.352\ F = 22.707$$

where ECP is the percentage cut in school appropriations.

The revenue loss clearly influences the size of the cut in educational budgets. As with total appropriations, the first-year revenue loss has a stronger and larger effect than total revenue loss, strengthening the impression that localities may not plan ahead with a comprehensive adjustment strategy, but rather adjust on an *ad hoc* basis. The earlier finding that the size of total appropriations cuts was only slightly −− although positively−− related to the size of the revenue losses also suggests the absence of a relatively uniform systematic adjustment strategy involving expenditure levels.

Neither community characteristics nor past trends are responsible for the relationship between school cuts and revenue losses. The latter retains its direct influence in unchanged size and degree. Indeed, the apparent weak link between locality size and school cuts would appear to be an artifact of the true link between revenue loss and school cuts. Here too, first-year revenue loss has the same stronger and larger effect on school cuts as total revenue loss.

As a check on this pattern of findings, the same analysis was performed using changes in per capita school appropriations as the dependent variable instead of the percentage change in such appropriations. The relationship between the revenue losses and school cuts is the same as before, although somewhat weaker, and it is not explained by community characteristics or trend. Again, first-year loss is a better predictor than total loss, but the difference in strength and size is greater than for percentage school cuts.

This analysis suggests that school appropriations were reduced in direct response to the revenue effects of Proposition 2 1/2, not in response to internal educational considerations. But why did such a large part of the overall appropriation response to Proposition 2 1/2 rest on education, a percentage far in excess of its proportion of total expenditures? The immense American concern with public education scarcely intimates that education is considered an unimportant, fringe, or elitist value that has low social priority. A combination of the loss of school committee autonomy, trend factors, scale considerations and -- paradoxically -- the very importance of education as a social value, may explain the heavy burden on this sector. The population of school age children has been declining in most communities for some years, but reducing basic capacity in accordance with this trend is difficult. School closings and the bargaining frictions with teachers' unions caused by dismissing teachers make such action politically difficult. Overall this reflects the public's deep commitment to education. So educational expenditures continued to grow through 1980. Quite possibly, therefore, an accumulating overcapacity was felt to exist by elected officials along with a political inability to deal with it resolutely. The extremeness and publicness of the revenue constraint imposed by Proposition 2 1/2 could have acted as a trigger to justify significant cuts that elected officials might have wanted to make earlier. Once basic capacity cuts became politically safe, the various sector scale factors dicussed above could make it politically attractive to go beyond this into cuts involving qualitative issues -- variety, special programs, etc. The size and complexity of the educational system would disguise the loss of genuine educational quality, and the cuts could be publicly viewed as simply scaling down redundancy. This is only speculative, but it would explain why education has been accorded the dubious role of overwhelmingly supporting a public response to Proposition 2 1/2.

## Alternative Revenue Sources

It has been noted that many communities in Massachusetts were severely affected by property tax and motor vehicle excise tax revenue losses in fiscal

1982. Although State aid helped somewhat to offset these losses, it is clear that many of the more severely impacted communities were left with a significantly smaller volume of revenue even after aid. Yet the analysis of appropriations suggests that the percentage change in total appropriations is only slightly related to the post–State–aid percentage of revenue lost due to Proposition 2 1/2. The ability of local governments to tap alternative sources of revenue is obviously a crucial issue here. Unfortunately, there is little current data to help understand what has happened with user charges and Federal aid in the first year of Proposition 2 1/2.

There is little information on the size of the revenue potential of increased reliance on user charges; data are available for five of the ten cities studied by the IMPACT: 2 1/2 Project (see Chapter 25 of this volume). In Springfield, officials expected water and sewer charges to provide an additional $10 million (179 percent of the post–aid, first–year revenue loss) in revenue in FY82. This explains why Springfield could increase appropriations by 1.6 percent with a post–aid, first–year revenue loss of 8.9 percent. Water and sewer charges are estimated to provide $750,000 (16 percent of post–aid, first–year revenue loss) in additional revenue for the town of Arlington. Total user charge increases in Chelsea are expected to raise an additional $500,000 (99.4 percent of the post–aid, first–year revenue loss) (1), while revenue from fees and charges increased from $23.6 million in FY81 to $30.7 million in FY82 in Cambridge to make up 60 percent of the first–year, post–aid revenue loss (see Chapter 23 of this volume). Thus, user fees and charges have very significant potential to raise substantial amounts of revenue, at least in some of the cities and towns in Massachusetts. Although many user charges are not likely to generate much revenue, some have the productivity potential to constitute a major offset to Proposition 2 1/2 revenue losses.

The other major source of local government revenue in Massachusetts is Federal aid, which might have helped to offset revenue losses during the first year of Proposition 2 1/2. Unfortunately, there is currently no information available concerning the magnitude of Federal aid for the sample communities in FY82. There is, however, strong evidence that there was a substantial decline in reliance on Federal aid in Massachusetts communities in the period 1976–80 (see Chapter 5 of this volume). The decline occurred across most types of communities, but was particularly severe in low–income communities and, to a lesser extent, in those communities most severely impacted by Proposition 2 1/2. Lower–income communities lost an average of $19.91 in real per capita Federal aid from 1976 to 1980, while high–income municipalities gained an average of $2.36. During the same time period, communities severely impacted by Proposition 2 1/2 experienced an average decrease in real per capita Federal aid of $17.84, while those communities suffering no revenue loss from Proposition 2 1/2 lost an average of $9.95. Furthermore, it is evident that further decreases in Federal aid are on the agenda of the Reagan administration.

Recent estimates obtained from the Office of General Revenue Sharing, in fact, indicate that the allocation of general revenue sharing funds to Massachusetts is expected to decline in the next entitlement period (October 1, 1982 to September 30, 1983) by 2.4 percent. This decrease is due to two factors in the distribution formula. First of all, Massachusetts 1980 urbanized population increased by only 2.55 percent from 1970 to 1980, compared to a U.S. average increase of 15.34 percent. Second, the general tax effort factor computed by the Office of General Revenue Sharing declined by 4.83 percent, while the U.S. average was a decrease of 2.58 percent. Indeed, the tax limitation provisions of Proposition 2 1/2 may themselves serve to exacerbate this decrease in the tax effort factor used to calculate allocations of revenue sharing to Massachuetts in future entitlement periods.

Although the potential of Federal aid as an offset to revenue loss is in general limited, it is significant that some of the more severely impacted communities have been able to gain substantial offsets to revenue losses by increasing certain types of user fees and charges. Communities able to tap public works fees as a revenue offset are especially fortunate. These fees are available primarily to larger cities, and it is precisely in these cities that the impact of Proposition 2 1/2 has been most severe. Thus, user fees and charges may be an important ingredient in the overall adjustment to Proposition 2 1/2 in specific cases.

For the bulk of communities, most fees and charges can be expected to have only limited potential. In the face of expected further declines in Federal aid, a more carefully compensatory State aid formula and/or access to novel alternative revenue sources -- some perhaps not even presently permitted by the State to localities -- are required if even greater burden is not to fall on the provision of local services.

## Changes in Municipal Bond Ratings

Debt is another source of revenue to which impacted communities might turn to meet certain fiscal responsibilities. Unfortunately, there is little information available regarding debt levels for the sample jurisdictions in FY82, or on the amount of debt issued each year. The change in debt levels that occurred in the first year of Proposition 2 1/2 cannot, therefore, be analyzed. An alternative approach is to examine changes in the credit-worthiness of municipalities, i.e., in their ability to go to the bond market for funding should the need arise. Moody's municipal bond ratings for the sample of municipalities for pre-and post 2 1/2 years, provide evidence on this point. Table 28.5 presents 1980 and 1982 bond ratings for the 41 sample communities.

Shortly after the passage of Proposition 2 1/2, Moody's suspended the bond ratings of over 40 communities. This was done in order to review the financial status of these communities for possible revision of their bond ratings. This was a departure from Moody's standard procedure, in which ratings are reviewed for possible revision only when a community attempts to borrow. Thus, ratings may have changed in some of the 41 sample communities even if they have not attempted to go to the debt market since the passage of Proposition 2 1/2.

Bond ratings either improved slightly or remained unchanged from 1980 to 1982 in most of the jurisdictions studied. However, bond ratings did decline in some of the larger cities, from Aa to Baa in Cambridge, from Aa to A1 in Springfield, from Aa to A in Pittsfield, Salem and Watertown, from Baa to Ba in Quincy, and from A to Baa in Worcester. Thus, some of the communities most severely impacted by Proposition 2 1/2 have lost some of their credibility in the municipal bond market.

These preliminary findings suggest a disturbing pattern. It might be expected that capital expenditures would be one of the first things to suffer in times of fiscal stress and fiscal limitation. This may represent a conscious effort on the part of local decision-makers to eliminate spending that is considered postponable. The results of this paper suggest that some of the communities most severely affected by Proposition 2 1/2 may have less choice in deciding whether to defer capital expenditures since thay are likely to experience higher borrowing costs. The issue of the effects of Proposition 2 1/2 on the ability of localities to borrow merits more extensive research efforts.


## Summary

This concluding section can be brief. Proposition 2 1/2 mandated considerable revenue losses in localities on average, but these losses varied greatly among localities. In general, the losses increased directly with size of jurisdiction and inversely with property wealth and growth. In this regard the initial impacts were distributed dysfunctionally. State aid, including supplements instituted as an offset of Proposition 2 1/2 impacts, only mildly moderated the very large dispersion of ultimate effects and their dysfunctional pattern. Considerable net losses had to be coped with by many localities.

Full value reassessment was undertaken by a significant minority of jurisdictions, with considerable offset advantages, but it was not possible for communities suffering the largest revenue losses. Indeed, it may take several years to complete revaluation in the larger cities. Appropriations adjustments and an increase in alternative revenue sources were the major discretionary adjustments. Changes in appropriations were on average considerable, but differed significantly across expenditure categories. Differences among localities in both total and the mix were far greater, and patterns emerged. In general, the size of revenue loss only partially explained the size of appropriations cuts. A smattering of information concerning increased reliance on alternative revenue sources suggests that this was used as a genuine alternative to appropriations cuts. This helps to explain the weak relationship between revenue loss and budget reduction.

The mix of appropriations cuts was anything but uniform across categories. Some categories were definitely protected, or even favored: e.g., police and fire. Others were cut sharply, including parks, libraries and schools. As before, the variations among localities were far greater than variations across categories. What emerged most clearly was that the education category was called upon to bear the overwhelming proportion of total appropriations cuts, and, in some cases, was cut more than the total to permit an increase in categories such as police and fire.

The relationship of localities to the capital market can be variously affected by Proposition 2 1/2. First, the legal basis of a locality's responsibiliy for existing as well as future debt obligations may be compromised by the stringent revenue constraints imposed. This would adversly affect its access to the bond market. Second, present-mandated revenue losses and future restrictions may force communities to depend on borrowing to finance outlays. Early-induced issuance of debt could adversley affect the rate that must be paid for borrowing. Even the prospect of increased dependence could adversely affect credit-worthiness. Early results suggest that bond ratings have changed in a pattern consistent with both effects: ratings have worsened in direct relation to the size of the first-year revenue losses resulting from Proposition 2 1/2.

So all routes to an "easy" escape from the rigors of Proposition 2 1/2 have been effectively tightened. Since those rigors vary so markedly among communities, is it at all clear that the burdens have been wisely allocated by the electorate, or that provision has been appropriately made for adjusting them?

Examination of the early impacts of Proposition 2 1/2 provides an attractive opportunity to learn something about the way the Federal system responds to shock. In the spirit of this challenge, there is occasionally speculation here beyond the descriptive analysis in an effort to understand the kinds and sizes of adjustment by the different agents, State and localities. There has been a provocative pattern of mix in the budget cuts which may be explained by an analysis in terms of social preference and priorities, adjustment process lags, and differential political vulnerability among categories in the interplay between public officials and the electorate. These observations are not to be interpreted as a definitive explanation for the phenomena, but only as a set of initial surmises in the face of a fascinating and important social experiment. More considered work in this direction is certainly warranted.


### Notes for Chapter 28

A longer version of this paper appeared in the Winter 1982 issue of *Public Budgeting and Finance.*

The authors would like to thank Oscar Fernandez and Danny Dobryn for their invaluable assistance with the data analysis.

1. Revenue from fees and charges is an enormous percentage of first-year, post-aid revenue loss for Chelsea because that community received a very substantial amount of State aid in FY82.

## Table 28.1
## Selected Characteristics of Sample Communities

|  | Pop 1970 | Pop 1980 | % Change | EQV 1980 (p.c.) |
|---|---|---|---|---|
| Amesbury | 5290 | 13971 | 164 | 10772 |
| Arlington | 53524 | 48219 | -10 | 16278 |
| Burlington | 21980 | 23486 | 7 | 24785 |
| Cambridge | 100361 | 95322 | -5 | 13544 |
| Chelmsford | 31432 | 31174 | -1 | 17585 |
| Chelsea | 30625 | 25431 | -17 | 6209 |
| Clinton | 13383 | 12771 | -5 | 10078 |
| Concord | 16148 | 16293 | 1 | 29031 |
| Dalton | 7505 | 7505 | 0 | 13791 |
| Dartmouth | 18800 | 23966 | 27 | 16870 |
| Dennis | 6454 | 12360 | 92 | 47087 |
| Dover | 4529 | 4703 | 4 | 44333 |
| Dracut | 18214 | 21249 | 17 | 12057 |
| Everett | 42485 | 37195 | -12 | 23874 |
| Foxborough | 14218 | 14148 | -1 | 16766 |
| Framingham | 64048 | 65113 | 2 | 17631 |
| Georgetwon | 5290 | 5687 | 8 | 16388 |
| Gloucester | 27941 | 27768 | -1 | 20055 |
| Hatfield | 2825 | 3045 | 8 | 16493 |
| Ipswich | 10750 | 11158 | 4 | 17387 |
| Kingston | 5999 | 7362 | 23 | 16979 |
| Leicester | 9140 | 9446 | 2 | 10544 |
| Longmeadow | 15630 | 16301 | 3 | 20968 |
| Lynnfield | 5151 | 5424 | 5 | 33831 |
| Marshfield | 15233 | 20916 | 37 | 16934 |
| Norwood | 11680 | 11389 | -2 | 12020 |
| Palmer | 937 | 1112 | 19 | 17968 |
| Pelham | 57020 | 51974 | -9 | 12381 |
| Pittsfield | 87966 | 84743 | -4 | 13558 |
| Quincy | 40556 | 38220 | -6 | 15780 |
| Salem | 11116 | 12269 | 10 | 20042 |
| Seekonk | 6330 | 7382 | 17 | 14413 |
| Southwick | 163905 | 152319 | -7 | 8633 |
| Springfield | 4878 | 5976 | 23 | 19294 |
| Sturbridge | 30815 | 29711 | -4 | 17835 |
| Watertown | 39307 | 34384 | -13 | 17537 |
| Wayland | 13461 | 12170 | -10 | 28406 |
| Welleseley | 28051 | 27209 | -3 | 29501 |
| Wenham | 3849 | 3897 | 1 | 20570 |
| Whitman | 13059 | 13534 | 4 | 11829 |
| Worcester | 176572 | 161799 | -8 | 8832 |
| mean | 30158 | 29465 | 9 | 18509 |
| st. dev. | 39256 | 35968 | 31 | 8601 |
| median | 15233 | 16293 | 1 | 16934 |

The abbreviations used in Tables 28.2, 28.3A, 28.3B, 28.3C, and 28.4 are listed below:

```
TL   =   total property tax levy cut without revaluation/1981 levy.
YL   =   first year property tax levy cut without revaluation/1981 levy.
RTL  =   total levy cut after revaluation/1981 levy.
RYL  =   first year levy cut after revaluation/1981 levy.
MV   =   motor vehicle excise revenue loss/1981 levy.
RTR  =   total revenue loss (inc. MV) after revaluation/1981 levy.
RYR  =   first year revenue loss (inc. MV) after revaluation/1981 levy.
AT   =   state aid (first year)/RTR
AY   =   state aid (first year)/RYR
PRTL =   post-aid total levy change/1981 levy.
PRYL =   post-aid first year levy change/1981 levy.
PRTR =   post-aid total revenue change/1981 levy.
PRYR =   post-aid first year revenue change/1381 levy.
AL   =   state aid (first year)/1981 levy.
```

TABLE 28.2

REVENUE LOSSES MANDATED BY PROPOSITION 2 1/2, FY81-FY82

| | TL | YL | RTL | RYL | MV | RTR | RYR | AT | AY | PRTL | PRYL | PRTR | PRYR | |
|---|---|---|---|---|---|---|---|---|---|---|---|---|---|---|
| Amesbury | -34.7 | -15.0 | -15.0 | -15.0 | -07.8 | -22.8 | -22.8 | -41.3 | -41.3 | -05.6 | -05.6 | -13.4 | -13.4 | 09.4 |
| Arlington | -40.0 | -15.0 | -40.0 | -15.0 | -04.1 | -44.1 | -19.1 | -10.3 | -23.9 | -35.4 | -10.4 | -39.5 | -14.5 | 04.6 |
| Burlington | -30.0 | -15.0 | -30.0 | -15.0 | -04.0 | -34.0 | -19.0 | -06.8 | -12.1 | -27.7 | -12.7 | -31.7 | -16.7 | 02.3 |
| Cambridge | -56.0 | -15.0 | -56.0 | -15.0 | -01.9 | -57.9 | -16.9 | -03.6 | -12.5 | -53.9 | -12.9 | -55.8 | -14.8 | 02.1 |
| Chelmsford | -10.0 | -10.0 | -06.9 | -06.9 | -05.6 | -12.5 | -12.5 | -48.5 | -48.5 | -00.9 | -00.9 | -06.4 | -06.4 | 06.1 |
| Chelsea | -72.0 | -15.0 | -72.0 | -15.0 | -02.9 | -74.9 | -17.9 | -23.4 | -98.1 | -54.5 | 02.5 | -57.3 | -00.3 | 17.5 |
| Clinton | -32.0 | -15.0 | -32.0 | -15.0 | -05.5 | -37.5 | -20.5 | -41.5 | -76.0 | -16.4 | 0.06 | -21.9 | -04.9 | 15.6 |
| Concord | -12.4 | -12.4 | -03.6 | -03.6 | -03.7 | -07.3 | -07.3 | -27.2 | -27.2 | -01.6 | -01.6 | -05.3 | -05.3 | 02.0 |
| Dalton | -31.0 | -15.0 | -31.0 | -15.0 | -04.7 | -35.7 | -19.7 | -20.4 | -37.0 | -23.7 | -07.7 | -28.4 | -12.4 | 07.3 |
| Dartmouth | 02.5 | 02.5 | 02.5 | 02.5 | -06.2 | -03.7 | -03.7 | -234.3 | -234.3 | 11.2 | 11.2 | 05.0 | 05.0 | 08.7 |
| Dennis | 02.5 | 02.5 | 02.5 | 02.5 | -06.6 | -04.1 | -04.1 | -95.4 | -95.4 | 06.4 | 06.4 | -00.2 | -00.2 | 03.9 |
| Dover | 02.5 | 02.5 | 02.5 | 02.5 | -05.4 | -02.9 | -02.9 | -25.7 | -25.7 | 03.2 | 03.2 | -02.2 | -02.2 | 00.7 |
| Dracut | -12.4 | -12.4 | -03.6 | -03.6 | -06.2 | -09.8 | -09.8 | -101.1 | -101.1 | 06.3 | 06.3 | 00.1 | 00.1 | 09.9 |
| Everett | -29.0 | -15.0 | -29.0 | -15.0 | -02.6 | -31.6 | -17.6 | -03.6 | -06.5 | -27.8 | -13.8 | -30.5 | -16.5 | 01.2 |
| Foxborough | -15.0 | -15.0 | -04.6 | -04.6 | -05.6 | -10.2 | -10.2 | -61.7 | -61.7 | 01.7 | 01.7 | -03.9 | -03.9 | 06.3 |
| Framingham | -15.0 | -15.0 | -12.0 | -12.0 | -05.8 | -17.8 | -17.8 | -23.5 | -23.5 | -07.8 | -07.8 | -13.6 | -13.6 | 04.2 |
| Georgetwon | -01.6 | -01.6 | 02.5 | 02.5 | -06.6 | -04.1 | -04.1 | -01.6 | -01.6 | 02.6 | 02.6 | -04.1 | -04.1 | 00.1 |
| Gloucester | -10.1 | -10.1 | -01.1 | -01.1 | -04.1 | -05.2 | -05.2 | -58.8 | -58.8 | 02.0 | 02.0 | -02.2 | -02.2 | 03.1 |
| Hatfield | -15.0 | -15.0 | 02.5 | 02.5 | -07.0 | -04.5 | -04.5 | -139.9 | -139.9 | 08.7 | 08.7 | 01.8 | 01.8 | 06.2 |
| Ipswich | 02.5 | 02.5 | 02.5 | 02.5 | -05.9 | -03.4 | -03.4 | -140.7 | -140.7 | 07.3 | 07.3 | 01.4 | 01.4 | 04.8 |
| Kingston | -15.0 | -15.0 | -07.4 | -07.4 | -05.1 | -12.4 | -12.4 | -42.7 | -42.7 | -02.1 | -02.1 | 10.7 | -07.1 | 05.3 |
| Leicester | 02.5 | 02.5 | 02.5 | 02.5 | -09.6 | -07.1 | -07.1 | -249.8 | -249.8 | 20.3 | 20.3 | 10.7 | 10.7 | 17.8 |
| Longmeadow | -04.9 | -04.9 | 02.5 | 02.5 | -06.1 | -03.6 | -03.6 | -66.7 | -66.7 | 04.9 | 04.9 | 01.2 | -01.2 | 02.4 |
| Lynnfield | 02.5 | 02.5 | 02.5 | 02.5 | -06.5 | -04.0 | -04.0 | -103.9 | -103.9 | 06.6 | 06.6 | 00.2 | 00.2 | 04.1 |
| Marshfield | -15.0 | -15.0 | -12.4 | -12.4 | -05.2 | -17.6 | -17.6 | -32.6 | -32.6 | -06.7 | -06.7 | -11.9 | -11.9 | 05.7 |
| Norwood | -03.3 | -03.3 | 02.5 | 02.5 | -06.2 | -03.7 | -03.7 | -114.7 | -114.7 | 06.8 | 06.8 | 00.5 | 00.5 | 04.3 |
| Palmer | -02.7 | -02.7 | -02.7 | -02.7 | -07.4 | -10.0 | -10.0 | -214.7 | -214.7 | 18.9 | 18.9 | 11.5 | 11.5 | 21.5 |
| Pelham | -10.7 | -10.7 | 00.9 | 00.9 | -04.5 | -03.6 | -03.6 | -248.2 | -248.2 | 09.8 | 09.8 | 05.3 | 05.3 | 08.9 |
| Pittsfield | -41.0 | -15.0 | -41.0 | -15.0 | -04.0 | -45.0 | -19.0 | -16.9 | -39.9 | -33.4 | -07.4 | -37.4 | -11.4 | 07.6 |
| Quincy | -56.0 | -15.0 | -56.0 | -15.0 | -02.8 | -58.8 | -17.8 | -09.4 | -31.1 | -50.5 | -09.5 | -53.3 | -12.3 | 05.5 |
| Salem | -40.0 | -15.0 | -40.0 | -15.0 | -03.5 | -43.5 | -18.5 | -11.7 | -27.5 | -34.9 | -09.9 | -38.4 | -13.4 | 05.1 |
| Seekonk | 02.5 | 02.5 | 02.5 | 02.5 | -05.4 | -02.9 | -02.9 | -107.8 | -107.8 | 05.6 | 05.6 | 00.2 | 00.2 | 03.1 |
| Southwick | 0.06 | 0.6 | 02.5 | 02.5 | -06.4 | -03.9 | -03.9 | -212.0 | -212.0 | 10.8 | 10.8 | 04.4 | 04.4 | 08.3 |
| Springfield | -49.0 | -15.0 | -49.0 | -15.0 | -05.1 | -54.1 | -20.1 | -20.6 | -55.6 | -37.8 | -03.8 | -42.9 | -08.9 | 11.2 |
| Sturbridge | 00.0 | 00.0 | 02.5 | 02.5 | -05.7 | -03.2 | -03.2 | -269.5 | -269.5 | 11.1 | 11.1 | 05.4 | 05.4 | 08.6 |
| Watertown | -40.0 | -15.0 | -40.0 | -15.0 | -04.5 | -43.5 | -18.5 | -03.6 | -08.4 | -38.4 | -13.4 | -42.0 | -17.0 | 01.6 |
| Wayland | -05.9 | -05.9 | 02.5 | 02.5 | -04.4 | -01.9 | -01.9 | -117.4 | -117.8 | 04.7 | 04.7 | 00.3 | 00.3 | 02.2 |
| Wellesley | -04.6 | -04.6 | 02.5 | 02.5 | -05.7 | -02.0 | -02.0 | -137.8 | -137.8 | 05.3 | 05.3 | 00.8 | 00.8 | 02.8 |
| Wenham | 02.5 | 02.5 | 02.5 | 02.5 | -05.8 | -03.2 | -03.2 | -218.4 | -218.4 | 09.4 | 09.4 | 03.7 | 03.7 | 06.9 |
| Whitman | -38.0 | -15.0 | -41.0 | -15.0 | -05.8 | -46.8 | -20.8 | -21.2 | -47.6 | -31.1 | -05.1 | -36.9 | -10.9 | 09.9 |
| Worcester | -56.0 | -15.0 | -56.0 | -15.0 | -04.3 | -60.3 | -19.3 | -01.4 | -04.2 | -55.2 | -14.2 | -59.5 | -18.5 | 00.8 |
| mean | -19.0 | -08.7 | -15.6 | -05.8 | -05.2 | -20.9 | -11.0 | -81.2 | -88.2 | -09.3 | 0.05 | -14.5 | -04.7 | 06.3 |
| st.dev. | 20.6 | 07.3 | 22.2 | 08.0 | -01.5 | 21.2 | 07.3 | 82.4 | 78.3 | 22.2 | 09.0 | 21.1 | 08.0 | 04.9 |
| median | 12.4 | 12.4 | 03.6 | 03.6 | -05.4 | 10.0 | 10.0 | 42.7 | 58.8 | 01.7 | 02.0 | 04.1 | 03.9 | 05.3 |

TABLE 28.3A

PROPOSITION 2 1/2 REVENUE LOSSES FOR COMMUNITIES GROUPED BY SIZE (1980 POPULATION)

| | Group I (11 Communities) <9500 | | | Group 2 (9 Communities) 9500-15,999 | | | Group 3 (11 Communities) 16,000-31,999 | | | Group 4 (6 Communities) 32,000-79,999 | | | Group 5 (4 Communities) >80,000 | | |
|------|-------|-------|--------|-------|-------|--------|-------|-------|--------|-------|-------|--------|-------|-------|--------|
| | mean | stdev | median | mean | stdev | median | mean | stdev | median | mean | stdev | median | mean | stdev | median |
| TL | -5.7 | 10.9 | 0 | -13.4 | 17.1 | -5.9 | -15.6 | 20.5 | -10.1 | -34.2 | 10.4 | -40.0 | -54.3 | 3.5 | -56.0 |
| YL | -4.2 | 7.9 | 0 | -06.8 | 8.3 | -5.9 | -9.1 | 5.8 | -10.1 | -15.0 | 0 | -15.0 | -15.0 | 0 | -15.0 |
| RTL | -1.6 | 10.2 | 2.5 | -09.5 | 16.5 | -2.7 | -10.9 | 22.4 | -3.6 | -33.7 | 11.5 | -40.0 | -54.3 | 3.5 | -56.0 |
| RYL | -0.1 | 5.7 | 2.5 | -4.7 | 8.1 | -2.7 | -4.3 | 7.1 | -3.6 | -14.5 | 1.2 | -15.0 | -15.0 | 0 | -15.0 |
| MV | -6.1 | 1.4 | 5.7 | 6.0 | 1.1 | 5.8 | 5.0 | 1.2 | 5.2 | 3.9 | 1.1 | 3.8 | 3.5 | 1.4 | 3.6 |
| RTR | -7.7 | 9.7 | -4.0 | -15.5 | 16.6 | -10.0 | -15.9 | 21.6 | -7.3 | -37.6 | 10.9 | -43.5 | -57.8 | 2.7 | -58.3 |
| RYR | -6.2 | 5.3 | -4.0 | -10.7 | 8.5 | -10.0 | -9.3 | 6.4 | -7.3 | -18.4 | 0.6 | -18.5 | -18.5 | 1.4 | -18.6 |
| AT | -139.3 | 104.5 | -139.9 | -93.5 | 60.6 | -95.4 | -77.4 | 66.3 | -58.8 | -11.6 | 7.7 | -11.0 | -8.8 | 8.6 | -6.5 |
| AY | -140.8 | 102.7 | -139.9 | -100.3 | 54.1 | -95.4 | -84.7 | 63.4 | -66.7 | -21.6 | 12.5 | -23.7 | -25.8 | 22.8 | -21.8 |
| PRTL | 5.2 | 11.2 | 8.7 | -0.9 | 14.9 | 4.7 | -5.0 | 19.4 | 2.0 | -29.6 | 11.2 | -34.2 | -49.3 | 7.9 | -52.2 |
| PRYL | 6.6 | 7.5 | 8.7 | 3.8 | 7.4 | 4.7 | 1.5 | 6.8 | 2.5 | -10.5 | 2.7 | -10.2 | -10.1 | 4.6 | -11.2 |
| PRTR | -0.9 | 10.4 | 1.8 | -7.0 | 14.7 | -0.2 | -10.0 | 18.6 | -2.2 | -33.6 | 10.5 | -37.9 | -52.9 | 7.1 | -54.5 |
| PRYR | 0.5 | 6.6 | 1.8 | -2.2 | 7.3 | -0.2 | -3.4 | 6.3 | -1.2 | -14.4 | 2.1 | -14.1 | -13.6 | 4.0 | -13.5 |
| AL | 6.8 | 4.7 | 6.9 | 8.5 | 6.4 | 6.3 | 5.9 | 4.7 | 4.3 | 4.0 | 2.4 | 4.4 | 4.9 | 4.6 | 3.8 |

Note: See Table 28.2 for definition of variables.

TABLE 28.3B

PROPOSITION 2 1/2 REVENUE LOSSES FOR COMMUNITIES GROUPED BY WEALTH
(1980 PER CAPITA EQUALIZED VALUATION)

| | Group 1 (10 Communities) <$13,500 | | | Group 2 (12 Communities) $13,500-$16,999 | | | Group 3 (7 Communities) $17,000-$19,999 | | | Group 4 (12 Communities) >$20,000 | | |
|------|-------|-------|--------|-------|-------|--------|-------|-------|--------|-------|-------|--------|
| | mean | stdev | median | mean | stdev | median | mean | stdev | median | mean | stdev | median |
| TL   | -33.5 | 23.6 | -36.4 | -23.5 | 20.8 | -15.0 | -10.9 | 14.3 | -10.0 | -7.0 | 11.7 | -4.7 |
| YL   | -11.8 | 6.3  | -15.0 | -11.1 | 7.1  | -15.0 | -7.4  | 7.1  | -10.0 | -4.6 | 7.1  | -4.7 |
| RTL  | -31.0 | 25.3 | -36.5 | -19.8 | 23.3 | -9.9  | -7.2  | 15.5 | 0.9   | -3.6 | 12.2 | 2.5  |
| RYL  | -10.9 | 6.8  | -15.0 | -7.5  | 8.1  | -9.9  | -3.6  | 7.6  | 0.9   | -1.2 | 6.7  | 2.5  |
| MV   | 5.9   | 2.0  | 5.6   | 4.9   | 1.6  | 5.1   | 5.3   | 1.0  | 5.7   | 4.9  | 1.2  | 5.0  |
| RTR  | -36.8 | 23.5 | -41.2 | -24.7 | 21.8 | -15.0 | -12.5 | 14.8 | -3.7  | -8.6 | 11.4 | -3.8 |
| RYR  | -16.7 | 5.5  | -19.2 | -12.4 | 6.7  | -14.7 | -9.0  | 7.1  | -3.7  | -6.1 | 5.9  | -3.8 |
| AT   | -73.2 | 88.4 | -32.3 | -65.0 | 83.2 | -26.5 | -1.212 | 105.8 | -114.7 | -80.8 | 62.5 | -81.1 |
| AY   | -92.8 | 79.3 | -65.8 | -71.4 | 79.1 | -34.8 | -1.219 | 104.9 | -114.7 | -81.5 | 61.7 | -81.1 |
| PRTL | -18.9 | 28.1 | -23.8 | -14.3 | 24.1 | -4.4  | -1.7  | 17.5 | 6.8   | -0.7 | 12.9 | 4.8  |
| PRYL | 1.2   | 11.2 | -1.6  | -2.0  | 8.8  | -4.4  | 1.8   | 9.5  | 6.8   | 1.7  | 7.5  | 4.8  |
| PRTR | -24.7 | 26.3 | -29.4 | -19.3 | 22.6 | -9.5  | -7.1  | 16.8 | 0.5   | -5.7 | 12.1 | -0.7 |
| PRYR | -4.6  | 10.1 | -6.9  | -6.9  | 7.4  | -9.5  | -3.5  | 9.0  | 0.5   | -3.3 | 6.6  | -0.7 |
| AL   | 12.1  | 6.0  | 10.5  | 5.4   | 2.4  | 5.6   | 5.5   | 2.6  | 4.8   | 2.9  | 1.6  | 2.6  |

Note: See Table 28.2 for definitions of variables.

TABLE 28.3C
PROPOSITION 2 1/2 REVENUE LOSSES FOR COMMUNITIES GROUPED BY GROWTH
(PERCENTAGE CHANGE IN POPULATION, 1970 TO 1980)

| | Group 1 (15 Communities) < -2.0% | | | Group 2 (7 Communities) -2.0% to 2.0% | | | Group 3 (5 Communities) >2.0% but <5.0% | | | Group 4 (5 Communities) 5.0% to 14.9% | | | Group 5 (9 Communities) >15% | | |
|---|---|---|---|---|---|---|---|---|---|---|---|---|---|---|---|
| | mean | stdev | median | mean | stdev | median | mean | stdev | median | mean | stdev | median | mean | stdev | median |
| TL | -35.2 | 22.1 | -40.0 | -13.0 | 9.9 | -12.4 | -7.1 | 17.6 | 2.5 | -8.3 | 14.1 | -1.6 | -9.1 | 12.2 | -10.7 |
| YL | -12.1 | 5.0 | -15.0 | -10.7 | 6.2 | -12.4 | -2.5 | 7.7 | 2.5 | -5.3 | 9.0 | -1.6 | -6.9 | 8.1 | -10.7 |
| RTL | -33.7 | 24.3 | -40.0 | -8.1 | 11.1 | -4.6 | -6.2 | 19.5 | 2.5 | -4.0 | 14.5 | 2.5 | -3.1 | 7.0 | 0.9 |
| RYL | -10.7 | 7.5 | -15.0 | -5.8 | 6.1 | -4.6 | -1.0 | 7.8 | 2.5 | -1.0 | 7.8 | 2.5 | -3.1 | 7.0 | 0.9 |
| MV | 4.2 | 1.4 | 4.1 | 5.0 | 0.8 | 5.6 | 6.6 | 1.7 | 5.9 | 5.9 | 1.2 | 6.5 | 6.0 | 1.0 | 6.2 |
| RTR | -37.9 | 23.4 | -43.5 | -13.1 | 11.1 | -10.2 | -12.8 | 19.1 | -3.6 | -9.9 | 13.5 | -4.1 | -9.0 | 7.2 | -4.1 |
| RYR | -14.9 | 6.8 | -17.9 | -10.8 | 6.2 | -10.2 | -7.6 | 7.6 | -3.6 | -6.9 | 6.8 | -4.1 | -9.0 | 7.2 | -4.1 |
| AT | -48.7 | 65.4 | -16.9 | -65.5 | 69.5 | -48.5 | -100.8 | 96.1 | -66.7 | -72.0 | 63.5 | -103.9 | -141.9 | 98.0 | -101.1 |
| AY | -64.6 | 61.1 | -39.9 | -67.9 | 68.0 | -48.5 | -106.1 | 91.2 | -66.7 | -73.1 | 62.2 | -103.9 | -141.9 | 98.0 | -101.1 |
| PRTL | -26.8 | 24.9 | -34.9 | -3.0 | 10.5 | -0.9 | 0.9 | 19.1 | 4.9 | -0.8 | 15.2 | 5.6 | 4.6 | 7.4 | 6.4 |
| PRYL | -3.8 | 9.8 | -7.4 | -0.7 | 6.0 | -0.9 | 6.1 | 9.2 | 4.9 | 2.2 | 8.6 | 5.6 | 4.6 | 7.4 | 6.4 |
| PRTR | -31.0 | 23.8 | -38.4 | -8.0 | 10.4 | -5.3 | -5.6 | 18.2 | -1.2 | -6.7 | 14.1 | 0.2 | -1.4 | 7.6 | 0.1 |
| PRYR | -8.0 | 8.8 | -11.4 | -5.7 | 6.0 | -5.3 | -0.4 | 7.7 | -1.2 | -3.7 | 7.6 | 0.2 | -1.4 | 7.6 | 0.1 |
| AL | 6.9 | 6.5 | 4.6 | -5.1 | 2.0 | 6.1 | 7.1 | 6.9 | 4.8 | 3.2 | 2.3 | 3.1 | 7.6 | 2.1 | 8.6 |

Note: See Table 28.2 for definitions of variables.

TABLE 28.4
APPROPRIATION CHANGES BY CATEGORY, 1981-1982

| | | Mean | St. Dev. | Median | Minimum | Maximum | Percentage of Total Appropriations Cut | | |
| --- | --- | --- | --- | --- | --- | --- | --- | --- | --- |
| | | | | | | | Mean | St. Dev. | Median |
| Schools | AC | -6.5 | 5.8 | -6.2 | -20.3 | 5.0 | 161.4 | 334.1 | 73.3 |
| | TR | 10.8 | 11.5 | 8.4 | -10.1 | 57.3 | | | |
| Police | AC | -0.5 | 18.1 | 1.5 | -94.7 | 40.8 | -28.0 | 166.3 | 0.4 |
| | TR | 11.5 | 7.8 | 9.2 | 1.7 | 45.4 | | | |
| Fire | AR | -4.2 | 15.3 | 0.7 | -68.0 | 10.0 | -3.1 | 54.2 | 0.2 |
| | TR | 15.9 | 21.2 | 10.0 | -0.3 | 106.1 | | | |
| Streets | AR | -10.6 | 20.7 | -8.0 | -85.5 | 20.0 | 14.8 | 57.2 | 6.8 |
| | TR | 14.2 | 23.9 | 8.8 | -4.6 | 149.6 | | | |
| Parks | AR | -22.9 | 25.1 | -12.0 | -99.8 | 3.4 | -0.5 | 27.1 | 1.7 |
| | TR | 21.2 | 25.9 | 15.5 | -32.9 | 91.8 | | | |
| Sanitation | AR | -4.2 | 37.3 | 0.0 | -100.0 | 69.0 | 3.5 | 17.8 | 0.6 |
| | TR | 41.6 | 142.9 | 5.9 | -17.9 | 740.9 | | | |
| Libraries | AR | -10.1 | 13.7 | -6.4 | -76.5 | 4.2 | 0.9 | 11.3 | 1.2 |
| | TR | 11.9 | 17.4 | 8.8 | -20.7 | 83.6 | | | |
| Total | AR | -5.6 | 7.7 | -4.1 | -35.2* | 6.5 | | | |
| | TR | 10.8 | 10.4 | 8.0 | -3.5 | 50.9 | | | |

Notes: AC = percentage appropriations change, 1981-82; TR = 5-year trend (mean annual percentage change, 1976-80).
* Hospital and junior college budgets were removed from Quincy's municipal budget.

## Table 28.5
## Municipal Bond Ratings, 1980 and 1982

| Community | 1980 Bond Rating | 1982 Bond Rating |
|---|:---:|:---:|
| Amesbury | Baa | A |
| Arlington | Aa | Aa |
| Burlington | Baa | A |
| Cambridge | Aa | Baa |
| Chelmsford | A | A 1 |
| Chelsea | B | Baa |
| Clinton | Baa | A |
| Concord | Aa | Aa |
| Dalton | Baa | A |
| Dartmouth | Baa | A |
| Dennis | A | A 1 |
| Dover | * | * |
| Dracut | Baa | A |
| Everett | Aa | Aa |
| Foxborough | A | A 1 |
| Framingham | Aa | Aa |
| Georgetown | Baa | A |
| Gloucester | A | A 1 |
| Hatfield | Baa | A |
| Ipswich | A | A 1 |
| Kingston | Baa | A |
| Leicester | Baa | A |
| Longmeadow | Aa | Aa |
| Lynnfield | Baa | A |
| Marshfield | Baa | A |
| Palmer | Aa | Aa |
| Pelham | * | * |
| Pittsfield | Aa | A |
| Quincy | Baa | Ba |
| Salem | Aa | A |
| Seekonk | Baa | A |
| Southwick | Baa | A |
| Springfield | Aa | A 1 |
| Sturbridge | Baa | A |
| Norwood | Aa | Aa |
| Watertown | Aa | A |
| Wayland | A | A 1 |
| Wellesley | Aaa | Aaa |
| Wenham | A | A 1 |
| Whitman | Baa | A |
| Worcester | A | Baa |

Source:  Moody's Investors Service, Inc.

# Epilogue

Proposition 2 1/2 has had many impacts on the cities and towns of Massachusetts in the first year following its enactment. It forced substantial cutbacks in local spending, particularly in the state's largest cities and towns. It accelerated the pace at which cities and towns proceeded toward 100% revaluation of property. It encouraged the state government to increase financial assistance to cities and towns (although the state did not take the imposed cutbacks into account in distributing additional aid). It forced substantial reduction in the size of the public workforce at both the local and state levels. It encouraged cities and towns to seek new nonproperty tax sources of revenue which in turn led to the adoption of new fees and charges. It reversed the trend toward ever-increasing property tax rates (although it did not lower all or even most residential tax bills). Finally, it altered political relationships in most municipalities -- reducing the ability of the average citizen to influence local budget priorities while enhancing the power of a few elected and appointed officials.

Whether Proposition 2 1/2 diminished the quality of any or all state and local services is unclear at this writing since spending reductions do not necessarily cause service level reductions. If Proposition 2 1/2 encourages local governments (through reorganization, regionalization, or a redefinition of employee responsibilities) to enhance productivity, service levels may even be increased. However, the evidence to date suggests that productivity has not been enhanced. In cities and towns facing severe spending rollbacks, it is likely that many public services have been reduced. Will the private sector or individual homeowners find ways to offset these cutbacks? It is not likely since there were few, if any, tax savings (only the rate of increase in property taxes was halted) for industry or homeowners to reallocate. Moreover, new fees and charges offset most tax rollbacks in communities where they did occur.

We don't yet know whether reductions in service levels and property tax rates have been or will be reflected in future housing and land prices. It is extremely difficult to trace the capitalization of tax reductions. We don't yet know whether employee morale in the public sector has been so adversely affected that service quality will deteriorate beyond the level implied by capital spending reductions. We don't yet know whether the cap on annual spending increases imposed by Proposition 2 1/2 will cause some communities to adopt a no-growth posture. Finally, we don't yet know whether the rapid decline in levels of capital spending in most cities and towns will cause irreparable harm to the state's basic infrastructure.

Some of the impacts of Proposition 2 1/2, substantial though they may be, will dissipate within a year or two, especially if the state government can continue to substitute increased state aid for lost property tax revenue. Other impacts of Proposition 2 1/2 will take a decade or more to become clear -- especially the long-term impacts of cutbacks in capital spending. It is too soon, therefore, to offer an overall assessment of Massachusetts' tax-cutting measure. Indeed, an overall assessment may elude us indefinitely as shifting circumstances and macro-economic trends foil attempts to isolate the specific impacts of Proposition 2 1/2.

The IMPACT: 2 1/2 Staff will continue its monitoring efforts. We will look at the second-year impacts of Proposition 2 1/2, particularly in large cities that must still make 15% annual cuts until they achieve the required 2.5% real tax rate. We will try to analyze the effects of reduced appropriation levels on both municipal services and user fees and charges. We will examine the actual distribution of state aid to cities and towns as well as local attempts to enhance public sector productivity. We will attempt to sort out the impacts of simultaneous federal budget cuts. Finally, we will continue to monitor shifts in the distribution of political power and changes in the local budget process in order to keep track of state-local relationships to see whether localities become more or less dependent on the state as a result of Proposition 2 1/2.

# Appendix
## Selected Data for Massachusetts Communities with Population Greater than 10,000

The data presented in this appendix have been abbreviated as follows:

| | |
|---|---|
| Expend | total municipal expenditures |
| Revenue | total municipal general revenue |
| FedAid | federal aid revenue |
| StAid | state aid revenue |
| FTEmp | total full-time municipal employees |
| PTEmp | total part-time municipal employees |
| Hshlds | number of households, 1970 |
| AvInc | average income, 1970 |
| %Res | percent residential property in the tax base, 1970 |
| Pop80 | 1980 population |
| %Change | percentage change in population between 1970 and 1980 |
| ATax80 | 1980 actual tax rate |
| ETax80 | 1980 effective tax rate |
| EQV | equalized property valuation, 1980 |
| Gap | 1981 Proposition 2 1/2 revenue gap |

The data for expenditures (Expend), revenue (Revenue), federal aid (FedAid), and state aid (StAid) are given in millions of dollars.

An asterisk (*) denotes a missing value.

|              | Expend  | Revenue | FedAid | StAid   | FTEmp | PTEmp | Hshlds |
|--------------|---------|---------|--------|---------|-------|-------|--------|
| Abington     | 9.498   | 8.955   | 0.019  | 3.021   | 347   | 143   | 3588   |
| Acton        | 14.119  | 13.888  | 0.072  | 1.813   | 324   | 103   | 4113   |
| Agawam       | 15.348  | 16.561  | 0.451  | 3.900   | 559   | 151   | 7025   |
| Amesbury     | 16.266  | 15.891  | 0.712  | 4.032   | 558   | 188   | 3815   |
| Amherst      | 13.100  | 12.755  | 0.635  | 2.718   | 388   | 166   | 17536  |
| Andover      | 23.251  | 25.123  | 0.092  | 3.879   | 817   | 176   | 7232   |
| Arlington    | 49.045  | 41.751  | 0      | 9.271   | 1307  | 229   | 18346  |
| Athol        | 2.826   | 2.552   | 0.019  | 0.837   | 292   | 141   | 3856   |
| Attleboro    | 25.162  | 5.137   | 5.137  | 2.835   | 1080  | 164   | 10598  |
| Auburn       | 10.994  | 11.718  | 0.466  | 2.829   | 388   | 178   | 4574   |
| Barnstable   | 28.539  | 29.445  | 2.601  | 4.590   | 886   | 55    | 7210   |
| Bedford      | 12.300  | 13.057  | 0.339  | 2.165   | 427   | 75    | 3597   |
| Bellingham   | 10.125  | 10.047  | 0      | 4.833   | 421   | 139   | 3635   |
| Belmont      | 24.668  | 23.537  | 0.732  | 3.412   | 723   | 230   | 9982   |
| Beverly      | 29.156  | 29.286  | 0.025  | 4.866   | 964   | 196   | 12919  |
| Billerica    | 30.139  | 33.125  | 1.171  | 8.880   | 1089  | 253   | 8146   |
| Boston       | 862.762 | 909.851 | 94.847 | 256.889 | 24187 | 3808  | 269220 |
| Bourne       | 11.348  | 10.922  | 1.061  | 2.569   | 442   | 78    | 4006   |
| Braintree    | 31.649  | 32.721  | 0.194  | 5.173   | 1107  | 97    | 9876   |
| Bridgewater  | 7.886   | 9.984   | 0.157  | 2.422   | 299   | 114   | 3484   |
| Brocton      | 92.595  | 87.187  | 14.428 | 20.864  | 3323  | 0     | 28627  |
| Brookline    | 57.037  | 59.122  | 2.670  | 6.111   | 1550  | 463   | 29855  |
| Burlington   | 23.681  | 25.601  | 0.011  | 4.454   | 762   | 261   | 5394   |
| Cambridge    | 133.849 | 121.003 | 19.312 | 13.265  | 4040  | 262   | 53482  |
| Canton       | 15.043  | 15.855  | 0      | 2.634   | 510   | 112   | 4753   |
| Chelmsford   | 24.157  | 24.938  | 0.027  | 7.286   | 1012  | 95    | 8513   |
| Chelsea      | 34.521  | 34.814  | 2.571  | 17.456  | 818   | 128   | 9773   |
| Chicopee     | 38.138  | 41.685  | 2.836  | 16.236  | 1634  | 564   | 22794  |
| Clinton      | 9.482   | 8.285   | 0.593  | 3.335   | 288   | 62    | 4373   |
| Concord      | 19.250  | 16.630  | 0.286  | 2.067   | 430   | 111   | 4481   |
| Danvers      | 33.391  | 32.140  | 0.061  | 3.050   | 1078  | 372   | 7554   |
| Dartmouth    | 16.723  | 13.754  | 1.255  | 3.218   | 551   | 122   | 6113   |
| Dedham       | 20.948  | 20.082  | 0.173  | 3.142   | 680   | 104   | 5789   |
| Dennis       | 7.827   | 8.003   | 0.039  | 0.438   | 131   | 51    | 2522   |
| Dracut       | 12.322  | 12.849  | 0.005  | 5.146   | 521   | 151   | 7312   |
| Duxbury      | 11.973  | 13.056  | 0.409  | 2.435   | 377   | 212   | 2327   |
| E.Longmeadow | 10,123  | 10,405  | 0.206  | 2.137   | 374   | 157   | 3764   |
| Easthampton  | 8.625   | 9.441   | 0.047  | 3.168   | 356   | 136   | 4449   |
| Easton       | 11.179  | 11.861  | 0      | 3.027   | 482   | 107   | 1531   |
| Everett      | 35.940  | 34.838  | 0.542  | 4.707   | 1307  | 164   | 14364  |
| Fairhaven    | 9.614   | 10.108  | 0.439  | 3.605   | 427   | 217   | 5463   |
| Fall River   | 84.852  | 92.279  | 14.240 | 45.622  | 3031  | 394   | 34552  |
| Falmouth     | 20.256  | 19.194  | 0.052  | 4.116   | 752   | 292   | 5550   |
| Fitchburg    | 30.891  | 32.069  | 3.446  | 8.266   | 978   | 261   | 15522  |
| Foxborough   | 11.364  | 11.567  | 0.035  | 3.098   | 412   | 130   | 3920   |
| Framingham   | 53.848  | 58.879  | 1.855  | 10.441  | 1895  | 374   | 21308  |
| Franklin     | 15.748  | 15.362  | 0.670  | 4.630   | 447   | 134   | 5260   |
| Gardner      | 11.450  | 11.454  | 0.254  | 4.814   | 410   | 149   | 6677   |
| Gloucester   | 22.426  | 23.556  | 0      | 4.781   | 841   | 132   | 9535   |
| Grafton      | 7.463   | 8.230   | 0.387  | 2.715   | 226   | 130   | 3210   |

| AvInc | %Res | Pop80 | %Change | ATax80 | ETax80 | EQV | Gap |
|-------|------|-------|---------|--------|--------|-----|-----|
| 11071 | 80 | 13517 | 9.6 | 33.7 | 33.7 | 152917 | -15 |
| 15131 | 81 | 17544 | 18.8 | 29.4 | 29.4 | 359173 | 3 |
| 10662 | 72 | 26271 | 21.0 | 48.5 | 32.0 | 301278 | -11 |
| 8947 | 61 | 13971 | 22.7 | 69.0 | 50.4 | 110019 | -15 |
| 4104 | 81 | 33229 | 26.2 | 28.2 | 28.2 | 246004 | -15 |
| 14541 | 69 | 26370 | 11.3 | 64.0 | 34.6 | 511270 | -6 |
| 10636 | 91 | 48219 | -9.9 | 81.0 | 47.8 | 613963 | -15 |
| 8990 | 58 | 10634 | -4.9 | 61.0 | 14.0 | 78004 | -15 |
| 10484 | 64 | 34196 | 3.9 | 72.4 | 42.7 | 368351 | -15 |
| 11141 | 65 | 14845 | -3.3 | 38.9 | 34.2 | 190909 | -15 |
| 9510 | 66 | 30898 | 55.7 | 21.3 | 19.3 | 935740 | 3 |
| 13908 | 61 | 13067 | -3.3 | 95.0 | 34.2 | 264731 | * |
| 10605 | 85 | 14300 | 2.4 | 43.5 | 34.8 | 123210 | -9 |
| 14893 | 88 | 26100 | -7.7 | 67.0 | 37.5 | 469200 | -6 |
| 10618 | 73 | 37655 | -1.8 | 83.1 | 43.2 | 467885 | -15 |
| 11127 | 73 | 36727 | 16.1 | 312.0 | 46.8 | 434833 | -15 |
| 6150 | 35 | 650142 | -11.6 | 254.9 | 114.7 | 3862222 | -15 |
| 8347 | 72 | 13874 | 9.8 | 19.7 | 19.7 | 305134 | -7 |
| 12758 | 59 | 36337 | 3.7 | 43.8 | 42.0 | 579615 | -15 |
| 9580 | 78 | 17202 | 33.2 | 43.3 | 42.4 | 153334 | -15 |
| 8645 | 65 | 95172 | 6.9 | 61.8 | 55.6 | 840139 | -15 |
| 8678 | 80 | 55062 | -6.2 | 98.0 | 60.8 | 704911 | -15 |
| 13096 | 54 | 23486 | 6.9 | 69.0 | 40.7 | 460668 | -15 |
| 5436 | 42 | 95322 | -5.0 | 188.4 | 69.7 | 924459 | -15 |
| 13571 | 65 | 18182 | 6.3 | 58.0 | 41.2 | 279459 | -15 |
| 13837 | 81 | 31174 | -0.8 | 53.0 | 35.5 | 426730 | -10 |
| 7728 | 35 | 25431 | -17.0 | 238.0 | 102.3 | 136416 | -15 |
| 7895 | 57 | 55112 | -17.3 | 184.0 | 42.3 | 469566 | -15 |
| 9452 | 49 | 12771 | -4.6 | 230.0 | 29.9 | 133846 | -15 |
| 19089 | 78 | 16293 | 0.9 | 35.2 | 34.1 | 382508 | -12 |
| 11534 | 64 | 24100 | -7.8 | 74.0 | 34.8 | 431915 | -9 |
| 10647 | 72 | 23966 | 27.5 | 32.0 | 26.9 | 320464 | 3 |
| 11902 | 65 | 25298 | -6.1 | 59.8 | 40.1 | 399971 | -10 |
| 9291 | 77 | 12360 | 91.5 | 13.0 | 13.0 | 471512 | 3 |
| 11203 | 81 | 21249 | 16.7 | 190.0 | 38.0 | 177900 | -12 |
| 14398 | 88 | 11807 | 54.6 | 37.8 | 37.8 | 226807 | -15 |
| 15228 | 72 | 12905 | -1.0 | 37.7 | 31.3 | 210513 | -4 |
| 9639 | 75 | 15580 | 19.7 | 34.0 | 34.0 | 154307 | -15 |
| 4531 | 80 | 16623 | 36.7 | 25.0 | 24.8 | 199660 | -15 |
| 9366 | 54 | 37195 | -12.5 | 141.2 | 42.4 | 715640 | -15 |
| 8989 | 68 | 15759 | -3.5 | 184.0 | 35.0 | 148984 | -15 |
| 6685 | 76 | 92574 | -4.5 | 160 | 60.8 | 481458 | -15 |
| 9593 | 64 | 23640 | 48.3 | 18.0 | 18.0 | 753971 | 0 |
| 8352 | 59 | 39580 | -8.7 | 46.9 | 46.9 | 351927 | -15 |
| 11546 | 60 | 14148 | -0.5 | 73.3 | 35.9 | 197325 | -15 |
| 10604 | 69 | 65113 | 1.7 | 67.0 | 42.9 | 904063 | -15 |
| 9616 | 79 | 18217 | 2.2 | 83.0 | 45.7 | 186176 | * |
| 9026 | 68 | 17900 | -9.4 | 50.3 | 40.7 | 137926 | -15 |
| 9338 | 63 | 27768 | -0.6 | 87.0 | 42.6 | 386094 | -10 |
| 11091 | 74 | 11238 | -3.6 | 44.8 | 35.4 | 114541 | 0 |

|              | Expend | Revenue | FedAid | StAid  | FTEmp | PTEmp | Hshlds |
|--------------|--------|---------|--------|--------|-------|-------|--------|
| Greenfield   | 18.004 | 16.003  | 0.542  | 5.864  | 537   | 155   | 6586   |
| Hanover      | 10.771 | 10.340  | 0.049  | 2.450  | 368   | 149   | 2719   |
| Harvard      | 3.319  | 3.805   | 0.001  | 0.567  | 120   | 48    | 7392   |
| Haverhill    | 50.382 | 50.365  | 3.655  | 11.611 | 1951  | 399   | 16122  |
| Hingham      | 17.605 | 18.096  | 0      | 3.295  | 741   | 137   | 5393   |
| Holbrook     | 9.484  | 9.095   | 0.419  | 2.313  | 317   | 117   | 3222   |
| Holden       | 8.574  | 8.260   | 0.001  | 1.770  | 262   | 177   | 3878   |
| Holliston    | 10.032 | 10.699  | 0.031  | 2.667  | 364   | 246   | 3238   |
| Holyoke      | 52.970 | 46.875  | 10.463 | 22.026 | 1622  | 156   | 18034  |
| Hudson       | 12.352 | 12.433  | 0.066  | 3.732  | 452   | 108   | 4553   |
| Ipswich      | 8.456  | 8.787   | 0.261  | 1.713  | 334   | 147   | 3602   |
| Lawrence     | 55.140 | 49.626  | 5.961  | 19.732 | 3245  | 117   | 23889  |
| Leominster   | 23.122 | 22.997  | 0.490  | 8.098  | 902   | 158   | 10467  |
| Lexington    | 32.195 | 32.788  | 0.070  | 5.750  | 879   | 313   | 9121   |
| Longmeadow   | 14.576 | 14.906  | 0      | 2.723  | 510   | 212   | 4927   |
| Lowell       | 84.919 | 77.578  | 13.948 | 28.634 | 2221  | 359   | 32772  |
| Ludlow       | 12.389 | 12.663  | 0.539  | 3.661  | 470   | 91    | 5227   |
| Lynn         | 85.340 | 80.786  | 7.792  | 28.817 | 2377  | 280   | 32081  |
| Lynnfield    | 9.520  | 8.995   | 0      | 1.800  | 301   | 207   | 3028   |
| Malden       | 61.102 | 51.059  | 9.170  | 13.468 | 1292  | 381   | 19408  |
| Mansfield    | 10.453 | 10.488  | 0.159  | 2.326  | 407   | 83    | 2983   |
| Marblehead   | 19.480 | 20.133  | 0.239  | 2.236  | 663   | 216   | 7405   |
| Marlborough  | 24.494 | 26.613  | 1.107  | 6.270  | 837   | 297   | 8849   |
| Marshfield   | 25.836 | 25.174  | 6.241  | 5.411  | 650   | 304   | 4173   |
| Medfield     | 9.459  | 9.677   | 0.543  | 2.084  | 284   | 142   | 2469   |
| Medford      | 49.687 | 46.996  | 2.485  | 14.217 | 1405  | 221   | 21814  |
| Melrose      | 25.346 | 25.473  | 1.603  | 5.661  | 861   | 132   | 10418  |
| Methuen      | 23.953 | 24.792  | 0.244  | 7.300  | 870   | 137   | 11184  |
| Middleborough| 11.893 | 11.010  | 0.215  | 3.123  | 510   | 158   | 4244   |
| Milford      | 19.204 | 16.629  | 0.005  | 6.334  | 672   | 71    | 6202   |
| Millbury     | 8.941  | 8.532   | 0.057  | 3.641  | 274   | 201   | 3710   |
| Milton       | 20.419 | 19.234  | 0      | 2.598  | 640   | 186   | 8929   |
| N. Adams     | 13.903 | 13.335  | 1.997  | 5.827  | 516   | 85    | 6884   |
| N.Andover    | 12.464 | 12.327  | 0.093  | 2.318  | 437   | 157   | 5607   |
| N.Attleborough| 19.570| 18.349  | 5.093  | 3.544  | 561   | 176   | 5942   |
| N.Reading    | 9.386  | 9.573   | 0.017  | 2.434  | 347   | 101   | 3054   |
| Natick       | 25.485 | 26.241  | 0.159  | 4.763  | 925   | 164   | 9292   |
| Needham      | 34.460 | 33.220  | 0.183  | 3.485  | 1148  | 359   | 8846   |
| New Bedford  | 77.597 | 80.404  | 9.055  | 35.187 | 3016  | 496   | 37039  |
| Newburyport  | 12.488 | 12.658  | 1.196  | 2.664  | 463   | 83    | 5311   |
| Newton       | 99.828 | 100.271 | 2.921  | 20.252 | 2444  | 1316  | 33504  |
| Northampton  | 22.080 | 25.970  | 3.284  | 10.120 | 618   | 246   | 11752  |
| Northborough | 9.368  | 9.636   | 1.848  | 1.516  | 212   | 126   | 2531   |
| Northbridge  | 7.289  | 7.470   | 0.117  | 3.309  | 231   | 124   | 3787   |
| Norton       | 8.916  | 9.205   | 0.055  | 2.858  | 350   | 68    | 3793   |
| Norwood      | 23.085 | 25.860  | 0.146  | 4.791  | 842   | 148   | 9417   |
| Oxford       | 8.953  | 9.073   | 0.844  | 3.910  | 306   | 198   | 2853   |
| Palmer       | 9.893  | 9.136   | 2.726  | 1.956  | 212   | 91    | 3863   |
| Peabody      | 46.917 | 45.556  | 1.328  | 5.348  | 1633  | 265   | 14455  |
| Pembroke     | 8.953  | 8.823   | 0      | 2.113  | 222   | 83    | 3043   |

| AvInc | %Res | Pop80 | %Change | ATax80 | ETax80 | EQV | Gap |
|-------|------|-------|---------|--------|--------|-----|-----|
| 8915 | 66 | 18436 | 1.8 | 38.8 | 38.8 | 230145 | * |
| 12529 | 70 | 11358 | 12.4 | 34.5 | 34.5 | 191277 | -15 |
| 5549 | 84 | 12170 | -2.6 | 26.0 | 26.0 | 98037 | 0 |
| 9546 | 59 | 46865 | 1.6 | 170.4 | 46.0 | 398600 | -15 |
| 14807 | 81 | 20339 | 7.9 | 77.0 | 37.7 | 351249 | -15 |
| 11109 | 79 | 11140 | -5.4 | 89.5 | 43.0 | 131429 | -15 |
| 13144 | 86 | 13336 | 6.2 | 39.3 | 30.3 | 173353 | 3 |
| 13210 | 79 | 12622 | 4.6 | 38.5 | 38.5 | 184429 | -15 |
| 7020 | 51 | 44678 | -10.8 | 102.0 | 42.8 | 262607 | -15 |
| 10970 | 79 | 16408 | 2.0 | 59.0 | 43.7 | 170439 | -15 |
| 10081 | 82 | 11158 | 3.8 | 73.0 | 35.0 | 158542 | 3 |
| 7514 | 51 | 63175 | -5.6 | 162.7 | 48.8 | 388303 | -15 |
| 10316 | 66 | 34508 | 4.8 | 55.0 | 35.8 | 332826 | -15 |
| 17334 | 70 | 29479 | -7.6 | 87.6 | 35.0 | 671053 | 2 |
| 19541 | 91 | 16301 | 4.3 | 49.0 | 34.8 | 287397 | -5 |
| 7312 | 60 | 92418 | -1.9 | 180.8 | 52.4 | 590566 | -15 |
| 11407 | 72 | 18150 | 3.3 | 75.0 | 35.3 | 207672 | -5 |
| 7736 | 53 | 78471 | -13.1 | 166.5 | 79.9 | 565419 | -15 |
| 17147 | 88 | 11267 | 4.1 | 26.6 | 26.3 | 236457 | 3 |
| 8487 | 59 | 53386 | -4.9 | 199.3 | 51.8 | 460546 | -15 |
| 10378 | 63 | 13453 | 35.4 | 76.8 | 32.3 | 172052 | -6 |
| 15452 | 89 | 20126 | -5.5 | 63.0 | 28.4 | 475424 | 3 |
| 10408 | 58 | 30617 | 9.6 | 208.0 | 43.7 | 346010 | -15 |
| 12670 | 84 | 20916 | 37.4 | 91.0 | 38.2 | 312757 | -15 |
| 15604 | 89 | 10220 | 4.1 | 73.1 | 38.8 | 149206 | * |
| 8816 | 73 | 58076 | -9.8 | 215.0 | 47.3 | 605096 | -15 |
| 12067 | 89 | 30055 | -9.4 | 68.8 | 48.8 | 339837 | -15 |
| 10147 | 74 | 36701 | 3.5 | 226.0 | 38.4 | 381412 | -10 |
| 9070 | 67 | 16404 | 20.6 | 93.0 | 40.0 | 157049 | -10 |
| 9617 | 61 | 23390 | 20.9 | 84.0 | 39.5 | 229787 | * |
| 9940 | 59 | 11808 | -1.5 | 252.0 | 42.8 | 95371 | -15 |
| 14902 | 83 | 25860 | -4.9 | 193.4 | 38.7 | 393540 | -15 |
| 7650 | 56 | 18063 | -5.9 | 55.5 | 38.3 | 119035 | -9 |
| 10453 | 59 | 20129 | 23.6 | 187.0 | 28.1 | 315640 | 3 |
| 10361 | 78 | 21095 | 13.0 | 37.8 | 34.4 | 226915 | -14 |
| 12210 | 75 | 11455 | 1.7 | 81.0 | 34.8 | 172056 | -7 |
| 12706 | 65 | 29461 | -5.1 | 103.0 | 41.2 | 484195 | -15 |
| 16823 | 73 | 27901 | -6.2 | 57.6 | 32.8 | 583214 | 1 |
| 6540 | 67 | 98478 | -3.2 | 141.6 | 53.8 | 601753 | -15 |
| 8780 | 72 | 15900 | 0.6 | 83.0 | 42.3 | 182437 | -15 |
| 11143 | 79 | 83622 | -8.4 | 169.2 | 50.8 | 1356860 | -15 |
| 7404 | 66 | 29286 | -1.3 | 31.5 | 31.5 | 331000 | -15 |
| 12066 | 74 | 10568 | 14.7 | 73.0 | 35.8 | 150945 | -7 |
| 9239 | 72 | 12246 | 3.8 | 45.0 | 32.9 | 101789 | 3 |
| 7104 | 76 | 12690 | 33.8 | 44.0 | 44.0 | 133353 | -15 |
| 12198 | 66 | 29711 | -3.6 | 48.0 | 36.5 | 423421 | -3 |
| 10070 | 80 | 11680 | 12.9 | 34.0 | 33.7 | 111910 | -15 |
| 9459 | 59 | 11389 | -2.5 | 32.0 | 29.4 | 128567 | -3 |
| 11264 | 71 | 45976 | -4.4 | 78.5 | 48.7 | 564465 | -15 |
| 10902 | 79 | 13487 | 20.5 | 32.9 | 32.9 | 188669 | * |

|              | Expend  | Revenue | FedAid | StAid  | FTEmp | PTEmp | Hshlds |
|--------------|---------|---------|--------|--------|-------|-------|--------|
| Pittsfield   | 44.481  | 41.621  | 0.956  | 11.753 | 1783  | 275   | 19060  |
| Plymouth     | 28.812  | 28.048  | 0.626  | 3.903  | 719   | 309   | 6602   |
| Quincy       | 116.072 | 113.070 | 3.022  | 21.997 | 3730  | 1055  | 30421  |
| Randolph     | 23.839  | 22.465  | 0.028  | 6.341  | 848   | 74    | 7501   |
| Reading      | 17.985  | 18.547  | 0.103  | 4.375  | 728   | 120   | 6652   |
| Revere       | 36.961  | 35.085  | 0      | 10.426 | 1165  | 162   | 14490  |
| Rockland     | 19.919  | 18.850  | 4.856  | 5.988  | 417   | 126   | 4256   |
| S.Hadley     | 11.126  | 11.096  | 1.437  | 2.889  | 364   | 131   | 6508   |
| Salem        | 38.632  | 41.797  | 2.276  | 6.802  | 1297  | 425   | 14985  |
| Saugus       | 20.306  | 19.500  | 0.022  | 4.190  | 640   | 278   | 7388   |
| Scituate     | 21.950  | 20.029  | 3.338  | 3.605  | 613   | 82    | 4735   |
| Seekonk      | 8.441   | 8.836   | 0.112  | 1.885  | 327   | 119   | 3318   |
| Sharon       | 11.961  | 12.309  | 0      | 2.403  | 383   | 139   | 3400   |
| Shrewsbury   | 15.789  | 14.379  | 0.025  | 3.181  | 559   | 237   | 5967   |
| Somerset     | 16.009  | 15.825  | 0.225  | 2.261  | 584   | 179   | 5492   |
| Somerville   | 61.081  | 63.717  | 3.603  | 26.271 | 1864  | 452   | 31709  |
| Southbridge  | 10.470  | 10.869  | 0.549  | 4.967  | 405   | 159   | 5869   |
| Spencer      | 4.865   | 5.384   | 0.017  | 2.462  | 167   | 182   | 2838   |
| Springfield  | 152.922 | 123.555 | 2.022  | 49.955 | 5441  | 2000  | 59406  |
| Stoneham     | 16.965  | 16.628  | 0.038  | 3.016  | 590   | 133   | 6617   |
| Stoughton    | 19.965  | 19.622  | 0.392  | 4.167  | 713   | 259   | 6545   |
| Sudbury      | 14.152  | 13.836  | 0      | 1.823  | 342   | 106   | 3433   |
| Swampscott   | 14.241  | 13.869  | 0.244  | 1.693  | 387   | 78    | 4481   |
| Swansea      | 8.947   | 9.346   | 0.092  | 2.819  | 331   | 78    | 3781   |
| Taunton      | 32.131  | 31.619  | 1.403  | 12.365 | 1385  | 234   | 13720  |
| Tewksbury    | 18.792  | 18.885  | 0.363  | 5.178  | 689   | 91    | 5394   |
| W.Springfield| 20.375  | 19.890  | 1.017  | 3.405  | 716   | 153   | 9651   |
| Wakefield    | 21.207  | 20.726  | 0.142  | 4.559  | 751   | 197   | 7957   |
| Walpole      | 18.924  | 16.407  | 0      | 3.808  | 502   | 213   | 4915   |
| Waltham      | 55.184  | 52.148  | 3.510  | 9.640  | 1609  | 138   | 21984  |
| Wareham      | 16.785  | 15.657  | 2.728  | 2.197  | 514   | 90    | 3809   |
| Watertown    | 38.162  | 31.696  | 0.453  | 6.882  | 806   | 76    | 13554  |
| Wayland      | 13.543  | 14.077  | 0.408  | 2.092  | 499   | 86    | 3754   |
| Webster      | 11.160  | 10.366  | 1.636  | 3.584  | 295   | 207   | 5259   |
| Wellesley    | 30.883  | 28.061  | 0.254  | 3.744  | 962   | 145   | 10517  |
| Westborough  | 11.214  | 10.726  | 0.019  | 1.843  | 375   | 67    | 3491   |
| Westfield    | 23.535  | 22.199  | 1.110  | 6.651  | 1067  | 162   | 10844  |
| Westford     | 9.777   | 10.020  | 0.060  | 2.867  | 359   | 105   | 2803   |
| Weston       | 13.700  | 13.804  | 0.046  | 2.015  | 365   | 180   | 3833   |
| Westport     | 7.705   | 8.200   | 0.007  | 2.800  | 303   | 27    | 3051   |
| Westwood     | 14.573  | 14.523  | 0.190  | 2.076  | 414   | 79    | 3597   |
| Weymouth     | 48.131  | 49.490  | 4.201  | 12.485 | 1675  | 295   | 16227  |
| Whitman      | 8.367   | 8.982   | 0.042  | 2.561  | 346   | 71    | 3826   |
| Wilbraham    | 10.827  | 11.025  | 1.605  | 1.673  | 267   | 144   | 3421   |
| Wilmington   | 18.160  | 17.822  | 0.865  | 3.471  | 519   | 162   | 4528   |
| Winchester   | 20.193  | 20.846  | 0.057  | 3.325  | 710   | 104   | 6831   |
| Winthrop     | 12.463  | 12.550  | 0.183  | 4.330  | 466   | 127   | 6693   |
| Woburn       | 28.683  | 31.002  | 0.065  | 6.360  | 1055  | 165   | 10946  |
| Worcester    | 190.757 | 183.781 | 13.225 | 63.013 | 6584  | 1486  | 66099  |
| Yarmouth     | 11.028  | 11.155  | 0      | 0.719  | 197   | 105   | 4548   |

| AVInc | %Res | Pop80 | %Change | ATax80 | ETax80 | EQV | Gap |
|---|---|---|---|---|---|---|---|
| 8905 | 57 | 51974 | -8.9 | 79.0 | 42.7 | 602357 | -15 |
| 9241 | 43 | 35913 | 93.0 | 22.0 | 22.0 | 937782 | 2.5 |
| 9076 | 57 | 84743 | -3.7 | 224.0 | 62.7 | 995536 | -15 |
| 12081 | 72 | 28218 | 4.4 | 85.0 | 41.6 | 320602 | -15 |
| 12210 | 75 | 11455 | 1.7 | 81.0 | 34.8 | 172056 | -7 |
| 9621 | 61 | 42423 | -1.7 | 227.6 | 63.7 | 356250 | -15 |
| 10034 | 77 | 15695 | 0.1 | 88.0 | 46.6 | 145164 | -15 |
| 8290 | 76 | 16399 | -3.7 | 40.0 | 33.6 | 174042 | -6 |
| 8400 | 43 | 38220 | -5.7 | 202.0 | 50.5 | 479744 | * |
| 11347 | 67 | 24746 | -1.5 | 55.9 | 36.9 | 366414 | -15 |
| 13321 | 88 | 17317 | 2.0 | 91.0 | 41.0 | 278420 | -15 |
| 11950 | 68 | 12269 | 10.4 | 41.0 | 29.9 | 191412 | 3 |
| 15560 | 84 | 13601 | 10.0 | 56.5 | 42.4 | 208057 | * |
| 12347 | 76 | 22674 | 18.1 | 47.1 | 31.1 | 281156 | 3 |
| 10697 | 62 | 18813 | 4.0 | 25.0 | 24.5 | 513190 | -1 |
| 7608 | 67 | 77372 | -12.9 | 245.8 | 63.9 | 536065 | -15 |
| 9314 | 65 | 16665 | -2.3 | 34.0 | 32.0 | 133286 | 3 |
| 9114 | 79 | 10774 | 22.7 | 44.0 | 27.8 | 80952 | 3 |
| 7343 | 52 | 152319 | -7.1 | 87.0 | 57.4 | 103876 | -15 |
| 11953 | 78 | 21424 | 3.4 | 43.3 | 38.9 | 301633 | -15 |
| 11173 | 77 | 26710 | 13.9 | 60.1 | 38.5 | 329928 | -15 |
| 17152 | 80 | 14027 | 3.9 | 57.5 | 36.2 | 294844 | -12 |
| 15680 | 87 | 13837 | 1.9 | 81.5 | 43.2 | 226249 | -15 |
| 10024 | 80 | 15461 | 22.3 | 49.0 | 31.4 | 171369 | * |
| 8964 | 62 | 45001 | 2.9 | 116.0 | 46.4 | 319875 | -15 |
| 11459 | 76 | 24635 | 8.3 | 49.5 | 41.1 | 287052 | -15 |
| 10326 | 54 | 27042 | -5.0 | 49.5 | 34.7 | 386231 | -11 |
| 12112 | 72 | 24895 | -2.0 | 173.0 | 43.3 | 338652 | -15 |
| 13083 | 69 | 18859 | 3.9 | 69.8 | 39.1 | 269643 | -13 |
| 8393 | 53 | 58200 | -5.5 | 63.0 | 41.6 | 821499 | -15 |
| 7952 | 65 | 18457 | 60.6 | 52.0 | 35.4 | 247579 | -8 |
| 10512 | 58 | 34384 | -12.5 | 224.0 | 51.5 | 427178 | -15 |
| 18026 | 81 | 12170 | -9.6 | 44.6 | 38.4 | 260022 | -6 |
| 8610 | 67 | 14480 | -2.9 | 127.0 | 35.6 | 112821 | -7 |
| 15879 | 82 | 27209 | -3.0 | 30.5 | 30.5 | 667423 | -5 |
| 12114 | 62 | 13619 | 8.1 | 43.0 | 31.4 | 230984 | 1 |
| 9219 | 68 | 36465 | 16.0 | 65.0 | 30.6 | 394381 | -15 |
| 11597 | 83 | 13434 | 29.6 | 68.4 | 34.9 | 170722 | -15 |
| 21637 | 91 | 11169 | 2.8 | 48.5 | 31.5 | 319950 | 3 |
| 9068 | 77 | 13763 | 40.6 | 63.2 | 26.5 | 189024 | -4 |
| 18158 | 69 | 13212 | 3.6 | 66.8 | 35.4 | 300008 | -15 |
| 10298 | 73 | 55601 | 1.8 | 79.2 | 46.7 | 630770 | -15 |
| 10465 | 77 | 13534 | 3.6 | 37.5 | 37.5 | 149371 | -15 |
| 14184 | 84 | 12053 | 0.6 | 33.7 | 33.0 | 194291 | -10 |
| 11253 | 55 | 17471 | 2.2 | 77.0 | 41.6 | 284489 | -15 |
| 17052 | 87 | 20701 | -7.0 | 74.8 | 41.9 | 370145 | -14 |
| 10572 | 87 | 19294 | -5.1 | 36.6 | 36.2 | 182803 | -15 |
| 11221 | 59 | 36626 | -2.1 | 40.2 | 40.2 | 543480 | -13 |
| 7399 | 61 | 161799 | -8.4 | 164.4 | 65.8 | 1145218 | -15 |
| 9018 | 78 | 18449 | 53.3 | 18.3 | 17.4 | 507761 | 3 |

# Index

# Contributors

STEPHEN AMBERG is a doctoral candidate in the Department of Political Science at the Massachusetts Institute of Technology.

REBECCA BLACK is economic development coordinator at Allston-Brighton Community Development Corporation and received the master of city planning degree from the Massachusetts Institute of Technology.

KATHERINE BRADBURY is an economist at the Federal Reserve Bank of Boston.

THOMAS CAMPBELL is a staff member of the Committee on Economic Development for the Washington State Legislature and received the master of city planning degree from the Massachusetts Institute of Technology.

CLAIRE CHRISTOPHERSON is assistant professor at Smith College.

MELVYN COLON is a housing planner at Nuestra Communidad Development Corporation in Roxbury, Massachusetts and received the master of city planning degree from the Massachusetts Institute of Technology.

RANDALL CRANE is a doctoral candidate in the Department of Urban Studies and Planning at the Massachusetts Institute of Technology.

SHERRY TVEDT DAVIS is a research associate at Public Systems Evaluation in Cambridge, Massachusetts and received the master of city planning degree from the Massachusetts Institute of Technology.

DANIEL DOBRYN is a member of the Undergraduate Research Opportunities Program at the Massachusetts Institute of Technology.

OSCAR FERNANDEZ is on the staff of Oxfam-America, an international development agency, and received the master of city planning degree from the Massachusetts Institute of Technology.

JANICE GOLDMAN is a doctoral student in the Department of Urban Studies and Planning at the Massachusetts Institute of Technology.

JOHN M. GREINER is senior research associate at the Urban Institute in Washington D.C.

HARRY P. HATRY is director of the State and Local Government Research Program at the Urban Institute in Washington D.C.

DANIEL HOLLAND is professor of finance at the Sloan School of Management at the Massachusetts Institute of Technology.

CYNTHIA HORAN is a doctoral candidate in the Department of Urban Studies and Planning at the Massachusetts Institute of Technology.

KARL E. KIM is a doctoral candidate in the Department of Urban Studies and Planning at the Massachusetts Institute of Technology.

JOHN C. KLENSIN is principal research scientist at the Laboratory of Architecture and Planning at the Massachusetts Institute of Technology.

HELEN F. LADD is associate professor at the John F. Kennedy School of Government at Harvard University.

ANDREW LAING is a doctoral student in the Department of Urban Studies and Planning at the Massachusetts Institute of Technology.

JAN LAWRENCE is manager of Public Information and Communication at the Maryland Center on Productivity and the Quality of Working Life at College Park, Maryland and received the master of city planning degree from the Massachusetts Institute of Technology.

PATRICIA McCARNEY is a doctoral student in the Department of Urban Studies and Planning at the Massachusetts Institute of Technology.

DONNA McDANIEL is the editor of the IMPACT: 2 1/2 Newsletter.

KARI MOE is issues coordinator for the Harold Washington mayoral campaign in Chicago and received the master of city planning degree from the Massachusetts Institute of Technology

MATT ROGERS is a member of the Undergraduate Research Opportunities Program at the Massachusetts Institute of Technology.

JEROME ROTHENBERG is professor of economics at the Massachusetts Institute of Technology.

JEROME RUBIN is executive director of Coalition for a Better Acre, a housing rehabilitation program in Lowell, Massachusetts and received the master of city planning degree from the Massachusetts Institute of Technology.

JANE FOUNTAIN SERIO is coordinator of the IMPACT: 2 1/2 Project.

PAUL SMOKE is a doctoral candidate in the Department of Urban Studies and Planning at the Massachusetts Institute of Technology.

LAWRENCE SUSSKIND is associate professor in the Department of Urban Studies and Planning at the Massachusetts Institute of Technology and director of the IMPACT: 2 1/2 Project.

ALAN TOSTI is a fiscal analyst at the Massachusetts Municipal Association.

CHRISTINE WOELFEL is a member of the Undergraduate Research Opportunities Program at the Massachusetts Institute of Technology.

# IMPACT: 2 1/2 Staff and Associates

Project Director
 Lawrence Susskind, Department of Urban Studies and Planning,
  Massachusetts Institute of Technology

Director, Human Services Monitoring
 Langley Keyes, Department of Urban Studies and Planning,
  Massachusetts Institute of Technology

Project Coordinator
 Jane Fountain Serio, Laboratory of Architecture and Planning,
  Massachusetts Institute of Technology

Massachusetts Institute of Technology
 Daniel Holland, Sloan School of Management
 Emma Jackson, Political Science
 Dr. John Klensin, Principal Research Scientist, Laboratory of Architecture
 and Planning
 Thomas Kochan, Sloan School of Management
 Michael Lipsky, Political Science
 Robert McKersie, Sloan School of Management
 Jerome Rothenberg, Economics
 William Wheaton, Urban Studies and Planning, Economics

The following are doctoral students in the Department of
Urban Studies and Planning:
 Randy Crane
 Janice Goldman
 Cynthia Horan
 Karl Kim
 Andrew Laing
 Patricia McCarney
 Paul Smoke

Harvard University
 H. James Brown, Kennedy School of Government
 Helen F. Ladd, Kennedy School of Government
 Jerome Murphy, School of Education
 Oliver Oldman, School of Law

Lincoln Institute of Land Policy
 Arlo Woolery, Executive Director
 Charles Cook, Director of Research and Education

Babson College
 Oskar Harmon, Economics
 Natalie Taylor, Management

Boston University
Greg Topakian, Economics

Simmons College
Deborah Kolb, Management

Tufts University
Andrew Reschovsky, Economics

University of Massachusetts, Amherst
Joseph R. Luro, Urban and Regional Management Program
George McDowell, Director, Center for Massachusetts Data
Craig Moore, School of Business Administration
Joel Naroff, School of Business Administration
Sidney Sufrin, School of Business Administration

University of Massachusetts, Harbor Campus
Franklin Patterson, Director, University Center for Studies in
  Policy and the Public Interest
Padraig O'Malley, Senior Policy Analyst

Wellesley College
Karl Case, Economics